THE WAITE GROUP®

PERL 5
HOW-TO

Mike Glover, Aidan Humphreys, Ed Weiss

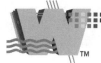

Waite Group Press™
A Division of Sams Publishing
Corte Madera, CA

Publisher: *Mitchell Waite*
Editor-in-Chief: *Charles Drucker*

Acquisitions Editor: *Jill Pisoni*

Editorial Director: *John Crudo*
Managing Editor: *Dan Scherf*
Content Editor: *Heidi Brumbaugh*
Copy editor: *Deirdre Greene*
Technical Reviewer: *Tom Christiansen*

Production Director: *Julianne Ososke*
Production Manager: *Cecile Kaufman*
Cover Design: *Sestina Quarequio*
Cover Illustration: *Jeff Koegel*
Design: *Karen Johnston*
Production: *Judith Levinson, Bill Romano*
Illustrations: *Larry Wilson*

© 1996 by The Waite Group, Inc.®
Published by Waite Group Press™, 200 Tamal Plaza, Corte Madera, CA 94925.

Waite Group Press™ is a division of Sams Publishing.

Waite Group Press™ is distributed to bookstores and book wholesalers by Publishers Group West, Box 8843, Emeryville, CA 94662, 1-800-788-3123 (in California 1-510-658-3453).

Printed in the United States of America
96 97 98 99 • 10 9 8 7 6 5 4 3 2 1

Library of Congress Cataloging-in-Publication Data
Glover, Mike.
    Perl 5 how-to / Mike Glover, Aidan Humphreys, Ed Weiss.
        p.   cm.
    Includes index.
    ISBN: 1-57169-058-1
    1. Perl (Computer program language) 2. Object-oriented
programming (Computer science) I. Humphreys, Aidan.   II. Weiss,
Ed. III. Title.
QA76.73.P33G56   1996
005.13'3--dc20   96-7074
                                                                                        CIP

DEDICATION

I would like to dedicate this book to Christina for being patient enough with
me to endure the nine months of 'fun' it took to put this book together. I would
also like to dedicate this book to the Patterson family because they have
given me so much over the years; this dedication is a small thank you for
all the support and love you have shown.
—Mike Glover

For Marie, Isabel, Anne-Louise, and Joya.
—Aidan Humphreys

To Sue, for her endless understanding.
—Ed Weiss

Message from the
Publisher

WELCOME TO OUR NERVOUS SYSTEM

Some people say that the World Wide Web is a graphical extension of the information superhighway, just a network of humans and machines sending each other long lists of the equivalent of digital junk mail.

I think it is much more than that. To me, the Web is nothing less than the nervous system of the entire planet—not just a collection of computer brains connected together, but more like a billion silicon neurons entangled and recirculating electro-chemical signals of information and data, each contributing to the birth of another CPU and another Web site.

Think of each person's hard disk connected at once to every other hard disk on earth, driven by human navigators searching like Columbus for the New World. Seen this way the Web is more of a super entity, a growing, living thing, controlled by the universal human will to expand, to be more. Yet, unlike a purposeful business plan with rigid rules, the Web expands in a nonlinear, unpredictable, creative way that echoes natural evolution.

We created our Web site not just to extend the reach of our computer book products but to be part of this synaptic neural network, to experience, like a nerve in the body, the flow of ideas and then to pass those ideas up the food chain of the mind. Your mind. Even more, we wanted to pump some of our own creative juices into this rich wine of technology.

TASTE OUR DIGITAL WINE

And so we ask you to taste our wine by visiting the body of our business. Begin by understanding the metaphor we have created for our Web site—a universal learning center, situated in outer space in the form of a space station. A place where you can journey to study any topic from the convenience of your own screen. Right now we are focusing on computer topics, but the stars are the limit on the Web.

If you are interested in discussing this Web site or finding out more about the Waite Group, please send me e-mail with your comments, and I will be happy to respond. Being a programmer myself, I love to talk about technology and find out what our readers are looking for.

Sincerely,

Mitchell Waite

Mitchell Waite, C.E.O. and Publisher

200 Tamal Plaza
Corte Madera, CA 94925
415-924-2575
415-924-2576 fax

Website:
http://www.waite.com/waite

CREATING THE HIGHEST QUALITY COMPUTER BOOKS IN THE INDUSTRY

Waite Group Press
Waite Group New Media

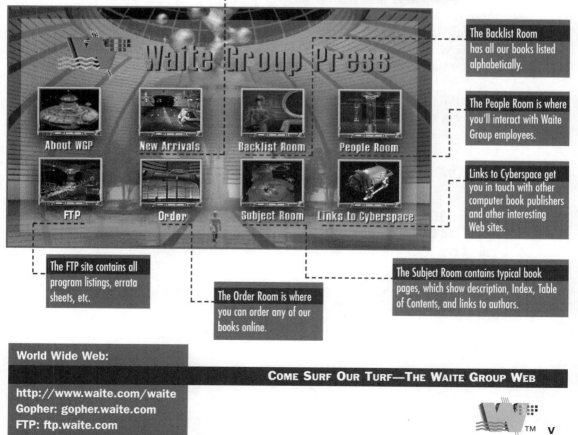

Mike Glover has been working as a computer consultant in the greater Toronto area for the last four years. His specialty is Unix system administration, system programming, and mission critical installations. Although he does everything from network installations to kernel hacking to vacuuming — if he's asked nicely — he doesn't do windows! Mike got his start with Unix systems at the University of Toronto Erindale College computer center, where he learned how to maintain and repair Unix systems and angry users. Mike is still working on trying to fix angry users. In his off time he teaches karate, but if you were to ask Christina, she would tell you that Mike doesn't have "off" time.

Aidan Humphreys received his M.S. in Information Technology from the University of London, 1988. He currently works as a systems integrator based in Frankfurt, Germany. Perl is an essential tool for his work implementing client/server systems for financial institutions across Europe. Aidan owes his fast motorcar to several crucial Perl programs.

Ed Weiss is a professional consultant who has extensive experience working on software development environments, designing and maintaining large computer networks, and integrating new technology. His most recent work has been helping corporations utilize object-oriented technology on very large projects. Ed discovered computers way back in the 1970s, although he won't admit it if you ask him. He maintained and supported Perl throughout AT&T Bell Laboratories for many years. Ed has been teaching computer courses since 1979.

TABLE OF CONTENTS

CONTENTS

ACKNOWLEDGMENTS

I would like to thank a number of people who have helped me along the way to get where I am today, the first being Robert Dick. Robert taught me how to yell at a machine to get it to work and where to hit it if it didn't listen. I would also like to thank the Erindale College CC. This is where I was given enough freedom to work on everything but my homework. The Pelly family also deserves my thanks for being a constant source of entertainment — everything from Dave Sr.'s constant attempts at cheating to Shelly's long-winded explanations of roundhouses to Paul and all the hours we have wasted playing video games. Last but definitely not least, Gord Cook, for being my friend and nemesis for over seven years.

—Mike Glover

I would like to thank Dan for cracking the whip when we needed it; Tom Christiansen for his acerbic and accurate criticisms of the first draft; John, Dave, and Barry for excusing their fellow Anglophone's prolonged absence from the Kneipen of Frankfurt.

—Aidan Humphreys

I must thank my wife Sue for her patience, understanding, and support. I sometimes believe it took more effort on her part than mine to produce my portion of this book. Many others were instrumental in creating this book, but none (sorry all) were more helpful.

—Ed Weiss

HOW TO USE THE CD-ROM

The companion CD-ROM contains all of the code for the How-To's in the book, as well as the Comprehensive Perl Archive Network (CPAN)—which contains Perl source and binaries, modules, and libraries. The CPAN tree is covered by the GNU General Public License, which you can read in Appendix C.

NOTE: Several assumptions and conditions are associated with this CD-ROM. It is assumed that you installed Perl in the /usr/local/bin directory. Most all of the scripts follow this convention. If you have Perl installed in another directory or if a script points to another path, you will need to modify the Perl script accordingly. In general, Perl scripts call modules using an initial capital letter. When you copy the .pm files from the CD-ROM to your hard drive, you'll need to make them initial capped for the supplied scripts to work correctly. Due to strict adherence to the ISO 9660 standard, the symbolic links are unresolved on this CD-ROM. Please check the file 00whois.html if you have trouble finding something. The file /ARCHIVE/CPAN.TGZ contains the CPAN tree in its entirety with all of the links resolved as of this writing. The CPAN is a constantly evolving archive; changes and updates are inevitable. The URL ftp://ftp.funet.fi is the link to the primary CPAN site.

Since all of the code for the How-To's in this book are on the companion CD-ROM, there is no need to type the code if you want to use it for your own projects. We will illustrate how to copy the files from the companion CD-ROM to your hard drive.

There are a few operating systems that work with Perl. This section will walk you through the steps necessary for the most popular ones: DOS/Windows 3.x, Windows 95, and various flavors of UNIX. Each operating system will be discussed in turn.

NOTE: For the following examples, we are going to assume that the CD-ROM drive you want to copy files from is the D: drive and the hard drive you want to copy files to is the C: drive. If your system is set up differently, please substitute the appropriate drive letters for your system.

DOS

These instructions for DOS assume you have no familiarity with DOS commands. If you feel uncomfortable with DOS and are using these instructions from the Windows DOS Prompt, please exit and follow the instructions for your version of Windows.

1. Move to the drive that you want to copy the files to. If you want to copy the files onto the C: drive, type

```
C:
```

and press [ENTER]. Ensure you are at the root directory by typing

```
CD \
```

and pressing [ENTER].

2. Create the directory you would like to store your files into. If you want to store the files into the PERL5HT directory, type

```
MD PERL5HT
```

and press [ENTER].

3. Move to that directory. If you created a directory called PERL5HT, move to that directory by typing

```
CD PERL5HT
```

and press [ENTER].

4. If you want to copy individual subdirectories from the CD-ROM to your hard drive, skip to step 5. If you want to copy the entire DOS-specific portion of the CD-ROM to your hard drive in this directory, type

```
XCOPY D:\SOURCE\DOS\*.* /V /S
```

and press [ENTER]. Notice there are some switches after the xcopy command. These switches are required to successfully copy the contents of the CD-ROM to your hard drive; /v tells xcopy to verify the files, and /s tells xcopy to copy the subdirectories.

5. To copy individual subdirectories from the CD-ROM to your hard drive, you must create the chapter directories before you copy the contents. For example, if you wanted to copy the code for Chapters 2, 5, and 7, you would type

```
MD CHAP_02
MD CHAP_05
MD CHAP_07
```

and press [ENTER] after each line. Then you would type

```
CD \PERL5HT\CHAP_02
XCOPY D:\SOURCE\DOS\CHAP_02 /V /S
```

continued on next page **xix**

continued from previous page

```
CD \PERL5HT\CHAP_05
XCOPY D:\SOURCE\DOS\CHAP_05 /V /S

CD \PERL5HT\CHAP_07
XCOPY D:\SOURCE\DOS\CHAP_07 /V /S
```

and press ENTER after each line.

Because the uncompressed CPAN tree is case-sensitive and has long filenames, you will need to use the compressed CPAN tree provided in the directory called ARCHIVE on the CD-ROM; it is named CPAN.TGZ. This file is tarred and gzipped, which are UNIX archive and compression terms, respectively. There are two GNU programs that will allow you to untar and ungzip this file for you: GNU untar and GNU ungzip. If you have access to Windows 3.x, WinZip 6.0a is a great utility that will also help you extract this file.

Windows 3.x

The following steps are for the use of Windows 3.x with short filenames.

1. Open the File Manager.

2. In File Manager, locate the drive you want to copy to and click on it.

3. If you have a directory to copy the files to, skip to step 4. Otherwise, create a new directory by selecting File, Create Directory. Type

```
PERL5HT
```

or a directory name of your choice and press ENTER or click on the OK button.

4. Click on PERL5HT or the directory you created.

5. Select the drive letter of your CD-ROM drive.

6. Double-click on the D: drive icon. You should see three directories: ARCHIVE, CPAN, and SOURCE. Double-click on the SOURCE directory and locate the WINDOWS directory. Double-click on this directory and drag the contents to the destination drive. If you only want to copy a few directories, control-click on the directories and drag the selection to the destination drive. Depending on how fast your computer is and also depending on the options set for your computer, the copying process may take a few moments to a few minutes.

The CPAN tree is provided in the directory called ARCHIVE on the CD-ROM and is named CPAN.TGZ. This file is tarred and gzipped, which are UNIX archive and compression terms, respectively. WinZip 6.0a is a great utility that will help you extract this file.

NOTE: When Windows copies a CD-ROM, it does not change the Read Only attribute for the files it copies. You can view the files, but you cannot edit them until you remove this attribute. To change it on all of the files, select the top-most directory with the files in it. In File Manager, select File, Properties and click on the Read Only checkbox to deselect it and click on OK.

Windows 95

The easiest way to copy files using Windows 95 is by using the desktop.

1. Double-click on the My Computer icon. Your drives will appear in a window on the desktop.

2. Double-click on your hard drive and create a new folder, such as Perl 5 How-To, by selecting File, New, Folder from the window menu. A folder called New Folder will be created on your hard drive with the name highlighted. Type in the name you want and press ENTER.

3. Go back to your drive window and double-click on the icon that represents your CD-ROM. You will see a window that has three folders in it: ARCHIVE, CPAN, and SOURCE.

4. Double-click on the SOURCE folder. You will see a window with four folders in it: DOS, WINDOWS, Win95, and Unix.

5. Double-click on the Win95 folder. Select the directories you want to copy (CTRL - click on the folders if you're not copying all of them) and drag your selection to the directory you created on your hard drive. You might need to reposition your windows to make the window for your hard drive visible. Depending on your system's performance, this may take a few moments to a few minutes.

The CPAN tree can be found in uncompressed format in the CPAN directory off the root. If you want to copy the entire CPAN tree to your hard drive—and if you have a lot of space on your hard drive—just drag the CPAN folder to your hard drive. Since the CPAN tree is over 230 megabytes in size, this operation will take some time.

NOTE: When Windows (any version) copies a CD-ROM, it does not change the Read Only attribute for the files it copies. You can view the files, but you cannot edit them until you remove this attribute. To change it on all of the files, select the topmost directory with the files in it. In Explorer, select File, Properties and click on the Read Only checkbox to deselect it and click on OK.

UNIX

Depending on the version of UNIX you are running, there can be several ways to mount the CD-ROM. This section will outline how to mount and copy files from a CD-ROM from most UNIX platforms.

NOTE: These UNIX examples assume you will be using the mount point /cdrom. If that is not the mount point you will be using, please substitute your mount point with the one in the example. In all cases, the mount point must exist or an error will occur. If the mount point directory does not exist, create the directory using the mkdir command and try remounting the CD-ROM.

Linux

This section will outline the steps you will need to follow if you are using the Linux operating system.

1. The mounting options in Linux are dependent on the contents of your /etc/fstab file. Steps a and b outline the different mount options if you have your CD-ROM described in your /etc/fstab file, and Step c outlines what to do if you do not have your CD-ROM described in the /etc/fstab file.

   a. To mount the CD-ROM in Linux, you do not need to be root if you have the following entry in your /etc/fstab file.

```
/dev/sbpcd  /cdromiso9660  user,noauto,so
```

   The CD-ROM device /dev/sbpcd reflects the specific CD-ROM drive type you have. This will be different from machine to machine. Then just mount the CD-ROM as any user with the following command.

```
mount /cdrom
```

   b. To mount the CD-ROM in Linux, you do not need to be root if you have the following entry in your /etc/fstab file.

```
/dev/sbpcd  /cdromiso9660  user,so
```

   The CD-ROM device /dev/sbpcd reflects the specific CD-ROM drive type you have. This will be different from machine to machine. This entry in the /etc/fstab file auto-mounts the CD-ROM to /cdrom so the mount command does not need to be issued.

   c. If you do not have an entry in the /etc/fstab for the /cdrom mount point, then you will have to mount the CD-ROM by hand. The following command will mount a CD-ROM to the mount point /cdrom. Note that you must be root to use the mount command, unless the suid permission has been set on the mount command.

```
mount /dev/cdrom -t iso9660 /cdrom
```

2. If you are using a file manager, refer to the instructions on how to copy directories with the file manager. If you are not using a file manager, then you can copy the contents of the CD-ROM to a directory using the cp command. To copy a directory named Unix from the CD-ROM to a local directory, type the following command at the UNIX prompt.

```
cp -r /cdrom/unix .
```

Solaris

Solaris has a volume manager, so floppy disks and CD-ROMs will be recognised and mounted automatically. To verify that the volume manager is running, type the following command.

```
ps -eaf | grep vol
```

If you get the /usr/bin/vold process from the ps command, then the volume manager is running. Skip to step 2. If the volume manager is not running, then continue with step 1.

1. In order to start the volume manager, you need to be root. The following command starts the Solaris volume manager.

```
/etc/init.d/volmgt start
```

2. Open the CD-ROM door and put in the CD-ROM. Close the door and wait a couple of seconds. You can access the CD-ROM contents by changing directories into the directory /cdrom/cdrom0. If the CD-ROM drive is the second CD-ROM on the machine, then the directory would be /cdrom/cdrom1.

3. If you are using a file manager, refer to the instructions on how to copy directories from the file manager. If you are not using a file manager, then you can copy the contents of the CD-ROM to a directory using the cp command. To copy a directory named Unix from the CD-ROM to a local directory, type the following command at the UNIX command prompt.

```
cp -r /cdrom/cdrom0/unix .
```

SUN/OS

In order to mount a CD-ROM under SUN/OS, you need to be root. Either log in as root or su (switch user) into root.

1. To mount the CD-ROM, the following command must be issued at the UNIX command prompt. This will mount the CD-ROM under the mount point /cdrom.

```
mount -f hsfs /dev/cdrom /cdrom
```

2. Once the CD-ROM has been mounted, then you can copy the contents of the CD-ROM to a local directory. If you are using a file manager, refer to the instructions on how to copy directories from the file manager. If you are not using a file manager, then you can copy the contents of the CD-ROM to a directory using the cp command. To copy a directory named Unix from the CD-ROM to a local directory, type the following command at the UNIX command prompt.

```
cp -r /cdrom/unix .
```

CHAPTER 1
PERL BASICS

PERL BASICS

Perl's popularity can be attributed to many things, one of which is the ease with which programs can be built. Unlike C or any other compiled language, Perl is interpreted, which greatly reduces development time. This allows the programmer to build larger and more complex programs in less time. Unfortunately, this reduction in time has a negative side effect: Some programmers do not give themselves enough time to get to know the language. This speedy development process can lead to inferior and inefficient code. The more complex the programs become, the more important it is to understand the syntax and semantics of the language.

3

This chapter will introduce the syntax and semantics of the Perl programming language so programmers new to Perl can get a good foundation for building effective Perl programs. Anyone familiar with Perl 4 should look through this chapter; this is an introduction to Perl 5, not just to Perl.

Throughout this book, the phrases *scalar context* and *array context* are used. Scalar context means that a function is being called and the return value of the function is a scalar value. The following example demonstrates calling a function named scalarContextFunction in a scalar context.

```
$returnValue = scalarContextFunction();
```

The result of the call to scalarContextFunction is stored in the scalar variable named $returnValue. A scalar is Perl's most basic data type.

When a function is called in an array context, the function returns a list. The following example demonstrates calling a function in an array context.

```
@returnValue = arrayContextFunction();
```

The variable *@returnValue* is the array that contains the information returned from the call to the function arrayContextFunction.

Some functions, such as the values and keys functions, can be used in both a scalar context and an array context. This means these functions have multiple personalities. For example, when the keys function is used in a scalar context, it returns the number of elements of the given associative array. When keys is called in an array context, it returns a list of all the keys of the given associative array.

1.1 Scalar Data Types

The scalar is the most basic of all of Perl's data types. This section will describe what a scalar is, how to use it, and how Perl actually looks at different scalar variables.

1.2 Arrays

An array can be defined as a list of ordered elements. Given this, Perl has a data type that is a list of scalars. This section will demonstrate how to manipulate and interrogate a Perl scalar array both as a list and as a stack.

1.3 Associative Arrays

Associative arrays are scalar arrays that are indexed by string instead of by numeric value. This section will show how to use Perl's associative arrays.

1.4 References

References were introduced with Perl 5 and are akin to C pointers. References allow you to construct complex data types. This section will demonstrate the basic use, and possible complex use, of Perl's references.

1.5 Regular Expressions

Perl has one of the most comprehensive and powerful pattern-matching capabilities of any programming language. This section will outline how to use Perl's regular expressions to match any given pattern.

1.6   Operators: Numeric and String

To perform mathematical, logical, or qualitative checks on variables, a language needs operators. This section will demonstrate Perl's operators and how to use them.

1.7   Control Statements

Every written, spoken, or logical language requires some sort of control to maintain correct flow of a conversation (or program). This section will outline Perl's flow control statements.

1.8   Subroutines, Packages, and Modules

The ability to create portable and modular code makes any language more viable to programmers. Perl has packages and modules that make Perl code portable. This section will discuss them.

1.9   Variable Localization

To create complex programs, a programmer needs a method of localizing variables to blocks of code. This section will outline how to localize a variable in Perl.

1.10   Special Variables

Perl has several special predefined global variables that change the behavior of Perl. This section will outline those variables and what each does.

1.1 Scalar Data Types

The *scalar data type* is the most basic form of a data container Perl has. A *scalar variable* can reference a string value or an integer value. In fact, Perl has three contexts in which it will interpret a scalar variable: string context, numeric context, and miscellaneous context. The latter of the three contexts is discussed in Section 1.4.

Perl treats strings and integers with almost the same regard. Almost, but not completely. There is a visible difference. To define or assign a scalar variable in a Perl script, you need to create a scalar variable and assign it a value. For example, the following three lines

```
$name="Gizmo";
$age=3;
$height=4.5;
```

define three scalar variables. One scalar variable, *$name,* contains a string data value; *$age* contains a double data value; *$height* contains a float value. When a scalar variable is assigned, the syntax of the assignment assists the Perl interpreter in deciding the variable type. If the value of the variable is surrounded in single or double quotes, then Perl treats the variable as a string. If there are no quotes, then Perl has to decide if the value is a string or a numeric value. This is demonstrated in the following Perl script.

```
#!/usr/local/bin/perl -w
```

continued on next page

continued from previous page

```
$firstName=Gizmo;
$lastName="Senegal";
$age="3";
```

If you were to run this script, you would get a warning about an unquoted string.

% **chap_01/howto01/bareword.pl**

Output

```
Unquoted string "Gizmo" may clash with future reserved word at bareword.pl
line 3
```

End Output

The warning is telling you that the bare word Gizmo may be a future reserved word like a function name, which may change the context of the assignment if a function named Gizmo is added to Perl. Take notice of the assignment of the variable *$age*. The assignment of *$age* uses quotes, which means that Perl will initially treat this scalar value as a string instead of a numeric value. Although this is acceptable, this should be considered poor style and should be avoided.

1.2 Arrays

Perl has a data structure that is strictly known as an array of scalars; this structure is more commonly known as an array or a list. Perl's arrays can be used as a simple list, a stack, or even the skeleton of a complex data structure. This section outlines Perl's arrays so you can gain an understanding of how to use arrays in various ways. Perl's array of scalars can be declared by any number of methods. One common method is to define an array to be empty, as in the following example.

```
@myList = ();
```

Keep in mind that Perl does not always require variables, including arrays, to be defined before use. The above example is provided merely as an example of how to define an empty array or how to empty an existing array. The above example defines an empty array of scalars named @myList.

Using Arrays as an Indexed List

The most common method of using an array as an indexed list is to directly assign the array all of its values at once, if possible. The following example sets the array variable *@months* to the months of the year.

```
@months = qw (JUNK Jan Feb March April May June July Aug Sept Oct Nov Dec);
```

There are two items to mention regarding the above example: the space holder JUNK and the keyword qw. Because arrays start at index 0, JUNK is used as a space holder. The list entry of $months[0] is filled with JUNK so Jan can be referenced at $months[1], June at $months[6], and Dec at $months[12]. The qw keyword was introduced with Perl 5. The two following lines of Perl code assign the same values to the list @array.

```
@array = qw (a b c d e);
@array = ("a", "b", "c", "d", "e");
```

The qw keyword is a shortened form used to extract individual words from a string. In the above case, the individual words are the names of the months, and the result of running qw on them is stored in the array @*months*. If the array cannot be assigned all at once, you can set the individual array elements on an individual basis. For example, you could have set the @*months* array in the following fashion.

```
$months[0] = "JUNK";
$months[1] = "Jan";
$months[2] = "Feb";
...
$months[12] = "Dec";
```

The ellipses are included for brevity; the rest of the @*months* array would have to be assigned in the same fashion. The above piece of code sets the value of $months[0] to the string value of "JUNK", $months[1] to "Jan", $months[2] to "Feb", etc. Notice when you assign the array elements directly, you use the $ character, not the @ character. The $ character at the beginning of an array tells Perl that one individual element of the array, not the complete array, is to be assigned. You can extract the information from an array in multiple ways. One of the most common is to index the array elements directly. The following script demonstrates directly indexing an array's contents.

```
#!/usr/local/bin/perl -w

my @months = qw (JUNK Jan Feb March April May June July Aug Sept Oct Nov
Dec);

for ($x=0; $x <= $#months; $x++)
{
    print "Index[$x] = $months[$x]\n";
}
```

The word $#months is actually a Perl convention that tells you the value of the largest subscript of an array. If $#months returns -1, the array is empty.
Run this script.

```
% chap_01/howto02/list.pl
```

Output

```
Index[0] = JUNK
Index[1] = Jan
Index[2] = Feb
Index[3] = March
Index[4] = April
Index[5] = May
Index[6] = June
Index[7] = July
Index[8] = Aug
Index[9] = Sept
Index[10] = Oct
Index[11] = Nov
Index[12] = Dec
```

End Output

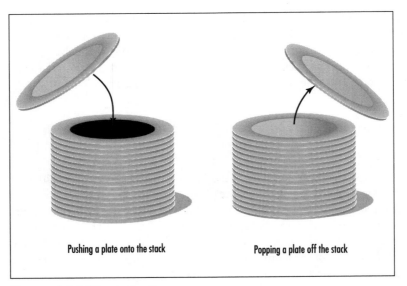

Pushing a plate onto the stack   Popping a plate off the stack

Figure 1-1 LIFO stack diagram

Using Arrays as Stacks

You can store information in an array using several methods. One method is to use the push function to push information onto the top of the array, treating the array as a stack.

```
push (@myList, "Hello");
push (@myList, "World!");
```

The above example pushes two strings, "Hello" and "World!", onto the array variable *@myList*. Because you used the push function, the variable *@myList* is being used as a last in first off (LIFO) stack. A LIFO stack works much like a dish stack in a cafeteria. Dishes are pushed onto the top of the stack and all the other dishes are pushed down. When dishes are removed from the stack, they are removed from the top and all the other dishes move toward the top of the stack. Figure 1-1 represents a LIFO stack using the dish stack analogy.

To get information off the top of the stack, use the pop function. Using the example above, if you were to call pop on the array *@myList,* the value "World!" would be returned because it was the last element pushed on the stack. The following script demonstrates how to use an array as a stack.

```
#!/usr/local/bin/perl -w

push (@myList, "Hello");
push (@myList, "World!");
push (@myList, "How");
push (@myList, "Are");
push (@myList, "You?");
```

```
while ( $index = pop(@myList) )
{
    print "Popping off stack: $index\n";
}
```

Run this script.

```
% chap_01/howto02/stack.pl
```

Output

```
Popping off stack: You?
Popping off stack: Are
Popping off stack: How
Popping off stack: World!
Popping off stack: Hello
```

End Output

Notice that elements are popped off in reverse order. This is the effect of the LIFO stack. When an element is popped off, the item is actually removed; once all the elements have been popped, the stack is empty.

1.3 Associative Arrays

Associative arrays are arrays that are indexed by string value instead of by integer index value. Figure 1-2 outlines the component elements of a standard list. Figure 1-3 outlines what an associative array could look like. To make things a little clearer, we will

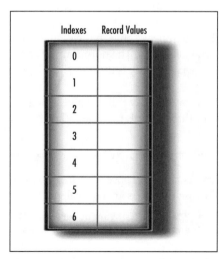

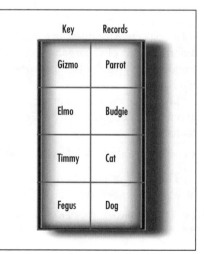

Figure 1-2 Component elements of a standard list

Figure 1-3 Outline of an associative array

compare a regular array against an associative array. If you have an array named @scalarArray and you want to print out the first element of the array, you would use the following syntax.

```
print $scalarArray[0];
```

Associative arrays, unlike scalar arrays, do not have a sense of order; there is no true first addressable element. This is because the indexes of the associative array are strings and the information is not stored in a predictable order. To retrieve a value from an associative array, you must know the key. If you know a key of the associative array *%associativeArray* and you want to print out the value, you would use the following syntax.

```
print $associativeArray{'mike'};
```

This example prints out the value of a key named mike in the associative array named *%associativeArray*.

Many programming languages, including C, do not have native associative array capabilities. Perl is an exception to this rule. This section demonstrates how to propagate and investigate Perl's associative array of scalars.

Perl's associative array of scalars can be declared using any number of methods. A common one is to declare an empty associative array, as in the following example.

```
%cities = ();
```

Populating an Associative Array

Keep in mind that Perl does not require variables, including associative arrays, to be defined before use. The above example is provided as an example of how to define an empty associative array or how to empty an existing array. It creates an empty associative array of scalars named %cities, which maintains a list of cities and their respective locations in Canada. Note the differences between the definition of a normal array of scalars and an associative array of scalars. The normal array is distinguished by the @ character, whereas the associative array is distinguished by the % character.

Much like the normal array, an associative array can have all its values assigned at once. The following piece of Perl code assigns three records to the associative array %cities.

```
%cities = ("Toronto" => "East", "Calgary" => "Central", "Vancouver" => 'West');
```

The operator => is equivalent to a comma; its main purpose is to create a visual association between pairs. Thus, the following two lines are equivalent.

```
%cities = ("Toronto" => "East", "Calgary" => "Central", "Vancouver" => 'West');
%cities = ("Toronto", "East", "Calgary", "Central", "Vancouver", 'West');
```

Like the standard array, the associative array can be populated by individual elements as well. For example, the following lines of Perl code populate the associative array %cities with the same values listed above.

```
$cities{'Toronto'} = "East";
$cities{'Vancouver'} = "West";
$cities{'Calgary'} = "Central";
```

Extracting Information from an Associative Array

You can list the contents of an associative array using one of three functions: keys, values, or each. The keys function returns a list of the keys of the given associative array when used in a list context and the number of keys when used in a scalar one. The keys returned from the keys function are merely indexes into the associative array. The keys function is the most common function used to extract information from an associative array. When used in a list context, the keys function returns a list of all the keys of the given associative array. The following Perl script lists the contents of an associative array.

```perl
#!/usr/local/bin/perl -w

my %cities = ("Toronto" => "East", "Calgary" => "Central", "Vancouver" =>
'West');

for $key (keys %cities)
{
    print "Key: $key Value: $cities{$key} \n";
}
```

Run this script.

```
% chap_01/howto03/keys.pl
```

─ Output

```
Key: Toronto Value: East
Key: Calgary Value: Central
Key: Vancouver Value: West
```

End Output

If you are interested only in the values of the associative array, then you could use the values function instead. The following script lists the contents of an associative array using the values function.

```perl
#!/usr/local/bin/perl -w

my %cities = ("Toronto" => "East", "Calgary" => "Central", "Vancouver" =>
'West');

for $value (values %cities)
```

continued on next page

continued from previous page

```
{
    print "Value: $value \n";
}
```

Run this script.

```
% chap_01/howto03/values.pl
```

Output

```
Value: East
Value: Central
Value: West
```

End Output

The obvious advantage of using the keys function over the values function is that with the keys function you can also get the values of the associative array. The third method you can use to list the contents of an associative array is to use the each function. This function returns a key-value pair from the associative array. The following script demonstrates the each function.

```
#!/usr/local/bin/perl -w

my %cities = ("Toronto" => "East", "Calgary" => "Central", "Vancouver" =>
'West');

while ( ($key, $value) = each %cities )
{
    print "Key: $key Value: $value \n";
}
```

Run this script.

```
% chap_01/howto03/each.pl
```

Output

```
Key: Toronto Value: East
Key: Calgary Value: Central
Key: Vancouver Value: West
```

End Output

1.4 References

References are a data type introduced with Perl 5. Calling a reference a data type is a very loose use of the term data type. A reference is more a generic entity that can point to any given data type, native or generated. For the C programmers reading this, a reference is nothing more than a pointer.

One of the biggest complaints about Perl 4 was that creating a complex data type was almost impossible. Even creating a simple matrix was something the gurus did because they knew what potions to brew. With references, potions need not be brewed, incantations need not be uttered, and little bags of tricks can be used for marbles. References fill the void in Perl 4.

Creating a Reference

When a reference is created, a new instance of the reference is created and stored in the receiving scalar. This is done so that if the original reference disappears, the scalar reference will still have a copy of the original. The following script demonstrates the creation of a reference.

```
#!/usr/local/bin/perl -w

# Set up the data types.
my $scalarVar = "Gizmo was here.";

# Create the reference to $scalarVar
my $scalarRef = \$scalarVar;
```

This example creates a reference named $scalarRef to a scalar variable named $scalarVar. There are several different types of references; they are outlined below.

Dereferencing a Reference

Perl's references do not automatically dereference themselves when used. References are scalars; if you were to print out a reference without trying to dereference it, then the scalar would print out information about itself. For example, say you type in the following script.

```
#!/usr/local/bin/perl -w

# Set up the data types.
my $scalarVar = "Gizmo was here.";
my @arrayVar = qw (Sunday Monday Tuesday Wednesday Thursday Friday
Saturday);
my %hashVar = ("Toronto" => "East", "Calgary" => "Central", "Vancouver" =>
'West');

# Create the references
my $scalarRef = \$scalarVar;
my $arrayRef = \@arrayVar;
my $hashRef = \%hashVar;

# Print out the references.
print "$scalarRef \n";
print "$arrayRef \n";
print "$hashRef \n";
```

The script, when run, would print out something like the following.

```
% chap_01/howto04/ref.pl
```

```
SCALAR(0xaddc4)
ARRAY(0xadec0)
HASH(0xade30)
```

The next seven sections demonstrate how to create and dereference scalar references, array references, hash references, code references, anonymous array references, anonymous hash references, and anonymous subroutine references.

Scalar References

A scalar reference is created by using the backslash operator on an existing scalar variable. The following example creates a reference to the variable *$scalarVariable*.

```
$scalarRef = \$scalarVariable;
```

To dereference the scalar reference, add a $ to the beginning of the reference. This means the variable will have two $ signs before the variable name when you are printing out the contents of the scalar reference. If the reference variable is called *$scalarRef*, use the following syntax to print out the contents of the reference.

```
print $$scalarRef;
```

The following code segment creates a reference to a scalar, then prints out the contents of the reference.

```
#!/usr/local/bin/perl -w

# Create the scalar variable
my $scalarVariable = "Gizmo was here.";

# Create the scalar reference
my $scalarRef = \$scalarVariable;

# Print out the contents of the scalar variable
print "Var: $scalarVariable\n";

# Print out the contents of the scalar reference.
# Note the double $$
print "Ref: " . $$scalarRef . "\n";
```

Run this script.

```
% chap_01/howto04/scalar.pl
```

```
Var: Gizmo was here.
Ref: Gizmo was here.
```

Array References

One way to create an array reference is to use the backslash operator on an existing array variable. The following script creates a reference to an array variable named @*months*, then prints out the contents of the array reference.

```perl
#!/usr/local/bin/perl -w

# Create the array
my @months = qw (Jan Feb March April May June July Aug Sept Oct Nov Dec);

# Create the array reference.
My $arrayRef = \@months;

# Print out the contents of the array reference.
for $month (@$arrayRef)
{
    print "Month: $month \n";
}
```

Run the above script.

```
% chap_01/howto04/array.pl
```

Output

```
Month: Jan
Month: Feb
Month: March
Month: April
Month: May
Month: June
Month: July
Month: Aug
Month: Sept
Month: Oct
Month: Nov
Month: Dec
```
End Output

Hash References

One way to create a hash reference is to use the backslash operator on an existing hash variable. The following script creates a reference to a hash variable named %*who* and then prints out the contents of the hash reference.

```perl
#!/usr/local/bin/perl -w

# Create the associative array
my %who = ('Name' => 'Gizmo', 'Age' => 3, 'Height' => '10 cm', 'Weight' =>
'10 gm');

# Create the hash reference
my $hashRef = \%who;
```

continued on next page

continued from previous page

```perl
    # Print out the contents of the associative array.
for $key (sort keys %$hashRef)
{
    $value = $hashRef->{$key};
    printf "Key: %10s Value: %-40s\n", $key, $value;
}
```

Run the above script.

```
% chap_01/howto04/array.pl
```

Output

```
Key:         Age Value: 3
Key:      Height Value: 10 cm
Key:        Name Value: Gizmo
Key:      Weight Value: 10 gm
```

End Output

Code References

A code reference is a reference to a subroutine. Code references are mainly used for callback functions. One way to create a code reference is to use the backslash operator on a function name. The following script creates a reference to a subroutine named callBack and then dereferences the reference to call the subroutine.

```perl
#!/usr/local/bin/perl -w

# Define the callback function.
sub callBack
{
    my ($mesg) = @_;

    print "$mesg\n";
}

# Create the code reference
my $codeRef = \&callBack;

# Call the callback function with different parameters.
&$codeRef ("Hi Mike!");
&$codeRef ("How Are You?");
```

Run the above script.

```
% chap_01/howto04/code.pl
```

Output

```
Hi Mike!
How Are You?
```

End Output

Anonymous Array References

An anonymous array is an array without a name. This means the array has been defined and stored into a reference instead of an array. Anonymous arrays are one of the best additions, in our opinion, to Perl 5. There will be times when you may want to create a temporary array but don't feel like creating a new array name. When you use an anonymous array, Perl creates the name space for the array. This means Perl picks the name of the array instead of the programmer; this appeals to most people's lazy side. According to Larry Wall, the author of Perl, the three great virtues of a programmer are "laziness, impatience, and hubris." (*Programming Perl*, p. xiv)

To create an anonymous array, use square brackets around a list. The following script creates an anonymous array and prints out some of the contents.

```
#!/usr/local/bin/perl -w

# Create the anonymous array reference.
My $arrayRef = [[1,2,3,4], 'a', 'b', 'c', 'd', 'e', 'f'];

# Print out some of the array
print $arrayRef->[0][0] . "\n";
print $arrayRef->[0][1] . "\n";
print $arrayRef->[1] . "\n";
```

Run the above script.

```
% chap_01/howto04/aaref.pl
```

Output

```
1
2
a
```

End Output

Notice that the above example creates an anonymous array inside an anonymous array. This is a way to create a matrix in Perl 5. Chapter 16 shows how to create complex data structures using references.

Anonymous Hash References

Anonymous hash references are created the same way anonymous array references are created. The hash is created and the reference is stored directly into the reference. Anonymous hash references have the same appeal as anonymous array references: The programmer does not need to create a name for the array. The following script makes a hash reference and prints out some of the contents.

```
#!/usr/local/bin/perl -w

my $hashRef = {'Name' => 'Gizmo', 'Age' => 3, 'Height' => '10 cm'};

print $hashRef->{'Name'} . "\n";
print $hashRef->{'Age'} . "\n";
print $hashRef->{'Height'} . "\n";
```

Run the above script.

```
% chap_01/howto04/ahash.pl
```

Output

```
Gizmo
3
10 cm
```

End Output

Anonymous Subroutine References

An anonymous subroutine is a subroutine that has been defined without a name. The following script creates a reference to an anonymous function.

```perl
#!/usr/local/bin/perl -w

my $codeRef = sub { my $mesg = shift; print "$mesg\n"; };

&$codeRef ("Hi Mike");
&$codeRef ("How Are You?");
```

Run the above script.

```
% chap_01/howto04/acode.pl
```

Output

```
Hi Mike
How Are You?
```

End Output

1.5 Regular Expressions

Regular expressions are used to search for patterns. The stronger the pattern-matching abilities, the more valuable the programming language becomes. Compared to other programming languages, compiled and interpreted, Perl has one of the most powerful pattern-matching capabilities. This section outlines the syntax of Perl's regular expressions and demonstrates Perl's powerful pattern-matching capabilities. This section is broken into two subsections: Regular Expression Syntax and Pattern-Matching Operators. The Regular Expression Syntax section outlines the syntax of Perl's regular expressions; the Pattern-Matching Operators section takes the rules defined in the Regular Expressions section and applies them to basic examples.

Regular Expression Syntax

Perl's regular expressions are so vast that a complete book could be dedicated to them. Because we don't have that luxury, this section outlines some of the more commonly used expressions and expression syntaxes.

The most common operator used when using regular expressions on strings is what Perl calls a *pattern-binding operator*. The pattern-binding operator looks like =~ or !~. The syntax of the pattern-binding operator is

```
$string =~ /regular expression/expression modifier
```

The regular expression can be anything from a basic scalar value to a complex regular expression looking for a complex pattern. The expression modifier is an optional element to the regular expression. If you were to look for a pattern of Hello in a scalar named $sentence, the syntax would look like the following.

```
$sentence =~ /Hello/;
```

If $sentence contains the value of Hello, then the above statement would return True. To take full advantage of Perl's regular expressions, you need to understand the syntax of the expressions. This subsection outlines everything from expression modifiers to expression quantifiers to predefined character patterns.

Modifiers

An expression modifier can be added to most regular expressions to modify the behavior of the expression. Table 1-1 lists the expression modifiers and what they do.

MODIFIER NAME	PURPOSE
i	Makes the search case-insensitive.
m	If the string has new-line characters embedded within it, the metacharacters ^ and $ will not work correctly. This modifier tells Perl to treat this line as a multiple line.
s	The character . matches any character except a new line. This modifier treats this line as a single line, which allows . to match a new-line character.
x	Allows white space in the expression.

Table 1-1 Regular expression modifiers

For example, if you were to perform a basic case-insensitive search, you would use the I modifier. The following example demonstrates how to use a modifier on a regular expression.

```
#!/usr/local/bin/perl -w

# Create a basic string.
my $string = "Hello World!";

if ($string =~ /"Hello World!"/)
{
    print "Case Match!\n";
}

if ($string =~ /"hello WORLD!"/i)
{
    print "Case insensitive Match!\n";
```

continued on next page

continued from previous page

```
}
```

      Run the above script.

```
% chap_01/howto05/modify.pl
```

─┤Output├──

```
Case Match!
Case insensitive Match!
```

┤End Output├───

Metacharacters

A *metacharacter* is a character that carries a special meaning. Metacharacters are used to make searches more specific so very complicated search patterns can be constructed. Table 1-2 outlines Perl's regular expression metacharacters and their meanings.

METACHARACTER	PURPOSE
\	Tells Perl to accept the following character as a regular character; this removes special meanings from any metacharacter.
^	Matches the beginning of the string, unless /m is used.
.	Matches any character except a new line character, unless /s is used.
$	Matches the end of the string, unless /m is used.
		Expresses alternation. This means the expressions will search for multiple patterns in the same string.
()	Groups expressions to assist in alternation and back referencing.
[]	Looks for a set of characters.

Table 1-2 Regular expression metacharacters

      The following example performs a very specific spell check on a text file. It looks for misspelled instances of the words "language" and "expression."

```
#!/usr/local/bin/perl -w

while (<STDIN>)
{
    # Look for incorrect spelling of 'language' and 'expression'.
    print if ( /(L|l)angau[gG]e|(E|e)xprestion/ );
}
```

      Use the following text file as input for the script. The misspelled words are highlighted.

```
Perl is an interpreted langauge optimized for scanning arbitrary
text files, extracting information from those text files, and
printing reports based on that information.  It's also a good
langauGe for many system management tasks.  The langauge is
```

intended to be practical (easy to use, efficient, complete) rather
than beautiful (tiny, elegant, minimal). It combines (in the author's
opinion, anyway) some of the best features of C,
sed, awk, and sh, so people familiar with those **langauges** should
have little difficulty with it. (**Langauge** historians will also note
some vestiges of csh, Pascal, and even BASIC-PLUS.) **Exprestion**
syntax corresponds quite closely to C **exprestion** syntax.

Run the above script.

```
% chap_01/howto05/meta.pl < chap_01/howto05/meta.txt
```

Output

```
Perl is an interpreted langauge optimized for scanning arbitrary
langauGe for many system management tasks.  The langauge is
sed, awk, and sh, so people familiar with those langauges should
have little difficulty with it. (Langauge historians will also note
some vestiges of csh, Pascal, and even BASIC-PLUS.)  Exprestion
syntax corresponds quite closely to C exprestion syntax.
```

End Output

Pattern Quantifiers

A *pattern quantifier* allows the programmer to write dynamic regular expressions without having to write out each possible instance of the pattern explicitly. Table 1-3 outlines each quantifier and its purpose.

QUANTIFIER	PURPOSE
*	Matches 0 or more times.
+	Matches 1 or more times.
?	Matches 0 or 1 times.
{n}	Matches exactly n times.
{n,}	Matches at least n times.
{n,m}	Matches at least n times but no more than m times.

Table 1-3 Regular expression pattern quantifiers

The following example scans an array of numbers looking for a number that starts with 870 and is followed by three 2s in a row.

```perl
#!/usr/local/bin/perl -w

my @numbers = qw (870226980 870222428 870222315 870641520 870222318);

for (@numbers)
{
    if ( /^8702{3}/)
    {
        print $_ . "\n";
    }
}
```

Run the above script.

```
% chap_01/howto05/quantify.pl
```

Output

```
870222428
870222315
870222318
```

End Output

Character Patterns

Perl uses a number of character patterns to look for special instances of patterns. Table 1-4 lists sequences of special characters and their purpose.

SEQUENCE	PURPOSE
\w	Matches an alphanumeric character. Alphanumeric also includes _.
\W	Matches a nonalphanumeric character.
\s	Matches a white space character. This includes space and tab.
\S	Matches a non-white space character.
\d	Matches a digit.
\D	Matches a nondigit character.
\b	Matches a word boundary.
\B	Matches a nonword boundary.
\A	Matches only at beginning of string.
\Z	Matches only at end of string.
\G	Matches only where previous m//g left off.

Table 1-4 Regular expression character patterns

The following example gets the current date in the UNIX date format and looks for the hours, minutes, and seconds.

```perl
#!/usr/local/bin/perl -w

# Get the date in the standard date format. (ex: Tue Oct 24 19:03:03 1995 )
my $date = localtime();

# Search through the date looking for the hour, minute, and second.
if ($date =~ /(\d\d):(\d\d):(\d\d)/)
{
    # Save the information.
    my $hours = $1;
    my $minutes = $2;
    my $seconds = $3;
```

```
    print "Hours   : $hours \n";
    print "Minutes: $minutes \n";
    print "Seconds: $seconds \n";
}
```

Run the above script.

```
% chap_01/hwoto05/charpatt.pl
```

Output

```
Hours   : 19
Minutes: 08
Seconds: 04
```
End Output

Pattern-Matching Operators

Pattern-matching operators are the keywords in Perl that perform pattern matches. The difference between regular expression syntax and pattern-matching operators is that regular expressions allow the programmer to build complex expressions, whereas pattern-matching operators allow the programmer to perform the searches. This subsection outlines Perl's pattern-matching operators and how to use them.

The syntax used to perform a pattern match on a string is

```
$string =~ /regular expression/expression modifier (optional)
```

The operator =~ performs a search looking for the regular expression within the given string. For example, the following Perl script scans text looking for the word "the."

```
#!/usr/local/bin/perl -w

while (<STDIN>)
{
    print if ($_ =~ /the/);
}
```

Run the above script on some sample text.

```
% chap_01/howto05/search.pl < chap_01/howto05/meta.txt
```

Output

```
intended to be practical (easy to use, efficient, complete) rather
(in the author's opinion, anyway) some of the best features of C,
```
End Output

Notice that the word "rather" was selected as well. Because the search looks for the pattern "the," any word that contains the pattern will be selected.

1.6 Operators: Numeric and String

Perl, like other programming languages, has a number of operators for both strings and numeric values. The operators can be broken down into four distinct groups: string operators, numeric operators, assignment operators, and equivalence operators. The next two subsections, String Operators and Numeric Operators, outline all the string and numeric operators and what should be expected when the operators are used.

String Operators

Perl has a number of string operators that do everything from basic string concatenation to case conversion. Perl can even increment string values. The most often used string operators are assignment operators and equivalence checks. Unfortunately, the most common mistake is made when trying to perform an equivalence check on a string value; many programmers use numeric operators instead. The following two statements demonstrate the right and wrong ways to perform an equivalence check on a string.

```perl
# Wrong!!!
if ($string == "Hello")
{
    # Do something...
}


# Right!
if ($string eq "Hello")
{
    # Do something...
}
```

The following script demonstrates the correct use of three of the operators listed in Table 1-5: eq, lt, and gt.

```perl
#!/usr/local/bin/perl -w

# Do this forever.
for (;;)
{
    # Get the information from the user.
    print "Enter a word: ";
    my $word1 = <STDIN>; chomp $word1;
    print "Enter another word: ";
    my $word2 = <STDIN>; chomp $word2;

    # Perform some basic string operations
    if ($word1 eq $word2)
    {
        print "The two phrases are equivalent.\n";
    }
    elsif ($word1 lt $word2)
    {
        print "<$word1> is alphabetically less than <$word2>\n";
    }
```

```
    elsif ($word1 gt $word2)
    {
        print "<$word1> is alphabetically greater than <$word2>\n";
    }
}
```

Run the above script.

```
% chap_01/howto06/strop.pl
```

Output

```
Enter a word: Hello
Enter another word: There
<Hello> is alphabetically less than <There>
Enter a word: Xenophobia
Enter another word: Hiccup
<Xenophobia> is alphabetically greater than <Hiccup>
Enter a word: This is the end.
Enter another word: This is the end.
The two phrases are equivalent.
```

End Output

Table 1-5 outlines Perl's string operators and the purpose of each.

OPERATOR	PURPOSE
x	Returns a string consisting of the string on the left of the operand, repeated the number of times of the right operand.
.	Concatenates the two strings on both sides of the operator.
eq	Returns True if the two operands are equivalent, False otherwise.
ne	Returns True if the two operands are not equal, False otherwise.
le	Returns True if the operand on the left is stringwise less than the operand on the right of the operator. Returns False otherwise.
lt	Returns True if the operand on the left is stringwise less than or equal to the operand on the right of the operator. Returns False otherwise.
ge	Returns True if the operand on the left is stringwise greater than or equal to the operand on the right of the operator. Returns False otherwise.
gt	Returns True if the operand on the left is stringwise greater than the operand on the right of the operator. Returns False otherwise.
cmp	Returns -1, 0, or 1 if the left operand is stringwise less than, equal to, or greater than the right operand.
,	Evaluates the left operand, then evaluates the right operand. It returns the result of the right operand.
++	Increments the string by one alphabetic value.

Table 1-5 String operators

Numeric Operators

Perl has the standard set of numeric operators plus a few extras. The following example demonstrates some of the more basic operators. Note that the equivalence operations performed on the values parallel those of the string equivalence example.

```perl
#!/usr/local/bin/perl -w

# Do this forever.
for (;;)
{
    # Get the information from the user.
    print "Enter a number: ";
    my $num1 = <STDIN>; chomp $num1;
    print "Enter another number: ";
    my $num2 = <STDIN>; chomp $num2;

    # Perform some basic numeric operations
    my $sum = $num1 + $num2;
    my $diff = $num1 - $num2;

    print "The sum of $num1 and $num2 is $sum\n";
    print "The difference of $num1 and $num2 is $diff\n";

    if ($num1 == $num2)
    {
        print "Both numbers are equal.\n";
    }
    elsif ($num1 < $num2)
    {
        print "$num1 is numerically less than $num2\n";
    }
    elsif ($num1 > $num2)
    {
        print "$num1 is numerically greater than $num2\n";
    }
}
```

Run the above script.

```
% chap_01/howto06/numop.pl
```

Output

```
Enter a number: 1
Enter another number: 2
The sum of 1 and 2 is 3
The difference of 1 and 2 is -1
1 is numerically less than 2
Enter a number: 42
Enter another number: 5
The sum of 42 and 5 is 47
The difference of 42 and 5 is 37
42 is numerically greater than 5
Enter a number: 68
Enter another number: 68
```

```
The sum of 68 and 68 is 136
The difference of 68 and 68 is 0
Both numbers are equal.
```

End Output

Table 1-6 lists Perl's numeric operators and their purpose.

OPERATOR	PURPOSE
+	Computes the additive value of the two operands.
-	Computes the difference between the two operands.
*	Computes the multiplication of the two operands.
/	Computes the division between the two operands.
%	Computes the modulus (remainder) of the two operands.
==	Returns True if the two operands are equivalent, False otherwise.
!=	Returns True if the two operands are not equal, False otherwise.
<=	Returns True if the operand on the left is numerically less than or equal to the operand on the right of the operator. Returns False otherwise.
<	Returns True if the operand on the left is numerically less than the operand on the right of the operator. Returns False otherwise.
=>	Returns True if the operand on the left is numerically greater than or equal to the operand on the right of the operator. Returns False otherwise.
>	Returns True if the operand on the left is numerically greater than the operand on the right of the operator. Returns False otherwise.
<=>	Returns -1 if the left operand is less than the right, +1 if is it greater than, and 0 (False) otherwise.
&&	Performs a logical AND operation. If the left operand is False, the right operand is not evaluated.
||	Performs a logical OR operation. If the left operand is True, then the right operator is not evaluated.
&	Returns the value of the two operators bitwise ANDed.
|	Returns the value of the two operators bitwise ORed.
^	Returns the value of the two operators bitwise XORed.
++	Increment operator. Increments the variable's value by 1.
--	Decrement operator. Decrements the variable's value by 1.
**	Computes the power of the left-hand value to the power of the right-hand value.
+=	Adds the value of the right-hand operand to the value of the left-hand operand.

continued on next page

continued from previous page

OPERATOR	PURPOSE
-=	Subtracts the value of the right-hand operand from the value of the left-hand operand.
*=	Multiplies the value of the left-hand operand with the value of the right-hand operand.
>>	Shifts the left operand right by the number of bits that is specified by the right operand.
<<	Shifts the left operand left by the number of bits that is specified by the right operand.
~	Performs a 1s complement of the operator. This is a unary operator.

Table 1-6 Numeric operators

When using arithmetic operators, precedence plays a large role. A general rule of thumb is to use parentheses wherever possible to force precedence. Using parentheses also helps the reader fully understand what you intend. The following example demonstrates the dangers of not using parentheses around operations.

```perl
#!/usr/local/bin/perl -w

# Get the values from the user.
print "Enter the first number : ";
my $num1 = <STDIN>; chomp $num1;
print "Enter the second number: ";
my $num2 = <STDIN>; chomp $num2;
print "Enter the third number : ";
my $num3 = <STDIN>; chomp $num3;

# Calculate:   A*B-C
my $answer = $num1 * $num2 - $num3;
print "$num1 * $num2 - $num3 = $answer \n";

# Calculate:   (A*B)-C
$answer = ($num1 * $num2) - $num3;
print "($num1 * $num2) - $num3 = $answer \n";

# Calculate:   A*(B-C)
$answer = $num1 * ($num2 - $num3);
print "$num1 * ($num2 - $num3) = $answer \n";
```

Run the above script.

```
% chap_01/howto06/bedmas.pl
```

Output

```
Enter the first number : 2
Enter the second number: 3
Enter the third number : 4
2 * 3 - 4 = 2
(2 * 3) - 4 = 2
2 * (3 - 4) = -2
```

End Output

Notice that Perl follows standard arithmetic precedence; it multiplies before it adds or subtracts. This is fine if that is what you intended. If not, you will end up with a drastically different answer. The first of the three operations performs an operation using standard precedence. As a result, the calculation performed is (A * B)

- C, which is exactly the same calculation as the second operation. The third operation performs A * (B-C), which reveals a completely different answer.

1.7 Control Statements

When talking about flow control with respect to programming languages, we are talking about the control the programmer has over the way the program behaves. Without flow control, a program will not loop, cycle, or iterate to perform repetitive tasks. This section outlines Perl's flow control statements and shows how to use them effectively. This section is broken into three subsections: conditional control statements, loop control statements, and labels.

Conditional Control Statements

There are two conditional control statements in Perl: the *if* statement and the *unless* statement. The *if* statement performs a task if the expression given to it is True. The syntax of an *if* statement is

```
if (Expression) {Code Segment}
if (Expression) {Code Segment} else {Code Segment}
if (Expression) {Code Segment} elsif {Code Segment} ... else {Code Segment}
```

The code segment can be anything from a simple line of Perl code to several hundreds of lines (yuck!). When either the *else* or *elsif* statement is used, it means if the expression given to the *if* is not True, then the respective code segment will be run. The following Perl script demonstrates the use of the *if* statement, using both the *elsif* and *else* statements.

```perl
#!/usr/local/bin/perl -w

while (<STDIN>)
{
    chomp;

    if ($_ < 10)
    {
        print "$_ is less than 10.\n";
    }
    elsif ($_ < 20)
    {
        print "$_ is between the values of 10 and 19.\n";
    }
    else
    {
        print "$_ is greater than or equal to 20.\n";
    }
}
```

Run the above script interactively and type in any number while the script is running.

```
% chap_01/howto07/if.pl
```

Output

```
10
10 is between the values of 10 and 19.
9
9 is less than 10.
11
11 is between the values of 10 and 19.
19
19 is between the values of 10 and 19.
20
20 is greater than or equal to 20.
22
22 is greater than or equal to 20.
```

End Output

The *unless* statement works the opposite of the *if* statement. The *unless* statement will only perform a task if the resultant operation is False. This is a little backwards sometimes, which is why we avoid the *unless* statement. Using the *unless* statement can make the code hard to understand. The following example outlines the use of the *unless* statement.

```
#!/usr/local/bin/perl -w

while (<STDIN>)
{
    chop;
    print "I have found what I'm looking for: <$_>\n" unless $_ ne "Gizmo";
}
```

The script is looking for the string "Gizmo"; when it finds it, it prints out a message. The whole of the intelligence is on the line

```
print "I have found what I'm looking for: <$_>\n" unless $_ ne "Gizmo";
```

The *unless* statement twists the logic so that the operation on the left side of the *unless* statement will be evaluated only if the operation on the right side evaluates to False. In the above example, the message is printed only if the variable $_ is equal to "Gizmo". Because the right side has to evaluate to False for the print statement to run, you need to check if the value is not equal to "Gizmo". When it is equal to "Gizmo", the string check evaluates to False, and the message is printed out. (Confused yet?) This is why we avoid the *unless* statement unless it lends itself to the situation, which it can. Run the above script and give it information.

```
% chap_01/howto07/unless.pl
```

Output

```
Hi There
Good morning.
Gizmo
I have found what I'm looking for: <Gizmo>
```

End Output

Loop Control Statements

Loop control statements allow you to create loops within the flow of the program. One of the most often used statements is the *for* loop. The *for* loop allows you to create a loop that will loop for a predetermined number of times. This could be anything from counting from 1 to 10 to cycling through an array and printing out the contents. An example of a *for* loop is the following script, which prints out the numbers from 1 to 10.

```
#!/usr/local/bin/perl -w

for ($x=1; $x <= 10; $x++)
{
    print $x . ", ";
}
print "\n";
```

The above example can be rewritten to list the numeric values explicitly. Modify the above script and change the lines

```
for ($x=1; $x <= 10; $x++)
{
    print $x . ", ";
}
```

to

```
for (1..10)
{
    print $_ . ", ";
}
```

The *for* loop is also used to create *infinite* loops. To create an *infinite* loop using a *for* loop, remove the loop conditions from the statement. The following example demonstrates how to create an *infinite* loop using a *for* loop.

```
#!/usr/local/bin/perl -w

for (;;)
{
    print "This is the loop that never ends, it goes on and on my
friends...\n";
}
```

The *foreach* statement is very much like the *for* loop except it iterates through list values. The following is an example of a *foreach* loop.

```
#!/usr/local/bin/perl

# Create a list of the days of the week.
@days = qw (Monday Tuesday Wednesday Thursday Friday Saturday Sunday);

# Cycle through the loop, and print out the contents.
foreach $day (@days)
{
    print "$day\n";
}
```

Run the script.

```
% chap_01/howto07/foreach.pl
```

Output

```
Monday
Tuesday
Wednesday
Thursday
Friday
Saturday
Sunday
```

End Output

In the above example, the variable *$day* is created locally to the *foreach* loop. If the variable *$day* is not specified, then $_ will be used.

The other popular control statement is the *while* loop. The *while* loop is a little different than the *for* loop in that it evaluates a conditional statement before entering the loop. The *while* loop is mainly used to create a loop that ends on a conditional statement. The following script counts from 1 to 10 using a *while* loop.

```perl
#!/usr/local/bin/perl

# Set the value of x
$x=1;

while ($x <= 10)
{
    print $x++ . ", ";
}
print "\n";
```

Run the script.

```
% chap_01/howto07/while.pl
```

Output

```
1, 2, 3, 4, 5, 6, 7, 8, 9, 10
```

End Output

Labels

Labels are used when you want to jump to a specific location within the code. This type of action is normally shunned by experienced programmers because using it can make it difficult to follow the flow of the program and it can also raise the heated discussion of the *goto* statement. Be that as it may, Perl has this ability, and it should be discussed. So far, we have not been totally honest about the true syntax of the *for*, *foreach*, and *while* statements. An optional label can be appended to these statements so jumps to their specific location can be made. Following is the true syntax of the *for*, *foreach*, and *while* statements.

```
Label while (Conditional Expression) Code Block
Label while (Conditional Expression) Code Block Continue Code Block
Label for (Expression; Expression; Expression) Code Block
Label foreach Variable (Array or List) Code Block
Label Code Block Continue
```

When a label is defined, a block has to be defined. This means that if a label is defined, then a pair of braces needs to be used to encapsulate the associated code segment. The best purpose for labels is if the program has to break out of several blocks at one time. The following example uses the last keyword to break out of nested *for* loops.

```
#!/usr/local/bin/perl -w

# Define the label name.
EXIT:
{
    # Create an infinite loop to demonstrate how last will
    # break out of multiple code blocks.
    for (;;)
    {
        my $x = 0;
        for (;;$x++)
        {
            print "$x, \n";
            last EXIT if $x >= 5;
        }
    }
}
print "Out of for loops.\n";
```

Run this script.

```
% chap_01/howto07/label.pl
```

Output

```
1, 2, 3, 4, 5,
Out of for loops.
```

End Output

1.8 Subroutines, Packages, and Modules

Subroutines, packages, and modules give programmers the ability to write modular code. A *subroutine* is a block of code that performs a specific task that can be referenced by name. *Packages* and *modules* are blocks of code that, in most cases, perform a specific task. They allow programmers to create variables under different name spaces. A name space is, effectively, where variables reside. As a default, any variables defined globally are put into the main name space. A variable in a package named "Foo" would reside under the "Foo" name space.

Subroutines

A subroutine is defined by the sub keyword and the block of code that follows. A block of code is contained with the {} characters. The syntactical definition of a Perl subroutine is

```
sub NAME { CODE }
```

where NAME is the name of the subroutine and CODE is the block of code. The following example demonstrates a subroutine declaration and calling the subroutine.

```perl
#!/usr/local/bin/perl -w

# Declare the subroutine named usage
sub usage
{
    my ($program, $exitCode) = @_;

    print "Usage: $program [-v] [-h]\n";
    exit $exitCode;
}

usage ($0, 1);
```

Run the script.

```
% chap_01/howto08/sub.pl
```

── Output ──────────────────────────────────────

```
Usage: chap_01/howto08/sub.pl [-v] [-h]
```

End Output ─────────────────────────────────────

When a subroutine is called with parameters, the parameters follow the subroutine name in list format. The example above calls the subroutine with the program name, $0, and an integer value that represents the exit value of the script. When a subroutine is called with parameters, the subroutine must somehow get the options being sent to it. This is done by using the special array @_. The line

```perl
my ($program, $exitCode) = @_;
```

creates two local variables, $program and $exitCode, from the global array @_. In Perl 4, to call a subroutine, an ampersand must proceed the subroutine name. In Perl 5, this is no longer necessary. Don't worry; this is still supported for backwards compatibility.

Packages

A package is nothing more than a separate name space for variables to reside in. The package provides a place for the programmer to hide, but not protect, private data. When a subroutine or variable is defined outside of a package, it is actually placed in the main package. To declare a package, use the package keyword. To define a package, use the syntax

```
package NAME;
```

where NAME is the name of the package. The scope of the package declaration is from the declaration to the end of the enclosing block. This means if a package is declared at the top of a script, then everything in the script is considered to be part of the package. The following example is a package named Nothing and a subroutine within the package named doNothing.

```
package Nothing;

sub doNothing
{
    print "This package does nothing!\n";
}

1;
```

The 1; is needed so that the *require* or *use* statements do not report an error when they try to include this package. If the 1; is omitted, the *require* statement returns a zero value, which is False, which also happens to be an error. To avoid this, force the package to return a nonzero value through the use of 1;. To include this package in a Perl script, use the require keyword. The following example requires the package created above and calls the subroutine declared within it.

```
#!/usr/local/bin/perl -w

# Use the package nothing.
require "Nothing.pl";

# Call the subroutine doNothing inside the package Nothing.
Nothing::doNothing();
```

Run the script.

```
% chap_01/howto08/package.pl
```

Output

```
This package does nothing!
```

End Output

As it stands, packages are being degraded by modules.

Modules

Modules are nothing more than packages with some extra frills. Modules behave the same way packages do; they hide data and subroutines and allow programmers to create portable code. Why use a module? Modules and packages do not pollute name spaces: the only time a variable gets quashed is because you, not the module, stepped on it. A module is equivalent to a constructor when you use the begin keyword and is equivalent to a destructor when you use the end keyword. Perl also has a concept of classes, which allows programmers to create objects. With the addition of classes comes methods, which means that objects can be created and methods can be defined for those objects. All in all, C++ programmers should be pleased.

Like packages, a module is defined by the package keyword; the scope of the module declaration is from the package keyword to the end of the block. The following example is a module that reads the password file and stores the account information in an object.

```perl
package Acctinfo;

# Set up internal variables.
sub new
{
    my $self = {};
    my ($loginId, $passwd, $uid, $gid, $quota);
    my ($comment, $gcos, $home, $shell);
    my $login = getlogin();

    # Get information from the passwd file.
    ($loginId, $passwd, $uid, $gid, $quota, $comment, $gcos, $home, $shell) =
getpwnam($login);

    # Store information in the object.
    $self->{'login'} = $login;
    $self->{'uid'} = $uid;
    $self->{'gid'} = $gid;
    $self->{'home'} = $home;
    $self->{'shell'} = $shell;

    # Bless this object...
    return bless $self;
}

# Return the user's login id.
sub getloginid
{
    my $self = shift;
    return $self->{'login'};
}

# Return the user's uid
sub getuid
{
    my $self = shift;
    return $self->{'uid'};
}

# Return the user's gid
sub getgid
{
    my $self = shift;
    return $self->{'gid'};
}
```

```
# Return the user's home
sub gethome
{
    my $self = shift;
    return $self->{'home'};
}

# Return the user's shell
sub getshell
{
    my $self = shift;
    return $self->{'shell'};
}

1;
```

As a convention, modules are given the extension .pm. The following example uses the module defined above and calls one of the methods defined.

```
#!/usr/local/bin/perl -w

# Use the account information module.
use Acctinfo;

# Call the new method.
my $passwordObject = new Acctinfo();

# Get the uid.
my $uid = $passwordObject->getuid();

# Print out the results.
print "UID: $uid \n";
```

Run the script

```
% chap_01/howto08/module.pl
```

Output

```
UID: 501
```

End Output

To include a Perl 5 module, use the keyword use. Notice that the .pm extension is not needed when using the use keyword. Modules are covered in greater depth in Chapter 14.

1.9 Variable Localization

To be able to create complex programs, you must be able to control variables and specify where and how long they survive. This ability is called *variable localization*.

When a variable is defined in Perl, the variable is created in the global variable name space by default. In actuality, variables are placed in the name space of the package in which they are defined. Because the default package is called main, all variables that are not specifically defined in a named package or subroutine are defined in the main package. To demonstrate this, the following example creates a global variable $myvar$ and prints out the global instance of the variable and the package-specific variable.

```perl
#!/usr/local/bin/perl -w

# Define a variable.
$myvar = "Hello";

# Print out the global variable.
print "Global   : $myvar \n";

# Print out the package specific variable.
print "Specific: $main::myvar \n";
```

Run the above script.

```
% chap_01/howto09/global.pl
```

Output

```
Global   : Hello
Specific: Hello
```
End Output

There are two keywords to localize a variable in Perl: LOCAL and MY. The local keyword is Perl 4's method of localizing a variable. Perl 5 can use both local and a new keyword, MY. The local keyword makes the variable local to the enclosed block, whereas MY totally hides the variable from the outside world. In any case, the use of MY is strongly encouraged. To demonstrate how to use MY, the following function creates a global variable named xxx and prints out the value. A function is called that defines a variable with the same name. If Perl had no concept of variable localization, then this new definition would clobber the existing value of xxx. The last print statement verifies that the global value of xxx has not been changed.

```perl
#!/usr/local/bin/perl -w

# Define a basic subroutine.
sub myFunction
{
    # Define $xxx locally within this function.
    my $xxx = 5;

    # Print out the local value of $xxx
    print "Inside the function \$xxx = $xxx \n";
}

# Set the variable $xxx
my $xxx = 1;

# Print out the global value of the variable
print "Before function \$xxx = $xxx \n";
```

```
# Call the function.
myFunction();

# Print out the global value of the variable
print "After function \$xxx = $xxx \n";
```

Run the script.

```
% chap_01/howto09/local.pl
```

```
Before function $xxx = 1
Inside the function $xxx = 5
After function $xxx = 1
```

There are some restrictions on which variables can and cannot be localized. Trying to localize the global variable $_ will not work.

1.10 Special Variables

Perl has over 50 predefined variables that are set or can be set when a Perl script is running. These variables can affect everything from the starting index in an array to the output field separator. The only problem with having so many predefined variables is that most of them are a mystery. This section outlines Perl's predefined variables. Table 1-7 provides details on the default value of the variables and a short description of what each variable does. The names of the predefined variables are cryptic; the English.pm module was created to help remove this cryptic element. The following example demonstrates how to use the English.pm module.

```
#!/usr/local/bin/perl -w

use English;

# Print out the process id using the standard variable.
print "PID          : Standard: $$ ";

# Print out the process id using the English value assigned.
print "English: $PROCESS_ID\n";

# Print out the real user ID using the standard variable.
print "Real User ID: Standard: $< ";

# Print out the real user id using the English value assigned.
print "English: $REAL_USER_ID\n";

# Print out the Perl version using the standard variable.
print "Perl Version: Standard: $] ";

# Print out the Perl version using the English value assigned.
```

continued on next page

continued from previous page

```
print "English: $PERL_VERSION\n";
```

Run the above script.

Output

```
PID            : Standard: 238 English: 238
Real User ID   : Standard: 501 English: 501
Perl Version   : Standard: 5.001 English: 5.001
```

End Output

Table 1-7 lists Perl's special variables and what they do.

VARIABLE	DEFAULT VALUE	DESCRIPTION
$_	N/A	The default input and pattern-searching space.
$digit	N/A	Contains the subpattern from a successful parentheses pattern match.
$&	N/A	The string from the last successful pattern match.
$`	N/A	The preceding string to the last successful pattern match.
$'	N/A	The string following the last successful pattern match.
$+	N/A	The last bracket matched from the last search pattern.
$*	0	Controls internal string multiline pattern matching.
$.	N/A	The current input line number of last filehandle read.
$/	\n	The input record separator.
$|	0	If set to nonzero, forces a flush of the currently selected stream after every write.
$,	N/A	The output field separator for the print command.
$"	Space	The separator that joins elements of arrays interpolated in strings.
$\	N/A	The output record separator for the print command.
$;	\034	The subscript separator for multidimensional array emulation. This special variable should be superseded by correct array emulation in Perl 5.
$#	N/A	The output format for printed numbers.
$%	N/A	The page number of the currently selected output stream.
$=	60	The page length of the currently selected output stream.
$-	N/A	The number of lines left on the current page.
$~	filehandle	The name of the current report format for the currently selected output stream.

VARIABLE	DEFAULT VALUE	DESCRIPTION
$^	filehandle	The name of the current top of page format for the currently selected output stream.
$:	\n-	The characters used to fill a continuation field.
$^L	\f	The default form feed character.
$?	N/A	The status value returned from the last system, pipe close, or backtick command.
$!	N/A	Contains the current value of errno.
$@	N/A	The Perl syntax error from the last eval statement.
$$	N/A	The process ID (PID) of the current running Perl script.
$<	N/A	The real user ID (UID) of the current running process.
$>	N/A	The effective UID of the current running process.
$(	N/A	The real group ID (GID) of the current running process.
$)	N/A	The effective GID of the current running process.
$0	N/A	The name of the file of the Perl script.
$[	0	The index of the first element of an array. This is very dangerous to change. Only use it if absolutely necessary.
$]	N/A	The string printed out when Perl is run with the -v command line option.
$^A	N/A	The accumulator for form line and write operations.
$^D	N/A	The current value of the debugging flags.
$^F	2	The maximum number of system file descriptors.
$^I	N/A	Contains the current value of the in-place editing flag.(i.e.: -i).
$^P	N/A	Internal debugging flag.
$^T	N/A	The time in which the script began running. The time is in seconds since January 1, 1970.
$^W	N/A	The current value of the warning switch.
$^X	N/A	The name of the Perl binary that was executed.
$ARGV	N/A	The name of the current file when reading from <>.

Table 1-7 Perl's special variables

Table 1-8 lists all of Perl's special arrays and what they do.

ARRAY	DESCRIPTION
@ARGV	The command line arguments issued when the script was started.
@EXPORT	The list of methods the package will export by default.
@EXPORT_OK	The list of methods the package will export by request.
@INC	The include path of directories to search looking for libraries or Perl scripts that are to be evaluated by the do command.
@ISA	The list of base classes of the package.
@_	The parameter array for subroutines.
%ENV	This associative array contains your current environment.
%INC	This associative array contains a record for each entry that has been required using do or require.
%OVERLOAD	Used to overload operators in a package.
%SIG	This associative array contains signal handlers for various signals. This is set by the programmer, so initially there are no signals trapped unless the programmer has explicitly stated them in the script.

Table 1-8 Perl's special arrays

C H A P T E R 2
CREATING PERL PROGRAMS

CREATING PERL PROGRAMS

How do I...

There is a gulf between understanding a programming language and creating working programs. Programs must be engineered so they can execute under a target operating system, understand invocation options, and conform to the standards set by other programs in that environment.

This chapter discusses how to create an executable Perl program under UNIX and DOS, how the program should obtain its arguments and options from the operating system, and how the program should patch over some of the inadequacies of Perl-unfriendly systems such as DOS.

2.1 Make My UNIX Perl Script into an Executable Program

This UNIX-oriented How-To will demonstrate how to use the #! method of invoking a script-based program.

2.2 Make My DOS Perl Script an Executable Program

This How-To will show you how to run a Perl script under the PC operating system DOS.

2.3 Make DOS Treat My Perl Script as a Real Command

DOS divides programs into two families: binary commands and scripts. Unfortunately, script-based programs are second-class citizens in the DOS world. Only binaries are allowed to interact with the operating system fully. This How-To will explain how to circumvent these limitations using a special DOS program called Pound-Bang-Perl.

2.4 Perform Consistent Command Line Parsing

The command line interface is still a powerful method of computing. Once your program is running under your chosen operating system, how do you give it the capability of understanding a set of flexible command line options? This How-To will show you how, using the Perl 5 library module Getopt::Std.

2.5 Process Complex Command Lines

This How-To will demonstrate an alternative approach to command line parsing that allows you to give options meaningful names rather than cryptic single letters. It uses the Perl 5 library module Getopt::Long.

COMPLEXITY
BEGINNING

2.1 How do I...
Make my UNIX Perl script into an executable program?

COMPATIBILITY: UNIX

Problem

I would like to invoke my Perl script as if it were an executable program. I would like Perl to launch itself automatically and interpret the script when I enter the script filename on the command line.

Technique

All modern UNIX operating systems support a notation, known as the #! (pronounced as pound-bang) notation, that automatically invokes an interpreter to evaluate a script. This means that a script can behave as an executable program. This How-To first demonstrates #! in Perl scripts and then describes a method to emulate #! on systems that don't support it.

Steps

1. Create a file named pmessage.pl with your favorite text editor.

2. Type the following Perl script and save it.

```
print "Perl message!\n";
```

3. Modify the file permissions associated with the file to make the script executable. Enter the command

```
chmod u+x pmessage.pl
```

Check that the file has execute permission with the ls -l command. You should see output similar to this:

```
-rwxrw--r--- pmessage.pl
```

The x indicates that the script has execute permission.

4. Test the script by entering the command

```
perl pmessage.pl
```

You won't be surprised to see the following output.

Output ──

Perl message!

End Output ──

5. Now edit the script. Insert the #! line as the first line of the file.

```
#!/usr/local/bin/perl
print "Perl message!\n";
```

We assume /usr/local/bin is the path to your copy of the Perl interpreter. If your version is installed elsewhere, change that line accordingly. Check Perl's location on your system with the which command if you need to.

```
which perl
/usr/bin/perl -w
```

6. Now test the script with the following command.

```
pmessage.pl
```

The script will now execute directly. You don't need to designate Perl as the script interpreter on the command line.

7. If your program needs to run on many different types of UNIX systems, including those that don't support the #! method, then some more subterfuge is required. Edit the file.

```
#!/usr/local/bin/perl
eval   "exec /usr/local/bin/perl -S $0 $*"
       if  0;
print "Perl message!\n";
```

8. Test the script both on the system that supports #! and the system that doesn't. You should see the same output in both cases.

How It Works

On systems that support #! invocation, the following occurs. When a file with executable permission is invoked from a command, UNIX examines the first 2 bytes of the file. If those bytes are #!, then the system identifies the program specified after the #! and passes the whole file to the program for interpretation. You can think of the system as a command translator. When the file script containing the first line

```
#!/path/interpreter -switches
```

is invoked as a command

```
script arg1 args2
```

then the system translates the command to

```
/path/interpreter -switches script arg1 arg2
```

On systems that don't support this method, you must use a shell to do the same work. This is how Step 7 works. The system pays no attention to the #! line and invokes the Bourne shell /bin/sh as the default interpreter. Every UNIX interpreter recognizes lines beginning with # as comments, so the Bourne shell ignores the first line. The second line is a valid Bourne shell command that performs precisely the same command translation just described. Now the Bourne shell invokes Perl as the script interpreter. Perl compiles and syntax checks the program before executing it.

The Perl syntax checker validates the second and third lines because they are both valid Bourne shell and valid Perl. Because the line appears to Perl as a conditional with a False condition (0 is always False), the syntax checker skips the line and then executes the rest of the script. We said subterfuge was needed!

The -S switch causes Perl to search for the script using the directories specified by the PATH environment variable. This avoids the need to include the script file's full path in the command.

Comments

This technique can be extended to cover the case where one script may have to execute on several different machines. The downside of the #! method is that it is not always portable. If your Perl binary is installed in /usr/bin on a Sun/Solaris machine

and in /usr/local/bin on an Alpha/OSF1, then which path do you specify after the #! ?
If you use the shell invocation discussed above, you can specify the path to your Perl
in an environment variable and ensure the script will execute on both installations.

COMPLEXITY
INTERMEDIATE

2.2 How do I...
Make my DOS Perl script an executable program?

COMPATIBILITY: DOS

Problem

I would like to run my Perl script on a DOS PC as if it were a DOS program. That
is, I would like to have my script invisibly invoke the Perl interpreter so I can type
myprog arg1 arg2 rather than c:\bin\perl myprog.pl arg1 arg2.

Technique

How-To 2.1 describes a UNIX method for invoking scripts as programs. Unfortunately,
DOS has some severe limitations in the way it treats scripts. To have DOS run your
Perl script as a program, you have to convince the operating system that the script
is a .BAT file. BAT files, such as AUTOEXEC.BAT, are lists of DOS commands. This
How-To examines some approaches for getting around these limitations and per-
suading DOS to execute your script without specifying the Perl interpreter.

Steps

In this How-To, you will use the script cat.pl. This script is a simple replacement
for the notorious DOS command TYPE.

 Enter the following code.

```
# usage: cat [-n] <files>

require "getopts.pl";
Getopts('nu');

do {print "Usage:\tcat [-u]\n\tcat [-n] <files>\n";
    exit;
} if $opt_u;

while (<>) {
    $ln++;
    printf "%4ld: ", $ln if $opt_n;
    print;
}
```

Execute the script under the Perl interpreter. Because cat.pl requires a file-name argument, run the script on itself. Type the following command.

```
perl cat.pl -n cat.pl
```

The program prints out its own text, complete with line numbering.

3. Convert the script into a program that can be directly executed by DOS. Edit the script. Insert the following lines as the first three lines of the file.

```
@REM=("
@perl %0.bat %1 %2 %3 %4 %5 %6 %7 %8 %9
@goto end ") if 0 ;
# cat4dos
# usage: cat [-n] <files>

require "getopts.pl";
Getopts('nu');

do {print "Usage:\tcat [-u]\n\tcat [-n] <files>\n";
    exit;
} if $opt_u;

while (<>) {
    $ln++;
    printf "%4ld: ", $ln if $opt_n;
    print;
}
```

The line beginning with @perl assumes PERL.EXE is on your path. It should be!

Skip over the Perl statements and add the two lines in bold to the end of the file.

```
...
while (<>) {
    $ln++;
    printf "%4ld: ", $ln if $opt_n;
    print;
}

@REM=(qq!
:end !) if 0 ;
```

4. Before you quit your editor, save the file under a new filename. Name the file CAT.BAT.

5. Now test the script with the following command.

```
cat CAT.BAT
```

The script is now directly executable without designating the interpreter on the command line.

How It Works

This technique is really a variant of the UNIX approach described in How-To 2.1. The code inserted like brackets around the Perl program fools COMMAND.COM,

(DOS's batch file interpreter) into passing the script to the Perl interpreter; at the same time, it jumps over the Perl code without trying to interpret it. It works like this. You invoke the Perl script as if it were a batch file. The batch file processor sees the first line as a comment line or remark. The second line uses the value of %0 to create the Perl command

```
perl CAT.BAT
```

This Perl script expects arguments. Up to 10 of these are substituted for the %1 ... batch file variables. The batch file interpreter then calls Perl to execute the script. To Perl, the DOS batch code appears to be valid, if rather obscure, Perl code. The first lines of the script appear to Perl to be a conditional assignment of an array where the condition is False, so the assignment is never made. Perl skips over these lines and begins executing the script proper. When it reaches the last two lines of the file, Perl sees another conditional assignment with a False condition and therefore terminates. The batch file processor resumes execution at the third line, which looks like a GOTO instruction to the label END. The batch processor jumps to the final line in the file and exits. Figure 2-1 illustrates the Perl wrapper function.

Comments

The utility commands supplied with standard DOS (and Windows-based emulators) are notoriously limited. The DOS command TYPE lists a file given as an argument. If you use a wildcard argument such as *.*, meaning the set files in the current directory, TYPE looks for a file named *.*. Most DOS users could use some better tools. Using this BAT command and Perl script in one file technique allows you to build up a set of Perl-based utilities to patch over the limitations of the DOS commands.

Windows NT and Windows 95 users are able to use the file association mechanism to have the Perl interpreter execute scripts that have .pl suffixes.

```
@ REM=("
@ perl %0.bat %1 %2 %3 %4 %5 %6 %7 %8 %9
@ goto end ") if 0 ;

#
# ... Perl Code ...
#

@ REM=(qq!
:end !) if 0 ;
```

Figure 2-1 DOS sees the Perl wrapper as a BAT file code

COMPLEXITY
INTERMEDIATE

2.3 How do I ...
Make DOS treat my Perl script as a real command?

COMPATIBILITY: | PERL 4 | PERL 5 | DOS |

Problem

Although I can embed my Perl scripts in batch files, I have problems with the limitations that MS-DOS puts on batch file commands. BAT commands can't take their input from a pipe, for example. Is there any way to make my Perl script a first-class citizen under DOS?

Technique

Although DOS supports UNIX-derived features such as pipes, STDIO, and redirection, only binary executables<197>.EXE or .COM files<197> can take advantage of them. DOS treats batch commands similarly to the VMS or CP/M operating systems, where concepts such as pipes and redirection don't exist. Under DOS, batch files are truly second-class citizens.

Fortunately, John Dollman (jgd@cix.compulink.co.uk) has created a neat little program called #!PERL.EXE (Pound-Bang-Perl) that gets around the problem. Pound-Bang-Perl provides Perl scripts with their own individual binary front end.

Steps

The first step demonstrates the problem. If you worked through How-To 2.2, you will have a .BAT program named CAT.BAT that lists files, somewhat in the manner of the UNIX program cat. If you didn't step through How-To 2.2, take the time to enter the code given in that section and save the file as cat.bat.

1. Use CAT.BAT to list itself. Issue the command

```
cat -n CAT.BAT
```

The CAT.BAT program lists out its own file with line numbering.

Suppose you want to use CAT.BAT to add line numbering to any arbitrary input. The easiest way to do that would be to use the cat command in a pipe. The command would read the input from stdin, insert a line number at the start of each line, and write the output to stdout. Sadly, this won't work under DOS. Try it.

```
type CAT.BAT | cat -n
```

The program hangs around waiting for input. The type command generates data, but DOS arranges that CAT.BAT will never see it.

To return to the DOS prompt, send CAT.BAT an end of file (hold down CTRL-Z, followed by ENTER).

2. Create a Perl program called cat1 using Pound-Bang-Perl, which is supplied on the CD. Create a copy of the binary #!PERL.EXE. This new binary will be the unique front-end program associated with the Perl script. Copy the file #!PERL.EXE to cat1.exe.

Copy #!PERL.EXE cat1.exe3. Copy the file cat.bat to the new file cat1.pl.

```
copy ex2-1.pl cat1.pl
```

3. Remove the special lines of DOS invocation code that begin and end the file.

```
@REM=("
@perl %0.bat %1 %2 %3 %4 %5 %6 %7 %8 %9
@goto end ") if 0 ;
...
@REM=(qq!
:end !) if 0 ;
```

4. Edit cat1.pl, adding the following as the first line of the file:

```
#!PERL.EXE
```

Substitute the actual location of PERL.EXE if it is not on your path. For example,

```
#!C:\BIN\PERL
```

Save the file.

5. Copy cat1.exe and cat1.pl to a directory on your path.

6. Test cat1 with the following command.

```
type CAT.BAT | cat1 -n
```

The cat program can use all the piping features of DOS.

How It Works

The program #!PERL.EXE is a front end for DOS Perl. Because it is an EXE program, DOS treats it as a "real" program, just as UNIX does with a Perl script. DOS provides it with stdin and stdout streams; when #!PERL.EXE launches the Perl interpreter, the interpreter inherits these streams and can read and write them.

#!PERL has three tasks to perform:

1. Find out its own name. If it is called cat1.exe, it attempts to locate a .pl script with the same name, cat1.pl. It searches sequentially in the following locations:

● The directory where it is installed

● In order, any directory named in the environment variables *PERLSCRIPTS, PERLLIB, PERL*
● Along the *PATH*

2. When #!PERL.EXE finds its script, it examines the first line of the file for a UNIX-style #! directive. This directive indicates the location of the Perl interpreter and may include switches to be passed to Perl.

3. #!PERL.EXE attempts to mimic the behavior of the UNIX command processors. When it finds the #! directive, it attempts to run the Perl interpreter named after the #!; otherwise, it searches for a PERL.EXE in the same locations as above. When it finds an interpreter, it executes it, passing on any options from the #! line, the script name, and any arguments given in the original command. Figure 2-2 shows how Perl executes scripts in DOS.

Comments

#!PERL provides a neat solution to many of the problems that come from writing Perl programs for DOS platforms. The .EXE file is very small; having several copies for several programs does not waste too much disk space. You are free to distribute #!PERL under the same terms that govern the distribution of the Perl kit.

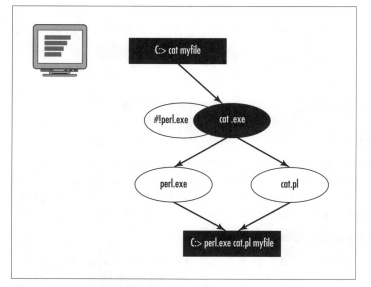

Figure 2-2 How #!PERL.EXE invokes Perl to execute a given script in DOS

COMPLEXITY
INTERMEDIATE

2.4 How do I ...
Perform consistent command line parsing?

COMPATIBILITY: UNIX DOS

Problem

I need to have a standard way of processing command line switches in my Perl scripts. The script should interpret the switches supplied on the command line and modify behavior accordingly.

For example, invoking the script with the -d switch will activate a diagnostic trace option; the -h switch will display help text; and -f with a filename immediately following will make the script read from the named file. The method should be simple, flexible, portable, and reusable.

Technique

Many programs modify their behavior in response to options specified by the user. In noninteractive programs, these options are supplied to the program as switches: the UNIX standard switch syntax is a single letter preceded by a minus sign. DOS and VMS programs commonly use the / character in place of the minus sign, with DOS using either switch inconsistently.

The user types switches at the command prompt after the name of the program. A sorting utility, for example, will normally sort its input by alphabetical order. If the same program is invoked with a -n switch, it will sort in numeric order.

For the very simplest cases, it is not hard to code a command line parser. Perl makes it easy to access the command line. The array @ARGV contains a list of the switches and arguments that the user typed at the prompt when he or she invoked the script. But what if the script attains new features during its lifetime? Then the parser must be elaborated to handle the new switches. What begins as a simple command line parser can soon become a piece of code more complex than the rest of the script.

So much for the simple case. It can be tricky (and tedious) to write code to parse and process complex sets of switches. Some commands allow multiple switches to be clustered together behind one symbol. Some switches are Boolean: They are either present or not. Other switches require arguments such as filenames or values.

One of the greatest allies of the Perl programmer is the Perl library. The library, which is part of the Perl distribution, contains many modules (self-contained units of Perl code) that take care of many common Perl programming tasks. It is no surprise then that the Perl 5 library supplies a module Getopt::Std to abstract the details of argument processing. Unless you have some very special requirements, writing elaborate switch-processing code is a waste of your time and effort. The routine Getopt::Std::getopt can simplify and standardize switch processing in even small scripts.

Steps

This script demonstrates processing a single Boolean switch. To use the getopt routine, the script must load the library file getopts.pl using the *require* statement.

 Create a new executable script called optdemo. Enter the lines of code in the listing below.

```
#!/usr/local/bin/perl -w
use 'Getopt::Std';

getopt('de');
print "Debug trace switch on\n" if $opt_d;
print "Extra debug trace switch on\n" if $opt_e;
print "No (more) switches specified\n";
```

The line beginning with *use* calls the routine getopt, supplying a quoted string as a parameter. In this case, the string contains the letters d and e. These letters will be used as Boolean switches for the script.

2. Add lines 5 through 7 and save the script as optdemo. Make it executable.

Invoke the script with various options shown below. You will see the following interaction:

 # optdemo

Output

```
No (more) switches specified
```

End Output

 # optdemo -d

Output

```
Debug trace switch on
No (more) switches specified
```

End Output

 # optdemo -e

Output

```
Extra debug trace switch on
No (more) switches specified
```

End Output

 # optdemo -x

Output

```
Unknown option: x
No (more) switches specified
```

End Output

Notice that the getopt routine issues an error message when the user invokes the program with an invalid option.

3. Edit the executable script called optdemo. This script will demonstrate processing a switch that takes an argument or parameter. The user will supply the name of a file on the command line after the -f switch.

Modify the call to getopt and replace the two following lines. Delete line 7.

```
getopt('f:');
print "Switch f set to $opt_f\n" if $opt_f;
print "No (More) switches specified\n";
```

Notice the colon in the string supplied to getopt. Think of the colon as a place marker indicating that a parameter is expected following the -f switch. Run the script again, supplying a real or fictitious filename as a parameter. You will see the following output.

```
# optdemo -f foo.bar
```

— Output —————————————————————————————————————

```
Switch f set to foo.bar
No (More) switches specified
```

— End Output ————————————————————————————————————

Getopt allows the space between the -f switch and the argument foo.bar to be optional. The user can type -ffoo.bar and the script will still work correctly. Try it.

4. Several switch characters clustered behind a single - are equivalent to the same switches supplied as individual dash-character pairs. In the following program, d and e switches take arguments. The other switches don't. Any of the Boolean switches can be clustered.

Modify the file to contain the following lines.

```
#!/usr/local/bin/perl -w
use 'Getopt::Std'

getopt('abcd:ef:');
print "Switch a is on\n" if $opt_a;
print "Switch b is on \n" if $opt_b;
print "Switch c is on \n" if $opt_c;
print "Debug switch set to $opt_d\n" if $opt_d > 5;
print "Switch e is on\n" if $opt_e;
if ($opt_f) {
   print "Cannot locate file $opt_f\n" unless -e $opt_f;
}

for $I (1..5) {
   print "Value of I is $I\n" if $opt_d;
}

print "No (more) switches specified\n";
```

5. Run the program and observe the output.

```
optdemo -cb -d 6 -f foo.bar
```

Output

```
Switch b is on
Switch c is on
Debug switch set to 6
Cannot locate file foo.bar
Value of I is 1
Value of I is 2
Value of I is 3
Value of I is 4
Value of I is 5
No (more) switches specified
```

End Output

How It Works

For each x switch specified in the parameter string, getopt defines an equivalent variable called $opt_x. Getopt sets the value of the variable to indicate whether the switch was specified on the command line.

At Step 2, switch d was associated with a variable called $opt_d. If the user specifies switch -d on the command line, then the value of $opt_d will be 1; if no switch -d is specified, $opt_d will be False. Switch e will similarly be associated with $opt_e and so on. A script can therefore easily determine whether a switch was specified by the user. All it must do is examine the value of the switch's associated variable.

At Step 4, a letter colon pair was supplied in the getopt parameter string. Such arguments are commonly filenames or a numeric value. The value of the supplied argument is then assigned to the equivalent $opt_ variable. You may supply as many or as few colon switches as you desire in the string. The order is unimportant because the sequence specified by the string does not imply that the user must follow that sequence when supplying switches.

Step 5, the last version of optdemo, demonstrates some common applications of switch processing. Each switch selects an optional function inside a Perl script.

Remember, the value of $opt_ variable tests False if the equivalent switch isn't supplied on the command line. Combining this with the postfix *if* statement provides a clean way of printing diagnostics from a program without clouding its logic. A more advanced use of this conditional diagnostic method prevents actions from being performed unless the switch variable is greater than some threshold value. See this in action with the -d switch above.

The -f switch demonstrates how the script can test user-supplied filenames for validity. The unless -e conditional tests True only where the supplied filename does not exist. The program then prints out a warning message.

Comments

The library function Getopt::Std::getopt is a lightweight solution to option processing. You can incorporate it into even simple scripts because the module contains less than 60 lines of code and so incurs little overhead. Getopt::Std::getopt does have its limits. Some programs require more sophistication in the way they parse options.

Getopt::Std::getopt cannot type-check command line arguments. Neither can it deal with optional arguments.

Probably its most noticeable limitation is that it understands only single-letter switches. Some developers believe bundles of single-letter switches are too cryptic and compromise the ease of use of their programs. It is becoming common to see programs that take full-word switches such as -file -host.

The Perl library recognizes that some programs require a power solution to switch parsing. The solution is a heavyweight alternative to Getopt::Std, Getopt::Long. The facilities offered by this module are considered in the next How-To.

COMPLEXITY
INTERMEDIATE

2.5 How do I ...
Process complex command lines?

COMPATIBILITY: UNIX DOS

Problem

I need to add command-line processing to my script. The script invocation options include

- Full word switches such as -file and -debug

- Switches that may take optional arguments and switches that must take arguments

- Switches that check the type of their arguments

Technique

How-To 2.4 mentions the limitations of Getopt::Std, the option-processing light module. This How-To shows how to use the more sophisticated facilities of the library module Getopt::Long.

Steps

1. Create a file with your text editor or take file 21-9.pl and make it executable.

2. Enter the listing below.

```perl
#!/usr/local/bin/perl -w

use Getopt::Long;

# $Getopt::Long::debug = 1;
# $Getopt::Long::autoabbrev = 1;

@optl = ("loglevel:i","file=s","trace!");
```

continued on next page

continued from previous page

```perl
die "Usage. $0 [-loglevel[<int>][-file <name>][-[no]trace]\n"
    unless GetOptions @optl;
print "Trace active\n"
    if $opt_trace;
print "No Trace\n"
    unless $opt_trace;
print "Log file is $opt_file\n"
    if $opt_file;
print "Loglevel value $opt_loglevel\n"
    if $opt_loglevel > 0;
```

3. Test the program with several options arguments. Try the following.

21-9.pl -trace
```
Trace active
```

21-9.pl -notrace
```
No Trace
$: 21-9.pl
No Trace
```

21-9.pl -file foo
```
No Trace
Log file is foo
```

21-9.pl -file
```
Option file requires an argument
Usage. 21-9.pl [-loglevel [<int>] [-file <name>] [-trace|-notrace]
```

21-9.pl -loglevel 3
```
No Trace
Loglevel value 3
```

4. Remove the comment symbol from the beginning of line six so that it reads

```perl
$Getopt::Long::autoabbrev = 1;
```

Test the program with abbreviated switches.

$: 21-9.pl -l 3 -f foo -t

─ Output ├───

```
Trace active
Log file is foo
Loglevel value 3
```
─ End Output ├──

The entire output on an Emacs screen can be seen in Figure 2-3.

How It Works

GetOptions adds a number of new features (see Table 2-1) to the option processing methods discussed in How To 2.4. There are three main differences:

    GetOptions accepts long option names.

```
alpha% longopt.pl -trace
Trace active
alpha% longopt.pl -notrace
No Trace
alpha% longopt.pl -file foo
No Trace
Log file is foo
alpha% longopt.pl -file
Option file requires an argument
Usage. longopt.pl [-loglevel[<int>]][-file <name>][-[no]trace]
alpha% longopt.pl -loglevel 3
No Trace
Loglevel value 3
alpha%
alpha%
```

Figure 2-3 Emacs output of longopt.pl

- GetOptions accepts options with optional arguments. They may, and only may, take arguments.

- GetOptions type-checks arguments if a type specification is present in the configuration string.

ARGUMENT	TYPE SPECIFICATION
=s	Takes a mandatory string argument.
:s	Takes an optional string argument.
=i	Takes a mandatory integer argument.
:i	Takes an optional integer argument.
=f	Takes a mandatory real number argument.
:f	Takes an optional real number argument.
!	May be negated with "no." No argument.

Table 2-1 Summary of GetOptions arguments

GetOptions responds to erroneous command arguments by printing an explanatory error message on STDERR and returning a nonzero value. The line below shows how to trap an error and print out a usage message.

```
die "Usage. $0 [-loglevel[<int>][-file <name>][-[no]trace]\n"
    unless GetOptions @optl;
```

Comments

How do you choose between Getopt::Std and Getopt::Long? If you need simple switch processing, or you want to be able to bundle switches, or your target computer is slow enough that minimizing start-up time is a priority, then use Getopt::Std. Getopt::Long contains four times as much code.

Some features to note:

- If the variable *$Getopt::Long::autoabbrev* is set, which it is by default, then you don't need to supply the full spelling of each option name. Unique abbreviations will be accepted.

- By default, Getopt::Long options are case-insensitive. Set *$Getopt::Long::ignorecase* to 1 if you want options such as -file and -File to be indistinguishable.

CHAPTER 3
FILE MANIPULATION

FILE MANIPULATION

How do I...

3.15   Determine the page count of a file?

3.16   Randomly access a file?

3.17   Get new data from a growing file?

The How-To's in this chapter demonstrate Perl's ability to manipulate and modify files and directories. In addition to standard shell programming, Perl has the ability to read in a file, manipulate the contents, and save the information to a new file. Perl also has the ability to query files for statistical information, something most shell programming currently cannot do easily. File manipulation in Perl is one of the most important topics.

3.1   Check If a File Exists

One of the most basic yet important pieces of knowledge is how to look for a file. This How-To will demonstrate how to determine if a file exists and many other file check operations.

3.2   Read from a File

Knowing how to scan through a file or read the contents of the file is something that is performed in almost every Perl script. This How-To will show you how to do this.

3.3   Write to a File

Like the other tasks in this chapter, writing to a file is a fundamental piece of knowledge. This How-To will show you how to read in a file and write out a modified version of the information.

3.4   Append to an Existing File

When writing to a file such as a common log file, you need to append new information to the end of the file. Normally, a new file is created or an existing file is overwritten when you open a file. This How-To will demonstrate how to append information to the end of a file.

3.5   Delete a File

Many Perl scripts create temporary files that should be removed when the script ends. This How-To will show how to remove a file from a Perl script using native Perl functions.

3.6   Determine a File's Permissions

A common task is checking if a file has correct permissions. This How-To will demonstrate how to do this.

3.7   Change a File's Permissions

This How-To is not as straightforward as it first seems. This How-To will show how to change a file's octal permissions from within a Perl script.

3.8   Get the Basename of a File

The basename of a file is the singular filename of a complete path. This How-To will outline a script that strips a given pathname and returns the filename at the end of the path.

3.9   Get the Dirname from a Filename

The dirname of a filename is the path of a given pathname. This How-To will outline a script that returns the path of a given pathname.

3.10   List All the Files in a Directory

Listing all the files is one of the most common tasks performed on a directory. This How-To will demonstrate how to do this using filename globbing.

3.11   Determine the Contents of a Directory Tree

This How-To will demonstrate how to create a list of all the files under a given directory tree.

3.12   Create a Directory Tree

This How-To will demonstrate a useful module that is shipped with Perl 5. The module, File::Path, has a couple of subroutines that assist in the creation and deletion of directory trees. This How-To will show how to create a directory tree in a Perl script.

3.13   Remove a Directory Tree

This How-To will demonstrate how to remove the directory tree created in How-To 3.12.

3.14   Rename a Group of Files with a Common Extension

More often than not, renaming a group of files with a common extension is performed by hand. This How-To will outline a script that performs this tedious task on any set of files with any extension.

3.15   Determine the Page Count of a File

The script that will be presented in this How-To is a good script to have if you pay for your printing. This How-To will outline a small script that returns the number of printed pages a file will generate.

3.16   Randomly Access a File

Perl allows more than just sequential access to flat text files. The Perl script demonstrated in this How-To takes the words of Larry Wall and mutates them.

3.17   Get New Data from a Growing File

Getting data from a growing file is more popularly known as *doing a tail -f*. If the UNIX command tail is run with the option *-f*, then the tail will display any new information added to the file. This How-To will show you how to do this.

Most of the How-To's presented in this chapter have a Perl 5 compatibility. The scripts that use only the GetOpts::Long module can be easily converted to Perl 4 if you use the Perl 4 getopts.pl library instead. A script that uses any other module is strictly a Perl 5 script.

COMPLEXITY
BEGINNING

3.1 How do I...
Check if a file exists?

COMPATIBILITY: PERL 5   UNIX

Problem

I need to check to see if a file exists before I do anything to it. How do I do this in Perl?

Technique

The script accepts a filename from the command line; using the *-f* file test operator, the script determines if the file exists. Perl has file test operators to test anything from the existence of a file to a file's permissions. Table 3-1 lists all the file test operators and what they test.

OPERATOR	DESCRIPTION
-A	Age of file in days from the last access time.
-B	Checks if the file is a binary file.
-C	Age of file in days from the last inode change.
-M	Age of file in days when script started.
-O	Checks if the file is owned by the real user ID (UID).
-R	Checks if the file is readable by real UID or group ID (GID).
-S	Checks if the file is a socket.
-T	Checks if the file is a text file.
-W	Checks if the file is writable by real UID or GID.
-X	Checks if the file is executable by real UID or GID.
-b	Checks if the file is a block special file.
-c	Checks if the file is a character special file.
-d	Checks if the file is a directory.
-e	Checks if the file exists.
-f	Checks if the file is a plain file.
-g	Checks if the file has setgid bit set.
-k	Checks if the file has sticky bit set.

OPERATOR	DESCRIPTION
-l	Checks if the file is a symbolic link.
-o	Checks if the file is owned by effective UID.
-p	Checks if the file is a named pipe.
-r	Checks if the file is readable by effective UID or GID.
-s	Checks if the file has nonzero size and returns the size of the file.
-t	Checks if the filehandle is opened to a TTY.
-u	Checks if the file has setuid bit set.
-w	Checks if the file is writable by effective UID or GID.
-x	Checks if the file is executable by effective UID or GID.
-z	Checks if the file has zero size.

Table 3-1 File test operators

Steps

This How-To demonstrates one of the file check operators listed in Table 3-1. This is accomplished by using an *if* statement and a file check operator.

1. Create a new file called chkfile.pl and enter the following script into it.

```
#!/usr/local/bin/perl -w

# Purpose
#    Determines if a file exists.

use Getopt::Long;

# Set up the command line to accept a filename.
my $ret = GetOptions ("f|filename:s");
my $filename = $opt_f || die "Usage: $0 -f filename\n";

# Check if the file exists
if (-e $filename)
{
    print "The file $filename exists.\n";
}
else
{
    print "The file $filename does not exist.\n";
}
```

2. Run the script with a file that exists.

```
% chkfile.pl -f /etc/passwd
```

Output

```
The file /etc/passwd exists.
```

End Output

3. Run the script with a file that does not exist.

```
% chkfile.pl -f /etc/nonexistentfile
```

Output

```
The file /etc/nonexistentfile does not exist.
```
End Output

How It Works

The *if* statement

```
if (-e $filename)
```

returns True if the file specified by the variable *$filename* exists. If so, then the message stating the file has been found is printed on the screen.

Comments

The file test operator *-s* returns the size of the requested file.

COMPLEXITY
BEGINNING

3.2   How do I...
Read from a file?

COMPATIBILITY: PERL 5   UNIX

Problem

I need to be able to open a file and read the contents. How do I do this?

Technique

Use the open command in Perl to open the file. The syntax of the open command is

```
open (FILEHANDLE, EXPRESSION)
```

The FILEHANDLE is the filehandle that is returned from the open command. This allows you to read from and write to the actual file. The EXPRESSION is an expression and the name of the file to open. Several expressions tell Perl to open the file for reading or writing. Table 3-2 is an outline of the open command and legal expressions and their effects.

EXPRESSION	EFFECT
open (FH, "<filename")	Opens filename for reading.
open (FH, "+<filename")	Opens filename for both reading and writing.
open (FH, ">filename")	Opens filename for writing.

EXPRESSION	EFFECT
open (FH, "+>filename")	Opens filename for both reading and writing.
open (FH, ">>filename")	Appends to filename.
open (FH, "command|")	Runs the command and pipes its output to the filehandle.
open (FH, "|command")	Pipes the output along the filehandle to the command.
open (FH, "-")	Opens STDIN.
open (FH, ">-")	Opens STDOUT.
open (FH, "<&=N")	Where N is a number, this performs the equivalent of C's fdopen for reading.
open (FH, ">&=N")	Where N is a number, this performs the equivalent of C's fdopen for writing.

Table 3-2 Open command expressions

There is no need to check whether the file exists before opening because open will return an error if the file could not be opened. Once the file has been opened, read from the file descriptor created.

Steps

The script in the How-To opens a file using Perl's open command.

1. Create a new file called openfile.pl and enter the following script into it.

```perl
#!/usr/local/bin/perl -w

# Purpose
#    Reads from a file.

use Getopt::Long;

# Set up the command line to accept a filename.
my $ret = GetOptions ("f|filename:s");
my $filename = $opt_f || die "Usage: $0 -f filename\n";

# Open the file.
open (INPUT, "$filename") || die "Could not open file $filename : $!\n";

# Start reading from the file.
while (<INPUT>)
{
    chop;
    print "Line $. = <$_>\n";
}

# Close the file
close (INPUT);
```

2. Run the script with the following example input.

```
% openfile.pl -f openfile.pl
```

```
Line 1 = <#!/usr/local/bin/perl -w>
Line 2 = <>
Line 3 = <# Purpose>
Line 4 = <# Reads from a file.>
Line 5 = <>
Line 6 = <use Getopt::Long;>
Line 7 = <>
Line 8 = <# Set up the command line to accept a filename.>
Line 9 = <my $ret = GetOptions ("f|filename:s");>
Line 10 = <my $filename = $opt_f || die "Usage: $0 -f filename\n";>
Line 11 = <>
Line 12 = <# Open the file.>
Line 13 = <open (INPUT, "$filename") || die "Could not open file $filename
: $!\n";>
Line 14 = <>
Line 15 = <# Start reading from the file.>
Line 16 = <while (<INPUT>)>
Line 17 = <{>
Line 18 = <    chop;>
Line 19 = <    print "Line $. = <$_>\n";>
Line 20 = <}>
Line 21 = <>
Line 22 = <# Close the file>
Line 23 = <close (INPUT);>
```

How It Works

The open command opens the file specified by the variable *$filename*. There is no need to check to see whether the file exists; the open command will do this. Notice that there is a die command logically ORed after the open command. Perl borrows this syntax from the Bourne shell so commands or variables can be assigned or run given the success of the previous command. For example, the command

```
open (INPUT, "$filename") || die "Error: ($filename) $!\n";
```

tries to open the file specified in the variable *$filename*. If the file can be opened, not just found, then the open is successful and the program continues to the next line in the script. If the open fails, then the die command is run. This behavior is specified by the double pipe symbol (||), which is a logical OR. The format of the logical OR is A || B; this states that if A is True, then ignore B; otherwise, run B. In this case, it means if the open fails, run the die command and inform the user that the file could not be opened. The special variable *$!* contains information about the failure of the open.

Comments

As in any logical statement, the OR chain can be extended to include as many statements as possible. So it is possible to have A || B || C || D || E, where E would run only if A, B, C, and D were all False.

COMPLEXITY
BEGINNING

3.3 How do I...
Write to a file?

COMPATIBILITY: PERL 5 | UNIX

Problem

I need to open a file to store information from a Perl script, but I don't know how to do it. How do you open a file for writing?

Technique

Using the same open command from the last section, you will add in a modifier in the expression field so you can write to the file. To open a file for writing, use either one greater-than sign (>), two greater-than signs (>>), or the plus sign (+) in combination with > or <. The following line of Perl code opens a file for writing.

```perl
open (FH, ">testfile.txt");
```

This command will create the file if it does not already exist. If the file does exist, then the file is emptied of its information.

The following line of Perl code opens a file for writing. If the given file exists, then this method will write to the end of the existing file.

```perl
open (FH, ">>testfile.txt");
```

The last of the three methods mentioned opens a file for both reading and writing using the plus expression.

```perl
open (FH, "+>testfile.txt");
```

Steps

The script in this How-To opens a file for reading and opens a file for writing. The input file is read and written to the output file. When done, both files are closed.

1. Create a new file called write.pl and enter the following script into it.

```perl
#!/usr/local/bin/perl -w

# Purpose
#    Writes to a file.

use Getopt::Long;

# Set up the command line to accept a filename.
my $ret = GetOptions ("i|input:s", "o|output:s");
my $input = $opt_i || die "Usage: $0 -i Input filename -o Output filename\n";
my $output = $opt_o || die "Usage: $0 -i Input filename -o Output filename\n";
```

continued on next page

continued from previous page

```perl
# Open the input file.
open (INPUT, "$input") || die "Could not open file $input : $!\n";

# Open the output file.
open (OUTPUT, ">$output") || die "Could not open file $output : $!\n";

# Start reading from the input file.
while (<INPUT>)
{
    chop;

    # Write to the output filename.
    print OUTPUT "Line $. = <$_>\n";
}

# Close the files.
close (INPUT);
close (OUTPUT);
```

2. Run the script with the following input.

```
% write.pl -i write.pl -o write.out
```

3. Inspect the file write.out.

```
% cat write.out
```

Output

```
Line 1 = <#!/usr/local/bin/perl -w>
Line 2 = <>
Line 3 = <use Getopt::Long;>
Line 4 = <>
Line 5 = <# Set up the command line to accept a filename.>
Line 6 = <my $ret = GetOptions ("i|input:s", "o|output:s");>
Line 7 = <my $input = $opt_i || die "Usage: $0 -i Input filename -o Output
filename\n";>
Line 8 = <my $output = $opt_o || die "Usage: $0 -i Input filename -o Output
filename\n";>
Line 9 = <>
Line 10 = <# Open the input file.>
Line 11 = <open (INPUT, "$input") || die "Could not open file $input :
$!\n";>
Line 12 = <>
Line 13 = <# Open the output file.>
Line 14 = <open (OUTPUT, ">$output") || die "Could not open file $output :
$!\n";>
Line 15 = <>
Line 16 = <# Start reading from the input file.>
Line 17 = <while (<INPUT>)>
Line 18 = <{>
Line 19 = <    chop;>
Line 20 = <>
Line 21 = <    # Write to the output filename.>
Line 22 = <    print OUTPUT "Line $. = <$_>\n";>
Line 23 = <}>
Line 24 = <>
Line 25 = <# Close the files.>
```

```
Line 26 = <close (INPUT);>
Line 27 = <close (OUTPUT);>
```
End Output

How It Works

All this script does is read in a file and write it out to a new file with some extra information tagged onto each line. Writing to the file takes place on the line

```
print OUTPUT "Line $. = <$_>\n";
```

which writes the information taken from the input file and adds the prefix Line XXXX = to each line. The variable $. is an internal Perl variable that holds the current line number of the last filehandle read.

Comments

There are quite a few modifiers that can be put in the expression field of the open command to perform different tasks.

COMPLEXITY
BEGINNING

3.4   How do I...
Append to an existing file?

COMPATIBILITY: PERL 5   UNIX

Problem

I want my Perl script to write information to a file, but I don't want the file to be erased each time it does. How do I do this?

Technique

The Perl open command can take a number of expressions that allow you to open the file a number of different ways. One way is to append to an existing file. The syntax needed to append to a file is

```
open (INPUT, ">>testfile.txt");
```

This script tries to open the file testfile.txt. If the file exists, subsequent writes to the file will be appended to the end of the existing contents.

Steps

This script is a modification of the script in How-To 3.3. The open call changes, but nothing else.

1. Make a copy of the script from How-To 3.3 and call it append.pl.

```
% cp chap_03/howto03/write.pl chap_03/howto04/append.pl
```

2. Edit append.pl and modify it. The final script is listed below with the changes highlighted in bold.

```perl
#!/usr/local/bin/perl -w

# Purpose
#    Appends to a file.

use Getopt::Long;

# Set up the command line to accept a filename.
my $ret = GetOptions ("i|input:s", "o|output:s");
my $input = $opt_i || die "Usage: $0 -i Input filename -o Output⇒
filename\n";
my $output = $opt_o || die "Usage: $0 -i Input filename -o Output filename\n";

# Open the input file.
open (INPUT, "$input") || die "Could not open file $input : $!\n";

# Open the output file.
open (OUTPUT, ">>$output") || die "Could not open file $output : $!\n";

# Start reading from the input file.
while (<INPUT>)
{
   chomp;
# Write to the output filename.
   print OUTPUT "Line $. = <$_>\n";
}

# Close the files.
close (INPUT);
close (OUTPUT);
```

3. Create a text file named input1.txt and add the following text to it.

```
This is the original file
in its full length.
```

4. Copy input1.txt to input2.txt.

```
% cp input1.txt input2.txt
```

5. Run the above script with the following input.

```
% append.pl -i input1.txt -o input2.txt
```

6. Look at the file input2.txt.

```
% cat input2.txt
```

Output

```
This is the original file
in its full length.
```

```
Line 0 = <This is the original file>
Line 1 = <in its full length.>
```

End Output

How It Works

The difference between the script in How-To 3.3 and this script is the line

```
open (OUTPUT, ">>$output") || die "Error: ($output) $!\n";
```

The double greater-than sign opens the file in append mode. This means if the file exists when the file opens, then the file is appended to. The open command will not succeed if the user has no permissions to open the file.

Comments

The output file does not have to exist when appending to a file. If it does not exist, it will be created.

COMPLEXITY
BEGINNING

3.5   How do I...
Delete a file?

COMPATIBILITY: PERL 5   UNIX

Problem

I created a temporary file in my Perl script, and I want the script to clean up after itself before it exits. How do I delete a file in Perl?

Technique

The script uses the Perl function unlink. The syntax of the unlink function is as follows.

```
$count = unlink (LIST);
```

The LIST is a list of files to be deleted; $count is a count of the number of files deleted. Perl's unlink function is the same as the standard C unlink function.

Steps

The script accepts a filename from the command line and tries to delete it using unlink. A file check is performed to make sure the file exists before trying to unlink it.

1. Edit a new file named delete.pl and enter the following script into it.

```
#!/usr/local/bin/perl -w
```

continued on next page

continued from previous page

```
# Purpose
#    Deletes a file.

use Getopt::Long;

# Set up the command line to accept a filename.
my $ret = GetOptions ("f|filename:s");
my $filename = $opt_f || die "Usage: $0 -f filename\n";

# Check if the file exists
if (-e $filename)
{
    # Delete the file.
    if (unlink ($filename))
    {
        print "The file $filename has been deleted.\n";
    }
    else
    {
        print "The file $filename was not deleted: $!\n";
    }
}
else
{
    print "The file $filename does not exist.\n";
}
```

2. Create an empty file named empty.

```
% touch empty
```

3. Get a listing of the current directory.

```
$ ls -l
```

Output

```
-rwxr-xr-x    1 glover    users           408 Oct  3 18:33 delete.pl
-rw-r--r--    1 glover    users             0 Oct  6 19:31 empty
```

End Output

4. Run the above script with the following input.

```
% chap_03/howto05/delete.pl -f empty
```

5. Get a listing of the current directory.

```
$ ls -l
```

Output

```
-rwxr-xr-x    1 glover    users           408 Oct  3 18:33 delete.pl
```

End Output

How It Works

The file is first checked for with the *if* statement. The *if* statement checks only if the file exists, not if the file can be deleted. The call to unlink tries to delete the file. The unlink function returns a True value if the file can be deleted, False otherwise. If the file cannot be deleted, the special variable *!$* contains detailed information about why the unlink call fails.

Comments

The *if* statement really isn't needed because if the file does not exist before you try to delete the file, unlink will fail.

COMPLEXITY
BEGINNING

3.6 How do I...
Determine a file's permissions?

COMPATIBILITY: PERL 5   UNIX

Problem

I need more detailed information about a file. I need the actual octal permission bits so I can see the permissions of the file. How do I do this?

Technique

UNIX operating systems use a system of octal-based permission bits to set read, write, and execute permissions of individual files. Each file has 12 bits that determine who can do what to the file. Figure 3-1 outlines the permission bits.

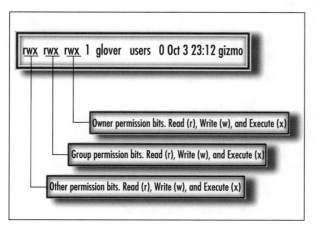

Figure 3-1 Permission bits

The permission bits are grouped into three groups: user, group, and other. Each permission group has 3 bits: read, write, and execute. These bits grant access to the user, the user's group, or the world for read, write, or execute access. Each bit group can be represented by an octal value because each bit in each group has an assigned value. For example, read has a value of 4, write has a value of 2, and execute has a value of 1. To translate the permissions bits to an octal value, add up all the values of the permission bits for each group. Table 3-3 outlines sample permission bits and their octal value.

PERMISSION BITS	OCTAL EQUIVALENT	
-rwx———	0700	
-rw-rw-rw-	0666	
-rwxrw———	0760	
-rw-r——r—	0644	
-rw——w——w-	0622	

Table 3-3 Sample permission bits

This example uses the stat function, which returns a 13-element array; 1 element is the permission mode of the given file. The syntax of the stat command is

```
($dev, $ino, $mode, $nlink, $uid, $gid, $rdev, $size, $atime, $mtime,
$ctime, $blksize, $blocks) = stat ($filename):
```

Table 3-4 lists the elements returned from the stat command in their respective order.

ELEMENT	DESCRIPTION	
dev	ID of device containing a directory entry for this file.	
ino	Inode number.	
mode	File permission mode.	
nlink	Number of links.	
uid	User ID of the file's owner.	
gid	Group ID of the file's group.	
rdev	ID of device. This is defined only for character of block special files.	
size	File size in bytes.	
atime	Time of last access in seconds since the epoch.	
mtime	Time of last modification in seconds since the epoch.	
ctime	Time of last status change in seconds since the epoch.	
blksize	Preferred I/O block size. Valid only on BSD type systems.	
blocks	Number of blocks allocated for file. Valid only on BSD systems.	

Table 3-4 File statistics returned from the stat command

The permission mode returned is in base two (binary) and you need to print it out in base eight. To do this, the printf command will be used, and the format argument %o will be used to print the permissions out in an octal format.

Steps

This script takes the name of a file and runs the stat command on it. Taking the file mode returned from the stat command, the script then displays the octal permissions of the file.

1. Create a new file called chkmode.pl and enter the following script into it.

```
#!/usr/local/bin/perl -w

# Purpose
#    Checks the permissions of a file.

use Getopt::Long;

# Set up the command line to accept a filename.
my $ret = GetOptions ("f|filename:s");
my $filename = $opt_f || die "Usage: $0 -f filename\n";

# Check if the file exists
if (! -e $filename)
{
    print "The file $filename does not exist.\n";
    exit;
}

# Perform a stat on the file.
my $perms = (stat ($filename))[2] & 07777;
printf "The octal permissions of the file $filename are %o\n", $perms;
```

2. Determine the permissions of a known file.

```
% ls -l gizmo
```

Output
```
-rw-r--r--   1 glover    users         0 Oct  3 19:53 gizmo
```
End Output

3. Run the above script with the filename of the file that was inspected.

```
% chkmode.pl -f gizmo
```

Output
```
The octal permissions of the file gizmo are 644
```
End Output

How It Works

Almost all the work is performed on the line

```
my $perms = (stat ($filename))[2] & 07777;
```

This line runs the stat command on the file specified by the variable *$filename*. You need only the third element of the stat command, so the stat command is wrapped in parentheses and the mode value is extracted from this. This is done by the segment (stat ($filename))[2]. This value is then bitwise ANDed with a mask of 07777. This strips off any extra information that stat may have returned. The command

```
my $perms = (stat ($filename))[2] & 07777;
```

runs the stat command on the file represented by *$filename*; the file mode is extracted and masked with 07777.

To print the permission bit as an octal value, the printf command is used with the option %o, which prints out a base eight value.

Comments

The permissions outlined in this How-To are strictly UNIX file-based permission bits.

COMPLEXITY
BEGINNING

3.7   How do I...
Change a file's permissions?

COMPATIBILITY: PERL 5   UNIX

Problem

I need to change a file's permission bits from inside a Perl script. I've been told that the chmod function changes a file's permission bits, but I can't seem to get the chmod function to work correctly. Why not?

Technique

Perl has a chmod function built into it to perform permission modifications. The chmod function takes a new file mode, a list of files, and returns the number of files successfully modified. The syntax is as follows:

```
$count = chmod $mode, LIST
```

A common problem is that people are familiar with permissions in base eight representation, not base ten. So the value given needs to be converted from base eight representation to base ten representation. Before you pass along the permission value to the chmod function, you need to convert the base; this is done with the oct function. The oct function takes a value, assumed to be in base eight, and returns the base ten equivalent value. Then you call the chmod function with the base ten equivalent value. If you do not understand UNIX octal-based file permissions, How-To 3.6 presents a basic discussion of them.

Steps

The script accepts a filename and an octal permission mode from the command line. The octal permission value is converted using the oct function; chmod is then called with the filename and the base ten representation of the octal permission.

1. Create a new file called chmod.pl and enter the following script into it.

```perl
#!/usr/local/bin/perl -w

# Purpose
#    Changes a files permissions.

use Getopt::Long;

# Set up the command line to accept a filename.
my $ret = GetOptions ("f|filename:s", "p|permission:s");
my $filename = $opt_f || die "Usage: $0 -f filename -p Permission\n";
my $newPerm = $opt_p || die "Usage: $0 -f filename -p Permission\n";

# Does the file exist?
if (! -e $filename)
{
    print "The file $filename does not exist.\n";
    exit;
}

# Translate the string mode to an octal value
my $mode = oct($newPerm);

# Change the permissions of the file.
if ((chmod $mode, $filename) != 1)
{
    print "Error: Could not change permissions on $filename : $!\n";
}
```

2. Create an empty file.

```
% touch gizmo
```

3. Check the new file's permissions.

```
% ls -l gizmo
```

Output

```
-rw-r--r--   1 glover   users            0 Oct  3 23:12 gizmo
```

End Output

4. Run the above script with the name of the empty file and the octal permissions.

```
% chmod.pl -f gizmo -p 0777
```

5. List the file's permissions.

```
% ls -l gizmo
```

Output

```
-rwxrwxrwx   1 glover   users           0 Oct  3 23:12 gizmo
```

End Output

How It Works

The script assumes that the permission mode will be given in the standard octal format. The base ten equivalent value is determined by calling the oct function in the following line.

```
$mode = oct($newPerm);
```

The oct function takes an assumed octal value, like the permission mode, and returns the equivalent base ten value. Changing the permission of the file is simply a matter of calling the chmod function with the filename and the base ten equivalent permission.

```
$count = chmod $mode, $filename;
```

Comments

The chmod function returns a scalar value representing the number of files that were successfully changed.

COMPLEXITY
BEGINNING

3.8 How do I...
Get the basename of a file?

COMPATIBILITY: PERL 5   UNIX   DOS

Problem

I want to get the filename from a complete pathname. How do I do this?

Technique

An absolute filename can be broken into two distinctive parts: the dirname and the basename. The dirname is the path to the file while the basename is the filename. Figure 3-2 outlines the basename and dirname of a filename.

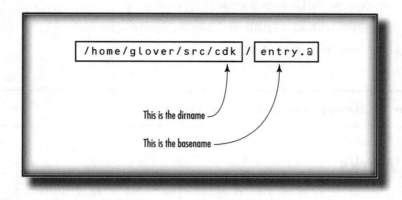

Figure 3-2 The two parts of a filename

A new module is provided with Perl 5 called File::Basename.pm. This module has a subroutine called basename that takes a pathname and returns the filename from the given path.

```
$base = basename($filename, $extension);
```

The $extension value is the extension of the file, which can be stripped from the filename. If you were to run the basename function with the following parameters, you would get the answer below. You will use this module to return the basename of a given path.

Steps

The script accepts a pathname from the command line and returns the basename of the given pathname using the File::Basename subroutine basename.

1. Create a new file called basename.pl and enter the following script into it.

```
#!/usr/local/bin/perl -w

# Purpose
#     Takes an absolute pathname and returns the basename of the filename.

use File::Basename;
use Getopt::Long;

# Set up the command line to accept a filename.
my $ret = GetOptions ("f|filename:s");
my $filename = $opt_f || die "Usage: $0 -f filename\n";

# Return the basename of the given filename.
my $base = basename($filename, "");
```

continued on next page

continued from previous page
```
print "The basename of $filename is $base\n";
```

2. Run the script with a long pathname, like the following input.

```
% basename.pl -f /home/glover/testfile
```

Output

```
The basename of /home/glover/testfile is testfile
```
End Output

How It Works

The basename function acts like the Free Software Foundation (FSF) basename command. The FSF basename command accepts a pathname and an optional extension and strips off the complete pathname and the extension. The Perl basename function requires the same two arguments. In the example above, the extension is passed as an empty string. Not passing an extension preserves the filename.

Comments

The File::Basename.pm module works on DOS, VMS, Mac, and UNIX platforms.

COMPLEXITY
BEGINNING

3.9 How do I...
Get the dirname from a filename?

COMPATIBILITY: PERL 5   UNIX   DOS

Problem

I have a pathname to a file and I need to split off the pathname from the filename. How do I do this?

Technique

This script is very similar to that of How-To 3.8. This script uses the File::Basename module to strip the pathname and return the complete path. This module has a function named dirname that accepts a pathname and returns the full path to the file. Following is a typical call to the dirname function.

```
$name = dirname ("/home/glover/waite/chap_03/howto09/dirname.pl");
```

The value of /home/glover/waite/chap_03/howto09 is stored in the variable *$name*.

Steps

This script accepts a pathname from the command line and returns the path of the given pathname. When the pathname is determined, the pathname is passed to the dirname function and the result is printed out.

 Make a copy of the file chap_03/howto08/basename.pl and copy it to the file chap_03/howto09/dirname.pl.

Change the lines

```
my $base = basename($filename, "");
print "The basename of $filename is $base\n";
```

to

```
my $dirname = dirname($filename);
print "The directory name of $filename is $dirname\n";
```

2. Here is the modified script with the changes in bold.

```
#!/usr/local/bin/perl -w

# Purpose
#   Takes an absolute pathname and returns the dirname of the filename.

use File::Basename;
use Getopt::Long;

# Set up the command line to accept a filename.
my $ret = GetOptions ("f|filename:s");
my $filename = $opt_f || die "Usage: $0 -f filename\n";

# Return the dirname of the given filename.
my $dirname = dirname($filename);
print "The directory name of $filename is $dirname\n";
```

3. Run this script with the following input.

```
% dirname.pl -f /home/glover/testfile
```

Output

```
The directory name of /home/glover/testfile is /home/glover
```
End Output

How It Works

All the work is actually performed in the File::Basename module. The pathname is stripped apart and everything but the filename is returned.

Comments

The File::Basename module also has a function called fileparse that takes a full pathname and returns both the pathname and the filename.

3.10 How do I...
List all the files in a directory?

COMPATIBILITY: PERL 4   PERL 5   UNIX   DOS

Problem

I need to know which files are in the current directory. How do I do this?

Technique

The script in this example uses file globbing within the Perl script. *Globbing* is when a wildcard character is used to match a set of filenames. Globbing is typically used when a person performs a typical directory listing. The following example uses the asterisk character to glob all files that end in .pl.

```
% ls *.pl
file1.pl file2.pl file3.pl
```

The globbing is performed by the Perl function appropriately named glob. The glob function takes the globbed expression and returns a list of all the files that match the glob. The syntax of the glob command is

```
@list = glob (EXPR);
```

The Perl script uses a wildcard character to generate a listing of all the files in the current directory.

Steps

This script uses file globbing to list all the files in the current directory. For each file found, the script prints out the filename.

1. Create a new file called listdir.pl and enter the following script into it.

```
#!/usr/local/bin/perl -w

# Purpose
#    Lists all the files in the current directory.

while (glob("*"))
{
    print "File: $_\n";
}
```

2. Run the script.

```
% listdir.pl
```

Output

```
File: aaa
File: bbb
File: ccc
File: ddd
File: eee
File: fff
File: ggg
File: listdir.pl
```

End Output

How It Works

The glob function takes an expression to match to files and returns a list of files. The example above looks for all the files under the current directory, as specified by the asterisk (*).

An understanding of UNIX file globbing becomes very handy when reading a directory and being selective about which files to manipulate. To make this script more selective, change the glob pattern. For example, to look for all files that end with the extension .pl, modify the script like this:

```perl
#!/usr/local/bin/perl -w

# Purpose
#    Lists all the files in the current directory.

while (glob("*.pl"))
{
    print "File: $_\n";
}
```

Comments

The only problem when using globbing is that the glob may match too many files and an error like *Argument List Too Long* could ensue. If you run into this situation, use the functions opendir, readdir, and closedir to perform the same task. The above script could be modified like this:

```perl
#!/usr/local/bin/perl -w

# Open the current directory using opendir.
opendir (DIRHANDLE, ".");

# Read in the contents of the current directory using the readdir function.
@filelist = readdir (DIRHANDLE);

# Close the directory handle.
closedir (DIRHANDLE);

# Start cycling through the file list.
```

continued on next page

continued from previous page

```
foreach $file (@filelist)
{
    print "File: $file\n";
}
```

We prefer globbing, but this is a preference, not a choice made by careful reasoning. To learn more about the details of opendir, readdir, and closedir, read How-To 3.14.

COMPLEXITY
INTERMEDIATE

3.11 How do I...
Determine the contents of a
directory tree?

COMPATIBILITY: PERL 5   UNIX

Problem

I need a listing of a directory tree. How do I do this?

Technique

The phrase *directory tree* is used to describe all of the files and directories under a directory. Directory structures can be visualized as inverted trees with the roots at the top and the leaves and branches at the bottom. Figure 3-3 demonstrates the tree using a UNIX file system as an example.

Using the Perl 5 module File::Find, this script calls the find function. The find function accepts two parameters: the starting point of the tree and a reference to a callback function.

```
find(\&wanted, $directory);
```

When find is called and a file is found, find calls the callback function. Two variables are created inside the callback; they are listed in Table 3-5.

VARIABLE NAME	CONTENTS	
$dir	The current directory name	
$_	The current filename within that directory	

Table 3-5 Find function side effect variables

The call-back routine is where all the processing takes place; this call-back routine prints out all the files found.

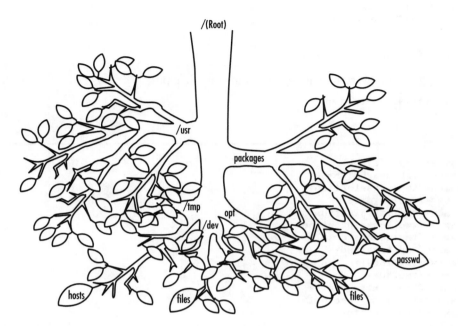

Figure 3-3 An example of the UNIX file system

Steps

Write the script so it will accept the name of the directory to traverse. This directory name is then passed to the find function, which is a function of the File::Find module.

1. Create a new file named listtree.pl and enter the following script into it.

```perl
#!/usr/local/bin/perl -w

# Purpose
#    Lists all the files under a directory tree.

use Getopt::Long;
use File::Find;

# Set up the command line to accept a filename.
my $ret = GetOptions ("d|directory:s");
my $directory = $opt_d || die "Usage: $0 -d directory\n";

#
# This performs actions on the files we have found.
#
sub wanted
{
    print "Dir =<$dir>\n";
    print "Name=<$name>\n";
```

continued on next page

continued from previous page
```
    print "File=<$_>\n";
}

find(\&wanted, $directory);
```

2. Run this script with the following sample input.

```
% listtree.pl -d /tmp
```

Output

```
Name=</tmp/vfstab>
Name=</tmp/caaa001W5>
Name=</tmp/winselection>
Name=</tmp/ps_data>
Name=</tmp/ttyselection>
Name=</tmp/lockcenterline>
Name=</tmp/localstart>
Name=</tmp/localend>
Name=</tmp/local>
Name=</tmp/X0>
Name=</tmp/textsw_shelf>
Name=</tmp/find_core.dat>
Name=</tmp/cccinfo>
```

End Output

How It Works

When the find function is called, it is passed two parameters: the directory to traverse and a function name. The function, which is passed as a reference, is the find function call-back routine. For example, the above callback function is called "wanted." When the find function finds a file, the wanted subroutine is called for processing.

Comments

For complex file finds, use the find2perl script. The find2perl script accepts the same parameters as the standard UNIX find command. As a result, it prints out a Perl script that performs the given find command. If you do not know how to use the UNIX find command, read the manual page for more details.

COMPLEXITY
INTERMEDIATE

3.12 How do I...
Create a directory tree?

COMPATIBILITY: PERL 5   UNIX

Problem

I have an installation script, written in Perl, that needs to create a directory tree. How do I do this?

Technique

This script uses the module File::Path to create the directory tree. The File::Path module has a subroutine called mkpath that takes a list of directories, a verbose flag, and the permission mode the directories are given when created.

```
mkpath(\@list, $verboseFlag, $permissionMode);
```

All the work resides in the mkpath subroutine.

Steps

This script uses the @ARGV array for the list of directories to create. After using the File::Path module, the subroutine mkpath is called with a reference to @ARGV.

1. Create a new file called mktree.pl and enter the following script into it.

```
#!/usr/local/bin/perl -w

# Purpose
#    Creates a complete directory tree.

use File::Path;

# Use the command line for the list of the new directory trees.
my $count = mkpath(\@ARGV, 1, 0711);
print "The number of directories created is $count\n";
```

2. Run this script with the following sample input.

```
% mktree.pl a b/c/d e/f/g
```

Output

```
mkdir a
mkdir b
mkdir b/c
mkdir b/c/d
mkdir e
mkdir e/f
mkdir e/f/g
```
End Output

How It Works

The subroutine mkpath accepts three arguments: a reference to an array containing a list of directories to create, a Boolean flag, and a file mode. The Boolean flag states whether the directory creation will be verbose or not. The mode is the permission mode of the directories to be created. Listing the directories created above:

```
Output
drwx--x--x   2 glover    users        1024 Oct   4 20:59 a
drwx--x--x   3 glover    users        1024 Oct   4 20:59 b
drwx--x--x   3 glover    users        1024 Oct   4 20:59 e
End Output
```

reveals that the permissions are octal 711, which is what is stated in the script. If any of the directories already exists, then mkpath does not try to create the tree.

Comments

The subroutine mkpath also returns the number of directories created. If you are interested in knowing how many directories have been created, remove the line

```
mkpath(\@ARGV, 1, 0711);
```

and add the following lines:

```
$count = mkpath(\@ARGV, 1, 0711);
print "The number of directories created is $count\n";
```

COMPLEXITY
INTERMEDIATE

3.13 How do I...
Remove a directory tree?

COMPATIBILITY: PERL 5   UNIX

Problem

I need to remove a complete directory tree in Perl and I don't want to write a complicated script or use a system call to perform this task. How do I do this?

Technique

This script uses the module File::Path to remove the directory tree. The File::Path module has a subroutine called rmtree that takes a list of directories to remove, a verbose flag, and a flag that skips any directories that you don't have write permission for.

```
$count = rmtree(\@list, $verboseFlag, $skipDirs);
```

All the work resides in the rmtree subroutine.

Steps

This script uses the @ARGV array for the list of directories to remove. After using the File::Path module, it calls the subroutine rmtree with a reference to @ARGV.

1. Create a new file called rmtree.pl and enter the following script into it.

```
#!/usr/local/bin/perl -w

# Purpose
```

```
#    Removes a complete directory tree.

use File::Path;

# Use the command line for the list of the directory trees to remove.
my $count = rmtree(\@ARGV, 1, 1);
print "There were $count files removed.\n";
```

2. Run this script with the following sample input. These directories were created in the previous How-To.

```
% rmtree.pl a b e
```

Output

```
rmdir a
rmdir b/c/d
rmdir b/c
rmdir b
rmdir e/f/g
rmdir e/f
rmdir e
There were 7 files removed.
```
End Output

How It Works

The subroutine rmtree takes three arguments: a reference to an array containing a list of all the directories to be deleted; a Boolean flag that, when set to True, causes rmtree to be verbose; and a Boolean flag that, when set to True, causes rmtree to skip any directories for which you do not have write permission. The subroutine rmtree also returns the number of directories deleted.

Comments

The rmtree subroutine is analogous to the UNIX command rm -r.

COMPLEXITY
INTERMEDIATE

3.14 How do I...
Rename a group of files with a common extension?

COMPATIBILITY: PERL 5   UNIX

Problem

I have a group of files with the same extension and I would like to rename them all to remove the extension. I don't want to do it by hand. How do I do this?

Technique

The script renames all the files with a common extension. Get a list of all the files in the current directory. The script accepts an extension of the files that are to be renamed. Using the module File::Basename, call basename on each file that has the extension to be removed. Refer to How-To 3.8 if you do not know how to use the basename function. With the stripped-down filename, use the function rename to rename the file. The rename function has the following syntax.

```
rename $original, $destination
```

Steps

This script accepts the extension of the common files from the command line. Using opendir, the script generates a list of all the files in the current directory with the given extension. Then each file has both the pathname and extension removed by the basename function. Rename is then called with the original name and the new name to move the file.

1. Create a new file called mvgrp.pl and enter the following script into it.

```perl
#!/usr/local/bin/perl -w

# Purpose
#    This renames a group of files with a common extension.

use Getopt::Long;
use File::Basename;

my $ret = GetOptions ("e|extension:s");
my $ext = $opt_e || die "Usage: $0 -e Extension\n";
my $filename;

# Open the directory using opendir.
opendir (DIR, ".") || die "Can't open directory . $! \n";
my @filelist = grep (/$ext$/, readdir (DIR));
closedir (@filelist);

# For each file, strip off the extension and rename it.
for $filename (@filelist)
{
    my $base = basename($filename, $ext);
    print "Renaming $filename -> $base\n";
    if (!rename $filename, $base)
    {
        print "Could not rename file $filename : $!\n";
    }
}
```

2. Create a group of files with the same extension. The following command line creates a group of files with a common extension of .bak.

```
% touch a.bak b.bak c.bak d.bak
```

3. Verify the contents of the current directory.

```
% ls -l
```

Output

```
-rw-r--r--    1 glover    users          0 Oct   4 22:19 a.bak
-rw-r--r--    1 glover    users          0 Oct   4 22:19 b.bak
-rw-r--r--    1 glover    users          0 Oct   4 22:19 c.bak
-rw-r--r--    1 glover    users          0 Oct   4 22:19 d.bak
```

End Output

4. Run the script.

```
% mvgrp.pl -e .bak
```

Output

```
Renaming a.bak -> a
Renaming b.bak -> b
Renaming c.bak -> c
Renaming d.bak -> d
```

End Output

5. Verify the contents of the current directory.

```
% ls -l
```

Output

```
-rw-r--r--    1 glover    users          0 Oct   4 22:20 a
-rw-r--r--    1 glover    users          0 Oct   4 22:20 b
-rw-r--r--    1 glover    users          0 Oct   4 22:20 c
-rw-r--r--    1 glover    users          0 Oct   4 22:20 d
```

End Output

How It Works

The opendir function opens the directory for reading. This gives you access to functions that enable you to treat the directory like a file by allowing random access to the directory. The random access directory functions are listed in Table 3-6.

FUNCTION	PURPOSE
opendir	Opens the directory and returns a directory handle.
readdir	Reads a directory when given a directory handle. Returns a list, if used in a list context, of files in the directory. If used in a scalar context, then returns the next file in the directory. If there are no more files, then returns an undefined value.
telldir	Returns the current position of the readdir routine on the given directory handle.
seekdir	Moves the given directory handle to the given position.

continued on next page

continued from previous page

FUNCTION	PURPOSE	
rewinddir	Moves the given directory to the beginning of the directory.	
closedir	Closes the directory.	

Table 3-6 Random access directory functions

The readdir function call is embedded within a grep function call. The grep is actually seeking through the list that readdir returned, looking for files that end in the given extension. This creates a list of all the files in the current directory with the given extension.

For each file in the list, run the basename function. Calling the basename function with a filename and an extension will return the basename of the filename without the extension. With this filename, call the rename function to rename the file to a filename without the extension.

Comments

A script comes with the Perl 5 distribution named "rename" in the eg directory. This script takes a regular expression for the files to rename.

COMPLEXITY
INTERMEDIATE

3.15 How do I...
Determine the page count of a file?

COMPATIBILITY: PERL 5   UNIX

Problem

I want to know how many printed pages a file is going to be before I print it out. How do I determine this information?

Technique

Open the file and, for each line, increment a counter. When the counter reaches the number of lines in a printed page, then increment the page counter. If there is a forced page feed character in the file, then increment the page count and reset the counter.

Steps

This script accepts a filename and an optional parameter that controls the number of lines per page. The default value for the number of lines per page is set to 66 in case the script is called without this option being set. The file is then opened and read in. Each line read in is searched for a form feed character; if one is found, then the page count is incremented and the line count is set to zero. When the file has been scanned, the result is printed out.

1. Create a new file called pgcount.pl and enter the following script into it.

```perl
#!/usr/local/bin/perl -w

# Purpose
#    Counts the number of pages of a file.

use Getopt::Long;

# Set up the command line to accept a filename.
my $ret = GetOptions ("f|filename:s","l|lines:i");
my $filename = $opt_f || die "Usage: $0 -f filename [-l lines per page]\n";
my $linesPerPage = $opt_l || 66;
my $line=0;
my $pages=1;
my $count=0;

# Open the file.
open (INPUT, "$filename") || die "Can't open file $filename : $!\n";

# Start reading the file.
while (<INPUT>)
{
    chomp;

    # Is there a forced page feed?
    if ($count = tr/\f//)
    {
        $line = 0;
        $pages += $count;
        next;
    }

    # Are we at a new page?
    if ($line == $linesPerPage)
    {
        $line = 0;
        $pages++;
    }
    else
    {
        $line ++;
    }
}

# Close the file.
close (INPUT);

# Print out the number of pages.
print "Page Count $pages\n";
```

2. Create a text file with the following input. For the lines that say (Page Break), type in CTRL-L instead.

```
This is a test
(Page Break)
of the pgcount.pl
```

continued on next page

continued from previous page
```
(Page Break)
perl script.
```

3. Run the script with the input file created.

```
% pgcount.pl -f pgcount.dat
```

Output
_____

Page Count 3

End Output
_____

How It Works

The script opens the input file and reads through the file line by line via the *while* statement. Each line is scanned for forced form feed characters by the line

```
if ($count = tr/\f//)
```

This line counts the number of form feed characters on the current line by substituting the form feed characters via the tr command. The segment

```
tr/\f//
```

calls the tr command to substitute the pattern \f, which is a form feed character. The tr command returns the number of characters substituted. If no form feed characters are found, then tr returns zero, which makes the *if* statement

```
if ($count = tr/\f//)
{
    $line = 0;
    $pages += $count;
    next;
}
```

fail. If the substitution returns a nonzero value, then the current line variable *$line* is set to zero, the page count variable *$pages* is incremented by the number of form feed characters found, and the next line is read via the next command.

If no form feed characters are found, then the next *if* statement is executed.

```
if ($line == $linesPerPage)
{
    $line = 0;
    $pages++;
}
else
{
    $line ++;
}
```

This *if* statement checks if the end of the page has been reached; if so, the current line count is set to zero and the page count is incremented. If not, the current line counter is incremented.

Comments

This script could be modified to count the number of words, characters, or any other statistic about a file.

COMPLEXITY
INTERMEDIATE

3.16 How do I...
Randomly access a file?

COMPATIBILITY: PERL 5 | UNIX | DOS

Problem

I need to be able to move around in a file while the file is open. How do I do this?

Technique

To do this, use the Perl functions seek and read. The seek function moves the file descriptor around within the file. The seek function has the following syntax.

```
seek (FILEHANDLE, POSITION, RELATIVE OFFSET VALUE);
```

The filehandle parameter is the descriptor associated with the open file. The position offset parameter is controlled by the offset value parameter. If the offset value is zero, the position movement is relative to the beginning of the file. If the offset value is one, the position movement will be relative to its current position. If the offset value is two, the position movement is relative to the end of the file.

The read function uses the file descriptor pointer that seek set to read information from the file. The read function has the following syntax.

```
read (FILEHANDLE, SCALAR, LENGTH, OFFSET);
```

The filehandle parameter is the descriptor associated with the open file. The scalar parameter is the variable in which the information read is stored. The length parameter tells the read function how many characters to read from the file. The offset parameter tells the read function where in the open file to read to. The offset parameter is an optional parameter.

The script takes a section of the perlfunc manual page and misquotes Larry Wall.

Steps

The script in this How-To uses a sequence of seek and read function calls to extract segments of text from the input file. The script scans its way through a section of the perlfunc manual page to create a misquote.

1. Create a new file called misquote.pl and enter the following script into it.

```
#!/usr/local/bin/perl -w

# Purpose
#    Randomly accesses a file.

use Getopt::Long;

# Set up the command line to accept a filename.
my $ret = GetOptions ("f|filename:s");
my $filename = $opt_f || die "Usage: $0 -f filename\n";
my $quote1 = "";
my $quote2 = "";
my $quote3 = "";
my $quote4 = "";

# Open the file.
open (INPUT, "$filename") || die "Can't open file $filename : $!\n";

# Seek to a location from the start of the file.
seek (INPUT, 800, 0);
read (INPUT, $quote1, 17);

# Seek to a location relative to the current position.
seek (INPUT, -445, 1);
read (INPUT, $quote2, 24);
seek (INPUT, 941, 1);
read (INPUT, $quote3, 20);

# Seek from the end of the file.
seek (INPUT, -41, 2);
read (INPUT, $quote4, 13);

# Close the file
close (INPUT);

# OK, misquote Larry.
print "$quote1, $quote2 $quote3 $quote4\n";
```

Below is the segment of the perlfunc manual page. The elements that were used in constructing the misquote from the input file are underlined for clarity.

2. Examine the input file.

```
Perl is an interpreted language optimized for scanning arbitrary text
files, extracting information from those text files, and printing reports
based on that information.  It's also a good language for many system
management tasks.  The language is intended to be practical (easy to use,
efficient, complete) rather than beautiful (tiny, elegant, minimal).
It combines (in the author's opinion, anyway) some of the best features of
C, sed, awk, and sh, so people familiar with those languages should have
little difficulty with it. (Language historians will also note some
vestiges of csh, Pascal, and even BASIC-PLUS.)  Expression syntax
corresponds quite closely to C expression syntax. Unlike most Unix
utilities, Perl does not arbitrarily limit the size of your data--
if you've got the memory, Perl can slurp in your whole file as a single
string.  Recursion is of unlimited depth.  And the hash tables used by
```

associative arrays grow as necessary to prevent degraded performance. Perl uses sophisticated pattern-matching techniques to scan large amounts of data very quickly. Although optimized for scanning text, Perl can also deal with binary data, and can make dbm files look like associative arrays (where dbm is available). Setuid Perl scripts are safer than C programs through a dataflow tracing mechanism which prevents many stupid security holes. If you have a problem that would ordinarily use sed or awk or sh, but it exceeds their capabilities or must run a little faster, and you don't want to write the silly thing in C, then Perl may be for you. There are also translators to turn your sed and awk scripts into Perl scripts.

But wait, there's more...

3. Run the above script on the above text segment.

```
% misquote.pl -f misquote.txt
```

─ Output ──

Perl can slurp in, in the author's opinion, many stupid security Perl scripts.

End Output ──

How It Works

The file is opened; then the file descriptor pointer is moved around within the file by calling the seek function. For example, the first seek/read pair moves the pointer of the file descriptor INPUT to the 800th character in the file.

```
seek (INPUT, 800, 0);
```

The seek function takes three arguments: the file descriptor, the offset value, and the relative starting point. Table 3-7 outlines the result of combinations of seek operations.

COMMAND	RESULT
seek (FD, 10, 0)	The file descriptor pointer moves to the 10th character from the beginning of the file.
seek (FD, 5, 1)	The file descriptor pointer moves five characters forward from its current position.
seek (FD, -5, 1)	The file descriptor pointer moves five characters backward from its current position.
seek (FD, -10, 2)	The file descriptor is moved 10 characters from the end of the file.

Table 3-7 File seek operations

After the seek, 17 characters are read in from the INPUT file descriptor and stored in the variable *$quote1*.

```
read (INPUT, $quote1, 17);
```

Each successive seek/read pair moves the pointer and reads in a segment of text, storing the segment into a new variable. When each seek and read has been performed, the "quote" is constructed and printed out.

Comments

We should have been lawyers.

COMPLEXITY
INTERMEDIATE

3.17   How do I...
Get new data from a growing file?

COMPATIBILITY: PERL 5   UNIX

Problem

I have an ever-growing log file and I need to display any new data that gets append-ed to the end of the file. How do I do this?

Technique

You can solve this problem in UNIX by using the tail command. The tail command has an -f option that displays any new data added to a file. If a file constantly grows, like a system log file, tail will display the newest lines. To mimic this, you need to mimic the tail code. This is done by opening the file and seeking to the end of the file. The following lines of code open the file and immediately move the file point-er 400 characters from the end.

```
# Open the file.
open (INPUT, "$filename") || die "Error: $!\n";

# Move the pointer 400 characters from the end of the file.
seek (INPUT, -400, 2);
```

After the file pointer has been moved, wait a few moments and try to read more information from the file descriptor. If the file has been modified, then you will be able to read information from the file. Once all the information has been read, force the file descriptor to the end of the file again and continue the loop.

Steps

The script accepts the filename to monitor from the command line. The file is opened using the open function; the last 400 characters of the file are displayed on the screen. Then the pointer to the file descriptor is moved to the end of the file, and the script waits 3 seconds. When the script wakes again, it looks for more information at the end of the file. If the pointer to the file descriptor can move, it reads in more and displays it. The pointer to the file descriptor is forced to the end of the file again, and it goes back to sleep.

1. Create a new file called tail.pl and enter the following script into it.

```perl
#!/usr/local/bin/perl -w

# Purpose
#    Gets new data from a growing file.

use Getopt::Long;

# Set up the command line to accept a filename.
my $ret = GetOptions ("f|filename:s");
my $filename = $opt_f || die "Usage: $0 -f filename\n";

# Open the file.
open (INPUT, "$filename") || die "Can't open file $filename : $!\n";

# Seek to the last 400 characters of the file.
seek (INPUT, -400, 2);

# Using the for loop, we will get the current position of the file
# pointer and try to read some information.
for (;;)
{
    for ($curpos = tell(INPUT); $_ = <INPUT>; $curpos = tell(INPUT))
    {
        # Print out the information if we have it.
        print "$_";
    }

    # Sleep for three seconds.
    sleep 3;

    # Move the pointer to the end of the file.
    seek(INPUT, $curpos, 0);
}
```

2. Examine the input file.

Perl is an interpreted language optimized for scanning arbitrary text files, extracting information from those text files, and printing reports based on that information. It's also a good language for many system management tasks. The language is intended to be practical (easy to use, efficient, complete) rather than beautiful (tiny, elegant, minimal). It combines (in the author's opinion, anyway) some of the best features of C, sed, awk, and sh, so people familiar with those languages should have little difficulty with it. (Language historians will also note some vestiges of csh, Pascal, and even BASIC-PLUS.) Expression syntax corresponds quite closely to C expression syntax. Unlike most Unix utilities, Perl does not arbitrarily limit the size of your data-- if you've got the memory, Perl can slurp in your whole file as a single string. Recursion is of unlimited depth. And the hash tables used by associative arrays grow as necessary to prevent degraded performance. Perl uses sophisticated pattern-matching techniques to scan large amounts of data very quickly. Although optimized for scanning text, Perl can also deal with binary data, and can make dbm files look like associative arrays (where dbm is available). Setuid Perl scripts are safer than C programs through a dataflow tracing mechanism which prevents many stupid security

continued on next page

continued from previous page

```
holes. If you have a problem that would ordinarily use sed or awk or sh,
but it exceeds their capabilities or must run a little faster, and you
don't want to write the silly thing in C, then Perl may be for you.
There are also translators to turn your sed and awk scripts into Perl
scripts.

But wait, there's more...
```

3. Run this script with the following input.

```
% tail.pl -f tail.txt
```

4. Open a new shell and concatenate information to the input file while the script is running.

```
% cat append.txt >> tail.txt
```

5. Look at the running script; you will notice new information has arrived. The new information is highlighted in bold.

Output

```
as a single string.  Recursion is of unlimited depth.  And the hash
tables used by associative arrays grow as necessary to prevent
degraded performance.  Perl uses sophisticated pattern-matching
techniques to scan large amounts of data very quickly.  Although
optimized for scanning text, Perl can also deal with binary data,
and can make dbm files look like associative arrays (where dbm is
available).  Setuid Perl scripts are safer than C programs through
a dataflow tracing mechanism which prevents many stupid security
holes.  If you have a problem that would ordinarily use sed or awk
or sh, but it exceeds their capabilities or must run a little
faster, and you don't want to write the silly thing in C, then Perl
may be for you.  There are also translators to turn your sed and
awk scripts into Perl scripts.

But wait, there's more...
If you have a problem that would ordinarily use sed or awk or sh, but it
exceeds their capabilities or must run a little faster, and you don't want
to write the silly thing in C, then Perl may be for you. There are also
translators to turn your sed and awk scripts into Perl scripts.

But wait, there's more...
```

End Output

How It Works

The script opens the given filename and immediately seeks to 400 characters from the end of the file. This mimics the tail command, which displays a number of lines of the file on startup. The value of 400 is an arbitrary value; the script can be modified to accept this value, or an abstraction of this value, from the command line.

Inside the *infinite* loop is another loop. This loop tries to read information from the file. Because the file descriptor is assumed to be at the end of the file, if the file has grown, then there is information to read. There are two elements of the internal *for* loop marking the current cursor position inside the file

```
$curpos = tell (INPUT),
```

and reading from the file.

```
$_ = <INPUT>.
```

If the cursor has changed positions, the second assignment of *$curpos* marks the cursor position and uses that to move the cursor position via the seek function call. After the internal *for* loop, there is a 3-second delay. This is more to conserve resources than a necessary element of the script. The final seek moves the cursor to the position in the file relative to the beginning of the file. This is possible because the variable *$curpos*, which is used to do this, maintains the cursor position of the last read.

Comments

In the Perl FAQ, there are two suggestions to solve this problem. One solution says to perform a seek to the last position. This can be accomplished by calling seek in the following fashion.

```
seek (FD, 0, 1)
```

This implementation is subject to the implementation of the stdio library on your machine, however. Because this is the least portable solution, we went with the one that didn't seem to have any limitations.

## CHAPTER 4

ENVIRONMENT VARIABLES AND COMMANDS

ENVIRONMENT VARIABLES AND COMMANDS

How do I...

Many Perl programs interact with their environment through the use of environment variables and external commands. Environment variables can be used to customize a script or import data. Many times you can use existing commands (operating system, shell, or locally provided) to provide the functionality you need. Being able to launch and interact with these commands is an integral part of Perl.

4.1 Read and Set Environment Variables

The ability to access environment variables is built into Perl and simple to use. You can manipulate these variables as if they were normal Perl variables. This section will show you how.

4.2 Determine If a Command Is in My PATH

The PATH environment variable describes where executable programs should be found. A command can be executed if it is found in your PATH. This section will show you how to determine if this is the case, so you can safely launch commands and not have to worry that the error *Command not found* will occur.

4.3 Set an Environment Variable from a Command File

You might wish to change environment variables by running a command. For the cases where this is not directly possible, this section will show you a way to make it happen.

4.4 Launch Other Commands

Perl has the ability to start other commands running. It is often better to use existing commands than to develop the functionality from scratch. This section will demonstrate this timesaving feature.

4.5 Launch a Process on Another Machine

You can start a command from Perl that knows how to run processes on another machine. (The command to do this is system-specific. On UNIX, the command is usually rsh.) This section will show you how.

4.6 Read Input from Another Program

Once you have started external programs, you may want to be able to interact with them. One common thing to do is to read the output of those programs. This How-To will show you how to do this.

4.7 Send Output to Another Program

Once you can read the output of a program, you will discover a need to be able to write to a running command. This How-To will show you how.

4.8 Save Output from a Command

Sometimes you do not need to read the output of a command. Instead, you need to designate where the output should go. This section will demonstrate two methods of doing this.

4.9 Check If a Process Is Already Running

By now you should be reading and writing to programs. How do you determine if a specific command is currently running? This section will show you how.

COMPLEXITY
BEGINNING

4.1 How do I...
Read and set environment variables?

COMPATIBILITY: PERL 4 | PERL 5 | UNIX | DOS

Problem

I need to access environment variables in my Perl scripts. How do I access and modify the environment?

Technique

Environment variables are named strings that can be used to affect program behavior. For example, the PATH variable determines where the system looks for commands to be executed.

Perl provides the %ENV associative array for access to environment variables. (See Chapter 1 for more information on associative arrays.) The key to this array is the variable name; the value is the environment variable's value. The Env module provides a second way to access the environment. This module makes Perl variables out of the environment variables. Access is then as easy as reading and setting regular Perl variables.

Steps

The first example reads and sets an environment variable using the %ENV associative array. The second example uses the Env module. The last example shows the equivalence of the two methods.

1. Create a script called env1.pl. Add the following code to it. The PATH variable is printed, appended to itself, and printed again.

```
print "\$ENV{'PATH'} = $ENV{'PATH'}\n";

$ENV{'PATH'} .= ":/new/path";

print "\$ENV{'PATH'} = $ENV{'PATH'}\n";
```

2. Run the script. The output will be similar to the following.

```
$ENV{'PATH'} = /usr/local/bin:/usr/bin:/bin
$ENV{'PATH'} = /usr/local/bin:/usr/bin:/bin:/new/path
```

3. Create a second script called env2.pl. This script uses the Env module to import the PATH variable. Add the following lines to the script.

```
use Env qw(PATH);

print "\$PATH = $PATH\n";
```

continued on next page

continued from previous page

```
$PATH.=":/and/another/path";

print "\$PATH = $PATH\n";
```

4. The output of the script is something like this:

```
$PATH = /usr/local/bin:/usr/bin:/bin
$PATH = /usr/local/bin:/usr/bin:/bin:/and/another/path
```

5. Create a third script to access two environment variables. This script will access the TEMP environment variable through the Env module and by accessing the ENV associative array directly. Call the script env3.pl and add the following lines.

```
use Env qw(PATH TEMP);

print "\$PATH = $PATH\n";
print "\$TEMP = $TEMP\n";
print "\$ENV{'TEMP'} = $ENV{'TEMP'}\n";

$TEMP = "e:\\temp";

print "\$TEMP = $TEMP\n";
print "\$ENV{'TEMP'} = $ENV{'TEMP'}\n";
```

6. Run the script. The output will be something like the following.

─┤Output├──

```
$PATH = /usr/local/bin:/usr/bin:/bin
$TEMP =
$ENV{'TEMP'} =
$TEMP = e:\temp
$ENV{'TEMP'} = e:\temp
```

─┤End Output├───

How It Works

The %ENV associative array is magic. Any time this array is read, it will access the environment. Any time it is set, the environment will be changed.

The Env module uses the tie function to define how access to a given variable takes place. In other words, the Env module controls use of the $PATH and $TEMP variables. When one of these variables is read, the module accesses the appropriate environment variable (through %ENV) and returns the result. When a value is stored in these variables, the %ENV array is updated appropriately.

Comments

Please refer to Figure 4-1 to see the output of all three Perl scripts. Notice the \s before a number of $s. This prevents Perl from treating the $ as the first character of a variable. Instead, it treats it as a printable character.

```
                birdofprey /home/spock/Waite/chap_04/howto01
> ls -CF
env1.pl  env2.pl  env3.pl
> cat env1.pl
print "\$ENV{'PATH'} = $ENV{'PATH'}\n";

$ENV{'PATH'} .= ":/new/path";

print "\$ENV{'PATH'} = $ENV{'PATH'}\n";
> perl -w env1.pl
$ENV{'PATH'} = /home/spock/tools/x86/bin:/usr/bin:/bin
$ENV{'PATH'} = /home/spock/tools/x86/bin:/usr/bin:/bin:/new/path
> cat env2.pl
use Env qw(PATH);

print "\$PATH = $PATH\n";

$PATH.=":/and/another/path";

print "\$PATH = $PATH\n";
> perl -w env2.pl
$PATH = /home/spock/tools/x86/bin:/usr/bin:/bin
$PATH = /home/spock/tools/x86/bin:/usr/bin:/bin:/and/another/path
> cat env3.pl
use Env qw(PATH TEMP);

print "\$PATH = $PATH\n";
print "\$TEMP = $TEMP\n";
print "\$ENV{'TEMP'} = $ENV{'TEMP'}\n";

$TEMP = "e:\\temp";

print "\$TEMP = $TEMP\n";
print "\$ENV{'TEMP'} = $ENV{'TEMP'}\n";
> perl -w env3.pl
$PATH = /home/spock/tools/x86/bin:/usr/bin:/bin
$TEMP = /tmp
$ENV{'TEMP'} = /tmp
$TEMP = e:\temp
$ENV{'TEMP'} = e:\temp
>
```

Figure 4-1 Output of the scripts

In each of the examples, the Env module is called with arguments. If no arguments are given, the entire environment is imported. This can cause trouble if you are using Perl variables with the same names as environment variables. It is usually best to import only the environment variables you need.

The use command and the Env module are Perl 5 specific. In Perl 4, the environment should be accessed through the ENV associative array.

COMPLEXITY
INTERMEDIATE

4.2   How do I...
Determine if a command is in my PATH?

COMPATIBILITY: PERL 4   PERL 5   UNIX   DOS

Problem

Sometimes I need to know whether a command is in my PATH before I run it. How can I check?

Technique

The easiest way to see if a command is in your PATH is to loop through all the directories in your PATH looking for the existence of the command file. A slightly more challenging script checks for the existence of a file that matches a pattern.

Steps

Two scripts are created. The first checks for the existence of a command in the PATH. If the command is found, it is checked to see if it is executable. If it is, the path to the command is printed and the script exits. The second script checks for commands in the PATH that match a pattern. If a file matching the pattern is found in a PATH directory and it is executable, it is printed.

1. Create a file called where1.pl. Add the following lines to set operating system-specific variables.

```
$DOS = 0; # set to 1 if under DOS
if ($DOS) {
    $PathSep = ";";
    $DirSep  = "\\";
} else {
    $PathSep = ":";
    $DirSep  = "/";
}
```

2. Initialize a variable with the name of the command to be found. Create an array of directories by splitting the PATH environment variable.

```
$File = "perl";
$Path = $ENV{'PATH'};
@Path = split($PathSep/,$Path);
```

3. Loop through each directory. If a directory is null, check the current directory. If a regular file with the command name exists in the directory and it is executable, print its name and exit. If the command is not found, print a message.

```
foreach $Dir (@Path) {
    $Dir = '.' if $Dir eq '';
    if (-f "$Dir$DirSep$File" && -x _) {
        print "Found $Dir$DirSep$File\n";
        exit 0;
    }
}
print "Not Found\n";
exit 1;
```

4. The entire script looks like this:

```
$DOS = 0; # set to 1 if under DOS
if ($DOS) {
    $PathSep = ";";
    $DirSep  = "\\";
} else {
    $PathSep = ":";
    $DirSep  = "/";
}

$File = "perl";
$Path = $ENV{'PATH'};
@Path = split($PathSep/,$Path);
foreach $Dir (@Path) {
    $Dir = '.' if $Dir eq '';
    if (-f "$Dir$DirSep$File" && -x _) {
        print "Found $Dir$DirSep$File\n";
        exit 0;
    }
}
print "Not Found\n";
exit 1;
```

5. Run the command. Your output will be similar to this:

Output

```
# Set up the command line
Found /usr/local/bin/perl
```

End Output

6. Copy the script into a file called where2.pl. Modify this script to search for a pattern. The operating system-specific code is the same. (This time we will assume that you are running under DOS.)

```
$DOS = 1; # set to 0 if under UNIX
if ($DOS) {
    $PathSep = ";";
    $DirSep  = "\\";
} else {
    $PathSep = ":";
    $DirSep  = "/";
}
```

7. Create a subroutine that returns an array of all the files that exist in a directory that is passed in as an argument.

```
sub DirFiles {
    my $Dir = $_[0];
    my @files;

    opendir(DIR,$Dir) || return ();
    @files = readdir(DIR);
    closedir(DIR);
    @files;
}
```

8. Create a variable to hold the pattern. If the script is running under DOS, all executables contain a . and a suffix. If the pattern does not contain a ., add it and allow it to be followed by any characters.

```
$FilePat = ".*win.*";

$DOS and $FilePat !~ /\\\./ and $FilePat .= "\\\..*";
```

9. Add another loop to the loop checking each directory. This second loop will iterate through each file in the directory to see if it matches the pattern. If it does, the file can be checked to see if it is a valid command. Create a variable called *ReturnCode* that will be used to see if a valid executable is found.

```
$Path = $ENV{'PATH'};
@Path = split($PathSep/,$Path);
$ReturnCode = 1;
foreach $Dir (@Path) {
    $Dir = '.' if $Dir eq '';
    foreach $DirFile (&DirFiles($Dir)) {
        if ($DirFile =~ /^$FilePat$/o) {
            if (-f "$Dir$DirSep$DirFile" && -x _) {
                print "Found $Dir$DirSep$DirFile\n";
                $ReturnCode = 0;
            }
        }
    }
}
$ReturnCode && print "Not Found\n";
exit $ReturnCode;
```

10. The entire script should now look like the following.

```
$DOS = 1; # set to 0 if under UNIX
if ($DOS) {
    $PathSep = ";";
    $DirSep  = "\\";
} else {
    $PathSep = ":";
    $DirSep  = "/";
}

sub DirFiles {
```

```
    my $Dir = $_[0];
    my @files;

    opendir(DIR,$Dir) || return ();
    @files = readdir(DIR);
    closedir(DIR);
    @files;
}

$FilePat = ".*win.*";

$DOS and $FilePat !~ /\\\./ and $FilePat .= "\\\..*";

$Path = $ENV{'PATH'};
@Path = split(/$PathSep/,$Path);
$ReturnCode = 1;
foreach $Dir (@Path) {
    $Dir = '.' if $Dir eq '';
    foreach $DirFile (&DirFiles($Dir)) {
        if ($DirFile =~ /^$FilePat$/o) {
            if (-f "$Dir$DirSep$DirFile" && -x _) {
                print "Found $Dir$DirSep$DirFile\n";
                $ReturnCode = 0;
            }
        }
    }
}
$ReturnCode && print "Not Found\n";
exit $ReturnCode;
```

11. Run the script. The output will look something like this:

Output

```
Found c:\bin\wingif.exe
Found c:\windows\win.com
Found c:\windows\winfile.exe
Found c:\windows\winhelp.exe
Found c:\windows\winmine.exe
Found c:\windows\wintutor.exe
Found c:\windows\winver.exe
```

End Output

How It Works

These scripts break the problem down into simple steps. First, the PATH is broken into its component directories. Second, for each directory, the script checks to see if the command exists in that directory. Then it checks to see if a file matching a pattern is a simple extension of the original problem.

The scripts need to check if the file(s) that is being looked for is a regular file. (This is done through the use of the *-f* check.) Under UNIX, directories can be marked as executable, so simply checking for existence of the file is not sufficient. (The executable designation means that the directory is searchable to those who have the execute permission.)

Comments

Remember that the \ character is special in Perl. You need to escape it to make sure that it is taken as the backslash character and not the escape character.

To check to see if a file is executable (using -x), use the special "_" character. This is an optimization. The "_" says to check the same file as the last time a file was checked. This allows Perl to use the information that Perl already has about the file without having to go to the file system a second time to gather this information.

The @_ array exists in a subroutine only if arguments are passed to that subroutine. If they are, @_ contains one array element for each argument passed.

The line

```
$DOS and $FilePat !~ /\\\./ and $FilePat .= "\\\..*";
```

is needed in the second script to create a pattern that will match an executable under DOS. This is because all files that are executable in DOS end in "." something (e.g., .exe). Although this pattern will match anything after the ., the -x check will succeed only if it is one of the valid executable suffixes.

The second script will only work under Perl 5. To make it work under Perl 4, the mys needs to be changed to locals and the ands needs to be changed to ||. The Perl 4 script is below.

```
$DOS = 1; # set to 0 if under UNIX
if ($DOS) {
    $PathSep = ";";
    $DirSep  = "\\";
} else {
    $PathSep = ":";
    $DirSep  = "/";
}

sub DirFiles {
    local ($Dir) = $_[0];
    local (@files);

    opendir(DIR,$Dir) || return ();
    @files = readdir(DIR);
    closedir(DIR);
    @files;
}

$FilePat = ".*win.*";

$DOS || ($FilePat !~ /\\\./) || ($FilePat .= "\\\..*");

$Path = $ENV{'PATH'};
@Path = split(/$PathSep/,$Path);
$ReturnCode = 1;
foreach $Dir (@Path) {
    $Dir = '.' if $Dir eq '';
```

```
    foreach $DirFile (&DirFiles($Dir)) {
    if ($DirFile =~ /^$FilePat$/o) {
        if (-f "$Dir$DirSep$DirFile" && -x _) {
        print "Found $Dir$DirSep$DirFile\n";
        $ReturnCode = 0;
        }
    }
    }
}
$ReturnCode && print "Not Found\n";
exit $ReturnCode;
```

COMPLEXITY
INTERMEDIATE

4.3 How do I...
Set an environment variable from a command file?

COMPATIBILITY: PERL 4 PERL 5 UNIX DOS

Problem

I would like to run a Perl script that modifies my environment. Is this possible?

Technique

It is not normally possible to affect your environment from a program. However, you can do this with some cooperation from the shell. The shell commands needed are specific to the type of shell being used.

Steps

The Perl script will print the command that the shell uses to change the environment. A short shell script is then constructed to call the Perl script and use its output to modify the environment.

 Create a script called set.pl. Add the following lines. A line is printed based on which shell is being used.

```
$Shell  = "sh"; # or "csh" or "DOS"

if($Shell eq "sh") {
    print "PATH=/bin:/usr/bin; export PATH\n";
} elsif($Shell eq "csh") {
    print "setenv PATH /bin:/usr/bin\n";
} elsif($Shell eq "DOS") {
    print "\@echo off";
    print "set PATH=c:\\bin;c:\\dos\n";
} else {
    die "Bad shell type\n";
}
```

2. Create a shell script that first runs this program and then redirects its output to a file. After that, the shell script needs to cause the commands in that file to be executed.

3. For sh, the script will look like this:

```
perl set.pl > /tmp/EnvCommands
/tmp/EnvCommands
```

4. For csh, the script will look like this:

```
perl set.pl > /tmp/EnvCommands
source /tmp/EnvCommands
```

5. And for DOS, the script will look like this:

```
perl set.pl > c:\temp\env.bat
c:\temp\env.bat
```

6. Both sh and csh can get the same results by doing this:

```
eval `perl set.pl`
```

7. There is no output generated by these scripts. The environment is silently changed.

How It Works

When shells execute commands, they start those commands in a copy of the current environment. Any changes to that copy are not seen by the originating shell. To change the current environment, the current shell must execute the environment-changing commands. The Perl code is straightforward. All it does is print commands the shell can interpret. The additional step is to get the shell to run those commands. The most general way to accomplish this is to put those commands into a file and then have the shell execute those commands. The method for doing that is shell-specific.

Comments

The DOS version of Perl cannot affect the current environment, although a .BAT file can. This occurs because the .BAT file is run by the current shell.

COMPLEXITY
BEGINNING

4.4   How do I...
Launch other commands?

COMPATIBILITY: PERL 4   PERL 5   UNIX   DOS

Problem

How do I run existing commands (operating system, shell, or locally provided) from my Perl script? For example, how do I run the date command from my script?

Technique

There are three ways to run commands from Perl. They vary in what happens to the output and the flow of control. The three ways are using the Perl command system, using exec, and putting a command between back-ticks.

Steps

The following scripts call the date command using the three possible methods. The output shows the difference between the calling methods.

1. Create a script called run1.pl. Add the following lines. The script will first turn off output buffering and then call the date command twice, using the Perl system command. The output will go to wherever the standard output is currently going. Execution continues in the script at the next line when the date command completes.

```
$| = 1;

print "The time is now: ";
system "date";

sleep 5;

print "Now it is: ";
system "date";
```

2. Run the script. The output will be similar to the following.

Output

```
The time is now: Mon Jan 01 09:07:03 CST 2001
Now it is: Mon Jan 01 09:07:08 CST 2001
```

End Output

3. Copy the script to a file called run2.pl. Change the system command to the exec command.

```
$| = 1;

print "The time is now: ";
exec "date";

sleep 5;

print "Now it is: ";
exec "date";
```

4. Run the script. The output will look like the following.

Output

```
The time is now: Mon Jan 01 09:07:08 CST 2001
```

End Output

5. Notice that only the first date command ran. This is because execution terminates when the command specified in the *exec* statement finishes. If you ran the script using the -w option

```
perl -w run2.pl
```

the following warning would have been printed.

─ Output ──

```
Statement unlikely to be reached at run2.pl line 6.
(Maybe you meant system() when you said exec()?)
```
End Output

6. The third form of executing a command is to run that command between back-ticks (`). Execution continues at the next statement, but output is redirected. The standard output is returned as the value of the statement. It can then be assigned to a variable or used like any other value. Create the following script and call it run3.pl. ("date 1" is an invalid use of *date*. It will generate an error message.)

```
$output = `date`;
print "\$output='$output'\n";

$output = `date 1`;
print "\$output='$output'\n";

$output = `date 1 2>&1`;
chop $output;
print "\$output='$output'\n";
```

7. The output follows. Notice that that error output is not saved unless it is redirected, as in the third call to the date command.

─ Output ──

```
$output='Mon Jan 01 09:07:04 CST 2001
'
$output=''
$output='date: invalid date `1''
```
End Output

How It Works

The system command runs the command as a child process of the script. It waits for the command to complete and then continues. The exec command replaces the Perl executable with the command. This means that there is no Perl script left to continue executing. Thus, an exec statement will be the last command executed in any Perl program.

The back-tick method of running a command will bring the output of the command back into the script itself. Only the standard output of the command is captured. Any output to standard error is sent to wherever standard error would usually go. As can be seen in the third example, the standard error output can be captured as well by redirecting it to standard out (by using 2>&1.)

Comments

DOS does not have standard error, so it can be safely ignored.

When using shell redirection in these commands, remember that /bin/sh is used. So make sure not to use any csh syntax.

Unlike the shell, Perl does not strip the end-of-line character when the output is captured. Use chop to remove it, as in

```
chop $Output;
```

COMPLEXITY
BEGINNING

4.5   How do I...
Launch a process on another machine?

COMPATIBILITY:

Problem

Can I run a command from Perl that will cause a command to be executed on another machine?

Technique

The method of doing this is the same as in the previous How-To. In this case, a system-dependent command must be run.

Steps

1. Create a script called rsh.pl that contains the following line.

```
system "rsh -n OtherMachine who";
```

How It Works

The usual Perl method for launching commands is used. The command being executed must know how to start a command on another machine.

Comments

rsh is a UNIX-specific command. You can substitute any command that is appropriate. All three methods from the previous How-To are available. Only system was used to show the system-specific command.

COMPLEXITY
INTERMEDIATE

4.6   How do I...
Read input from another program?

COMPATIBILITY: PERL 4 PERL 5 UNIX DOS

Problem

Occasionally, I would like to launch a program from Perl and be able to process its output. How can I do this without having to put all the output into one variable?

Technique

You can open a command as if it were a file. This is done by opening a string that contains the command to run; the string must end in a | character. The presence of that final character is how Perl knows that it is a command and not a filename.

Steps

The example shows how to run the who command and count the number of times a user is logged on. The output of the who command contains lines that have the user's login followed by some additional information. There is one line for each login. Only the login name is needed for this script.

 1. Create a file called read.pl. Add the following lines to import the English module and to define the command to be run.

```
use English;

$Cmd = "who";
```

2. Open a filehandle called IN to receive the output of the command.

```
open(IN,"$Cmd |") or die "Can't run command '$Cmd', $OS_ERROR\n";
```

3. Loop through each line of output. Split the line on white space, saving only the first token (the login name). Use an associative array to count the number of times this user has been seen.

```
while($line = <IN>) {
    ($who) = split(/\s+/,$line);
```

```
    $Cnt{$who}++;
}
```

4. Close the filehandle. Print a message and exit if the process returned an error when it finished.

```
close(IN);
die "$Cmd returned error: $CHILD_ERROR\n" if $CHILD_ERROR;
```

5. Print the number of times a user is logged on. Sort the output alphabetically by user name.

```
for $user (sort keys %Cnt) {
    print "User $user is logged in $Cnt{$user} times\n";
}
```

6. The entire script follows.

```
use English;

$Cmd = "who";
open(IN,"$Cmd |") or die "Can't run command '$Cmd', $OS_ERROR\n";
while($line = <IN>) {
    chop $line;
    ($who) = split(/\s+/,$line);
    $Cnt{$who}++;
}
close(IN);
die "$Cmd returned error: $CHILD_ERROR\n" if $CHILD_ERROR;
for $user (sort keys %Cnt) {
    print "User $user is logged in $Cnt{$user} times\n";
}
```

7. Run the script. The output will be similar to the following.

Output

```
User root is logged in 1 times
User spock is logged in 2 times
```

End Output

A screen dump of the execution of the script can be seen in Figure 4-2.

How It Works

The method of opening a command that ends in a | symbol is similar to reading from a pipe. Instead of reading the output of a pipe from standard input, a filehandle is created to read the data. If the command exits with a failure code, this is noticed when the filehandle is closed. Other than those differences, reading from a command is the same as reading data from a file.

Comments

When a never-before-referenced variable is accessed in Perl, the value of this variable will be zero or a null string. This allows the program to do the counting in the line

```
$Cnt{$who}++;
```

```
birdofprey /home/spock/Waite/chap_04/howto06

> cat read.pl
use English;

$Cmd = "who";
open(IN,"$Cmd |") or die "Can't run command '$Cmd', $OS_ERROR\n";
while($line = <IN>) {
    ($who) = split(/\s+/,$line);
    $Cnt{$who}++;
}
close(IN);
die "$Cmd returned error: $CHILD_ERROR\n" if $CHILD_ERROR;
for $user (sort keys %Cnt) {
    print "User $user is logged in $Cnt{$user} times\n";
}
> who
spock     tty1      Feb 29 04:40
root      tty2      Feb 29 14:41
spock     ttyp9     Feb 29 14:42 (localhost)
> perl -w read.pl
User root is logged in 1 times
User spock is logged in 2 times
>
```

Figure 4-2 Output of read

The script needs to be modified to run under Perl 4. The use of the English module must be removed and the *or* must be changed to ||.

```
$Cmd = "who";
open(IN,"$Cmd |") || die "Can't run command '$Cmd', $!\n";
while($line = <IN>) {
    ($who) = split(/\s+/,$line);
    $Cnt{$who}++;
}
close(IN);
die "$Cmd returned error: $?\n" if $?;
for $user (sort keys %Cnt) {
    print "User $user is logged in $Cnt{$user} times\n";
}
```

COMPLEXITY
INTERMEDIATE

4.7   How do I...
Send output to another program?

COMPATIBILITY: PERL 4   PERL 5   UNIX   DOS

Problem

I need to send some of the output of my Perl script to another command. Because I need only some of the output to go to the command, I cannot pipe the script directly to the command. Is there a way to do this?

Technique

This is very similar to the previous How-To. In this case, a filehandle is opened that will be used to write data to a command instead of being used to read data. The open command is passed a string that starts with a | character, followed by the command to read the data.

Steps

This example outputs a sequence of numbers and their cubes. The command that will receive this data is egrep. This is a contrived example, but it illustrates the method to write data to a command quite simply.

1. Create a file called out.pl. Add the following lines to use the English module and to create a variable to hold the command that will receive the output.

```
use English;

$Cmd = "egrep '^3 '";
```

2. Open a filehandle called OUT that will send data to the command. Print the first five cubes to the filehandle.

```
open(OUT,"| $Cmd") or die "Can't run command '$Cmd', $OS_ERROR\n";
for $Cnt (1..5) {
    print OUT "$Cnt cubed is ", $Cnt ** 3, "\n";
}
```

3. Close the filehandle and check the exit status of the command.

```
close(OUT);
die "$Cmd returned error: $CHILD_ERROR\n" if $CHILD_ERROR;
```

4. The entire script looks like this:

```
use English;

$Cmd = "egrep '^3 '";
open(OUT,"| $Cmd") or die "Can't run command '$Cmd', $OS_ERROR\n";
for $Cnt (1..5) {
    print OUT "$Cnt cubed is ", $Cnt ** 3, "\n";
}
close(OUT);
die "$Cmd returned error: $CHILD_ERROR\n" if $CHILD_ERROR;
```

5. Run the command. The output follows.

Output

```
3 cubed is 27
```
End Output

How It Works

Opening a file that starts with a | character tells Perl that the data written to this file-handle will be sent to the standard input of the command that makes up the rest of the string. This is very similar to using pipes from the shell.

Comments

Be careful of commands that do not exit with a successful return code. They can make the script appear to fail.

The script needs to be modified to run under Perl 4. The use of the English module must be removed and the or must be changed to ||.

```
$Cmd = "egrep '^3 '";
open(OUT,"| $Cmd") || die "Can't run command '$Cmd', $!\n";
for $Cnt (1..5) {
    print OUT "$Cnt cubed is ", $Cnt ** 3, "\n";
}
close(OUT);
die "$Cmd returned error: $?\n" if $?;
```

COMPLEXITY
INTERMEDIATE

4.8 How do I...
Save output from a command?

COMPATIBILITY:

Problem

I need to run a command from Perl and have control of where its output goes.

Technique

There are two ways to exert control over where the output of a command will go. The first method lets the shell handle it. The second method has Perl change where the standard filehandles are directed to.

Steps

The first example lets the shell redirect the output of a command. The second example changes where standard error and standard output are going before the command is run. The command will then inherit the new locations.

1. Create a file called date1.pl containing the following line.

```
system "date >date1.out 2>date1.err";
```

2. Run the script. No output will appear and date1.err will be empty. date1.out will contain something like this:

```
Mon Jan 01 09:07:04 CST 2001
```

3. Create a second script called date2.pl. The location that standard output and standard error are being written to is modified by opening their file-handles to point to another location. The date command will then use those locations when it is run.

```
$StdOut = "date2.out";
$StdErr = "date2.err";
open(STDOUT,">$StdOut") || die "Can't open STDOUT to $StdOut, $!\n";
open(STDERR,">$StdErr") || die "Can't open STDERR to $StdErr, $!\n";
system "date";
```

4. Run the script. The output will be the same as the first script.

5. Copy date2.pl to a file called date3.pl. Add lines to save and restore where standard output and standard error are going.

```
$StdOut = "date3.out";
$StdErr = "date3.err";

open(SAVESTDOUT, ">&STDOUT") || die "Can't save STDOUT, $!\n";
open(SAVESTDERR, ">&STDERR") || die "Can't save STDERR, $!\n";

open(STDOUT,">$StdOut") || die "Can't open STDOUT to $StdOut, $!\n";
open(STDERR,">$StdErr") || die "Can't open STDERR to $StdErr, $!\n";

system "date";

open(STDOUT, ">&SAVESTDOUT");
open(STDERR, ">&SAVESTDERR");
```

6. Run the script. The output is the same as before. If this script were to continue, standard output and standard error would be going to their original locations.

How It Works

If shell redirection is used, Perl does not need to be involved in setting the destination of the output. To control this from Perl, you must change where the standard file-handles point. When the command runs, it inherits these filehandles. The use of >& in an open string tells Perl to make the filehandle a copy of the filehandle following those characters. In this way, filehandles can be copied, saved, and restored.

Comments

When a single string is executed as an external command from a UNIX version of Perl, it is checked for shell metacharacters (such as < and >). If any are found, the string is passed to /bin/sh to be executed. Otherwise, it is passed directly to UNIX for execution. Remember that it is passed to /bin/sh, not to whatever shell you are currently using.

When a program is running under DOS, there is no separation of standard error and standard output. The DOS shell will honor the use of the output redirect (>) character.

COMPLEXITY
INTERMEDIATE

4.9 How do I...
Check if a process is already running?

COMPATIBILITY: PERL 4   PERL 5   UNIX

Problem

Sometimes the actions my Perl script needs to take are determined by whether a certain command is running or not. How do I determine this?

Technique

The determination of whether a command is running or not is greatly simplified if the command's process number is known. If so, the UNIX kill command can check for the existence of that process. If not, the UNIX ps command can be run to try to find the command among all the processes currently running. The first script also shows how to create a child process to a script. A sample of ps output from a Linnx System can be seen in Figure 4-3.

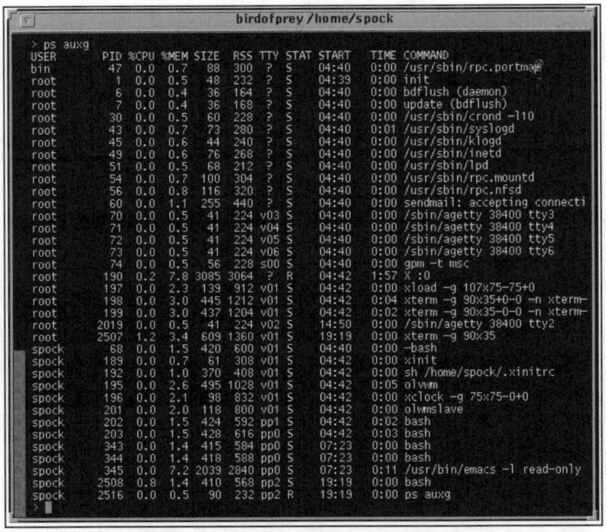

Figure 4-3 A list of processes using the ps command

Steps

The first example creates a child process and then uses the kill command to check if that process is alive. The child process executes the sleep command. This causes the child to wait five seconds before exiting. The child process should still be alive when the parent process checks it. The second example uses the ps command to see if a Perl process is running.

1. Create a file called running1.pl. Add the following lines to it. The command first forks, creating a child process running the same code. The value returned from the fork gives the child's process ID (PID) to the parent and zero to the child. If the process is the parent ($pid is not zero), call kill with the zero signal and the child's PID. The zero signal just checks to see if the child is alive. Print a message telling whether the child is alive. (It should be.)

```
$Cmd = "sleep 5";

$pid = fork;
if ($pid) {
    $rc = kill 0, $pid;
    if ($rc) {
        print "Child $pid running\n";
    } else {
        print "Child $pid not running\n";
    }
```

2. Now wait for the child process to finish and check to see if the child is alive again. (It better not be.)

```
    wait;
    $rc = kill 0, $pid;
    if ($rc) {
        print "Child $pid running\n";
    } else {
        print "Child $pid not running\n";
    }
```

3. If the return was zero after the fork, the child process is running. Execute the command to sleep five seconds.

```
} else {
    exec $Cmd;
}
```

4. The entire script follows.

```
$Cmd = "sleep 5";

$pid = fork;
if ($pid) {
    $rc = kill 0, $pid;
    if ($rc) {
        print "Child $pid running\n";
    } else {
```

continued on next page

continued from previous page

```
            print "Child $pid not running\n";
    }
    wait;
    $rc = kill 0, $pid;
    if ($rc) {
        print "Child $pid running\n";
    } else {
        print "Child $pid not running\n";
    }
} else {
    exec $Cmd;
}
```

5. Run the script. The output will look something like this:

Output
───

```
Child 1271 running
Child 1271 not running
```
End Output
───

6. Create a second script to use ps to determine if a process is running. Call the script running2.pl. First, add a line that contains a system-specific ps command. (The options will vary on different UNIX machines.)

```
$PsCmd = "ps auxg";
```

7. Next, set the command to be searched for and open the ps command. Loop through each line of the ps output looking for the command. If the command is found, increment a counter that contains the number of times it was seen.

```
$RunningCmd = "perl";
$Running = 0;

open(IN,"$PsCmd |") or die "Can't run $PsCmd\n";
while(<IN>) {
    /\b$RunningCmd\b/o or next;
    $Running++;
}
close(IN);
```

8. Print a message depending on the number of times the command was seen.

```
if ($Running == 0) {
    print "$RunningCmd is not running\n";
}elsif ($Running == 1) {
    print "$RunningCmd is running\n";
}else {
    print "$RunningCmd is running multiple times\n";
}
```

9. The entire script should now look like this:

```
$PsCmd = "ps auxg";
```

```
$RunningCmd = "perl";
$Running = 0;

open(IN,"$PsCmd |") or die "Can't run $PsCmd\n";
while(<IN>) {
    /\b$RunningCmd\b/o or next;
    $Running++;
}
close(IN);
if ($Running == 0) {
    print "$RunningCmd is not running\n";
}elsif ($Running == 1) {
    print "$RunningCmd is running\n";
}else {
    print "$RunningCmd is running multiple times\n";
}
```

10. Run the script. The output may look something like this:

Output

```
perl is running multiple times
```
End Output

How It Works

When the PID is known, the kill 0 command checks if the process is running. It returns 1 if it is and 0 if it is not. (On some systems, kill 0 will not work. If that is the case, try the second method.) Without knowing the PID, you will find it harder to solve the problem, which cannot always be reliably solved. Check the process list and see if the command can be picked out using a string match. The problem is that the command name might not be in the list or, worse, it could be an argument to another command (like this one). Be careful when applying this technique.

Comments

The \b in the regular expression provides a way to make sure that the name of the command being searched for is not a substring of another command name. The \b matches a "word boundary."

FILE HANDLING

FILE HANDLING

How do I...

Perl provides many standard features when it comes to file handling. Most of the time, you will just want the default behavior. However, there are cases when you may need to alter this behavior to get the appropriate results. When dealing with filehandles, manipulating them can sometimes be confusing. Simple examples are given in this chapter to help you understand the approaches involved.

5.1   Separate Error and Standard Output

UNIX allows error output from a command to go to a different location than the normal output. The ability to process the different outputs in a dissimilar way can often be quite useful. This section will demonstrate this technique.

5.2   Unbuffer Output

Output is normally buffered to achieve efficiency. However, there may be times when you need to see data in a finer granularity than blocks. This section will show you a straightforward way to accomplish this.

5.3   Localize a Filehandle

The ability to make filehandles local to a subroutine can make a subroutine more modular, functional, and reentrant. This section will demonstrate how.

5.4   Pass a Filehandle to a Function

Once filehandles can be made local to a subroutine, it is nice to be able to pass them to subroutines as you would any other argument. You will see a method for getting this effect in this section.

COMPLEXITY
INTERMEDIATE

5.1   How do I...
Separate error and standard output?

COMPATIBILITY:

Problem

UNIX allows error output from a command to go to a different location than the normal output. Sometimes when I launch commands from Perl, I need to be able to access the outputs separately. How can I achieve this?

Technique

Perl allows you to read the output of a command as if it were a file (see Chapter 4). However, you can only open one filehandle for this output. This means you can see standard out, standard error, or both combined. To see both output streams, you need to write at least one of them to a file. Once the output is in a file, you can read it normally.

Filehandles can be duplicated (saved) by using the following syntax.

```
open(SAVEFILEHANDLE, ">&FILEHANDLE") || die "Can't save FILEHANDLE, $!\n";
```

The >&FILEHANDLE tells Perl to duplicate that filehandle into the new filehandle.

Steps

In this example, the current destinations of STDOUT and STDERR are saved, directed to new locations, used, and then restored to their original state.

1. Create a file called sep1.pl. Add the following lines to it. First define the new locations of the outputs. Then save the current destinations of STDOUT and STDERR.

```
$StdOut = "sep1.std";
$StdErr = "sep1.err";

open(SAVESTDOUT, ">&STDOUT") || die "Can't save STDOUT, $!\n";
open(SAVESTDERR, ">&STDERR") || die "Can't save STDERR, $!\n";
```

2. Next, redirect the output locations and use them.

```
open(STDOUT,">$StdOut") || die "Can't open STDOUT to $StdOut, $!\n";
open(STDERR,">$StdErr") || die "Can't open STDERR to $StdErr, $!\n";

print "to STDOUT\n";
print STDERR "to STDERR\n";

system "date";
```

3. Then restore the output locations and print something to them to verify that they have been restored.

```
open(STDOUT, ">&SAVESTDOUT");
open(STDERR, ">&SAVESTDERR");

print "back to original STDOUT\n";
print STDERR "back to original STDERR\n";
```

4. The entire script follows.

```
$StdOut = "sep1.std";
$StdErr = "sep1.err";

open(SAVESTDOUT, ">&STDOUT") || die "Can't save STDOUT, $!\n";
open(SAVESTDERR, ">&STDERR") || die "Can't save STDERR, $!\n";

open(STDOUT,">$StdOut") || die "Can't open STDOUT to $StdOut, $!\n";
open(STDERR,">$StdErr") || die "Can't open STDERR to $StdErr, $!\n";

print "to STDOUT\n";
print STDERR "to STDERR\n";

system "date";

open(STDOUT, ">&SAVESTDOUT");
open(STDERR, ">&SAVESTDERR");

print "back to original STDOUT\n";
print STDERR "back to original STDERR\n";
```

5. Run the script. The output to the terminal should look like this:

```
Output
back to original STDERR
back to original STDOUT
End Output
```

6. sep1.std will contain something like this:

```
Mon Jan 01 12:31:28 CST 2001
to STDOUT
```

7. sep1.err will contain this:

```
to STDERR
```

8. Notice that the lines in sep1.std appear to be in the wrong order.

9. Copy sep1.pl to sep2.pl. Make the following modifications to fix the output order.

```perl
use FileHandle;

$StdOut = "sep2.std";
$StdErr = "sep2.err";

open(SAVESTDOUT, ">&STDOUT") || die "Can't save STDOUT, $!\n";
open(SAVESTDERR, ">&STDERR") || die "Can't save STDERR, $!\n";

open(STDOUT,">$StdOut") || die "Can't open STDOUT to $StdOut, $!\n";
open(STDERR,">$StdErr") || die "Can't open STDERR to $StdErr, $!\n";

STDOUT->autoflush(1);
STDERR->autoflush(1);

print "to STDOUT\n";
print STDERR "to STDERR\n";

system "date";

open(STDOUT, ">&SAVESTDOUT");
open(STDERR, ">&SAVESTDERR");

print "back to original STDOUT\n";
print STDERR "back to original STDERR\n";
```

10. Run this second script. The output to the terminal will look like this:

`Output`
```
back to original STDOUT
back to original STDERR
```
`End Output`

11. sep2.std will now contain something like this:

```
to STDOUT
Mon Jan 01 12:31:28 CST 2001
```

12. sep2.err will be the same.

How It Works

When Perl launches commands, the commands inherit the standard filehandles (STDIN, STDOUT, STDERR). By changing where these filehandles point, you can affect the output (and input) of a command.

Why did the output seem to come out in the wrong order in the first example? STDOUT is buffered by default. That means that nothing is written until a block of output is accumulated. When more than one process is writing to the same filehandle, this can be a problem. In the first example, the first line was buffered. Then the date command was run and its output was also buffered. Whenever a process completes, it flushes its output. Because date finished first, its output was written first! The solution to this is to turn on autoflush before two processes can have the same filehandle open.

Comments

In the second example, autoflush was turned on for STDERR. This is usually not necessary because STDERR is supposed to have this turned on automatically by the operating system. But it is best to be safe.

The second example will not work under Perl 4 because the FileHandle module is not available. To create a Perl 4 script, remove the line with that module and make the following changes. The select lines change the current filehandle, turn on autoflush, and then return to the original filehandle.

```
$StdOut = "sep2.std";
$StdErr = "sep2.err";

open(SAVESTDOUT, ">&STDOUT") || die "Can't save STDOUT, $!\n";
open(SAVESTDERR, ">&STDERR") || die "Can't save STDERR, $!\n";

open(STDOUT,">$StdOut") || die "Can't open STDOUT to $StdOut, $!\n";
open(STDERR,">$StdErr") || die "Can't open STDERR to $StdErr, $!\n";

select((select(STDOUT), $| = 1)[0]);
select((select(STDERR), $| = 1)[0]);

print "to STDOUT\n";
print STDERR "to STDERR\n";

system "date";

open(STDOUT, ">&SAVESTDOUT");
open(STDERR, ">&SAVESTDERR");

print "back to original STDOUT\n";
print STDERR "back to original STDERR\n";
```

COMPLEXITY
INTERMEDIATE

5.2 How do I...
Unbuffer output?

COMPATIBILITY: PERL 4 PERL 5 UNIX DOS

Problem

Sometimes I like to be able to watch the progress of a script that is creating a file. The problem is that the data in the file is only written in blocks. I would like to watch the file grow, line by line. Is this possible?

Technique

Most output to a file is buffered. This is a performance enhancement because the file does not need to be updated as often and the data can be written in big chunks. It is easy to defeat this. Each filehandle contains an indication of whether it should buffer or not. The autoflush method of the filehandle can alter this behavior.

To turn on autoflush, use the FileHandle module. The autoflush method can then be used on any filehandle. To turn on autoflush for STDOUT, use the following syntax.

```
STDOUT->autoflush(1);
```

Steps

The example prints a line to both STDOUT and STDERR, turns on autoflush, and then prints another line to each output.

1. Create a file called unbuffer.pl. Add the following lines to it.

```
use FileHandle;

print "to STDOUT\n";
print STDERR "to STDERR\n";

STDOUT->autoflush(1);
STDERR->autoflush(1);

print "to STDOUT\n";
print STDERR "to STDERR\n";
```

2. Run the script and redirect both outputs to a file. (The syntax may vary, depending on which shell you are using. This example assumes /bin/sh.)

```
perl -w unbuffer.pl4 > unbuffer.out 2>&1
```

3. The output will look like this:

Output

```
to STDERR
to STDOUT
to STDOUT
to STDERR
```

End Output

4. Notice that the output is not in the same order as the lines were printed.

How It Works

Autoflush tells Perl to force out the data after every call to print. Normally, the data is not written out until a full block of data is accumulated or the filehandle is closed.

Comments

The example output will have the lines printed in the wrong order only if the output is redirected to a file. This occurs because STDOUT is not buffered if the output is directed to a terminal. STDERR is unbuffered in any case. (Thus, autoflush did not have to be turned on for it.)

The buffering of a filehandle can be turned on and off at will. It is best to buffer the output whenever possible. Unbuffer only when necessary. Turn buffering back on when it will not affect the outcome of your script.

DOS does not distinguish between STDOUT and STDERR. The use of autoflush is the same.

The example will not work under Perl 4 because the FileHandle module is not available. To create a Perl 4 script, remove the line with that module and make the following changes. The select lines change the current filehandle, turn on autoflush, and then return to the original filehandle.

```
print "to STDOUT\n";
print STDERR "to STDERR\n";

select((select(STDOUT), $| = 1)[0]);
select((select(STDERR), $| = 1)[0]);

print "to STDOUT\n";
print STDERR "to STDERR\n";
```

COMPLEXITY
ADVANCED

5.3 How do I...
Localize a filehandle?

COMPATIBILITY: PERL 4 PERL 5 UNIX DOS

Problem

I have a subroutine that needs to have a local filehandle. If I try to declare one, I get an error message. Can I do this?

Technique

Unfortunately, filehandles are not first-class citizens. You cannot make one local to a subroutine in a straightforward way. To get the effect you are looking for, you need to use type globs. In Perl, there can be many different variables with the same name. You can have a scalar variable named "var," an array named "var," an associative array named "var," and even a filehandle named "var." The collection of these is known as a type glob. Basically, a type glob is a pointer to a symbol table entry that contains the information about each of these variables.

You cannot declare a filehandle to be local to a subroutine, but you can declare a type glob to be local to one. By doing this, you are declaring all the variables with that name to be local to the subroutine. It's not pretty, but it does allow filehandles to be made local. To create a local type glob, use the following syntax.

```
local(*FILE);
```

Steps

The example contains a script that can read a file that references other files and outputs the expansion. This will be very familiar to anyone who has used nroff. If a line starts with .so, the rest of the line is taken as a file to be "sourced" in at that point.

1. Create five input files. The first is nroff.da1.

```
In file 1
\" Include file 2
.so nroff.da2
\" Include file 5
.so nroff.da5
```

2. The second is nroff.da2.

```
In file 2
\" Include file 3
.so nroff.da3
\" Include file 4
.so nroff.da4
```

3. The third is nroff.da3.

```
In file 3
```

4. The fourth is nroff.da4.

```
In file 4
```

5. The fifth is nroff.da5.

```
In file 5
```

6. Expanding nroff.da1 should produce the following.

| Output |

```
--Start nroff.da1--
In file 1
\" Include file 2
--Start nroff.da2--
In file 2
\" Include file 3
--Start nroff.da3--
In file 3
--End nroff.da3--
\" Include file 4
```

```
--Start nroff.da4--
In file 4
--End nroff.da4--
--End nroff.da2--
\" Include file 5
--Start nroff.da5--
In file 5
--End nroff.da5--
--End nroff.da1--
```
End Output

7. Create a file called nroff.pl. First, add lines to create a subroutine that takes a filename as the first argument, creates a local type glob, and prints the filename.

```perl
sub SoElim {
    my $file = $_[0];
    local(*FILE);

    print "--Start $file--\n";
```

8. Open the file that was passed as an argument using the type glob name as a filehandle. Loop through each line of the file looking for lines that start with .so. Call the subroutine recursively if such a line is found; otherwise, print the line.

```perl
open(FILE,$file) || die "Can't open $file, $!\n";
while(<FILE>) {
    if(/^\.so\s+([^><|\s]+)/) {
        SoElim($1);
    } else {
        print;
    }
}
```

9. Close the file and print a message.

```perl
close(FILE);
print "--End $file--\n";
}
```

10. The main body of the script calls the subroutine with the first filename.

```perl
SoElim("nroff.da1");
```

11. The entire script follows.

```perl
sub SoElim {
    my $file = $_[0];
    local(*FILE);

    print "--Start $file--\n";

    open(FILE,$file) || die "Can't open $file, $!\n";
    while(<FILE>) {
        if(/^\.so\s+([^><|\s]+)/) {
```

continued on next page

continued from previous page

```
                SoElim($1);
        } else {
            print;
        }
    }
    close(FILE);
    print "--End $file--\n";
}

SoElim("nroff.da1");
```

12. Run the script. The output should be the same as above.

How It Works

Every time local(*FILE) is executed, a new symbol table entry is created for all the variables whose names are FILE. This allows a new filehandle to be created that has the same name as other filehandles. When the subroutine is exited, the symbol table entry is freed and those variables are deleted.

Comments

When declaring a type glob to be local to a subroutine, be careful not to expect other variables with the same name to stay global. It is best to use unique names for each variable.

You must use local to make type globs local to a subroutine. If you try use my, Perl will flag the use as an error. Be careful: If you call other subroutines from a subroutine that declares a local type glob, they will see the new version of those variables, not the global ones.

Notice that the regular expression that matches the .so lines seems a bit more complicated than it needs to be.

```
/^\.so\s+([^><|\s]+)/
```

This is to protect against a .so line containing the characters special to the open command. If the .so line looked like

```
.so >/etc/passwd
```

it could clobber an existing file.

The script will only work under Perl 5. To make it work under Perl 4, the my needs to be turned into a local, and the subroutine calls need to be prepended with a &.

```
sub SoElim {
    local($file) = $_[0];
    local(*FILE);

    print "--Start $file--\n";

    open(FILE,$file) || die "Can't open $file, $!\n";
    while(<FILE>) {
        if(/^\.so\s+([^><|\s]+)/) {
```

```
            &SoElim($1);
        } else {
            print;
        }
    }
    close(FILE);
    print "--End $file--\n";
}

&SoElim("nroff.da1");
```

COMPLEXITY
ADVANCED

5.4 How do I...
Pass a filehandle to a function?

COMPATIBILITY: PERL 4   PERL 5   UNIX   DOS

Problem

I would like to make my Perl scripts more modular. I have tried to pass filehandles to subroutines without success. Is there a way to do this?

Technique

This problem is almost equivalent to the one in the last How-To, where you needed to localize filehandles. You need to pass a type glob to the subroutine. This is because filehandles are not normal variables. See the previous How-To for more discussion of the problem.

Steps

The example contains a script that can read a file that references other files and outputs the expansion. This will be very familiar to any one who has used nroff. If a line starts with .so, the rest of the line is taken as a file to be "sourced" in at that point. This example performs the same function as the previous How-To. Instead of opening the files local to the subroutine, filehandles (globs) will be passed.

1. Create five input files. The first is nroff.da1.

```
In file 1
\" Include file 2
.so nroff.da2
\" Include file 5
.so nroff.da5
```

2. The second is nroff.da2.

```
In file 2
\" Include file 3
.so nroff.da3
```

continued on next page

continued from previous page
```
\" Include file 4
.so nroff.da4
```
3. The third is nroff.da3.
```
In file 3
```
4. The fourth is nroff.da4.
```
In file 4
```
5. The fifth is nroff.da5.
```
In file 5
```
6. Expanding nroff.da1 should produce the following.

--- Output ---
```
--Start nroff.da1--
In file 1
\" Include file 2
--Start nroff.da2--
In file 2
\" Include file 3
--Start nroff.da3--
In file 3
--End nroff.da3--
\" Include file 4
--Start nroff.da4--
In file 4
--End nroff.da4--
--End nroff.da2--
\" Include file 5
--Start nroff.da5--
In file 5
--End nroff.da5--
--End nroff.da1--
```
--- End Output ---

7. Create a file called nroff.pl. First create a subroutine that takes a type glob and a filename as arguments. Then declare a local type glob and print the filename.
```
sub SoElim {
    local(*FILEIN) = $_[0];
    my($FileName) = $_[1];
    local(*FILE);

    print "--Start $FileName--\n";
```
8. Loop through each line of the file looking for lines that start with .so. If such a line is found, open the filename mentioned on the line and call the subroutine recursively. Otherwise, print the line.
```
while(<FILEIN>) {
        if(/^\.so\s+([^><|\s]+)/) {
```

```
                open(FILE,$1) || die "Can't open $1, $!\n";
                SoElim(*FILE,$1);
                close(FILE);
            } else {
                print;
            }
        }
    print "--End $FileName--\n";
}
```

9. The main body of the script opens the top level file and calls the subroutine.

```
$file_main = "nroff.da1";
open(FILE_MAIN,$file_main) || die "Can't open $file_main\n";
SoElim(*FILE_MAIN,$file_main);
close(FILE_MAIN);
```

10. The entire script should look like this:

```
sub SoElim {
    local(*FILEIN) = $_[0];
    my($FileName) = $_[1];
    local(*FILE);

    print "--Start $FileName--\n";
    while(<FILEIN>) {
        if(/^\.so\s+([^><|\s]+)/) {
            open(FILE,$1) || die "Can't open $1, $!\n";
            SoElim(*FILE,$1);
            close(FILE);
        } else {
            print;
        }
    }
    print "--End $FileName--\n";
}

$file_main = "nroff.da1";
open(FILE_MAIN,$file_main) || die "Can't open $file_main\n";
SoElim(*FILE_MAIN,$file_main);
close(FILE_MAIN);
```

How It Works

If filehandles were treated the same as a normal variable, this script would look like any other script in which arguments are passed. Because type globs are the only way to localize a filehandle, they must be used in recursive subroutines. In Perl 5, type globs can be passed by reference to subroutines that will use them as filehandles. This is sure to become the preferred method of passing filehandles. Type globs can always be passed directly, as in this example.

Comments

The filename is passed to the subroutine only so informational messages can be printed. It would not normally be needed.

The passing of a filehandle as a reference to a type glob can be seen in this code:

```perl
sub MyPrint {
    my $FileHandle = $_[0];
    my $Value = $_[1];

    print $FileHandle $Value;
}

MyPrint(\*STDOUT,"Hi Mom\n");
```

The nroff.pl script will only work under Perl 5. To make it work under Perl 4, the my needs to be turned into a local, and the subroutine calls need to be prepended with a &.

```perl
sub SoElim {
    local(*FILEIN) = $_[0];
    local($FileName) = $_[1];
    local(*FILE);

    print "--Start $FileName--\n";
    while(<FILEIN>) {
        if(/^\.so\s+([^><|\s]+)/) {
            open(FILE,$1) || die "Can't open $1, $!\n";
            &SoElim(*FILE,$1);
            close(FILE);
        } else {
            print;
        }
    }
    print "--End $FileName--\n";
}

$file_main = "nroff.da1";
open(FILE_MAIN,$file_main) || die "Can't open $file_main\n";
&SoElim(*FILE_MAIN,$file_main);
close(FILE_MAIN);
```

CHAPTER 6
ADVANCED CONTROL STRUCTURES

ADVANCED CONTROL STRUCTURES

How do I...

Perl provides many methods for controlling the execution of code. This makes it easy to manipulate data structures and other data. Most of these control structures involve looping. There are numerous ways to loop and various ways to alter the control flow in the loops. In addition, you can usually apply these methods to sequences of code that do not loop.

6.1   Loop Through a List

One of the more basic functions you can perform is looping through an array, acting on one data element at a time. This section will show you how.

6.2   Loop Through an Associative Array

Looping through an associative array is not easy. An associative array does not have an index, so Perl provides commands that facilitate looping. This section will demonstrate these commands.

6.3   Exit a Loop

It is not always desirable to execute a loop all the way to completion. This How-To will provide you with a method for exiting a loop.

6.4   Skip to the Next Iteration of a Loop

Sometimes the function a loop is providing does not apply to all the elements present in the data structure being acted upon. This section will show you a method of going to the next iteration of a loop without having to execute all the code in a loop.

6.5   Use Multiple Iterators in a Loop

An *iterator* is a variable used to index through an array. While acting on multiple data structures in parallel, it is often necessary to have multiple iterators. This How-To will provide two methods for accomplishing this.

6.6   Write a *switch* Statement

Often it is necessary to perform some actions based on the value of a variable. Perl has many methods of achieving this but does not provide a *switch* statement. Nevertheless, there are a number of ways to get the functionality of a *switch* statement. This How-To will show you a few of those ways.

COMPLEXITY
BEGINNING

6.1   How do I...
Loop through a list?

COMPATIBILITY: PERL 4 PERL 5 UNIX DOS

Problem

I have to create a list. How do I loop through each element of the list?

Technique

In Perl, lists and arrays are similar. To loop through an array, use an array index to access each element. To loop through a list, use the *foreach* statement to loop through each value. Use the *foreach* statement on arrays when you need just the values of the array. The array indexes will be ignored. The *foreach* loop looks like this:

```
foreach $Var (@list) {
}
```

The *foreach* loop is executed once for each element in the list (or array.) Each time through the loop, the *$Var* variable takes on the next element in the list.

Steps

The examples build an array of the first ten cubes and then access each number in turn.

1. Create a file called loop1.pl. Create a *foreach* loop that builds the first ten cubes. Remember that array indexes start with 0 in Perl.

```
foreach $Index (1..10) {
    $i = $Index - 1;
    $Array[$i] = $Index ** 3;
}
```

2. Create a second loop to print each value in the array.

```
foreach $Index (0..9) {
    print "The cube of ", $Index + 1, " is $Array[$Index]\n";
}
```

3. The entire script looks like this:

```
foreach $Index (1..10) {
    $i = $Index - 1;
    $Array[$i] = $Index ** 3;
}

foreach $Index (0..9) {
    print "The cube of ", $Index + 1, " is $Array[$Index]\n";
}
```

4. Run the script. The output follows.

| Output |

```
The cube of 1 is 1
The cube of 2 is 8
The cube of 3 is 27
The cube of 4 is 64
The cube of 5 is 125
The cube of 6 is 216
The cube of 7 is 343
The cube of 8 is 512
The cube of 9 is 729
The cube of 10 is 1000
```

| End Output |

5. If you do not need to use the array index, just access the values of the array. Because the *foreach* loop loops though the set of values given inside the parentheses, specify the array there. Copy loop1.pl to loop2.pl. Change the *foreach* loop to loop through the values, not the indexes.

```
foreach $Index (1..10) {
```

continued on next page

continued from previous page

```
    $i = $Index - 1;
    $Array[$i] = $Index ** 3;
}

print "The first 10 cubes are:";
foreach $Element (@Array) {
    print " $Element";
}
print "\n";
```

6. Run the script. The output follows.

Output

```
The first 10 cubes are: 1 8 27 64 125 216 343 512 729 1000
```
End Output

How It Works

The *foreach* loop loops through a set of values. These values can be specified as a set of indexes or a set of values. If indexes are used, the index can be used to access each element of an array. If an array is specified, each time though the loop the next array value will be accessed.

In list context, the .. operator will expand the sequence of numbers listed on either side of it. 1..10 will expand to the first 10 whole numbers.

Comments

The *foreach* loop is required only if you are looping through the array values. When using indexes, you can use other Perl constructs to loop through an array, for example, the *while* loop shown below.

```
$Index = 0;
while ($Index < 10) {
    print "The cube of ", $Index + 1, " is $Array[$Index]\n";
    $Index++;
}
```

Perl uses the @ character as the first character of an array variable. Use it when you need to refer to more than one element of an array. Use the $ character when accessing a single scalar variable. This is the method used to access single array elements. So @Array is the whole array, $Array[0] is the first element of the array, and @Array[0..2] is the first three elements of the array.

The example uses the fact that Perl arrays start with an index of 0. It is possible to change this with the $[variable. If you set this to 1, all arrays will start with an index of 1. This is a compiler directive in Perl 5, so it will be in effect only for the current source file. Its use is discouraged.

The keyword foreach is just an alias for *for*. Feel free to use either one.

Using 1..N where N is a large number can take up a great deal of space. It is better to loop through an array's values if possible. If that is not possible, a *while* loop that increments the index would be more efficient.

When accessing the entire range of an array's indexes, it is best to use the value

```
$#Array
```

instead of a fixed number. This construct gives the last index of an array. It can be used like

```
foreach $Index (0..$#Array) {
```

Using this method, you will not need to modify the script if the size of the array changes.

COMPLEXITY
INTERMEDIATE

6.2 How do I...
Loop through an associative array?

COMPATIBILITY: PERL 4   PERL 5   UNIX   DOS

Problem

I can loop through normal arrays using indexes. How do I loop through associative arrays?

Technique

Perl provides a number of commands to create lists of an associate array's values and/or keys. By using these commands, you can access each element of an associative array using a *foreach* loop. The commands are keys, values, and each.

Steps

The examples use an associative array that contains headers from a mail message. The input file contains one header per line. The header consists of a header keyword followed by a colon and the value of that header.

1. Create a file called aloop1.in. Add the following headers to it.

```
From: spock
To: someone@perl.com
Cc: somebody@perl.com
Subject: Just testing
```

2. Create a file called aloop1.pl. Add to it a *while* loop that reads a line from standard input and removes the new line character. Split the line into header and value, and save these values in an associative array. Limit the split command to two values in case the line has other colons in it.

```
while(<>) {
    chop;
    ($Header, $Value) = split(/:/,$_,2);
    $Value =~ s/^\s+//;              # remove trailing whitespace
    $Heading{$Header} = $Value;
}
```

3. Generate a list of the keys to the %Heading associative array by using the keys command. Sort the keys to give better looking output. Use a *foreach* loop to loop through each key. Print the key and the associative array value.

```
foreach $Head (sort keys %Heading) {
    print "$Head --> $Heading{$Head}\n";
}
```

4. The whole example follows.

```
while(<>) {
    chop;
    ($Header, $Value) = split(/:/,$_,2);
    $Value =~ s/^\s+//;              # remove trailing whitespace
    $Heading{$Header} = $Value;
}

foreach $Head (sort keys %Heading) {
    print "$Head --> $Heading{$Head}\n";
}
```

5. Run the script on the input file.

```
perl -w aloop1.pl aloop1.in
```

6. The output follows.

─ Output ├───

```
Cc --> somebody@perl.com
From --> spock
Subject --> Just testing
To --> someone@perl.com
```
End Output ├───

7. Another method for looping through an associative array is to use the each command. The each command returns both a key and a value. When used in a loop, it will return every pair in the associative array. Copy aloop1.pl to aloop2.pl. Change the loop to use the each command.

```
while(<>) {
    chop;
    ($Header, $Value) = split(/:/,$_,2);
    $Value =~ s/^\s+//;              # remove trailing whitespace
    $Heading{$Header} = $Value;
}
```

```
while ( ($Head,$Val) = each %Heading) {
    print "$Head --> $Val\n";
}
```

8. Run the script. The output should look like the following. (There is no sorting this time.)

Output

```
Subject --> Just testing
To --> someone@perl.com
From --> spock
Cc --> somebody@perl.com
```

End Output

9. Instead of using each to generate a key-value pair, assign the keys to one array and the values to a different array. Copy aloop2.pl to aloop3.pl. Create two arrays using the keys and values commands. Change the loop to use the values in those arrays.

```
while(<>) {
    chop;
    ($Header, $Value) = split(/:/,$_,2);
    $Value =~ s/^\s+//;              # remove trailing whitespace
    $Heading{$Header} = $Value;
}

@Heads = keys %Heading;
@Vals = values %Heading;

while ($Head = shift(@Heads)) {
    $Val = shift(@Vals);
    print "$Head --> $Val\n";
}
```

10. Run the script. The output should be the same as the last example.

How It Works

The approach is to generate a list using the keys command and then use a loop construct to access the items one at a time. Use the key to access the value of the associative array corresponding to that key.

The each command returns both the key and the value. In this case, the value is returned and thus the associative array does not need to be accessed to retrieve it. This also applies when using the values command.

The each, keys, and values commands generate a list of values. These values will be in a seemingly random sequence. However, the sequence will always be the same, unless the associative array is changed, and the values will always come out in the same order as the keys. (In other words, the first key will correspond to the first value, and so on.)

The use of while(<>) is special. If no files are given on the command line, standard input is read. If there are files on the command line, they are concatenated and read as if they were one big file. Each time through the *while* loop, the next line is assigned to the $_ variable. This is the default variable for most operators. For example, the chop command removes the last character of the $_ variable if no variable is given.

The *while* loop tests the return value of the statement inside the parentheses. The value of an assignment statement is the value that was assigned. When assigning from an array, when there is nothing left to return, False is returned and the *while* loop terminates.

Comments

Associative arrays do not preserve order. If you need to preserve the exact order of the elements, use a regular array. (Possibly two: one for the keys and one for the values.) In Perl 5, you can create an array of lists. Each list can contain both the key and value.

Both the key and value of each element of the associative arrays above were used. This does not have to be the case. You can use the preceding techniques to access just the keys or values.

COMPLEXITY
BEGINNING

6.3 How do I...
Exit a loop?

COMPATIBILITY: PERL 4 PERL 5 UNIX DOS

Problem

Sometimes I need to exit a loop before the loop would normally terminate. How do I do this?

Technique

Perl supplies the last command to exit a loop. Execution continues at the statement following the loop.

Steps

The first example looks for the first occurrence of a string in a file. The second example performs the same task with a label added to the loop.

1. Create a file called exit1.pl. Add the following lines to hold a pattern and filename. Then open the file for input.

```
$Pattern = "perl";
$File = "exit1.in";
open (FILE,$File) || die "Can't open $File, $!\n";
```

2. Loop through each line of the file checking for the pattern. If found, print it and exit the loop.

```perl
while(<FILE>) {
    if (/$Pattern/o) {
        print "$File: $_";
        last;
    }
}
close(FILE);
```

3. The entire script looks like this:

```perl
$Pattern = "perl";
$File = "exit1.in";
open (FILE,$File) || die "Can't open $File, $!\n";
while(<FILE>) {
    if (/$Pattern/o) {
        print "$File: $_";
        last;
    }
}
close(FILE);
```

4. Create an input file called exit1.in. Add the following lines to it.

```
Hi
bye
perl
mom
```

5. Run the script on the input file.

```
perl -w exit1.pl exit1.in
```

6. The output will be the following.

Output
---

exit1.in: perl

End Output
---

7. Modify the script to use a label. Copy exit1.pl to exit2.pl. Add a label.

```perl
$Pattern = "perl";
$File = "exit1.in";
open (FILE,$File) || die "Can't open $File, $!\n";
FileLoop:
while(<FILE>) {
    if (/$Pattern/o) {
        print "$File: $_";
        last FileLoop;
    }
}
close(FILE);
```

8. Run the new script. The output is the same as before.

How It Works

The last command exits the innermost loop enclosing it. Given a label, it exits the loop that has that label. Use a label when trying to exit from nested loops. It shows which loop is being exited and is the way to exit an outer loop.

Comments

The regular expression has an o appended to it.

```
/$Pattern/o
```

This speeds up Perl by telling it that the pattern will not change during the execution of the script. (Compile the pattern once.)

When you are reading lines into Perl and assigning them to a variable, make sure that the variable will contain the entire line including the end-of-line character(s). That is why there is no new-line character specified in the *print* statement. The new line already exists in the $_ variable.

COMPLEXITY
BEGINNING

6.4 How do I...
Skip to the next iteration of a loop?

COMPATIBILITY: PERL 4   PERL 5   UNIX   DOS

Problem

I need to be able to go to the next iteration of a loop without having to complete all the steps in a loop. Is this possible?

Technique

Perl supplies the next command to resume execution of a loop at the next iteration.

Steps

The example lists all the regular and readable files in a directory on one output line.

1. Create a file called skip1.pl. First add the following lines to open a directory. Use the current directory if no argument exists.

```
$Dir = ".";
$Dir = $ARGV[0] if defined($ARGV[0]);
opendir(DIR,$Dir) || die "Can't open directory '$Dir', $!\n";
```

2. Loop through each file in the directory. Check to see if the file is a regular file and if it is readable. If either one is not True, go to the next file.

```perl
while($File = readdir(DIR)) {
    -f "$Dir/$File" || next;
    -r _             || next;
```

3. Keep count of the number of files printed. The first file should not have a space prepended.

```perl
    $cnt++;
    if ($cnt == 1) {
        print "$File";
    } else {
        print " $File";
    }
}
```

4. Finish up by printing a new line and closing the directory.

```perl
print "\n";
closedir(DIR);
```

5. The entire script follows.

```perl
$Dir = ".";
$Dir = $ARGV[0] if defined($ARGV[0]);
opendir(DIR,$Dir) || die "Can't open directory '$Dir', $!\n";
while($File = readdir(DIR)) {
    -f "$Dir/$File" || next;
    -r _             || next;
    $cnt++;
    if ($cnt == 1) {
        print "$File";
    } else {
        print " $File";
    }
}
print "\n";
closedir(DIR);
```

6. Run the script.

```perl
perl -w skip1.pl
```

7. The output should look like the following.

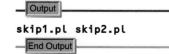

Output

skip1.pl skip2.pl

End Output

8. The next statement applies to the innermost loop enclosing it. To exit a higher-level loop, use a label. Modify this example to use next with a label. Copy skip1.pl to skip2.pl. Add a label to the loop.

```
$Dir = ".";
$Dir = $ARGV[0] if defined($ARGV[0]);
opendir(DIR,$Dir) || die "Can't open directory '$Dir', $!\n";
DirLoop:
while($File = readdir(DIR)) {
    -f "$Dir/$File" || next DirLoop;
    -r _              || next DirLoop;
    $cnt++;
    if ($cnt == 1) {
        print "$File";
    } else {
        print " $File";
    }
}
print "\n";
closedir(DIR);
```

9. Run the script. The output will be the same as before.

How It Works

The *next* statement causes execution to resume at the top of the loop. It has the same effect as if the statement were the last one in the loop.

The test to see if the file is readable looks like this:

```
-r _ || next;
```

The filename is not specified. An _ is given instead. This tells Perl to test the same file as the last file test. This can speed up the script because Perl will not need to go to the file system again to find out the information. (Perl caches the last file lookup.)

Comments

$Dir/$File is used when checking the status of a file. $File cannot be used because the file may be in a different directory. ($Dir may not be ".".)

When using *next* in a *for* loop, increment and test execute before the *next* iteration starts. This is normally the desired effect because that is what happens when a new iteration starts after finishing all the statements in the *for* loop.

The line

```
$Dir = $ARGV[0] if defined($ARGV[0]);
```

is just a variation on the *if* statement. It is equivalent to

```
if (defined($ARGV[0])) {
    $Dir = $ARGV[0];
}
```

All variables in Perl start with the value 0 or "". That is why $cnt can be incremented without being assigned an initial value. Normally, it is a good practice to do that initial assignment.

COMPLEXITY
INTERMEDIATE

6.5   How do I...
Use multiple iterators in a loop?

COMPATIBILITY:  PERL 4   PERL 5   UNIX   DOS

Problem

I can use a *for* loop to iterate though an array. Occasionally, I need to loop through two arrays in the same loop. How can I do this?

Technique

It is possible to increment multiple iterators in a *for* loop. The trick involves using the comma operator. The comma operator allows two statements to be executed where one is usually performed. Because the *for* loop allows only one statement to be executed as part of the increment, the comma operator allows two different increments. Thus, you can say

```
for($i = 0, $j = 0;($i <= 9) && ($j <= 9);$i++,$j++)
```

A more elegant way involves using the *continue* statement in conjunction with a *while* loop. The *continue* statement is executed each time an iteration through the *while* loop completes. Multiple statements can appear in the *continue* statement.

Steps

The examples try to determine if one of the two arrays passed is a subarray of the other. To simplify the example, assume that the arrays contain sorted integers. The arrays are passed in as arguments, with each element separated by white space.

1. Create a file called mult1.pl. First, store the input arrays into two Perl arrays. Next, determine which array is larger. Remember which array is larger; then make @ArrayA be the larger array.

```
@ArrayA = split(/\s+/,$ARGV[0]);
@ArrayB = split(/\s+/,$ARGV[1]);

if ($#ArrayA < $#ArrayB) {
    $BigArray = "Array2";
    $SmallArray = "Array1";
    @TmpArray = @ArrayA;
    @ArrayA = @ArrayB;
    @ArrayB = @TmpArray;
} else {
    $BigArray = "Array1";
    $SmallArray = "Array2";
}
```

2. Because @ArrayA is larger, you need to check to see if @ArrayB is a subarray. If @ArrayB is a subarray, its first element must match one of @ArrayA's elements. Start with both array indexes at 0 and loop through the elements of @ArrayA looking for a match with the first element of @ArrayB.

```
$Aindex = 0;
$Bindex = 0;
for ($i=0;$i<=$#ArrayA;$i++) {
    if ($ArrayB[$Bindex] <= $ArrayA[$i]) {
        $Aindex = $i;
        last;
    }
}
```

3. Once you have found the start of the match, compare the elements in the two arrays to see if they match.

```
$SubArray = 1;
for(;($Aindex <= $#ArrayA) && ($Bindex <= $#ArrayB);$Aindex++,$Bindex++) {
    if ($ArrayA[$Aindex] != $ArrayB[$Bindex]) {
        $SubArray = 0;
        last;
    }
}
```

4. Print the results.

```
if ($SubArray && ($Bindex > $#ArrayB)) {
    print "$SmallArray is a subarray of $BigArray\n";
} else {
    print "$SmallArray is not a subarray of $BigArray\n";
}
```

5. Here is the finished script:

```
@ArrayA = split(/\s+/,$ARGV[0]);
@ArrayB = split(/\s+/,$ARGV[1]);

if ($#ArrayA < $#ArrayB) {
    $BigArray = "Array2";
    $SmallArray = "Array1";
    @TmpArray = @ArrayA;
    @ArrayA = @ArrayB;
    @ArrayB = @TmpArray;
} else {
    $BigArray = "Array1";
    $SmallArray = "Array2";
}
$Aindex = 0;
$Bindex = 0;
for ($i=0;$i<=$#ArrayA;$i++) {
    if ($ArrayB[$Bindex] <= $ArrayA[$i]) {
        $Aindex = $i;
        last;
    }
}

$SubArray = 1;
for(;($Aindex <= $#ArrayA) && ($Bindex <= $#ArrayB);$Aindex++,$Bindex++) {
    if ($ArrayA[$Aindex] != $ArrayB[$Bindex]) {
```

```
            $SubArray = 0;
            last;
        }
    }

if ($SubArray && ($Bindex > $#ArrayB)) {
    print "$SmallArray is a subarray of $BigArray\n";
} else {
    print "$SmallArray is not a subarray of $BigArray\n";
}
```

6. Run the script on two arrays.

```
perl -w mult1.pl '1 2 3 4' '2 3 4'
```

7. The output follows.

Output

Array2 is a subarray of Array1

End Output

---

8. To use the *while* loop with the *continue* statement instead, remove the increments from the *for* loop and change it to a *while* loop.

```
@ArrayA = split(/\s+/,$ARGV[0]);
@ArrayB = split(/\s+/,$ARGV[1]);

if ($#ArrayA < $#ArrayB) {
    $BigArray = "Array2";
    $SmallArray = "Array1";
    @TmpArray = @ArrayA;
    @ArrayA = @ArrayB;
    @ArrayB = @TmpArray;
} else {
    $BigArray = "Array1";
    $SmallArray = "Array2";
}
$Aindex = 0;
$Bindex = 0;
for ($i=0;$i<=$#ArrayA;$i++) {
    if ($ArrayB[$Bindex] <= $ArrayA[$i]) {
        $Aindex = $i;
        last;
    }
}

$SubArray = 1;
while(($Aindex <= $#ArrayA) && ($Bindex <= $#ArrayB)) {
    if ($ArrayA[$Aindex] != $ArrayB[$Bindex]) {
        $SubArray = 0;
        last;
    }
} continue {
    $Aindex++;
    $Bindex++;
```

continued on next page

continued from previous page
```
}

if ($SubArray && ($Bindex > $#ArrayB)) {
    print "$SmallArray is a subarray of $BigArray\n";
} else {
    print "$SmallArray is not a subarray of $BigArray\n";
}
```

9. Run the second script. The output will be the same.

How It Works

The comma operator is merely a way of joining two statements into one large one. The result of the larger statement is the result of the second statement. The result of the first statement is ignored.

The *continue* statement allows an arbitrary number of statements to be executed at the end of a *while* loop. This makes it easy to use the *while* loop as a *for* loop. By using a *while* loop in this manner, you may be able to express the sometimes messy statements inside the *for* loop parentheses more clearly.

The standard way of turning a *for* loop into a *while* loop is to put the initialization portion before the beginning of the *while* loop. The condition goes into the *while* loop parentheses and the iteration portion goes into the *continue* block.

Comments

Multiple comma operators can be used in the same statement. This makes it possible to increment more than two iterators at once.

The variable used as an incrementor in a *for* loop is local to the *for* loop body unless it was declared previously. It is necessary to save this value in another variable if you wish to use it after the end of the *for* loop.

COMPLEXITY
ADVANCED

6.6 How do I...
Write a switch statement?

COMPATIBILITY: PERL 4   PERL 5   UNIX   DOS

Problem

I need to be able to execute different code based on the value of a variable. I cannot find a *switch* statement in my Perl manual. Is there one?

Technique

There is not a *switch* (case) statement in Perl. However, there are many ways to perform the same function. Because Perl is very efficient at optimizing the way it executes code, most ways to switch cases in Perl end up being just as efficient as if there were a *switch* statement.

Steps

The examples show a way to evaluate options passed to a program. The options are DOS-like: a / followed by some characters, optionally followed by some values. This example is not complete. It just shows how to execute code based on the current option being evaluated.

The first example uses syntax that makes it look like a *switch* statement in other languages. The second example uses an *if* statement; most of the time an *if* statement is easier to write and just as efficient.

1. Create a file called switch1.pl. Add the following lines to it. First, shift off any options on the command line and store them in a variable. (This will strip away any white space between options.)

```
$Args = "";
while (@ARGV) {
    $ARGV[0] =~ m%^/% || last;
    $Args .= shift;
}
```

2. Remove the leading slash and then split the option variable into the individual options. Loop over the options, evaluating one at a time.

```
$Args =~ s%^/%%;
foreach $Arg (split("/",$Args)) {
```

3. Because each option can have an optional value part, match on the option name. Store the name in $_.

```
$Arg =~ /\w+/;
$_ = $&;
```

4. Create a block of statements with a label. Check for the A option. The default variable to check a regular expression against is the $_ variable; we have already assigned the option to that. If the match succeeds, execute the *do* block. The last statement in the *do* block is the last command. It will cause the *switch* statement to be exited.

```
CASE: {
        /^A$/ && do {
                print "Found A\n";
                last CASE;
            };
```

5. Do the same thing for the other options.

```
        /^B$/ && do {
                print "Found B\n";
                last CASE;
            };
        /^C$/ && do {
                print "Found C\n";
                last CASE;
            };
        /^HELP$/ && do {
```

continued on next page

continued from previous page

```
                        print "Found HELP\n";
                        last CASE;
                };
```

6. If no option has matched, print that fact.

```
        print "Unknown option found: /$Arg\n";
    }
}
```

7. The whole example should now look like this:

```perl
$Args = "";
while (@ARGV) {
    $ARGV[0] =~ m%^/% || last;
    $Args .= shift;
}

$Args =~ s%^/%%;
foreach $Arg (split("/",$Args)) {
    $Arg =~ /\w+/;
    $_ = $&;
    CASE: {
        /^A$/ && do {
                        print "Found A\n";
                        last CASE;
                };
        /^B$/ && do {
                        print "Found B\n";
                        last CASE;
                };
        /^C$/ && do {
                        print "Found C\n";
                        last CASE;
                };
        /^HELP$/ && do {
                        print "Found HELP\n";
                        last CASE;
                };
        print "Unknown option found: /$Arg\n";
    }
}
```

8. Run the script.

```
perl -w switch1.pl /A/C /HELP /B /Foo/Bar:3
```

9. The output follows.

Output

```
Found A
Found C
Found HELP
Found B
Unknown option found: /Foo
Unknown option found: /Bar:3
```

End Output

10. The solution could just as well use an *if* statement. Copy switch1.pl to switch2.pl. Change the "switch" code to use an *if* statement instead.

```perl
$Args = "";
while (@ARGV) {
    $ARGV[0] =~ m%^/% || last;
    $Args .= shift;
}

$Args =~ s%^/%%;
foreach $Arg (split("/",$Args)) {
    $Arg =~ /\w+/;
    $_ = $&;
    if (/^A$/) {
        print "Found A\n";
    } elsif  (/^B$/) {
        print "Found B\n";
    } elsif  (/^C$/) {
        print "Found C\n";
    } elsif  (/^HELP$/) {
        print "Found HELP\n";
    } else {
        print "Unknown option found: /$Arg\n";
    }
}
```

11. Run the script. The output will be the same.

How It Works

The functionality of a *switch* statement is available in many forms in Perl. A *switch* statement is just a fancy way of checking a variable against a set of possible values. Both examples check for the possible values and execute code when one is found. The first example needs to make sure that no additional checking is attempted once a match is found. This is accomplished using the last command to jump out of the code that was checking values.

A block of code (code between {}) can be treated like a loop that executes just once. The next, last, and redo operators will work in that block. A label is needed for the last statement because it was also enclosed in a *do* block.

Comments

The first *while* loop's check was @ARGV. @ARGV in this context (scalar context) returns the number of elements in the array. This is true of any array. Using an array in list context (as in a *foreach* loop) causes all the values of the array to be returned.

Use a *do* block in places where you want to execute multiple statements, but only one is available (such as after the && operator). Notice that the shift operator uses @ARGV by default. This is unusual because most operators use $_ by default.

When matching values with regular expressions, remember that substring matches are successful. If, when trying to match the A option, the regular expression had been /A/, any option that contained an A would have successfully matched.

That is why the regular expression contained the beginning of line (^) and end of line ($) characters (/^A$/). If all the matched are going to be on the full value, using the eq operator may be more clear. If not, be careful of the order in which the regular expressions are tried. (Check /AE/ before /A/.)

The normal pattern-matching string is the regular expression surrounded by /s, such as /A/. However, if the pattern contains a slash, it is often easier to use a different character to express the pattern. The m command allows this. The next character after the m is taken to be the pattern delimiter (e.g., m%^/%). The substitution command also allows any character (s%/%%).

USER INPUT

USER INPUT

How do I...

Many Perl scripts need to collect and process user input. This chapter shows you various ways to collect that input, along with ways to manipulate it. Perl allows you to interact with the operating system to access its many input modes. This allows you to write scripts that provide different methods of interacting with the user.

7.1 Read a Line of Input from the Keyboard

The simplest interaction with the user is to collect a single line of input. This section will show you how.

7.2 Read a Single Character from the Keyboard

Sometimes the interaction with the user should be at the character level instead of the line level. This How-To will show how to tell the operating system to return each character one at a time.

7.3 Read a Password Without Echoing It

Passwords and occasionally other data should not be visible on the screen. This prevents onlookers from observing that data. This section will show you how to turn off the echoing.

7.4 Convert Mixed-Case Input

When the case of the input is not important, you can convert it to all lowercase or all uppercase. This How-To will show you how.

7.5 Validate Input

Verifying that entered data is valid can be a complicated job. Perl provides many ways of dealing with the input. You can check both the format and the validity of fields. This section will show you how.

7.6 Implement a Simple Menu Interface

If there is a well-defined number of responses that a user can enter, you might want to provide a menu. The program can check a user's choice from the menu; if the choice is invalid, the user can be prompted to make a correct choice. This How-To will show you how to do this.

COMPLEXITY
BEGINNING

7.1 How do I...
Read a line of input from the keyboard?

COMPATIBILITY: | PERL 4 | PERL 5 | UNIX | DOS |

Problem

I need to query the user for input. How can I do this?

Technique

By default, all input to a Perl program comes from standard input. This input is received from the keyboard unless it is redirected by the user. Therefore, getting input from the keyboard is usually easier than getting it from anywhere else.

The first example shows a simple way to retrieve one line of input from standard input. This script reads data from the keyboard as long as no files are passed to the script as arguments. If they are, standard input will come from those files instead of from the keyboard. The second script shows a method of retrieving input from the keyboard even if standard input is coming from a file.

Steps

1. Create a file called input1.pl. Add the following lines to unbuffer standard output, prompt the user, and retrieve a line of input. Then remove the new-line character and print the input.

```perl
$| = 1;
print "Please enter data here: ";
$Input = <>;
chop $Input;
print "Input = $Input\n";
```

2. Run the script. You will get a prompt like this:

```
Output
```

```
Please enter data here:
```

```
End Output
```

3. Enter "hi." The result of the entire session follows.

```
Output
```

```
Please enter data here: hi
Input = hi
```

```
End Output
```

4. If standard input is not coming from the keyboard, you need to open it. The name of the device to open depends on the operating system. Copy input1.pl into input2.pl. Add a variable that tells whether UNIX or DOS is the current operating system and select the correct device to open for input.

```perl
$DOS = 0;

if ($DOS) {
    $Console = "con";
} else {
    $Console = "/dev/tty";
}
open(IN,"$Console") || die "Can't open $Console, $!\n";

$| = 1;
print "Please enter data here: ";
$Input = <IN>;
chop $Input;
print "Input = $Input\n";

close(IN);
```

5. Run the script. The input and output should be the same as before.

How It Works

Many Perl scripts operate on standard input. The language makes it easy to use that input. Perl opens standard input for you before a script starts executing. The use of <> means that one line should be read from "the usual place." That place is standard input if no files were passed to the script as arguments. If there are files on the command line, <> will read each line from each file one at a time. Perl takes care of opening and closing each of the files.

In the second example, <IN> is used to read a line from the filehandle IN. This is the standard method of reading from any filehandle.

Comments

If you wish to access standard input, even if files are passed as arguments, the construct <STDIN> will do this. It does not have the magical properties that <> does. Be aware that standard input can be redirected away from the keyboard by the user.

If <> (or any <filehandle>) is used in an array context, the lines are not read one by one, but all the lines are read and each line is assigned to an array element. For example:

```
@Lines = <>;
```

Each line is assigned from standard input or the input files to the array. This can be useful when performing operations that depend on the context in which a specific line is found.

COMPLEXITY
ADVANCED

7.2 How do I...
Read a single character from the keyboard?

COMPATIBILITY: PERL 4 | PERL 5 | UNIX | DOS

Problem

I have an application where I want to retrieve one character from the user and then provide feedback. Requiring the user to enter a new line after each character seems excessive. Can I get the character without the new line being entered?

Technique

Most operating systems improve system performance by returning only complete lines to a read operation. The system must be told to return individual characters if that is the desired functionality. This is very system-dependent. A Perl 5 module called ReadKey was created to hide these details. If this module exists on your system, the functionality you want is easy to achieve. If not, there are some system-dependent tricks that you can try. These may or may not work on any given system. Only a trial of the given script will reveal if the trick will work on your system. If you do not have the ReadKey module (or another module) and would like to get it, see Appendix A.

Steps

The first two scripts show the use of the ReadKey module. The third script uses the Curses module. Try this module if the ReadKey module is not available. If neither of these modules is available or only Perl 4 is available, the last two scripts show some operating-system-dependent tricks that can be tried.

1. Create a file called char1.pl. Add the following lines to import the ReadKey module, set cbreak mode on standard input, and read a character.

```
use Term::ReadKey;

print "Please enter character here: ";
ReadMode("cbreak",STDIN);
$Input = getc(STDIN);
ReadMode("original",STDIN);
print "$Input\nInput = $Input\n";
```

2. Run the script. You will be prompted for a character.

Output

```
Please enter character here:
```
End Output
---

3. Enter "a." The entire output will then look like this:

Output

```
Please enter character here: a
Input = a
```
End Output
---

4. A problem can occur with the first example. What if the user interrupts the script before the second call is made to ReadMode? To make sure that the input modes are reset in case of an interrupt, put the reset call into the END subroutine and catch all possible interrupts. Now if the user interrupts the script, the signal will be caught and the script will exit normally. Now the modes will be reset even if the script is interrupted. Copy char1.pl into char2.pl. Add the END subroutine and catch the signals.

```perl
use Term::ReadKey;
sub GotSig {
    exit;
}

$SIG{"INT"}  = "GotSig";
$SIG{"QUIT"} = "GotSig";
$SIG{"TERM"} = "GotSig";

print "Please enter character here: ";
ReadMode("cbreak",STDIN);
$Input = getc(STDIN);
print "$Input\nInput = $Input\n";

sub END {
    ReadMode("original",STDIN);
}
```

5. Run the script. Interrupt it before entering a character. The modes are reset.

6. If the ReadKey module is not present, you can try the Curses module. (The Curses cbreak mode leaves echoing on.)

```perl
use Curses;

sub GotSig {
    exit;
}

$SIG{"INT"}  = "GotSig";
$SIG{"QUIT"} = "GotSig";
$SIG{"TERM"} = "GotSig";

print "Please enter character here: ";
&cbreak;
$Input = getc(STDIN);
print "\nInput = $Input\n";

sub END {
    &nocbreak;
}
```

7. Run the script. It should behave just like the ReadKey script.

8. If neither module exists on your system or you are using Perl 4, you can try one of the following two scripts. This first script is for UNIX systems. The method of turning on cbreak mode depends on which version of UNIX is being run. Copy char3.pl into char4.pl.

```perl
sub GotSig {
    exit;
}

$SIG{"INT"}  = "GotSig";
$SIG{"QUIT"} = "GotSig";
$SIG{"TERM"} = "GotSig";

$Bsd = -f "/vmunix";
```

```
print "Please enter character here: ";
if ($Bsd) {
    system "stty cbreak < /dev/tty > /dev/tty 2>&1";
} else {
    system "stty -icanon eof ^a";
}
$Input = getc(STDIN);
print "\nInput = $Input\n";

sub END {
    if ($Bsd) {
        system "stty -cbreak < /dev/tty > /dev/tty 2>&1";
    } else {
        system "stty icanon eof ^d";
    }
}
```

9. Run the script. It will behave as before.

10. The DOS method of allowing single-character input is also very magical. If the ioctl command is supported in your version of Perl, the following should work. Copy char4.pl to char5.pl. Make the following changes.

```
$IoctlSave = ioctl(STDIN,0,0);
$IoctlSave &= 0xff;

sub GotSig {
    exit;
}

$SIG{"INT"}  = "GotSig";
$SIG{"QUIT"} = "GotSig";
$SIG{"TERM"} = "GotSig";

print "Please enter character here: ";
ioctl(STDIN,1,$IoctlSave | 32);
sysread(STDIN,$Input,1);
print "\nInput = $Input\n";

sub END {
    ioctl(STDIN,1,$IoctlSave);
}
```

11. Run the script. Again the script behaves like before.

How It Works

The operating system needs to be told that input is desired character by character. Each operating system has its own way of setting this mode. The ReadKey module makes this transparent to a Perl script. Unfortunately, the ReadKey module is not yet a standard part of the Perl distribution. If it exists on your system or you can get it, this is the best way of handling single-character input. The Curses module can also be helpful, but again, it is not standard.

If neither module can be found, you will need to access the operating system directly. This is system-dependent. Under UNIX, use the stty command to modify the characteristics of the terminal. The options for stty vary by the version and provider of the operating system. You may need to read up on stty to get the proper arguments. Under DOS, you can try to use the ioctl command to modify the terminal characteristics. This is highly magical and may not work.

Comments

An easy method of determining whether a module is loaded on your system is to try a one-line script that has the use command in it. If this script does not fail, the module is available.

In addition to telling the operating system to return individual characters, cbreak mode turns off special character processing. For example, the delete character will no longer delete the previous character, but it will be returned from a read just like any other character. The cbreak mode of ReadKey also turns off the echoing of characters. If you want the user to see the character(s) entered, you will need to print them.

The END subroutine is a special one in Perl 5. This routine is called whenever a Perl script exits. This is a good place to do clean up. By trapping signals and calling exit from the signal handler, the END subroutine will run in even abnormal situations.

Be careful if you use sysread to input data. Mixing that call with the normal inputting functions can cause the input to be read in an incorrect order. It is best not to mix input reading types. If no mixing is done, the data will always be read in the proper order.

Modules are not available in Perl 4. Because the last two examples do not use modules, they can be compatible with Perl 4. The END subroutine is not called when a Perl 4 script exits. You can add this call manually. For example, modify char4.pl to call the END subroutine.

```perl
sub GotSig {
    &END;
    exit;
}

$SIG{"INT"}  = "GotSig";
$SIG{"QUIT"} = "GotSig";
$SIG{"TERM"} = "GotSig";

$Bsd = -f "/vmunix";

print "Please enter character here: ";
if ($Bsd) {
    system "stty cbreak < /dev/tty > /dev/tty 2>&1";
} else {
    system "stty -icanon eof ^a";
}
$Input = getc(STDIN);
print "\nInput = $Input\n";
&END;
```

```
sub END {
    if ($Bsd) {
        system "stty -cbreak < /dev/tty > /dev/tty 2>&1";
    } else {
        system "stty icanon eof ^d";
    }
}
```

COMPLEXITY
BEGINNING

7.3   How do I...
Read a password without echoing it?

COMPATIBILITY:

Problem

I need to prompt the user for a password. Normal input is echoed to the screen; that is not appropriate for this task. Can I turn off the echoing?

Technique

The operating system must be told not to echo input. This is operating system-dependent. The Perl 5 module ReadKey can hide the operating-system details. Unfortunately, ReadKey is not a standard part of Perl 5. If you do not have it and wish to get it, see Appendix A.

Steps

The first two examples show the use of ReadKey to turn off input echoing. If ReadKey is not available or Perl 4 is being used, use the the third example to turn off echoing under UNIX.

1. Create a file called noecho1.pl. Add the following lines to it. First import the ReadKey module and tell standard input not to echo. Read the password and reset the input mode. To verify that it works, print the password.

```
use Term::ReadKey;

ReadMode("noecho",STDIN);
print "Enter your password: ";
$Password = <>;
chop $Password;
print "\n";
ReadMode("original",STDIN);

print "$Password\n";
```

Run the script. When prompted for a password, enter "PassWord." The output will look like this:

— Output ——

```
Enter your password:
PassWord
```
End Output ———

3. If the user breaks out of the script without entering a password, the system will be left in the noecho state. To prevent this, put the restore of the input modes into the END subroutine and catch all the possible signals. In this way, the input modes are restored even if the script is interrupted. Copy noecho1.pl to noecho2.pl. Make the following changes.

```perl
use Term::ReadKey;

sub GotSig {
    exit;
}

$SIG{"INT"}  = "GotSig";
$SIG{"QUIT"} = "GotSig";
$SIG{"TERM"} = "GotSig";

ReadMode("noecho",STDIN);
print "Enter your password: ";
$Password = <>;
chop $Password;
print "\n";

print "$Password\n";

sub END {
    ReadMode("original",STDIN);
}
```

4. Run the script. Interrupt it before entering a password. Echoing will be turned back on.

5. If the ReadKey module is not available, the next script can be used under UNIX to get the same behavior. Copy noecho2.pl to noecho3.pl. Make the following changes.

```perl
sub GotSig {
    exit;
}

$SIG{"INT"}  = "GotSig";
$SIG{"QUIT"} = "GotSig";
$SIG{"TERM"} = "GotSig";

system "stty -echo";
print "Enter your password: ";
```

```
$Password = <>;
chop $Password;
print "\n";

print "$Password\n";

sub END {
    system "stty echo";
}
```

6. Run the script. It should behave exactly like the previous script.

How It Works

The operating system must be told to turn off input character echoing. The ReadKey module provides an operating system-independent method of doing this. Unfortunately, ReadKey may not be available on your system. If it is not, the UNIX command stty can be issued to turn echoing on and off.

Comments

The use of the string Term::ReadKey to access ReadKey means that ReadKey is part of a grouping of modules under a parent module. In this case, the parent module is Term. Other modules exist under Term that provide other terminal accessing functionality.

Passwords should never be printed. These scripts do so to show that they are operating correctly. Do not do this except for debugging; even then, use phony passwords.

The END subroutine is a special one in Perl 5. This routine is called whenever a Perl script exits. This is a good place to do cleanup. By trapping signals and calling exit from the signal handler, the END subroutine will run even in abnormal situations.

Modules are not available in Perl 4. The last example does not use modules, so it can be compatible with Perl 4. The END subroutine is not called when a Perl 4 script exits. You can add this call manually. For example, you can modify noecho3.pl to call the END subroutine.

```
sub GotSig {
    &END;
    exit;
}

$SIG{"INT"}  = "GotSig";
$SIG{"QUIT"} = "GotSig";
$SIG{"TERM"} = "GotSig";

system "stty -echo";
print "Enter your password: ";
$Password = <>;
chop $Password;
print "\n";
```

continued on next page

continued from previous page
```
print "$Password\n";
&END;

sub END {
    system "stty echo";
}
```

COMPLEXITY
BEGINNING

7.4   How do I...
Convert mixed-case input?

COMPATIBILITY: PERL 4 | PERL 5 | UNIX | DOS

Problem

I have an input file that contains data in mixed case. How can I convert it to a single case so I can work with it?

Technique

Perl provides a number of methods of converting data to a single case. A mixed-case string can be converted to lowercase or uppercase. The first method is to use special characters in a string to tell Perl to convert the case of the string. The second method is to call the Perl 5 functions that do case conversion.

Steps

The first example changes the case of input and tries to match the input against some strings. The second example changes the case of any input given to it.

1. Create a file called mixed1.pl. First create a loop to read in the data. Print the input line while surrounding it with the \L and \E special characters. Any characters after the \L are converted to lowercase. This change of case continues until the \E character is seen. You do not need the \E special character if the case conversion continues until the end of the string.

```
while ($Input = <>) {
    print "\L$Input\E";
    print "\L$Input";
```

2. Use the special characters to compare the input with some strings.

```
chop $Input;
if ("\L$Input" eq "lowercase") {
    print "Found lowercase\n";
}
print "\U$Input\n";
if ("\U$Input" eq "UPPERCASE") {
    print "Found UPPERCASE\n";
}
}
```

3. The entire script looks like this:

```perl
while ($Input = <>) {
    print "\L$Input\E";
    print "\L$Input";
    chop $Input;
    if ("\L$Input" eq "lowercase") {
        print "Found lowercase\n";
    }
    print "\U$Input\n";
    if ("\U$Input" eq "UPPERCASE") {
        print "Found UPPERCASE\n";
    }
}
```

4. Create an input file called mixed1.in. Add the following lines to it.

```
Hi Mom
uppercase
LOWERCASE
```

5. Run the script on this input file. The output follows.

Output

```
hi mom
hi mom
HI MOM
uppercase
uppercase
UPPERCASE
Found UPPERCASE
lowercase
lowercase
Found lowercase
LOWERCASE
```
End Output
---

6. Perl 5 provides access to the functions that do the case conversion. These functions take a string as a parameter and return the same string with the case converted. The function lc converts the string to lowercase, whereas the function uc changes the string to uppercase. Create a file called mixed2.pl to use these functions. Add the following lines.

```perl
while ($Input = <>) {
    print lc($Input);
    print uc($Input);
}
```

7. Run this script on mixed1.in. The output follows.

Output

```
hi mom
HI MOM
uppercase
```

continued on next page

continued from previous page
```
UPPERCASE
lowercase
LOWERCASE
```
End Output

How It Works

Perl provides functions that change the case of a string. These functions can be called directly in Perl 5. In both Perl 5 and Perl 4, these functions can be accessed by embedding special characters in a string.

Comments

The case-converting functions have no effect on any characters that are not alphabetic.

COMPLEXITY
INTERMEDIATE

7.5   How do I...
Validate input?

COMPATIBILITY: `PERL 4` `PERL 5` `UNIX` `DOS`

Problem

When reading input, I need to verify that the data conforms to a set of criteria. How can I do this?

Technique

There are many ways to process data in Perl. The input can be checked to verify that it is in a certain format, and each individual piece of data can be checked to see if it is valid. These functions are achieved by using Perl's pattern-matching and comparison functions.

The examples show how to verify some simple input. The same techniques can be used for very complex data.

Steps

The first example checks the format of some data. The second example checks the format and then verifies that some fields of that data meet specific criteria.

1. Create a file called valid1.pl. First read in an input line. Then verify the format of the line. In this case, the input lines should contain a number followed by a string followed by another number. If the data is valid, save the individual fields and print *Success*. Otherwise, print an error message.

```perl
while ($Input = <>) {
    chop($Input);
    if ($Input =~ /^(\d+)\s+(\w+)\s+(\d+)$/) {
```

```
        $Num1 = $1;
        $String = $2;
        $Num2 = $3;
        print "'$Input' is valid\n";
    } else {
        print "Bad Data\n";
    }
}
```

2. Create an input file called valid1.pl. Add the following lines to it.

```
1 abc 4
a b c
11 abc 9
11 ValidData1 9
```

3. Run the script against this file. The output follows.

```
'1 abc 4' is valid
Bad Data
'11 abc 9' is valid
'11 ValidData1 9' is valid
```

4. If a string can take on only a fixed number of values, you can create an associative array that contains those values as a key. Set the value of each entry in the associate array to 1 to show that that key is valid. Copy valid1.pl into valid2.pl. Add a check of the value of the first number. Then add an associative array of valid values for the string. Validate the string using the associative array.

```
%Valid = (
    "ValidData1" => 1,
    "ValidData2" => 1,
    "ValidData3" => 1,
);

while ($Input = <>) {
    chop($Input);
    if ($Input =~ /^(\d+)\s+(\w+)\s+(\d+)$/) {
        $Num1 = $1;
        $String = $2;
        $Num2 = $3;
        if ($Num1 <= 10) {
            print "First Field must be greater than 10\n";
        } elsif (defined($Valid{$String})) {
            print "'$Input' is valid\n";
        } else {
            print "String invalid\n";
        }
    } else {
        print "Bad Data\n";
    }
}
```

5. Run the script on the same input file as before. The output follows.

Output

```
First Field must be greater than 10
Bad Data
String invalid
'11 ValidData1 9' is valid
```

End Output

How It Works

The pattern-matching ability of Perl is powerful. It can verify that a string (line of input) is in a certain format. As a side effect, field values are saved in variables. This makes it quite easy to verify and collect data from a string. Once the fields are broken out of an input line, these fields can be checked for validity.

To see how regular expressions work, consider the regular expression used in the script.

```
/^(\d+)\s+(\w+)\s+(\d+)$/
```

The regular expression starts at the beginning of the line (^). Then it matches a number (\d+). Next it verifies that the number is separated from the next field by at least one white space character (\s+). A word must come after the space (\w+). More white space must follow, and then another number. The regular expression then checks for the end of line after the second number to verify that there are no more fields on the line ($). The parentheses around the various matches, groups the matches for later use. The data matched in the first set of parentheses is assigned to the variable $1, the data matched in the second set of parentheses is assigned to $2, and so on.

The defined function is used to see if the associative array has a key that matches the input string. Because the associate array has only valid values as keys, if the entry exists, the value must be valid.

Comments

Regular expressions in Perl can contain many special characters. In this example, you saw \d, which matches any digit. The + after that character tells the regular expression that there must be one or more of those characters. In this case, that means there must be one or more digits. The \w character matches any alphanumeric or underscore character. The \s character matches any white space: any space, tab, or new-line character.

The => string in Perl 5 is very similar to a comma. In fact, it is the same except that it forces the value on the left side to be a string. The => string makes it easier when defining an associative array to see which value is the key and which value is the key's value.

Because => is valid in Perl 5 only, change the =>s in the second script to commas to run the script under Perl 4.

```
%Valid = (
    "ValidData1",1,
    "ValidData2",1,
    "ValidData3",1,
);

while ($Input = <>) {
    chop($Input);
    if ($Input =~ /^(\d+)\s+(\w+)\s+(\d+)$/) {
        $Num1 = $1;
        $String = $2;
        $Num2 = $3;
        if ($Num1 <= 10) {
            print "First Field must be greater than 10\n";
        } elsif (defined($Valid{$String})) {
            print "'$Input' is valid\n";
        } else {
            print "String invalid\n";
        }
    } else {
        print "Bad Data\n";
    }
}
```

COMPLEXITY
INTERMEDIATE

7.6 How do I...
Implement a simple menu interface?

COMPATIBILITY: PERL 4 PERL 5 UNIX DOS

Problem

I need to let the user select among a number of choices. How can I create a simple menu to get the choice?

Technique

In this How-To, you create a subroutine to print a menu of choices and return the selection. The input to the subroutine is an array of strings. Each string represents one choice. The routine prints each choice and prompts the user to select one of them. The subroutine then returns both the array index and the string of the user's choice.

Steps

1. Create a file called menu.pl. First create a subroutine called MenuChoice. The input is an array of menu choices. Create an *infinite* loop to prompt the user for a valid menu choice.

```
sub MenuChoice {
    my(@Menu) = @_;
    my($Item,$Choice);

    while (1) {
        print "Please choose one of the following: \n";
        foreach $Item (0..$#Menu) {
            print "\t", $Item, ": $Menu[$Item]\n";
        }
```

2. Read the choice. Check that it is a number and is in the proper range. If not, print a message and let the loop repeat. Otherwise, exit the loop and return both the choice number and the menu value.

```
        $Choice = <>;
        chop $Choice;
        if ($Choice =~ /^\d+$/) {
            if (($Choice < 0) || ($Choice > $#Menu)) {
                print "$Choice not valid, please try again\n";
            } else {
                last;
            }
        } else {
            print "Please enter a number, try again\n";
        }
    }
    ($Choice, $Menu[$Choice]);
}
```

3. Create a menu and call the subroutine. Print the results.

```
@MyMenu = (
            "Choice A",
            "Choice B",
            "Choice C",
            "Choice D",
            );

($Num,$String) = &MenuChoice(@MyMenu);
print "$Num=$String\n";
```

4. The entire script follows.

```
sub MenuChoice {
    my(@Menu) = @_;
    my($Item,$Choice);

    while (1) {
        print "Please choose one of the following: \n";
        foreach $Item (0..$#Menu) {
            print "\t", $Item, ": $Menu[$Item]\n";
        }
        $Choice = <>;
        chop $Choice;
        if ($Choice =~ /^\d+$/) {
            if (($Choice < 0) || ($Choice > $#Menu)) {
                print "$Choice not valid, please try again\n";
            } else {
```

```
                    last;
                }
            } else {
                print "Please enter a number, try again\n";
            }
        }
    ($Choice, $Menu[$Choice]);
}

@MyMenu = (
            "Choice A",
            "Choice B",
            "Choice C",
            "Choice D",
            );

($Num,$String) = &MenuChoice(@MyMenu);
print "$Num=$String\n";
```

5. Run the script. You will be prompted for a choice.

Output

```
Please choose one of the following:
        0:  Choice A
        1:  Choice B
        2:  Choice C
        3:  Choice D
```

End Output

6. Enter "1."

7. The script will then print.

Output

```
1=Choice B
```

End Output

How It Works

The script uses an array of strings to generate a simple menu. Each string represents one choice. The subroutine uses this array to print out a list of choices. The user's choice is validated and the results are returned from the subroutine. Because the subroutine returns an index and a string, either can be used to select the function the user requested.

Comments

There are a number of ways to get the size of an array in Perl. Using $# in front of the array name ($#Menu) returns the last valid array index. This will be the number of entries in the array minus 1. This is because the array indexes start at 0. Use the scalar function to get the number of entries in the array. When an array is passed to this function, the number of array entries is returned (scalar(@Menu)).

Input to a subroutine is always passed through the @_ array. The last command exits the enclosing loop.

Change the "my"s to "local"s to create a script that will run under Perl 4.

```perl
sub MenuChoice {
    local(@Menu) = @_;
    local($Item,$Choice);

    while (1) {
        print "Please choose one of the following: \n";
        foreach $Item (0..$#Menu) {
            print "\t", $Item, ": $Menu[$Item]\n";
        }
        $Choice = <>;
        chop $Choice;
        if ($Choice =~ /^\d+$/) {
            if (($Choice < 0) || ($Choice > $#Menu)) {
                print "$Choice not valid, please try again\n";
            } else {
                last;
            }
        } else {
            print "Please enter a number, try again\n";
        }
    }
    ($Choice, $Menu[$Choice]);
}
@MyMenu = (
            "Choice A",
            "Choice B",
            "Choice C",
            "Choice D",
            );

($Num,$String) = &MenuChoice(@MyMenu);
print "$Num=$String\n";
```

MATCHING, FILTERING, AND TRANSFORMING

MATCHING, FILTERING, AND TRANSFORMING

How do I ...

8.13   Shuffle a file?

8.14   Convert DOS text files to UNIX text files and vice versa?

This chapter is about text processing. Perl is such a powerful text-processing engine that many of the programs presented here are one-line commands. Don't underestimate the potential of such programs. A one-line Perl command is often sufficient to transform gigabytes of files or pinpoint a unique byte amidst all that data. If the title of the chapter doesn't sound too exciting, subtitle it "Realm of the Killer One-Liners."

Single-line programs have another area of application. They can be used as commands or components of commands within a batch or shell script. Used in this context, they can be helpful in processing the output of other commands or filtering streams of data flowing down a pipe. If you deal with shell scripts regularly, you will recognize that this is a context in which the UNIX programs sed and awk have often been used.

8.1   Make Perl Emulate awk

This How-To will show you how to discover how to use Perl command line switches to process text files. Perl can be as easy to use as specialized text manipulation tools, such as the awk language.

8.2   Select Fields from Input Data

Consider how easily a spreadsheet program allows you to select and move columns of data. This How-To will explain how Perl can perform similar transformations on an ordinary text file.

8.3   Exclude Fields from Input Data

This How-To will decribe a simple method for removing columns of data from a text file.

8.4   Select Certain Fields from Fixed Field-Length Input

Text files usually consist of words or fields separated by spaces. Files of fixed-length data have no separator characters. This How-To will illustrate processing fixed field-length data.

8.5   Select Lines from Input Data

Previous How-To's have demonstrated filtering columns from files. This How-To will demonstrate a method for filtering lines from a file.

8.6   Exclude Lines from Input Data

This How-To will teach you how to use Perl pattern matching to remove specific lines from a file.

8.7   Process Comma-Separated Files

This How-To will teach you how to process files that use commas or other nonwhite space characters to separate words or fields.

8.8   Replace a String in a Number of Files

One of the most common (and most tedious) tasks at the computer is replacing a word in a large number of files. Read this How-To to learn how to write Perl programs that will do all the work for you.

8.9   Match a Pathname Containing Slash Characters

The Perl match operator is commonly expressed with two forward-slash characters. Protecting forward-slash characters in patterns with back-slashes can lead to cryptic, error-prone programs. This How-To will teach you how to avoid escape characters in patterns.

8.10   Reference the Data That Matches Parts of a Regular Expression

When a successful match has occurred, how can you access sections of the string that matched specific components of your pattern? This How-To will demonstrate the Perl technique in action.

8.11   Match Multiline Patterns

Perl patterns are normally assumed to lie within a single line of a file. This How-To will illustrate a method for matching within paragraphs or other blocks of data.

8.12   Display a Window of Text Around a Matching Line

This How-To will show a simple program that searches a file and prints the matching lines in context, surrounded by a window of adjacent text.

8.13   Shuffle a File

This How-To will explain how you can juggle lines of a file into a completely random sequence.

8.14   Convert DOS Text Files to UNIX Text Files and Vice Versa

This How-To will explain how you can remove those nasty ^M characters from DOS files under UNIX and how you can reestablish the format of UNIX files on DOS computers.

COMPLEXITY:
BEGINNING

8.1 How do I ...
Make Perl emulate awk?

COMPATIBILITY: UNIX   DOS

Problem

Many day-to-day tasks at the computer involve manipulating text data: filtering certain lines, selecting columns of text, and so on. Perl has powerful text-processing features, but I have to work harder to use them than I do with "dedicated" text-processing tools such as awk. Is there any way to make Perl text processing as easy to handle as it is in a dedicated text-processing language?

Technique

Most of the programs presented in this chapter draw upon the paradigm of a text file matrix. This paradigm originated in the UNIX program sed and was greatly extended by the awk programming language. If you haven't met awk, don't worry—awk is simply a language for processing text files. In many ways, Perl has superseded it because Perl builds upon and surpasses awk's features. When we talk about emulating awk in this chapter, we mean processing using the text matrix model.

A programmer thinks of an input file as a two-dimensional matrix of fields arranged into rows and columns. Each complete line of text, ending in a carriage return or line feed, corresponds to a record. The file shown in Figure 8-1 contains six records. Each word within the line corresponds to a field within the record. The first line shown in Figure 8-1 has four fields.

A music notation based	
upon groups of lines and	
spaces was first popularized	
by a Benedictine monk named	
Guidio d'Aresso in the eleventh	
century.	

Figure 8-1 A simple text file

In Figure 8-2, you can pinpoint the line containing the word "monk" as record [3] and the word "monk" itself by its field coordinates [3][3]. Because the data is mapped out like a spreadsheet, you can easily specify transformation procedures by which records and fields are exchanged, deleted, or selected for further processing. SQL databases organize data in a similar way.

	0	1	2	3	4
0	A	music	notation	based	
1	upon	groups	of	lines	and
2	spaces	was	first	popularized	
3	by	a	Benedictine	monk	named
4	Guidio	d'Aresso	in	the	eleventh
5	century.				

Figure 8-2 A text file viewed as a matrix

Perl doesn't exactly have an awk emulation mode, but it has something pretty close: the switch combination -l -a -n -e. We will get into the details of what each switch does in the How It Works section. For now, just regard the -lane switch clusters as meaning "text matrix mode on."

Steps

1. Enter the following command and observe the output.

```
perl -lane 'print length @F' myfile1
```

How It Works

When you invoke Perl with the -lane switches, each file in the command is read line by line. Each line read is automatically split into fields. By default, Perl uses white space as a field separator. Individual fields are stripped of surrounding white space. These fields are stored in the @F array. The @F array is then processed by the Perl code given as a parameter to the -e switch. Switch -e is, of course, the last component of the -lane cluster. Remember, the file processing and record splitting are all performed by Perl without programming effort. All you have to do is supply some code for -e. Table 8-1 lists Perl's text-processing switches.

SWITCH	DESCRIPTION
- n	Embed the script within this loop:
	```while(<>){```
	```...```
	```}```
- p	As -n but automatically print $_ after each iteration.
	Equivalent to wrapping the script in:
	```while(<>){```
	```...```
	```}continue{```
	```print $_;```
	```}```

continued on next page

continued from previous page

SWITCH	DESCRIPTION	
-a	Auto Split mode. Split input line on current field separator (default is white space) and store the results in @F.	
-l	Automatic line-ending mode. Strips the end-of-line terminator on input. Restores it for output.	
-F regular-expression	Specifies an alternate pattern to use as field separator if -a (auto-split) mode is active.	

Table 8-1 Perl text-processing switches

Comments

Consider how much effort would be involved if you were to write an equivalent program in C.

COMPLEXITY
BEGINNING

8.2 How do I...
Select fields from input data?

COMPATIBILITY: UNIX DOS

Problem

I need to select columns of fields from an input file or a data stream generated from another program. I cannot assume that the data has fixed field lengths. Fields are separated by spaces or tabs.

As a variation, I would like to select multiple columns, both adjacent and separated.

Technique

The -lane switch allows you to write this program in one line. Consequently, you will write it as a command rather than as a script.

Steps

1. To select the first column, enter the command

```
perl -pale 'shift(@F)' file.txt
```

2. To select any column, column 3, enter

```
perl -lane 'print $F[3]' file.txt
```

3. To select the last column, enter

```
perl -lane 'print pop(@F)' file.txt
```

4. To select the second column from the right, enter

```
perl -lane 'print pop pop(@F)' file.txt
```

5. To select columns 2 through 4, enter

```
perl -lane 'print "@F[2..4]"' file.txt
```

How It Works

The -a switch makes Perl activate its auto split mode. Perl automatically executes

```
@F = split;
```

whenever it reads a new line of text. Wherever Perl finds a default field separator, it splits the line into fields. The result is a list of fields held in the @F array. You can manipulate these fields freely, rather like the cells in a spreadsheet row.

Comments

Be careful with one-line commands if you are using Perl for DOS. Although they have the potential to greatly enrich the spartan DOS command set, one-line commands often fall victim to the inadequate quoting available from the COMMAND.COM shell. You could consider using one of the replacement shells available, such as 4DOS.COM, to avoid these problems.

In UNIX, remember to single-quote the Perl program to prevent the shell from becoming confused by the $ symbols.

Although the -l switch makes Perl restore the end-of-line character, \n, when it prints the record, Perl has no automatic means of restoring field separator characters or white space. If you need the white space to distinguish output fields, you can insert white-space field separators between the $F[n] variables.

COMPLEXITY
BEGINNING

8.3   How do I...
Exclude fields from input data?

COMPATIBILITY:

Problem

I need to filter out fields from an input file or data stream generated from another program. The data cannot be assumed to have fixed field lengths. Fields are separated by spaces or tabs.

As a variation, I would like to select multiple columns, both adjacent and separated.

Technique

Remember that the -lane switch cluster makes Perl read each line of each file supplied on the command line, split the line into @F, and apply the -e command. Using the -lane switch, this program can be written in one line. Consequently, you will write it as a command rather than as a script.

Steps

1. To remove the first column, enter the command

```
perl -lane 'shift(@F); print "@F"' file.txt
```

2. To remove the last column, enter the command

```
perl -lane 'pop(@F); print "@F"' file.txt
```

3. To remove arbitrary columns, say the first and second, enter the command

```
perl -lane 'splice(@F, 1, 2); print "@F"' file.txt
```

How It Works

The first two steps should be clear. The @F array contains a list of fields from the input line. The Perl shift function removes the first element of the list. The pop function removes the last element of the list.

Step 3 may be puzzling. The splice function is usually used to insert elements into lists. Here you used it to delete elements. The splice command (@F, 1, 2) means remove two elements of array @F starting at offset 1; because you did not provide a fourth argument to the function, you are instructing splice to replace them with nothing. More succinctly, you are deleting elements 1 and 2 from the list @F.

Comments

If you are an awk user, remember when you read the code that Perl regards 0 as the index of column 1 and $F[0] as the first field. Starting at 1, awk indexes the fields. If you cannot live with the Perl convention that fields start at offset 0, you can make Perl work with arrays where the first element is at offset 1 by assigning the Perl start of index variable $[.

```
$[ = 1;
```

Use this command with caution, as it does not make for easy-to-understand programs.

COMPLEXITY
INTERMEDIATE

8.4   How do I...
Select certain fields from fixed field-length input?

COMPATIBILITY: UNIX   DOS

Problem

I need to select columns of fields from an input file or data stream generated from another program. The data is formatted into fixed-length fields. There is no field separator character.

I would also like to select multiple columns, both adjacent and separated.

Technique

This is a simpler problem to solve than when you have separate fields (see How-To's 8.2 and 8.3)—although it doesn't have such an elegant solution. You can treat each record as a string even if the data is binary. Because there is no field separator character present in the input, you cannot split the data using the -a auto-split switch. However, because the data is in fixed-length fields, you can assume that each field extends between two character positions within the record. You can extract individual fields with substring operations or unpack templates.

Steps

1. To select characters 10 through 14, enter the command

```
perl -lne 'print substr($_, 10, 5); ' myfile
```

2. To select multiple adjacent columns, use an unpack template. Generate a binary data file by executing makedata.pl, the program listed below.

```
#!/usr/local/bin/perl
$data = pack("ia10LA8",2019,"Wipke",906491,"Stolze");
print "$data\n";
```

```
makedata.pl > datafile.dat
```

3. Use the program below, getdata.pl, to extract the ASCII fields. Enter the script and make it executable.

```
#!/usr/local/bin/perl
($x, $name, $y, $locale) = unpack("i a10 L A8",$_);
print "$name, $locale\n";
```

4. Run the program with this command and observe the output.

```
perl -ln getdata.pl datafile.dat
```

Output
```
Wipke       ,Stolze
```
End Output

How It Works

The Perl substring operator will extract data from a string between two specified character offsets. If you know the offset position of the column of data you are interested in, then you can use the method illustrated in Step 1 to obtain it.

The second approach, illustrated in Step 3, uses a more powerful tool to extract multiple columns of data, the unpack template. The Perl unpack function takes a structure or string of binary data and coverts it into a list according to a set of type templates. Unpack is the reverse of the pack function, which created the binary data from the input values in Step 2.

The first format template is an i character, denoting a signed integer value. The unpack function extracts the appropriate number of bytes from the input string and assigns them to the variable $x. The format a10 denotes a fixed-length ASCII string of 10 characters, including the null character. This becomes the value of $name. L is an unsigned long value; it is followed by a template A8, which denotes a non-null terminated string of 8 characters. This becomes the value of $locale.

Comments

The pack and unpack operations support more than 20 data format templates and are generally more efficient that the substr function. Read the perlfunc manual page for a full specification of how these functions operate.

COMPLEXITY
BEGINNING

8.5   How do I...
Select lines from input data?

COMPATIBILITY: UNIX   DOS

Problem

I would like to select specific lines from an input file or data stream generated from another program. For example, I would like to select all lines that begin with a capital letter.

Technique

The Perl match operator m// takes a regular expression as an argument and returns True if the input it is examining matches the regular expression. You can use the Perl match operator to test if the input line of text matches an arbitrary regular expression and print only those lines that match.

Steps

1. To select lines that begin with an initial capital letter (see Figure 8-3) from the file textfile.in, enter the command

```
$ perl -ne 'print if m/^[A-Z]/;' textfile.txt
```

This produces the following output.

Output

```
A music notation based
Guidio d'Aresso in the eleventh
```

End Output

	0	1	2	3	4
0	A	music	notation	based	
1	upon	groups	of	lines	and
2	spaces	was	first	popularized	
3	by	a	Benedictine	monk	named
4	Guidio	d'Aresso	in	the	eleventh
5	century.				

Figure 8-3 Selecting lines beginning with capital letter

How It Works

The -n flag, as you saw earlier in this chapter, automates the file-processing loop, loading each line of the file into the default variable $_. Each line is printed only if it matches the regular expression after the *if*. Notice that you do not explicitly state that the current line is the target of the m// match. Remember that m// will match against the default variable $_ if no explict argument is given.

The ^ symbol is a location assertion. It means that the expression that follows must be the first item on the line. To locate the end of line, use $ immediately after your expression. To locate your expression at a word boundary, use the location assertion \b.

The expression [A-Z] means a set of characters in the range A through Z; in other words, the expession will match any capital letter.

Comments

If your system has a grep command available, you might want to use it in this situation instead of Perl. The disadvantage of grep is that it does not support all of Perl's rich regular expression language so you cannot expect it to be available if your script is run on non-UNIX systems.

Perl supports alternatives in regular expressions. The following will match lines containing any one of the names of three different computer manufacturers.

```
print if m/Sun|DEC|Intel/;
```

The example above uses a character range, or character class, to indicate the set of capital letters. Perl has several shorthand versions for common character classes. Below are some useful and commonly used examples.

 The symbol \d will match the class [0-9]. It means digit.

- The symbol \D will match the class [^0-9]. It means nondigit.

- The symbol \w will match any character-matching class [0-9a-z_A-Z]. It means word character.

- The symbol \W will match any character not matching \w, such as "?", space, and "-".

- The symbol \s will match any one of the white-space characters in the class [\t\n\r\f].

- The symbol \S will match the class [^ \t\n\r\f]. It means nonwhite-space character.

See Table 1-4 for a complete list of character class symbols.

COMPLEXITY
BEGINNING

8.6 How do I...
Exclude lines from input data?

COMPATIBILITY: UNIX DOS

Problem

I would like to filter out certain lines from the input. The context of the line may be significant. For example, I want to remove blank lines from a file only if they occur after a section heading. How can I implement this kind of filter?

Technique

You can exclude lines from the input following the approach of How-To 8.5. All you need to do is use an *unless* keyword. The syntax of an *unless* statement is exactly the same as the syntax of an *if* statement, but *unless* (condition) means *if* (not condition).

Steps

1. To reject lines that begin with an initial capital letter, enter the command

```
$ perl -ne 'print unless /^[A-Z]/;' textfile.txt
```

```
upon groups of lines and
spaces was first popularized ...
```

2. To remove blank lines that occur after some specific previous line, list the file cfrfile.cfr.

```
[Chess]

BackGround=00408080
BlackSquare=00008000
...
```

3. There is a blank line following the heading [Chess]. Remove it (but no other blank lines) by issuing the following command.

```
perl -ne 'print unless /^$/  && $p; $p = m/^\[/;' cfrfile.cfr
[Chess]
BackGround=00408080
BlackSquare=00008000
...
```

How It Works

The command in Step 3 has a condition that reads "print the current line unless the line is empty (/^$/) and $p is set." The variable $p contains the result of matching the previous line against the pattern /^\[/. This is how the program tests the current line in a context determined by the previous line.

Read the pattern /^\[/ as matching lines beginning with a left square-bracket character. This pattern will match section header lines such as this:

```
[Chess]
```

Comments

Matching lines in the context of previous lines is one thing you certainly can't do with a grep command!

COMPLEXITY
BEGINNING

8.7   How do I...
Process comma-separated files?

COMPATIBILITY: UNIX DOS

Problem

I would like to select columns of fields from a comma-separated file produced by a spreadsheet. Alternatively, I might be using a similar type of file where the field separator is some special character other than white space.

Technique

The -lane method of processing word-oriented data is also good for comma-separated files. Word-oriented files use white space as a field delimiter. All you need do to process a comma-separated file is to tell Perl about the new field-separator character.

Steps

1. Create a file containing comma-separated data. Save it as comma.in. List the file.

```
Roman,fixed,formal typeface
Script,proportional,hand written
Courier,fixed,typewriter
Sans-serif,proportional,headings and titles
Draft,fixed,teletype and terminals
```

2. To select the last column of each line, enter the command

```
perl -F, -lane 'print pop @F;' comma.in
```

Observe the following output.

Output

```
formal typeface
hand written
typewriter
headings and titles
teletype and terminals
```

End Output

How It Works

The -F option, when used in combination with the -a auto split option, allows you to specify a different character (or characters) as field separators. If you specify -F as a separator, each field is split on the comma character and made available in the @F array.

Comments

Don't forget you can use a group of characters or a regular expression as a field separator. You are not limited to single-character separators. See How-To's 1.5 and 8.5 for discussion of regular expressions.

COMPLEXITY
BEGINNING

8.8 How do I...
Replace a string in a number of files?

COMPATIBILITY: UNIX   DOS

Problem

I would like to substitute new text for each occurrence of a string in a large number of files. The operation is similar to the search and replace functions provided by interactive editors. I would like to modify the file in place but keep a backup for safety.

Technique

This How-To introduces a new Perl switch, the in-place switch -i. This switch allows files to be edited in place. This means that any substitutions performed on the data within the file will be written back to the original, changing the file permanently.

Because you modify your source file directly, it is vital that you keep a backup copy. You can do this with the same -i switch. Perl will create a backup file if you supply a file suffix as an argument to the -i switch. The name of the backup file is generated by appending the suffix to the name of the original.

Steps

1. Demonstrate the -i option by replacing the string "music" with the string "MUSIC" in a text file. For input, reuse data file 8-1.in from How-To 8.1. Enter the following command.

```
perl -p -i.bak -e 's/music/MUSIC/' 8-1.in
```

2. Cat the file 8-1.txt to check that the modification has taken effect.

```
cat 8-1.in
A MUSIC notation based
upon groups of lines and ...
```

3. List the directory to check that the backup file has been created. Use the command ls if you are working with UNIX or the command dir if you are working with DOS.

```
ls
8-1.bak
8-1.txt
```

4. Cat the backup file to check that it is intact.

```
cat 8-1.bak
A music notation based
upon groups of lines and ...
```

How It Works

When Perl is invoked with the switches -p -i -e, it places a special processing wrapper around the command supplied with the -e switch. Perl translates the command -e /music/MUSIC/ into this program.

```
#!/usr/bin/perl
while (<>){
  rename($ARGV, $ARGV . '.bak');
  open(OUT, ">$ARGV");
  s/music/MUSIC/;
}
continue {
  print OUT;
}
```

Comments

Any Perl program that processes files with the <> operator can use the -i switch. If your program has the structure

```
while(<>) {
  s/old/new/;
  print;
}
```

and you want to commit the changes to the input file, then you can use the -i switch in the #!line, like this:

```
#!/usr/bin/perl -i.bak
```

COMPLEXITY
BEGINNING

8.9 How do I...
Match a pathname containing slash characters?

COMPATIBILITY: UNIX DOS

Problem

Regular expressions can become difficult to understand when they require numerous back-slash escape characters. This commonly arises when I have to match pathnames. How can I simplify the syntax of my regular expressions?

Technique

UNIX pathnames use the forward-slash character as a separator for subdirectories. Perl conventionally uses the forward-slash character as a pattern delimiter. If you want to match path /usr/local/lib/, you must use a cryptic expression that looks like this:

```
/\/usr\/local\/lib\//
```

Perl allows you to resolve the conflict by escaping each forward-slash with a backslash. This can become clumsy and lead to unreadable patterns and difficult-to-spot programming errors. There is a better way. Perl allows you to use alternative pattern-delimiter characters.

Steps

Demonstrate the use of alternative pattern delimiters by matching a pathname against a cryptic escaped pattern and then against an alternative pattern that uses the # character as a pattern delimiter. To demonstrate that input matches the expression, use the substitute command s// to replace the string /usr/local with the string /usr/share/.

1. Enter the command

```
# perl -pale "s/\/usr\/local/\/usr\/share/"
```

Type the pathname below. The program responds by printing the modified input.

/usr/local/bin/perl
/usr/share/bin/perl

Type the end-of-file character to terminate the program.

2. Enter an equivalent command that uses a clearer pattern delimited by # characters.

```
# perl -pale "s#/usr/local#/usr/share#"
```

Type in a pathname, as below.

/usr/local/bin/perl

If input matches, the program responds by echoing.

/usr/share/bin/perl

How It Works

Perl allows you to use any nonalphanumeric character (except for white-space characters) as a pattern delimiter. The comma is usually a good choice, as is the # symbol. There are some characters you should use with caution, however. The ! symbol makes a good visual delimiter but can upset some UNIX shells. The ' character can lead to confusion if you are already quoting your command from the shell. Do not use ' characters where your pattern contains a variable or back-slash expression. It will prevent interpolation.

Comments

The two commands above produce equivalent results. Yet the second is clearer and you are less likely to make a mistake while typing it. Note that although we used a substitution command here, the technique applies equally to the match operator m//.

```
m,/usr/l.+,
```

will match input /usr/local and /usr/lib.

COMPLEXITY
INTERMEDIATE

8.10 How do I...
Reference the data that matches parts of a regular expression?

COMPATIBILITY: UNIX   DOS

Problem

I have matched a Perl pattern against a string. How can I extract the portions of the string that match components of the pattern?

Technique

If you are familiar with the UNIX command sed, you will know about match references. Surrounding part of a regular expression in parentheses allows you to refer back to the portion of text that matches the parenthesized component. Perl, similarly, provides a neat way of referring back to portions of strings that match a component of a pattern using number variables, such as $1, $2, ...

Steps

1. Enter the following command.

```
perl -ne 's/(.*) pats (.*)/\u$2 bites \1$1/,print'
```

2. Type the following line and observe the response. Press CTRL-C to terminate the program.

```
Man pats dog
```

Output

```
Dog bites man
```

End Output

How It Works

You can refer back to the portion of text that matches the first expression in parentheses in your pattern with the variable $1, to the second with $2, and so forth. You can use these variables to construct the replacement string dynamically by referring to them on the right side of the substitution command. Figure 8-4 illustrates data manipulation with matched parts from a Perl pattern.

Comments

These variables are block-scoped and can be referenced within the same block of code in which they are first used. They behave just like an ordinary variable except in one respect: Each new successful match will clobber the previous value. If you

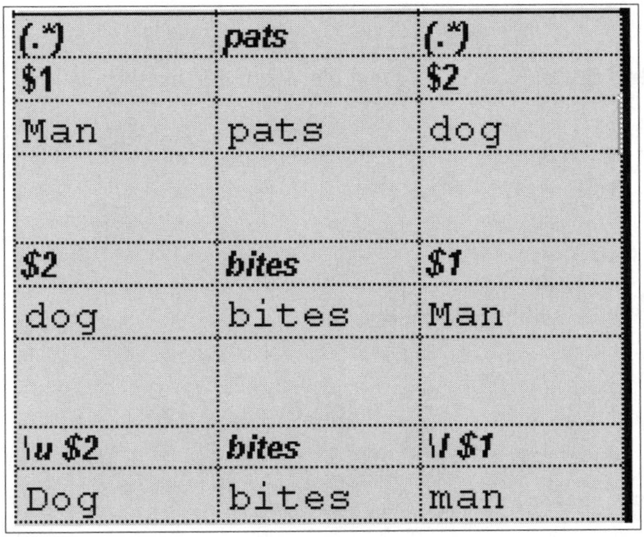

(.*)	pats	(.*)
$1		$2
Man	pats	dog

$2	bites	$1
dog	bites	Man

\u $2	bites	\l $1
Dog	bites	man

Figure 8-4 Manipulation of the data that matched parts of a Perl pattern

need to keep the matching segments intact, then assign the value of $1 to a normal variable.

```
s/(.*)good(.*)/$1bad$2/;
$subject = $1; $predicate = $2;
```

COMPLEXITY
INTERMEDIATE

8.11 How do I...
Match multiline patterns?

COMPATIBILITY: PERL 4   PERL 5

Problem

I want to match a pattern that occurs in a free format text file. I cannot guarantee that the pattern is contained on one line. It may be split over two lines. Is there any way to match a text pattern that is spread over two or more lines?

Technique

Normally, Perl pattern matching works on the assumption that the target is a string terminated with a new line. You can modify this assumption by coding the match operator with an s option and altering the special variable, $/, which sets paragraph mode. The paragraph allows Perl's <> operator to read in text a paragraph at a time, and the s option allows matching to extend beyond new-line characters.

Steps

You will search for the words "lines and spaces" in a text file, assuming that they lie on different lines.

1. List the input file textfile.in.

```
A music notation based
upon groups of lines and
spaces was first popularized ...
```

2. Enter the following code as program splitpat.pl.

```perl
#!/usr/local/bin/perl -w
use strict;

$/ = "";    # Paragraph mode

while(<>) {
   print $1 if /(lines.*\n.*spaces)/s;
}
```

3. Match a pattern that is spread over more than one line. Enter the following command.

```
splitpat.pl "lines.*spaces"textfile.in

lines and
spaces
```

How It Works

To match patterns spanning multiple lines of text, you have to stop Perl from chopping the text into lines before you can process it. By default, the normal Perl end-of-record symbol is a new-line character. You can set any character or string to be an end-of-record delimiter by assigning it to the system variable $/.

Perl shifts into paragraph mode if you assign a magic value, the null string, to $/. That is, each time you read from <>, you will receive a paragraph of text rather than a line. Perl understands a paragraph to be a chunk of text delimited by two or more new-line characters. You set $/ to the empty string "" with this line:

```
$/ = "";    # Paragraph mode
```

Now you can set multiline match mode on by using the s option of the pattern match operator. This causes the pattern match operator to treat new-line characters as normal characters within the matched string.

Comments

Some programs store records organized into multiline blocks. A common example of this is the CFR format. MS-Windows uses CFR format files to store program configurations. A typical entry looks something like this:

```
[Chess]

BackGround=00408080
BlackSquare=00008000
WhiteSquare=00C0C0C0
BlackPiece=000000FF
WhitePiece=00FFFFFF
Text=00000000
```

You can process these files easily if you use paragraph mode to load each record block as a single string.

COMPLEXITY
INTERMEDIATE

8.12 How do I...
Display a window of text around a matching line?

COMPATIBILITY: PERL 4 PERL 5

Problem

I would like to search through a file for lines that match a regular expression. When a line matches, Perl should print it out, together with a window of lines that surround it.

Technique

Sometimes it is useful not only to see the lines that match a pattern but also to see the matching line in context. In this section, you create a program called wgrep.pl - window grep. Invoke the program with two arguments, a pattern and a filename. The pattern can be any arbitrary Perl pattern.

```
wgrep.pl <pattern> <filename>
```

This program searches through the file, attempting to match each line against the pattern. If a line matches, wgrep.pl prints out the line and the three lines preceding and following it.

Steps

1. Enter the following program as wgrep.pl.

```
#!/usr/local/bin/perl -w
use strict;

#Usage: wgrep pattern [files...]

$WINDOWSZ = 3;

$regexp = shift;
$regexp =~ s,/,\\/,g;
```

continued on next page

continued from previous page

```perl
$_ = <>;
push(@queue,$_);

for (1.. $WINDOWSZ) {
    unshift(@queue, '');
    push(@queue, $_) if $_ = <>;
}

while ($queue[$WINDOWSZ])
{
    if ($queue[$WINDOWSZ] =~ /$regexp/o)
    {
        print "-" x 64, "\n";
        print "@queue\n";
    }
    shift(@queue);
    $_ = <> if $_;
    push(@queue,$_);
}
```

2. Run the program on itself. Enter the following command.

```
wgrep.pl while wgrep.pl
```

```perl
    push(@queue, $_) if $_ = <>;
 }

 while ($queue[$WINDOWSZ])
 {
     if ($queue[$WINDOWSZ] =~ /$regexp/o)
     {
```

The program prints out a window of the three lines of text surrounding the line that matches the first argument of the program.

How It Works

As the program scans through the input, it maintains a window of seven lines of text stored in @queue. Why seven lines? Three lines on either side of the line current line plus the current line.

Each time around the *while* loop, the program tries to match the current line against the pattern supplied as the first argument. If it matches, it prints the entire array @queue with a separating line of dashes. It then purges the oldest line from the queue, pulls in a new line, appends it to the front of the queue, and loops again.

Comments

Notice the use of the o option of the match operator. If Perl sees a match expression containing a variable, it will runtime compile the expression on each iteration of the loop. Because the variable does not change value during the program, you should use the o option to tell Perl to compile the match expression once only.

A more robust and full-featured version of this context-grep program, cgrep, developed by Lutz Prechelt, is available on the CD.

COMPLEXITY
INTERMEDIATE

8.13 How do I...
Shuffle a file?

COMPATIBILITY: UNIX DOS

Problem

I would like to take a sorted file and shuffle it so that the sequence of lines it contains is completely random.

Technique

Because of Perl's built-in memory management, you can safely slurp a whole file into a data structure in memory and manipulate the data internally. (Of course, you can do this only if you have enough memory available.) This is the simplest approach to solving this problem.

Once you have the data stored in an array, the program has random access to each line from the file.

Steps

1. Create the following program, save it as shuffle.pl, and make it executable.

```
#!/usr/local/bin/perl -w
# Randomize input lines

srand;  # make the rand function random

while(<>){
    push @lines, $_;
}

while(@lines) {
  print splice(@lines, rand @lines, 1);
}
```

2. Invoke the program, using the file textfile.in as a data source.

```
shuffle.pl textfile.in
```

The program shuffles each line of the file, producing output like this:

Output
```
spaces was first popularized
century.
upon groups of lines and
A music notation based
Guidio d'Aresso in the eleventh
by a Benedictine monk named
```
End Output

How It Works

The srand function sets a random seed, based on the system clock, for the randomization rand function. The first *while* loop reads the whole input in the array @lines. The second *while* loop iterates, selecting a line from the array using the splice function. Splice returns a line at a random offset within @lines and deletes it. Deleting the line ensures it cannot be chosen again.

Comments

You can easily extend this approach to sorting the individual fields of each line in a random order.

COMPLEXITY
INTERMEDIATE

8.14 How do I...
Convert DOS text files to UNIX text files and vice versa?

COMPATIBILITY: PERL 4   PERL 5

Problem

How can I convert a text file from a DOS system to UNIX format, losing the additional ^M character at the end of each line? Similarly, how can I convert a UNIX file with a lone new-line character at the end of each line to use the new-line, carriage-return pair expected by DOS?

Technique

If you work regularly on both DOS and UNIX computers, you are familiar with the irritation of copying files between the systems only to find that in a UNIX editor, a DOS file displays a ^M character at the end of each line, and that each line in a UNIX file begins where the previous line ended when listed at a DOS machine.

You can correct the problem very simply with a one-line Perl command. The command deletes new-line carriage-return pairs using a substitution statement and allows Perl to replace the end-of-line terminator automatically when you call the *print* statement. The command keeps a backup copy of the original file with a suitable file suffix.

Steps

1. To convert a DOS file to UNIX format on a UNIX machine:

```
perl -pe -i.lfcr "s/[\012\015]//;" file
```

2. To convert a UNIX file to DOS format on a DOS machine:

```
perl -pe -i.lf "s/[\012]//;" file
```

How It Works

When you invoke Perl with the -p option, it embeds your substitution statement within a file-processing loop that automatically reads the next line of input, executes the given command, and prints the resulting line. The s// function deletes the end-of-line character; the automatic print that follows adds an end-of-line terminator suitable to the machine that you are running the program on.

Comments

Do not try to "convert" files containing binary data because you will corrupt them. You may want to protect yourself against corrupting binary files. You can test whether a file contains binary data by using -B operator. Here is an example:

```
die "Cannot convert a binary file\n" if (-B $file);
```

WRITING REPORTS IN PERL

WRITING REPORTS IN PERL

How do I...

The ability to write reports in Perl is a distinguishing factor between Perl and C, and Perl and the Bourne shell; C and the Bourne shell do not have the report-writing facility that Perl has. The strength of Perl's report-writing facility lies in the ability to create a clear and readable report. The How-To's in this chapter build on each other. How-To 9.2 takes the script written in How-To 9.1 and builds on it; How-To 9.3 does the same with the script in How-To 9.2. The scripts presented in this chapter have a Perl 5 twist because they use modules instead of requiring libraries. The scripts can be easily fitted to Perl 4 syntax if necessary.

9.1   Align Fields on a Report

Knowing how to align fields is the most important piece of information needed to create complex reports simply. This How-To will show how to left-justify, right-justify, and center individual fields on a report.

9.2   Split a Long Field over Multiple Lines

If a field is too long for the physical page, your script will need to split up the field. This How-To will demonstrate how to split a lengthy field over as many lines as needed.

9.3   Attach a Header to a Report

For a report to be truly readable, it must have a field header so the reader understands the information being presented. This also holds true when the report spans more than one page. This How-To will demonstrate how to attach a header to a report.

9.4   Put a Variable in the Report Header

If a report spans more than one page, a page number is an added extra. This How-To will show you how to include the page number variable in the top of the file header form.

9.5   Attach a Footer to a Report

As with the header, the footer becomes increasingly important as the information presented becomes more complicated. This How-To will show you how to attach a footer to your report.

9.6   Switch Between Multiple Report Formats

The more complicated the data, the greater your desire may become to present the same piece of information in two different formats for full effect. This How-To will demonstrate how to accomplish this.

COMPLEXITY

BEGINNING

9.1 How do I...
Align fields on a report?

COMPATIBILITY: PERL 5   UNIX   DOS

Problem

I want to be able to use the Perl report-writing facility, but I don't know how.

Technique

To create a report, define a report "picture" to give the report shape and substance. This is done by using the format keyword. The format keyword allows you to create a picture based on an output stream or filehandle. Within the format picture, you define fields using the at symbol (@) followed by the less-than (<), greater-than (>), number sign (#), or pipe character (|). Table 9-1 demonstrates the possible field formats and what they represent.

FIELD PICTURE	DESCRIPTION
@<<<<<	A left-justified 6-character-wide field.
@>>>>>>>>>	A right-justified 10-character-wide field.
@|||||	A centered 5-character-wide field.
@###.##	A float field broken into 5 integer characters and 2 fractional characters.
^<<<<<<<<<<<<<<	A left-justified 15-character field. The caret character (^) signifies that this
	field is a split line field. The contents of this field can be split across multiple lines.

Table 9-1 Report field pictures

This How-To uses the @ARGV array as input. If the script is run with a list of filenames, then the script will use these files as input. If no filename is specified, then the script will use the STDIN stream for the source of the information. The write command is used in conjunction with the format keyword to create the final report.

Steps

1. Create a new file named align.pl and type the following script into it.

```
#!/usr/local/bin/perl -w

# Do this until there are no more records.
while (<ARGV>)
{
    chomp;
```

continued on next page

continued from previous page

```perl
    # Split the line on the pipe symbol.
    ($number,$type,$name,$price,$desc) = split (/\|/);

    # Print out the item information.
    write;
}

format STDOUT =
@>>> @|||||| @<<<<<<<<< @<<<<<<<<<<<<< $@####.##
@<<<<<<<<<<<<<<<<<<<<<<<<<<<<<<<<<<<<<<<<<<
$.,$number,$type,$name,$price,$desc
.
```

2. Create a data file named align.dat and type the following into it.

```
101|Hardware|Hammer|25.00|A thing to hit nails with.
121|Hardware|Nail|0.15|A thing to be hit by a hammer. (see hammer)
142|Hardware|Sander|10.15|Used to sand all sorts of things, except sand.
206|Household|Kitchen Sink|100.00|Lost the last time I went on vacation.
(next time I won't check it in)
210|Household|Windows|45.00|User friendly and does not need to be plugged
in.
242|Household|Vacuum|300.00|I'm not sure what this is used for, but people
seem to have them anyway.
266|Household|Microwave|100.00|Kitchen item. (also see hot water heater)
312|Garden|Rake|25.00|Used to rake leaves, cut grass and break noses if
left lying on the ground.
344|Garden|Gravel|30.00|Why bother - the dog is going to dig through it
again anyway.
362|Garden|Top Soil|10.00|Is there such a thing as "Bottom Soil?"
384|Garden|Mosquitos|0.00|Some are large as a dog and will carry you away.
500|Sports|Hockey Stick|10.00|Used to push the puck around.
501|Sports|Bike|400.00|Sits in the garage and collects dust.
556|Sports|First Aid Kit|25.00|Used more times than not, unfortunately.
601|Misc|Dog Food|1.50|The stuff the cat eats.
623|Misc|Cat Food|0.75|The stuff the dog eats.
644|Misc|Socks|1.00|What both the dog and cat destroy.
```

3. Run the program using align.dat as the input file.

```
%chap_09/howto01/align.pl chap_09/howto01/align.dat
```

Output

```
0  101  Hardware   Hammer        $ 25.00  A thing to hit nails with.
1  121  Hardware   Nail          $  0.15  A thing to be hit by a hammer.
                                          (see hammer)
2  142  Hardware   Sander        $ 10.15  Used to sand all sorts of
                                          things, except sand.
3  206  Household  Kitchen Sink  $100.00  Lost the last time I went on
                                          vacation. (next time I
                                          won t check it in)
4  210  Household  Windows       $ 45.00  User friendly and does not
                                          need to be plugged in.
5  242  Household  Vacuum        $300.00  I'm not sure what this is
                                          used for, but people seem to
                                          have them anyway.
6  266  Household  Microwave     $100.00  Kitchen item. (also see hot
                                          water heater)
```

```
 7  312   Garden     Rake            $ 25.00   Used to rake leaves, cut grass
                                                and break noses if left lying
                                                on the ground.
 8  344   Garden     Gravel          $ 30.00   Why bother - the dog is going
                                                to dig through it again anyway.
 9  362   Garden     Top Soil        $ 10.00   Is there such a thing as
                                                "Bottom Soil?"
10  384   Garden     Mosquitos       $  0.00   Some are large as a dog and
                                                will carry you away.
11  500   Sports     Hockey Stick    $ 10.00   Used to push the puck around.
12  501   Sports     Bike            $400.00   Sits in the garage and
                                                collects dust.
13  556   Sports     First Aid Kit   $ 25.00   Used more times than not,
                                                unfortunately.
14  601   Misc.      Dog Food        $  1.50   The stuff the cat eats.
15  623   Misc.      Cat Food        $  0.75   The stuff the dog eats.
16  644   Misc.      Socks           $  1.00   What both the dog and cat
                                                destroy.
```

End Output

How It Works

Inside the *while* loop, the variables *$number, $type, $name, $price,* and *$desc* hold the values that are to be displayed through the report writer. Every time the write command is called, the STDOUT format is used to display the record. The record picture has to define a field for each piece of information to be displayed. The record format

```
@>>> @|||||| @<<<<<<<<< @<<<<<<<<<<<<< $@####.##
@<<<<<<<<<<<<<<<<<<<<<<<<<<<<<<<<<<<<<<<<<<<<<<
```

states that there are to be six fields are to be displayed for each record. The specific format of each field is defined at the start of the field by the @ sign, and the alignment is dictated by < (align to the left), > (align to the right), and | (align to the center). The @####.## field specifies a number field (float field) of five integer characters and two decimal characters that is right-adjusted. Use the # format only to line up decimal points.

Comments

The variables used within the format picture should not be declared as local. Because the format picture is usually defined within the global space of the script, the variables referenced within the format areas should be also.

COMPLEXITY
BEGINNING

9.2   How do I...
Split a long field over multiple lines?

COMPATIBILITY: PERL 5   UNIX   DOS

Problem

I have a field to be displayed in a format record, but the contents of the field are too long to fit on a single line.

Technique

Use the caret character (^) instead of the at symbol (@). The caret character tells Perl that this one field may be too long to fit in a single field and may need to be split.

Steps

1. Copy the Perl script from How-To 9.1 into a file named split.pl.

2. Modify the script split.pl. The following example demonstrates the modified script split.pl. The modifications are highlighted in bold.

```
#!/usr/local/bin/perl -w

# Do this until there are no more records.
while (<ARGV>)
{
    chomp;

    # Split the line on the pipe symbol.
    ($number,$type,$name,$price,$desc) = split (/\|/);

    # Print out the item information.
    write;
}

format STDOUT =
@>>>> @||||||| @<<<<<<<<< @<<<<<<<<<<<<< $@####.##
^<<<<<<<<<<<<<<<<<<<<<<<
$,,$number,$type,$name,$price,$desc
~
^<<<<<<<<<<<<<<<<<<<<<<<
$desc
~
^<<<<<<<<<<<<<<<<<<<<<<<<<
$desc
.
```

3. Run the script using the input file from How-To 9.1.

```
% chap_09/howto02/split.pl chap_09/howto01/align.dat
```

Output

```
 0  101  Hardware   Hammer       $ 25.00  A thing to hit nails with.
 1  121  Hardware   Nail         $  0.15  A thing to be hit by a hammer.
                                          (see hammer)
 2  142  Hardware   Sander       $ 10.15  Used to sand all sorts of
                                          things, except sand.
 3  206  Household  Kitchen Sink $100.00  Lost the last time I went on
                                          vacation. (next time I won't
                                          check it in)
 4  210  Household  Windows      $ 45.00  User friendly and does not
                                          need to be plugged in.
 5  242  Household  Vacuum       $300.00  I'm not sure what this is used
                                          for, but people seem to have
                                          them anyway.
 6  266  Household  Microwave    $100.00  Kitchen item. (also see hot
                                          water heater)
 7  312  Garden     Rake         $ 25.00  Used to rake leaves, cut grass
                                          and  break noses if left lying
                                          on the  ground.
 8  344  Garden     Gravel       $ 30.00  Why bother - the dog is going
                                          to dig through it again anyway.
 9  362  Garden     Top Soil     $ 10.00  Is there such a thing as
                                          "Bottom Soil?"
10  384  Garden     Mosquitos    $  0.00  Some are large as a dog and
                                          will carry you away.
11  500  Sports     Hockey Stick $ 10.00  Used to push the puck around.
12  501  Sports     Bike         $400.00  Sits in the garage and
                                          collects dust.
13  556  Sports     First Aid Kit $ 25.00 Used more times than not,
                                          unfortunately.
14  601  Misc.      Dog Food     $  1.50  The stuff the cat eats.
15  623  Misc.      Cat Food     $  0.75  The stuff the dog eats.
16  644  Misc.      Socks        $  1.00  What both the dog and cat
                                          destroy.
```

End Output

How It Works

In a Perl report format, the caret character (^) signifies the beginning of a split field. The tilde character (~) at the beginning of the line suppresses blank lines of output. This means that if the value in the description variable is not long enough to fill all three lines, then the extra lines will not be printed.

Note that a line field will split on a word unless the word is longer than the length of the field.

Comments

If the tilde characters were removed, then each record would be three lines long, regardless. The following example demonstrates what the first three lines of output would look like.

```
Output
    0   101    Hardware    Hammer        $ 25.00    A thing to hit nails with.

    1   121    Hardware    Nail          $  0.15    A thing to be hit by a
                                                    hammer. (see hammer)

    2   142    Hardware    Sander        $ 10.15    Used to sand all sorts
                                                    of things, except sand.
End Output
```

COMPLEXITY
BEGINNING

9.3   How do I...
Attach a header to a report?

COMPATIBILITY: PERL 5   UNIX   DOS

Problem

I generated a report and it spans more than one page. A top-of-form header would make the report look more professional. How do I add a top-of-form header to my report?

Technique

To add a top-of-form header to a report, a format name must be defined with _TOP appended to the name of the format name. In this example, you will be using the format name of STDOUT, so the format name will be STDOUT_TOP.

Steps

1. Copy the Perl script from How-To 9.2 into a file named header.pl.

2. Modify the script header.pl. The following example demonstrates the modified script header.pl. The modifications are highlighted in bold.

```perl
#!/usr/local/bin/perl -w

# Do this until there are no more records.
while (<ARGV>)
{
    chomp;

    # Split the line on the pipe symbol.
    ($number,$type,$name,$price,$desc) = split (/\|/);
```

```
     # Print out the item information.
     write;
}

format STDOUT_TOP=
Count Item #  Item Type  Item Name       Price      Description
===============================================================================
.

format STDOUT=
@>>>> @|||||| @<<<<<<<<< @<<<<<<<<<<<< $@####.##
^<<<<<<<<<<<<<<<<<<<<<<<<<
$.,$number,$type,$name,$price,$desc
~
^<<<<<<<<<<<<<<<<<<<<<<<<<
$desc
~
^<<<<<<<<<<<<<<<<<<<<<<<<<
$desc
.
```

3. Run the script using the input file from How-To 9.1.

```
% chap_09/howto03/header.pl chap_09/howto01/align.dat
```

Output

Count	Item #	Item Type	Item Name	Price	Description
0	101	Hardware	Hammer	$ 25.00	A thing to hit nails with.
1	121	Hardware	Nail	$ 0.15	A thing to be hit by a hammer. (see hammer)
2	142	Hardware	Sander	$ 10.15	Used to sand all sorts of things, except sand.
3	206	Household	Kitchen Sink	$100.00	Lost the last time I went on vacation. (next time I won't check it in)
4	210	Household	Windows	$ 45.00	User friendly and does not need to be plugged in.
5	242	Household	Vacuum	$300.00	I'm not sure what this is used for, but people seem to have them anyway.
6	266	Household	Microwave	$100.00	Kitchen item. (also see hot water heater)
7	312	Garden	Rake	$ 25.00	Used to rake leaves, cut grass and break noses if left lying on the ground.
8	344	Garden	Gravel	$ 30.00	Why – bother the dog is going to dig through it again anyway.
9	362	Garden	Top Soil	$ 10.00	Is there such a thing as "Bottom Soil?"
10	384	Garden	Mosquitos	$ 0.00	Some are large as a dog and will carry you away.
11	500	Sports	Hockey Stick	$ 10.00	Used to push the puck around.
12	501	Sports	Bike	$400.00	Sits in the garage and

continued on next page

continued from previous page

```
                                              collects dust.
  13   556   Sports     First Aid Kit   $  25.00   Used more times than not,
                                              unfortunately.
  14   601   Misc.      Dog Food        $   1.50   The stuff the cat eats.
  15   623   Misc.      Cat Food        $   0.75   The stuff the dog eats.
  16   644   Misc.      Socks           $   1.00   What both the dog and cat
                                              destroy.
```

End Output

How It Works

Whenever a new page is started, Perl looks for a header statement for the current filehandle. It prints out the header line(s) and then starts printing out each record row. If the report spans more than one page, a form feed character is added as well.

Comments

So far, all the scripts presented in this chapter have used the STDOUT stream. Many people confuse the STDOUT filehandle name space and the STDOUT format name space. As a default, Perl uses the name of the report stream stored in the variable $~, which is set to the name of the currently selected filehandle. When write is called without a format name space, Perl uses the value in the variable $~ for the report format name. When a top-of-form header needs to be printed and a format name was not provided in the *write* statement, Perl uses the value in the variable $^ as the current format name.

COMPLEXITY
INTERMEDIATE

9.4 How do I...
Put a variable in the report header?

COMPATIBILITY: PERL 5 | UNIX | DOS

Problem

The script I wrote generates output that spans across numerous pages. I want to be able to have the page number on the top-of-form header on each page. How do I do this?

Technique

You need to put a format field and the variable name that is going to fill the field in the header handle.

Steps

1. Copy the Perl script created in How-To 9.3 into a file named variable.pl.

2. Modify the script variable.pl. The following example demonstrates the modified script variable.pl. The modifications are highlighted in bold.

```perl
#!/usr/local/bin/perl -w

use English;

# Do this until there are no more records.
while (<ARGV>)
{
    chomp;

    # Split the line on the pipe symbol.
    ($number,$type,$name,$price,$desc) = split (/\|/);

    # Print out the item information.
    write;
}

format STDOUT_TOP=
Count Item #  Item Type  Item Name      Price      Description    Page
@>>>>>>
$FORMAT_PAGE_NUMBER
==============================================================================
.

format STDOUT=
@>>>> @||||||  @<<<<<<<<< @<<<<<<<<<<<<< $@####.##
^<<<<<<<<<<<<<<<<<<<<<<<<<
$.,$number,$type,$name,$price,$desc
~
^<<<<<<<<<<<<<<<<<<<<<<<<<
$desc
~
^<<<<<<<<<<<<<<<<<<<<<<<<<
$desc
.
```

3. Run the script using the input file from How-To 9.1.

```
% chap_09/howto04/variable.pl chap_09/howto01/align.dat
```

___Output_____

```
Count Item # Item Type  Item Name      Price   Description        Page      1
==============================================================================
    0  101    Hardware   Hammer         $ 25.00 A thing to hit nails with.
    1  121    Hardware   Nail           $  0.15 A thing to be hit by a
                                                hammer. (see hammer)
    2  142    Hardware   Sander         $ 10.15 Used to sand all sorts of
                                                things, except sand.
    3  206    Household  Kitchen Sink   $100.00 Lost the last time I went
                                                on vacation. (next time
                                                I won't check it in)
    4  210    Household  Windows        $ 45.00 User friendly and does not
                                                need to be plugged in.
```

continued on next page

continued from previous page

5	242	Household	Vacuum	$300.00	I'm not sure what this is used for, but people seem to have them anyway.
6	266	Household	Microwave	$100.00	Kitchen item. (also see hot water heater)
7	312	Garden	Rake	$ 25.00	Used to rake leaves, cut grass and break noses if left lying on the ground.
8	344	Garden	Gravel	$ 30.00	Why bother - the dog is going to dig through it again anyway.
9	362	Garden	Top Soil	$ 10.00	Is there such a thing as "Bottom Soil?"
10	384	Garden	Mosquitos	$ 0.00	Some are large as a dog and will carry you away.
11	500	Sports	Hockey Stick	$ 10.00	Used to push the puck around.
12	501	Sports	Bike	$400.00	Sits in the garage and collects dust.
13	556	Sports	First Aid Kit	$ 25.00	Used more times than not, unfortunately.
14	601	Misc.	Dog Food	$ 1.50	The stuff the cat eats.
15	623	Misc.	Cat Food	$ 0.75	The stuff the dog eats.
16	644	Misc.	Socks	$ 1.00	What both the dog and cat destroy.

End Output

How It Works

The field format @>>>>>>> on the title line specifies the format for the page number; in this case, the page number is right-justified. The variable $FORMAT_PAGE_NUMBER is created by the Engligh.pm module. It is an alias for the special variable $%. Whenever a new page is encountered, the top-of-form header is read and expanded so the page number will be displayed on the top-right corner of the page.

Comments

A variable in the top-of-form header can be used for many things: a name, a phone number, or any other miscellaneous information.

COMPLEXITY
INTERMEDIATE

9.5 How do I...
Attach a footer to a report?

COMPATIBILITY: PERL 5 UNIX DOS

Problem

I am creating a report and would like to add both a header and a footer to each page. How-To 9.3 demonstrates how to use the _TOP keyword to add a header to a report. There is no corresponding _BOTTOM keyword. How do I add a footer to a report?

Technique

The basic technique is to create the footer manually. Pay attention to the current line being printed; when the report is nearing the end of the page, print out the footer, and force the page to end. This tricks Perl into thinking the report has printed out a full page, and the next page will begin.

Steps

1. Copy the Perl script created in How-To 9.4 into a file named footer.pl.

2. Modify the script footer.pl. The following example demonstrates the modified script footer.pl. The modifications are highlighted in bold.

```perl
#!/usr/local/bin/perl -w
use English;

# Set the count to zero.
$pageCount = 0;
$pageItemCount = 0;

# Set the page to be 20 lines long.
# (This is only for demonstration purposes)
$FORMAT_LINES_PER_PAGE = 20;

# Do this until there are no more records.
while (<ARGV>)
{
    chomp;

    # Split the line on the pipe symbol.
    ($number,$type,$name,$price,$desc) = split (/\|/);

    # Print out the item information.
    write;

    # Increment the item count.
    $pageCount++;
    $pageItemCount++;

    # Check if we are near the bottom of the page.
    if ($FORMAT_LINES_LEFT <= 3)
    {
        # Print out the footer.
        print "------------\n";
        print "Item Count For This Page $pageItemCount\n";
        $pageItemCount = 0;

        # Set the line value to zero.
        $FORMAT_LINES_LEFT = 0;
    }
}

# Print out any residual information.
print "------------\n";
```

continued on next page

continued from previous page

```
print "Item Count For This Page $pageItemCount\n";
exit;

#
# Start of format 'pictures'
#
format STDOUT_TOP=
Count Item #  Item Type  Item Name      Price      Description    Page
@>>>>>>
$FORMAT_PAGE_NUMBER
=============================================================================
.

format STDOUT=
@>>>> @|||||| @<<<<<<<<< @<<<<<<<<<<<<< @####.##
^<<<<<<<<<<<<<<<<<<<<<<<<
$pageCount,$number,$type,$name,$price,$desc
~
^<<<<<<<<<<<<<<<<<<<<<<<<
$desc
~
^<<<<<<<<<<<<<<<<<<<<<<<<
$desc
.
```

3. Run the script using the input file from How-To 9.1.

```
% chap_09/howto05/footer.pl chap_09/howto01/align.dat
```

Output

Count	Item #	Item Type	Item Name	Price	Description	Page	1
0	101	Hardware	Hammer	$ 25.00	A thing to hit nails with.		
1	121	Hardware	Nail	$ 0.15	A thing to be hit by a hammer. (see hammer)		
2	142	Hardware	Sander	$ 10.15	Used to sand all sorts of things, except sand.		
3	206	Household	Kitchen Sink	$100.00	Lost the last time I went on vacation. (next time I won't check it in)		
4	210	Household	Windows	$ 45.00	User friendly and does not need to be plugged in.		
5	242	Household	Vacuum	$300.00	I'm not sure what this is used for, but people seem to have them anyway.		
6	266	Household	Microwave	$100.00	Kitchen item. (also see hot water heater)		

```
-------------
Item Count For This Page 7
(Page Break)
```

Count	Item #	Item Type	Item Name	Price	Description	Page	2
7	312	Garden	Rake	$ 25.00	Used to rake leaves, cut grass and break noses if left lying on the ground.		
8	344	Garden	Gravel	$ 30.00	Why bother — the dog is		

```
                                        going to dig through it
                                        again anyway.
    9  362   Garden    Top Soil     $ 10.00  Is there such a thing as
                                        "Bottom Soil?"
   10  384   Garden    Mosquitos    $  0.00  Some are large as a dog and
                                        will carry you away.
   11  500   Sports    Hockey Stick $ 10.00  Used to push the puck
                                        around.
   12  501   Sports    Bike         $400.00  Sits in the garage and
                                        collects dust.
   13  556   Sports    First Aid Kit $ 25.00  Used more times than not,
                                        unfortunately.
-------------
Item Count For This Page 7
(Page Break)
Count  Item # Item Type Item Name    Price   Description       Page   3
===============================================================================
   14  601   Misc.     Dog Food     $  1.50  The stuff the cat eats.
   15  623   Misc.     Cat Food     $  0.75  The stuff the dog eats.
   16  644   Misc.     Socks        $  1.00  What both the dog and cat
                                        destroy.
-------------
Item Count For This Page 3
```
End Output

How It Works

The intelligence of the script resides in the line

```
if ($FORMAT_LINES_LEFT <= 3)
```

which checks to see how many lines are left in the current page. If there are less than 3, then add the footer and end the page. You look for 3 lines because the split line field takes 3 lines. If the report were nearing the end of the page and the full description field was going to be used, the variable $FORMAT_LINES_LEFT would decrement by 3. Which means that if you check if the number of lines left is equal to 3, it is possible that the variable $FORMAT_LINES_LEFT could go from 4 to 1 on one record, and the footer for the current page would not be printed out. Once the footer is printed out, the end of page is forced by setting the variable $FORMAT_LINES_LEFT to 0.

Comments

The _BOTTOM addition to Perl is currently in the works; the problem, Larry says, is that it is difficult to determine the number of lines of the footer. Until then, you'll have to create the footer manually.

COMPLEXITY
INTERMEDIATE

9.6 How do I...
Switch between multiple report formats?

COMPATIBILITY: PERL 5   UNIX   DOS

Problem

I have a script that reads an input file and creates two separate reports from the given data. I don't want to create two scripts to perform similar tasks. How can I have the same script write two reports at the same time?

Technique

As a default, report output is usually sent to the screen, which means many programmers use the STDOUT filehandle stream. To switch between filehandles, use the select command; as a side effect, the values of the variables $^ and $~ change as well. This does not mean that you have to switch filehandles to switch reports. All you need to do is redefine the values of $^ and $~ to reflect the correct report format. This How-To uses the variables $FORMAT_NAME and $FORMAT_TOP_NAME, which are defined by the English.pm module, to select the reports.

Steps

1. Create a new file named reports.pl and type the following script into it.

```perl
#!/usr/local/bin/perl -w

# Make the script more readable...
use English;
use FileHandle;

# Set the page to be 20 lines long.
# (This is only for demonstration purposes)
$FORMAT_LINES_PER_PAGE = 20;

# Set some variables.
my $TAXRATE=0.15;
my $totalCost=0;
my $totalTax=0;
my $totalPrice=0;

# Select the 'INVOICE' picture.
$FORMAT_NAME = "INVOICE";
$FORMAT_TOP_NAME = "INVOICE_TOP";

# Do this until there are no more records.
```

```
while (<ARGV>)
{
    chomp;

    # Split the line on the pipe symbol.
    ($code,$name,$price,$quantity) = split (/\|/);

    # Determine the cost of this item.
    $cost = $price * $quantity;
    $tax = $cost * $TAXRATE;
    $finalCost = $cost + $tax;

    # Keep a running tab.
    $totalPrice += $cost;
    $totalTax += $tax;
    $totalCost += $finalCost;

    # Spit out the information.
    write;
}

# Select the 'TOTAL' picture.
$FORMAT_NAME = "TOTAL";

# Write out the totals.
write;

# This format 'picture' is for the invoice.
format INVOICE_TOP =
Quantity Name                          Code    Price    Tax      Cost
========================================================================
.

format INVOICE =
@<<<<<<< @<<<<<<<<<<<<<<<<<<<<<< @<<<<<< $@#####.## $@###.## $@#####.##
$quantity,$name,$code,$price,$tax,$cost
.

format TOTAL =
========================================================================
                                        $@#####.## $@###.## $@#####.##
$totalPrice,$totalTax,$totalCost
.
```

2. Create an input file named reports.dat and type the following into it.

```
101|Hammer|25.00|2
121|Nail|0.15|200
142|Sander|10.15|2
206|Kitchen Sink|100.00|1
242|Vacuum|300.00|1
266|Microwave|100.00|1
312|Rake|25.00|4
344|Gravel|30.00|7
384|Mosquitos|0.00|10000
500|Hockey Stick|10.00|10
```

3. Run the script with the input file.

```
% chap_09/howto06/reports.pl  chap_09/howto06/reports.dat
```

─── Output ───

Quantity	Name	Code	Price	Tax	Cost
2	Hammer	101	$ 25.00	$ 7.50	$ 50.00
200	Nail	121	$ 0.15	$ 4.50	$ 30.00
2	Sander	142	$ 10.15	$ 3.04	$ 20.30
1	Kitchen Sink	206	$ 100.00	$ 15.00	$ 100.00
1	Vacuum	242	$ 300.00	$ 45.00	$ 300.00
1	Microwave	266	$ 100.00	$ 15.00	$ 100.00
4	Rake	312	$ 25.00	$ 15.00	$ 100.00
7	Gravel	344	$ 30.00	$ 31.50	$ 210.00
10000	Mosquitos	384	$ 0.00	$ 0.00	$ 0.00
10	Hockey Stick	500	$ 10.00	$ 15.00	$ 100.00
			$ 1010.30	$ 151.55	$ 1161.85

─── End Output ───

How It Works

When this script is run, the input file is read and printed out using the INVOICE format section, even though the output of the script is using the STDOUT stream. This is accomplished by the two lines

```
$FORMAT_NAME = "INVOICE";
$FORMAT_TOP_NAME = "INVOICE_TOP";
```

The two variables, $FORMAT_NAME and $FORMAT_TOP_NAME, are defined by the English.pm module and are aliases for the built-in Perl variables $~ and $^, respectively. When these variables are given a new value, a write command is called the next time without a format name; the values in the variables $~ and $^ contain the report picture to use. In this How-To, the body of the report is defined by the INVOICE and INVOICE_TOP format pictures. This report picture is used to display an itemized list of purchases, and lists all the elements of the individual items "bought." When all the items have been "rung in," the total needs to be displayed. The total is defined in the TOTAL format name and is selected by the line

```
$FORMAT_NAME = "TOTAL";
```

Then write is called and the total is printed out using the TOTAL report format.

Comments

This script demonstrates the mass confusion Perl programmers suffer regarding file-handle name space and report name space. This confusion arises because the values of $^ and $~ are set when select is called, and most Perl programmers think they need to use select to change format names.

DBM FILES

DBM FILES

How do I...

Database management (DBM) files are a specific format file, the only purpose of which is to act as a reservoir for databases of information. DBM files were created for programs that use or require large databases of information. Some examples of this are the B News and C News history files. Since their inception, DBM files have been used more as a basic tool to store and fetch information. One of the few, noticeable changes from Perl 4 to Perl 5 is the way Perl manipulates DBM files. Perl 4 uses the commands dbmopen and dbmclose to open and close DBM files. Perl 5 uses the dbmopen/dbmclose method as well, but introduces a new method to interact with DBM files. Perl

5 uses the methods tie and untie to create a binding between an object and a DBM file. The tie function opens a DBM file and returns a reference object that is used to call methods such as get and put to interact with the DBM file.

The scripts presented in this chapter demonstrate how to open DBM files, manipulate internal DBM data, and close DBM files using both the dbmopen and tie methods. There should be enough information in this chapter to make even the most novice Perl programmer comfortable using DBM files.

10.1   Create a DBM File Using Perl

This How-To will demonstrate how to create a DBM file from a flat ASCII text file using the old method of dbmopen.

10.2   Display the Contents of a DBM File

How to display the contents of a DBM file is one of the most frequently asked questions about DBM files. This How-To will present the answer: using the new tie/untie pair.

10.3   Modify Records Inside a DBM File

This section will use the DBM file created in How-To 10.1 and modify several of the records.

10.4   Delete Records from a DBM File

Many experienced Perl programmers still make a mistake when trying to delete records from a DBM file. This section will outline how to delete records correctly.

10.5   Empty a DBM File

There are many ways to empty a DBM file. This How-To will demonstrate one of the most accepted methods.

10.6   Merge Two DBM Files Together

Merging two DBM files together is not as simple as you may first think. This How-To will take two DBM files and create a third, merged DBM database file.

10.7   Perform a "Sounds-Like" Match

Performing vague pattern searches is a common task for all database engines. This How-To will create a script that can perform approximate pattern searches on the records of a DBM database file.

10.8   Maintain a Sorted DBM File

The larger a DBM file gets, the more important it becomes to keep a sorted and ordered DBM file. This How-To will demonstrate how to maintain an ordered DBM file using the new tie function.

COMPLEXITY
INTERMEDIATE

10.1 How do I...
Create a DBM file using Perl?

COMPATIBILITY: PERL 5 UNIX

Problem

I have a program that needs a large database of information to run. Using a flat text file as a database is too difficult and slow. I understand using a DBM file would speed up the script; the only problem is, I don't know how to create a DBM file using Perl. How do I do this?

Technique

The script opens a named ASCII file and starts reading through it. At the same time, it opens a DBM file for writing. The following line of Perl code opens a DBM file:

```perl
dbmopen (%inventory, $database, 0700);
```

When a DBM file is opened using the dbmopen function, it takes three parameters. The first, %inventory in this example, is the name of the hash the DBM file will be accessed through. The second is the name of the DBM file. In the example provided, the name of the file is contained in the variable *$database*. The third parameter is the permissions the DBM file is opened with. In the example, the DBM file is opened with 0700. The value is a standard UNIX file permission octal value. The value of 0700 states the file will be opened with read, write, and execute access for the owner and nothing else for world and groups.

Once the DBM file is opened and can be accessed through the hash %inventory, you can start writing records into the DBM file. The first thing to determine is the key value of the hash. Hashes require some sort of key as an index. You must determine what field will be suitable for an index key value. The example provided uses the stock inventory number. Because the stock inventory number is a unique value, it is the best candidate. All you need to do is to scan through the text file and store the information into the DBM file. Once this is done, close the DBM file using the dbmclose command.

Steps

1. Create a new file named convert.pl and type the following script into it.

```perl
#!/usr/local/bin/perl -w

# Use the DBM module.
use Getopt::Long;
use DB_File;

# Set up the command line options.
```

continued on next page

continued from previous page

```perl
my      $ret     = GetOptions ("f|filename:s", "d|database:s");
my $filename    = $opt_f || die "Usage: $0 -f filename -d database\n";
my $database    = $opt_d || die "Usage: $0 -f filename -d database\n";
my %inventory;

# Open the input file.
open (INPUT, "$filename") || die "Can not open the file $filename : $!\n";

# Open the DBM database file.
dbmopen (%inventory, $database, 0700) || die "Can not open the DBM database
$database : $!\n";

# Loop through the input file and put it into the DBM database.
while (<INPUT>)
{
    chomp;

    # Split the line
    my ($number,$type,$name,$price,$desc) = split (/\|/);

    # Save the information into the DBM file.
    $inventory{$number} = "${type}|${name}|${price}|${desc}";
}

# Close the dbm database
dbmclose %inventory;

# Close the input file.
close (INPUT);
```

2. Create a text file named convert.dat and type in the following information.

```
100|Hardware|Hammer|25.00|A thing to hit nails with.
122|Hardware|Nail|0.15|A thing to be hit by a hammer. (see hammer)
142|Hardware|Sander|10.15|Used to sand all sorts of things, except sand.
206|Household|Kitchen Sink|100.00|Lost the last time I went on vacation.
(next time I won't check it in)
210|Household|Windows|45.00|User friendly and does not need to be plugged
in.
242|Household|Vacuum|300.00|I'm not sure what this is used for, but people
seem to have them anyway.
266|Household|Microwave|100.00|Kitchen item. (also see hot water heater)
312|Garden|Rake|25.00|Used to rake leaves, cut grass and break noses if
left lying on the ground.
344|Garden|Gravel|30.00|Why bother - the dog is going to dig through it
again anyway.
362|Garden|Top Soil|10.00|Is there such a thing as "Bottom Soil?"
384|Garden|Mosquitos|0.00|Some are large as a dog and will carry you away.
500|Sports|Hockey Stick|10.00|Used to push the puck around.
502|Sports|Bike|400.00|Sits in the garage and collects dust.
556|Sports|First Aid Kit|25.00|Used more times than not, unfortunately.
602|Misc|Dog Food|1.50|The stuff the cat eats.
624|Misc|Cat Food|0.75|The stuff the dog eats.
644|Misc|Socks|1.00|What both the dog and cat destroy.
```

3. Run the script using the above text file as an input file.

```
% chap_10/howto01/convert.pl -f chap_10/howto01/convert.dat -d
chap_10/howto01/convert.dbm
```

4. This script produces no visible output. To ensure that the script ran correctly, check that the file chap_10/howto01/convert.dbm exists.

```
% ls chap_10/howto01/
```

Output

```
convert.pl   convert.dat convert.dbm
```

End Output

All the other examples in this chapter use the DBM file generated from this How-To.

How It Works

When the DBM file is opened, the hash %inventory is tied to the DBM file. A unique index key value is chosen and pertinent information associated with that key is stored into the hash. The following line of Perl code demonstrates how to store more than one piece of information for a given key.

```
$inventory{$number} = "${type}|${name}|${price}|${desc}";
```

The key of the hash is in the variable *$number*, but you need to keep several pieces of information for each key. This example keeps information about the item type, the name of the item, the price of the item, and a description of the item. The information is stored with the pipe symbol (|) as a delimiter. Thus, when the record is read, you can split the record on the pipe symbol to get the individual record elements. This works only if the stored fields do not contain any of the chosen delimiters. Once all the data from the text file has been read and the hash has been filled, the DBM file needs to be closed using the dbmclose function. Because the DBM file was opened using the dbmopen function, you have to close it with the dbmclose function. The dbmclose function takes one argument: the name of the hash that contains the data. In this case, you would call dbmclose as follows.

```
dbmclose (%inventory);
```

Comments

Of all the enhancements and changes to Perl, DBM file manipulation is one of the most noticeable. It is also one of the few places where Perl 4 scripts, which use the dbmopen function, may not work without some intervention to bring the script up to Perl 5 compatibility.

10.2 How do I...
Display the contents of a DBM file?

COMPATIBILITY: PERL 5   UNIX

Problem

I have a DBM file. How do I display its contents?

Technique

This How-To demonstrates how to use the new the tie/untie pair of commands to manipulate a DBM file. Get the name of the DBM file to open, either by the command line or using standard input. The script in this How-To uses the command line for this information.

The DBM file is opened using the tie function. The tie function is a new addition to Perl; its purpose is to create an association between a package and a variable. The package provides a means to manipulate the named package using the variable. The syntax of the tie function is as follows:

```
Variable = tie Variable, Package Name, Argument List
```

Because tie is a generic function, different packages that use tie will have different argument lists. The value that tie returns is an object, which should allow another method of manipulating the package information.

Currently, there are three different methods to call the tie function with respect to Berkeley DBM files. The first of the three is

```
$db = tie %hash,  DB_File, $filename [, $flags, $mode, $DB_HASH] ;
```

The %hash parameter is the name of a hash variable, associative array. The second parameter is the package name: DB_File. This states that you want to use the Berkeley DBM file type. Because there are several different DBM file types, this is important. The third parameter, $filename, is the name of the DBM file. The $flags parameter is the flags to use when attempting to open the DBM file. Several flags can be used when trying to open a DBM file. The module Fcntl.pm contains a list of open flags that can be used when attempting to open a DBM file; this is why the script in this How-To uses the Fcntl.pm module. Table 10-1 lists all the flags supplied by the Fcntl.pm module for use with DBM files.

FLAG NAME	DESCRIPTION
O_APPEND	Appends information to the given file.
O_CREAT	Creates a new file.
O_EXCL	When used with O_CREAT, if the file already exists, the open will fail.

FLAG NAME	DESCRIPTION
O_NDELAY	The file is opened without blocking. This means that any reads or writes to the file will not cause the process to wait.
O_NONBLOCK	The file is opened without blocking. This means that any reads or writes to the file will not cause the process to wait.
O_RDONLY	Opens the file read only.
O_RDWR	Opens the file both read and write.
O_TRUNC	Opens the file. If it exists already, it is truncated.
O_WRONLY	Opens the file write only.

Table 10-1 File access flags

The $mode parameter is the permissions of the file to be created if the DBM file is new. The permissions are in the standard UNIX file permissions format. The last parameter, $DB_HASH, states that the file is a Berkeley DBM file type. The last three arguments, $flags, $mode, and $DB_HASH, are optional and are not needed to open a Berkeley DBM file in hash format.

A second method for opening a DBM file is used when manipulating a DBM file that has been stored as a B-Tree. This method is the same as the method used to open a hash-type DBM file, except the last argument is $DB_BTREE and all the arguments are required. The syntax needed to open a B-Tree DBM file using the tie function is

```
$db = tie %hash,  DB_File, $filename, $flags, $mode, $DB_BTREE ;
```

The B-Tree type DBM file is discussed in How-To 10.8. The third method to open a DBM file using tie is

```
$db = tie @array, DB_File, $filename, $flags, $mode, $DB_RECNO ;
```

This DBM file type allows both fixed-length and variable-length flat text files to be manipulated using the same interface type as both the DB_HASH and DB_BTREE tie interfaces. Notice that the first parameter @array is a list and not a hash.

In this How-To, the records of the DBM file are listed using the each function. The each function returns a key-value pair. The key is the index to the current record; the value is the content of the current record. Using the each function is preferred to using the functions keys or values. If the hash is large, then the functions keys and values will return a huge array of values.

Steps

1. Open a new file named listdb.pl and type the following script into it.

```
#!/usr/local/bin/perl -w

# Use the DBM module.
use Getopt::Long;
```

continued on next page

continued from previous page

```
use English;
use DB_File;

# Set up the command line options.
my $ret       = GetOptions ("d|database:s");
my $database  = $opt_d || die "Usage: $0 -d database\n";
my (%contents,$count,$type,$name,$price,$desc,$record);

# Open the DBM database file.
dbmopen (%contents, $database, 0700) || die "Could not open DBM file
$database : $!\n";

# Force the top of page.
$FORMAT_LINES_LEFT = 0;
$count = 0;

# Start printing out the dbm information.
for $number (sort keys %contents)
{
    # Get the contents from the hash.
    $record = $contents{$number};

    # Split up the record.
    ($type,$name,$price,$desc) = split (/\|/, $record);
    $count++;

    # Write it...
    write;
}

# Close the DBM database.
dbmclose %contents;

# Top of picture formats.
format STDOUT_TOP=
Count Item #  Item Type  Item Name      Price      Description    Page
@>>>>>>
$FORMAT_PAGE_NUMBER
===========================================================================
.


format STDOUT=
@>>>> @|||||| @<<<<<<<<< @<<<<<<<<<<<<< $@####.##
^<<<<<<<<<<<<<<<<<<<<<<<<<
$count,$number,$type,$name,$price,$desc
~
^<<<<<<<<<<<<<<<<<<<<<<<<<
$desc
~
^<<<<<<<<<<<<<<<<<<<<<<<<<
$desc
.
```

2. Run the script using the DBM file created in How-To 10.1.

```
$ chap_10/howto02/listdb.pl -d chap_10/howto01/convert.dbm
```

Output

Count	Item #	Item Type	Item Name	Price	Description	Page	1
=====	======	=========	=========	=====	===========	====	=
1	100	Hardware	Hammer	$ 25.00	A thing to hit nails with.		
2	122	Hardware	Nail	$ 0.15	A thing to be hit by a hammer. (see hammer)		
3	142	Hardware	Sander	$ 10.15	Used to sand all sorts of things, except sand.		
4	206	Household	Kitchen Sink	$100.00	Lost the last time I went on vacation. (next time I won't check it in)		
5	210	Household	Windows	$ 45.00	User friendly and does not need to be plugged in.		
6	242	Household	Vacuum	$300.00	I'm not sure what this is used for, but people seem to have them anyway.		
7	266	Household	Microwave	$100.00	Kitchen item. (also see hot water heater)		
8	312	Garden	Rake	$ 25.00	Used to rake leaves, cut grass and break noses if left lying on the ground.		
9	344	Garden	Gravel	$ 30.00	Why bother – the dog is going to dig through it again anyway.		
10	362	Garden	Top Soil	$ 10.00	Is there such a thing as "Bottom Soil?"		
11	384	Garden	Mosquitos	$ 0.00	Some are large as a dog and will carry you away.		
12	500	Sports	Hockey Stick	$ 10.00	Used to push the puck around.		
13	502	Sports	Bike	$400.00	Sits in the garage and collects dust.		
14	556	Sports	First Aid Kit	$ 25.00	Used more times than not, unfortunately.		
15	602	Misc	Dog Food	$ 1.50	The stuff the cat eats.		
16	624	Misc	Cat Food	$ 0.75	The stuff the dog eats.		
17	644	Misc	Socks	$ 1.00	What both the dog and cat destroy.		

End Output

How It Works

The bulk of the work takes place in the *while* loop. The following line of Perl code calls the each function, which returns a two-element array from the hash %inventory.

```
($key,$record) = each %inventory
```

The two-element array consists of the index value of the current record and the record value. The index is stored in the variable *$key* and the record is stored in the variable *$record*. Each record returned has to be split up on the delimiter (chosen in How-To 10.1) to get the individual elements from the record. This is done by the line

```
($type,$name,$price,$desc) = split (/\|/, $record);
```

All that remains to be done is to display the information, which is what the write command does.

Comments

This script may be one of the most useful scripts you write. It might be a good idea to keep a copy around; at the least, fully understand the components of this script so you can reproduce it.

COMPLEXITY
INTERMEDIATE

10.3 How do I...
Modify records inside a DBM file?

COMPATIBILITY: PERL 5 | UNIX

Problem

I have a DBM file and I need to modify the information in it. How do I do this?

Technique

To modify a record in a DBM file, you need to open the DBM file with read/write access. This script uses the tie/untie pair to open and close the DBM file. To learn more about the syntax of the tie/untie pair and their parameters, read How-To 10.2. Once opened, records are selected by their index and modified. Once all the modifications have been done, the DBM file is closed.

Steps

1. Create a new file named modifydb.pl and type the following script into it.

```perl
#!/usr/local/bin/perl -w

# Use the DBM module.
use Getopt::Long;
use DB_File;
use Fcntl;

# Set up the command line options.
my $ret      = GetOptions ("d|database:s", "i|index:s");
my $database = $opt_d || die "Usage: $0 -d database -i index\n";
my $index    = $opt_i || die "Usage: $0 -d database -i index\n";
my %inventory;

# Open the DBM database file.
tie %inventory, DB_File, $database, O_RDWR|O_CREAT, 0700 || die "Could not
open DBM file $database : $!\n";

# Does the record exist?
die "$0: Record key $index does not exist in the database.\n" if (! defined
$inventory{$index});
```

```
# Change the record.
$inventory{$index} = uc $inventory{$index};

# Close the dbm database
untie %inventory;
```

2. Copy the DBM file generated in How-To 10.1 into a new file named modify.dbm.

```
% cp chap_10/howto01/convert.dbm chap_10/howto03/modify.dbm
```

3. Using the script from How-To 10.2, list the contents of the DBM file.

```
% chap_10/howto02/dumpdbm.pl -d chap_10/howto03/modify.dbm
```

Output

Count	Item #	Item Type	Item Name	Price	Description	Page	1
1	100	Hardware	Hammer	$ 25.00	A thing to hit nails with.		
2	122	Hardware	Nail	$ 0.15	A thing to be hit by a hammer. (see hammer)		
3	142	Hardware	Sander	$ 10.15	Used to sand all sorts of things, except sand.		
4	206	Household	Kitchen Sink	$ 100.00	Lost the last time I went on vacation. (next time I won't check it in)		
5	210	Household	Windows	$ 45.00	User friendly and does not need to be plugged in.		
6	242	Household	Vacuum	$300.00	I'm not sure what this is used for, but people seem to have them anyway.		
7	266	Household	Microwave	$100.00	Kitchen item. (also see hot water heater)		
8	312	Garden	Rake	$ 25.00	Used to rake leaves, cut grass and break noses if left lying on the ground.		
9	344	Garden	Gravel	$ 30.00	Why bother - the dog is going to dig through it again anyway.		
10	362	Garden	Top Soil	$ 10.00	Is there such a thing as "Bottom Soil?"		
11	384	Garden	Mosquitos	$ 0.00	Some are large as a dog and will carry you away.		
12	500	Sports	Hockey Stick	$ 10.00	Used to push the puck around.		
13	502	Sports	Bike	$400.00	Sits in the garage and collects dust.		
14	556	Sports	First Aid Kit	$ 25.00	Used more times than not, unfortunately.		
15	602	Misc	Dog Food	$ 1.50	The stuff the cat eats.		
16	624	Misc	Cat Food	$ 0.75	The stuff the dog eats.		
17	644	Misc	Socks	$ 1.00	What both the dog and cat destroy.		

End Output

4. Run the above script on the same DBM file.

```
$ chap_10/howto03/modifydb.pl -d chap_10/howto03/modify.dbm -i 556
```

5. Using the script from How-To 10.2, list the contents of the DBM file. The difference between the original listing and this listing is highlighted in bold.

```
% chap_10/howto02/dumpdbm.pl -d chap_10/howto03/modify.dbm
```

─ Output ───

Count	Item #	Item Type	Item Name	Price	Description	Page	1
1	100	Hardware	Hammer	$ 25.00	A thing to hit nails with.		
2	122	Hardware	Nail	$ 0.15	A thing to be hit by a hammer. (see hammer)		
3	142	Hardware	Sander	$ 10.15	Used to sand all sorts of things, except sand.		
4	206	Household	Kitchen Sink	$100.00	Lost the last time I went on vacation. (next time I won't check it in)		
5	210	Household	Windows	$ 45.00	User friendly and does not need to be plugged in.		
6	242	Household	Vacuum	$300.00	I'm not sure what this is used for, but people seem to have them anyway.		
7	266	Household	Microwave	$100.00	Kitchen item. (also see hot water heater)		
8	312	Garden	Rake	$ 25.00	Used to rake leaves, cut grass and break noses if left lying on the ground.		
9	344	Garden	Gravel	$ 30.00	Why bother - the dog is going to dig through it again anyway.		
10	362	Garden	Top Soil	$ 10.00	Is there such a thing as "Bottom Soil?"		
11	384	Garden	Mosquitos	$ 0.00	Some are large as a dog and will carry you away.		
12	500	Sports	Hockey Stick	$ 10.00	Used to push the puck around.		
13	502	Sports	Bike	$400.00	Sits in the garage and collects dust.		
14	**556**	**SPORTS**	**FIRST AID KIT**	**$ 25.00**	**USED MORE TIMES THAN NOT, UNFORTUNATELY.**		
15	602	Misc	Dog Food	$ 1.50	The stuff the cat eats.		
16	624	Misc	Cat Food	$ 0.75	The stuff the dog eats.		
17	644	Misc	Socks	$ 1.00	What both the dog and cat destroy.		

End Output ───

How It Works

This script uses the tie/untie pair, which is a new method of opening DBM files. The tie function is not strictly for DBM files; its main purpose is to bind variables to packages. The packages provide methods for retrieval, storage, or manipulation via the variables; DBM files happen to be a very good application of this theory. When tie is called, it returns an instance of the type of object being bound to. The following line creates the bind between a DBM file and a variable using the tie function.

```
tie %inventory, DB_File, $database, O_RDWR|O_CREAT, 0700 || die "Could not
open DBM file $database : $!\n";
```

The tie function takes several parameters, one of which is the object type; in this case, it is DB_File. The fourth parameter, O_RDWR|O_CREAT, tells tie to try to open the DBM file with read and write permissions; if it can't, then a new DBM file is created. Before you try to modify the record in the DBM file, check to make sure the record exists. This is done with the following line.

```
die "$0: Record key $index does not exist in the database.\n" if (! defined
$inventory{$index});
```

If the record does not exist, the script exits with a message stating that the record to be modified does not exist. If the record does exists, then the contents of the record are casted to uppercase.

```
$inventory{$index} = uc $inventory{$index};
```

The uc function takes a scalar value and returns the uppercase of the same value. After this, the DBM file is closed using the untie function.

Comments

The benefit of using DBM files as opposed to flat files is that record searches are linear. To check if a record exists, simply check to see if the key value exists in the hash. Performing searches this way uses up fewer system resources.

COMPLEXITY
INTERMEDIATE

10.4   How do I...
Delete records from a DBM file?

COMPATIBILITY: PERL 5   UNIX

Problem

I need to be able to delete a record from the DBM file. How do I do this?

Technique

This script opens a DBM file using the tie function and deletes a record using the delete function; then it closes the DBM file using the untie function.

Steps

1. Create a new file named deletedb.pl and type the following script into it.

```perl
#!/usr/local/bin/perl -w

# Use the DBM module.
use Getopt::Long;
use English;
use DB_File;
use Fcntl;

# Set up the command line options.
my $ret      = GetOptions ("d|database:s", "i|index:s");
my $database = $opt_d || die "Usage: $0 -d database -i index\n";
my $index    = $opt_i || die "Usage: $0 -d database -i index\n";

# Open the DBM database file.
tie (%inventory, DB_File, $database, O_RDWR|O_CREAT, 0700) || die "Could
not open DBM file $database : $!\n";

# Does the record exist?
die "$0: Record key $index does not exist in the database.\n" if (! defined
$inventory{$index});

# Remove the original record from the database.
delete $inventory{$index};

# Close the dbm database
untie %inventory;
```

2. Copy the DBM file generated in How-To 10.1 into a new file named delete.dbm.

```
% cp chap_10/howto01/convert.dbm chap_10/howto04/delete.dbm
```

3. Using the script from How-To 10.2, list the contents of the DBM file.

```
% chap_10/howto02/dumpdbm.pl -d chap_10/howto04/delete.dbm
```

Output

Count	Item #	Item Type	Item Name	Price	Description	Page 1
1	100	Hardware	Hammer	$ 25.00	A thing to hit nails with.	
2	122	Hardware	Nail	$ 0.15	A thing to be hit by a hammer. (see hammer)	
3	142	Hardware	Sander	$ 10.15	Used to sand all sorts of things, except sand.	
4	206	Household	Kitchen Sink	$100.00	Lost the last time I went on vacation. (next time I won't check it in)	

5	210	Household	Windows	$ 45.00	User friendly and does not need to be plugged in.
6	242	Household	Vacuum	$300.00	I'm not sure what this is used for, but people seem to have them anyway.
7	266	Household	Microwave	$100.00	Kitchen item. (also see hot water heater)
8	312	Garden	Rake	$ 25.00	Used to rake leaves, cut grass and break noses if left lying on the ground.
9	344	Garden	Gravel	$ 30.00	Why bother – the dog is going to dig through it again anyway.
10	362	Garden	Top Soil	$ 10.00	Is there such a thing as "Bottom Soil?"
11	384	Garden	Mosquitos	$ 0.00	Some are large as a dog and will carry you away.
12	500	Sports	Hockey Stick	$ 10.00	Used to push the puck around.
13	502	Sports	Bike	$400.00	Sits in the garage and collects dust.
14	556	Sports	First Aid Kit	$ 25.00	Used more times than not, unfortunately.
15	602	Misc	Dog Food	$ 1.50	The stuff the cat eats.
16	624	Misc	Cat Food	$ 0.75	The stuff the dog eats.
17	644	Misc	Socks	$ 1.00	What both the dog and cat destroy.

`End Output`

4. Run the above script on the DBM file.

```
% chap_10/howto04/deletedb.pl -d chap_10/howto04/delete.dbm -I 556
```

5. Using the script from How-To 10.2, list the contents of the DBM file.

```
% chap_10/howto02/dumpdbm.pl -d chap_10/howto04/delete.dbm
```

`Output`

Count	Item #	Item Type	Item Name	Price	Description	Page	1
==
1	100	Hardware	Hammer	$ 25.00	A thing to hit nails with.		
2	122	Hardware	Nail	$ 0.15	A thing to be hit by a hammer. (see hammer)		
3	142	Hardware	Sander	$ 10.15	Used to sand all sorts of things, except sand.		
4	206	Household	Kitchen Sink	$100.00	Lost the last time I went on vacation. (next time I won't check it in)		
5	210	Household	Windows	$ 45.00	User friendly and does not need to be plugged in.		
6	242	Household	Vacuum	$300.00	I'm not sure what this is used for, but people seem to have them anyway.		
7	266	Household	Microwave	$100.00	Kitchen item. (also see hot water heater)		

continued on next page

continued from previous page

8	312	Garden	Rake	$ 25.00	Used to rake leaves, cut grass and break noses if left lying on the ground.
9	344	Garden	Gravel	$ 30.00	Why bother – the dog is going to dig through it again anyway.
10	362	Garden	Top Soil	$ 10.00	Is there such a thing as "Bottom Soil?"
11	384	Garden	Mosquitos	$ 0.00	Some are large as a dog and will carry you away.
12	500	Sports	Hockey Stick	$ 10.00	Used to push the puck around.
13	502	Sports	Bike	$400.00	Sits in the garage and collects dust.
14	602	Misc	Dog Food	$ 1.50	The stuff the cat eats.
15	624	Misc	Cat Food	$ 0.75	The stuff the dog eats.
16	644	Misc	Socks	$ 1.00	What both the dog and cat destroy.

End Output

Notice that record 556, which existed in the first listing, is missing from this listing.

How It Works

The DBM file is opened using the tie function; notice that the only file mode used is O_RDWR. To remove records from a hash, you must delete a record using the delete function. Unfortunately, many people think that the undef function will work as well. It doesn't. The following line deletes the record at index $index in the hash %inventory.

```
delete $inventory{$index};
```

The big difference between the undef function and the delete function is that the delete function deletes the reference of the variable. This means that the variable no longer exists as far as Perl is concerned. The undef function, on the other hand, sets the variable to a null value. How does this affect DBM files? Well, because DBM files are usually tied to hashes, if a record is "removed" using undef, the record still exists in the hash, but it has an empty value. For example, if a hash named %demo has a record in the position specified by the $index variable, then performing a defined function call on $demo{$index} would result in True.

```
if ( defined $demo{$index} ) { print "Hello"; }
```

In this case, Hello will be printed. If the record at $index is removed via undef

```
undef $demo{$index}
```

and the same check is run, Hello will still be printed. This is because the variable $demo{$index} is still defined. However, if the record is removed using delete,

```
delete $demo{$index}
```

then Hello will not be printed out. The delete function actually removes the variable instance from its name space; hence, the variable is no longer defined.

Why mention this point? Many Perl programmers, new and old, make this mistake; it can cause hours of frustration.

Comments

The tie function returns an object that has methods that allow you to access the information in the DBM file. Some people believe that using the object methods is a mistake. Until everyone can agree on this situation, we suggest doing it the way described in this chapter.

COMPLEXITY
INTERMEDIATE

10.5 How do I...
Empty a DBM file?

COMPATIBILITY: PERL 5   UNIX

Problem

I need to delete the contents of a DBM file without deleting the file itself. How do I do this?

Technique

This can be done one of two ways: by opening the DBM file and cycling through the records of the DBM file or by opening the DBM file and calling undef on the hash associated with the DBM file. This How-To outlines the latter method because it is quicker and cleaner.

Steps

1. Create a new file named emptydb.pl and type the following script into it.

```perl
#!/usr/local/bin/perl -w

# Use the DBM module.
use Getopt::Long;
use DB_File;
use Fcntl;

# Set up the command line options.
my $ret     = GetOptions ("d|database:s");
my $database  = $opt_d || die "Usage: $0 -d database\n";
my %inventory;

# Open the DBM database file.
tie (%inventory, DB_File, $database, O_RDWR, 0700) || die "Could not open
DBM file $database : $!\n";
```

continued on next page

continued from previous page

```
# Print out the DBM record count.
my $recordCount = keys %inventory;
print "Before: DBM database record count = $recordCount\n";

# Remove all the records from the database.
undef %inventory;

# Print out the DBM record count.
$recordCount = keys %inventory;
print "After : DBM database record count = $recordCount\n";

# Close the dbm database
untie %inventory;
```

2. Copy the DBM file generated in How-To 10.1 into a new file named delete.dbm.

```
% cp chap_10/howto01/convert.dbm chap_10/howto05/empty.dbm
```

3. Run the above script on the DBM file.

```
$ chap_10/howto05/emptydb.pl -d chap_10/howto05/empty.dbm
```

Output

```
Before: DBM database record count = 17
After : DBM database record count = 0
```
End Output

How It Works

The call

```
tie (%inventory, DB_File, $database, O_RDWR, 0700) || die "Could not open
DBM file $database : $!\n";
```

opens the DBM file specified by the variable *$database* and ties the variable *%inventory* to the DBM file. The DBM file is then erased by the line

```
undef %inventory;
```

which removes all the elements in the hash *%inventory*. The DBM file is then closed with no records in the hash.

Comments

Do not confuse the example in this How-To with the example in How-To 10.4. This example uses undef to empty the complete hash; the example in How-To 10.4 uses delete to delete a specific record in a DBM file. undef works because it sets the whole hash reference to an empty element.

COMPLEXITY
INTERMEDIATE

10.6 How do I...
Merge two DBM files together?

COMPATIBILITY: PERL 5 UNIX

Problem

I have two DBM files that have the exact same internal structure. I need the records from both the DBM files merged into one single file. How do I do this?

Technique

Using the tie function once again, this How-To shows you how to open and read both source DBM files. As the source DBM files are being read, the records are inserted into the common hash variable that is tied to the resultant DBM file. Once the two DBM files have been read, all three DBM files are closed.

Steps

1. Create a new file named mergedb.pl and type the following script into it.

```perl
#!/usr/local/bin/perl -w

# Use the DBM module.
use Getopt::Long;
use English;
use DB_File;
use Fcntl;

# Set up the command line options.
my $ret     = GetOptions ("db1:s", "db2:s", "result:s");
my $db1     = $opt_db1 || die "Usage: $0 --db1 database --db2 database --
result database\n";
my $db2     = $opt_db2 || die "Usage: $0 --db1 database --db2 database --
result database\n";
my $result = $opt_result || die "Usage: $0 --db1 database --db2 database -
-result database\n";
my (%inv1, %inv2, %resultant, $key);

# Open the first DBM file.
tie (%inv1, DB_File, $db1, O_RDONLY, 0700) || die "Could not open DBM
file $db1 : $!\n";

# Open the second DBM file.
tie (%inv2, DB_File, $db2, O_RDONLY, 0700) || die "Could not open DBM
file $db2 : $!\n";

# Open the resultant DBM file.
tie (%resultant, DB_File, $result, O_RDWR|O_CREAT, 0700) || die "Could
not open DBM file $result : $!\n";
```

continued on next page

continued from previous page

```
# Merge in the first DBM file.
for $key (keys %inv1)
{
    if (defined $resultant{$key})
    {
        print "Error: The key $key already exists in the final DBM file.
Ignoring record.\n";
    }
    else
    {
        $resultant{$key} = $inv1{$key};
    }
}

# Merge in the second DBM file.
for $key (keys %inv2)
{
    if (defined $resultant{$key})
    {
        print "Error: The key $key already exists in the final DBM file.
Ignoring record.\n";
    }
    else
    {
        $resultant{$key} = $inv2{$key};
    }
}

# Close all the databases.
untie %inv1;
untie %inv2;
untie %resultant;
```

2. Make a copy of the file chap_10/howto06/db1.dbm from the CD-ROM to a local directory.

3. List the contents of the DBM file chap_10/howto06/db1.dbm using the script from How-To 10.2.

```
% chap_10/howto02/dumpdbm.pl -d chap_10/howto06/db1.dbm
```

Output

Count	Item #	Item Type	Item Name	Price	Description	Page	1
1	142	Hardware	Sander	$ 10.15	Used to sand all sorts of things, except sand.		
2	206	Household	Kitchen Sink	$100.00	Lost the last time I went on vacation. (next time I won't check it in)		
3	384	Garden	Mosquitos	$ 0.00	Some are large as a dog and will carry you away.		
4	500	Sports	Hockey Stick	$ 10.00	Used to push the puck around.		
5	644	Misc	Socks	$ 1.00	What both the dog and cat destroy.		

End Output

4. Make a copy of the file chap_10/howto06/db2.dbm from the CD-ROM to a local directory.

5. List the contents of the DBM file chap_10/howto06/db2.dbm using the script from How-To 10.2.

```
% chap_10/howto02/dumpdbm.pl -d chap_10/howto06/db2.dbm
```

Output

```
Count  Item #  Item Type   Item Name      Price    Description          Page      1
====================================================================================
   1    121    Hardware    Nail           $  0.15  A thing to be hit by a
                                                   hammer. (see hammer)
   2    243    Household   Vacuum         $300.00  I'm not sure what this is
                                                   used for, but people seem
                                                   to have them anyway.
   3    365    Garden      Top Soil       $ 10.00  Is there such a thing as
                                                   "Bottom Soil?"
   4    557    Sports      First Aid Kit  $ 25.00  Used more times than not,
                                                   unfortunately.
   5    623    Misc        Cat Food       $  0.75  The stuff the dog eats.
```

End Output

6. Run the above script with the following command line arguments.

```
% chap_10/howto06/mergedb.pl --db1 db1.dbm --db2 db2.dbm --result db3.dbm
```

7. Check that the new database file exists by listing the contents of the directory.

```
% ls chap_10/howto06/
```

Output

```
db1.dbm db2.dbm    db3.dbm    mergedb.pl
```

End Output

8. List the contents of the new DBM file chap_10/howto06/db3.dbm using the script from How-To 10.2.

```
% chap_10/howto02/dumpdbm.pl -d chap_10/howto06/db3.dbm
```

Output

```
Count  Item #  Item Type   Item Name      Price    Description          Page      1
====================================================================================
   1    121    Hardware    Nail           $  0.15  A thing to be hit by a
                                                   hammer. (see hammer)
   2    142    Hardware    Sander         $ 10.15  Used to sand all sorts of
                                                   things, except sand.
   3    206    Household   Kitchen Sink   $100.00  Lost the last time I went
                                                   on vacation. (next time I
                                                   won't check it in)
   4    243    Household   Vacuum         $300.00  I'm not sure what this is
                                                   used for, but people seem
                                                   to have them anyway.
```

continued on next page

continued from previous page

5	365	Garden	Top Soil	$ 10.00	Is there such a thing as "Bottom Soil?"
6	384	Garden	Mosquitos	$ 0.00	Some are large as a dog and will carry you away.
7	500	Sports	Hockey Stick	$ 10.00	Used to push the puck around.
8	557	Sports	First Aid Kit	$ 25.00	Used more times than not, unfortunately.
9	623	Misc	Cat Food	$ 0.75	The stuff the dog eats.
10	644	Misc	Socks	$ 1.00	What both the dog and cat destroy.

End Output

How It Works

All three DBM files are opened using the tie function. The two source DBM files are opened read only, as specified by the file mode flag O_RDONLY. The destination DBM file is opened with the file mode permissions of O_RDWR|O_CREAT, which opens the DBM file with read/write permissions if the DBM file exists or creates a new DBM file if one does not already exist. Once all the DBM files have been opened, the first DBM file is read and merged into the destination DBM file. To cycle through the DBM file, an array of the keys of the DBM file is generated with the code segment

```
keys %inv2
```

The keys function returns a list of all the keys of the given hash. Using this list, you can cycle through all the elements of the hash.

The contents of the first DBM file are merged in so records in the destination DBM file are not clobbered. To check if a record exists in a DBM file, the following line is used.

```
if (defined $resultant{$key})
```

This checks if the record at the index specified at $key is already defined. If there is a record at this location, then an error message is printed to the screen and the record is not modified. If the record does not already exist, then the record is stored into the destination hash with the following line.

```
$resultant{$key} = $inv2{$key};
```

This line stores the record at index $key from the hash %inv2 into the record at index $key in hash %resultant. The hash %resultant is the destination hash for the merge. Once the first DBM file has been merged into the destination hash, the second DBM file is merged in exactly the same way. Once this is done, all three DBM files are closed via the untie function.

Comments

This script can easily be modified to take a list of source DBM files and a destination DBM file and merge the list into a single DBM file. The destination files must be able to accept the list of source DBM files from the command line and you must write a function that merges the hashes. The script named chap_10/howto06/mergexdb.pl does this.

COMPLEXITY
INTERMEDIATE

10.7 How do I...
Perform a "sounds-like" match?

COMPATIBILITY: PERL 5   UNIX

Problem

A "sounds-like" match is an operation that searches a string looking for a vague pattern. This type of search is performed on every conceivable type of database, including DBM files. How do I perform a sounds-like pattern match on records in a DBM file?

Technique

To do this, use a *pattern-binding operator*. A pattern-binding operator allows you to search a string with little effort looking for a pattern. The syntax of the pattern-binding operator is

```
$string =~ /pattern/
```

This operation will result in True if the given pattern is contained within the variable named *$string*. The pattern can be anything from a basic scalar string to a complex regular expression. The example provided in this How-To uses a basic string value that is given from the command line. To perform a comprehensive search of the DBM file, the string value scans each record for the given pattern.

Steps

1. Create a new file named pattern.pl and type the following script into it.

```perl
#!/usr/local/bin/perl -w

# Purpose:
#    This script demonstrates how to perform a
#  'sounds-like' pattern match on a DBM file.

# Use the DBM module.
use Getopt::Long;
use DB_File;
use Fcntl;

# Set up the command line options.
my $ret        = GetOptions ("d|database:s", "p|pattern:s");
my $database    = $opt_d || die "Usage: $0 -d database -p pattern\n";
my $pattern = $opt_p || die "Usage: $0 -d database -p pattern\n";
my ($key, %inventory);
```

continued on next page

continued from previous page

```
# Open the DBM database file.
tie (%inventory, DB_File, $database, O_RDONLY, 0700) || die "Could not open
DBM file $database : $!\n";

# Start looking for the pattern we were given.
for $key (keys %inventory)
{
    # Look for the 'sounds-like' pattern...
    if ($inventory{$key} =~ $pattern)
    {
        print "Match found ($pattern) =~ <$inventory{$key}>\n";
    }
}

# Close the dbm database
untie %inventory;
```

2. List the contents of the DBM file chap_10/howto01/convert.dbm, using the script from How-To 10.2.

```
% chap_10/howto02/dumpdbm.pl -d chap_10/howto01/convert.dbm
```

Output

Count	Item #	Item Type	Item Name	Price	Description	Page	1
=========	=========	=========	=========	=========	=========	=========	=========
1	100	Hardware	Hammer	$ 25.00	A thing to hit nails with.		
2	122	Hardware	Nail	$ 0.15	A thing to be hit by a hammer. (see hammer)		
3	142	Hardware	Sander	$ 10.15	Used to sand all sorts of things, except sand.		
4	206	Household	Kitchen Sink	$100.00	Lost the last time I went on vacation. (next time I won't check it in)		
5	210	Household	Windows	$ 45.00	User friendly and does not need to be plugged in.		
6	242	Household	Vacuum	$300.00	I'm not sure what this is used for, but people seem to have them anyway.		
7	266	Household	Microwave	$100.00	Kitchen item. (also see hot water heater)		
8	312	Garden	Rake	$ 25.00	Used to rake leaves, cut grass and break noses if left lying on the ground.		
9	344	Garden	Gravel	$ 30.00	Why bother — the dog is going to dig through it again anyway.		
10	362	Garden	Top Soil	$ 10.00	Is there such a thing as "Bottom Soil?"		
11	384	Garden	Mosquitos	$ 0.00	Some are large as a dog and will carry you away.		
12	500	Sports	Hockey Stick	$ 10.00	Used to push the puck around.		
13	502	Sports	Bike	$400.00	Sits in the garage and collects dust.		

14	556	Sports	First Aid Kit	$ 25.00	Used more times than not unfortunately.
15	602	Misc	Dog Food	$ 1.50	The stuff the cat eats.
16	624	Misc	Cat Food	$ 0.75	The stuff the dog eats.
17	644	Misc	Socks	$ 1.00	What both the dog and cat destroy

End Output

3. Run the above script on the DBM file chap_10/howto01/convert.dbm.

```
% chap_10/howto07/pattern.pl -d chap_10/howto01/convert.dbm -p the
```

Output

```
Match found (the) =~ <Household|Kitchen Sink|100.00|Lost the last time I
went on vacation. (next time I won't check it in)>
Match found (the) =~ <Household|Vacuum|300.00|I'm not sure what this is
used for, but people seem to have them anyway.>
Match found (the) =~ <Garden|Rake|25.00|Used to rake leaves, cut grass and
break noses if left lying on the ground.>
Match found (the) =~ <Misc|Dog Food|1.50|The stuff the cat eats.>
Match found (the) =~ <Misc|Cat Food|0.75|The stuff the dog eats.>
Match found (the) =~ <Misc|Socks|1.00|What both the dog and cat destroy.>
Match found (the) =~ <Garden|Gravel|30.00|Why bother - the dog is going to
dig through it again anyway.>
Match found (the) =~ <Garden|Top Soil|10.00|Is there such a thing as
"Bottom Soil?">
Match found (the) =~ <Sports|Hockey Stick|10.00|Used to push the puck
around.>
Match found (the) =~ <Sports|Bike|400.00|Sits in the garage and collects
dust.>
```

End Output

How It Works

The DBM file is opened using the tie function and cycled through using a *for* loop. The sounds-like pattern match is performed by the lines

```
if ($inventory{$key} =~ $pattern)
{
    print "Match found ($pattern) =~ <$inventory{$key}>\n";
}
```

The above lines actually say *If the pattern (which is contained in the variable* $pattern) *is contained in the record (which is contained in the variable* $inventory{$key}) *then print out the match.* When all the records have been searched, the DBM file is closed using the untie function.

Comments

Perl's pattern-binding operators and regular expressions are very powerful elements. How-To 1.4 is dedicated to explaining regular expressions and pattern-binding operators.

COMPLEXITY
INTERMEDIATE

10.8 How do I...
Maintain a sorted DBM file?

COMPATIBILITY: PERL 5   UNIX

Problem

As DBM files grow, the need to keep an ordered database grows. How can I keep a balanced and ordered DBM file in Perl?

Technique

Using the new tie function, apply one of the new DBM file types: a sorted *B-Tree*. A B-Tree is a balanced multiway tree, which means by design the tree is ordered. This allows you to keep an ordered DBM file. To tell the tie to use the B-Tree type database file, use the following syntax to open the database.

```
$db = tie %hash,  DB_File, $filename, $flags, $mode, $DB_BTREE ;
```

The last option, $DB_BTREE, tells the tie function that the database has been stored as a B-Tree. The only disadvantage of using the DB_BTREE type is that it is not the standard DBM file type, and to retrieve information from it, you must know that the DBM database is of type DB_BTREE.

Steps

1. Create a script that writes a DBM file in B-Tree format. The following script does just this. Create a new file named btree.pl and type the following script into it.

```
#!/usr/local/bin/perl -w

use Getopt::Long;
use DB_File;
use Fcntl;

# Set up the command line options.
my $ret      = GetOptions ("f|filename:s", "d|database:s");
my $filename   = $opt_f || die "Usage: $0 -f filename -d database\n";
my $database   = $opt_d || die "Usage: $0 -f filename -d database\n";
my %inventory;

# Open the input file.
open (INPUT, "$filename") || die "Error: Can not open the file $filename :
$!\n";

# Open the DBM database file.
tie %inventory, DB_File, $database, O_RDWR|O_CREAT, 0700, $DB_BTREE ||
die "Error: Can not open the DBM database $database : $!\n";
```

```perl
# Loop through the input file and put it into the DBM database.
while (<INPUT>)
{
    chomp;

    # Split the line
    my ($number,$type,$name,$price,$desc) = split (/\|/);

    # Save the information into the DBM file.
    $inventory{$number} = "${type}|${name}|${price}|${desc}";
}

# Close the dbm database
untie %inventory;

# Close the input file.
close (INPUT);
```

2. Create a B-Tree type DBM file using the ASCII file from How-To 10.1.

```
% chap_10/howto08/btree.pl -f /chap_10/howto01/convert.dat -d
chap_10/howto08/btree.dbm
```

3. Verify that the new DBM file exists.

```
% ls chap_10/howto08
```

Output

btree.dbm   btree.pl

End Output

---

4. Next you need a script that displays the contents of a B-Tree type DBM
database file. Create a new file named dumpbt.pl and enter the following
script into it.

```perl
#!/usr/bin/perl -w

# Use the DBM module.
use Getopt::Long;
use English;
use DB_File;
use Fcntl;

# Set up the command line options.
my $ret       = GetOptions ("d|database:s");
my $database  = $opt_d || die "Usage: $0 -d database\n";
my (%contents,$count,$type,$name,$price,$desc,$record);

# Open the DBM database file.
tie %contents, DB_File, $database, O_RDWR|O_CREAT, 0700, $DB_BTREE ||
die "Could not open DBM file $database : $!\n";

# Force the top of page.
$FORMAT_LINES_LEFT = 0;
$count = 0;
```

continued on next page

continued from previous page

```perl
# Start printing out the dbm information.
for $number (keys %contents)
{
    # Get the contents from the associative array.
    $record = $contents{$number};

    # Split the record up.
    ($type,$name,$price,$desc) = split (/\|/, $record);
    $count++;

    # Write it...
    write;
}

# Close the DBM database.
untie %contents;

# Top of picture formats.
format STDOUT_TOP=
Count Item #  Item Type  Item Name        Price        Description    Page
@>>>>>>
$FORMAT_PAGE_NUMBER
===========================================================================
.

format STDOUT=
@>>>> @||||||| @<<<<<<<<< @<<<<<<<<<<<<< $@####.##
^<<<<<<<<<<<<<<<<<<<<<<<<
$count,$number,$type,$name,$price,$desc
~
^<<<<<<<<<<<<<<<<<<<<<<<<
$desc
~
^<<<<<<<<<<<<<<<<<<<<<<<<
$desc
.
```

5. Verify the B-Tree DBM file is, in fact, sorted by running dumpbt.pl on the B-Tree type DBM file created.

```
Output
```

Count	Item #	Item Type	Item Name	Price	Description	Page	1
1	100	Hardware	Hammer	$ 25.00	A thing to hit nails with.		
2	122	Hardware	Nail	$ 0.15	A thing to be hit by a hammer. (see hammer)		
3	142	Hardware	Sander	$ 10.15	Used to sand all sorts of things, except sand.		
4	206	Household	Kitchen Sink	$100.00	Lost the last time I went on vacation. (next time I won't check it in)		
5	210	Household	Windows	$ 45.00	User friendly and does not need to be plugged in.		
6	242	Household	Vacuum	$300.00	I'm not sure what this is used for, but people seem to have them anyway.		

```
 7   266   Household   Microwave      $100.00   Kitchen item. (also see hot
                                                water heater)
 8   312   Garden      Rake           $ 25.00   Used to rake leaves, cut
                                                grass and break noses if
                                                left lying on the ground.
 9   344   Garden      Gravel         $ 30.00   Why bother - the dog is
                                                going to dig through it
                                                again anyway.
10   362   Garden      Top Soil       $ 10.00   Is there such a thing as
                                                "Bottom Soil?"
11   384   Garden      Mosquitos      $  0.00   Some are large as a dog and
                                                will carry you away.
12   500   Sports      Hockey Stick   $ 10.00   Used to push the puck around.
13   502   Sports      Bike           $400.00   Sits in the garage and
                                                collects dust.
14   556   Sports      First Aid Kit  $ 25.00   Used more times than not,
                                                unfortunately.
15   602   Misc        Dog Food       $  1.50   The stuff the cat eats.
16   624   Misc        Cat Food       $  0.75   The stuff the dog eats.
17   644   Misc        Socks          $  1.00   What both the dog and cat
                                                destroy.
```

End Output

How It Works

All the work is performed in the DBM B-Tree implementation. When the DBM file is opened using the tie function with the $DB_BTREE option, the manipulation of the DBM file is the same as if it were a normal unbalanced DBM file.

Comments

To make a generic DBM file read, you can supply an option from the command line that gives an indication of the type of DBM file. This is a simple modification because the way you interact with a balanced DBM file is exactly the same as how you interact with an unbalanced DBM file.

## CHAPTER 11

PROGRAM AUTOMATION

PROGRAM AUTOMATION

How do I...

You will find tools and utilities such as word processors and spreadsheets on most computer systems. These tools are rarely customized to specific needs, however. Perl allows you to create your own scripts that do exactly what is needed. Sometimes the standard tools supplied by an operating system rely on a user interacting with them. Creating scripts that interact with these tools is usually quite difficult. Perl provides a way to emulate a user interacting with these tools.

It is possible to automate many routine tasks with Perl's capabilities. Perl is especially useful for tasks that are repetitive and long. You can create scripts that perform common functions and design them to take options that will customize their behavior. This allows one script to be used even if the task being automated has numerous variations. For example, a script to create user accounts can be given an option to create the user's home directory in a nonstandard location.

11.1 Perform Expect Processing Without Expect

The UNIX command expect is used to emulate a user interacting with a program. It waits for specific output from a command and responds to that output with the appropriate input. This How-To will show you how to use Perl's library that supplies this same functionality.

11.2 Automate ftp

ftp is a protocol that is designed to transfer files from one location to another. Normally, a user needs to give the ftp program commands. This How-To will show you how to use Perl's library that allows a program to act as a user to retrieve files and perform other ftp functions.

11.3 Log in to a Remote System Automatically

The act of logging into a remote system can involve many steps. These same steps need to be done each time a login occurs. The section will show you how to automate the login process and then allow the user to interact with the remote system.

11.4 Mix Interactive and Automatic Processing in a Chat Script

Some interactions with programs are very routine. You can intersperse the usual steps with some unique interplay. This section will show you how to build a script to intermix the two.

11.5 Set Up 50 New User Accounts

A common task for system administrators is to add new users. This involves many steps and details. The ability to automate this process can save time and eliminate a very repetitive set of tasks. This How-To will show you how.

COMPLEXITY
INTERMEDIATE

11.1 How do I...

Perform expect processing without expect?

COMPATIBILITY: PERL 4   PERL 5   UNIX

Problem

I would like to automate the use of an interactive program. Because the program was designed to communicate with a user directly, it is not easy to write a simple script to do this interaction. I would normally use expect for this. Can this be done in Perl instead?

Technique

Almost all scripts communicate with other commands by using standard input and standard output. Some programs read and write directly to a terminal, however. It is not possible to create a normal script that interacts with such a command. expect is a UNIX utility that is used to communicate with these commands.

A Perl library called chat provides expect-like functionality. chat provides functions to start programs locally and to connect to services on other machines. Once a connection is made to a program, there are functions to read from and write to it.

The typical example is the passwd program. Because passwd will only talk directly to a terminal, normal scripts will not work. chat allows the interaction to be conducted through a pseudo-tty. This allows a chat script to interact with programs that think they are talking to a real terminal.

Steps

This example shows a chat session with the passwd program to change a user's password. Run the script as the root user to allow it to change any user's password.

1. Create a file called passwd.pl. Add the following lines to import the chat library, set the user and new password, and start the passwd program. The open_proc function returns a handle to be used to communicate with passwd.

```
require "chat2.pl";

$User = "janeuser";
$NewPasswd = "password";
$Handle = &chat::open_proc("passwd $User");
```

2. Create an expect call that times-out in 10 seconds and verifies that the passwd program has started. Passwd should print a message about changing the password for the user. Execute the null command when the pattern is seen. This step just verifies that the command started.

```
&chat::expect($Handle,10,
            "for $User.*",      ';',
            'EOF',              '&Eof;',
            'TIMEOUT',          '&TimeOut');
```

3. The next line from the passwd program should be a prompt to supply the new password. Call expect to look for the prompt. When seen, send the new password to the program. Use the print function to send data to the program. The first argument is the handle of the program. The next argument is the string to send to the program.

```
&chat::expect($Handle,10,
            '.*assword:.*',     '&chat::print($Handle, "$NewPasswd\n");',
            'EOF',              '&Eof;',
            'TIMEOUT',          '&TimeOut');
```

4. The passwd program should then prompt for the new password to be repeated. This is to verify that the password was typed in correctly. When this second prompt is seen, send the new password again.

```
&chat::expect($Handle,10,
               'assword:.*',         '&chat::print($Handle, "$NewPasswd\n");',
               'EOF',                 '&Eof;',
               'TIMEOUT',             '&TimeOut');
```

5. The password should have been changed and the passwd program should be completed. Check for this by calling expect with only the TIME-OUT regular expression. If the expected end of file (EOF) is seen, the expect call will return. This is because there is no EOF regular expression in the expect call. If more data is returned from the passwd program, the time-out will occur because the returned data was not matched. After verifying the completion of the passwd program, close the chat handle.

```
&chat::expect($Handle,10,
               'TIMEOUT',             '&TimeOut');

&chat::close($Handle);
```

6. Create two subroutines to handle unexpected actions from the passwd program.

```
sub Eof {
    print "Unexpected end of file\n";
    exit 1;
}

sub TimeOut {
    print "Unexpected timeout\n";
    exit 2;
}
```

7. The entire script follows.

```
require "chat2.pl";

$User = "janeuser";
$NewPasswd = "password";
$Handle = &chat::open_proc("passwd $User");

&chat::expect($Handle,10,
               "for $User.*",         ';',
               'EOF',                 '&Eof;',
               'TIMEOUT',             '&TimeOut');

&chat::expect($Handle,10,
               '.*assword:.*',        '&chat::print($Handle, "$NewPasswd\n");',
               'EOF',                 '&Eof;',
               'TIMEOUT',             '&TimeOut');

&chat::expect($Handle,10,
               'assword:.*',          '&chat::print($Handle, "$NewPasswd\n");',
               'EOF',                 '&Eof;',
               'TIMEOUT',             '&TimeOut');
```

```
&chat::expect($Handle,10,
              'TIMEOUT',              '&TimeOut');

&chat::close($Handle);

sub Eof {
    print "Unexpected end of file\n";
    exit 1;
}

sub TimeOut {
    print "Unexpected timeout\n";
    exit 2;
}
```

8. Run the script. You will not see any output unless there are errors.

How It Works

You can automate interaction with programs by using the chat library. It allows you to start, read from, and write to external programs. Pseudo-ttys are used when running programs locally. There is also a function provided for opening ports on other systems. This function is open_port. It takes two arguments: the server and the port number. A handle is returned. The normal chat function can then be used to interact with the service on the handle.

The chat function for reading data from the process is expect. This function takes a variable number of arguments. The first argument is the handle, and the second is a time-out in seconds. If the expected data is not returned in that time period, the function will return anyway. The rest of the arguments are optional and come in pairs. The first argument in a pair is a regular expression telling what data is trying to be matched. The second argument in a pair is the action to be taken when that data is seen. The regular expressions are checked in the order they are placed in the function call. Once data is matched, it is discarded by chat. The data can be accessed by the variables that are set as a side effect of pattern matching ($&, $1, $2, ...).

There are two special regular expressions that the expect function uses: EOF and TIME-OUT. They are used to check for error conditions. EOF is matched if end of file is seen. EOF is also matched when errors are encountered. In the example, the Eof function is called if EOF is seen. The second special pattern is TIME-OUT, which is matched if expect times-out after waiting to match any of the regular expressions. The example script calls the TimeOut subroutine if this happens.

The chat library is defined in a package called chat. To access the variables and functions in that package, use the :: symbol. Access to a variable or function is available only by prepending the variable or function with the package name and the :: symbol.

Comments

Be careful with the order in which regular expressions are listed in an expect call. Put the most specific expressions first. Otherwise, a more general expression may match the string first. It is usually best to put the arguments in an expect call inside single quotes. This will prevent any variable interpretation in the wrong context.

If you are trying to write portable programs, watch out for slight changes in the output of the processes being run. For example, the case of a word may change. The above script does not try to match the "p" in password. This will allow the match to happen if the letter is in either case.

The chat library is not very portable and may not work on your machine. Another library called Comm.pl is available. Try this library if you cannot get chat to work. It provides most of the same functionality as chat. The Comm.pl library can be found on the Internet with all the Perl sources, libraries, and modules. See Appendix A for information on how to find this library.

Perl 4 uses the single quote character instead of ::. This script will work under Perl 4 if those symbols are changed. Remember to put a backslash before each single quote when it is embedded inside a string delimited by single quotes.

```perl
require "chat2.pl";

$User = "janeuser";
$NewPasswd = "password";
$Handle = &chat'open_proc("passwd $User");

&chat'expect($Handle,10,
                "for $User.*",      ';',
                'EOF',              '&Eof;',
                'TIMEOUT',          '&TimeOut');

&chat'expect($Handle,10,
                '.*assword:.*',     '&chat\'print($Handle, "$NewPasswd\n");',
                'EOF',              '&Eof;',
                'TIMEOUT',          '&TimeOut');

&chat'expect($Handle,10,
                'assword:.*',       '&chat\'print($Handle, "$NewPasswd\n");',
                'EOF',              '&Eof;',
                'TIMEOUT',          '&TimeOut');

&chat'expect($Handle,10,
                'TIMEOUT',          '&TimeOut');

&chat'close($Handle);

sub Eof {
    print "Unexpected end of file\n";
    exit 1;
}

sub TimeOut {
    print "Unexpected timeout\n";
    exit 2;
}
```

COMPLEXITY
INTERMEDIATE

11.2 How do I...
Automate ftp?

COMPATIBILITY: PERL 4 | PERL 5 | UNIX

Problem

I use ftp to transfer files between two of my computers. I run the same ftp job quite often. Is there any way to automate this?

Technique

ftp is a protocol that is designed to transfer files from one location to another. Normally, a user needs to give the ftp program commands. Perl provides a way to automate otherwise interactive programs. The library that is provided to do this is called chat. Built on top of chat is another library called ftp. This library makes it easy to automate ftp sessions.

Steps

The example script uses the ftp library to connect to a machine, lists some files on that machine, and retrieves a version of the Perl source code.

1. Create a file called runftp.pl. First add lines to import the ftp library and define the host to connect to.

```
require "ftp.pl";

$FtpHost = "ftp.metronet.com";
```

2. Use the ftp library's open command to connect to the host. This function takes four arguments: the host name, the ftp port number, a Boolean that tells whether to make multiple attempts to connect, and an attempt count. For this example, do not allow retries. Make sure to set the attempt count to 1. The open command returns 1 for success and 0 for failure. Print a message and exit if the connection cannot be established.

```
if (&ftp::open($FtpHost,21,0,1) != 1) {
    die "Can't open $FtpHost\n";
}
```

3. After the connect, the script must log into the remote host. Use the login function to do this. The first argument is the user name and the second is the password. The site being connected to allows anonymous connections. Use a user name of "anonymous" and a password that contains your mail address. The login function returns 1 for success and 0 for failure.

```
if (&ftp::login("anonymous","joe\@somewhere.com") != 1) {
    die "Can't login to $FtpHost\n";
}
```

4. The ftp library provides a pwd function to list the current directory of the ftp process. Get that value and print it.

```
if (($Pwd = &ftp::pwd) eq "") {
    die "Can't get current directory\n";
}

print "pwd=$Pwd\n";
```

5. Create a variable to contain the directory you want to change to. Call the cwd command to change to that directory. The command returns 1 for success and 0 for failure.

```
$NewCwd = "/pub/perl/source";
if (&ftp::cwd($NewCwd) != 1) {
    die "Can't cwd to $NewCwd\n";
}
```

6. The ftp process allows the listing of the contents of the current directory. To get this listing, the directory must first be opened. Use the dir_open command.

```
if (&ftp::dir_open != 1) {
    die "Can't open directory for reading\n";
}
```

7. The directory is read one line at a time. Use the read function to read each line. As long as the function returns a value greater than 0, a line has been read. A value of 0 means that the listing is complete. Loop through all the lines of the listing. Store each line in the variable $buf as it is read. Print this variable.

```
print "Directory listing for $NewCwd:\n";
while (&ftp::read() > 0 ) {
    print $ftp::buf;
}
```

8. Once all the lines of the listing have been read, close the directory. If the close fails, print a message and exit.

```
if (&ftp::dir_close != 1) {
    die "Can't close directory read\n";
}
```

9. The ftp process has two modes for exchanging data: ASCII and image (binary). These modes are represented by the characters "A" and "I" respectively. The mode can be changed by passing the character to the type function. This function returns 1 for success and 0 for failure. Turn on the ASCII mode. Print a message and exit if it does not succeed.

```
if (&ftp::type("A") != 1) {
    die "Can't change type to ASCII\n";
}
```

10. The data that is to be retrieved is in binary format. The above call to type was just to show the change to ASCII. Change the mode to image so that binary data can be retrieved.

```
if (&ftp::type("I") != 1) {
    die "Can't change type to binary\n";
}
```

11. Create a variable with the name of the file to be retrieved.

```
$File = "perl5.002.tar.gz";
print "Getting $File\n";
```

12. Files are retrieved using the get command. This routine takes one or two arguments. The first argument is the name of the file to be retrieved. The second optional argument is the name to store the file under on the local system. Without the second argument, the file is saved under the same name as the remote system. The comment shows how to use get for two arguments. Get the file using the same name as the remote system.

```
#if (&ftp::get($File,"NewName") != 1) {
if (&ftp::get($File) != 1) {
    die "Can't get $File\n";
}
```

13. When all ftp processing is done, close the connection.

```
&ftp::close;
```

14. The full script follows.

```
require "ftp.pl";

$FtpHost = "ftp.metronet.com";
if (&ftp::open($FtpHost,21,0,1) != 1) {
    die "Can't open $FtpHost\n";
}
if (&ftp::login("anonymous","joe\@somewhere.com") != 1) {
    die "Can't login to $FtpHost\n";
}

if (($Pwd = &ftp::pwd) eq "") {
    die "Can't get current directory\n";
}

print "pwd=$Pwd\n";

$NewCwd = "/pub/perl/source";
if (&ftp::cwd($NewCwd) != 1) {
    die "Can't cwd to $NewCwd\n";
}

if (&ftp::dir_open != 1) {
    die "Can't open directory for reading\n";
}

print "Directory listing for $NewCwd:\n";
```

continued on next page

continued from previous page

```perl
while (&ftp::read() > 0 ) {
    print $ftp::buf;
}

if (&ftp::dir_close != 1) {
    die "Can't close directory read\n";
}

if (&ftp::type("A") != 1) {
    die "Can't change type to ASCII\n";
}
if (&ftp::type("I") != 1) {
    die "Can't change type to binary\n";
}

$File = "perl5.002.tar.gz";
print "Getting $File\n";
#if (&ftp::get($File,"NewName") != 1) {
if (&ftp::get($File) != 1) {
    die "Can't get $File\n";
}

&ftp::close;
```

15. Run the script. The output will be similar to the following.

```
pwd=/
Directory listing for /pub/perl/source:
total 19222
-rw-r--r--   1 1000      200            2719 Oct 31 21:55 .gncache
-rw-r--r--   1 1000      200         1300096 Apr 25  1995 Mac_Perl_418_appl.bin
-rw-r--r--   1 1000      200          482794 Jun  6  1994 bperl3x.zip
-rw-r--r--   1 1000      200            1452 Oct 31 21:54 index.html
-rw-r--r--   1 1000      200            1834 Oct 31 21:55 menu
-rw-r--r--   1 1000      200             989 Sep  6 20:00 ntperl5.001l.announce
-rw-r--r--   1 1000      200          121022 Mar 31  1994 perl.exe-z
-rw-r--r--   1 1000      200         1305327 Jun  6  1994 perl4.036.tar.Z
-rw-r--r--   1 1000      200          300394 Mar 31  1994 perl4.zip
-rw-r--r--   1 1000      200         1190621 Oct 31 21:53 perl5.001n.tar.gz
-rw-r--r--   1 1000      200         1287814 Nov 21 23:02 perl5.002.tar.gz
-rw-r--r--   1 1000      200            1430 Sep  6 20:03 perl5.vms.announce
Getting perl5.002.tar.gz
```

How It Works

The ftp library provides a high-level interface to the ftp process. Commands are supplied that let you connect to a remote machine, change directories, get directory listings, retrieve files, put files, rename files, etc. The library provides a function to perform each of these activities.

The ftp library is implemented in a package. This allows the variable and functions in the package to be hidden from all other packages. To access the variables and functions in the package, the package name and a :: must be prepended to the variable or function.

Comments

The require command includes the file given as an argument. If the same file is required a second time, the require command will notice this and not include it.

The standard port number for ftp is 21. This is hard-coded into the script. It is not likely that this number will change. If it does, make it a variable.

Because ftp.pl depends on chat and chat is not very portable, ftp may not work on your machine. For other options, see the comments section of How-To 11.1.

This script will work under Perl 4 with a few minor changes. Change the ::s to single quotes and change $ftp::buf to $ftp::ftpbuf.

```perl
require "ftp.pl";

$FtpHost = "ftp.metronet.com";
if (&ftp'open($FtpHost,21,0,1) != 1) {
    die "Can't open $FtpHost\n";
}
if (&ftp'login("anonymous"," joe\@somewhere.com ") != 1) {
    die "Can't login to $FtpHost\n";
}

if (($Pwd = &ftp'pwd) eq "") {
    die "Can't get current directory\n";
}

print "pwd=$Pwd\n";

$NewCwd = "/pub/perl/source";
if (&ftp'cwd($NewCwd) != 1) {
    die "Can't cwd to $NewCwd\n";
}

if (&ftp'dir_open != 1) {
    die "Can't open directory for reading\n";
}

print "Directory listing for $NewCwd:\n";
while (&ftp'read() > 0 ) {
    print $ftp'ftpbuf;
}

if (&ftp'dir_close != 1) {
    die "Can't close directory read\n";
}

if (&ftp'type("A") != 1) {
    die "Can't change type to ASCII\n";
}
if (&ftp'type("I") != 1) {
    die "Can't change type to binary\n";
}

$File = "perl5.002.tar.gz";
print "Getting $File\n";
#if (&ftp'get($File,"NewName") != 1) {
```

continued on next page

continued from previous page

```
if (&ftp'get($File) != 1) {
    die "Can't get $File\n";
}

&ftp'close;
```

COMPLEXITY
INTERMEDIATE

11.3 How do I...
Log in to a remote system automatically?

COMPATIBILITY: PERL 4   PERL 5   UNIX

Problem

Every time I log in to a certain system, I have to execute the exact same commands. Can I automate this?

Technique

The chat library allows you to automate what would normally be an interactive session. This ability allows you to execute the commands that are usually run when logging in to a machine. The tricky part happens when you want to resume manual control over the interaction. The way to do this is to have your script forward the input to the remote machine and show the output from the remote machine on the local machine.

Steps

The example script logs in to a remote system and then lets the user interact with the remote session.

1. Create a file called remote.pl. First add lines to include the chat library and the ReadKey library and to catch any signals. If a signal is caught, call exit. This will allow normal exit processing to occur. (The END subroutine will execute.)

```
require "chat2.pl";
use Term::ReadKey;

sub GotSig {
    exit;
}

$SIG{"INT"}  = "GotSig";
$SIG{"QUIT"} = "GotSig";
$SIG{"TERM"} = "GotSig";
```

2. Change STDOUT to be unbuffered. Call chat's open_proc function to open a connection with a local shell process. A handle to this process is returned. Use this handle in all interactions with the shell process.

```
$| = 1;

$Handle = &chat::open_proc("/bin/sh");
```

3. Use some expect calls to verify that the shell has started. When it has, send
a command to the shell telling it to turn off echoing. Use the chat print
command to send input to the shell. The print command's first argument is
the handle of the process to send input to. The rest of the arguments are
strings that are to be used as input. Turn off echoing to make it easier to
automate this script.

```
&chat::expect($Handle,10,
              '\$\s',           '&chat::print($Handle, "stty -echo\n");',
              'EOF',            '&Eof;',
              'TIMEOUT',        '&TimeOut');
```

4. Verify that echo is turned off. Then when a shell prompt is seen, log in to
the remote machine. Append an exit command to the login command. This
will cause the local shell to exit when the remote one does. If a password is
needed, send it when prompted.

```
&chat::expect($Handle,10,
              'stty -echo',     ';',
              'EOF',            '&Eof;',
              'TIMEOUT',        '&TimeOut');
&chat::expect($Handle,10,
              '\$\s', &chat::print($Handle, "rlogin SomeMachine;exit\n");',
              'EOF',            '&Eof;',
              'TIMEOUT',        '&TimeOut');
# &chat::expect($Handle,10,
#              'Password:',      '&chat::print($Handle, "passwd\n");',
#              'EOF',            '&Eof;',
#              'TIMEOUT',        '&TimeOut');
```

5. Turn off all processing of input from the local terminal. These actions are
necessary to allow the remote shell to do all the processing of characters.
Data from the local terminal will be sent in raw mode to the remote
machine.

```
ReadMode("ultra-raw",STDIN);
```

6. Start an infinite loop processing the input to and output from the remote
machine. Call select with no time-out, STDIN, and the process handle. Data
on standard input will be used to send to the process. Output from the
process will be seen on the process handle.

```
while (1) {
    @Ready = &chat::select(undef,STDIN,$Handle);
```

7. Check the ready handles to see if standard input is ready. If STDIN is not in
the @Ready array, nothing will be returned from the grep and the *if* will fail.
Otherwise, STDIN will be returned and the *if* will succeed. If there is input
available from STDIN, read it. Use the sysread command so that data can be

read that is not on line boundaries. If nothing is read, end of file has been
seen, so exit the loop. Write any data read to the remote process.

```
if (grep($_ eq 'STDIN', @Ready)) {
    $Count = sysread(STDIN,$InBuffer,1024);
    ($Count >= 1) || last;
    &chat::print($Handle, $InBuffer);
}
```

8. Check to see if the process is ready to return data and read it if it is. If no
data is returned, exit the loop because the process has ended. Pass the pattern that will match any character(s) to the expect function. The command
that is executed is the variable that holds the data that the regular expression matched. This is then returned from the expect function and assigned
to $OutBuffer. Print the data returned.

```
if (grep($_ eq $Handle, @Ready)) {
    ($OutBuffer = &chat::expect($Handle,0,'[\s\S]+','$&')) || last;
    print $OutBuffer;
}
}
```

9. When the loop finishes, close the process handle to clean up.

```
&chat::close($Handle);
```

10. Define an END subroutine that resets the terminal's modes. In Perl 5, this
subroutine will be executed whenever the script finishes.

```
sub END {
    ReadMode("original",STDIN);
}
```

11. Define the Eof subroutine to be called if an expect call receives an unexpected end of file or error. Create a TimeOut function. This will be called
from expect if the time-out expires.

```
sub Eof {
    print "Unexpected end of file\n";
    exit 1;
}

sub TimeOut {
    print "Unexpected timeout\n";
    exit 2;
}
```

12. The complete script looks like this.

```
require "chat2.pl";
use Term::ReadKey;

sub GotSig {
    exit;
}

$SIG{"INT"}  = "GotSig";
```

```perl
$SIG{"QUIT"} = "GotSig";
$SIG{"TERM"} = "GotSig";

$| = 1;

$Handle = &chat::open_proc("/bin/sh");

&chat::expect($Handle,10,
                '\$\s',              '&chat::print($Handle, "stty -echo\n");',
                'EOF',               '&Eof;',
                'TIMEOUT',           '&TimeOut');
&chat::expect($Handle,10,
                'stty -echo',        ';',
                'EOF',               '&Eof;',
                'TIMEOUT',           '&TimeOut');
&chat::expect($Handle,10,
                '\$\s',              '&chat::print($Handle, "rlogin
                                     'SomeMachine;exit\n");',
                'EOF',               '&Eof;',
                'TIMEOUT',           '&TimeOut');
# &chat::expect($Handle,10,
#               'Password:',          '&chat::print($Handle, "passwd\n");',
#               'EOF',                '&Eof;',
#               'TIMEOUT',            '&TimeOut');

ReadMode("ultra-raw",STDIN);

while (1) {
    @Ready = &chat::select(undef,STDIN,$Handle);
    if (grep($_ eq 'STDIN', @Ready)) {
        $Count = sysread(STDIN,$InBuffer,1024);
        ($Count >= 1) || last;
        &chat::print($Handle, $InBuffer);
    }
    if (grep($_ eq $Handle, @Ready)) {
        ($OutBuffer = &chat::expect($Handle,0,'[\s\S]+','$&')) || last;
        print $OutBuffer;
    }
}
&chat::close($Handle);

sub END {
    ReadMode("original",STDIN);
}

sub Eof {
    print "Unexpected end of file\n";
    exit 1;
}

sub TimeOut {
    print "Unexpected timeout\n";
    exit 2;
}
```

13. Run the script. An example session follows.

```
> perl remote.pl
Linux 1.2.13. (POSIX).
$ w
  4:37pm   up   7:30,   1 user,   load average: 0.05, 0.02, 0.00
User       tty        from              login@  idle   JCPU   PCPU   what
spock      tty1                         9:06am  7:28    14            (bash)
$ exit
logout
rlogin: connection closed.
>
```

How It Works

The chat library supplies all the commands needed to interact with a remote process. The process can be started automatically and then control can be returned to manual. This is achieved by having the script read data from the user and send it to the process and by reading the data from the process and printing it to the user. The chat function select provides the means for implementing this.

The chat expect function takes a variable number of arguments. The first argument is the handle and the second is a time-out in seconds. If the expected data is not returned in that time period, the function will return anyway. The rest of the arguments are optional and come in pairs. The first argument in a pair is a regular expression telling what data is trying to be matched. The second argument in a pair is the action to be taken when that data is seen. The regular expressions are checked in the order they are placed in the function call. Once data is matched, it is discarded by chat. The data can be accessed by the variables that are set as a side effect of pattern matching ($&, $1, $2, ...). expect takes two special patterns to check for error conditions. EOF is matched if end of file is seen and when errors are encountered. TIME-OUT is matched if expect times-out.

Use the chat print command to send input to the shell. The print command's first argument is the handle of the process to send input to. The rest of the arguments are strings that are to be used as input.

chat supplies a select function to interact with multiple file and process handles. The function takes a variable number of arguments. The first argument is the time-out period. The rest of the arguments are handles to check. If data becomes ready to read on one or more of the handles, the function returns the handle(s) that has data available. select will also return if the time-out period expires. A time-out period of undef tells select not to time-out.

The grep command evaluates the first argument on each element of the second argument. During the evaluation, $_ is set to the element being evaluated. If the evaluation returns True, the element is returned from the grep command.

ReadMode is described in Chapter 7. It is used to modify the characteristics of the terminal.

Comments

For a more basic description of the chat library, see How-To 11.1.

The command used to log in to a remote machine is dependent on your operating system and environment.

The regular expression [\s\S] will match any possible character, including a new line. This pattern says to match a white space character or a non-white space character. This covers all possible characters.

The interaction with the remote shell will look just as if the user had manually logged in to the system. The echoing and other interaction will be normal. The echoing was only disabled in the local system. The remote system will do the echoing for the interaction.

The chat library is not very portable and may not work on your machine. Another library called Comm.pl is available. Try this if you cannot get chat to work. It provides most of the same functionality as chat. The Comm.pl library can be found on the Internet with all the Perl sources, libraries, and modules. See Appendix A for information on how to find this library.

This script can be converted to Perl 4 with a few changes. Change all package references using :: to a single quote. Remember to add a backslash if the single quote is going inside a string delimited by single quotes. The END subroutine is not called automatically by Perl 4. Add a call to it at the end of the script and in the signal handler. The ReadKey module is not available in Perl 4. Replace it with calls to the operating system. The particular command to use will be specific to your system. See Chapter 7 for more information on this topic.

```perl
require "chat2.pl";

sub GotSig {
    &END;
    exit;
}

$SIG{"INT"}  = "GotSig";
$SIG{"QUIT"} = "GotSig";
$SIG{"TERM"} = "GotSig";

$| = 1;

$Handle = &chat'open_proc("/bin/sh");

&chat'expect($Handle,10,
            '\$\s',                '&chat\'print($Handle, "stty -echo\n");',
            'EOF',                 '&Eof;',
            'TIMEOUT',             '&TimeOut');
&chat'expect($Handle,10,
            'stty -echo',          ';',
            'EOF',                 '&Eof;',
            'TIMEOUT',             '&TimeOut');
&chat'expect($Handle,10,
            '\$\s',  '&chat\'print($Handle,"rloginSomeMachine;exit\n");',
            'EOF',                 '&Eof;',
            'TIMEOUT',             '&TimeOut');
# &chat'expect($Handle,10,
#            'Password:',          '&chat\'print($Handle, "passwd\n");',
```

continued on next page

continued from previous page

```
#                'EOF',                '&Eof;',
#                'TIMEOUT',            '&TimeOut');

system "stty cbreak raw -echo > /dev/tty";

while (1) {
    @Ready = &chat'select(undef,STDIN,$Handle);
    if (grep($_ eq 'STDIN', @Ready)) {
        $Count = sysread(STDIN,$InBuffer,1024);
        ($Count >= 1) || last;
        &chat'print($Handle, $InBuffer);
    }
    if (grep($_ eq $Handle, @Ready)) {
        ($OutBuffer = &chat'expect($Handle,0,'[\s\S]+','$&')) || last;
        print $OutBuffer;
    }
}
&chat'close($Handle);
&END;

sub END {
    system "stty -cbreak -raw echo > /dev/tty";
}

sub Eof {
    print "Unexpected end of file\n";
    exit 1;
}

sub TimeOut {
    print "Unexpected timeout\n";
    exit 2;
}
```

COMPLEXITY
ADVANCED

11.4 How do I...
Mix interactive and automatic processing in a chat script?

COMPATIBILITY: PERL 4 PERL 5 UNIX

Problem

I have a chat script that automates an interaction with a remote program. I would like to be able to return manual control back to the user in various spots. I know how to turn control back to the user as the last operation in a script, but how can I have the user return control back to automatic multiple times?

Technique

chat is a Perl library that allows you to interact with programs that normally communicate directly to a terminal. How-To 11.1 provides an introduction to it.

chat's ability is an extension of the function that allows interaction to be returned the user at the end of a script. This ability is seen in How-To 11.3. This How-To builds on that functionality. The user is able to return control to automatic by typing in the end-of-file character ([CTRL]-[D]). The script then can perform more operations and return control to the user.

Steps

This script logs the user into the remote machine as root. The script then returns control back to the user so he or she can type in the password. (Some systems may require multiple passwords.) The user can then type [CTRL]-[D] and return to the script. The script can then set up the environment for the root user and again return control to the user.

1. Copy remote.pl from How-To 11.3 and call the new file inter.pl. Change the command to log into the remote machine to log in as root.

```perl
require "chat2.pl";
use Term::ReadKey;

sub GotSig {
    exit;
}

$SIG{"INT"}  = "GotSig";
$SIG{"QUIT"} = "GotSig";
$SIG{"TERM"} = "GotSig";

$| = 1;

$Handle = &chat::open_proc("/bin/sh");

&chat::expect($Handle,10,
               '\$\s',              '&chat::print($Handle, "stty -echo\n");',
               'EOF',               '&Eof;',
               'TIMEOUT',           '&TimeOut');
&chat::expect($Handle,10,
               'stty -echo',        ';',
               'EOF',               '&Eof;',
               'TIMEOUT',           '&TimeOut');
&chat::expect($Handle,10,
               '\$\s',
                 '&chat::print($Handle,"rlogin-LrootSomeMachine;exit\n");',
               'EOF',               '&Eof;',
               'TIMEOUT',           '&TimeOut');

ReadMode("ultra-raw",STDIN);
```

2. Add a call to an Interact subroutine. This will allow the user to input the password(s). Once the password(s) has been entered, the user can type CTRL-D and the subroutine will return. Next, set up the environment. Assume that there is a command called Setup to do this. Then return control to the user to allow the user to interact with the program as root.

```
&Interact($Handle);
&chat::print($Handle, "source /etc/Setup\n");
&Interact($Handle);
&chat::close($Handle);
```

3. Put the *while* loop that reads from both the user and the process into the Interact subroutine. Make all the local variables local by declaring them in *my* statements. Add the check for CTRL-D (\004) to the standard input portion. When this character is seen, exit the *while* loop that will then exit the subroutine.

```
sub Interact {
    my($Ihandle) = @_;
    my(@Ready,$Count,$InBuffer,$OutBuffer);

    while (1) {
        @Ready = &chat::select(undef,STDIN,$Ihandle);
        if (grep($_ eq 'STDIN', @Ready)) {
            $Count = sysread(STDIN,$InBuffer,1024);
            ($Count >= 1) || last;
            ($InBuffer =~ /\004/) && last;
            &chat::print($Ihandle, $InBuffer);
        }
        if (grep($_ eq $Ihandle, @Ready)) {
            ($OutBuffer = &chat::expect($Ihandle,0,'[\s\S]+','$&')) ||last;
            print $OutBuffer;
        }
    }
}

sub END {
    ReadMode("original",STDIN);
}

sub Eof {
    print "Unexpected end of file\n";
    exit 1;
}

sub TimeOut {
    print "Unexpected timeout\n";
    exit 2;
}
```

4. The entire modified script follows.

```
require "chat2.pl";
use Term::ReadKey;
```

```
sub GotSig {
    exit;
}

$SIG{"INT"}  = "GotSig";
$SIG{"QUIT"} = "GotSig";
$SIG{"TERM"} = "GotSig";

$| = 1;

$Handle = &chat::open_proc("/bin/sh");

&chat::expect($Handle,10,
                '\$\s',              '&chat::print($Handle, "stty -echo\n");',
                'EOF',               '&Eof;',
                'TIMEOUT',           '&TimeOut');
&chat::expect($Handle,10,
                'stty -echo',        ';',
                'EOF',               '&Eof;',
                'TIMEOUT',           '&TimeOut');
&chat::expect($Handle,10,
                '\$\s',
                   '&chat::print($Handle,"rlogin-lrootSomeMachine;exit\n");',
                'EOF',               '&Eof;',
                'TIMEOUT',           '&TimeOut');

ReadMode("ultra-raw",STDIN);

&Interact($Handle);
&chat::print($Handle, "source /etc/Setup\n");
&Interact($Handle);
&chat::close($Handle);

sub Interact {
    my($Ihandle) = @_;
    my(@Ready,$Count,$InBuffer,$OutBuffer);

    while (1) {
        @Ready = &chat::select(undef,STDIN,$Ihandle);
        if (grep($_ eq 'STDIN', @Ready)) {
            $Count = sysread(STDIN,$InBuffer,1024);
            ($Count >= 1) || last;
            ($InBuffer =~ /\004/) && last;
            &chat::print($Ihandle, $InBuffer);
        }
        if (grep($_ eq $Ihandle, @Ready)) {
            ($OutBuffer = &chat::expect($Ihandle,0,'[\s\S]+','$&')) ||last;
            print $OutBuffer;
        }
    }
}

sub END {
    ReadMode("original",STDIN);
}
```

continued on next page

continued from previous page

```
sub Eof {
    print "Unexpected end of file\n";
    exit 1;
}

sub TimeOut {
    print "Unexpected timeout\n";
    exit 2;
}
```

5. Run the script. The session will look something like the following.

```
> perl inter.pl
Password:
SunOS Release 4.1.4 (GENERIC)
# source /etc/Setup
Env initialized
# exit
# logout
Connection closed.
>
```

How It Works

The loop that allows for direct user interaction can be modified to check for certain conditions. In this case, the check is for a specific character that tells the subroutine to return control to the script.

Comments

Because the terminal has been put into raw mode, the check for user input to return control back to the script is done on a single character. If you wish to check for a string instead, the check will be more complicated. This is because the characters can come in one at a time or in groups.

This script can be made to work with Perl 4 by changing the same items as in How-To 11.3. In addition, the my declarations need to be converted to local commands.

```
require "chat2.pl";

sub GotSig {
    &END;
    exit;
}

$SIG{"INT"}  = "GotSig";
$SIG{"QUIT"} = "GotSig";
$SIG{"TERM"} = "GotSig";

$| = 1;

$Handle = &chat'open_proc("/bin/sh");

&chat'expect($Handle,10,
```

```
                    '\$\s',                  '&chat\'print($Handle, "stty -echo\n");',
                    'EOF',                   '&Eof;',
                    'TIMEOUT',               '&TimeOut');
&chat'expect($Handle,10,
                    'stty -echo',           ';',
                    'EOF',                   '&Eof;',
                    'TIMEOUT',               '&TimeOut');
&chat'expect($Handle,10,
                    '\$\s',
                     '&chat\'print($Handle, "rlogin -l root SomeMachine;exit\n");',
                    'EOF',                   '&Eof;',
                    'TIMEOUT',               '&TimeOut');

system "stty cbreak raw -echo > /dev/tty";

&Interact($Handle);
&chat'print($Handle, "source /etc/Setup\n");
&Interact($Handle);
&chat'close($Handle);
&END;

sub Interact {
    local($Ihandle) = @_;
    local(@Ready,$Count,$InBuffer,$OutBuffer);

    while (1) {
        @Ready = &chat'select(undef,STDIN,$Ihandle);
        if (grep($_ eq 'STDIN', @Ready)) {
            $Count = sysread(STDIN,$InBuffer,1024);
            ($Count >= 1) || last;
            ($InBuffer =~ /\004/) && last;
            &chat'print($Ihandle, $InBuffer);
        }
        if (grep($_ eq $Ihandle, @Ready)) {
            ($OutBuffer = &chat'expect($Ihandle,0,'[\s\S]+','$&')) || last;
            print $OutBuffer;
        }
    }
}

sub END {
    system "stty -cbreak -raw echo > /dev/tty";
}

sub Eof {
    print "Unexpected end of file\n";
    exit 1;
}

sub TimeOut {
    print "Unexpected timeout\n";
    exit 2;
}
```

COMPLEXITY
ADVANCED

11.5 How do I...
Set up 50 new user accounts?

COMPATIBILITY: PERL 4   PERL 5   UNIX

Problem

I need to add many users to my system. It is very time-consuming to do each one individually. How can I automate this?

Technique

You can create a script to automate the creation of user accounts. It will be a long script because of all the steps involved. This script assumes that an input file contains a list of login names to be added. Alternatively, this information can be typed in as standard input. Each user name needs to be on a separate line. Each line can contain additional information, including the user's real name, a password, a user ID (UID), a group ID (GID), a home directory, and a preferred shell. If this data is not entered, the script will use default values. This data must be presented in a specific order and separated by colons.

Steps

1. Create a file called adduser.pl. Add the following lines to it. Because the script is run as root, certain precautions must be taken. First, if the IFS environment variable is set, change it to the null string. Additionally, set the PATH to a known value and set the umask. Unbuffer standard output to allow all output to be seen, even in cases of failure.

```
if ($ENV{"IFS"}) {
    $ENV{"IFS"} = "";
}
$ENV{"PATH"} = "/bin:/usr/bin:/usr/ucb";
umask(022);
$| = 1;
```

2. Verify that the script is running as root and change to /etc directory. Random numbers will be needed to generate passwords. The srand function seeds the random number generator. To get a nonpredictable seed, srand uses the current time with the current process number.

```
($> == 0) || die "Must be running as root\n";

chdir "/etc" || die "Can't cd to /etc, $!\n";

srand(time|$$);
```

3. Create an array containing all the characters that can be used to create passwords. The space character is left out so that it is easier to communicate the password to the user. The sprintf function takes a number and converts it to a character and returns it. Determine the size of the password array. Create an array of characters that can be used as salts for the crypt command.

```perl
for $i (33..126) {
    push (@Pchars,sprintf ("%c",$i));
}
$Psize = scalar(@Pchars);
@Schars = ("a".."z","A".."Z","0".."9",".","/");
$Ssize = scalar(@Schars);
```

4. Set up the Perl script to catch signals sent to it. The value assigned to the SIG associative array is a function to be called when the signal (i.e., the key to the array) is received. This will allow the script to clean up temporary files in the file system.

```perl
$SIG{"INT"} = "ABORT";
$SIG{"QUIT"} = "ABORT";
$SIG{"HUP"} = "ABORT";
$SIG{"PIPE"} = "ABORT";
```

5. The passwd file needs to be locked to prevent multiple processes from trying to change it at the same time. To do that, create a file called /etc/ptmp. The open system call is not guaranteed to be atomic, so it cannot be used for this purpose. The link call will be atomic. Create a file that can be linked to ptmp.

```perl
$PtmpTmp = "ptmp$$";
open(PTMPTMP,">$PtmpTmp") || die "Can't create temporary passwd file\n";
close(PTMPTMP);
```

6. Loop up to 60 times trying to get the lock. If the link call was successful, you have the lock. Remove the temporary file that is linked to ptmp. If the link was not made and this is the first time through the loop, print a message. Each time through the loop, print a dot. This will give the user feedback that something is happening. If a dot has been printed, print a new line when the lock is acquired. Wait 1 second before trying the link again. If the lock could not be acquired, call the ABORT function to print a message and exit.

```perl
$PtmpTmp = "ptmp$$";
open(PTMPTMP,">$PtmpTmp") || die "Can't create temporary passwd file, $!\n";
close(PTMPTMP);
for ($i=1;$i<=60;$i++) {
    $GotPtmp = link($PtmpTmp,"ptmp");
    if ($GotPtmp) {
        unlink $PtmpTmp;
        ($i == 1) || print "\n"; # If no dots, no newline
        last;
    }
```

continued on next page

continued from previous page

```
        ($i == 1) && print "Waiting for lock on /etc/passwd\n";
        print ".";
        sleep 1;
}
$GotPtmp || &ABORT("\nCan't get lock on /etc/passwd");
```

7. Some systems set a limit on the lowest number UID and GID that can be assigned. Create two variables to make the limit 100 for each. Open the passwd file for reading, and open the ptmp file to hold a copy of the changes to the passwd. When the script is done, this file will become the new passwd file. Open the group file for reading and open a temporary group file. This temporary file will eventually become the new group file.

```
$SmallestUid = 100;
$SmallestGid = 100;
open(PASSWD,"passwd") || &ABORT("Can't open /etc/passwd, $!");
open(PTMP,">ptmp") || &ABORT("Can't open /etc/ptmp, $!");
open(GROUP,"group") || &ABORT("Can't open /etc/group, $!");
open(GTMP,">gtmp") || &ABORT("Can't open /etc/gtmp, $!");
```

8. Create two arrays to hold the UIDs and GIDs that currently exist. Create two indexes for these arrays. These arrays will be used to find available IDs to use. Loop through the passwd file gathering information and writing the data to the new passwd file. Split up the line and save the first four fields. Save the login name in an associative array. This will be used to make sure duplicate login IDs are not created. Save the UID for the same purpose. If the UID is not less than the minimum, save it in a UID array. This is the array that will be referenced if a new unique UID is needed. After all the lines in the passwd file have been read, close the passwd file.

```
$UidIndex = 0;
$GidIndex = 0;
while (<PASSWD>) {
    print PTMP;
    ($Login,$Passwd,$Uid,$Gid) = split(":",$_,5);
    $LoginSeen{$Login} = 1;
    $UidSeen{$Uid} = 1;
    if ($Uid >= $SmallestUid) {
        $Uids[$UidIndex++] = $Uid;
    }
}
close(PASSWD);
```

9. Loop through the group file, gathering the same type of information that was retrieved from the passwd file. The temporary group file is not created at this time. There may be new users to add to existing groups. This will not be known until later. Get the individual fields from each group file line. Save the group name and the GID. When all the lines have been read, close the file.

```
while (<GROUP>) {
    ($Group,$Passwd,$Gid,$Members) = split(":");
```

```
    $GroupSeen{$Group} = 1;
    $GidSeen{$Gid} = 1;
    if ($Gid >= $SmallestGid) {
        $Gids[$GidIndex++] = $Gid;
    }
}
close(GROUP);
```

10. Read from a file or standard input all the new users to add. Each line of the input can have multiple fields delimited by colons. All but the first field are optional. The second field (the user's real name) should be supplied. Defaults will be assigned to any field not supplied. Split the line into the individual fields. If no login is present, it must be a blank line. Skip to the next line. Check to see if the login name is already in use. If so, print a message and skip to the next line. Save the new login name in the associative array holding the names of the existing logins.

```
while(<>) {
    chop;
    ($Login,$RealName,$ClearPasswd,$Shell,$Home,$Uid,$Gid) = split(":");
    $Login || next;
    if ($LoginSeen{$Login}) {
        print "$Login already in use .. skipping\n";
        next;
    }
    $LoginSeen{$Login} = 1;
```

11. Check for a password. If there is no password, create one from eight random characters. Generate a salt so that the password may be encrypted. Retrieve two random characters from the salt characters array and assign them to the salt. Encrypt the password.

```
if (! $ClearPasswd) {
        for $i (1..8) {
            $ClearPasswd .= $Pchars[int(rand($Psize))];
        }
    }
    $Salt = "$Schars[int(rand($Ssize))]$Schars[int(rand($Ssize))]";
    $Passwd = crypt($ClearPasswd,$Salt);
```

12. If no shell is supplied, use the default one. If no home directory is specified, assign one in the /home directory.

```
if (! $Shell) {
        $Shell = "/bin/sh";
    }
    if (! $Home) {
        $Home = "/home/$Login";
    }
```

13. Check to see if a UID was supplied. If the UID was supplied, check to see that it is not in use. If no UID was supplied, one will need to be generated. To find the smallest available UID, start with the smallest possible one. Sort the existing UIDs and loop through each one at a time. If the current try at

a new UID is not the same as the entry from the sorted list, a new one has
been found. If the UID is in use, increment the candidate UID and try
again. Save the new UID in the associative array holding the existing UIDs.
Save the UID in the array used to generate new UIDs.

```
if (defined($Uid) && ($Uid ne "")) {
        if ($UidSeen{$Uid}) {
                print "$Uid alread in use .. skipping $Login\n";
                next;
        }
    } else {
        $Uid = $SmallestUid;
        for $u (sort @Uids) {
                ($u == $Uid) || last;
                $Uid++;
        }
        $UidSeen{$Uid} = 1;
        push(@Uids,$Uid);
    }
```

14. Check to see if a GID was supplied. No check is needed for an existing GID
because users can be put into the same group. Start looking for a unique
GID if one was not supplied, starting with the smallest possible one.
Because multiple logins can have the same GID, the array that keeps track
of the used GIDs can have duplicate entries. Ignore these. Set the last seen
GID to an invalid number to start. Loop through a sorted list of existing
GIDs. If the existing GID is the same as the last GID looked at, go to the
next one. This will weed out duplicate entries. If the candidate GID is different from the current existing one, a unique one has been found, so exit
the loop. Otherwise, increment the candidate GID and save the last seen
existing GID. Save the new GID in the array of existing GIDs.

```
if ((! defined($Gid)) || ($Gid eq "")) {
        $Gid = $SmallestGid;
        $OldG = $SmallestGid - 1;
        for $g (sort @Gids) {
                ($g == $OldG) && next;
                ($g == $Gid) || last;
                $Gid++;
                $OldG = $g;
        }
    }
    push(@Gids,$Gid);
```

15. Check to see if the GID is one of the ones in the current group file. If so,
the new login is being added to an existing group. Use an associative array
to save these new logins. Check to see if another new login has been added
to the group. If so, separate the two by a comma; otherwise, just add the
login name. A new group is being created if the GID was not seen in the
group file. An associative array is being used to hold the logins being added
to a new group. Check to see if another new login has already been seen
that is being added to this group. If so, separate the logins with a comma.

Otherwise, this is the first login to be added to a new group. Check to see if the login name is already being used as a group name. If so, skip this login and go onto the next one. Save the login name in the new group associative array.

```
if ($GidSeen{$Gid}) {
    if ($ExistingGroupInfo{$Gid}) {
        $ExistingGroupInfo{$Gid} .= ",$Login";
    } else {
        $ExistingGroupInfo{$Gid} = "$Login";
    }
} else {
    if ($NewGroupInfo{$Gid}) {
        $NewGroupInfo{$Gid} .= ",$Login";
    } else {
        if ($GroupSeen{$Login}) {
            print "$Login already used as a group name .. skipping\n";
            next;
        }
        $NewGroupInfo{$Gid} = "$Login";
    }
}
```

16. The new home directories will be created later. Save the UID and GID for the home directory in an associative array. Write the passwd file entry for the new login. Print out the login and the password assigned. It is not usually a good idea to print passwords, but the password needs to be communicated to the user. Once all the new logins have been processed, close the new passwd file.

```
$Homes{$Home} = "$Uid:$Gid";

print PTMP "$Login:$Passwd:$Uid:$Gid:$RealName:$Home:$Shell\n";
print "$Login has passwd ->$ClearPasswd<-\n";
}
close(PTMP);
```

17. The new group file needs to be generated. Open the existing group file to copy data from it. Loop through each entry in the group file, getting all the fields from each line. Check if new logins are being added to the current group. If there are existing members to be added to, append a comma to separate them from the new entries. Append the new members to the group. Print out the group to the new group file. Once all the lines in the existing group file have been processed, close the file.

```
open(GROUP,"group") || &ABORT("Can't open /etc/group, $!");
while (<GROUP>) {
    chop;
    ($Group,$Passwd,$Gid,$Members) = split(":");
    if ($ExistingGroupInfo{$Gid}) {
        if ($Members ne "") {
            $Members .= ",";
```

continued on next page

continued from previous page

```
        }
        $Members .= $ExistingGroupInfo{$Gid};
    }
    print GTMP join(":",$Group,$Passwd,$Gid,$Members), "\n";
}
close(GROUP);
```

18. All the new group entries must be added to the new group file. Loop through a sort list of the new GIDs. Get the first login in the list of logins for this new GID. This login will be used as the group name. Add the new group to the new group file. When all the new groups have been added, close the new group file.

```
for $Gid (sort keys %NewGroupInfo) {
    ($Group) = split(",",$NewGroupInfo{$Gid},2);
    print GTMP join(":",$Group,"*",$Gid,$NewGroupInfo{$Gid}), "\n";
}
close(GTMP);
```

19. Save the existing group file under a new name and install the new group file. Save the existing passwd file and install the new passwd file. Because the ptmp file will no longer exist, the lock on the passwd file has now been removed.

```
rename("group","group.old");
rename("gtmp","group") || &ABORT("Can't install new group file, $!");
rename("passwd","passwd.old");
rename("ptmp","passwd") || &ABORT("Can't install new passwd file, $!");
```

20. The new home directories need to be created. Loop through each new directory creating the new home directory. If it cannot be made, print a message and go on to the next one. Get the UID and GID to be used on the home directory. Change the owner and group on the home directory to the new values. Change the modes on the directory. These modes can be made more restrictive. At this time, you may want to copy in some standard files into the home directory. After the home directories are created, the script is done.

```
for $Home (keys %Homes) {
    if (! (mkdir ($Home, 0755))) {
        print "Can't create $Home\n";
        next;
    }
    ($Uid,$Gid) = split(":",$Homes{$Home});
    if (! (chown $Uid, $Gid, $Home)) {
        print "Can't set ownership on $Home, $!\n";
        next;
    }
    chmod 0755, $Home || print "Can't change modes on $Home, $!\n";
    # Copy in standard file to $Home?
}
exit 0;
```

21. Define the ABORT subroutine. This routine will clean up in case of error or interruption. Save a possible message passed in as an argument. If the ptmp lock file has been created, remove it. If the temporary ptmp file exists, delete it. If the new group file exists, remove it. If there was a message, print it. Then print a message and exit.

```perl
sub ABORT {
    local($msg) = @_;

    $GotPtmp && unlink "ptmp";
    -f $PtmpTmp && unlink $PtmpTmp;
    -f "gtmp" && unlink "gtmp";
    $msg && print "$msg";
    print "\n\nAborting\n";
    exit 1;
}
```

22. The entire script follows.

```perl
if ($ENV{"IFS"}) {
    $ENV{"IFS"} = "";
}
$ENV{"PATH"} = "/bin:/usr/bin:/usr/ucb";
umask(022);
$| = 1;

($> == 0) || die "Must be running as root\n";

chdir "/etc" || die "Can't cd to /etc, $!\n";

srand(time|$$);
for $i (33..126) {
    push (@Pchars,sprintf ("%c",$i));
}
$Psize = scalar(@Pchars);
@Schars = ("a".."z","A".."Z","0".."9",".","/");
$Ssize = scalar(@Schars);

$SIG{"INT"} = "ABORT";
$SIG{"QUIT"} = "ABORT";
$SIG{"HUP"} = "ABORT";
$SIG{"PIPE"} = "ABORT";


$PtmpTmp = "ptmp$$";
open(PTMPTMP,">$PtmpTmp") || die "Can't create temporary passwd file, $!\n";
close(PTMPTMP);
for ($i=1;$i<=60;$i++) {
    $GotPtmp = link($PtmpTmp,"ptmp");
    if ($GotPtmp) {
        unlink $PtmpTmp;
        ($i == 1) || print "\n"; # If no dots, no newline
        last;
    }
    ($i == 1) && print "Waiting for lock on /etc/passwd\n";
    print ".";
    sleep 1;
```

continued on next page

continued from previous page

```
}
$GotPtmp || &ABORT("\nCan't get lock on /etc/passwd");
$SmallestUid = 100;
$SmallestGid = 100;
open(PASSWD,"passwd") || &ABORT("Can't open /etc/passwd, $!");
open(PTMP,">ptmp") || &ABORT("Can't open /etc/ptmp, $!");
open(GROUP,"group") || &ABORT("Can't open /etc/group, $!");
open(GTMP,">gtmp") || &ABORT("Can't open /etc/gtmp, $!");

$UidIndex = 0;
$GidIndex = 0;
while (<PASSWD>) {
    print PTMP;
    ($Login,$Passwd,$Uid,$Gid) = split(":",$_,5);
    $LoginSeen{$Login} = 1;
    $UidSeen{$Uid} = 1;
    if ($Uid >= $SmallestUid) {
        $Uids[$UidIndex++] = $Uid;
    }
}
close(PASSWD);

while (<GROUP>) {
    ($Group,$Passwd,$Gid,$Members) = split(":");
    $GroupSeen{$Group} = 1;
    $GidSeen{$Gid} = 1;
    if ($Gid >= $SmallestGid) {
        $Gids[$GidIndex++] = $Gid;
    }
}
close(GROUP);

while(<>) {
    chop;
    ($Login,$RealName,$ClearPasswd,$Shell,$Home,$Uid,$Gid) = split(":");
    $Login || next;
    if ($LoginSeen{$Login}) {
        print "$Login already in use .. skipping\n";
        next;
    }
    $LoginSeen{$Login} = 1;
    if (! $ClearPasswd) {
        for $i (1..8) {
            $ClearPasswd .= $Pchars[int(rand($Psize))];
        }
    }
    $Salt = "$Schars[int(rand($Ssize))]$Schars[int(rand($Ssize))]";
    $Passwd = crypt($ClearPasswd,$Salt);
    if (! $Shell) {
        $Shell = "/bin/sh";
    }
    if (! $Home) {
        $Home = "/home/$Login";
    }
    if (defined($Uid) && ($Uid ne "")) {
        if ($UidSeen{$Uid}) {
```

```
                print "$Uid alread in use .. skipping $Login\n";
                next;
            }
    } else {
        $Uid = $SmallestUid;
        for $u (sort @Uids) {
            ($u == $Uid) || last;
            $Uid++;
        }
        $UidSeen{$Uid} = 1;
        push(@Uids,$Uid);
    }
    if ((! defined($Gid)) || ($Gid eq "")) {
        $Gid = $SmallestGid;
        $OldG = $SmallestGid - 1;
        for $g (sort @Gids) {
            ($g == $OldG) && next;
            ($g == $Gid) || last;
            $Gid++;
            $OldG = $g;
        }
    }
    push(@Gids,$Gid);
    if ($GidSeen{$Gid}) {
        if ($ExistingGroupInfo{$Gid}) {
            $ExistingGroupInfo{$Gid} .= ",$Login";
        } else {
            $ExistingGroupInfo{$Gid} = "$Login";
        }
    } else {
        if ($NewGroupInfo{$Gid}) {
            $NewGroupInfo{$Gid} .= ",$Login";
        } else {
            if ($GroupSeen{$Login}) {
                print "$Login already used as a group name .. skipping\n";
                next;
            }
            $NewGroupInfo{$Gid} = "$Login";
        }
    }
    $Homes{$Home} = "$Uid:$Gid";

    print PTMP "$Login:$Passwd:$Uid:$Gid:$RealName:$Home:$Shell\n";
    print "$Login has passwd ->$ClearPasswd<-\n";
}
close(PTMP);

open(GROUP,"group") || &ABORT("Can't open /etc/group, $!");
while (<GROUP>) {
    chop;
    ($Group,$Passwd,$Gid,$Members) = split(":");
    if ($ExistingGroupInfo{$Gid}) {
        if ($Members ne "") {
            $Members .= ",";
        }
        $Members .= $ExistingGroupInfo{$Gid};
```

continued on next page

continued from previous page

```
        }
        print GTMP join(":",$Group,$Passwd,$Gid,$Members), "\n";
    }
    close(GROUP);

    for $Gid (sort keys %NewGroupInfo) {
        ($Group) = split(",",$NewGroupInfo{$Gid},2);
        print GTMP join(":",$Group,"*",$Gid,$NewGroupInfo{$Gid}), "\n";
    }
    close(GTMP);

    rename("group","group.old");
    rename("gtmp","group") || &ABORT("Can't install new group file, $!");
    rename("passwd","passwd.old");
    rename("ptmp","passwd") || &ABORT("Can't install new password file, $!");

    for $Home (keys %Homes) {
        if (! (mkdir ($Home, 0755))) {
            print "Can't create $Home\n";
            next;
        }
        ($Uid,$Gid) = split(":",$Homes{$Home});
        if (! (chown $Uid, $Gid, $Home)) {
            print "Can't set ownership on $Home, $!\n";
            next;
        }
        chmod 0755, $Home || print "Can't change modes on $Home, $!\n";
        # Copy in standard file to $Home?
    }
    exit 0;

    sub ABORT {
        local($msg) = @_;

        $GotPtmp && unlink "ptmp";
        -f $PtmpTmp && unlink $PtmpTmp;
        -f "gtmp" && unlink "gtmp";
        $msg && print "$msg";
        print "\n\nAborting\n";
        exit 1;
    }
```

23. Create an input file called adduser.in. Add the following lines.

```
john
mary
joan
fred:fred jones:passwd::/OtherHome/fred
kim:kim smith:passwd::/OtherHome/kim::10
don:don brown:passwd:/bin/bash::150:10
```

24. Run the script on the input file. The output will look like the following.

```
john has passwd ->:Y(";AS9<-
mary has passwd ->fblUe~X><-
joan has passwd ->Sw*?d<4f<-
fred has passwd ->passwd<-
kim has passwd ->passwd<-
```

```
don has passwd ->passwd<-
```

How It Works

New users can be added to a system by creating a number of entries in the correct files and creating a home directory for the user. Take care to prevent duplicate entries from being made in the password and group files. Because this work is being done on a multiprocessing system, the files must be locked to prevent multiple updates from affecting the critical files.

Comments

This script is long, but that is only because the amount of work to be done is large. Each section of the script can be examined individually to see what is happening. Understanding the total script will help in your understanding of the power of Perl.

A new user's GID is not stored in the %GidSeen associative array because the new data is being stored in two arrays: one for existing groups and one for new groups. The %GidSeen array is being used to tell the two groups apart.

Salts are used in the encryption so that if there are two identical passwords, their encrypted forms will be different. The method for finding a new UID or GID can be made much more efficient. If this script is run often, you may want to do that. Because passwords were generated for the users, it is a good idea to have users change those passwords as soon as possible.

CHAPTER 12
INTERPROCESS COMMUNICATIONS

INTERPROCESS COMMUNICATIONS

How do I ...

This chapter deals with one of the most intriguing aspects of programming, process creation, and communication. Most of the programs you write have simple two-dimensional lives. They accept input, process it, and send the results to the output. Other programs reach into the third dimension. They interact with other processes on the system, create new processes themselves, and delegate tasks to other processes. A system running lots of processes is rather like an ant hill. The system is full of autonomous entities, not so intelligent individually yet capable of working together to create a complex social interaction.

Interprocess communications formerly was an area of programming shrouded in mystique. Perl strips away much of that mystique. Although Perl is commonly viewed as a language for data processing, you can use Perl as high-level development language to create long-lived processes. You can often express the code more elegantly with Perl than with a C equivalent. The resulting processes are just as powerful and flexible in the way they access system services. This makes Perl an excellent language for exploring the previously esoteric area of process programming.

This chapter will chiefly interest UNIX users because the models of concurrency and process creation described here are primarily those of the UNIX system.

12.1   Spawn a Child Process from a Perl Script

This How-To will describe a general technique you can use for Perl process creation.

12.2   Send Data to an Exec'ed Process Using a Pipe

This How-To will show you how to communicate with a new process and have it carry out tasks on your behalf.

12.3   Create a Daemon Process in Perl

This section will illustrate the special programming methods needed for developing very long-lived processes.

12.4   Read and Write to Shared Memory

This section will show you how to implement and use the fastest form of interprocess communication.

12.5   Use Semaphores in Perl

When two or more processes are attempting to use a shared resource, they must synchronize their activities. This How-To will show you how to implement a semaphore to safeguard a common resource from unwanted concurrent access.

COMPLEXITY
INTERMEDIATE

12.1   How do I ...
Spawn a child process from a Perl script?

COMPATIBILITY: UNIX

Problem

I want to create a Perl script that can delegate some of its tasks to child processes. The main script should not allow itself to become tied up in a task. Rather, the main process should create a child process and delegate any significant processing to it. Both processes should run concurrently. How do I spawn a process in Perl?

Technique

Multitasking and multithreading operating systems such as OS/2, Windows NT, and UNIX allow a number of processes to run parallel on one machine. If you type the ps command on a heavily loaded UNIX system, you may see more than 100 processes running simultaneously.

You can think of the relationship between these processes as a family tree. One particular process can create any number of new processes; each of those in turn can create new processes of their own. The terminology of parallel processes relies heavily on this family tree metaphor. When a process creates one more process, we describe the original as a *parent* and the other as a *child*. The generation of new processes is often referred to as *spawning*.

Perl provides more than one method for spawning new processes. You may be surprised to think of some of these examples in terms of process creation.

$foo = `program`

The parent process executes program as a synchronous child process. The main program waits for program to terminate before assigning its output to a variable and continuing.

system("program");

The parent process executes program as a synchronous child process—synchronous because the main program waits for program to terminate before continuing.

open(FOO,"program|");

The parent process executes program as an asynchronous process, piping its input to the parent.

open(FOO,"|program");

The parent process executes program as an asynchronous child process. Output on filehandle FOO is piped to the child.

fork()

This command is the fundamental process-creation routine. All the other techniques implicitly use the fork call. The example in this How-To shows the fork function in action.

If you are unfamiliar with process creation, you need some background before you look at the example. The UNIX system implements process creation with a system service called fork. The Perl function fork executes the same system call. When any program calls fork, the system creates an identical copy of the program and starts to execute it.

The new process is an exact clone of the parent. It has the same data and variable values as the parent. It even shares the same file descriptors as the parent. It doesn't start its execution from the first instruction in the program text, but continues with the next statement after the call to fork.

This leads to an intriguing problem. If the parent and child are perfect clones, how does the child know it is a child and the parent know it is the parent?

The only way to tell is to have each process immediately examine the return value of the fork call. In the parent, a successful fork returns the process identifier (PID) of the new child. In the child, fork can return only a nominal value of 0. If fork should fail for some reason, it returns -1. The processes should check for this value as well. Table 12-1 summarizes the values.

> 0	You are the parent. The value is the PID of your child.	
0	You are a new child process. The value 0 is nominal.	
undef	Oops! Fork error. You failed to spawn a child.	

Table 12-1 Interpreting the values returned from the fork call

The behavior of fork may seem a little counterintuitive if you are meeting it for the first time. The key to understanding it is to think in terms of processes rather than programs.

Normally, when you produce a Perl program, you think of each line of the text being executed in a predictable sequence. When you think of processes, you have to think of each instance of your program behaving as an independent entity. Each process may share the same program text, but after forking, each process may pursue a completely different route through the program.

Certainly, a parent process is responsible for the children it spawns, just like a real parent (Table 12-2). Yet you normally think of the child outliving its parent. In the case of processes, the parent is expected to outlive the child. This is because once the child terminates, the parent has the job of deleting all record of it from the system. The final act of a parent is to wait for the last child to terminate and perform a clean-up operation. This operation is described as *reaping the child*. If the parent fails to perform this duty, then the kernel retains the record of the child after it has terminated. In the worst case, the system may run out of resources for new processes. Unreaped child processes show up in ps output marked as <defunct>. A <defunct> entry represents the remnants of a process that has terminated without being reaped by the parent. Such processes are referred to as *zombies*.

Reaping a child is easy in Perl. To reap a specific child, you have to call the waitpid function, supplying the PID as an argument; normally the second argument is 0. Call the wait function if your process has created only one child. The wait function does not require arguments.

Check the fork status after spawning.	
Wait on the child before exiting.	

Table 12-2 Responsibilities of parent processes

Now let's look at the child process (Table 12-3). The child is not limited to executing the same program text as its parent. The child may replace itself with another program. In Perl, you do this by calling the exec function with the path of the new program as an argument. Try not to think of the process calling the other program. The process becomes the other program. All trace of the original is obliterated and the new program starts executing at the first instruction in its text.

Check they are child processes created by fork.	
Replace their program text by another if required.	

Table 12-3 Responsibilities of child processes

Steps

1. Create a new program called forknew.pl or pull the file off the *Perl 5 How-To* CD.

2. Enter the following code into it.

```perl
#!/usr/local/bin/perl
# example to demonstrate how to fork a child process
#

$child_id = fork();
die "fork failed: $!" unless defined $child_id;

if ($child_id ) {
    # Parent
      waitpid($child_id,0);
      print "The parent reaped child $child_id, with status $?\n"
}
else {
    # Child
    #Execute cal
    exec "/usr/bin/cal" || die "Exec $!";
    exit 0;
}
```

3. Execute the program.

forknew.pl

Output

```
    October 1995
S   M Tu  W Th  F   S
1   2  3  4  5  6   7
8   9 10 11 12 13 14
15 16 17 18 19 20 21
22 23 24 25 26 27 28
29 30 31

The parent reaped child 10210, with status 0
```
End Output

How It Works

The example has no great intrinsic functionality, but it enables you to explore a programming technique you can apply later to more realistic examples.

The call to fork is embedded within an *if* statement that checks the return value for error. This is a typical method of spawning processes in Perl. If all is well, the fork succeeded and there are now two clone processes executing the same script. Now each must determine its status, parent or child, by checking the value returned by fork. In the parent, fork returns a value and so the *if* condition is True. The parent executes the *then* branch. The child finds fork returned a 0 or False value and executes the *else* branch. The processes are already behaving independently.

The child now encounters an instruction to exec another program, cal. The first argument of the exec call is the path of the cal program. Exec asks the operating system to overwrite the child text with the cal program. The cal binary simply prints out a monthly calendar and terminates. That is the end of the child process.

The parent finds it has no more to do than to reap the child when it terminates. The parent calls waitpid with the PID of the child, returned by the fork function as an argument. The second argument to waitpid is a flag, which in this case is set to 0. The waitpid function can perform more exotic forms of reaping if the flag is set to an appropriate value. You can get more information on this in the perlfunc manual pages.

The call to waitpid may block the process until the child terminates. If the child terminates before the call to waitpid, then waitpid will return immediately. The return value of the function indicates the child's exit status. In this example, the parent prints this information in a message and then terminates itself.

Comments

How-To 12.2 provides a practical example of how the flexible fork/exec spawning method can be used to implement a more complex interaction between parent and child when both processes run parallel.

COMPLEXITY
ADVANCED

12.2 How do I ...
Send data to an exec'ed process using a pipe?

COMPATIBILITY: UNIX

Problem

I want to send data through a pipe to a spawned process. Specifically, I want to have my Perl program send mail by spawning the UNIX mail utility and sending the text of the mail to the child process.

Technique

This How-To shows how you can send mail from a Perl program simply by borrowing the facilities of the UNIX mail system. The techniques you explore here are not limited to sending mail. They have a general application. This section shows you how to spawn a standard program so that it can be manipulated by a Perl script. This gives the parent program the ability to call up the services of many existing utilities and use them to perform services on its behalf. Don't duplicate—recycle!

Of course, Perl has high-level methods of launching other processes, but this How-To gives you the opportunity to explore some lower-level system-programming concepts in Perl.

Because a forked process is a true clone, it inherits the same filehandles as its parent. The technique is this: Have the parent set up a pipe file descriptor before forking. The child process will inherit that same pipe file descriptor. When the child prepares to exec another program, it attaches the pipe to its STDIN and executes the new program. The parent process can now talk directly to the utility program. It writes to the pipe, and the utility receives the data via STDIN.

Steps

1. Create a program called pmail.pl.

2. Enter the following code.

```perl
#!/usr/local/bin/perl
# Exec a child /bin/mail and send yourself a mail message
use POSIX;

MAIN:
{
  $username = getlogin() || die "$!" ;

  pipe(PRH, PWH) || die "pipe $!";

  $parent = fork();
  die "fork failed: $!" unless  defined $parent;

 unless ($parent )
 {
    # Child
    # Reader close write side
    close(PWH);

    # Make read side of the pipe our STDIN
    close(STDIN);
    open(STDIN,  ">&PRH");
    select(STDIN); $| = 1;

    #Execute mail username
    exec "/bin/mail", $username || die "Exec $!";
 }
 else
 {
    # Parent
    # Writer close the pipe read side.
    close(PRH);

    # Redirect STDOUT
    close(STDOUT);
    open(STDOUT, ">&PWH");
    select(STDOUT); $| = 1;
```

continued on next page

continued from previous page

```
    # Pour STDIN down the pipe.
    # Terminate message with a lone stop.
    undef $/;
    print <> . "\n.\n";
    close(STDOUT);
    #
    wait;
    open(STDOUT,">/dev/tty" );
    print "$0 exiting\n";
    exit(0);
  }
}
```

3. Before you run the program, check the status of your mail queue, using the mail utility.

mail

— Output ——————————————————————————————————————

```
No mail for perluser
```
End Output ——————————————————————————————————————

4. Create a data file, message.in.

cat > message.in

— Output ——————————————————————————————————————

```
This mail message was sent automatically by a Perl process.
Have a nice day.
```
End Output ——————————————————————————————————————

5. Execute the pmail.pl program in this way:

pmail.pl < message.in

— Output ——————————————————————————————————————

```
pmail.pl exiting
```
End Output ——————————————————————————————————————

6. Check your mail queue once again. You may need to wait for a minute or so for the mail to be propagated.

mail

— Output ——————————————————————————————————————

```
Mail version SMI 4.1-OWV3 Mon Sep 23 07:17:24 PDT 1991  ? for help.
"/usr/spool/mail/perluser": 1 message 1 new
>N  1 perluser              Sun Oct 15 18:25    13/368
```
End Output ——————————————————————————————————————

7. The mail has been delivered. You can read it by hitting ENTER at the next prompt. Then type D and Q to delete it and quit the mail utility.

```
{Mail}&
Message  1:
```

```
From perluser Sun Oct 15 18:25:41 1995

This mail message was sent automatically by a Perl process.

Have a nice day.

{Mail}& d
{Mail}& q
```

How It Works

First, the parent creates a pair of pipe file descriptors using the Perl function pipe. The pipe has a read-end PRH and a write-end PWH. You use this pipe to establish communications between two processes.

Once the pipe has been created, the program forks in the standard way. See How-To 12.1 for a description of forking.

The third step is for the parent and child process to prepare the pipe for communication. The parent is the generator of data, so it calls the Perl function close on the redundant read filehandle PRH. The child is a reader, so it closes the redundant write filehandle PHR. Parent and child are now linked by a pipe communication channel.

The fourth step is for the child to copy the pipe filehandle over its STDIN filehandle, so STDIN will actually read from the pipe. It accomplishes this by calling open with PRH as its second argument. Normally, the second argument to open is the name of a file, rather than an open filehandle. This form of the open function is referred to as *duping* because the STDIN filehandle is now a duplicate of PRH. STDIN reads data from PRH.

The fifth step is for the child to exec /bin/mail, the UNIX mail utility. It passes your user name as a command line argument. This tells the mail program to send mail to you. When the mail program reads from STDIN, it is reading from the child end of the pipe set up by the parent.

The final step is for the parent to transmit a message through the pipe to the mail program. Mail messages terminate with a lone dot character on a new line. Pmail automatically adds this sequence when it has no more data to send.

Comments

You don't have to work this hard if you want to send data to another program in Perl. Calling open with a filename beginning with a pipe character is the simplest way of achieving a similar effect. There is a lot of low-level programming in this How-To, but you can use the techniques to implement much more complex interaction between parent and child than is possible with simple pipe opens.

One possibilitiy is to have the parent and child as coprocesses, exchanging messages back and forth across two pipes or a socketpair. This would allow you to drive a standard program with another process. Even interactive programs could be driven this way. Take a look at the Perl library chat module for an example of this type of progamming.

COMPLEXITY
ADVANCED

12.3 How do I ...
Create a daemon process in Perl?

COMPATIBILITY: UNIX

Problem

I want to create a daemon, a long-running, noninteractive process, in Perl. The process should normally terminate only when the system is shut down. The daemon can offer services to other processes on the same machine or over the network, but it does not need to be interactive.

Technique

Running a process over one entire lifetime of a system means that your process has to be very well mannered. A daemon process cannot afford to indulge in any form of antisocial behavior because repetitious misdemeanors can have major consequences for other activities taking place on the system.

A Perl daemon has several responsibilities. First, it must fork and the parent must exit. This frees the process from the shell command that created it and allows the shell to continue.

Second, it must set its current working directory to / or /tmp or another specific directory. If the process uses the directory from which the user invoked it, then you, the programmer, have no control over several future possibilities. For example, a running daemon will prevent the device containing the working directory from being dismounted from the system. Root and /tmp are never normally dismounted. Another disk partition or network disk will report *device busy* if the administrator tries to dismount them while a daemon is running there. Keep in mind that, if the process crashes and dumps its core memory to disk, it will dump the file in the working directory. If the working directory location is not predictable, then you may encounter permission or disk space problems.

Set its umask, used for setting default file creation permissions, to 0. This allows the process to create files with any permissions it desires without being over-ruled by a umask inherited from the parent.

The daemon must write all error messages to a log file because it has no controlling terminal to send output to. You can achieve this by redirecting STDOUT and STDERR to a log file. Each time the daemon appends a message, it should open and close the log file. This forces a flush of output to the file. If the file is removed by some other system activity, the daemon is freed from the risk of crashing due to a write failure.

The daemon should call POSIX::setsid() to promote itself to process group leader and break connection with the controlling terminal of its parent.

The daemon must close all unneeded file descriptors inherited from the parent, freeing system resources.

Steps

1. Create the program file daemon.pl.

2. Enter the following text into it.

```perl
#!/usr/local/bin/perl -w
# Daemon Program

use strict;
use POSIX;

sub TIOCNOTTY { return 0x20007471};

sub log_message {
  my($msg) = @_;
  open(STDERR, ">>$main::logfile");
  print STDERR "$msg\n";
  close(STDERR);
}

sub daemon_actions {
    $0 = "daemon_child_of_$main::ppid";
    log_message "Changing process name to $0\n";
    sleep 60;
    exit;
}

MAIN:{
  $main::ppid = $$;
  $main::pid = fork();
  die "Fork failed: $!"
      unless defined $main::pid;

  SWITCH: {
    $main::pid > 0 && do {
        die "Created process $main::pid\nExiting ...\n" ;
    };
    $main::pid == 0 && do {
        close(STDIN);
        close(STDOUT);
        $main::logfile = ">/tmp/$0.log.$$";
        open(STDERR, $main::logfile) ||
                die "$0.$$ cannot open $main::logfile\n";

        chdir("/tmp");

        POSIX::setsid();

        open(TTY, "</dev/tty");
        ioctl(TTY,&TIOCNOTTY,0);
        close(TTY);
        daemon_actions();
    }
  }
}
```

3. Invoke the program.

```
daemon.pl
```

Output

```
Created process 9928
Exiting ...
```

End Output

4. Execute a ps command to show information from the process table. Notice that daemon.pl has spawned a new process, named daemon_child_of_9927, and has a single ? character entry under the TT column, indicating it has no controlling terminal (TTY).

```
ps -xj
```

Output

PPID	PID	PGID	SID	TT	TPGID	STAT	UID	TIME	COMMAND
1	9928	9928	9928	?	-1	S0	167	0:00	daemon_child_of_9927
8366	8367	8367	8367	p2	9929	SOE	167	0:05	-csh (csh)
8367	9929	9929	8367	p2	9929	RE	167	0:00	ps -xj

End Output

How It Works

When the user runs the program from a shell command, daemon.pl immediately forks a new process and has the parent die. In this script, you test for the parent or child status of each process using a Perl *switch* statement. Perl executes the first branch when the return value of the fork function is greater than 0, implying that this is a parent process. The parent calls the die function with a suitable diagnostic message. This immediate termination of the parent process separates daemon.pl from the command processor that invoked it.

The remaining process then gets busy severing its relationship with its inherited environment. The method proceeds as outlined in the Technique section.

The Process Checks That It Can Create a Log File

A daemon process must communicate with the outside world through a log file. There will be no possibility of writing to a terminal because the daemon process will shortly abandon the terminal from which it was invoked. You should choose the name of the log file to include a unique identifier for the process—in this case, the PID number.

The Process Closes All the Open Filehandles Inherited from the Parent

This task is performed in a *for* loop. Daemon.pl inherited the three standard filehandles. If the parent explicitly opens files, then you should add these to the loop list.

The Process Locates Its Working Directory at a Specific Location in the File System

On invocation, the process's working directory is the directory from which it was invoked. It is undesirable that the daemon have an arbitrary working directory because this can interfere with the administration of the file system. The programmer should set the current working directory to a defined location. You can achieve this with a call to chdir to set the working directory to /tmp.

The Daemon Calls setsid to Become a Process Group Leader

Normally, if a process spawns several subprocesses, signals sent to the parent will affect the children. To prevent this possibility, the daemon calls setsid with the session ID 0 as an argument. This promotes the process to be a process group leader in its own right and to be immune to propagated process group signals.

The Daemon Detaches Itself from Its Controlling Terminal Using ioctl

The process breaks its relationship with the controlling terminal by calling ioctl with the parameter &TIOCNOTTY. The example value is valid for Sun systems, but you should investigate the system include file sys/ioctl.h for the correct value for your computer.

The process is now without a controlling terminal and immune from SIGHUP signals. You must do this because the daemon will run continuously. It will run even when the user logs out, the window-based terminal is closed, or the physical terminal is disconnected from the system.

In Step 4, you check the status of the daemon child using the ps command. The values for the process group ID (PGID) and session ID (SID) are both equal to the process's own PID. The command displays the value for the controlling terminal (TT) as ? (none) and the parent of the process (PPID) is 1, indicating that the initial UNIX process init has adopted the child as a daemon.

Comments

If you are familiar with writing in a language like C, you may be surprised that you can write satisfactory daemon processes in Perl. Indeed, there are advantages to Perl. One of the biggest problems with long-running processes is memory management. In C, where the programmer has to manage memory resources, you must ensure that each chunk of memory is returned to the system when it is no longer required. If you slip up and fail to release memory, then your program has a memory leak. Even commonly used programs have this problem. Normally, this is not a disaster. The operating system guarantees to return all your allocated memory to the system when your program exits.

In the case of daemon processes that may execute for several hundred days, however, rigorous memory management is vital. Perl controls memory resources in the

Perl runtime system (in all but a few special cases). Perl memory management has been tested in production by many thousands of users. You should never have to worry about data typing, memory allocation, or memory leaks.

COMPLEXITY
ADVANCED

12.4 How do I ...
Read and write to shared memory?

COMPATIBILITY: UNIX

Problem

I want several Perl processes to share a common data area and to be able to read and write the information placed there. How can I create and access a shared memory segment from Perl?

Technique

You may be used to thinking of a data structure created by a program as being totally private to that program. Many operating systems provide shared memory segments to allow several processes to read and write to a common data structure. This How-To illustrates how the Perl functions shmctl, shmget, and shmread create, update, and access shared data structures that are accessible to several processes.

Steps

The program shm.pl creates and writes to a segment of shared memory.

1. Enter the following text into the program shm.pl.

```perl
#!/usr/local/bin/perl
# Create and update shared memory segment
require 5.000;

BEGIN {
  $IPC_PRIVATE = 0;
  $IPC_RMID = 0;
  $size = 2000;
  $id = shmget($IPC_PRIVATE, $size , 0777 );
  die if !defined($key);
}

END {
  print "deleting $key\n";
  shmctl($id ,$IPC_RMID, 0) || die "$!";
  exit;
}

print "Key is $key\n";
```

```
for($i = 0; $i < 6; $i++) {
  $message = "The time is: " . `date`;
  shmwrite($id, $message, 0, 60 ) || die "$!";
  sleep 10;
}
```

2. Create a second program, shmread.pl. This process will read from the same shared memory segment and print out the data written there by shm.pl.

```
#!/usr/local/bin/perl
# read from a shared memory segment
require 5.000;

BEGIN {
  $IPC_PRIVATE = 0;
  $IPC_RMID = 0;
  $size = 2000;
  $key = shift @ARGV ;
  die "Invalid SMEM ID\n" unless $key;
}

shmread($key,$buff,0,60) || die "$!";

print $buff,"\n";
```

3. Invoke the programs to run in the background. Type the command this way:

shm.pl &

Output

```
[1] 13030
 Key is 1203
```
End Output

4. Inspect the status of interprocess communications facilities on your system by invoking the ipcs command. In the listing below, notice that program shm.pl creates a shared memory segment with an ID of 1203.

ipcs

Output

```
IPC status from fireball as of Sun Oct 15 18:06:22 1995
T     ID   KEY        MODE        OWNER     GROUP
Message Queues:
Shared Memory:
m    1203 0x00000000 --rw-rw-rw-  ahumphr   GERMANY
Semaphores:
```
End Output

5. Invoke shmread.pl with the appropriate shared memory ID. In this case, the ID is 1203.

shmread.pl 1203

continued on next page

continued from previous page

—[Output]————————————————————————————

```
The time is: Sun Oct 15 18:06:29 MET 1995
```
[End Output]————————————————————————————

6. Wait a few seconds before checking that the shared memory is being
updated by shm.pl. Type the same shmread.pl command. The program
reads and prints out the latest data in the shared segment.

shmread.pl 1203

—[Output]————————————————————————————

```
The time is: Sun Oct 15 18:06:59 MET 1995
```
[End Output]————————————————————————————

7. When the shm.pl program terminates, it will remove the shared memory
segment it created. If the shm.pl program terminates abnormally for any
reason, you can remove the shared memory segment using the UNIX command ipcrm. Proceed as shown in the sequence of commands below.

ipcs

—[Output]————————————————————————————

```
IPC status from fireball as of Sun Oct 15 18:06:22 1995
T     ID    KEY         MODE        OWNER      GROUP
Message Queues:
Shared Memory:
m    1203 0x00000000 --rw-rw-rw-  ahumphr   GERMANY
Semaphores:
```
[End Output]————————————————————————————

ipcrm -m 1203

ipcs

—[Output]————————————————————————————

```
IPC status from fireball as of Sun Oct 15 18:07:24 1995
T     ID    KEY         MODE        OWNER      GROUP
Message Queues:
Shared Memory:
Semaphores:
```
[End Output]————————————————————————————

How It Works

The writer program shm.pl requests the operating system to put aside a segment of
memory that may be accessed by many processes. The operating system labels the
segment with an identifier, in this case 1203. It does this by calling the Perl
function shmget, supplying parameters indicating the size of the segment in bytes
and a set of chmod-like permissions. In this case, we use 777, to provide full rights
to any program. The IPC_PRIVATE parameter causes shmget to create the segment.

The program then loops, writing the current time into the segment every 10 seconds. Because the segment is sharable and updating regularly, you can easily check that the writer program shm.pl is running successfully.

In Step 2, you invoke the reader program, shmread.pl, to create a snapshot of the contents of the segment. The Perl function shmread reads from the memory segment identified by $key into the local memory buffer $buff. You then print out the contents of the snapshot buffer. This illustrates how one process can read from shared memory that is being updated by another program simultaneously.

Finally, shm.pl uses the END subroutine to remove the shared memory segment it created by calling the Perl function shmctl with the parameter IPC_RMID.

Comments

Nearly all modern UNIX systems support shared memory. You may find some older systems that cannot support it, and some support it only if the kernel is specially configured. Shared memory is a feature developed for UNIX System V, so you may find it referred to as System-V IPC in your manual.

There are two more things to mention about shared memory. First, shared memory IPC is faster than alternative interprocess communication methods and an order of magnitude faster than I/O activity such as writing to files. You should consider using shared memory if writing information to a file would cause unacceptable delays in your process.

Second, shared memory segments are persistent. They remain in the system until you explicitly remove them. Shared memory does not disappear when the process that created it terminates. This makes shared memory an interesting debugging tool. You can follow the actions of a failing program by having it write its status into a shared memory segment. The data will remain available for reading after the process crashes.

COMPLEXITY
ADVANCED

12.5   How do I ...
Use semaphores in Perl?

COMPATIBILITY: UNIX

Problem

I need to synchronize several processes trying to access a common resource so that only one process may access the resource at one time. My version of UNIX implements semaphores for this purpose. How is it possible to use semaphores in Perl?

Technique

Although the UNIX implementation of semaphores is unduly complex, a semaphore is really a very simple concept. A *semaphore* is a special variable that grants or denies access to a shared resource.

Each process must try to take the semaphore before it accesses the resource. If a process attempts a take while the resource is busy, it will be blocked, as if it were waiting for input. When the resource becomes available, each process that tried to take the semaphore is unblocked and tries to take the semaphore again. Once a process succeeds in taking the semaphore, it gains access to the resource. Once the activity is complete, the successful process provides the semaphore, indicating the resource is available for other processes.

As an analogy, think of a resource safeguarded by semaphores as being like a supermarket that admits only customers who have a shopping cart. If too many people try to use the shop at one time, they will exhaust the supply of carts. Thereafter, customers have to queue up and wait for a shopper to return a cart to the pool. Then one more customer can get into the store.

Steps

1. Create program semserv.pl, as shown below. This program sets up a semaphore that guards an exclusive resource. To keep the code simple, do not focus on the resource itself; it could be a printer or shared memory segment, but in this case is purely conceptual.

2. Type in the listing below and call the program semserv.pl.

```
#!/usr/local/bin/perl -w

require Semaphor;

$semid = Semaphor::create($$);

print "Created semaphore key: $$\n";
```

3. Each client program that needs to access the conceptual resource must first try to take the semaphore created by the server. The program uses a Perl package called Semaphor, contained in the file Semaphor.pm. The package provides three subroutines. Semaphor::create is a subroutine that creates a semaphore. It takes a key-value parameter and returns the ID of an initialized semaphore with the value 1. Semaphor::take is a subroutine that requests access to a resource by attempting to take the semaphore. Semaphor::give is a subroutine that indicates that the resource is returned to the pool by relinquishing the semaphore.

Create the file Semaphor.pm and type in this listing:

```
package Semaphor;

sub create {
  # Create a semaphore and initialize it.
  local($IPC_KEY) = @_;
  local($semid);
```

```perl
   $IPC_CREATE = 0001000;
   $semid = semget($IPC_KEY, 1, 0666 | $IPC_CREATE);
   die "Semaphor-semget failed" if !defined($semid);

   $semnum = 0;
   $semflag = 0;
   $opstring = pack("sss", $semnum, $semop = 1, $semflag);
   semop($semid,$opstring) || die "$!";

   return $semid;
}


sub take {
# Obtain the semaphore
   local($IPC_KEY) = @_;
   local($semid);
   $semid = semget($IPC_KEY,  0 , 0 );
   die if !defined($semid);

   $semnum  = 0;
   $semflag = 0;
   $opstring = pack("sss", $semnum, $semop = -1,  $semflag);

   semop($semid,$opstring) || die "$!";
}

sub give {
# Relinquish a semaphore
   local($IPC_KEY) = @_;
   local($semid);
   $semid = semget($IPC_KEY, 0, 0);
   die if !defined($semid);

   $semnum  = 0;
   $semflag = 0;
   $opstring = pack("sss", $semnum, $semop = 1, $semflag);

   semop($semid,$opstring) || die "$!";
}

1;
```

4. Create a client program to simulate a set of processes competing for access to the safeguarded resource. Create the following listing in the file semclnt.pl. Notice that it requires the same package of semaphore operations, semaphor.pm, as the server.

```perl
#!/usr/local/bin/perl -w
# semclnt.pl

require Semaphor;

BEGIN {
   # Check the IPC Key was supplied on the command line
   $IPC_KEY = shift @ARGV;
```

continued on next page

continued from previous page

```
    die "usage: $0 <IPC_KEY>\nQuitting " unless $IPC_KEY;
    $pid = ($$ % 2) ? "Alpha" : "Omega";
    srand($$);
    $debug = 0;
}


END {
    # This routine is called automatically on exit
    print "Bye from $pid!";
}


# This routine simulates an activity of random duration
# such as enqueuing a print job or writing to a file.
sub busy {
local($msg) = @_;
    print $msg;
    $| = 1;
    $k = rand(10);
    for($j=0; $j < $k ; $j++) {
       print ".";      # show activity by writing ... to the terminal
       sleep(1);
    };
    print "done!\n";
    $| = 0;
}


MAIN:
for($i = 0; $i < 5; $i++) {

    # Try to access the shared resource.
    # We will block if the resource is busy
    print "$pid trying semaphore\n" if $debug;
    semaphore::take($IPC_KEY);

    # We finally got access. Let's get busy.
    print "$pid using resource\n" if $debug;
    busy("$pid busy");

    # Finished, so time to relinquish the resource.
    print "$pid giving semaphore\n" if $debug;
    semaphore::give($IPC_KEY);

    # Do something else for a random period of time.
    sleep(rand(15));
}
```

5. Execute the program semserv.pl to create a semaphore and print its identifier at the terminal.

semserv.pl

| Output |

```
Created semaphore id: 9840
```

| End Output |

6. Check the status of the semaphore using the system ipcs command.

Notice that the semaphore has been created with a key value of 9840, or 0x02670 in hex.

ipcs

Output

```
IPC status from fireball as of Sat Oct 21 20:05:32 1995
T    ID    KEY          MODE        OWNER     GROUP
Message Queues:
Shared Memory:
Semaphores:
s    50 0x00002670 --ra-ra-ra-  ahumphr   GERMANY
```

End Output

7. You can simulate multiple processes attempting to access a shared resource by executing two instances of the client program semclnt.pl. For identification, one process will print its name as Alpha and the other will print its name as Omega. Both processes will attempt to take the semaphore at random intervals. When a process succeeds in taking the semaphore, it runs a routine called busy that prints the string Alpha busy... with an arbitrary number of trailing dots. This routine simulates the process monopolizing the protected resource. When it has completed its activities, the process prints out the string done! Once the processes have taken five turns each to use the resource, they terminate with a farewell message.

Enter the command exactly as shown below and observe the dialog as it evolves at your terminal. You may want to run this step several times to convince yourself that access to the conceptual resource is truly random and mutually exclusive.

semclnt.pl 9840 & ; semclnt.pl 9840 &

Output

```
[1] 9842
[2] 9843
Alpha busy..........done!
Omega busy.....done!
Omega busy.done!
Alpha busy.done!
Alpha busy.......done!
Omega busy.........done!
Alpha busy........done!
Omega busy......done!
Alpha busy..........done!
Omega busy.......Bye from Alpha!..done!
Bye from Omega!


[2]  + Done             semclnt.pl 9840
[1]  + Done             semclnt.pl 9840
```

End Output

8. Remove the semaphore from your system by executing the ipcrm command with the semaphore ID as a parameter to the -s option. You can obtain the ID with the ipcs command, as shown in Step 6.

```
ipcrm -s 50
```

How It Works

This How-To uses a simulation technique to illustrate the use of semaphores. You do not need to concern yourself with the implementation of semaphores and the blocking mechanism. The kernel will handle those intricacies for you.

Let's turn first to the creation of the semaphore by the server program semserv.pl. You create a semaphore in a way similar to creating shared memory. Start with some external names or values that will act as a key. This key can be shared as common knowledge among the processes that use the semaphore. Common choices for keys are filenames and PIDs. Here you use the PID of the server process.

You then call Semaphor::create, passing the key as a parameter. Semaphor::create handles all the details of semaphore creation and hands you back an IPC ID value to act as your handle to the semaphore. Any other process that knows about the key-value can obtain a handle to the same semaphore. The Perl function semget is called by Semaphor::create to have the kernel produce the semaphore structure. The semaphore value is then initialized to 1 using the Perl function semop.

The client program semclnt.pl is a simple example of a simulation program written in Perl. semclnt.pl acts as one of a number of processes attempting to access a resource guarded by the semaphore. To make the simulation more convincing, the activities semclnt.pl engages in take unpredictable periods of time. This is accomplished by calls to the Perl function sleep, with random duration generated by rand. The subroutine busy takes a random period of time to print a variable length string to the terminal.

Perl promises to run the special BEGIN subroutine "as early as possible." BEGIN initializes the program by reading the semaphore key supplied on the command line. It then sets its identifier to be either Alpha or Omega, depending on the oddness or evenness of the PID. It then calls srand() to randomize the number sequences it will use in the simulation.

The main procedure of semclnt.pl is a simple loop. First, it tries to take the semaphore. When it succeeds, it calls busy for an unpredictable length of time and then relinquishes the semaphore and simulates some other processing activity for up to 15 seconds. semclnt.pl quits after five iterations.

Comments

Semaphores can be more elaborate than shown in this How-To. The type of semaphore you implemented here is a binary semaphore. It may take the values 1 or 0, depending on whether the resource is free or in use. UNIX IPC semaphores are capable of many complex permutations. If the resources you are trying to guard are many, then the semaphore value can be greater than 1.

## CHAPTER 13

CLIENT-SERVER AND NETWORK PROGRAMMING

CLIENT-SERVER AND NETWORK PROGRAMMING

How do I ...

After reading this chapter, you should be able to write Perl programs that reach beyond your computer and contact other programs running in your local network at remote locations across a local area network (LAN) or the Internet.

13.1 Create an Internet Domain Socket in Perl

How do you create an Internet protocol socket so that your Perl program can talk to the Net? This How-To will explore a small package of Perl functions that create TCP or UDP protocol interface to a LAN or wide area network. You can use the library in your programs to simplify network access.

13.2 Write a TCP-based Client Program in Perl

What techniques are involved in programming a simple TCP client process? A TCP client can connect to a TCP-based server and request data from it. This

How-To will show you how to access the TCP daytime service that runs on most networked hosts.

13.3   Write a UDP-based Client in Perl

UDP is the Internet connectionless protocol. This How-To will explain some of the issues involved in using UDP-based requests.

13.4   Write a Concurrent, Nondeadlocking Client

One issue every socket program must face is the possibility of deadlock. *Deadlock* occurs when two processes become confused about the synchronization of data exchange and become blocked, each waiting for data from the other. This How-To will show how you can use subprocesses to avoid deadlock and to implement client process concurrency.

13.5   Create a Server Socket in Perl

The counterpart of the client socket library is the server socket library, discussed in this How-To. This section will provide details on how to implement a set of routines for creating a socket that will accept connections from TCP and UDP clients.

13.6   Write a Socket-based Network Server in Perl

This section will show you how to use a small library to implement a remote Perl server that allows remote processes to connect, evaluates submitted arithmetic expressions, and returns the result across the Net.

COMPLEXITY
INTERMEDIATE

13.1   How do I...
Create an Internet domain socket in Perl?

COMPATIBILITY: UNIX

Problem

How do I write a program that can exchange data with another program across the Internet using the TCP protocol?

Technique

You can include a small library in your code to write the client half of a client-server application. If you prefer to skip ahead and try out a few programs that use the library, do so; you don't have to know how the library works to use it. You can come back to this How-To when you feel a need to understand the details. For those of you who like to know the details, read on.

First, let us define what we mean by a *client*. A program is a client if it initiates an exchange of data with another program on a network by sending a request to the other process. The other program in this relationship is commonly called a *server*. A server provides an information service to other processes on the network. A server starts out as the passive partner in the relationship because it is always prepared to receive requests from another program but never initiates the exchange.

There are two alternative models of network communications commonly found on workstation networks: streams and sockets. The examples in this chapter deal exclusively with the socket interface from Berkeley UNIX.

There is a good deal of unwarranted mystique surrounding network programming and sockets. A *socket* is a standard application interface to network communications that first appeared with the early 1980s' BSD UNIX. Recently, the socket interface has become available in the Microsoft Windows environment due to the popular WinSock interface standard.

Let us dispel some of the mystique. A socket appears to the programmer to behave in the familiar manner of a read/write file descriptor. In Perl, you can write to a socket handle just as you would to a filehandle. The socket interface handles the transmission of the data you write across the network. Similarly, once your program has connected to a source of data across the network, you can read the data from the socket using the normal Perl input facilities.

The only complicated part of handling a socket-based program is the steps involved in the identification of the proposed network partner program. To access a remote service, the application must supply two pieces of information:

- The name of the remote host

- A port number or name associated with a service provider process on the remote machine

Because the code you need to write to do this is similar for every application, you can simplify each application by reusing a common set of functions. For this reason, the core code of each of the How-To's in this chapter is encapsulated in a small library consisting of two Perl packages. The routines factor out the standard code involved in preparing socket descriptors for connection with a network partner.

Once you have this code library available, you can write a simple network-aware program in a few lines of Perl code.

This is not to oversimplify the subject. Writing mission-critical network-based programs in Perl is possible, but robust network programming is complex. Applications must be prepared to trap numerous error conditions and exceptions. The library presented here keeps things simple—if an error occurs, the program aborts. Of course, you are free to add error-trapping code of your own.

Steps

1. Create a file named Csok.pm. Enter the code in the listing below.

```
# Package for client socket connections
# Csok.pm -- TCP/UDP client module
#
package Csok;
```

continued on next page

continued from previous page

```perl
require Exporter;
@ISA = 'Exporter';
@EXPORT = qw(connectTCP, connectUDP);

use Socket;

sub connectTCP {
  my($S, $host, $service) = @_;
  connectsok($S, $host, $service, 'tcp');
}


sub connectUDP {
  my($S, $host, $service) = @_;
  connectsok($S, $host, $service, 'udp');
}


sub connectsok {
  my($S, $rhost_name, $service_name, $protoc_name) = @_ ;
  my($port, $SOCK_TYPE, $protocol, $local_sok,
     $remote_ip_addr, $remote_sok, $remote_quad);

  $SOCK_TYPE =  $protoc_name eq 'tcp' ? SOCK_STREAM : SOCK_DGRAM ;
  $protocol = getprotobyname($protoc_name);

  # Create a socket descriptor
  socket($S, PF_INET, $SOCK_TYPE, $protocol) || die $!;
  print STDERR "socket descriptor ok\n"  if $debug ;

  # Bind the socket descriptor to a local socket address
  $local_sok = sockaddr_in(0, inet_aton($HOSTNAME));
  bind($S, $local_sok) || die "Bind call failed: $!" ;
  print STDERR "bind ok\n" if $debug;

  # Remote Service specified by name or port number?
  if ($service_name =~ /^\d+$/ ) {
    $port = $service_name;
  } else {
    $port = (getservbyname($service_name, $protoc_name))[2];
    die "Unknown service $service_name" unless $port;
  }
  print STDERR "service $service_name/$protoc_name on port $port\n"
    if $debug;

  # Attempt to connect to the remote socket address
  $remote_ip_addr = gethostbyname($rhost_name);
  $remote_sok = sockaddr_in($port, $remote_ip_addr);
  connect($S, $remote_sok) || die $!;
  $remote_quad = inet_ntoa($remote_ip_addr);
  print STDERR "$rhost_name($remote_quad:$port) connect ok \n" if $debug;

}


BEGIN {
  require 'hostname.pl';
  $HOSTNAME = hostname();
}
1;
```

2. To include the code into another program, insert the line

```
use Csok;
```

into the file. If the library is not in your local directory, add the path of the library to the variable @INC. The assignment must execute before the *use* statement. You should therefore place the @INC update in a *BEGIN* block preceding the *use* statement, because the *use* statement is itself an implicit *BEGIN* block.

3. To run your program with socket diagnostics activated, set the variable *$Csok::debug* to 1. Use this line in your application:

```
$Csok::debug = 1;
```

4. To turn diagnostics off, add this line to your application:

```
$Csok::debug = 0;
```

How It Works

The package Csok provides two access functions, connectTCP and connectUDP, through which the application program can create a socket connection to another network process. Both functions have similar calling arguments. The application supplies a filehandle name that will become the filehandle associated with the socket, the name of the remote host, and the name or port number of the remote service.

The routines connectUDP and connectTCP are wrapper routines that simplify the call to the routine that really does the work: connectsok. Looking at the code in subroutine connectsok, you can see the logic of forming a socket follows the pattern described in Table 13-1.

STEP	DESCRIPTION
1.	Specify the type and protocol of the new socket, TCP or UDP.
2.	Create a socket filehandle using the socket call.
3.	Create an IP address and port and pair for local machine.
4.	Attach the socket to this port address using the bind call.

Table 13-1 Creating an Internet domain socket for a client process

The Perl function getprotobyname converts the desired protocol name, UDP or TCP, into a system constant. The type of the socket must then be set to match the protocol: SOCK_STREAM for TCP and SOCK_DGRAM for the UDP protocol. Once you have this information, you can call the function socket to create the socket and associate the user-supplied filehandle with it.

```
socket($S, PF_INET, $SOCK_TYPE, $protocol) || die $!;
```

The subroutine checks the return value of socket to see if a system error occurred. If there was an error, connectsok calls die to terminate the program. If you don't want this (rather simple-minded) behavior, you should include some error-trapping code instead.

The next job is to fill in some of the information that the socket will require before it can be used to access the network. A connected socket is like a bidirectional pipe. Each end of the pipe needs to be associated with an Internet machine address and a port number.

The routine connectsok translates the name of the local host to an Internet address by calling the function Socket::inet_aton. You can request that the port number for the local end of the socket be dynamically allocated by specifying the port number as 0. The address and port information are packed into a special structure using the convenient routine Socket::sockaddr_in.

To complete the setup of the socket on the local machine, call the bind function to link the socket with the address you have specified, as specified in Table 13-2.

STEP	DESCRIPTION	
1.	Obtain the IP address of the remote machine.	
2.	Create a port and IP address pair for the remote machine.	
3.	Connect to the remote machine port using the connect call.	

Table 13-2 Connecting the socket to another process

The next stage is to set up the address of the remote machine and service and have the connect call manage the negotiation of a link across the Internet.

connectsok first checks its service name parameter to see if the service was specified by name or number. If the port address was specified as a name, then conectsok finds out the numeric value of the port by calling getservbyname. It then obtains the IP address of the remote machine by calling gethostbyname and packs the address and port into a structure using Socket::sockaddr_in.

Finally, you are ready to connect to the remote server. All you need to do is to call the function connect. connect will manage the negotiation with the network for you. If you have specified TCP as your protocol choice, connect will create a point-to-point connection between your process and the remote server. If you are using UDP, a connectionless protocol where each packet is transmitted independently without guarantee of sequence or delivery, then connect simply caches information about the remote host address.

Comments

Many of the function calls in connectsok are concerned with breaking the dependency between code and a specific system. You could code the same routine by using numeric constants as parameters to the calls bind, socket, and connect. The problem is that each system is free to define its own values for these constants, and the resulting code would not work on another computer that defines a different numeric value for, say, protocol type.

We used two methods to avoid system-specific coding. Package Csok uses the module Socket, which defines a symbolic name for various system-specific constants. These constants, imported from Socket.pm, are barewords such as SOCK_DGRAM. Second, the program makes heavy use of the Perl get functions. These functions, with names like getservbyname, return system-specific values for items such as services and hostnames. You could obtain a service port number by reading the /etc/services file, but then you would have a problem if you tried to run your program on a machine using the NIS package to declare service names. The get functions make your code portable because they guarantee to yield the appropriate value whatever the configuration of the machine.

Remember that, to obtain the address of a remote machine using gethostbyname, you must have access to a database of hostnames, either on your local Net or, if you are using a full Internet connection, through the Domain Name Service (DNS). If your system doesn't know about a remote machine, then it cannot tell you its address.

COMPLEXITY
INTERMEDIATE

13.2 How do I ...
Write a TCP-based client program in Perl?

COMPATIBILITY: UNIX

Problem

How do I write a program that can connect and exchange data with a server program across the Internet using the TCP protocol and the BSD socket interface?

Technique

This How-To demonstrates the client socket library described in How-To 13.1. As an example, we will demonstrate a simple client program connecting to another host across the network to obtain the remote host's idea of the time of day.

Steps

1. Enter the code below into a file called tcpdt.pl. Adjust the BEGIN line to reference the library containing the Csok.pm module described in How-To 13.1.

```
#!/usr/local/bin/perl
# daytime service access using TCP
#

BEGIN { push(@INC, "../lib");}
use Csok;
```

continued on next page

continued from previous page

```
$Csok::debug = 1;

sub TCPdaytime
{
  local($host) = @_;
  Csok::connectTCP(main::SD, $host, 'daytime');
  while(<SD>) {
    print "$_\n";
  }
}

MAIN:
TCPdaytime(shift || 'localhost');
```

2. Execute tcpdt.pl in this way:

```
tcpdt.pl beta
```

where beta is the name of another host on your network.

3. The following dialog shows tcpdt.pl being used to access the daytime service, first on the local computer, then on a machine called delta attached to the local net, and finally to access a computer in a different time zone via the Internet. Notice that the clocks on delta and localhost are not synchronized.

```
alpha% tcpdt.pl
```

Output

```
service daytime/tcp on port 13
socket descriptor ok
bind ok
localhost(127.0.0.1:13) connect ok
Sun Oct 29 18:16:34 1995
```

End Output

```
alpha% tcpdt.pl delta
```

Output

```
service daytime/tcp on port 13
socket descriptor ok
bind ok
delta(192.93.226.1:13) connect ok
Sun Oct 29 18:19:18 1995
```

End Output

```
alpha% tcpdt.pl beta
```

Output

```
service daytime/tcp on port 13
socket descriptor ok
bind ok
beta(193.32.167.128:13) connect ok
Sun Oct 29 12:16:35 1995
```

End Output

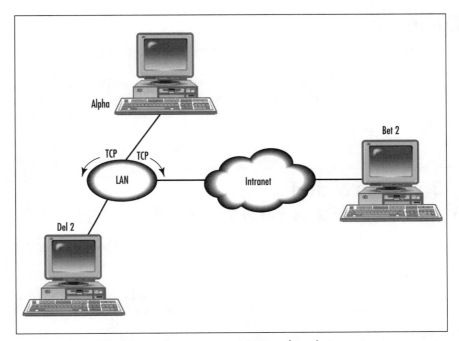

Figure 13-1 TCP connections over a LAN and an intranet

How It Works

After requiring the client socket package Csok, tcpdt.pl activates Csok diagnostics by setting the value of Csok::debug to 1. This tells you what is happening during the socket connection process and provides information to debug failures. The name of the compatible remote host is taken from the command line or, if no host is specified, the local machine is assumed. The name localhost always refers to the local machine. The TCP connections between an intranet and a LAN are illustrated in Figure 13-1.

The routine TCPdaytime( ) calls Csok::connectTCP, supplying the name of the server host and specifying the required service by name as daytime. The first argument to the function connectTCP is a filehandle named SD because the name SD is created in the package main and the socket is created in the package Csok. Remember to qualify the filehandle with the full name of the calling package. If you forget to do this, the socket will be created as Csok::SD.

The TCP daytime service is activated when a connection is established. You don't have to send a request to the remote server; it will detect when a client is connected and immediately send a time-of-day string, then close the socket.

In Perl, you can treat the socket handle as if it were any other filehandle. Simply read from it using the normal extract or read functions. End of file will detect when the server closes the other end of the socket.

Comments

Most networked workstations run a set of special minimal services for testing purposes. These services are managed by the process inetd, which is usually started at system boot time. The daytime service returns a human-readable string to the client via either TCP or UDP. To obtain a remote time value in a form more useful for an application, you should use the TIME service, which returns the number of seconds since midnight, January 1, 1900.

COMPLEXITY
INTERMEDIATE

13.3   How do I ...
Write a UDP-based client in Perl?

COMPATIBILITY: UNIX

Problem

How do I write a program that can connect and exchange data with a server program across the Internet using the UDP protocol and the BSD socket interface?

Technique

How-To 13.2 demonstrates a way in which the Csok package can contact a remote server using the TCP protocol. In this How-To, we look at the Internet datagram service UDP.

The simple socket program below uses another test service available on all Internet-aware platforms: the UDP echo service. An echo server simply receives a UDP datagram and returns it to the sender. This is useful behavior; if your program receives the echoed packet, then you know that a network route exists between your machine and the remote machine. The program here is called ping.pl, in honor of the ping utilities supplied with most IP software.

Steps

1. List the program ping.pl.

```
#!/usr/local/bin/perl -w
# simple udp ping
#

BEGIN { push(@INC, "../lib") }
use Csok;
use FileHandle;

$Csok::debug = 0;

sub alarm_h {
    close(SD);
}

sub UDPecho
```

```
{
  my($host) = @_;
  Csok::connectUDP('main::SD', $host, 'echo');

  autoflush SD 1;
  autoflush STDOUT 1;

  print SD "PING!\n";
  alarm $TIMEOUT;
  recv(SD,$response = "",64,0);
}
MAIN:
$TIMEOUT = 5;
$host = shift || 'localhost';
$SIG{'ALRM'} = \&alarm_h;
UDPecho($host);
if ($response) {
  print "$host returned our $response";
} else {
  print "No reply from $host\n";
}
```

2. Send a UDP packet to a remote machine like this (where beta is the name of a machine reachable from your network):

`ping.pl beta`

If the remote machine is up and on the network, the UDP echo server returns the packet. You will see a dialog resembling this:

`Output`

beta returned our PING!

`End Output`

3. If there is no route through the network to the remote machine, or the remote machine is down or malfunctioning, you will see a dialog similar to this:

`ping.pl meta`

`Output`

No reply from meta

`End Output`

How It Works

How-To 13.2 describes how to create a TCP daytime client. For the daytime service, you need only to create a socket and read data from it. For the echo service (as with most services), you need to create a socket, write to it, and then read back the response. If no response arrives, due to the remote machine being down or unreachable, then the client will block forever, waiting for data on the socket. You must set up a timeout to interrupt the socket read. If no data is available after a certain length of time, the read call aborts and avoids this potential deadlock. The mechanism is implemented with a call-back function, alarm_h, to be activated when the program receives a system alarm signal.

Create a UDP socket by calling the subroutine Csok::connectUDP, supplying a host name and the echo service as parameters. The first parameter becomes the Perl filehandle associated with the socket. Again, remember to qualify the name with the package in which you want to create the socket: package main, in this case. Remember, too, to set the socket descriptor to unbuffered mode using the autoflush method from the module FileHandle. If you don't do this, your program may buffer the data and never send it.

Then write the string PING! to the UDP socket. The IP software, running on the host, encapsulates the string into a UDP packet and transmits it to the remote computer. The program then requests that it should receive an alarm signal in $TIMEOUT seconds and tries to read a response from the socket.

Two things can happen at this point. The packet is echoed by the remote host and received on the socket—in this case, ping.pl prints out a success message and exits. Alternatively, the alarm signal is received by the program before the packet is received. This invokes the alarm_h handler, which terminates the read on the socket and makes the program print out a failure message.

Comments

From the socket-programming point of view, there is little difference in building a UDP socket and building a TCP socket. TCP is a stream-oriented protocol; it guarantees delivery and the correct ordering of long sequences of data. UDP is a datagram service, suitable for sending discrete transactions. UDP does not have any sequencing of packets and relies on the underlying network technology to deliver the packet of data to the intended recipient. There are no guarantees that the data will be received. If you need to guarantee that data will be received by the server, and in the correct sequence, you must program your own error correction or use TCP. TCP, however, is a much busier protocol and commands significantly more network bandwidth.

COMPLEXITY
INTERMEDIATE

13.4 How do I...
Write a concurrent, nondeadlocking client?

COMPATIBILITY: UNIX

Problem

How do I write a program that avoids blocking and deadlock while exchanging data with an Internet server?

Technique

In How-To 13.3, we touch upon the issue of client deadlock. If a client expects a packet to be delivered to it from the network, it will normally be in a read state. As you know, the read call blocks a process. If, for whatever reason, the server never sees a request packet, it will not respond. The client, therefore, will never return from its blocked read call and no more data exchange will be possible. Whenever a process must repeatedly write and read data from a socket, there is a chance that one single error in network transmission could block the client forever. This condition is known as *client deadlock*.

There are several techniques for avoiding deadlock situations. One method, demonstrated in How-To 13.3, is to set a time-out on read calls. A better solution is to break the synchronous nature of reading and writing by creating two separate processes to read and write to the socket independently.

Because the writer process executes separately from the reader process, it cannot become deadlocked by a blocked read call. It will continue to send more requests and, assuming the receive side delay or failure is transitory, the reader will unblock when more data arrives from the server.

We will use the UDP echo server as the example remote server. See How-To 13.3 for discussion of UDP echo.

Steps

1. Create the program udpecho.pl, listed below. Adjust the directory reference in the BEGIN line to point to the location of your Csok.pm module.

```perl
#!/usr/local/bin/perl -w
# Send and receive data from the UDP echo service
# using asynchronous processes
#

BEGIN { push(@INC, "../lib") }

use Csok;
use FileHandle;
$Csok::debug = 1;

sub reader {
    while( <SD>) {
        print
    }
}

sub writer {
    while(<>) {
        print SD
    }
}

sub UDPecho
{
    my($host) = @_;
    Csok::connectUDP('main::SD', $host, 'echo');
```

continued on next page

continued from previous page

```
    autoflush SD 1;
    autoflush STDOUT 1;

    $child_id = fork();
    die "fork failed: $!" unless defined $child_id;

    if ($child_id > 0) {
      # Parent - writes to server
      writer();

      # all done - tidy up
      sleep 3;
      shutdown(SD, 2);
      wait;
      exit 0;

    } else {
      # Child reads from server
      reader();
      print STDERR "Child exiting\n" if $debug;
    }
}

MAIN:
$debug = 1;
$host = shift || 'localhost' ;
UDPecho($host);
```

2. To run the program, invoke it with the name of the remote host and supply a file of input data for it to read from. We contact the host beta in this example. Substitute the name of a host on your network in place of beta. As input, use the file text.in, which contains a pictogram of a large friendly mammal.

```
udpecho.pl beta text.in
```

3. As the program udpecho.pl activates Csok diagnostics, you will see a dialog similar to this:

─| Output |──

```
service echo/udp on port 7
socket descriptor ok
bind ok
beta(195.32.167.128:7) connect ok
```

| End Output |──

How It Works

The method of creating a socket connection should be familiar from earlier How-To's in this chapter. The program calls Csok::connectUDP, supplying the name of the remote host and a filehandle identifier and specifying the echo service as parameters. You then set the socket to unbuffered mode so data is transmitted immediately as it is available. Then the program forks, creating a new clone process as illustrated in Figure 13-2.

The parent process takes the role of writer and the child takes the role of reader. The parent process writes input to the socket using the normal Perl *print* statement. The child process simultaneously begins to read the data returned on the socket by the remote machine. The data is output to the terminal. Because you now have two independent processes reading and writing to the socket, there is no possibility of client deadlock.

When the parent has sent all its data on the socket, it waits for a reasonable period of time and then starts the termination process. First, it calls close on the socket. This initiates closing the socket connection at remote and local end points. When close is activated, the child receives an end of file on its copy of the socket and terminates. The parent waits for the child to terminate and then exits itself.

Comments

Client deadlock is just one form of deadlock that can occur in client-server programming. The client can still become deadlocked if the server has problems, because the writer process blocks sending data to a nonwrite socket. This prevents the writer from completing data transfer and so halts the termination process. One way around this is

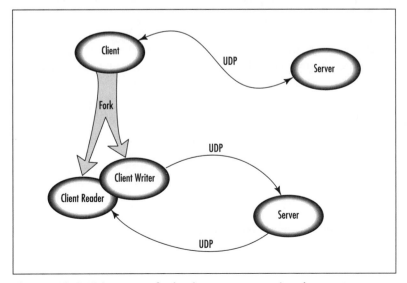

Figure 13-2 Using two-forked processes to implement a nondeadlocking client

to combine the reader and writer processes method with a time-out method. If everything becomes blocked by a failing server, then the time-out procedure should take appropriate action, terminating blocked writes and killing the child process.

COMPLEXITY
INTERMEDIATE

13.5 How do I...
Create a server socket in Perl?

COMPATIBILITY: UNIX

Problem

How do I create a server socket in Perl? A server socket will allow an arbitrary client program to connect to it and will then perform a service for the client, exchanging data using the UDP protocol and the BSD socket interface.

Technique

Just as with the client socket package Csok.pm, you don't have to understand how the server socket package works to use it. If you want to skip ahead to the next How-To to get a feel for the server package in action, then do so. Come back to this section when you want to get into the details.

Creating a server socket is not that different from creating a client socket. The difference is that, whereas the client socket is used to initiate connections and therefore knows the remote address it needs to connect to, a server socket must be ready to accept all comers. The server cannot know in advance which clients are going to seek connections with it. The server socket must therefore be placed in a mode where it is ready to react to an attempt by the client to connect. This mode is know as *passive mode*; a socket that is listening for attempts to connect is know as a *passive socket*.

Steps

1. Create the module Ssok.pl listed below or use the example from the CD.

```
# Package for creating a passive socket for TCP/UDP server
# Ssok.pm -- TCP/UDP server module
#
package Ssok;

require Exporter;
@ISA = 'Exporter';
@EXPORT = qw (passiveTCP, passiveUDP);

$QUEUE_LENGTH = 5;

use Socket;

sub passiveTCP {
```

```perl
  local($S, $service_name) = @_;
  passivesock($S, $service_name, 'tcp', $QUEUE_LENGTH);
}

sub passiveUDP {
  local($S, $service_name) = @_;
  passivesock($S, $service_name, 'udp', $QUEUE_LENGTH);
}

sub passivesock
{
    local($S, $service_name, $protoc_name, $qlen) = @_;
    my($port, $SOCK_TYPE);

    $SOCK_TYPE =  $protoc_name eq "tcp" ? SOCK_STREAM : SOCK_DGRAM ;
    $PROTOCOL = (getprotobyname($protoc_name))[2];

    # If the service name is numeric then assume it is a port spec.
    if( $service_name =~ /^\d+$/) {
      $port = $service_name;
    } else {
      $port = (getservbyname($service_name, $protoc_name))[2];
      die "Unknown service: $service_name" unless $port;
    }
    print "Rendezvous on port $port/$protoc_name\n" if $debug;

    # Create a socket descriptor
    socket($S, PF_INET, $SOCK_TYPE, $PROTOCOL) || die "socket: $!";
    print STDERR "socket descriptor ok\n"  if $debug ;

    # Identify the socket with the address
    # Create a socket address - let the protocol set the host address.

    $local_socket = sockaddr_in($port, inet_aton(INADDR_ANY) );
    bind($S, $local_socket) || die "bind: $!";

    # Set the socket as passive, await connections.
    listen($S, $qlen)
}

1;
```

2. To include the code in another program, insert the line

```perl
use Ssok;
```

into the file. If the Ssok.pm module is not in your local directory, add the path of the library to the variable *@INC*.

3. To run your program with socket diagnostics activated, set the variable *$Ssok::debug* to 1. Use this line in your application:

```perl
$Ssok::debug = 1;
```

4. To turn diagnostics off, add this line to your application:

```perl
$Ssok::debug = 0;
```

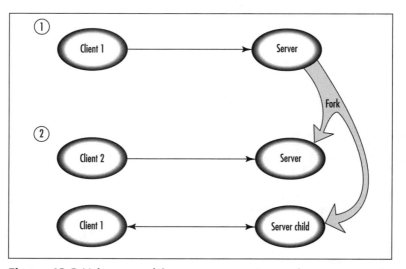

Figure 13-3 Using a multiprocess server to service concurrent clients

How It Works

The package Ssok.pm contains one main subroutine, passivesock, that automates each step in the creation of a server socket. passivesok can create either TCP or UDP sockets, according to which value is passed to it in the $protoc_name parameter. Two convenient subroutines called passiveTCP and passiveUDP act as wrapper routines, simplifying the calling interface of passivesok. Concurrent clients can be serviced by using a multiprocess server, as illustrated in Figure 13-3.

An application calls passiveTCP or passiveUDP, supplying as parameters the name of a file descriptor to associate with the socket and either the name of a service or a port number.

This service or port number is known as the *rendezvous port* of the server. The name or value of this port will be well known around the network as the address on which a client can meet the server. Once a client connects to the server rendezvous port, the two processes can negotiate a new port address over which to exchange data. The rendezvous then becomes free once more to receive new connections from other clients. A server socket can queue requests from clients to connect while this negotiation takes place.

The creation of the socket proceeds in the manner summarized in Table 13-3.

STEP	DESCRIPTION	
1.	Specify the type and protocol of the new socket, TCP or UDP.	
2.	Create a socket filehandle using the socket call.	
3.	Create a port and IP address pair for local machine.	
4.	Attach the socket to this port/address using the bind call.	

Table 13-3 Creating an Internet domain socket for a server process

The package determines the protocol type required by the calling program and sets the socket type to SOCK_STREAM or SOCK_DGRAM, accordingly. These constants are defined by the Socket.pm module from the Perl library. If the port is identified nonnumerically, then the routine assumes that the parameter is a service name and looks up the equivalent numeric value using getservbyname. With this information in place, the routine calls the Perl function socket to create a socket descriptor.

The bind call associates the descriptor with an Internet address/port structure. An Internet host address is standardized to four 1-byte numbers in the range of 1 to 254, known as the *quad notation*. Because this is the local end of the socket, you can let the protocol fill in the local host quad. Simply call Socket::sockaddr_in to pack the address INADDR_ANY with the port number identified by getservbyname. The subsequent call to bind replaces the INADDR_ANY with the real IP address of the local machine.

Setting the socket to passive mode is achieved by calling the Perl function listen. The listen function places the socket in a state in which it is ready to accept connections from remote clients. Several clients can attempt to connect simultaneously because connection requests are automatically queued. The number of simultaneously queued clients is set by $QUEUE_LENGTH, the second argument of the listen call. When the package is initialized, $QUEUE_LENGTH is set to 5. If five processes are already waiting to connect to the socket, a sixth process's attempts to connect will be rejected.

Comments

A server that uses the TCP protocol is described as *connection oriented*. A server that uses UDP is described as *connectionless*. Using TCP implies a reliable delivery of data to and from the client. If your server is to be accessible beyond your local LAN, then you should choose a TCP-based server. A server that uses UDP on a shared network should expect clients to experience packet loss. What then is the use of a UDP-based server?

UDP can do one thing that a TCP server cannot. TCP is a point-to-point protocol. Only one pair of processes can be connected on a TCP channel at one time. UDP, however, can broadcast data to the network by using the network broadcast address as the address of its partner. If your server intends to send the same or similar data to a large number of clients, then you should consider using UDP broadcasts. The disadvantage is that you will have to write error detection and request techniques into your application's data-handling logic.

COMPLEXITY
INTERMEDIATE

13.6 How do I...
Write a socket-based network server in Perl?

COMPATIBILITY: UNIX

Problem

How can I write a program that offers a service to the network? The server program will allow a client program to connect to it and request that data be transferred from the server to the client across the network.

Technique

This How-To implements a TCP server using the server socket library Ssok.pm, discussed in How-To 13.5. The server performs the task of a remote Perl arithmetic interpreter. It accepts a request from a client in the form of an arithmetic expression, evaluates the expression, and returns the result back to the client via a TCP channel.

Steps

1. Examine the code contained in the file tcpserv.pl. This code implements a Perl server process that evaluates arithmetic expressions over a network.

```perl
#!/usr/local/bin/perl -Tw
# Simple TCP based server

BEGIN { push(@INC, "../lib")}

use Socket;
use Ssok;
use FileHandle;

sub exit_handler
{
  local($sig) = @_ ;
  $SIG{'INT'} = $SIG{'QUIT'} = 'IGNORE';
  warn "Caught SIG $sig, exiting gracefully\n";
  sleep 2;
  close(S);
  close(NS);
  exit 1;
}

sub child_handler {
  wait;
}

MAIN:
$debug = 1;
```

```perl
$SIG{'INT'} = $SIG{'QUIT'} = \&exit_handler;
$SIG{'CHLD'} = \&child_handler;

$DEFAULT_PORT = 6499;
$_ = shift || $DEFAULT_PORT;
m/(\d*)/;
$port = $1;


Ssok::passiveTCP(main::S, $port);

autoflush S 1;
autoflush STDOUT 1;

printf("Server $0 up. Waiting for connections ...\n") if $debug;
for($con = 1; ;$con++) {
  ACCEPT: {
      ($addr = accept(NS, S)) || redo ACCEPT;
  }

  autoflush NS 1;

  $child = fork();
  die "fork failed: $!" unless defined $child;

  if( $child == 0) {
     #Child
     print "Accepted connection #$con \n" if $debug;

     ($_, $packed) = unpack_sockaddr_in($addr);
     $client_addr  = Socket::inet_ntoa($packed);
     print "from client ($client_addr:$port)\n" if $debug;

     while( <NS> ) {
       if ( m,(\d+)\s*([+*-/])\s*(\d+),) {;
            $op1 = $1; $op = $2; $op2 = $3;
            $_ = "$op1 $op $op2\n" ;
            print "$con: $_ " if $debug;
            $result = eval $_;
            print NS "$result\n" unless $@;
            print NS "$@\n" if $@;
       } else {
            print NS "Syntax Error\n";
       }
     }
     close(NS);
     exit 0;
  }
  #Parent, close NS and wait for next connection
  close(NS);
}
```

2. Create the file tcpclnt.pl. The code implements a concurrent client process that sends requests to the server and reads back the results.

```perl
#!/usr/local/bin/perl
# daytime service access using TCP
#
```

continued on next page

continued from previous page

```perl
BEGIN { push(@INC, "../lib"); }

use Csok;
$Csok::debug = 1;

sub TCPecho
{
  my($host, $port) = @_;
  Csok::connectTCP('main::SD', $host, $port);
  select(SD); $| = 1; select(STDOUT);

  $child = fork();
  die "fork failed: $!" unless defined $child;

  if ($child == 0) {

    #Parent writes
    while(<>) {
      print SD ;
    }
    sleep 3;
    kill $child;
    shutdown(SD,2);
    exit 0;
  } else {

    # Child reads
    while( <SD>) {
      print ;
    }
  }
}


MAIN:
$DEFAULT_PORT = 6499;
$host = shift || 'localhost' ;
$port = shift || $DEFAULT_PORT;
TCPecho($host, $port);
```

3. Copy the server software to a remote machine on the local network. The remote machine should run Perl. Log on to the machine and run the server, preferably on a windowing workstation. You will see the following initialization message.

Output
_____

```
Server tcpserv.pl up. Waiting for connections ...
```
End Output
_____

4. Either leave the server running in one window on your workstation or, if you are not running a Windowing shell, suspend the session and return to your local workstation.

5. Run the client in this way:

```
tcpclnt.pl
```

You will see the following diagnostics as the program connects to the remote server.

Output

```
socket descriptor ok
bind ok
service 6499/tcp on port 6499
alpha(192.93.226.3:6499) connect ok
```

End Output

6. Type in some simple arithmetic expressions. You should see results similar to those below. You will then see output similar to the following as the server evaluates the Perl expressions and returns the results to the client. The client prints the results on the terminal.

```
2 + 3
```

Output

```
5
```

End Output

```
92 / 8
```

Output

```
11.5
```

End Output

```
x + 1
```

Output

```
Syntax Error
```

End Output

```
56 * 47
```

Output

```
2632
```

End Output

How It Works

The server is a connection-based concurrent server. It uses one subprocess per connection to handle the data exchange between server and client. This allows the server to service many requests simultaneously and therefore support several client sessions. When a client terminates the connection, the server subprocess dies, and the parent process must interrupt itself and reap the child before continuing.

The server operates in this way. It arranges to create a socket at a rendezvous port using the server socket library Ssok.pm. The server then calls accept to have the socket wait for a client to connect to it. When a client connects to the rendezvous socket, accept creates another clone socket at a different port address. This is the port over which the server communicates with the client. The server then spawns a subprocess to handle the client dialog. The master process then closes its copy of the new socket and calls accept again to wait for more connections.

The child process then begins its work with the client, reading Perl expressions from the NS socket and returning the evaluated expression back to the client.

Comments

When the client has no more outstanding requests, it shuts down its side of the socket and the server subprocess terminates. This termination of an unpredictable number of child processes could cause a problem, unless the parent process removes the remnants of the defunct child from the process table. Yet the parent is busy waiting for connections on the socket. To make the server interrupt its accept call, you have to insert a signal handler in the server code. This is achieved by setting the value of the variable

```
$SIG{'CHLD'} = \&child_handler;
```

The subroutine child_handler is invoked whenever a child process dies. The routine calls the Perl function wait to remove the child from the process table. The problem is that the Perl function accept calls the similarly named system call; you have now interrupted the system call and returned to user mode. accept simply returns with an error status.

This is why the server has embedded accept in its own block.

```
ACCEPT: {
    ($addr = accept(NS, S)) || redo ACCEPT;
}
```

If accept returns with an error status, the server assumes that the call was interrupted by the death of a child. It restarts the call to accept, ready to obtain another connection. If accept returns with a positive value, the server has obtained a connection; the value returned by accept is the address of the client.

Finally, notice that the server program runs with the -T taint flag. All network servers should run with the flag because it provides some degree of security against abuse of the server facilities by malicious clients. Giving an arbitrary client the right to connect to a remote Perl interpreter and execute any arbitrary command is dangerous. The taint flag prohibits the direct use of externally supplied values in the Perl program. Each variable that has received a value from outside the program must be untainted before the value is used. Untainting a variable is achieved by dissembling the input using pattern matching and assigning the dissembled values to new variables. Here is an example of variable untainting from the server program.

```
if ( m,(\d+)\s*([+*-/])\s*(\d+), {;
        $op1 = $1; $op = $2; $op2 = $3;
```

Breaking up externally supplied values in this way ensures that the program is written with some check to ensure that values obtained from the network are legitimate input. The client cannot attempt to spoof the Perl interpreter into performing malicious commands.

FUNCTIONS, LIBRARIES, PACKAGES, AND MODULES

FUNCTIONS, LIBRARIES, PACKAGES, AND MODULES

How do I...

Perl functions (also called subroutines) provide a wide array of useful services. Functions can take a variable number of parameters and return multiple results. When functions are passed references, they can modify variables in the calling routine. References also allow arrays to be passed to and from functions.

Perl provides a number of ways to reuse Perl code. For example, you can create libraries and modules that can be used by multiple scripts. Perl uses a method of partitioning the name space. Packages allow libraries and modules to create and use variables in their own name spaces. With this ability, modules need not worry about reusing a variable name that is used in a different module.

You can use plain old documentation (POD) files to create documentation for scripts, libraries, and modules.

14.1   Pass Variables by Reference

Parameters can be passed to functions by reference. This allows the called function to modify variables in the calling function. Passing large data structures as references can significantly speed up the execution of a function. With references, the data structures do not have to be copied in and out of the function. This section will show you how to pass variables by reference.

14.2   Pass Multiple Arrays to a Function

All parameters to and return values from a function are passed as a list of scalar values. This prevents arrays from being passed to and from a function. With references, functions can operate on arrays passed as arguments. This How-To will demonstrate how to pass multiple arrays to a function.

14.3   Return More Than One Variable from a Function

There is no limit to the number of return values from a function. This section will show you an easy way to return multiple results.

14.4   Create and Use a Package

Packages allow the partitioning of Perl's name space. This allows multiple modules to use the same variable names without overwriting them. This How-To will demonstrate how to create and use a package.

14.5   Create and Use a Library

Perl libraries allow code to be loaded into a script. This promotes reuse and prevents code from being maintained in more than one location. This How-To will demonstrate how to create and use a library.

14.6   Create and Use a Module

Modules add to the ability of libraries. A script can specify what functionality it wants from the module. This allows selective importing of functions and variables into the current name space. This section will show you how to create and use a module.

14.7   Create a POD File

POD files can be used to create documentation for scripts, libraries, and modules. In fact, Perl scripts, libraries, and modules can become self-documenting by embedding POD directives in them. This How-To will demonstrate how to create a POD file.

COMPLEXITY
INTERMEDIATE

14.1   How do I...
Pass variables by reference?

COMPATIBILITY: PERL 4   PERL 5   UNIX   DOS

Problem

I would like to have the variables passed to a function reflect any changes made to them in the function. In other words, if I pass a variable v to a function and I change its value, I would like v to have the changed value when the function returns. How do I do this?

Technique

Scalar values passed to a Perl function are passed as an implicit reference. This means that in a function, $_[0] is an alias for the first argument, $_[1] is an alias for the second argument, and so on. All arguments to a function are expanded to a single list of values. This means that all arrays and associative arrays are expanded to be a list of their values. The fact that the values are part of any type of array is not known by the function. Use references to alleviate this problem; How-To 14.2 shows you how to do this.

This How-To passes scalar variables by reference. This provides a simple example of the technique of passing references. A reference is a value that points to another value. References can be used like any other value and they can be dereferenced. The act of dereferencing a reference exposes the variable that the reference points to. Once the reference has been dereferenced, the pointed-to value can be read, modified, deleted, etc. A reference to a normal variable is created by putting a back-slash in front of the variable.

```
$Ref = \$Var;
```

The reference is dereferenced by putting a dollar sign in front of it.

```
$$Var = 5;
print $$Var;
```

References can also be used to point at arrays and other Perl types.

```
@Array = (1, 2, 3);
$ArrayRef = \@Array;
@$ArrayRef = (5, 6, 7);
```

References can be passed to functions. Any changes to the value being referenced are seen in the calling function.

Steps

The example scripts show how to interchange the value of two variables. The first script creates a function that exchanges two integers. The second script shows that the same function can be used to exchange two strings.

1. Create a script called ref1.pl. First, add a line turn on strict checking. Next, add a function to take two variables and exchange their values.

```
use strict;

sub Switch {
    my($a,$b) = @_;

    print "Entering Switch. \$a = $$a, \$b = $$b\n";
    ($$a, $$b) = ($$b, $$a);
    print "Exiting Switch. \$a = $$a, \$b = $$b\n";
}
```

2. Add the following lines to use to test the script.

```
my($Var1) = 14;
my($Var2) = 35;

print "\$Var1 = $Var1, \$Var2 = $Var2\n";
&Switch(\$Var1,\$Var2);
print "\$Var1 = $Var1, \$Var2 = $Var2\n";
```

3. The entire script follows.

```
use strict;

sub Switch {
    my($a,$b) = @_;

    print "Entering Switch. \$a = $$a, \$b = $$b\n";
    ($$a, $$b) = ($$b, $$a);
    print "Exiting Switch. \$a = $$a, \$b = $$b\n";
}

my($Var1) = 14;
my($Var2) = 35;

print "\$Var1 = $Var1, \$Var2 = $Var2\n";
&Switch(\$Var1,\$Var2);
print "\$Var1 = $Var1, \$Var2 = $Var2\n";
```

4. Run the script. The output follows.

Output

```
$Var1 = 14, $Var2 = 35
Entering Switch. $a = 14, $b = 35
Exiting Switch. $a = 35, $b = 14
$Var1 = 35, $Var2 = 14
```

End Output

5. Copy ref1.pl to ref2.pl. Add a call to the function that passes two strings as arguments.

```perl
use strict;

sub Switch {
    my($a,$b) = @_;

    print "Entering Switch. \$a = $$a, \$b = $$b\n";
    ($$a, $$b) = ($$b, $$a);
    print "Exiting Switch. \$a = $$a, \$b = $$b\n";
}

my($Var1) = 14;
my($Var2) = 35;

print "\$Var1 = $Var1, \$Var2 = $Var2\n";
&Switch(\$Var1,\$Var2);
print "\$Var1 = $Var1, \$Var2 = $Var2\n";

print "\n";

$Var1 = "String1";
$Var2 = "String2";

print "\$Var1 = $Var1, \$Var2 = $Var2\n";
&Switch(\$Var1,\$Var2);
print "\$Var1 = $Var1, \$Var2 = $Var2\n";
```

6. Run this new script. Both the integers and strings are successfully interchanged.

Output
```
$Var1 = 14, $Var2 = 35
Entering Switch. $a = 14, $b = 35
Exiting Switch. $a = 35, $b = 14
$Var1 = 35, $Var2 = 14

$Var1 = String1, $Var2 = String2
Entering Switch. $a = String1, $b = String2
Exiting Switch. $a = String2, $b = String1
$Var1 = String2, $Var2 = String1
```
End Output

A screen dump of the execution of the script can be seen in Figure 14-1.

How It Works

References can be passed to a function like any other data type. When a reference is dereferenced in a function, the value being referenced can be accessed and modified.

```
birdofprey /home/spock/Waite/chap_14/howto01

> cat ref2.pl
use strict;

sub Switch {
    my($a,$b) = @_;

    print "Entering Switch. \$a = $$a, \$b = $$b\n";
    ($$a, $$b) = ($$b, $$a);
    print "Exiting Switch. \$a = $$a, \$b = $$b\n";
}

my($Var1) = 14;
my($Var2) = 35;

print "\$Var1 = $Var1, \$Var2 = $Var2\n";
&Switch(\$Var1,\$Var2);
print "\$Var1 = $Var1, \$Var2 = $Var2\n";

print "\n";

$Var1 = "String1";
$Var2 = "String2";

print "\$Var1 = $Var1, \$Var2 = $Var2\n";
&Switch(\$Var1,\$Var2);
print "\$Var1 = $Var1, \$Var2 = $Var2\n";
> perl -w ref2.pl
$Var1 = 14, $Var2 = 35
Entering Switch. $a = 14, $b = 35
Exiting Switch. $a = 35, $b = 14
$Var1 = 35, $Var2 = 14

$Var1 = String1, $Var2 = String2
Entering Switch. $a = String1, $b = String2
Exiting Switch. $a = String2, $b = String1
$Var1 = String2, $Var2 = String1
>
```

Figure 14-1 Output of ref2.pl

Comments

Both scripts start with the line

```
use strict;
```

This statement turns on strict checking of the script. It can catch the misuse of references, variables, and subroutines.

Perl 4 does not have references. Because scalar variables are passed by implicit reference, the values can be modified by modifying the implicit reference. Perl 4 also does not have my. The mys can be safely removed.

```
sub Switch {

    print "Entering Switch. \$a = $_[0], \$b = $_[1]\n";
    ($_[0], $_[1]) = ($_[1], $_[0]);
    print "Exiting Switch. \$a = $_[0], \$b = $_[1]\n";
}

$Var1 = 14;
$Var2 = 35;

print "\$Var1 = $Var1, \$Var2 = $Var2\n";
```

```
&Switch($Var1,$Var2);
print "\$Var1 = $Var1, \$Var2 = $Var2\n";

print "\n";

$Var1 = "String1";
$Var2 = "String2";

print "\$Var1 = $Var1, \$Var2 = $Var2\n";
&Switch($Var1,$Var2);
print "\$Var1 = $Var1, \$Var2 = $Var2\n";
```

COMPLEXITY
INTERMEDIATE

14.2 How do I...
Pass multiple arrays to a function?

COMPATIBILITY:

Problem

I would like to create a function that compares two arrays. Whenever I try this, only individual values are received by the function. How can I get two arrays passed into a function?

Technique

Perl passes only scalar values to functions. If arrays are passed to a function, the arrays are expanded to their individual values. Thus, the called function never knows that arrays were given as arguments. The method to get arrays passed to function is to pass them as references. A reference is a smart pointer to another variable. It is a normal scalar variable that contains a pointer to another variable. It can be dereferenced to get the variable pointed to. Create a reference by putting a back-slash in front of a variable. A reference is dereferenced by putting a dollar sign adjacent to the reference name.

```
$ArrayRef = \@Array;
print "@$ArrayRef\n";
```

See How-To 14.1 for a more in-depth description of references.

Steps

The example script contains a function to compare two arrays passed to it as references. The script also contains some code to test the function. The case where the arrays are the same and the case where the arrays are different are tested.

1. Create a file called array.pl. Add a subroutine that compares two arrays passed in as references. Save the array reference arguments in two local variables and create a local variable for the array comparison.

```perl
use strict;

sub ArrayCompare {
    my($Array1,$Array2) = @_;
    my($Index);
```

2. Make sure the arrays are of the same size. If not, return failure. Compare the arrays element by element. If any elements are different, return failure. If all the elements match, return success.

```perl
    if (@$Array1 != @$Array2) {
        return 0;
    }
    for $Index (0..$#$Array1) {
        if ($Array1->[$Index] != $Array2->[$Index]) {
            return 0;
        }
    }
    return 1;
}
```

3. Create two identical arrays to test the function. Call the function to verify that the function will return True. The back-slash in front of the arrays passes a reference.

```perl
my(@A1) = (1,2,3,4);
my(@A2) = (1,2,3,4);

if (&ArrayCompare(\@A1,\@A2)) {
    print "A1 = A2\n";
} else {
    print "A1 != A2\n";
}
```

4. Create two dissimilar arrays and call the function.

```perl
my(@A3) = (1,2,3,4);
my(@A4) = (1,2,7,4);

if (&ArrayCompare(\@A3,\@A4)) {
    print "A3 = A4\n";
} else {
    print "A3 != A4\n";
}
```

5. The entire script looks like this:

```perl
use strict;

sub ArrayCompare {
    my($Array1,$Array2) = @_;
    my($Index);
```

```
        if (a$Array1 != a$Array2) {
            return 0;
        }
        for $Index (0..$#$Array1) {
            if ($Array1->[$Index] != $Array2->[$Index]) {
                return 0;
            }
        }
        return 1;
}

my(aA1) = (1,2,3,4);
my(aA2) = (1,2,3,4);

if (&ArrayCompare(\aA1,\aA2)) {
    print "A1 = A2\n";
} else {
    print "A1 != A2\n";
}

my(aA3) = (1,2,3,4);
my(aA4) = (1,2,7,4);

if (&ArrayCompare(\aA3,\aA4)) {
    print "A3 = A4\n";
} else {
    print "A3 != A4\n";
}
```

6. Run the script. The output should look like the following.

Output

```
A1 = A2
A3 != A4
```

End Output

How It Works

References change only how variables are passed and accessed. The code is otherwise the same. Each time a reference needs to be dereferenced, a dollar sign needs to be attached to the reference name to access the underlying variable. When a reference needs to be created, a back-slash needs to be prepended to the variable.

Comments

Perl 4 does not have references. Both Perl 4 and Perl 5 have type globs. There can be many different variables with the same name in Perl. You can have a scalar variable named var, an array named var, an associative array named var, and even a filehandle named var. The collection of these is known as a type glob. Basically, a type glob is a pointer to a symbol table entry that contains the information about each of these variables.

To get reference-like behavior in Perl 4, use type globs. Change the script so it does not use *my* and uses type globs instead of references. Use the * character to get a type glob. The dereference of a type glob uses the normal syntax.

```
sub ArrayCompare {
    local(*Array1,*Array2) = @_;
    local($Index);

    if (@Array1 != @Array2) {
        return 0;
    }
    for $Index (0..$#Array1) {
        if ($Array1[$Index] != $Array2[$Index]) {
            return 0;
        }
    }
    return 1;
}

@A1 = (1,2,3,4);
@A2 = (1,2,3,4);

if (&ArrayCompare(*A1,*A2)) {
    print "A1 = A2\n";
} else {
    print "A1 != A2\n";
}

@A3 = (1,2,3,4);
@A4 = (1,2,7,4);

if (&ArrayCompare(*A3,*A4)) {
    print "A3 = A4\n";
} else {
    print "A3 != A4\n";
}
```

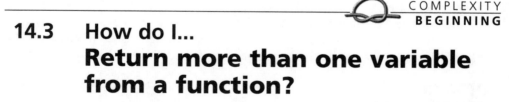

COMPLEXITY
BEGINNING

14.3 How do I...
Return more than one variable from a function?

COMPATIBILITY: PERL 4 | PERL 5 | UNIX | DOS

Problem

I would like to be able to return more than one variable from a function. How can I do this?

Technique

Perl allows any number of variables to be returned from a function. The return command takes 0 or more variables. Each of these variables is returned to the calling function. As long as the calling function assigns the return values to variables, the values are available. If no assignment is done, the values are ignored. If no return command is used at the end of a function, the last value or values evaluated in the function are returned.

Multiple variables are passed to a return command as a list.

```
return $Value1, $Value2;
```

or

```
return ($Value1, $Value2);
```

The values are assigned by the calling function by using a list.

```
($Return1, $Return2) = &Subroutine();
```

Steps

The first script creates two functions. The first takes an integer and returns 1; the second function takes two integers and returns 2. The second script shows how multiple values can be returned using an array instead of multiple scalar values.

1. Create a file called multi1.pl. Add a first function that takes one integer as input. If that integer is less than 100, multiply by 10; otherwise add 10. The last statement in the function is not necessary. It gives the value to be returned, but that is the last value used before the end of the function. By default, that is the value that would be returned anyway. To be clear, it is always a good idea to have a *return* statement.

```
sub ReturnOne {
    my($In) = @_;
    my($Out);

    if ($In < 100) {
        $Out = $In * 10;
    } else {
        $Out = $In + 10;
    }
    return($Out);
}
```

2. Call the function with two test values. Print the values returned.

```
$Output1 = &ReturnOne(5);
$Output2 = &ReturnOne(100);

print "$Output1 $Output2\n";
```

3. Create a second function that takes two integers, performs the same processing, and returns both results.

```
sub ReturnTwo {
    my($In1,$In2) = @_;
    my($Out1,$Out2);

    if ($In1 < 100) {
        $Out1 = $In1 * 10;
    } else {
        $Out1 = $In1 + 10;
    }
    if ($In2 < 100) {
        $Out2 = $In2 * 10;
    } else {
        $Out2 = $In2 + 10;
    }
    return($Out1, $Out2);
}
```

4. Call the second function and print the results.

```
($Output3,$Output4) = &ReturnTwo(5,100);

print "$Output3 $Output4\n";
```

5. The completed script follows.

```
sub ReturnOne {
    my($In) = @_;
    my($Out);

    if ($In < 100) {
        $Out = $In * 10;
    } else {
        $Out = $In + 10;
    }
    return($Out);
}

$Output1 = &ReturnOne(5);
$Output2 = &ReturnOne(100);

print "$Output1 $Output2\n";

sub ReturnTwo {
    my($In1,$In2) = @_;
    my($Out1,$Out2);

    if ($In1 < 100) {
        $Out1 = $In1 * 10;
    } else {
        $Out1 = $In1 + 10;
    }
    if ($In2 < 100) {
        $Out2 = $In2 * 10;
    } else {
        $Out2 = $In2 + 10;
    }
    return($Out1, $Out2);
}
($Output3,$Output4) = &ReturnTwo(5,100);
```

```
print "$Output3 $Output4\n";
```

6. Run the script. The output follows.

```
50 110
50 110
```

7. Change the second function to use an array for the results instead of two different variables.

```
sub ReturnOne {
    my($In) = @_;
    my($Out);

    if ($In < 100) {
        $Out = $In * 10;
    } else {
        $Out = $In + 10;
    }
    return($Out);
}

$Output1 = &ReturnOne(5);
$Output2 = &ReturnOne(100);

print "$Output1 $Output2\n";

sub ReturnTwo {
    my($In1,$In2) = @_;
    my(@Out);

    if ($In1 < 100) {
        $Out[0] = $In1 * 10;
    } else {
        $Out[0] = $In1 + 10;
    }
    if ($In2 < 100) {
        $Out[1] = $In2 * 10;
    } else {
        $Out[1] = $In2 + 10;
    }
    return(@Out);
}

($Output3,$Output4) = &ReturnTwo(5,100);

print "$Output3 $Output4\n";
```

8. The output is the same.

```
50 110
50 110
```

How It Works

Perl functions can return any number of values from a function. The calling function can assign any number of these return values to variables. If variables are not assigned, they are ignored.

Comments

Just as arrays cannot be passed to functions as arrays, they cannot be returned from functions as arrays. Only values can be passed or returned. References must be used to access true arrays. See How-To 14.2 to see how to do this.

Be careful when calling functions that return arrays. If you were to call the second function like this:

```
$Result = &ReturnTwo(5,100);
```

the value of $Result would always be 2. This is because, when you assign an array to a scalar variable, the variable receives the number of elements in the array, not the first element of the array.

Change all the mys to locals to allow the script to run under Perl 4. Here is the modified first script.

```
sub ReturnOne {
    local($In) = @_;
    local($Out);

    if ($In < 100) {
        $Out = $In * 10;
    } else {
        $Out = $In + 10;
    }
    return($Out);
}

$Output1 = &ReturnOne(5);
$Output2 = &ReturnOne(100);

print "$Output1 $Output2\n";

sub ReturnTwo {
    local($In1,$In2) = @_;
    local($Out1,$Out2);

    if ($In1 < 100) {
        $Out1 = $In1 * 10;
    } else {
        $Out1 = $In1 + 10;
    }
    if ($In2 < 100) {
        $Out2 = $In2 * 10;
    } else {
        $Out2 = $In2 + 10;
```

```
    } else {
        $Out2 = $In2 + 10;
    }
    return($Out1, $Out2);
}

($Output3,$Output4) = &ReturnTwo(5,100);

print "$Output3 $Output4\n";
```

COMPLEXITY
INTERMEDIATE

14.4 How do I...
Create and use a package?

COMPATIBILITY: PERL 4 | PERL 5 | UNIX | DOS

Problem

I have a set of routines that implement a vector. When I include these routines in a program, all the variables and subroutines are seen in the script. Because some of the variables and subroutine names can be used in other routines, different libraries can modify each other's variables. How can I prevent this?

Technique

Perl provides the concept of a package. This allows different name spaces to be used for different sets of routines. This means that the same variable name can be used, but it can be a different variable in each package. By default, all scripts start out in package Main. The package currently in use can be changed with the package command.

```
package Vector;
```

You can access variables and subroutines in other packages by prefixing their names with the package name and a double colon.

```
print "$Vector::Version\n"
```

or

```
&Vector::VecSubtract($Vec1,$Vec2);
```

Steps

The example is a small portion of a package that implements the functionality of a vector. The VecMult function is defined. Its first argument is a vector. If the second argument is another vector, the two vectors are multiplied and the resulting vector is returned. If the second argument is an integer, each element of the vector is multiplied by the integer and the result is returned. The vectors passed to and returned from the function are passed as references.

1. Create a file called vector.pl. Add a minimal package Vector that contains the VecMult function. First, change into the Vector package and add a version number. Create the VecMult function. Use the main:: prefix to put the function into the Main package. It can then be called without prefixing a package name.

```
use strict;

package Vector;

$Vector::Version = "0.01";

sub main::VecMult {
    my($Vec,$Mult) = @_;
    my($Element,$Index,@OutVec);
```

2. Check to see if the second argument is a reference. If it is, the argument should be a vector; otherwise, it should be an integer. The ref function returns False if its argument is not a reference. If it is a reference, verify that both vectors are the same size and then multiply them. Multiply the vector by the integer if the second argument is not a reference. Return the resulting vector.

```
    @OutVec = ();
    if (ref($Mult)) {
        if (@$Vec == @$Mult) {
            for $Index (0..$#$Vec) {
                $OutVec[$Index] = $Vec->[$Index] * $Mult->[$Index];
            }
        } else {
            die "Bad multiplier passed to VecMult\n";
        }
    } else {
        foreach $Element (@$Vec) {
            push(@OutVec, $Element * $Mult);
        }
    }
    return @OutVec;
}
```

3. Return to the package Main and print the vector package's version number. Create some test code to test multiplying a vector by an integer. Then test multiplying the vector by another vector.

```
package main;

print "Package Vector version = $Vector::Version\n";

my(@Vec) = (1,2,3);
my($Multiplier) = 3;
my(@NewVec) = &VecMult(\@Vec,$Multiplier);
print "(@Vec) * $Multiplier = (@NewVec)\n";

my(@Multiplier) = (2,4,6);
@NewVec = &VecMult(\@Vec,\@Multiplier);
print "(@Vec) * (@Multiplier) = (@NewVec)\n";
```

4. The entire script follows.

```perl
use strict;

package Vector;

$Vector::Version = "0.01";

sub main::VecMult {
    my($Vec,$Mult) = @_;
    my($Element,$Index,@OutVec);

    @OutVec = ();
    if (ref($Mult)) {
        if (@$Vec == @$Mult) {
            for $Index (0..$#$Vec) {
                $OutVec[$Index] = $Vec->[$Index] * $Mult->[$Index];
            }
        } else {
            die "Bad multiplier passed to VecMult\n";
        }
    } else {
        foreach $Element (@$Vec) {
            push(@OutVec, $Element * $Mult);
        }
    }
    return @OutVec;
}

package main;

print "Package Vector version = $Vector::Version\n";

my(@Vec) = (1,2,3);
my($Multiplier) = 3;
my(@NewVec) = &VecMult(\@Vec,$Multiplier);
print "(@Vec) * $Multiplier = (@NewVec)\n";

my(@Multiplier) = (2,4,6);
@NewVec = &VecMult(\@Vec,\@Multiplier);
print "(@Vec) * (@Multiplier) = (@NewVec)\n";
```

A screen dump of the execution of the script can be seen in Figure 14-2.

5. Run the script. The output follows.

Output

```
Package Vector version = 0.01
(1 2 3) * 3 = (3 6 9)
(1 2 3) * (2 4 6) = (2 8 18)
```

End Output

```
> cat Vector.pl
use strict;

package Vector;

$Vector::Version = "0.01";

sub main::VecMult {
    my($Vec,$Mult) = @_;
    my($Element,$Index,@OutVec);

    @OutVec = ();
    if (ref($Mult)) {
        if (@$Vec == @$Mult) {
            for $Index (0..$#$Vec) {
                $OutVec[$Index] = $Vec->[$Index] * $Mult->[$Index];
            }
        } else {
            die "Bad multiplier passed to VecMult\n";
        }
    } else {
        foreach $Element (@$Vec) {
            push(@OutVec, $Element * $Mult);
        }
    }
    return @OutVec;
}

package main;

print "Package Vector version = $Vector::Version\n";

my(@Vec) = (1,2,3);
my($Multiplier) = 3;
my(@NewVec) = &VecMult(\@Vec,$Multiplier);
print "(@Vec) * $Multiplier = (@NewVec)\n";

my(@Multiplier) = (2,4,6);
@NewVec = &VecMult(\@Vec,\@Multiplier);
print "(@Vec) * (@Multiplier) = (@NewVec)\n";
> perl -w Vector.pl
Package Vector version = 0.01
(1 2 3) * 3 = (3 6 9)
(1 2 3) * (2 4 6) = (2 8 18)
>
```

Figure 14-2 Output of vector.pl

How It Works

Perl provides a way to partition name spaces. Use the package command to change between name spaces. All scripts start out in the Main package. Variables and subroutines can be accessed in other name spaces by prepending the package name.

Comments

If the value returned by the ref function is not False, the value will be a string that tells which kind of reference it is.

Perl 4 has packages, but not references. The symbol to use in Perl 4 to access other packages is the single quote, not the double colon. To create a Perl 4 script that provides similar functionality, type globs need to be used instead of references. See How-To 14.2 to see how to do this. Perl 4 also does not have the ref command. Two multiply functions need to be created: one that multiplies vectors and one that multiplies a vector by an integer.

```
package Vector;

$Vector'Version = "0.01";

sub main'VecMult {
    local(*Vec,*Mult) = @_;
    local($Element,$Index,@OutVec);

    @OutVec = ();
    if (@Vec == @Mult) {
        for $Index (0..$#Vec) {
            $OutVec[$Index] = $Vec[$Index] * $Mult[$Index];
        }
    } else {
        die "Bad multiplier passed to VecMult\n";
    }
    return @OutVec;
}

sub main'VecScale {
    local(*Vec,$Scale) = @_;
    local($Element,@OutVec);

    @OutVec = ();
    foreach $Element (@Vec) {
        push(@OutVec, $Element * $Scale);
    }
    return @OutVec;
}

package main;

print "Package Vector version = $Vector'Version\n";

@Vec = (1,2,3);
$Multiplier = 3;
@NewVec = &VecScale(*Vec,$Multiplier);
print "(@Vec) * $Multiplier = (@NewVec)\n";

@Multiplier = (2,4,6);
@NewVec = &VecMult(*Vec,*Multiplier);
print "(@Vec) * (@Multiplier) = (@NewVec)\n";
```

COMPLEXITY
INTERMEDIATE

14.5 How do I...
Create and use a library?

COMPATIBILITY: PERL 4   PERL 5   UNIX   DOS

Problem

I have a vector package that I would like to be able to use in multiple programs. Can I do this without copying the code into each program?

Technique

Perl provides the require command to include source from a file into a script. The argument to the require command is the file to be included.

```
require "veclib.pl";
```

After the require command, the script behaves as if the source in the required file were included directly in the program. Usually, the source in the file is part of a package. This separates the name space of the script from that of the required file. This is not a requirement. See How-To 14.4 for the use of packages.

A library in Perl is a file that contains reusable Perl code. It is usually imported into a script using require.

Steps

The package from How-To 14.4 is put into its own file. This creates a vector library. This library is a partial attempt at a vector library. It contains only a vector multiply function. The main script imports this library and makes two calls to the multiply function to verify that it is working.

1. Create a file called veclib.pl. This file should contain the package from How-To 14.4. Add a final line to the end of the file. This tells the require command that the file was successfully loaded. If False is returned, require will fail and so will the script.

```
use strict;

package Vector;

$Vector::Version = "0.01";

sub main::VecMult {
    my($Vec,$Mult) = @_;
    my($Element,$Index,@OutVec);

    @OutVec = ();
    if (ref($Mult)) {
        if (@$Vec == @$Mult) {
```

```
                    for $Index (0..$#$Vec) {
                        $OutVec[$Index] = $Vec->[$Index] * $Mult->[$Index];
                    }
                } else {
                    die "Bad multiplier passed to VecMult\n";
                }
            } else {
                foreach $Element (@$Vec) {
                    push(@OutVec, $Element * $Mult);
                }
            }
            return @OutVec;
}

1;
```

2. Create a file called uselib.pl. Add lines to require the library and execute the multiply function. Perl contains an @INC array to hold the list of directories searched to look for the library. You can modify the directory list by using the use lib command. If the library is not in one of the "normal" places, add the correct directory to the array using this method:

```
use strict;

use lib ("/path/to/local/libs");

require "veclib.pl";

print "Package Vector version = $Vector::Version\n";

my(@Vec) = (1,2,3);
my($Multiplier) = 3;
my(@NewVec) = &VecMult(\@Vec,$Multiplier);
print "(@Vec) * $Multiplier = (@NewVec)\n";

my(@Multiplier) = (2,4,6);
@NewVec = &VecMult(\@Vec,\@Multiplier);
print "(@Vec) * (@Multiplier) = (@NewVec)\n";
```

3. Run the script. The output of the script follows.

Output

```
Package Vector version = 0.01
(1 2 3) * 3 = (3 6 9)
(1 2 3) * (2 4 6) = (2 8 18)
```

End Output

How It Works

A library in Perl is just a file that can be loaded into a script. By convention, the file contains routines and variables inside a package. The require command is used to bring the library into a script and to keep track of what has been loaded. If another attempt is made to require the file, it will be ignored because the code has already been loaded.

Comments

The "normal" places that Perl looks for library commands are system-dependent. These can be easily determined by writing a short script to list them.

```
print "@INC\n";
```

The library can be made to work under Perl 4 by making the same changes as in How-To 14.4.

```
package Vector;

$Vector'Version = "0.01";

sub main'VecMult {
    local(*Vec,*Mult) = @_;
    local($Element,$Index,@OutVec);

    @OutVec = ();
    if (@Vec == @Mult) {
        for $Index (0..$#Vec) {
            $OutVec[$Index] = $Vec[$Index] * $Mult[$Index];
        }
    } else {
        die "Bad multiplier passed to VecMult\n";
    }
    return @OutVec;
}

sub main'VecScale {
    local(*Vec,$Scale) = @_;
    local($Element,@OutVec);

    @OutVec = ();
    foreach $Element (@Vec) {
        push(@OutVec, $Element * $Scale);
    }
    return @OutVec;
}

1;
```

The script needs the same changes as in How-To 14.4 as well. In addition, modify the @INC array by pushing a new directory onto it.

```
push (@INC,"/path/to/local/libs");

require "veclib.pl4";

print "Package Vector version = $Vector'Version\n";

@Vec = (1,2,3);
$Multiplier = 3;
@NewVec = &VecScale(*Vec,$Multiplier);
```

```
print "(@Vec) * $Multiplier = (@NewVec)\n";

@Multiplier = (2,4,6);
@NewVec = &VecMult(*Vec,*Multiplier);
print "(@Vec) * (@Multiplier) = (@NewVec)\n";
```

COMPLEXITY
ADVANCED

14.6 How do I...
Create and use a module?

COMPATIBILITY: `PERL 5` `UNIX` `DOS`

Problem

I have been using libraries to encapsulate my reusable packages. Perl 5 provides modules. These seem to provide more control over importing variables and functions into the main package. How do I turn a library into a module?

Technique

Perl 5 modules are an extension of libraries. They allow a library and the script importing it to decide which variables and subroutines are to be imported into the script's name space. With libraries, the library decides what is imported into the calling script's name space. Libraries are loaded into a script using the require command. Modules are imported using the use command.

```
use Vector;
```

The use command does a require of a file, with the same name as the module being imported with a .pm extension. In the above case, it does a

```
require "Vector.pm";
```

It then calls the import method of the module. The import method is responsible for importing the correct variables and functions into the current package. The import method is usually supplied by the Exporter module. This module is required into the module and then the import method is inherited by the module. See Chapter 23 for information on inheritance. In this case, it just means that the import method in the Exporter module is callable by the module being defined.

Steps

The library from How-To 14.5 is turned into a module. This creates a vector module. This module is a partial attempt at a true vector module. It contains only a vector multiply function. The main script imports this module and makes two calls to the multiply function to verify that it is working.

1. Create a file called Vector.pm. This contains the library from How-To 14.5, modified to be a module. Add the require of the Exporter module. Inherit the Exporter module to make its import function available. The qw() syntax is a fancy way of creating a list of singly quoted words. Each word is separated by white space. Create an EXPORT array. This array contains the variables and functions that normally would go into the calling script's name space. It is used by the Exporter module. Change the subroutine name to prevent it from being put into the Main package.

```perl
use strict;

package Vector;
require Exporter;

@Vector::ISA = qw(Exporter);
@Vector::EXPORT = qw(VecMult);

$Vector::Version = "0.01";

sub VecMult {
    my($Vec,$Mult) = @_;
    my($Element,$Index,@OutVec);

    @OutVec = ();
    if (ref($Mult)) {
        if (@$Vec == @$Mult) {
            for $Index (0..$#$Vec) {
                $OutVec[$Index] = $Vec->[$Index] * $Mult->[$Index];
            }
        } else {
            die "Bad multiplier passed to VecMult\n";
        }
    } else {
        foreach $Element (@$Vec) {
            push(@OutVec, $Element * $Mult);
        }
    }
    return @OutVec;
}

1;
```

2. Create a file called mod.pl. Add the main script from How-To 14.5, with the require changed to use. This script exercises the vector module.

```perl
use strict;

use lib ("/path/to/local/libs");

use Vector;

print "Package Vector version = $Vector::Version\n";

my(@Vec) = (1,2,3);
my($Multiplier) = 3;
my(@NewVec) = &VecMult(\@Vec,$Multiplier);
print "(@Vec) * $Multiplier = (@NewVec)\n";
```

```
my(@Multiplier) = (2,4,6);
@NewVec = &VecMult(\@Vec,\@Multiplier);
print "(@Vec) * (@Multiplier) = (@NewVec)\n";
```

3. Run the script. The output follows.

Output

```
Package Vector version = 0.01
(1 2 3) * 3 = (3 6 9)
(1 2 3) * (2 4 6) = (2 8 18)
```

End Output

How It Works

Perl provides the use command to import modules into a script. This allows the importing script to specify what variables and functions are to be imported into the current name space. Most of the added functionality is provided by the Exporter module. Its import function performs the name space manipulation. It uses two arrays to decide what to import. The EXPORT array lists the variables and subroutines to be imported into the current name space if no list of imports is passed to the import method in the use command. The EXPORT_OK array specifies additional functions and variables that can be imported if the use command lists them. If a name is not in either array, it cannot be imported.

Comments

With libraries, functions are imported into the main package. With modules, functions are imported into the calling name space. It is a good idea to try to minimize the number of entries in the EXPORT array. This will prevent the pollution of the caller's name space.

Be careful that you use the use command on modules and not the require command. If require is used, the import method will not be called.

It is possible to make the functions in a module behave as if they were built-in commands. In general, it appears that way. However, when the die or warn commands are called, the line number from the module is reported in the message printed. This can be modified to print the line number of the calling routine. The Carp module supplies this functionality. This module supplies the carp, croak, and confess functions. carp and croak are used to replace the warn and die commands. confess is just like croak, but it also prints a stack backtrace. To see how to use this, import the Carp module and change the die call to a croak call.

The import of the Carp module uses the ability of scripts to specify to the module how the name space is to be modified. By passing a list to Carp, the only changes to the name space are the functions or variables supplied in the list. In this case, only the croak function is imported into the current name space. Normally, Carp exports croak, carp, and confess.

```perl
use strict;

package Vector2;
require Exporter;
use Carp qw(croak);

@Vector::ISA = qw(Exporter);
@Vector::EXPORT = qw(VecMult);

$Vector::Version = "0.01";

sub VecMult {
    my($Vec,$Mult) = @_;
    my($Element,$Index,@OutVec);

    @OutVec = ();
    if (ref($Mult)) {
        if (@$Vec == @$Mult) {
            for $Index (0..$#$Vec) {
                $OutVec[$Index] = $Vec->[$Index] * $Mult->[$Index];
            }
        } else {
            croak "Bad multiplier passed to VecMult\n";
        }
    } else {
        foreach $Element (@$Vec) {
            push(@OutVec, $Element * $Mult);
        }
    }
    return @OutVec;
}

1;
```

COMPLEXITY
INTERMEDIATE

14.7   How do I...
Create a POD file?

COMPATIBILITY: PERL 5   UNIX

Problem

I have heard of POD files, and I have heard that you can create manual pages and
HTML files from them. How do I create and translate POD files?

Technique

A plain old documentation (POD) file is nothing more than a basic text file with keywords placed in it for an interpreter to translate. In fact, a basic flat ASCII text file
could be used and translated into a HTML script or a manual page; it just would not
have any special effects.

Steps

1. Create a new file named example.pod and type the following into it.

```
=head1 NAME

Chapter 14 - Functions, Libraries, Packages, and Modules

=head1 DESCRIPTION

POD Files
```

This chapter covers information about how Perl packages programs and modules within Perl itself. This specific How-To demonstrates one of the newest elements, POD files. POD files are basic text files that have special formatting information in them so a basic POD translator can be written. Currently there are only three POD translators available. They are

```
=over 5

=item HTML

=item Standard Manual Pages

=item Tex Formatted Files

=back

=head2 HTML
```

The POD to HTML converter is aptly named pod2html. This perl script takes the POD file information based in the POD file and translates it to HTML code.

```
=head2 Standard Manual Pages
```

The POD to manual pages converter is named pod2man. This script creates standard nroff type files, which are converted into human readable format via nroff.

```
=head2 Tex Formatted Files
```

The POD to Tex formatter is named pod2latex. This creates LaTex formatted documents.

One can see the advantage that POD files create. A person would only need to know how to create a simple POD file and they would have the capability to create many different types of text formatted documents.

Aside from basic simplicity, POD files have some powerful abilities as well. Different text types can be specified directly within the POD files. For example, if I wanted I<italics>, then all I would do is add in the simple POD commands to tell the converted that the given text is to be in I<italics>. I can do the same for B<bold>.

Of course, there are limitations. For instance, italics for a manual page actually come out as an underline, because manual pages are ASCII based. HTML

continued on next page

continued from previous page

pages on the other hand would display the formats more true to nature.

I can also demonstrate straight text by enclosing them in a command that allows literal code to be displayed. This allows me to add in special characters like C<$%!*&> or anything else.

Links can also be established in the POD file. For example, if I wanted to create a link to another section in this POD file, like L<HTML>, then all I have to do is add it with the link command. There are a few types of links that create textual links to other files.

=head1 Summary

The following list outlines the possible commands in a POD file and what they do.

```
   B<text>          Bolds the embodied text.
   C<text>          Literal text.
   I<text>          Italicize the embodied text.
```

Figure 14-3 example.html

```
S<text>              Maintains the embodied text containing non-breaking spaces.
L<name>              Links to a manual page.
L<name/item>         References an item in another manual page.
L<name/section>      References a section in another manual page.
L<"sec">             References a section in this manual page.
F<filename>          Lists the filename.
Z<>                  A zero width character.
```

2. Create a HTML markup file by running the script pod2html.

```
% pod2html example.pod
```

```
Scanning pods...
Creating example.html from example.pod
```

3. Verify that the HTML script is accurate by starting a Web browser and loading the file example.html. Figure 14-3 demonstrates the example.html file, loaded into Netscape.

4. Create a manual page by running the script pod2man.

```
% pod2man example.pod > example.man
```

5. Create a LaTex document by running the script pod2latex.

```
% pod2latex example.pod
```

A LaTex document named example.tex is created from running this script.

How It Works

The POD files have a number of commands that dictate how the interpreter will treat the text. A POD file translator interprets the POD file and creates another text file format. POD files were introduced to create a common base for some of the different types of file text formats that currently exist. The currently supported formats include HTML, LaTex, and nroff.

Currently, there are three types of internal paragraphs for POD files: verbatim paragraphs, command paragraphs, and blocks of text. Within the blocks of text, there can be formatting commands.

One of the specific formats within a POD file is called a *verbatim paragraph*. A verbatim paragraph is defined by the fact that it is indented with some form of white space. A verbatim paragraph is used when text within the POD file needs to be untouched from the format interpreter.

A *command paragraph* is a paragraph that is given a specific type of display by the command identifier. There are five current command identifiers; each has a specific purpose and display type. Listing the different display types is difficult because the actual output of the display varies according to the level of software the user actually has. Table 14-1 lists all the current paragraph commands and what they do.

COMMAND	PURPOSE
=head1 text	The text that follows this command is labeled as major text heading.
=head2 text	The text that follows this command is labeled as the subheading.
=item text	The text that follows this command is considered part of a list.
=over N	Performs an indent by moving the text over N characters.
=back	Restores the indent to the default value.

Table 14-1 POD file paragraph commands

Commands can be embedded into the POD file to bold text, italicize text, and create links to other files or links to the current file. Because all the intelligence is in the POD file translator, do not be surprised if the number of commands expands. Table 14-2 lists all the current format commands and their purposes.

COMMAND	PURPOSE
B<text>	Bolds the embodied text.
C<text>	Literal text.
I<text>	Italicizes the embodied text.
S<text>	Maintains the embodied text containing nonbreaking spaces.
L<name>	Links to a manual page.
L<name/item>	References an item in another manual page.
L<name/section>	References a section in another manual page.
L<"sec">	References a section in this manual page.
F<filename>	Lists the filename.
Z<>	A zero-width character.

Table 14-2 POD file format commands

Comments

POD files are not too complex. They provide a simple interface to create multiple file formats from a single text file. Because POD files are simple, do not expect too much from them.

CHAPTER 15

HANDLING ASYNCHRONOUS EVENTS

HANDLING ASYNCHRONOUS EVENTS

How do I...

15.1   Handle signals in Perl?

15.2   Use signals to communicate with a running process?

15.3   Have a process wait for an event?

15.4   Write a time-out?

15.5   Schedule time-based events?

15.6   Handle exceptions gracefully?

In most of your Perl programs, you will never use asynchronous processing methods. A program is executed sequentially, one statement before the next. Yet many programs are more easily described as asynchronous processes. In the case of applications that use graphic interfaces, it is impossible to predict the sequence of button presses and menu-selection events. The interface must be ready to react asynchronously to any event the user throws at it, at any time, as illustrated in Figure 15-1.

This chapter looks at several models of Perl 5 asynchronous processing from designing processes that react to signals such as the CTRL-C interrupt from your keyboard, to call-back-based programming, to time-based events, to handling exceptions and unpredictable failures.

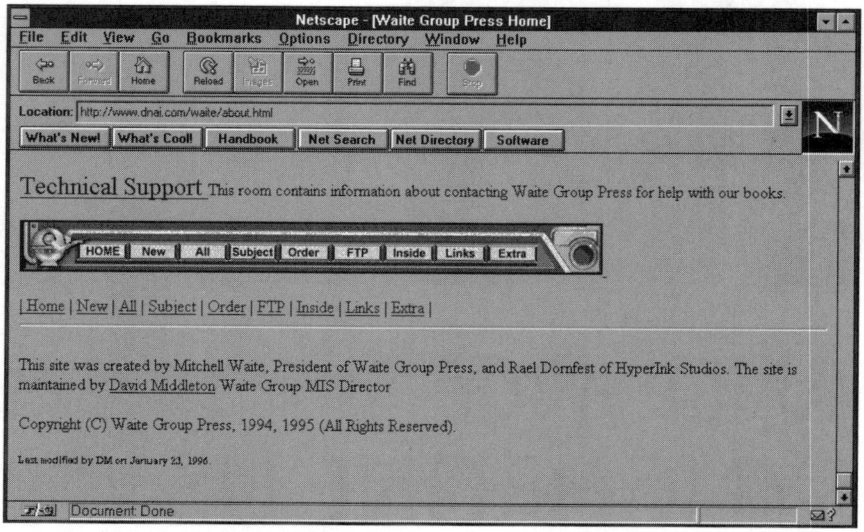

Figure 15-1 Graphic interfaces rely upon asynchronous processing techniques

Because the implementation of asynchronous behavior requires an operating system capable of multitasking, most of the examples in this chapter are incompatible with primitive single-process systems like DOS. As Windows 95 Perl implementations mature, you should be able to implement the ideas of this chapter under that operating system.

15.1   Handle Signals in Perl

Signals are operating-system interrupts that can be passed to a running process. This How-To will describe the basic model of handling signals in Perl.

15.2   Use Signals to Communicate with a Running Process

A process is an executing instance of a program. How can you communicate with it once it is up and running? The How-To will show an application of asynchronous processing that forces a process to issue a status report whenever it receives an operating-system signal.

15.3   Have a Process Wait for an Event

This How-To will discuss two methods of having a process idle while it waits for a signal. The second method also will show how to pause a process for periods of less than a second.

15.4   Write a Time-Out

You may have a login script or AUTOEXEC batch file that offers users a choice of actions whenever they begin a session on a computer. This is fine if the user always sits patiently in front of the terminal while the session initializes. Sometimes, however, the user may not want to wait around to answer questions. This section will show you how to write a program that waits for a reply. If the reply doesn't come within a few seconds, it proceeds with the processing using a default value. The value returned by the program can be used to determine which set of login options to execute.

15.5   Schedule Time-Based Events

This How-To will present a useful Perl package for scheduling events in your programs.

15.6   Handle Exceptions Gracefully

Languages such as Ada and C++ have constructs for handling exceptional events. Perl also has an exception-handling mechanism. The package exception.pl provides a neat method of preventing your program from blowing up when something unpredictable happens. This section will illustrate how to use it.

COMPLEXITY
INTERMEDIATE

15.1   How do I...
Handle signals in Perl?

COMPATIBILITY: UNIX

Problem

I want to add a facility to my program with which I can trap signals, such as the interrupt signal generated when the user presses CTRL-C on the keyboard. The program can then perform special housekeeping processing rather than simply terminating. How can I do this with Perl?

Technique

Perl provides an elegant method of defining handlers for signals. The associative array %SIG maps signal names to subroutines. If the program receives a mapped signal, then normal processing is interrupted and control jumps to the appropriate subroutine. This How-To defines a signal handler that is called when the program receives a keyboard interrupt.

Steps

1. Create a new file named keybsig.pl. Enter the following code and make the file executable.

```
#!/usr/local/bin/perl -w

use Config;
```

continued on next page

continued from previous page

```perl
sub sig_int_h {
    my($signal) = @_;
    $old_sig = $SIG{$signal};
        $SIG{$signal} = 'IGNORE';
    print "Caught $signal signal. Exit? [n]";
        $_ = <STDIN>;
    if(/[yY]/) {
            print "Terminating ...\n";
            exit(1);
    }
        $SIG{$signal} = $old_sig;
    return;
}


die "SIGINT not supported"
    unless $Config{'sig_name'} =~ /INT/;
warn "SIGQUIT not supported"
    unless $Config{'sig_name'} =~ /QUIT/;
$SIG{'INT'} = \&sig_int_h;
$SIG{'QUIT'} = 'IGNORE';
print "Press <Control-C> to interrupt\n";
for(;;){
    sleep 1;
}
```

2. Run the program. When you see the following prompt

Output

```
keybsig.pl
Press <Control-C> to interrupt
```

End Output

press the interrupt key on your keyboard (the interrupt is usually mapped
to CTRL-C; it might differ on some systems). The program asks if you want
to quit. Type yes.

Output

```
^CCaught INT signal. Exit? [n]y
Terminating...
```

End Output

Rerun the program, type the interrupt key, and then answer no. The program continues running.

3. If you are using UNIX, run the program and send a SIGQUIT from the keyboard. (The output from the command stty -a will show you which key is
mapped to SIGQUIT on your system. It is usually CTRL-\.) The default
action of a program is to dump a memory image to disk and terminate
when it receives a quit signal. As expected, the present program doesn't
respond to the signal.

How It Works

The mechanism for defining a nondefault signal handler should be clear from the program. Define a subroutine for the signal and store its address in the %SIG array as the value associated with the name of the signal. You can take the address of a subroutine using the \ operator.

```
$SIG{'INT'} = \&sig_int_h;
```

Signal names and the range of signals available differ from system to system. To find out which signals are defined on your system, load the module Config.pm with the following statement.

```
use Config;
```

You can determine which signals are supported by examining the string %Config{'sig_name'}, which contains the names of the effective signals on your system.

Each signal has a default action associated with it. You override this default action when you assign a subroutine address to the %SIG array. To restore the default action, use the special Perl value DEFAULT. This line of code restores the default action for the interrupt signal (usually to terminate the program).

```
$SIG{'INT'} = 'DEFAULT';
```

If you do not want your program to respond to certain signals, assign the special value IGNORE to the signal's entry in %SIG. This is how keybsig.pl ignores the quit signal.

Notice that the first line of code in the subroutine sig_int_h ignores further instances of the int signal and restores the status quo before it returns. This is to prevent the interrupt handler itself from being interrupted on operating systems without reliable signals. Figure 15-2 shows what happens when signal processing interrupts execution flow.

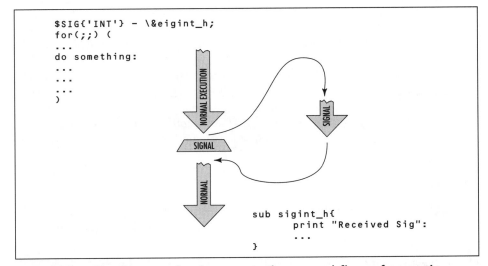

Figure 15-2 Signal processing interrupts the normal flow of execution

Comments

Signals that are ignored by a parent process are also ignored by a child process. Child processes are created when a program calls fork or when the program creates a process filehandle in an open call. Process creation techniques are covered in Chapter 12.

COMPLEXITY
INTERMEDIATE

15.2 How do I...
Use signals to communicate with a running process?

COMPATIBILITY: UNIX

Problem

I need a lightweight method of communicating with a running process so that I can notify it of certain events or modify its behavior while it executes. For example, I want to notify a daemon process that its configuration file has been modified and that it should reload it.

Technique

There are many ways of communicating with a running process. Most require fairly sophisticated programming and may involve intricate operating-system facilities such as sockets or semaphores. The simplest form of interprocess communication, the humble signal, often is enough to implement facilities of the kind contemplated here.

Some processes are designed to run as daemons. The difficulty in communicating with a daemon process is that it has broken its links with any controlling terminal and has closed all the standard filehandles that were open when the process was first launched. The daemon may perform services for clients, but because it lacks a terminal, it cannot communicate directly with a human agent. However, you can still communicate with the process by sending it signals.

This How-To implements a signal-based notification facility for running processes and explores an interesting technique for reporting a process status through the command line vector.

Steps

1. Enter the following code (or use example sigcom.pl supplied with the CD). This code implements a process that will run as a background task forever, using as little CPU as possible.

```
#!/usr/local/bin/perl -w
# sigcom.pl use signals to communicate with a process
#
```

```
use Config;

sub report {
    open(STATS, "netstat -rn |") || die "Cannot run netstat, $!\n";
    print "Net \t Use\n";
    while(<STATS>) {
      ($net,$_,$_,$_,$use,$_) = split;
      print "$net \t $use\n" if $use ;
    }
    close(STATS);
}

die "SIGHUP not supported"
        unless $Config{'sig_name'} =~ /HUP/;
$SIG{'HUP'} = \&report;

for(;;) {
  sleep(60);
}
```

 Make the file executable and run the script in the background like this:

sigcom.pl &
[1] 17812

> The ampersand character tells the shell to run the program in background mode so you are free to type new commands at the terminal while the program continues to execute. Here you are using the C shell. The numbers the shell prints after starting the script indicate the current job number—1 in this case—and the process ID of the Perl script—17812.

3. Now send a signal to the program. Most UNIX systems support a SIGHUP, hang-up signal. You can generate the signal with a kill command.

kill -HUP 17812

> The program responds by printing a report on the terminal. The report details each network the computer can access and the number of packets it has transmitted on that network. On our system, the report looks like this. You will probably see fewer networks listed on your machine.

─| Output |───

Net	Use
199.93.227.200	55436
127.0.0.1	839
199.93.227.2	94
136.0.0.0	9742
198.114.248.0	7
194.32.105.0	184
193.32.233.0	167
190.1.243.0	10162
194.55.42.0	11084
199.93.226.0	2286273
132.0.0.0	213

continued on next page

continued from previous page

199.93.228.0	129300
192.83.165.0	65153
199.93.229.0	487825
193.32.166.0	48000
199.93.230.0	17558
193.32.167.0	17514

End Output

 4. Because the process will run forever, you should now stop it. Terminate the process by typing the following command

```
kill 17812
```

where 17812 is the process number from step 2.

How It Works

The main program does three things. It defines a routine report and installs it as a signal-handler routine for the signal SIGHUP by assigning its address to the array element $SIG{'HUP'}. Then the process goes into a never-ending *for* loop, sleeping for 60 seconds during each iteration. The process sleeps in this way so as to consume as few processor resources as possible.

When the SIGHUP is received by the slumbering process, the subroutine designated in the %SIG array is activated as a handler for that signal report. The subroutine simply reports a condensed version of the output from the UNIX netstat command. If you don't have a netstat command on your system, you can redefine report to print out a text message or other system information.

Comments

Notice that in a strictly sequential reading of the program, the process is still executing the nonterminated *for* loop. The signal handler causes control to jump to the report subroutine in a manner that is asynchronous with the rest of the program statements. This style of programming is often called *call-back* or *event-based programming*.

Imagine that you are waiting for a visitor to arrive at your place of work. If the entrance to the building is out of sight, then you have a choice. Every few minutes you can wander down to the entrance hall and personally check to see if the visitor has arrived, or you can arrange with the receptionist to telephone when the visitor comes into the building. The second option is normally preferable because you don't have to waste your time walking back and forth. You simply arrange to be informed when the event occurs. When the event occurs, you can take the actions necessary. In the meantime, you can carry on with something else.

This situation is analogous to call-back programming. When you install the signal-handler report, you are arranging that the operating system will inform you when a certain event, represented by the signal, occurs. You have in effect asked the operating system to call back whenever that happens.

COMPLEXITY
INTERMEDIATE

15.3 How do I...
Have a process wait for an event?

COMPATIBILITY: UNIX

Problem

How can I have my Perl process wait for an event to occur without using significant system resources?

Technique

We discussed call-back techniques in How-To 15.2. A common approach to call-back processing is to have the process enter a *main* loop waiting for an event. When the event occurs, respond to it and then go back to waiting. This How-To describes how to implement that *main* loop.

The key issue is that if you write a *polling* loop that is computationally active, then you use resources to no effect. A loop like that shown below consumes as much CPU time as your machine has available.

```
MAIN_LOOP: for(;;) { 1; } # waste CPU resources
```

You need to implement a *waiting* loop, in which the process is blocked and computationally inactive until the event occurs. You can do this in two ways, using the Perl calls sleep and select.

Steps

1. To have a process sleep for some seconds, use the simple sleep command. To see its effect, enter the following command.

```
perl -e 'sleep(5)'
```

The command pauses for 5 seconds and then terminates. No significant CPU resources are consumed. Kill the program by pressing the interrupt key.

2. To implement a *main* loop using sleep, create a file called pause1.pl, enter the following code, and execute it. If you have a performance monitor program for your system, run it and confirm that pause1.pl uses no significant CPU time. Kill the program by pressing the interrupt key.

```
#!/usr/local/bin/perl -w
# pause indefinitely
for(;;) {
    sleep(10);
}
```

3. An alternative method of pausing for some period of time is to use a select call. Create a file named pause2.pl, enter the following code, and execute it.

```
#!/usr/local/bin/perl -w
for(;;) {
    select(undef, undef, undef, 10);
}
```

Check the CPU usage of your system while the program is running. Then kill pause2.pl by pressing the interrupt key.

How It Works

The sleep call instructs the operating system not to schedule the process for further execution until at least the specified number of seconds have elapsed. The process therefore lies dormant for that number of seconds.

The select call is usually used to detect if a set of filehandles is available for reading or writing. The first three arguments usually specify lists of filehandles. The last argument to select is a time-out value in seconds. The select call checks the filehandles for a period of time not less than that specified. It terminates when the time-out expires. Because you are not interested in monitoring filehandles, supply undef as an argument for the first three parameters. In this case, select behaves as a simple time-out function.

Comments

An interesting use of the select call time-out is to pause with a finer granularity than sleep allows. The function sleep can accept only integer arguments. The shortest period it can pause is consequently 1 second. The select function's time-out argument is a floating-point number, so pauses of less than a second are possible.

This statement causes a Perl script to pause for 100 milliseconds:

```
select(undef,undef,undef, 0.1);
```

Don't confuse this four-argument select function with the similarly named single-argument select that sets and returns the current filehandle. They are unrelated.

COMPLEXITY
INTERMEDIATE

15.4 How do I ...
Write a time-out?

COMPATIBILITY: UNIX

Problem

How can I prevent a process from waiting forever for an event? I want to have the process wait a certain number of seconds and then, if the event hasn't occurred, the process should return to other processing.

Technique

Many login scripts or AUTOEXEC.BAT files are designed to be interactive. When someone logs in at the console of a workstation, the login script may ask the person to select which of several alternative setups he or she wants to execute. This can become boring for the user, especially if he or she logs in each day. A better solution is to prompt the user for a selection, wait a few seconds, and then, if there is no response, select a default.

Later versions of DOS are supplied with a command that can do this. No such command is available on UNIX, but it is not hard to write one. This How-To demonstrates a method of implementing this facility in Perl using alarm signals.

Steps

1. Enter the following code into a file called ask.pl (or use example ask.pl from the CD).

```perl
#!/usr/local/bin/perl -w
# ask.pl, interactive prompt
#
$REPLY = "No\n";
use Getopt::Long ;

sub alarm_h {
    alarm(0);
    terminate();
}

sub terminate {
    print $REPLY;
    exit 0;
}

MAIN: {
    $opt_prompt = "";
    Getopt::Long::GetOptions("prompt=s","time=i") ||
        die "Usage:$0 -prompt <string> -time <seconds>\n";
    $SIG{'ALRM'} = \&alarm_h;
    alarm($opt_time ? $opt_time : 1);
    print STDERR "$opt_prompt ";
    $REPLY = <STDIN>;
    terminate();
}
```

2. Run the program like this:

```
ask.pl -p "Yes No Maybe?" -t 5
```

When the prompt "Yes No Maybe?" appears, reply by typing Maybe. The program responds by echoing your reply back to the terminal.

Output

```
Yes No Maybe? Maybe
Maybe
```

End Output

3. Now run the program again like this:
```
ask.pl -p "Yes No Maybe?" -t 5
```

— Output ————————————————————————————————————

Yes No Maybe?

End Output ————————————————————————————————————

This time, don't type a reply. Wait for 5 seconds, the time-out set by the -t option. The program responds:
```
ask.pl -p "Yes No Maybe?" -t 5
```

— Output ————————————————————————————————————

Yes No Maybe?
No

End Output ————————————————————————————————————

The default response is to print No to the terminal.

How It Works

The script first processes its command line using the Perl module Getopt::Long. (Take a look at Chapter 2 if you are unfamiliar with this form of command line processing; Getopt is discussed there.) Then it prints out the supplied prompt and waits for the user to type something. When the user presses the ENTER key, the program echoes the user's typed response back to stdout.

That's not all. Just before the program prints the prompt, it sets up a signal-handler routine, alarm_h, to respond to the UNIX timer-event signal SIGALRM. Then it sets its own alarm clock with a call to the alarm function.

The alarm function arranges for the operating system to send a process to a SIGALRM in some number of seconds. To receive a SIGALRM in, say, 10 seconds, the program must call alarm(10). The number supplied as an argument to alarm tells the operating system to deliver a SIGALRM to the calling process in that number of seconds. The operating system may be busy when the precise time arrives, so the timing cannot be guaranteed. The signal may be delayed for a moment or two longer than the period specified.

The routine alarm_h is invoked whenever the process receives the alarm signal. alarm_h simply returns a default reply of No and terminates the program.

This script has two outcomes: Either the user enters input in the specified time, in which case the program echoes the response and exits or, after waiting for a few seconds, the time-out expires and the program prints a default response to STDOUT.

Comments

Don't confuse the behavior of the function alarm with the function sleep. sleep puts the process into a dormant state. It arranges for the process to pause inactively for a specified period of time, during which no further instructions are executed. The alarm function does not pause the process. The alarm call is executed and control immediately returns to the next statement in the program. The asynchronous signal SIGALRM can be delivered many seconds later.

You might want to use the program within a C-shell login script like this:

```csh
#!/bin/csh
set ans=`ask.pl -p "Run window system O)penwin M)otif ?" -t 4`
echo $ans
if ( $ans == "O") then
  echo "run Openwindows - OK."
else if ( $ans == "M" ) then
  echo "run Motif - OK."
else
  echo "No response - using character terminal"
endif
```

COMPLEXITY
INTERMEDIATE

15.5 How do I...
Schedule time-based events?

COMPATIBILITY: UNIX

Problem

My program needs to schedule a number of tasks on a timed basis. I want to have the program run task A every X seconds and task B every Y seconds. I also want to be able to schedule nonrepeating tasks such as time-outs while waiting for input. How can I do this without complicating my program?

Technique

To solve this problem, write a Perl package to implement a scheduler module. Then centralize all the timer handling in the program within this package. The package is called TEvent.

Whenever the main program needs to perform a task on a timed basis, all it has to do is call the TEvent::RegisterActive subroutine with a request to perform tasks on a timed basis. Each request specifies three pieces of information:

● An interval of time to wait before executing the task

● The address of a Perl call-back subroutine that will carry out the task

● Whether the task will be repeated or happen only once

A periodic task is one that should be automatically rescheduled after each execution. A nonrepeating task is executed only once.

Once the timed event is registered, all the logic for handling the SIGALRM signals is hidden away from the main program.

Steps

1. Enter the following code or use the example TEvent.pm from the CD. This code implements the TEvent package.

```perl
#!/usr/local/bin/perl -w
# Timer Multiplex module;
# Dispatches tasks on a timed event basis

package TEvent;

require Exporter;
@ISA = 'Exporter';
@EXPORT = qw(Register,
             RegisterActive,
             Activate,
             Deactivate,
          DEBUG
            );

sub SigAlarmHandler {
    my($event);
    $TICKS++;
    for $event (@TEventList){
        print STDERR "TEvent: Checking $event->{Callback}\n" if $DEBUG;
        next unless $event->{Status};
        next unless ($TICKS % $event->{Schedule} == 0);
        $event->{Status} = 0 unless $event->{Repeat};
        $cb = $event->{Callback};
        print STDERR "TEvent: Firing $event->{Callback}\n" if $DEBUG;
        eval {&$cb};
    }
    alarm($ALARM_PERIOD);
    print STDERR "TEvent: Ticks = $TICKS\n" if $DEBUG;
    return;
}

sub RegisterEvent {
    my($cb, $schedule, $repeat) = @_;
    my($event);
    $event = {
    Callback => $cb,
    Schedule => $schedule,
    Repeat   => $repeat,
    Status   => 0
    };
    push(@TEventList, $event);
    print STDERR "TEvent: EventList added $event->{Callback}\n" if $DEBUG;
    return $event;
}

sub Register {
    my($cb, $schedule, $repeat) = @_;
    my($tag);
    $tag = RegisterEvent($cb, $schedule, $repeat);
    return $tag;
}
```

```perl
sub RegisterActive {
    my($cb, $schedule, $repeat) = @_;
    my($tag);
    $tag = RegisterEvent($cb, $schedule, $repeat);
    &Activate($tag);
    return $tag;
}

sub Activate {
    my($event) = @_;
    if (ref($event) eq "HASH") {
        $event->{Status} = 1;
    }else{
        warn "TEvent: Attempted activation unregistered event\n";
    }
}

sub Deactivate {
    my($event) = @_;
    if (ref($event) eq "HASH"){
        $event->{Status} = 0;
    }else{
        warn "TEvent: Attempted deactivation unregistered event\n";
    }
}

BEGIN {
    $TICKS = 0;
    $SIG{'ALRM'} = \&SigAlarmHandler;
    $ALARM_PERIOD = 1;
    alarm $ALARM_PERIOD;
}

END {
    alarm 0;
}

1;
```

2. Create a file pevent.pl to test the TEvent package.

```perl
#!/usr/local/bin/perl
# Demonstrate Tevent.pm module
#
use TEvent;

sub cb_1 { print "This is cb_1\n" }

sub cb_2 { print "This is cb_2\n" }

MAIN:
TEvent::RegisterActive(\&cb_1, 7, 1);
TEvent::RegisterActive(\&cb_2, 11, 1);
for(;;) {
  $_ = <STDIN>;
}
```

The main program declares two call-back routines and registers two timed events. Event one calls back subroutine cb_1 every 7 seconds; event two calls back subroutine cb_2 every 11 seconds. Once these events are registered, the main program can carry on with other activities. The TEvent module organizes the interruption of the main program whenever a scheduled event becomes due. In this case, the main program is busy reading from the STDIN filehandle.

3. Run the program in this way:

```
pevent.pl
```

Output

```
This is cb_1
This is cb_2
This is cb_1
This is cb_1
This is cb_2
This is cb_1
```

End Output

4. Press the interrupt key to terminate the program.

How It Works

The package TEvent has two tasks: to manage a list of events and to monitor the passing of time.

We represent a scheduled event with a data structure created by the subroutine RegisterActive. This routine creates an anonymous hash with four fields. Think of the anonymous hash as similar to a C struct or Pascal record type: a set of named fields with associated values. The field named Callback contains the name of a call-back routine associated with the event. Schedule contains an integer representing the periodicity of the event—the interval before the event occurs. Repeat is a True-False value. True indicates that the event is to be scheduled on a periodic basis. The Status field is provided to mark nonrepeating events as expired so you can activate and deactivate periodic events without reregistering them.

```
{
  Callback => $cb,
  Schedule => $schedule,
  Repeat => $repeat,
  Status => 0
};
```

The routines Activate and Deactivate can be used to set the status of a task. A convenience function, Register, is provided for events that are to be registered but marked inactive. The program can activate them at some subsequent time.

Once the event data is created, RegisterActive places it in a list of events named TEventList.

```
push(@TEventList, $event);
```

Time management is achieved by setting up a simple clock. The clock ticks every second; on tick, the module checks to see if any event is due. If it is, TEvent calls the routine associated with the event. The clock is implemented by TEvent registering its own SIGALRM call-back routine, SigAlarmHandler, and arranging to receive a steady tick of SIGALRM signals at the rate of one per second.

```
BEGIN {
    $TICKS = 0;
    $SIG{'ALRM'} = \&SigAlarmHandler;
    $ALARM_PERIOD = 1;
    alarm $ALARM_PERIOD;
}
```

When a tick is received, SigAlarmHandler scans the TEventList for active tasks awaiting execution. It then calls the associated subroutine and waits for it to terminate. If the event is nonrepeating, the subroutine changes the event status to expired— it is not considered again. SigAlarmHandler then examines the next event. Finally, when the whole event list is scanned, SigAlarmHandler calls alarm and arranges to receive another tick in 1 second.

You can see the whole process in action in the main program. First, the two simple call-back routines are defined: They merely announce their execution on stdout. Then the program registers two events with the TEvent package. The output from the program shows each routine being called every 7 and 11 seconds, respectively.

Figure 15-3 illustrates the TEvent module. The TEventList is scanned every time the ALRM signal is received. At this point events 2, 3, and 5 are eligible for execution. Event 2 has been processed. Event 3's associated call-back routine is executing. Event 5 will be handled next.

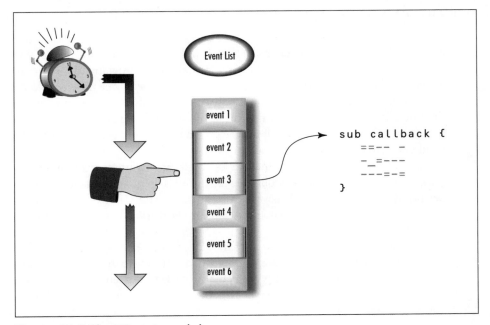

Figure 15-3 The TEvent module

Comments

There is one caveat to this approach. You shouldn't mix the TEvent module and other SIGALRM-related calls such as alarm. Both these calls set up a request for SIGALRM. When a SIGALRM is received by a process, there is no way for TEvent to realize that the signal was requested by another part of the program.

COMPLEXITY
INTERMEDIATE

15.6   How do I...
Handle exceptions gracefully?

COMPATIBILITY: UNIX

Problem

How can I write Perl code that handles exceptions: unpredictable events such as operating-system commands that fail, hardware failure, receiving invalid input from the user, reading corrupt information, and so on? What are the best ways of trapping exception events in Perl without clouding the logic of the main program?

Technique

In one sense, there is nothing very exceptional about exceptions. If you have written any Perl programs at all, you are already familiar with lines of code like this:

```
open(FILE1,">myfile") || die "Cannot open myfile: $!";
```

Good Perl programming dictates that you check each operating-system call, such as open, close, and fork, for success or failure. If the call fails for some reason, you should take some action or, in the extreme case, abort the program. The open call above could have been written without the || die component. The program would have worked correctly until myfile was deleted or given read-only permissions or the administrator dismounted the disk or the file system failed or.... If there was no exception-handling code after the || and the program had continued, then the results would be hard to predict.

You just saw the || die feature that allows you to trap failure status from system calls, but the main exception-handling facility in Perl is the *eval* statement. From one perspective, the eval function behaves in a way similar to the C++ try function: It lets you execute a small segment of code and trap even fatal errors that occur within the segment.

The eval function parses and executes the values returned by its arguments. The values may be an expression or a small Perl program. One way to think of eval's behavior is that it invokes a new Perl interpreter from within a Perl program. Any fatal runtime error produced by the eval'd code (even including *die* statements) causes an abort— not of the whole program, but just of the code interpreted by the *eval* statement. So the statement eval "die ;"; terminates the *eval* statement but not the program that called eval. *Eval* simply sets $@ to the error status and returns the undefined value. Your program can check the return of the *eval* statement and take appropriate action if an error occurs—even if that error would normally blow up your program.

The library file exception.pl, written by Tom Christiansen, lets you take this approach further, providing C++-like exception-processing facilities, including user-defined exceptions. The program below demonstrates exception.pl in action.

Steps

1. Enter the following code or use the example exect.pl from the CD. Make the resulting program executable for your operating system.

```perl
#!/usr/local/bin/perl

require "exceptions.pl";

sub get_input {
    $_ = <STDIN>;
    throw('bad_input') if /^$/;
    throw('not_a_number') unless m/^[0-9]+$/;

}

TRY: {
    print "Enter a number: ";
    if ($error = catch('get_input();',
                       'empty input','not a number')) {
        warn "Error during input: $error\n";
        redo;
    }
}
print "Input : $_";
```

2. Execute the program with the following input.
except.pl

```
Enter a number : 12xyz
Error during input: Not a number
Enter a number : 12
Input : 12
```

How It Works

This program calls the subroutine get_input to read some input from STDIN. If the input is valid, the program proceeds as normal; otherwise, it catches the error status, issues the appropriate error message, and calls get_input again. The Perl library package exception.pl enables this typical error-checking procedure to be handled without clouding the logic of the program.

Comments

Here are the two golden rules of programming for exceptions:

● Include exception-handling code wherever it conceivably could be needed. If something can go wrong, then sometime it will—the program must be able to deal with any anomalous situation.

● Don't cloud over the main logic of your program with reams of exception-handling code. Keep your exception-handling neat, succinct, and separate from the standard processing paths.

These two rules often conflict. You can see this clearly in programming languages such as C that don't offer much support for handling exceptions. If you are a C programmer, you have written code that looks something like this:

```
happened = something();
if ( this == happened ) {
  handle_this();
} else if ( that == happened ) {
    handle_that();
} else if ( this != happened ){
  do_the_right_thing();
} else {
  return in_abject_failure;
}
```

Be prepared to handle the occurrence of an exception that completely obscures the logic of the code—you really just want to do_the_right_thing().

Some programming languages such as C++ and Ada have exception-handling facilities as extra features of the language. Exception handlers enable the programmer to separate the execution-handling code from the main logic, keeping the code clean and maintainable. Perl has some neat exception-handling facilities, too, but instead of adding new features to the language, Perl uses its own interpreter accessible through the eval function to give you what you need.

CHAPTER 16
DATA STRUCTURES

DATA STRUCTURES

How do I...

Each Perl program uses data structures to hold the data it is processing. These data structures are often the simple, built-in types. When processing complex data, you need more advanced structures. You can construct these structures by combining the built-in types.

References were introduced in Perl 5. This new data type allows you to create nested data structures. Trees, graphs, and other structures can now be easily created. You can create these structures by embedding arrays and associative arrays into each other.

16.1   Build a Binary Tree

A binary tree is a useful construct for storing dictionary-type information. Data can be easily entered, removed, and searched for. The tree can easily grow to any size without any special handling. Access to the data is much quicker than access to data in an array. The structure of the tree can be used to store information on the relation of nodes to one another. This gives it advantages over associative arrays. This section will show you how to create a binary tree.

16.2 Process Nested Lists

Nested lists represent hierarchical information. This data can be stored as a tree structure in Perl. Once a tree has been built, the relationships between the data can be discovered from the position of the data in the tree. For example, subordinate data is below the more important data. This How-To will demonstrate how to process nested lists.

16.3 Build a Multitree

A multitree contains multiple branches from a node in a tree. This allows related data to be stored at the same level in a tree. You can use this data structure to represent more complicated relationships than you can represent with a binary tree. This section will show you how to build a multitree.

16.4 Represent a Graph

Many relationships between data can be represented by a graph. Each machine in a local area network can be thought of as a vertex in a graph. The connections between the machines and the network can be represented by arcs between the vertexes. With such a data structure, you can answer many questions about the network. This How-To will demonstrate how to represent such a graph.

COMPLEXITY
ADVANCED

16.1 How do I...
Build a binary tree?

COMPATIBILITY: PERL 5   UNIX   DOS

Problem

I need to build a symbol table of all the keywords seen in a program. I would like to do this using a binary tree. How do I create one in Perl?

Technique

A binary tree is a data structure built from nodes connected in a tree-like structure. Each node has three entries: the value of the node, a link to a left subtree, and a link to a right subtree. (See Figure 16-1 for an example binary tree.) You can store values in a binary tree as follows. If there are no nodes in the tree, create a new node as the base of the tree, with the value and subtree links undefined. If a tree already exists, compare the new value to the value in the top node of the tree. If the values are the same, the value is already in the tree and does not need to be entered. If the new value is less than the value in the node, examine the left subtree. If the value is greater, examine the right subtree. Then compare the value with the value in the node at the top of the subtree. Repeat this process until you find the value or the link to the next subtree is undefined. If you find an undefined subtree, the value is

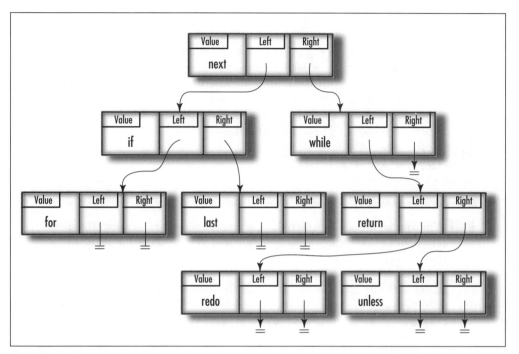

Figure 16-1 A binary tree

not in the tree. Create a new node with the value and undefined subtree links. Then link this node to the last node searched, replacing the subtree that was found to be undefined. Search for a value in the tree in the same way, except do not enter the value if it is not in the tree.

Steps

This script implements a binary tree. Use it to store keywords from a program. Store these keywords as strings in the value field of a node. Supply a subroutine that prints out the binary tree so you can verify that the tree is properly created. Implement the tree so that a node is a reference to an associative array that contains three entries: one for the value to be stored, two for the links to the subtrees. If no subtree exists, store the undefined value as the link. Otherwise, store a reference to the top node of the subtree.

1. Create a file called binary.pl to implement a binary tree. First, define a subroutine that compares two values. In this case, it compares two strings. If the strings are equal, return 0. If the first string is less than the second, return -1. Otherwise, return 1.

```
use strict;

sub AlphaCmp {
    return ($_[0] cmp $_[1]);
}
```

2. Create a common subroutine that will be used by both Search and Insert to determine if a value is already entered into the tree. The subroutine takes three arguments: a node, a new value, and a reference to a subroutine that does value comparison. Have it return an indication of success and the last node that was searched. The leading underscore denotes the fact that this is an internal routine. For the insert function to work, it needs to know the last node seen so it can enter a new node as a subtree of that node. Initialize a variable to hold that node with undefined.

```
sub _Search {
    my($Node,$Val,$Cmp) = @_;
    my($Previous,$Compare);

    $Previous = undef;
```

3. While nodes are still found in the tree, compare the new value with the current node's value. If they are the same, the search is successful. Return 1 to indicate success, and return the previous node. If the node does not contain the value, save the node and advance to the next subtree. If the value is not found in the tree, return failure and the last node examined.

```
    while (defined($Node)) {
        $Compare = &$Cmp($Node->{"Value"},$Val);
        if ($Compare == 0) {
            return (1,$Previous);
        }
        $Previous = $Node;
        if ($Compare > 0) {
            $Node = $Node->{"Left"};
        } else {
            $Node = $Node->{"Right"};
        }
    }
    return (0,$Previous);
}
```

4. Create the search function. Have it pass arguments to the internal search function and store only the first return value. This value is the one that tells whether the value was found in the tree.

```
sub Search {
    my($Result);

    ($Result) = _Search(@_);
    return $Result;
}
```

5. Put in an insert function. Have it take three arguments: the first node of a tree, a value, and a reference to a compare function. Have this function return the node passed in, unless the node is undefined. If so, return the new node that is created. This will allow the calling function to keep track of the top of the tree. Call the internal search function and save the results. If the value is found, return the node that was passed in.

```
sub Insert {
    my($Node,$Val,$Cmp) = @_;
    my($Result,$Insert,$Compare,$NewNode);

    ($Result,$Insert) = _Search($Node,$Val,$Cmp);
    if ($Result) {
        return $Node;
    }
```

6. If the value is not found, create a new node that contains the value and two undefined subtrees. If a node is returned from the unsuccessful search for the value, it is the node in which the reference to the new node should be inserted. Determine what subtree to insert it into by comparing the value with the one in the previous node. If no node is returned, the tree is empty. Return the new node as the base of the tree.

```
    $NewNode = {
        "Value" => $Val,
        "Left"  => undef,
        "Right" => undef
    };
    if (defined($Insert)) {
        if (&$Cmp($Insert->{"Value"},$Val) > 0) {
            $Insert->{"Left"} = $NewNode;
        } else {
            $Insert->{"Right"} = $NewNode;
        }
        return $Node;
    } else {
        return $NewNode;
    }
}
```

7. Use the binary tree to store some keyword strings. Start the tree as empty and then add the keywords. Then call the print function to show the state of the tree.

```
my($Top) = undef;
my($i);

for $i ("next","if","while","for","last","return","redo","unless") {
    $Top = Insert($Top,$i,\&AlphaCmp);
}

Print($Top);
```

8. Define a print function to show the values in the tree.

```
sub Print {
    my($n) = @_;

    defined($n) or return;
    print "$n->{'Value'}:";
    defined($n->{"Left"}) and print "$n->{'Left'}{'Value'}";
    print ":";
    defined($n->{"Right"}) and print "$n->{'Right'}{'Value'}";
```

continued on next page

continued from previous page

```perl
    print "\n";
    Print($n->{"Left"});
    Print($n->{"Right"});
}
```

   9. The entire script should look like the following.

```perl
use strict;

sub AlphaCmp {
    return ($_[0] cmp $_[1]);
}

sub _Search {
    my($Node,$Val,$Cmp) = @_;
    my($Previous,$Compare);

    $Previous = undef;
    while (defined($Node)) {
        $Compare = &$Cmp($Node->{"Value"},$Val);
        if ($Compare == 0) {
            return (1,$Previous);
        }
        $Previous = $Node;
        if ($Compare > 0) {
            $Node = $Node->{"Left"};
        } else {
            $Node = $Node->{"Right"};
        }
    }
    return (0,$Previous);
}

sub Search {
    my($Result);

    ($Result) = _Search(@_);
    return $Result;
}

sub Insert {
    my($Node,$Val,$Cmp) = @_;
    my($Result,$Insert,$Compare,$NewNode);

    ($Result,$Insert) = _Search($Node,$Val,$Cmp);
    if ($Result) {
        return $Node;
    }
    $NewNode = {
        "Value" => $Val,
        "Left"  => undef,
        "Right" => undef
    };
    if (defined($Insert)) {
        if (&$Cmp($Insert->{"Value"},$Val) > 0) {
            $Insert->{"Left"} = $NewNode;
```

```
            } else {
                $Insert->{"Right"} = $NewNode;
            }
            return $Node;
        } else {
            return $NewNode;
        }
}

my($Top) = undef;
my($i);

for $i ("next","if","while","for","last","return","redo","unless") {
    $Top = Insert($Top,$i,\&AlphaCmp);
}

Print($Top);

sub Print {
    my($n) = @_;

    defined($n) or return;
    print "$n->{'Value'}:";
    defined($n->{"Left"}) and print "$n->{'Left'}{'Value'}";
    print ":";
    defined($n->{"Right"}) and print "$n->{'Right'}{'Value'}";
    print "\n";
    Print($n->{"Left"});
    Print($n->{"Right"});
}
```

10. Run the script.

```
perl binary.pl
```

11. The output follows.

Output

```
next:if:while
if:for:last
for::
last::
while:return:
return:redo:unless
redo::
unless::
```

End Output

How It Works

The binary tree is created by linking together nodes by storing references to other nodes in each node. This allows you to walk through the tree looking for a value or to insert a new value. The tree that is built in the example is the same one shown in Figure 16-1.

Comments

A binary tree is useful for storing and searching for arbitrary values. The value stored in the value field does not need to be a simple scalar value. It can be a complex structure such as an address book entry. The value passed to the binary tree is a reference to the structure. Many fields can be stored, with one being used as the key field on which the comparisons are done. In the case of an address book, this would be a person's name. This script can be used in this manner by replacing the comparison subroutine with one that can compare address book entries.

COMPLEXITY
ADVANCED

16.2 How do I...
Process nested lists?

COMPATIBILITY: PERL 5 | UNIX | DOS

Problem

Sometimes I need to read data that is in the form of nested lists. How can I read in and process this data?

Technique

Tree-like data is often stored in a file as a set of nested lists. You can read in this data one list at a time and create a tree to hold it. Once the tree is built, you can walk through the tree to access the data. Because the lists are nested, use a recursive approach. Create a function to process a list. If, in the processing of a list, another list is encountered, call the function recursively.

The example script can process lists made up of zero or more entries. A list starts with a left parenthesis and is followed by the list elements. Each element is separated from the next by a comma. A list ends with a right parenthesis. A list element is either a string or another list. A string starts with a double quote and continues on until the next double quote. White space is ignored except when it is within a string. A string can contain any character except a double quote.

Store a list in an array that has one element for each list element. If the list element is a string, store the string directly in the array element. If the list element is another list, store a reference to the sublist in the array element. The result of parsing the highest-level list is a reference to the entire tree. Figure 16-2 shows a representation of some of the input data.

Steps

The functions used to create a tree from the input are generic. You can use these functions to process a more restrictive form of list. The data to be parsed is a nested list representing a subdirectory in a file system. Each list must start off with a string that

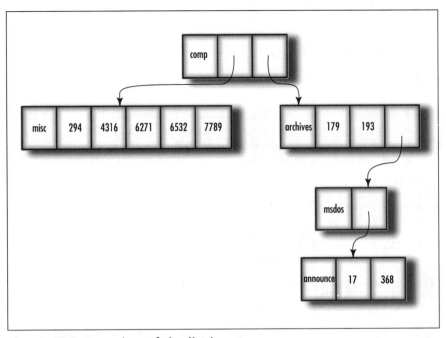

Figure 16-2 A portion of the list input

gives the name of the directory being described. Each element in the list after that is a file in the directory. If the element is a string, it is a normal file in the directory. If the entry is a list, it represents a subdirectory.

Check the validity of the input in two passes. In the first pass, create generic list-handling code that creates the tree structure. This pass verifies only that the data is a valid list made up of strings and sublists. Have the second pass walk through the tree. Verify that the lists contain the restricted form for saving file-system directories. Have the tree-walking code print out a visual representation of the directory.

1. Create a file named list.pl. First, create a subroutine to gather lines of input. The function takes one argument that tells whether data needs to be found. Have it read a line of input and remove the trailing new line. Return this data to the calling function. If data is required and the end of file is seen, print a message and exit. If data is not required, return the undefined value.

```
use strict;

sub GetLine {
    my($NeedInput) = @_;
    my($Line);

    $Line = <>;
    if (defined($Line)) {
        chomp($Line);
```

continued on next page

continued from previous page

```
        return $Line;
    }
    if ($NeedInput) {
        die "Incomplete Input\n";
    }
    return undef;
}
```

2. Enter the following subroutine to collect strings from the input. It is passed the current input data. Remove the leading double quote. If there is not a leading quote, print a message and exit. Collect input lines until the ending quote is found. Return the string and any data left on the input line.

```
sub GetString {
    my($Line) = @_;
    my($String,$Rest);

    $Line =~ s/\s*"// or die "Bad String passes as input\n";
    until ($Line =~ /"/) {
        $Line .= "\n" . GetLine(1);
    }
    ($String,$Rest) = $Line =~ /(.*?)"(.*)/s;
    return ($String,$Rest);
}
```

3. Define a subroutine to extract lists from the input. The input to this function is the current input. Remove the leading left parenthesis. If it is not there, print a message and exit. Create a reference to an array to hold the list data. The input does not start with a right parenthesis; read the elements in the list. Make sure that the input line contains some characters. If not, read input lines until some characters are found.

```
sub GetTuple {
    my($Line) = @_;
    my($Tuple,$SubTuple,$String);

    # Check for starting paren

    $Line =~ s/\s*\(\s*// or die "Bad Tuple passes as input\n";
    $Tuple = [];
    until ($Line =~ s/^\s*\)//) {            # go until ending paren
        while ($Line eq "") {
            $Line = GetLine(1);
            $Line =~ s/^\s*//;
        }
```

4. If the input starts with a double quote, the start of a string element has been found. Call the GetString function to retrieve the string. Store the string in the list array. If the input starts with a left parenthesis, a sublist has been found. Call this function recursively to retrieve the sublist. The input can also start with a right parenthesis. If so, skip to the next iteration of the loop to process the end of list. Any other input is an error. Print a message and exit.

```
        if ($Line =~ /^"/) {              # start of string
            ($String,$Line) = GetString($Line);
            push (@$Tuple,$String);
        } elsif($Line =~ /^\(/) {         # start of tuple
            ($SubTuple,$Line) = GetTuple($Line);
            push (@$Tuple,$SubTuple);
        } elsif($Line =~ /^\)/) {         # end of tuple, finish loop
            next;
        } else {
            die "Bad Tuple\n";
        }
```

5. Once the list element has been processed, remove any leading white space from the remaining input. Process the input until a character is found. If the next character is not a right parenthesis, it must be a comma separating list elements. If not, print a message and exit. Once the list has been processed, return the reference to the list array and any remaining input.

```
    $Line =~ s/^\s*//;
    while ($Line eq "") {
        $Line = GetLine(1);
        $Line =~ s/^\s*//;
    }

    # check for end of tuple or the start of another element

    ($Line =~ /^\)/) or ($Line =~ s/,\s*//)
            or die "Bad separator in Tuple\n";
    }
    return ($Tuple,$Line);
}
```

6. Enter a subroutine to process a directory tree entry. The input to this function is a string and a list entry. The string is prepended to any output. This is used to show the full path to any directory entries. If the list entry passed to the function is a reference, the entry must be a list. Call a function to process the directory. If the entry is not a reference, it must be a string. Call a function to process the file.

```
sub ProcessTree {
    my($Prefix,$Tuple) = @_;

    if (ref($Tuple)) {
        ProcessDir($Prefix,$Tuple);
    } else {
        ProcessFile($Prefix,$Tuple);
    }
}
```

7. Add a function to process a directory. The input is the output prefix and the reference to the directory array. If the reference is not to an array, an error has occurred. Print a message and exit. Get the directory name from the first element in the array. If it is a reference, it is not a string containing the directory name. This is an error. Print a message and exit. Otherwise, print the path to the directory. Loop through the remaining array elements and process them as entries in the current directory.

```
sub ProcessDir {
    my($Prefix,$Dir) = @_;
    my($Name,$Element);

    if (ref($Dir) ne "ARRAY") {
        die "Bad Directory Reference\n";
    }
    $Name = $Dir->[0];
    if (ref($Name)) {
        die "Directory didn't have a name\n";
    }
    print "$Prefix$Name\n";

    if ($#$Dir > 0) {
        for $Element (@$Dir[1..$#$Dir]) {
            ProcessTree("$Prefix$Name/",$Element);
        }
    }
}
```

8. Add a subroutine to process files. Print the full path to the file and return.

```
sub ProcessFile {
    my($Prefix,$File) = @_;

    print "$Prefix$File\n";
}
```

9. Start processing the input. If no data is present, print a message and exit. Look at the first character in the input. It must be the start of a string or list. Process the correct kind of entry by calling the proper function. If the input is invalid, print a message and exit.

```
my($Tuple,$Rest);

my($Input) = GetLine(0);
defined($Input) or die "No Input\n";

{
    if ($Input =~ /^\s*\(/) {
        ($Tuple,$Rest) = GetTuple($Input);
    } elsif ($Input =~ /^\s*"/) {
        ($Tuple,$Rest) = GetString($Input);
    } else {
        die "Bad Input\n";
    }
```

10. Call the ProcessTree function to walk through the directory tree created. The prefix string starts as null because this is the top of the tree. If there is input left, repeat this block to process the next string or list. Otherwise, read the next input line. If input exists, repeat the block. If the end of file is seen, the script should exit.

```
        ProcessTree("",$Tuple);
        $Rest and redo;
        while($Input = GetLine(0)) {
            $Input =~ s/^\s*//;
            $Input =~ /./ and last;
        }
        defined($Input) and redo;
}
```

11. The entire program follows.

```
use strict;

sub GetLine {
    my($NeedInput) = @_;
    my($Line);

    $Line = <>;
    if (defined($Line)) {
        chomp($Line);
        return $Line;
    }
    if ($NeedInput) {
        die "Incomplete Input\n";
    }
    return undef;
}

sub GetString {
    my($Line) = @_;
    my($String,$Rest);

    $Line =~ s/\s*"// or die "Bad String passes as input\n";
    until ($Line =~ /"/) {
        $Line .= "\n" . GetLine(1);
    }
    ($String,$Rest) = $Line =~ /(.*?)"(.*)/s;
    return ($String,$Rest);
}

sub GetTuple {
    my($Line) = @_;
    my($Tuple,$SubTuple,$String);

    # Check for starting paren

    $Line =~ s/\s*\(\s*// or die "Bad Tuple passes as input\n";
    $Tuple = [];
    until ($Line =~ s/^\s*\)//) {          # go until ending paren
        while ($Line eq "") {
            $Line = GetLine(1);
            $Line =~ s/^\s*//;
        }
        if ($Line =~ /^"/) {               # start of string
            ($String,$Line) = GetString($Line);
            push @$Tuple,$String;
        } elsif($Line =~ /^\(/) {          # start of tuple
```

continued on next page

continued from previous page

```perl
                ($SubTuple,$Line) = GetTuple($Line);
                push (@$Tuple,$SubTuple);
        } elsif($Line =~ /^\)/) {              # end of tuple, finish loop
            next;
        } else {
            die "Bad Tuple\n";
        }
        $Line =~ s/^\s*//;
        while ($Line eq "") {
            $Line = GetLine(1);
            $Line =~ s/^\s*//;
        }

        # check for end of tuple or the start of another element

        ($Line =~ /^\)/) or ($Line =~ s/,\s*//)
            or die "Bad separator in Tuple\n";
    }
    return ($Tuple,$Line);
}

sub ProcessTree {
    my($Prefix,$Tuple) = @_;

    if (ref($Tuple)) {
        ProcessDir($Prefix,$Tuple);
    } else {
        ProcessFile($Prefix,$Tuple);
    }
}

sub ProcessDir {
    my($Prefix,$Dir) = @_;
    my($Name,$Element);

    if (ref($Dir) ne "ARRAY") {
        die "Bad Directory Reference\n";
    }
    $Name = $Dir->[0];
    if (ref($Name)) {
        die "Directory didn't have a name\n";
    }
    print "$Prefix$Name\n";

    if ($#$Dir > 0) {
        for $Element (@$Dir[1..$#$Dir]) {
            ProcessTree("$Prefix$Name/",$Element);
        }
    }
}

sub ProcessFile {
    my($Prefix,$File) = @_;

    print "$Prefix$File\n";
}
```

```
my($Tuple,$Rest);

my($Input) = GetLine(0);
defined($Input) or die "No Input\n";

{
    if ($Input =~ /^\s*\(/) {
        ($Tuple,$Rest) = GetTuple($Input);
    } elsif ($Input =~ /^\s*"/) {
        ($Tuple,$Rest) = GetString($Input);
    } else {
        die "Bad Input\n";
    }

    ProcessTree("",$Tuple);
    $Rest and redo;
    while($Input = GetLine(0)) {
        $Input =~ s/^\s*//;
        $Input =~ /./ and last;
    }
    defined($Input) and redo;
}
```

12. Create an input file named list.in with the following data.

```
("comp",
  ("misc",
    "294",
    "4316",
    "6271",
    "6532",
    "7789"
  ),
  ("archives",
    "179",
    "193",
    ("msdos",
      ("announce",
        "17",
        "368"
      )
    )
  )
)
("org",
  ("usenix",
    "361"
  )
)
```

13. Run the script.

```
perl list.pl list.in
```

14. The output follows.

```
Output
comp
comp/misc
comp/misc/294
comp/misc/4316
comp/misc/6271
comp/misc/6532
comp/misc/7789
comp/archives
comp/archives/179
comp/archives/193
comp/archives/msdos
comp/archives/msdos/announce
comp/archives/msdos/announce/17
comp/archives/msdos/announce/368
org
org/usenix
org/usenix/361
End Output
```

How It Works

A general algorithm for reading in lists can be used many times (see How-To 16.3 for another example). With such a code base, you can address many list-type problems by reusing code. The specifics of a particular problem can be applied when walking through the generated tree.

Comments

The code presented here makes no attempt to recover from bad input. It was assumed that the input was machine-generated. A more robust approach would be needed for input being entered by a user. The error messages would also need enhancement. The context for the error could be displayed, giving the user a place to start looking for the error.

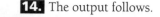

COMPLEXITY
ADVANCED

16.3 How do I...
Build a multitree?

COMPATIBILITY: PERL 5   UNIX   DOS

Problem

I need to create a tree that has multiple branches per node. How do I create and use a multitree?

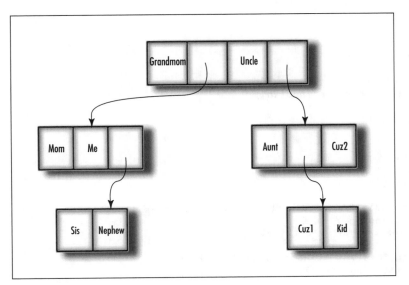

Figure 16-3 A multitree

Technique

The easiest way to represent a multitree in Perl 5 is to use references as the links between nodes. In this manner, subnodes are represented in the node as a reference to another node. How-To 16.2 reads in nested lists and creates a multitree. That How-To provides much of the information needed to use multitrees. The code is generic and is reused here to show how it can be easily modified. Only the tree-walking code needs to be modified. Figure 16-3 shows the multitree used in this How-To.

Steps

The input for this script is part of a family tree. Each list contains all the siblings in a specific generation. Each sibling is represented by two elements in the list. The first element is the sibling's name. The second element is a sublist listing all the siblings' offspring. An empty list denotes the fact that there are no children.

The family tree-specific code verifies that the siblings come in pairs and they are the correct type. For each list pair, print the family member's name and make a recursive call to the tree-walking routine to print the children.

1. Create a script called multi.pl to create a family tree. Copy the generic list-processing code from How-To 16.2.

```perl
use strict;

sub GetLine {
    my($NeedInput) = @_;
    my($Line);
```

continued on next page

continued from previous page

```perl
    $Line = <>;
    if (defined($Line)) {
        chomp($Line);
        return $Line;
    }
    if ($NeedInput) {
        die "Incomplete Input\n";
    }
    return undef;
}

sub GetString {
    my($Line) = @_;
    my($String,$Rest);

    $Line =~ s/\s*"// or die "Bad String passes as input\n";
    until ($Line =~ /"/) {
        $Line .= "\n" . GetLine(1);
    }
    ($String,$Rest) = $Line =~ /(.*?)"(.*)/s;
    return ($String,$Rest);
}

sub GetTuple {
    my($Line) = @_;
    my($Tuple,$SubTuple,$String);

    # Check for starting paren

    $Line =~ s/\s*\(\s*// or die "Bad Tuple passes as input\n";
    $Tuple = [];
    until ($Line =~ s/^\s*\)//) {          # go until ending paren
        while ($Line eq "") {
            $Line = GetLine(1);
            $Line =~ s/^\s*//;
        }
        if ($Line =~ /^"/) {               # start of string
            ($String,$Line) = GetString($Line);
            push (@$Tuple,$String);
        } elsif($Line =~ /^\(/) {          # start of tuple
            ($SubTuple,$Line) = GetTuple($Line);
            push (@$Tuple,$SubTuple);
        } elsif($Line =~ /^\)/) {          # end of tuple, finish loop
            next;
        } else {
            die "Bad Tuple\n";
        }
        $Line =~ s/^\s*//;
        while ($Line eq "") {
            $Line = GetLine(1);
            $Line =~ s/^\s*//;
        }

        # check for end of tuple or the start of another element

        ($Line =~ /^\)/) or ($Line =~ s/,\s*//)
```

```
                or die "Bad separator in Tuple\n";
        }
        return ($Tuple,$Line);
}
```

2. Add a subroutine to walk through the family tree. The function takes two arguments. The first argument is the string representing the family's ancestors. The second argument is the tree to process. Verify that the tree is really a tree and not an integral type. Loop through all the siblings, processing each sibling until they have all been processed. Get the first entry for a sibling. Verify that it is not a subtree and then print the name with the ancestor's path preceding it. Verify that an element exists for the sibling's offspring. If it is missing, print a message and exit. Process the offspring by calling this function recursively.

```
sub ProcessFamily {
    my($Prefix,$Family) = @_;
    my($Name,$Index);

    if (ref($Family) ne "ARRAY") {
        die "Bad Family Reference\n";
    }
    $Index = 0;
    while ($#$Family >= $Index) {
        $Name = $Family->[$Index++];
        if (ref($Name)) {
            die "Family member didn't have a name\n";
        }
        print "$Prefix$Name\n";

        if ($#$Family < $Index) {
            die "No Family members\n";
        }
        ProcessFamily("$Prefix$Name/",$Family->[$Index++]);
    }
}
```

3. Read the first line of input. If there is not any, print a message and exit. Use the generic list-reading function to retrieve a sibling list. Walk through the family tree, printing its members. Because this is the highest level of the tree, the ancestor string is empty. If there is more data, repeat the block to process another tree.

```
my($Tuple,$Rest);

my($Input) = GetLine(0);
defined($Input) or die "No Input\n";

{
    if ($Input =~ /^\s*\(/) {
        ($Tuple,$Rest) = GetTuple($Input);
    } else {
        die "Bad Input\n";
    }
```

continued on next page

continued from previous page

```
    ProcessFamily("",$Tuple);
    $Rest and redo;
    while($Input = GetLine(0)) {
        $Input =~ s/^\s*//;
        $Input =~ /./ and last;
    }
    defined($Input) and redo;
}
```

4. The entire script follows. The changes from How-To 16.2 are shown in bold.

```perl
use strict;

sub GetLine {
    my($NeedInput) = @_;
    my($Line);

    $Line = <>;
    if (defined($Line)) {
        chomp($Line);
        return $Line;
    }
    if ($NeedInput) {
        die "Incomplete Input\n";
    }
    return undef;
}

sub GetString {
    my($Line) = @_;
    my($String,$Rest);

    $Line =~ s/\s*"// or die "Bad String passes as input\n";
    until ($Line =~ /"/) {
        $Line .= "\n" . GetLine(1);
    }
    ($String,$Rest) = $Line =~ /(.*?)"(.*)/s;
    return ($String,$Rest);
}

sub GetTuple {
    my($Line) = @_;
    my($Tuple,$SubTuple,$String);

    # Check for starting paren

    $Line =~ s/\s*\(\s*// or die "Bad Tuple passes as input\n";
    $Tuple = [];
    until ($Line =~ /^\s*\)//) {          # go until ending paren
        while ($Line eq "") {
            $Line = GetLine(1);
            $Line =~ s/^\s*//;
        }
        if ($Line =~ /^"/) {              # start of string
            ($String,$Line) = GetString($Line);
```

```
                  push (@$Tuple,$String);
          } elsif($Line =~ /^\(/) {          # start of tuple
              ($SubTuple,$Line) = GetTuple($Line);
              push (@$Tuple,$SubTuple);
          } elsif($Line =~ /^\)/) {          # end of tuple, finish loop
              next;
          } else {
              die "Bad Tuple\n";
          }
          $Line =~ s/^\s*//;
          while ($Line eq "") {
              $Line = GetLine(1);
              $Line =~ s/^\s*//;
          }

          # check for end of tuple or the start of another element

          ($Line =~ /^\)/) or ($Line =~ s/,\s*//)
              or die "Bad separator in Tuple\n";
      }
      return ($Tuple,$Line);
}

sub ProcessFamily {
    my($Prefix,$Family) = @_;
    my($Name,$Index);

    if (ref($Family) ne "ARRAY") {
        die "Bad Family Reference\n";
    }
    $Index = 0;
    while ($#$Family >= $Index) {
        $Name = $Family->[$Index++];
        if (ref($Name)) {
            die "Family member didn't have a name\n";
        }
        print "$Prefix$Name\n";

        if ($#$Family < $Index) {
            die "No Family members\n";
        }
        ProcessFamily("$Prefix$Name/",$Family->[$Index++]);
    }
}


my($Tuple,$Rest);

my($Input) = GetLine(0);
defined($Input) or die "No Input\n";

{
    if ($Input =~ /^\s*\(/) {
        ($Tuple,$Rest) = GetTuple($Input);
    } else {
        die "Bad Input\n";
    }
```

continued on next page

continued from previous page

```
    ProcessFamily("",$Tuple);
    $Rest and redo;
    while($Input = GetLine(0)) {
        $Input =~ s/^\s*//;
        $Input =~ /./ and last;
    }
    defined($Input) and redo;
}
```

5. Create an input file called multi.in with the following data.

```
("Grandmom", (
  "Mom", (
    "Me", (),
    "Sis", (
      "Nephew", ()
    )
  ),
  "Uncle", (),
  "Aunt", (
    "Cuz1", (
      "Kid", ()
    ),
    "Cuz2", ()
  )
))
```

6. Run the script.

```
perl multi.pl multi.in
```

7. The output follows.

Output

```
Grandmom
Grandmom/Mom
Grandmom/Mom/Me
Grandmom/Mom/Sis
Grandmom/Mom/Sis/Nephew
Grandmom/Uncle
Grandmom/Aunt
Grandmom/Aunt/Cuz1
Grandmom/Aunt/Cuz1/Kid
Grandmom/Aunt/Cuz2
```

End Output

How It Works

The generic list-creation code from How-To 16.2 is used to read in a nested list representing a family tree. This code creates a multitree. Specific tree-handling code is added to process the tree.

Comments

The generic nested list-reading code is structured, so it is easy to add another list-element type. A new function is needed to process that type. Then you should add a check for the start character to the GetTuple routine. Once the special character is seen, the new function is called.

COMPLEXITY
ADVANCED

16.4 How do I...
Represent a graph?

COMPATIBILITY: PERL 5 | UNIX | DOS

Problem

I have data representing cities and the train routes between them. I need to process this data to answer questions such as, "Can I visit each city without having to visit a city more than once?" How can I do this in Perl?

Technique

Information of this sort is best thought of as a graph. Nodes (cities) are connected by arcs. Create an associative array that has an entry for each node. Use that entry to contain a reference to another associative array. Use this second array to contain each city that is connected to the original city.

Steps

The input to this program is one line per node. The first element in the line is the node name. The rest of the line contains the names of the nodes that are directly connected to this node. The connections between nodes are not directional. This means that node traversal can proceed in either direction: from node 1 to node 2 or from node 2 to node 1. The input does not list both connections. Store the connection in both nodes.

Once the graph is built, traverse the graph from each node. Do this to determine the longest path through the graph, starting at each node. The graph to be processed is shown in Figure 16-4.

1. Create a file called graph.pl. First, create a loop to read each line of the input and store it in an associative array. Split the line of white space to generate a list of nodes on the line. The first node on the line is the node that the rest of the nodes are connected to.

```
use strict;

my (%Nodes);

while(<>) {
    my($n);
    my($Node, @Line) = split;
```

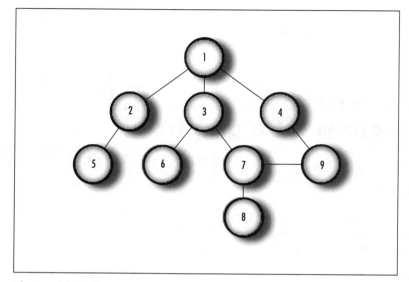

Figure 16-4 The example graph

2. Loop through each node on the line and create a connection between nodes. The Nodes associative array has an entry for each node. In each entry, store a reference to an associative array that has an entry for each node that is connected to the node. Set the value of this entry to 1 to denote that it exists. Because connections are bidirectional, update the node that is connected to the current node to show the connection.

```
for $n (@Line) {
    $Nodes{$Node}{$n} = 1;
    $Nodes{$n}{$Node} = 1;
}
}
```

3. To verify that the data was processed correctly, print the connections from each node. Then loop through each node and call a function to do a graph walk, starting at the node. This function returns the longest path that can be taken. Print this information.

```
my ($Node);
foreach $Node (keys %Nodes) {
    print "$Node: ", join(" ",sort keys %{$Nodes{$Node}}),"\n";
}

foreach $Node (sort keys %Nodes) {
    my(@Path) = ( $Node );
    @Path = Walk(@Path);
    print "Longest path starting at $Path[0] is: @Path\n";
}
```

4. Create the graph-walking function. The input to the function is an array representing an initial path. This function determines the longest path that can be made, starting from this initial path. Save the fact that each node in the initial path has already been visited. Save this path as the longest one seen so far.

```
sub Walk {
    my(@Path) = @_;
    my($Node,%Seen,$Next);
    my($Length,$NewLength);
    my(@NewPath,$Edge,@LongPath);

    for $Node (@Path) {
        $Seen{$Node} = 1;
    }
    $Length = scalar(@Path);
    @LongPath = @Path;
```

5. Start at the last node in the path and check to see if any of the nodes it is connected to have not been visited yet. If there are nodes that have not been visited, call this function recursively to determine the longest path that can be seen, starting with the current path with the connected node added. After the path is returned, check its size. If it is longer than the current longest path, save it as the new longest path. Once all connected nodes have been tried, the longest path has been determined.

```
    $Next = $Path[$#Path];
    for $Edge (sort keys %{$Nodes{$Next}}) {
        if (! $Seen{$Edge}) {
            @NewPath = Walk(@Path,$Edge);
        }
        $NewLength = scalar(@NewPath);
        if ($NewLength > $Length) {
            $Length = $NewLength;
            @LongPath = @NewPath;
        }
    }
    return @LongPath;
}
```

6. The entire script follows.

```
use strict;

my (%Nodes);

while(<>) {
    my($n);
    my($Node, @Line) = split;

    for $n (@Line) {
        $Nodes{$Node}{$n} = 1;
        $Nodes{$n}{$Node} = 1;
    }
}
```

continued on next page

continued from previous page

```
my ($Node);
foreach $Node (keys %Nodes) {
    print "$Node: ", join(" ",sort keys %{$Nodes{$Node}}),"\n";
}

foreach $Node (sort keys %Nodes) {
    my(@Path) = ( $Node );
    @Path = Walk(@Path);
    print "Longest path starting at $Path[0] is: @Path\n";
}

sub Walk {
    my(@Path) = @_;
    my($Node,%Seen,$Next);
    my($Length,$NewLength);
    my(@NewPath,$Edge,@LongPath);

    for $Node (@Path) {
        $Seen{$Node} = 1;
    }
    $Length = scalar(@Path);
    @LongPath = @Path;
    $Next = $Path[$#Path];
    for $Edge (sort keys %{$Nodes{$Next}}) {
        if (! $Seen{$Edge}) {
            @NewPath = Walk(@Path,$Edge);
        }
        $NewLength = scalar(@NewPath);
        if ($NewLength > $Length) {
            $Length = $NewLength;
            @LongPath = @NewPath;
        }
    }
    return @LongPath;
}
```

7. Create an input file called graph.in. Enter the following lines.

```
1 2 3 4
2 5
3 6 7
4 9
7 8 9
```

8. Run the script.

```
perl graph.pl graph.in
```

9. The output from the script follows.

```
Output
```

```
1: 2 3 4
2: 1 5
3: 1 6 7
4: 1 9
5: 2
6: 3
```

```
7:  3  8  9
8:  7
9:  4  7
Longest path starting at 1 is: 1 4 9 7 3 6
Longest path starting at 2 is: 2 1 4 9 7 3 6
Longest path starting at 3 is: 3 7 9 4 1 2 5
Longest path starting at 4 is: 4 9 7 3 1 2 5
Longest path starting at 5 is: 5 2 1 4 9 7 3 6
Longest path starting at 6 is: 6 3 7 9 4 1 2 5
Longest path starting at 7 is: 7 9 4 1 2 5
Longest path starting at 8 is: 8 7 9 4 1 2 5
Longest path starting at 9 is: 9 4 1 3 7 8
```
End Output

How It Works

A graph is represented by an associative array that contains an entry for each node. These entries contain a reference to another associative array. This second associative array contains one entry for each node that the first node is connected to. The walking of the node is done by starting at a node and following each of its connections, one at a time. The node that is connected is then processed. Its connections are also followed. By keeping track of which nodes have been visited in an associative array, you can prevent the walk from repeating a path.

Comments

The associative array holding the nodes connected to another node contains only the fact that there is a connection. This array could hold much more data. If this graph were holding the connections between cities, you could add the distance between the cities, the cost of shipping, and time schedules. This could be done by having all this information stored in an associative array and storing a reference to it in the connection array. This would allow for a more detailed analysis of the graph.

## CHAPTER 17

SORTING, SEARCHING, AND RECURSION

SORTING, SEARCHING, AND RECURSION

How do I...

Once data has been entered into a Perl program, you can manipulate it in many ways. You can sort and search the data. Your scripts can find data and rearrange it. You can search tree-like structures and traverse graphs in many different ways. You can do sorts on alphabetic data, numeric data, and any data for which you can define an ordering. Having numerous ways to process data allows you to extract the information you need easily.

17.1 Sort an Array

The sequence of the data in a data structure often does not matter. Humans, however, often prefer to see data in an accessible way, most commonly in a sorted form. This How-To will show you how to sort an array.

451

17.2   Sort an Array into Unique Elements

Programs sometimes need sorted data. By sorting data, you can discover duplicate data and use only the first occurrence of it. This section will demonstrate how to sort an array into unique elements.

17.3   Sort Nonscalar Data Types

Sorting is quite easy with numbers and strings. Sometimes, however, you need to sort records. This How-To will provide a way to define how any data structure is sorted.

17.4   Build a Concordance

Humans need help finding data in text. A *concordance* is a useful device for assisting a reader in finding information. It lists the line numbers where each word and term can be found in a document. This section will show you how to build a concordance.

17.5   Write Recursive Subroutines

You can elegantly code many algorithms using recursive subroutines. This How-To will demonstrate an easy method of doing this.

17.6   Perform a Depth and Breadth First Search

By searching a graph, you can gather information on how various elements relate. This section will show you two common ways of searching through a graph.

17.7   Perform a Topological Search

A directed graph can hold ordering information, such as what activity needs to be performed before another one. This section will use a topological sort of a graph to show an order in which all activities can be accomplished.

17.8   Perform an Infix, Prefix, and Postfix Traversal

You can visit each node in a tree in many different ways. This How-To will show you the three most common traversal methods.

COMPLEXITY
BEGINNING

17.1   How do I...
Sort an array?

COMPATIBILITY: PERL 4   PERL 5   UNIX   DOS

Problem

Sometimes I need to sort data in an array. I often end up with unsorted arrays because the input to the script is not sorted. How can I sort the array so I can process the data in the correct sequence?

Technique

Perl provides the sort command to arrange data in arrays or lists. You can tell the sort command the sorting sequence of the data. You can sort numeric, alphabetic, and other data.

Steps

The example script sorts numbers and strings. These sorts show the various ways the sort command is told to do the sorting.

1. Create a script called sorta.pl to test the various sorting methods. First, create an array of strings and sort them. An alphabetic sort is sort's default method. Print the sorted strings.

```
@Strings = ("Fred", "Jane", "Alice", "Harry");
@SortedStrings = sort @Strings;
print "@SortedStrings\n";
```

2. The sort command can be given a subroutine to use in comparing two values. Create a subroutine to compare two numbers. The sort command predefines two values for the subroutine: $a and $b. These are the two values that sort needs to compare. The subroutine must return -1 if $a is less than $b, 0 if they are the same, and 1 if $a is greater than $b. The <=> operator returns these values for two numbers.

```
sub ByNum {
    $a <=> $b;
}
```

3. Create an array of numbers. Call sort to sort the numbers using the above subroutine. Pass the subroutine name as the first argument to sort. Print the sorted numbers.

```
@Numbers = (1, 10, 4, 7, 3, 9);
@SortedNumbers = sort ByNum @Numbers;
print "@SortedNumbers\n";
```

4. The sort command can take a block of code as the first argument instead of a subroutine name. This block can contain the code to compare the two values. This is useful if the code is small. Sort the numbers using an inline block and then print them.

```
@SortedNumbers = sort { $a <=> $b } @Numbers;
print "@SortedNumbers\n";
```

5. If the numbers should be sorted in descending instead of ascending sequence, the reverse command can be used. This command takes an array and returns it in reverse order. Use reverse to sort the numbers in descending sequence. Print the result.

```
@SortedNumbers = reverse sort { $a <=> $b } @Numbers;
print "@SortedNumbers\n";
```

6. It is often faster to sort the numbers directly into the sequence needed rather than reversing the sorted array. Do this by having the sort block reverse the sense of the comparison. Then print the sorted numbers.

```
@SortedNumbers = sort { $b <=> $a } @Numbers;
print "@SortedNumbers\n";
```

7. You can use sort in this way to sort strings in descending order. Use the cmp operator to compare the strings. Print the sorted strings.

```
@SortedStrings = sort { $b cmp $a } @Strings;
print "@SortedStrings\n";
```

8. The entire script follows.

```
@Strings = ("Fred", "Jane", "Alice", "Harry");
@SortedStrings = sort @Strings;
print "@SortedStrings\n";

sub ByNum {
    $a <=> $b;
}

@Numbers = (1, 10, 4, 7, 3, 9);
@SortedNumbers = sort ByNum @Numbers;
print "@SortedNumbers\n";

@SortedNumbers = sort { $a <=> $b } @Numbers;
print "@SortedNumbers\n";

@SortedNumbers = reverse sort { $a <=> $b } @Numbers;
print "@SortedNumbers\n";

@SortedNumbers = sort { $b <=> $a } @Numbers;
print "@SortedNumbers\n";

@SortedStrings = sort { $b cmp $a } @Strings;
print "@SortedStrings\n";
```

9. Run the script.

```
perl sorta.pl
```

10. The output follows.

Output

```
Alice Fred Harry Jane
1 3 4 7 9 10
1 3 4 7 9 10
10 9 7 4 3 1
10 9 7 4 3 1
Jane Harry Fred Alice
```

End Output

A screen dump of the execution of the script can be seen in Figure 17-1.

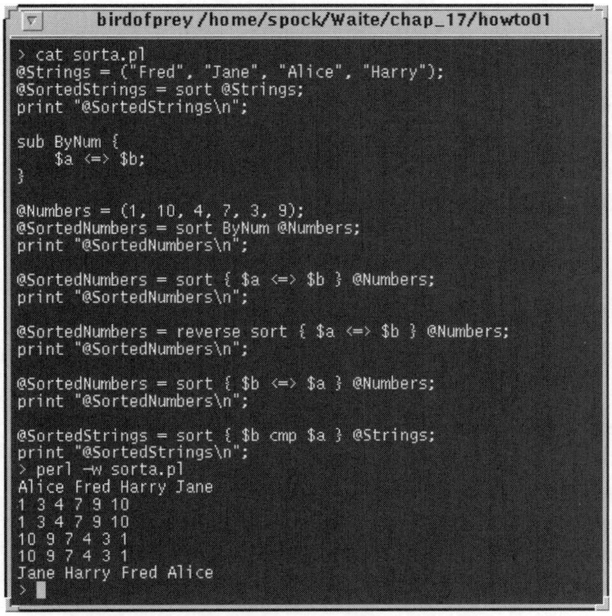

Figure 17-1 Output of sorta.pl

How It Works

The sort command is very flexible. It can be given a subroutine or block of code to use to compare two values in the array to be sorted. By varying this code, a sort can place values in any defined order.

Comments

The examples here compare only numeric and string data. To learn how to sort more complex data types, see How-To 17.3.

COMPLEXITY
BEGINNING

17.2 How do I...
Sort an array into unique elements?

COMPATIBILITY: PERL 4   PERL 5   UNIX   DOS

Problem

I can sort my arrays using sort, but I sometimes have duplicate entries in my arrays. How can I sort and retrieve only the unique elements?

Technique

By using the grep command with sort, you can sort an array and list only the unique
elements. The grep command takes two arguments. The first is an expression that
returns True or False. The second is an array. The result of the grep command is all
the elements of the array for which the expression returned True. In the expression
below, the variable $_ takes on each value of array.

Steps

The example script takes an array of strings and returns only the unique elements
in sorted order. The first method of doing this sorts the elements and then removes
the duplicates. The second method sorts only the unique elements.

1. Create a script called unique.pl to take an array and return the unique elements in sorted order. First, define an array to process. Use sort to sort the
array and pass the resulting array to grep. The first argument to grep is an
expression to remove duplicate entries. It compares the current element to
the previous one and returns True only if they are different. Print the resulting array.

```
@Strings = ("Fred", "Jane", "Alice", "Fred", "Harry", "Alice");

@SortedUnique = grep(($Last eq $_ ? 0 : ($Last = $_, 1)),sort @Strings);
print "@SortedUnique\n";
```

2. Create a call to grep that uses an associative array to remove the duplicate
entries in the array. Sort the output of the grep command. Print the resulting array.

```
@SortedUnique = sort grep((! $Seen{$_}++),@Strings);
print "@SortedUnique\n";
```

3. The entire script follows.

```
@Strings = ("Fred", "Jane", "Alice", "Fred", "Harry", "Alice");

@SortedUnique = grep(($Last eq $_ ? 0 : ($Last = $_, 1)),sort @Strings);
print "@SortedUnique\n";

@SortedUnique = sort grep((! $Seen{$_}++),@Strings);
print "@SortedUnique\n";
```

4. Run the script.

```
perl unique.pl
```

5. The output of the script follows.

Output

```
Alice  Fred  Harry  Jane
Alice  Fred  Harry  Jane
```

End Output

How It Works

The grep command is useful for selecting specific elements of an array. In this example, it is used to remove duplicate entries in an array. The first grep expression

```
grep(($Last eq $_ ? 0 : ($Last = $_, 1)),sort @Strings);
```

relies on the array being sorted before it is passed to grep. The expression compares the previous value to the current one. If they are the same, it returns False. If they are different, it saves the current value as the previous one and returns True. The result of the comma operator is the result of the expression on the right side of the comma. In this case, it is 1, or True.

The second call to grep

```
grep((! $Seen{$_}++),@Strings);
```

does not depend on the array being sorted before being passed to it. The expression checks an associative array to see if the value is a key to the array. If it is, the value of the array element is negated. Because only positive integers are saved as values, the negation returns False. This causes the grep command to ignore the entry. If the element does not exist in the associative array, the undefined value is returned and it is negated. This returns True to grep, causing the element to be put in the output of the grep command. The array element is always incremented. This causes it to exist and have a positive value after the first attempt to find it.

Comments

The use of grep in this example allows an array to be sorted and only the unique elements returned. The second use of grep allows the unique elements to be extracted without being sorted. This can be useful when you want to get the unique elements if they do not need to be sorted.

COMPLEXITY
INTERMEDIATE

17.3 How do I...
Sort nonscalar data types?

COMPATIBILITY: PERL 5 UNIX DOS

Problem

I know how to sort my arrays when they are made up of integers and strings. How do I sort a more complicated data structure?

Technique

Perl allows you to define a function or block of code that compares two values. The sort command then uses this routine to sort the array values. You can define the function to sort the array in any possible way.

Steps

The example program reads the input data into an array of references to associative arrays. The data describes countries and is sorted by population and land size (in square miles).

1. Create a script called nonscal.pl to sort the country data. First, read in the data. Each input line contains the country, its population, and its size. These entries are separated by commas. Put each country's data in an associative array and store a reference to that array in an array of countries.

```perl
use strict;

my(@Countries) = ();
while (<>) {
    chop;
    my($Country, $Population, $Size) = split(",",$_);
    push(@Countries, {
        Country    => $Country,
        Population => $Population,
        Size       => $Size,
    });
}
```

2. Loop through each country, sorting by population. The sort routine should contain a block to compare two populations. The block has two values predefined for it: $a and $b. These are the two values that sort needs to compare. The block must return -1 if $a is less than $b, 0 if they are the same, and 1 if $a is greater than $b. The <=> operator returns these values for two integers. Sort into descending sequence. Print each country name.

```perl
my($Country);

print "Countries by population\n";
for $Country (sort { ($::b->{Population}) <=> ($::a->{Population}) }
@Countries) {
    print "\t$$Country{Country}\n";
}
```

3. Sort and print the countries by size.

```perl
print "Countries by size\n";
for $Country (sort { ($::b->{Size}) <=> ($::a->{Size}) } @Countries) {
    print "\t$$Country{Country}\n";
}
```

4. The entire script follows.

```perl
use strict;

my(@Countries) = ();
while (<>) {
    chop;
    my($Country, $Population, $Size) = split(",",$_);
    push(@Countries, {
```

```
        Country      => $Country,
        Population => $Population,
        Size         => $Size,
    });
}

my($Country);

print "Countries by population\n";
for $Country (sort { ($::b->{Population}) <=> ($::a->{Population}) }
@Countries) {
    print "\t$$Country{Country}\n";
}

print "Countries by size\n";
for $Country (sort { ($::b->{Size}) <=> ($::a->{Size}) } @Countries) {
    print "\t$$Country{Country}\n";
}
```

5. Create an input file called nonscal.in with the following values.

```
Brazil,140440000,3286488
China,1069410000,3718783
India,773430000,1237062
Mexico,81230000,761605
United States,241960000,3679245
```

6. Run the script.

```
perl nonscal.pl nonscal.in
```

7. The output of the script follows.

Output

```
Countries by population
        China
        India
        United States
        Brazil
        Mexico
Countries by size
        China
        United States
        Brazil
        India
        Mexico
```

End Output

How It Works

You can configure sort by defining a block or subroutine that compares two values. Depending on how you do the comparison, the array can be sorted into almost any sequence. The variables in the sort block use the form $::a instead of $a. This is because $a and $b cannot be lexical variables (declared with a *my* statement). To keep "use strict" from issuing an error, qualify $a and $b with their package name. $::a is short-hand for $main::a.

Comments

You can use this technique on simple data as well as on complex data structures. For example, you could sort strings without considering case. Do this by converting the two values in the sort function to a common case and then comparing them.

COMPLEXITY
INTERMEDIATE

17.4 How do I...
Build a concordance?

COMPATIBILITY: | PERL 4 | PERL 5 | UNIX | DOS |

Problem

I have a paper that I would like to build a concordance from. How can I do this in Perl?

Technique

A concordance is a useful device for assisting a reader in finding information. It lists the line numbers where each word and term can be found in a document. Building a concordance is quite easy in Perl. It is easy to save each line and keep an entry for each word that tells which lines it was seen in. The Perl formatting commands (format and write) allow you to print this data in any form desired.

Steps

The example reads in lines of text and saves each line. It also keeps an associative array that stores the lines that a word was seen on. Certain common words are excluded. This information is then printed in a concordance format.

1. Create a script called concord.pl to create a concordance. First, set up the format strings.

```
use strict;

format STDOUT_TOP =
Word            Line #  Line
.

format STDOUT =
@<<<<<<<<<<<< @>>>>> @<<<<<<<<<<<<<<<<<<<<<<<<<<<<<<<<<<<<<<<<<<<<<<<<<<<
$::Word,        $::Line,  $::Lines[$::Line]
.
```

2. Create an associative array of the words that should be excluded from the concordance. Loop through each line of the input. Remove the new-line character from the end of the line and add the line to an array for later use.

```perl
my ($Word, %Exclude);
for $Word ("a", "an", "any", "and", "as", "be", "in", "it", "the") {
    $Exclude{$Word} = 1;
}

my(@Words,$Word,%Concord);
my($Line) = 0;

while(<>) {
    chop;
    $Line++;
    $::Lines[$Line] = $_;
```

3. Loop through each word on the line. If the word contains a number or is in the list of words to be excluded, skip it. Add the line number that the word was found on into the array referenced by the associative array entry for the current word.

```perl
    @Words = split(/\W+/);
    for $Word (@Words) {
        $Word =~ /\D/ or next;
        $Exclude{"\L$Word"} and next;
        push(@{$Concord{$Word}},$Line);
    }
}
```

4. Loop through a sorted list of all the words found. For each line that the word was found on, print the word, the line number, and the line. Set the word variable to null after each print. This will cause the word not to be printed repeatedly for each line it was found on.

```perl
for $::Word (sort keys %Concord) {
    for $::Line (@{$Concord{$::Word}}) {
        write;
        $::Word = "";
    }
}
```

5. The entire script follows.

```perl
use strict;

format STDOUT_TOP =
Word            Line #  Line
.

format STDOUT =
@<<<<<<<<<<< @>>>>>   @<<<<<<<<<<<<<<<<<<<<<<<<<<<<<<<<<<<<<<<<<<<<<<<<<<<<
$::Word,        $::Line, $::Lines[$::Line]
.

my ($Word, %Exclude);
for $Word ("a", "an", "any", "and", "as", "be", "in", "it", "the") {
    $Exclude{$Word} = 1;
}
```

continued on next page

continued from previous page

```
my(@Words,$Word,%Concord);
my($Line) = 0;

while(<>) {
    chop;
    $Line++;
    $::Lines[$Line] = $_;
    @Words = split(/\W+/);
    for $Word (@Words) {
        $Word =~ /\D/ or next;
        $Exclude{"\L$Word"} and next;
        push(@{$Concord{$Word}},$Line);
    }
}
for $::Word (sort keys %Concord) {
    for $::Line (@{$Concord{$::Word}}) {
        write;
        $::Word = "";
    }
}
```

6. Create an input file called concord.in with the following paragraph from the Perl manual.

```
Arbitrarily nested data structures
    Any scalar value, including any array element, may
    now contain a reference to any other variable or
    subroutine.   You can easily create anonymous
    variables and subroutines. Perl manages your
    reference counts for you.
```

7. Run the script.

```
perl concord.pl concord.in
```

8. The output follows.

Output

Word	Line #	Line
Arbitrarily	1	Arbitrarily nested data structures
Perl	5	variables and subroutines. Perl manages your
You	4	subroutine. You can easily create anonymous
anonymous	4	subroutine. You can easily create anonymous
array	2	Any scalar value, including any array element, may
can	4	subroutine. You can easily create anonymous
contain	3	now contain a reference to any other variable or
counts	6	reference counts for you.
create	4	subroutine. You can easily create anonymous
data	1	Arbitrarily nested data structures
easily	4	subroutine. You can easily create anonymous
element	2	Any scalar value, including any array element, may
for	6	reference counts for you.
including	2	Any scalar value, including any array element, may
manages	5	variables and subroutines. Perl manages your
may	2	Any scalar value, including any array element, may
nested	1	Arbitrarily nested data structures

```
now            3          now contain a reference to any other variable or
or             3          now contain a reference to any other variable or
other          3          now contain a reference to any other variable or
reference      3          now contain a reference to any other variable or
               6          reference counts for you.
scalar         2          Any scalar value, including any array element, may
structures     1    Arbitrarily nested data structures
subroutine     4          subroutine. You can easily create anonymous
subroutines    5          variables and subroutines. Perl manages your
to             3          now contain a reference to any other variable or
value          2          Any scalar value, including any array element, may
variable       3          now contain a reference to any other variable or
variables      5          variables and subroutines. Perl manages your
you            6          reference counts for you.
your           5          variables and subroutines. Perl manages your
```

End Output

How It Works

Building a concordance involves storing lines and breaking up those lines into the words contained in them. Store each line and build an array of lines that each word is in.

The line

```
push(@{$Concord{$Word}},$Line);
```

does a number of things. Its goal is to add a line to an array of lines. A reference to this array is stored in an associative array of words. If the word has not been seen yet, the entry to the associative array is created and a reference to an array containing the initial line is made.

Comments

For more information on formats, see Chapter 9. For more information on references, see Chapter 1.

The exclude list is not very extensive. One improvement to this script would be a better list. This list could be stored in a file, and the file could then be read in to initialize the exclude associative array. If you like numbers in the concordance, you can remove the line skipping them. The script will print nonalphabetic characters in the concordance. You can exclude these by adding another line like the one to skip numbers.

All the variables used in the format statement look like

```
$::Word
```

This is because they cannot be lexical variables (declared with a *my* statement). To keep "use strict" from issuing an error, qualify each of the variables with their package name. $::Word is shorthand for $main::Word.

It is difficult to write this script in Perl 4 because Perl 4 does not have references. Instead of having a reference to an array containing all line numbers that a word has been seen in, you would need to use a string instead. Change the array to a string by joining all the line numbers together, separated by a comma. When the values need to be accessed, split the string into an array. Also, remove the "use strict" and the ::s. Change the AND to a &&, and the OR to a ||.

```perl
format STDOUT_TOP =
Word            Line #  Line
.

format STDOUT =
@<<<<<<<<<<<< @>>>>> @<<<<<<<<<<<<<<<<<<<<<<<<<<<<<<<<<<<<<<<<<<<<<<<<<<<<<
$Word,         $Line, $Lines[$Line]
.

for $Word ("a", "an", "any", "and", "as", "be", "in", "it", "the") {
    $Exclude{$Word} = 1;
}

$Line = 0;

while(<>) {
    chop;
    $Line++;
    $Lines[$Line] = $_;
    @Words = split(/\W+/);
    for $Word (@Words) {
        $Word =~ /\D/ || next;
        $Exclude{"\L$Word"} && next;
        @LineNums = split(",",$Concord{$Word});
        push(@LineNums,$Line);
        $Concord{$Word} = join(",",@LineNums);
    }
}
for $Word (sort keys %Concord) {
    for $Line (split(",",$Concord{$Word})) {
        write;
        $Word = "";
    }
}
```

COMPLEXITY
BEGINNING

17.5   How do I...
Write recursive subroutines?

COMPATIBILITY: PERL 4   PERL 5   UNIX   DOS

Problem

I have an algorithm that calls for using recursive subroutines. How can I do this in Perl?

Technique

A recursive subroutine is one that calls itself. As long as a subroutine's variables are made local to the subroutine, any subroutine can be called recursively.

Steps

The example script takes an integer and returns its factorial.

1. Create a script called recurse.pl to return factorials. First, create a subroutine to compute factorials. If the argument is 2 or less, return that number. If it is greater than 2, multiply the argument by the factorial of 1 less than the argument.

```perl
sub Factorial {
    my($n) = @_;

    $n <= 2 and return $n;
    return $n * Factorial($n-1);
}
```

2. Print the first nine factorials.

```perl
for $i (1..9) {
    print "$i Factorial =\t", Factorial($i), "\n";
}
```

3. The entire script follows.

```perl
sub Factorial {
    my($n) = @_;

    $n <= 2 and return $n;
    return $n * Factorial($n-1);
}

for $i (1..9) {
    print "$i Factorial =\t", Factorial($i), "\n";
}
```

4. Run the script.

```perl
perl recurse.pl
```

5. The output follows.

```
Output
1 Factorial =    1
2 Factorial =    2
3 Factorial =    6
4 Factorial =    24
5 Factorial =    120
6 Factorial =    720
7 Factorial =    5040
8 Factorial =    40320
9 Factorial =    362880
End Output
```

How It Works

A Perl subroutine can call itself. The only precaution that you need to take is to make sure that new local variables are used on each invocation. The my declaration of a variable will cause this to happen.

```
my($n) = @_;
```

Comments

Perl 4 does not have the my declaration. The *local* statement can be used instead. This will have the same effect. However, using the *my* statement is more desirable. It will allow only the declared variables to be visible within the function. A *local* statement generates a new variable, but it can be seen by functions called from the function with the *local* statement.

Perl 4 does not have the AND conditional. Use && instead. Add a & in front of all subroutine calls. A Perl 4 version of the script follows.

```
sub Factorial {
    local($n) = @_;

    $n <= 2 && return $n;
    return $n * &Factorial($n-1);
}

for $i (1..9) {
    print "$i Factorial =\t", &Factorial($i), "\n";
}
```

COMPLEXITY
ADVANCED

17.6 How do I...
Perform a depth and breadth first search?

COMPATIBILITY: PERL 5   UNIX   DOS

Problem

I have a graph where the nodes are cities and the arcs are the connections between the cities. I need to search the graph to find the shortest distance between two cities. What is the best way of searching the graph?

Technique

There are two standard ways of searching a graph: depth first and breadth first. The first method starts at the initial node and goes as far as possible down a path before returning to try a different path. The second method looks at all the nodes closest to the initial node before starting to search nodes farther away.

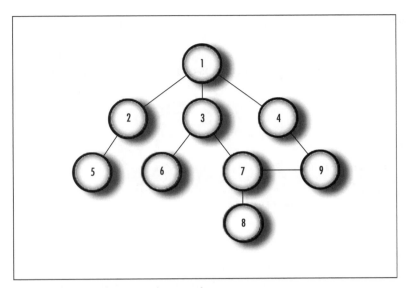

Figure 17-2 The example graph

How-To 16.4 describes a method of representing a graph in Perl. The same method is used here. The same data is used as well. The graph formed by this data is shown in Figure 17-2.

Steps

The example script creates a graph and traverses it depth first and then breadth first. Create a function for each type of search. Use a global associative array to keep track of which nodes have been visited. This is used to make sure that nodes are visited only once.

1. Create a script called search.pl to read in a graph and traverse it both depth first and breadth first. First, read in the node data from a file and store it in an associative array of associative arrays. Use the same code as in How-To 16.4.

```
use strict;

my (%Nodes);

while(<>) {
    my($n);
    my($Node, @Line) = split;

    for $n (@Line) {
        $Nodes{$Node}{$n} = 1;
        $Nodes{$n}{$Node} = 1;
    }
}
```

2. Create a function to print out the graph in depth-first order. This subroutine takes one argument, the initial node to search from. If this node has been visited, return. Otherwise, print the node, mark it visited, and call the function recursively for each node that is connected to the node argument.

```perl
my(%Seen);

sub Depth {
    my($Node) = @_;
    my($N);

    $Seen{$Node} and return;
    print "$Node ";
    $Seen{$Node}++;
    for $N (sort keys %{$Nodes{$Node}}) {
        Depth($N);
    }
}
```

3. Create a subroutine to do a breadth-first traversal. There should be a single argument, a node to start from. If this node has already been seen, return. Otherwise, push the node onto a queue of nodes to search. The queue will hold the closest nodes at the front of the queue. As more distant nodes are seen, put them on the end of the queue. In this manner, the closest nodes are visited first.

```perl
sub Breadth {
    my($Node) = @_;
    my(@Bqueue,$N);

    $Seen{$Node} and return;
    push(@Bqueue,$Node);
```

4. Create a loop to take a node off the front of the queue and process it. When there are no more nodes in the queue, exit the loop. If the node has already been visited, go to the next node. Otherwise, print the node and mark it visited. Push each node connected to the current node onto the queue. Do this only if a node has not been visited yet.

```perl
    while($Node = shift(@Bqueue)) {
        $Seen{$Node} and next;
        print "$Node ";
        $Seen{$Node}++;
        for $N (sort keys %{$Nodes{$Node}}) {
            $Seen{$N} || push(@Bqueue,$N);
        }
    }
}
```

5. Print out the graph data.

```perl
my($Node);

foreach $Node (keys %Nodes) {
    print "$Node: ", join(" ",sort keys %{$Nodes{$Node}}),"\n";
}
```

6. For each node in the graph, call the depth-first subroutine. Do this in case some parts of the graph are not connected to other parts. If the graph is fully connected, only the fist call results in a printout of nodes. This happens because all the nodes are marked visited on the first pass.

```perl
print "\nDepth first:\n";
foreach $Node (keys %Nodes) {
    Depth($Node);
}
```

7. Undefine the associative array holding the visited status. This allows a breadth-first search to start, with no nodes marked as visited. Call the breadth-first function for each node in the graph. As above, a fully connected graph produces output on the first call only.

```perl
undef %Seen;
print "\nBreadth first:\n";
foreach $Node (keys %Nodes) {
    Breadth($Node);
}
print "\n";
```

8. The entire script follows.

```perl
use strict;

my (%Nodes);

while(<>) {
    my($n);
    my($Node, @Line) = split;

    for $n (@Line) {
        $Nodes{$Node}{$n} = 1;
        $Nodes{$n}{$Node} = 1;
    }
}

my(%Seen);

sub Depth {
    my($Node) = @_;
    my($N);

    $Seen{$Node} and return;
    print "$Node ";
    $Seen{$Node}++;
    for $N (sort keys %{$Nodes{$Node}}) {
        Depth($N);
    }
}

sub Breadth {
    my($Node) = @_;
    my(@Bqueue,$N);
```

continued on next page

continued from previous page

```
        $Seen{$Node} and return;
        push(@Bqueue,$Node);
        while($Node = shift(@Bqueue)) {
            $Seen{$Node} and next;
            print "$Node ";
            $Seen{$Node}++;
            for $N (sort keys %{$Nodes{$Node}}) {
                $Seen{$N} || push(@Bqueue,$N);
            }
        }
}

my($Node);

foreach $Node (keys %Nodes) {
    print "$Node: ", join(" ",sort keys %{$Nodes{$Node}}),"\n";
}

print "\nDepth first:\n";
foreach $Node (keys %Nodes) {
    Depth($Node);
}

undef %Seen;
print "\nBreadth first:\n";
foreach $Node (keys %Nodes) {
    Breadth($Node);
}
print "\n";
```

9. Create an input file called search.in with the following data.

```
1 2 3 4
2 5
3 6 7
4 9
7 8 9
```

10. Run the script.

```
perl search.pl search.in
```

11. The output follows.

```
┌─ Output ────────────────────────────────────────────

1: 2 3 4
2: 1 5
3: 1 6 7
4: 1 9
5: 2
6: 3
7: 3 8 9
8: 7
9: 4 7

Depth first:
1 2 5 3 6 7 8 9 4
Breadth first:
1 2 3 4 5 6 7 9 8
└─ End Output ────────────────────────────────────────
```

How It Works

The depth-first search works by using recursion. Each time the function is called, it prints the current node and descends another level into the graph. This continues until all connected nodes are visited. The call stack then unwinds and another path is taken.

The breadth-first search uses a queue to store nodes to be visited. This allows the first nodes that are seen (the closest ones) to be printed first and the farther ones to be saved for later printing.

Comments

This script cannot be used in Perl 4 because Perl 4 does not have references.

COMPLEXITY
ADVANCED

17.7 How do I...
Perform a topological search?

COMPATIBILITY: PERL 5   UNIX   DOS

Problem

I have a directed graph of a project's activities. It shows what activities need to be done before another activity can start. How can I perform a topological search of this graph to show the sequence in which activities must be performed?

Technique

A directed graph is an excellent way to represent a set of activities that must be performed and the order in which they must be performed. How to represent a graph is seen in How-To 16.4. However, the graph in How-To 16.4 is not a directed graph. It assumes that if node A is connected to node B, node B is connected to node A. In a directed graph, the connection goes in one direction. With activities, a connection from node A to node B says that the activity represented by node A must be done before the activity represented by node B. See Figure 17-3 for the directed graph used in this How-To.

To perform a topological sort, the graph must not contain any loops. If it did, an activity could not be performed until after it was performed, which is impossible. In this example, a graph is represented in the same way as in How-To 16.4. The only change is that a reverse connection will not be established. So no link between node B and node A is made when the link between node A and node B is seen.

A topological sort is done by first listing all the nodes that are not being pointed to by other nodes. These nodes represent activities that have no prerequisites. These nodes are then removed from the graph. This represents the activities being completed. The process is then repeated until all nodes have been visited.

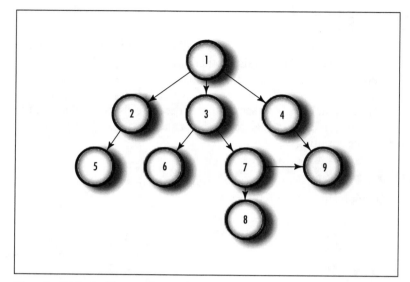

Figure 17-3 A directed graph

Steps

The example script reads in the data from How-To 16.4 and creates a directed graph. A topological sort of the graph is done, printing nodes as they are visited. In How-To 16.4, the %Node associative array holds the links from the node that is the key to the array to other nodes. Because the links are not directed, this array holds all the nodes. In a directed graph, there can be nodes that do not point to other nodes, so this array cannot be used to list all the nodes. In this script, the associative array %Vcount is used for that purpose. An associative array called %Count holds the number of nodes pointing to the node that is the key to the array.

1. Create a script called topo.pl to read in a directed graph and print out a topological sort of it. First, read in the graph as in How-To 16.4, but without the reverse link. Keep track of the number of links pointing to each node. Print out the data in the graph to show the connection between nodes.

```perl
use strict;

my(%Vcount,%Nodes,%Count);

while(<>) {
    my($n);
    my($Node, @Line) = split;

    $Vcount{$Node}++;
    for $n (@Line) {
        $Nodes{$Node}{$n} = 1;
        $Count{$n}++;
```

```
        $Vcount{$n}++;
    }
}

my($Node);
foreach $Node (keys %Nodes) {
    print "$Node: ", join(" ",sort keys %{$Nodes{$Node}}),"\n";
}
```

2. For each node, if it has no nodes pointing to it, add it to an array of orphan nodes.

```
my(@Orphans);

for $Node (sort keys %Vcount) {
    if ($Count{$Node} == 0) {
        push(@Orphans,$Node);
    }
}
```

3. Loop once for each node. Each time through the loop, remove a node from the orphan array. If there are no nodes in the array, there must be a loop in the graph. If so, print a message and exit. Print the node. For each node that the current node points to, decrement the pointed-to counter. If the count drops to 0, add the node to the orphan array.

```
my($i);

for $i (keys %Vcount) {
    $Node = shift @Orphans;
    if (! defined($Node)) {
        die "Cycle in the graph\n";
    }
    print "$Node ";

    my($n);
    for $n (sort keys %{$Nodes{$Node}}) {
        if(--$Count{$n} == 0) {
            push(@Orphans,$n);
        }
    }
}

print "\n";
```

4. The entire script follows.

```
use strict;

my(%Vcount,%Nodes,%Count);

while(<>) {
    my($n);
    my($Node, @Line) = split;

    $Vcount{$Node}++;
    for $n (@Line) {
        $Nodes{$Node}{$n} = 1;
```

continued on next page

continued from previous page

```
            $Count{$n}++;
            $Vcount{$n}++;
        }
}

my($Node);
foreach $Node (keys %Nodes) {
    print "$Node: ", join(" ",sort keys %{$Nodes{$Node}}),"\n";
}

my(@Orphans);

for $Node (sort keys %Vcount) {
    if ($Count{$Node} == 0) {
        push(@Orphans,$Node);
    }
}

my($i);

for $i (keys %Vcount) {
    $Node = shift @Orphans;
    if (! defined($Node)) {
        die "Cycle in the graph\n";
    }
    print "$Node ";

    my($n);
    for $n (sort keys %{$Nodes{$Node}}) {
        if(--$Count{$n} == 0) {
            push(@Orphans,$n);
        }
    }
}

print "\n";
```

5. Create an input file called topo.in with the following data.

```
1 2 3 4
2 5
3 6 7
4 9
7 8 9
```

6. Run the script.

```
perl topo.pl topo.in
```

7. The output of the script follows.

```
Output
1: 2 3 4
2: 5
3: 6 7
4: 9
7: 8 9
1 2 3 4 5 6 7 8 9
End Output
```

How It Works

The script creates an array that is used as a queue. Each node that does not have a node pointing to it is pushed onto the array. These nodes are then printed and removed from consideration. Each node that is pointed to by each of those nodes has its pointed-to counter decremented to represent the removal of the node. If any of these nodes now have no nodes pointing to them, they are pushed onto the queue. By removing nodes from the front of the queue, all the nodes are visited in topological order.

The loop through all the nodes uses a variable $i to hold each node. This variable is never used. The nodes are retrieved from the orphan array instead. The use of the loop in this manner is just a method of causing a loop to happen as many times as there are nodes. Because the loop prints one node each time through the loop, that is the correct number of times to iterate.

The value stored in each %Vcount entry is irrelevant. The only items of interest are the keys to the associative array. Incrementing the value of an existing array element has no effect on the keys. Incrementing a nonexistent array element causes the element to become defined. This adds the key to the array.

Comments

There is no real need for the sorting of arrays done in this script. This is done to make the output look better. When a choice of nodes is possible, the sort will cause the lower numbered one to print first.

COMPLEXITY
ADVANCED

17.8 How do I...
Perform an infix, prefix, and postfix traversal?

COMPATIBILITY: PERL 5   UNIX   DOS

Problem

I have a binary tree of program keywords that I need to traverse. How can I do that?

Technique

The three standard ways of traversing a tree are infix, prefix, and postfix. An *infix traversal* visits all the nodes in the left subtree of a node, the node itself, and then the nodes in the right subtree. A *prefix traversal* visits all the nodes in the left subtree, then the nodes in the right subtree, and lastly the node itself. A *postfix traversal* visits the node first, then the left subtree, and lastly the right subtree.

For more information on binary trees, see How-To 16.1. The binary tree used in this How-To is shown in Figure 17-4.

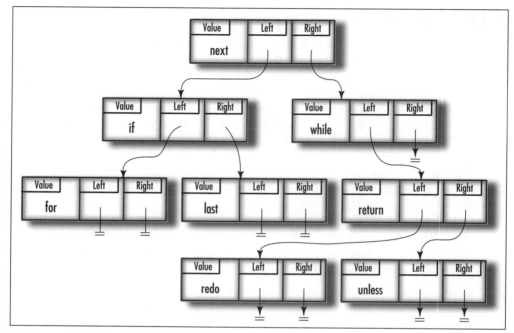

Figure 17-4 A binary tree

Steps

The example script prints out a binary tree using all three types of traversals. The method of storing a binary tree is seen in How-To 16.1. This same method is used here. In addition, all the searching and inserting functions from How-To 16.1 are used. Only the traversal functions are new.

1. Create a script called traverse.pl to create a binary tree and traverse it. First, copy the code from How-To 16.1 to implement a binary tree, the code to build one, and the code to display the built tree.

```
use strict;

sub AlphaCmp {
    return ($_[0] cmp $_[1]);
}

sub _Search {
    my($Node,$Val,$Cmp) = @_;
    my($Previous,$Compare);

    $Previous = undef;
    while (defined($Node)) {
        $Compare = &$Cmp($Node->{"Value"},$Val);
        if ($Compare == 0) {
```

```
                    return (1,$Previous);
            }
            $Previous = $Node;
            if ($Compare > 0) {
                $Node = $Node->{"Left"};
            } else {
                $Node = $Node->{"Right"};
            }
        }
        return (0,$Previous);
}

sub Search {
    my($Result);

    ($Result) = _Search(@_);
    return $Result;
}

sub Insert {
    my($Node,$Val,$Cmp) = @_;
    my($Result,$Insert,$Compare,$NewNode);

    ($Result,$Insert) = _Search($Node,$Val,$Cmp);
    if ($Result) {
        return $Node;
    }
    $NewNode = {
        "Value" => $Val,
        "Left"  => undef,
        "Right" => undef
    };
    if (defined($Insert)) {
        if (&$Cmp($Insert->{"Value"},$Val) > 0) {
            $Insert->{"Left"} = $NewNode;
        } else {
            $Insert->{"Right"} = $NewNode;
        }
        return $Node;
    } else {
        return $NewNode;
    }
}

my($Top) = undef;
my($i);

for $i ("next","if","while","for","last","return","redo","unless") {
    $Top = Insert($Top,$i,\&AlphaCmp);
}

Print($Top);

sub Print {
    my($n) = @_;
```

continued on next page

continued from previous page

```
    defined($n) or return;
    print "$n->{'Value'}:";
    defined($n->{"Left"}) and print "$n->{'Left'}{'Value'}";
    print ":";
    defined($n->{"Right"}) and print "$n->{'Right'}{'Value'}";
    print "\n";
    Print($n->{"Left"});
    Print($n->{"Right"});
}
```

2. Add a function to print the tree in infix form. The function should use recursion to print the subtrees. If the node passed to the function is not defined, return without printing anything. If it is defined, print the left subtree, the node itself, and the right subtree.

```
sub InFix {
    my($n) = @_;

    defined($n) or return;
    InFix($n->{'Left'});
    print "$n->{'Value'} ";
    InFix($n->{'Right'});
}
```

3. Add a function to print the tree in prefix form. This will be identical to the previous function, with only the order of printing changed.

```
sub PreFix {
    my($n) = @_;

    defined($n) or return;
    print "$n->{'Value'} ";
    PreFix($n->{'Left'});
    PreFix($n->{'Right'});
}
```

4. Add a postfix function.

```
sub PostFix {
    my($n) = @_;

    defined($n) or return;
    PostFix($n->{'Left'});
    PostFix($n->{'Right'});
    print "$n->{'Value'} ";
}
```

5. Print a traversal of the tree in all three forms.

```
print "\nInfix = ";
InFix($Top);
print "\n\nPrefix = ";
PreFix($Top);
print "\n\nPostfix = ";
PostFix($Top);
print "\n";
```

6. The entire script follows.

```perl
use strict;

sub AlphaCmp {
    return ($_[0] cmp $_[1]);
}

sub _Search {
    my($Node,$Val,$Cmp) = @_;
    my($Previous,$Compare);

    $Previous = undef;
    while (defined($Node)) {
        $Compare = &$Cmp($Node->{"Value"},$Val);
        if ($Compare == 0) {
            return (1,$Previous);
        }
        $Previous = $Node;
        if ($Compare > 0) {
            $Node = $Node->{"Left"};
        } else {
            $Node = $Node->{"Right"};
        }
    }
    return (0,$Previous);
}

sub Search {
    my($Result);

    ($Result) = _Search(@_);
    return $Result;
}

sub Insert {
    my($Node,$Val,$Cmp) = @_;
    my($Result,$Insert,$Compare,$NewNode);

    ($Result,$Insert) = _Search($Node,$Val,$Cmp);
    if ($Result) {
        return $Node;
    }
    $NewNode = {
        "Value" => $Val,
        "Left"  => undef,
        "Right" => undef
    };
    if (defined($Insert)) {
        if (&$Cmp($Insert->{"Value"},$Val) > 0) {
            $Insert->{"Left"} = $NewNode;
        } else {
            $Insert->{"Right"} = $NewNode;
        }
        return $Node;
    } else {
```

continued on next page

continued from previous page

```perl
            return $NewNode;
        }
}

my($Top) = undef;
my($i);

for $i ("next","if","while","for","last","return","redo","unless") {
    $Top = Insert($Top,$i,\&AlphaCmp);
}

Print($Top);

sub Print {
    my($n) = @_;

    defined($n) or return;
    print "$n->{'Value'}:";
    defined($n->{"Left"}) and print "$n->{'Left'}{'Value'}";
    print ":";
    defined($n->{"Right"}) and print "$n->{'Right'}{'Value'}";
    print "\n";
    Print($n->{"Left"});
    Print($n->{"Right"});
}

sub InFix {
    my($n) = @_;

    defined($n) or return;
    InFix($n->{'Left'});
    print "$n->{'Value'} ";
    InFix($n->{'Right'});
}

sub PreFix {
    my($n) = @_;

    defined($n) or return;
    print "$n->{'Value'} ";
    PreFix($n->{'Left'});
    PreFix($n->{'Right'});
}

sub PostFix {
    my($n) = @_;

    defined($n) or return;
    PostFix($n->{'Left'});
    PostFix($n->{'Right'});
    print "$n->{'Value'} ";
}

print "\nInfix = ";
InFix($Top);
print "\n\nPrefix = ";
```

```
PreFix($Top);
print "\n\nPostfix = ";
PostFix($Top);
print "\n";
```

7. Run the script.

```
perl traverse.pl
```

8. The output follows.

```
next:if:while
if:for:last
for::
last::
while:return:
return:redo:unless
redo::
unless::

Infix = for if last next redo return unless while

Prefix = next if for last while return redo unless

Postfix = for last if redo unless return while next
```

How It Works

The different methods of traversing a tree vary only in the order in which the subtrees are traversed and when the value in the node itself is used. Recursion is used to descend into the subtrees. This is a natural way for traversals to happen in the correct order.

Comments

These traversals can be performed on trees with more than two subtrees. The only difference is that multiple subtrees may be on the "left" and multiple subtrees may be on the "right."

SPECIAL FILE
PROCESSING

SPECIAL FILE
PROCESSING

How do I...

Perl makes it easy to process data files that come in many different formats. A file can be converted to an easily processed form and then the data can be processed. Sometimes it is easier to call an external program to create the processed form. A Perl script can call a program and read the converted data. The reverse is also true. An external program can take the output of a Perl script and change it into another format. Of course, sometimes it is easier and faster to have Perl do all the processing. This chapter will give you a feel for the numerous ways Perl can be used to process data files.

18.1   Process uuencoded Files

Files that have been uuencoded to be sent over a network can be uudecoded by Perl without invoking an external program. The section will show you how.

18.2 Process Compressed Files

Files that have been compressed to save space can be processed by Perl. It is possible to read these files without having to restore them on disk. This How-To will demonstrate this technique.

18.3 Encrypt Files

The output of a Perl script can be encrypted to keep the data secret. This section will show you how to encrypt files.

18.4 Extract Text from a Binary File

Binary files can be processed by Perl as easily as files with only printable data. This section will demonstrate how to print the strings inside a binary file.

18.5 Process Ethernet Packet Dumps

Many network problems can be solved by analyzing the individual packets being sent across a network. Perl makes it easy to extract data from the packets. This How-To will show you how to process Ethernet packet dumps.

COMPLEXITY
BEGINNING

18.1 How do I...
Process uuencoded files?

COMPATIBILITY: PERL 4 PERL 5 UNIX DOS

Problem

Someone sent me a uuencoded file. How can I read this file in Perl?

Technique

Files may be uuencoded so that they can be sent over a network. The uuencode program takes binary data and encodes it into ASCII characters. You can then safely send the encoded file over a network that does not allow certain binary data to be transmitted.

Perl provides the unpack function to take a string representing a structure and convert it into a list. (The pack function takes a list and converts it into a binary string.) The string in this case is a number of characters from the original file encoded into ASCII. pack/unpack knows about uuencoding and can convert a string to and from that format.

Steps

The example script reads in a uuencoded file and creates the original file from it. The uuencode program puts a line at the beginning of the encoded file that tells where the uuencoded data starts, what its filename should be, and what permissions that file should have. The data ends with a line that says "end."

The example data has been uuencoded. So, in effect, the script is re-creating itself!

1. Create a file called uudecode.pl. Add the following script to it. First, loop through the beginning of the file looking for the begin line. That line contains three data fields separated by white space. The first field is the string begin. The second field is an octal number representing the file permissions the recreated file should have. The last string is the name the restored file should have. The pattern that matches the begin line saves two values. (The values match inside parentheses.) Use these values to store the mode and filename. Remember the fact that the line was seen. If the begin line is not found, print a message and exit.

```
$Found = 0;
while (<>) {
    if (/^begin\s+(\d+)\s+(.*)/) {
        $Mode = $1;
        $FileName = $2;
        $Found = 1;
        last;
    }
}

$Found || die "No begin line\n";
```

2. Open the output file for writing. If the open fails, print a message and exit. Loop through the data one line at a time. If there is only white space on the line, skip it. The line must contain more than three characters (the end-of-line character, a size character, and some data). If there are less than three characters, skip the line. When the end-of-data line is seen, exit the loop. The end of data is denoted by the string end on a line by itself.

```
open (OUT,">$FileName") || die "Can't open $FileName\n";

while (<>) {
    /^\s*$/ && next;
    length() > 2 || next;
    /^end$/ && last;
```

3. Convert the uuencode line to the original string. The unpack function takes two arguments. The first is a string telling how the data is packed. In this case, the entire line is uuencoded, so use the letter u. The second argument is the string to be unpacked. A list is returned, but because there is only one string on each line, the uudecoded string can be stored in a scalar variable. Check to verify that the data was unpacked properly. If not, print a message and exit. Write the unpacked data into the output file.

```
    $Line = unpack("u",$_);
    defined($Line) || die "Invalid uuencoded string\n";
    print OUT $Line;
}
```

4. After all the data has been read, close the output file. Call chmod to change the permissions on the created file to be what was requested in the input. Remember that the mode is an octal number. It needs to be converted to decimal to be used by chmod.

```
close(OUT);
chmod oct($Mode), $FileName;
```

5. The entire script follows.

```
$Found = 0;
while (<>) {
    if (/^begin\s+(\d+)\s+(.*)/) {
        $Mode = $1;
        $FileName = $2;
        $Found = 1;
        last;
    }
}

$Found || die "No begin line\n";

open (OUT,">$FileName") || die "Can't open $FileName\n";

while (<>) {
    /^\s*$/ && next;
    length() > 2 || next;
    /^end$/ && last;
    $Line = unpack("u",$_);
    defined($Line) || die "Invalid uuencoded string\n";
    print OUT $Line;
}

close(OUT);
chmod oct($Mode), $FileName;
```

6. Create an input file called uudecode.in with the following data (or copy the file off the CD). This is the output of the script being run through uuencode.

`Output`

```
begin 644 uu.pl
M)$90=6YD(#0,/#L*=VAI;&4-("@\/CX@>PH)("`@("`@(&EF("@O7F)E9VEN
M9"LH+BDI*7-\X2@J*2\I('L*"0D)("`@("`@("`@)$UO9&4@/2`D,3L*"0D)
M"21&:6QE3F%M92`]("0R.PH)"0D@("`@("`@)$9O=6YD(#T@,3L*"0D)("`@
M;"01;F5X="QPH)"0DO7EQSO\ID@*"0D@("`@("`@;&%S=#L*"0D)"0E]"@D)?0H*
M)$9O=6YD('Q\(&1I92`B3F@@8F5G:6X@;&EN95QN(CL*"@IO<&5N("A/550L
M(CXD1FEL94YA;64B*2!\?"!D:64@(D-A;B=T(&]P96X@)$9I;&5.86UE7&XB
M.PH*=VAI;&4@*#P^*2![("`@("`@("`@("`@("`@("`@("`@("`@("`@("`@
M("`@("`@("`@("`@(&YE>'0["@D@("`@("`@("`@("`@("`@("`@("`@("`@
M("`@("`@("`@(&YE>'0["@D@("`@("`@("`@("`@("`@("`@("`@("`@("`@
M("`@("`@(&QA<W0["@D@("`@("`@("`@("`@("`@("`@("`@("`@("`@("`@
M("`@("`@('!R:6YT($]55"`D3&EN93L*?0H*8VQO<V4H3U54*3L*8VAM;V0@
`
end
```

`End Output`

7. Run the script.

```
perl uudecode.pl uudecode.in
```

8. The output of the script should be the script itself, saved under the name uu.pl.

How It Works

The fact that pack/unpack knows about uuencoded data makes this a simple program to write. Each line is given to unpack to be converted back to its original form.

Comments

If you receive mail that contains an uuencoded file, you do not need to strip the headers and text from the top and bottom of the message. The script skips to the beginning of the uuencoded data and stops at the end of it.

COMPLEXITY
BEGINNING

18.2 How do I...
Process compressed files?

COMPATIBILITY: PERL 4 PERL 5 UNIX DOS

Problem

I have a compressed file that I would like to use in a Perl program. How can I uncompress the file in my program?

Technique

Many operating systems allow files to be compressed. This usually results in doubling the amount of disk space available. Some compression programs compact just one file. Others allow many files to be compressed together (often called *archived*). To access a compressed file, you need to run an uncompress program to restore the original file. If this program can send the uncompressed data to standard output, Perl can read it and then process it.

The standard output of a command can be read by Perl, using a feature of the open command. Instead of giving a filename to open as the source of the data to be read, you can give a command line instead. If this command line ends in a pipe symbol (|), the command will be run and its standard output will be taken as the data to be read.

Steps

Two example scripts are given. Both scripts launch an uncompress program and read its output. This data is then printed. In your scripts, you can process the data any way you like. These scripts show how to access the uncompressed data. The first script assumes that the file was compressed using gzip. gzip is available on both UNIX and DOS systems. It takes a single file and compresses it. The program zcat takes a gzipped file and sends the uncompressed output to standard output. The script takes 0 or more compressed files as arguments. These files are uncompressed and printed. If no file is given as an argument to zcat, it will read from standard input.

The second script assumes that pkzip was used as the compress/archiver. It takes two arguments. The first argument is the file to be uncompressed. The second argument is the pkzip file that contains the archived file (and possibly others). The pkunzip program is used to extract the uncompress file. The -c option to pkunzip causes the output to be sent to standard output so that the Perl script can process it.

1. Create a file called uncomp1.pl. Enter the following script into it.

```
open(IN,"zcat @ARGV |") || die "Can't open $ARGV[0] ...\n";

while(<IN>) {
    print;
}

close(IN);
```

2. Create a file called uncomp2.pl. Add the following program into it.

```
if ($#ARGV != 1) {
    die "Incorrect number of arguments\n";
}

$File     = $ARGV[0];
$CompFile = $ARGV[1];

open(IN,"pkunzip -c $CompFile $File |") || die "Can't open $CompFile\n";

while(<IN>) {
    print;
}

close(IN);
```

How It Works

The pkzip-based script verifies that two arguments are passed to it. This makes sure that the pkunzip program is called correctly. Because the zcat program can take multiple compressed files as arguments, no argument checking is done. The script launches the uncompress program in the open command. If the open fails, a message is printed and the script exits. Once the command is running, the script can read the data from the input filehandle.

Comments

This technique can be extended to almost any compression program. If the uncompress program cannot send the file to standard output, the uncompressed file can be put in a temporary location. Then the script can open that file and process the data. When the script finishes, the temporary file is then deleted.

COMPLEXITY
BEGINNING

18.3 How do I...
Encrypt files?

COMPATIBILITY: PERL 4 | PERL 5 | UNIX | DOS

Problem

I have some sensitive data that I would like to keep secret. Can I output encrypted data to a file in Perl?

Technique

Perl does not provide a built-in encryption routine. However, data from a Perl script can be passed through any command before being written to a file. To encrypt data, the output can be sent to an encryption program. Perl can write to the standard input of a command by using a special form of the open command. Instead of opening a file to be written to, you can give a command line. The command line must start with a pipe symbol (|). This is how Perl knows to send the data to the command line instead of a file

The example script assumes that there is a program named crypt available. It takes data from standard input and writes an encrypted version to standard output. If an argument is given to the crypt command, it is taken as a password. If no password is supplied, the crypt command prompts for one.

Steps

The example script takes zero or more arguments. The first argument is the name of the encrypted file to be created. If no name is supplied, crypt.out is assumed to be the name. If additional arguments are given, they are names of files to be read. If no files are given, standard input is used. The input file(s) is read and sent to the crypt program to be encrypted.

1. Create a file named encrypt.pl. Add the following script to that file.

```
if ($#ARGV >=0) {
    $CryptFile = shift @ARGV;
} else {
    $CryptFile = "crypt.out";
}

open(OUT,"| crypt > $CryptFile") || die "Can't run crypt\n";

while(<>) {
    print OUT;
}
close(OUT);
```

How It Works

The script checks to see if there is at least one argument. If there is, it removes it from the argument list and saves it. The open command creates an output handle. Any data sent to that handle will be sent to the crypt program. The output of the crypt program is redirected into the appropriate output file. All the input is read and sent to the output filehandle.

The construct

```
while(<>) {
```

reads each line in the files listed in the @ARGV array. This array is where the input arguments are stored. If the array is empty, the data is read from standard input instead. Each time through the loop, one line is read and stored into the special variable $_. The body of the loop writes a line to the output filehandle. (The default data for the print statement is taken from $_.)

Comments

The crypt command may not be available on your system. This command is common on some UNIX platforms in the United States. However, government restrictions prevent its export abroad. You may be able to find a similar command on your system.

Because no password is given on the command line to crypt, the crypt program will prompt the user for one. The password could be supplied as part of the command line, such as

```
$Passwd = "pass_word";
open(OUT,"| crypt '$Passwd' > $CryptFile") || die "Can't run crypt\n";
```

This is not usually a good idea. A malicious user could discover the password by reading the script.

COMPLEXITY
INTERMEDIATE

18.4   How do I...
Extract text from a binary file?

COMPATIBILITY: | PERL 4 | PERL 5 | UNIX | DOS |

Problem

I have a number of executables for the same program. I want to find the newest version of the program. I know that there is a version number hidden inside the executable. How can I retrieve the strings stored in the executable files?

Technique

The ability to extract strings from a binary file is quite useful. Besides looking for version information, you can see error messages, options, file locations, and other data.

This information can be used to resolve problems with a program. Finding which files a program uses can be very helpful in finding where files related to the program are stored.

The way to extract strings from a binary file is to read the file as any other data file and then search for printable characters. The trick is to make sure that there are multiple printable characters in a row. This will help cut down on the number of times binary data is mistaken for real strings. A good choice for the number of characters in a row is four.

Steps

The example script reads from any files listed on the command line or standard input and output strings that are found. Any sequence of four or more printable characters in a row is assumed to be a string.

1. Create a file called strings.pl containing the following script.

```
$size = 4;

while (<>) {
    while (/[ -~]{$size,}/g) {
        print "$&\n";
    }
}
```

2. Run the script on the Perl executable.

```
perl strings.pl /usr/local/bin/perl
```

3. The first ten lines of output will look something like this:

```
Output
SVWh
perlmain.c
DynaLoader::boot_DynaLoader
DB_File::bootstrap
Fcntl::bootstrap
GDBM_File::bootstrap
ODBM_File::bootstrap
POSIX::bootstrap
SDBM_File::bootstrap
Socket::bootstrap
End Output
```

How It Works

Each line of the input is read and examined. A *while* loop looking for any printable character is run on each line. The construct

```
[ -~]
```

matches any character in the set of characters that is between the space character and the tilde character. In the case of the ASCII character set, these are all the printable characters. The pattern match then makes sure that there are four or more of these characters in a row by using the construct

```
{$size,}
```

The braces contain two numbers separated by a comma. The first number tells the minimum number of times the preceding character must be seen. In this case, there must be a minimum of four printable characters. The number after the comma is the maximum number of times to match. Because no maximum number is specified, there is no maximum.

Once a string is matched, it is printed. $& is the variable that holds the last successful pattern match.

Comments

The output given depends on the version of Perl you are running and the machine you are running it on. The output may not look anything like what was given.

The string length is hard-coded into this script. The length could be made an option, with four being the default. This would allow you to look for longer or shorter strings, depending on what is needed.

COMPLEXITY
ADVANCED

18.5 How do I...
Process Ethernet packet dumps?

COMPATIBILITY: PERL 4 PERL 5 UNIX DOS

Problem

My network is overloaded. I cannot find the source of all the packets. I can capture the packets, but how do I determine what is in them?

Technique

An Ethernet network sends data from one location to another location using an Ethernet packet. This packet is a sequence of bytes in a well-defined format.

The analysis of the contents of an Ethernet packet is a very complex undertaking. A book could be written describing how to do it. (There are such books!) The example given here builds a framework for printing out the fields of a packet. It looks at only some of the major fields. The script can be extended to look at other fields that may be of interest.

The script assumes that the packets are dumped into a file in hexadecimal format and the packets are separated by a blank line. The packet is read into an array, with each byte (two hexadecimal characters) stored into an array element. The fields of the packet are examined by looking at the appropriate bytes in the array. Because all fields are not on byte boundaries, the individual bits of a byte are sometimes examined.

An Ethernet packet consists of a 14-byte header followed by data. The first 6 bytes are the hardware address of the destination machine. The second 6 bytes are the hardware address of the source machine. The last 2 bytes of the header are used to determine the type of the packet.

If the packet is an Internet Protocol (IP) packet, the data in an Ethernet packet starts with an IP header. The format of this header is shown in Figure 18-1.

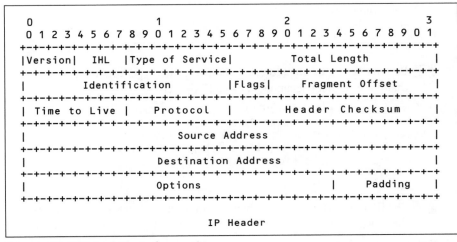

```
0                   1                   2                   3
0 1 2 3 4 5 6 7 8 9 0 1 2 3 4 5 6 7 8 9 0 1 2 3 4 5 6 7 8 9 0 1
+-+-+-+-+-+-+-+-+-+-+-+-+-+-+-+-+-+-+-+-+-+-+-+-+-+-+-+-+-+-+-+-+
|Version|  IHL  |Type of Service|         Total Length          |
+-+-+-+-+-+-+-+-+-+-+-+-+-+-+-+-+-+-+-+-+-+-+-+-+-+-+-+-+-+-+-+-+
|         Identification        |Flags|     Fragment Offset     |
+-+-+-+-+-+-+-+-+-+-+-+-+-+-+-+-+-+-+-+-+-+-+-+-+-+-+-+-+-+-+-+-+
| Time to Live  |    Protocol   |         Header Checksum        |
+-+-+-+-+-+-+-+-+-+-+-+-+-+-+-+-+-+-+-+-+-+-+-+-+-+-+-+-+-+-+-+-+
|                        Source Address                         |
+-+-+-+-+-+-+-+-+-+-+-+-+-+-+-+-+-+-+-+-+-+-+-+-+-+-+-+-+-+-+-+-+
|                      Destination Address                      |
+-+-+-+-+-+-+-+-+-+-+-+-+-+-+-+-+-+-+-+-+-+-+-+-+-+-+-+-+-+-+-+-+
|                    Options                     |    Padding    |
+-+-+-+-+-+-+-+-+-+-+-+-+-+-+-+-+-+-+-+-+-+-+-+-+-+-+-+-+-+-+-+-+

                           IP Header
```

Figure 18-1 IP header information

If the IP packet contains a TCP or UDP packet, the first 4 bytes of the IP data field contain the from and to ports.

Steps

The example script looks at some of the major fields of an Ethernet packet described above. There is a loop to process each packet. Within that loop is code to examine the individual fields.

1. Create a file called ether.pl. Insert the following code. First, include the Socket module to retrieve a constant used to look up machine names. Next, create a loop to process each packet. Assign each byte to an entry in an array. A byte consists of two hexadecimal digits.

```perl
use Socket;

$Eof = 0;
PACKET:
while (! $Eof) {
    my(@Packet);
    $i = 0;
    while ($In = <>) {
        chop($In);
        $In =~ s/\s+//g;
        $In =~ /./ || last;
        while ($In =~ s/^..//) {
            $Packet[$i++] = $&;
        }
        if ($In =~ /./) {
```

continued on next page

continued from previous page

```
            print "Bad packet string - skipping\n";
            next PACKET;
        }
    }
    if (! defined($In)) {
        $Eof = 1;
    }
    $i || next;
```

2. Remove the hardware addresses and the packet type from the packet. Verify that the Ethernet packet contains an IP packet.

```
@EtherTo = splice(@Packet,0,6);
@EtherFrom = splice(@Packet,0,6);
($EtherType1,$EtherType2) = splice(@Packet,0,2);
if ($EtherType1 ne "08" || $EtherType2 ne "00") {
    print "Not an IP packet - skipping\n";
    next;
}
```

3. The IP header is normally 20 bytes. Remove it and get the second 4 bits of the header. The real length of the header is four times the value in those bits.

```
$IpHeadLen = 20;
@IpHead = splice(@Packet,0,$IpHeadLen);
($IpVersion,$HeaderLen) = $IpHead[0] =~ /(.)(.)/;
$HeaderLen = hex($HeaderLen) * 4;
if ($HeaderLen - 20 > 0) {
    @Options = splice(@Packet,0,$HeaderLen - 20);
    $IpHeadLen = $HeaderLen;
}
```

4. Retrieve some of the fields from the IP header. In the case of the flags and the fragmentation offset, some bit manipulation is needed to extract the correct values.

```
$TypeOfService = $IpHead[1];
$Length = hex($IpHead[2]) * 0x100 + hex($IpHead[3]);
@Ident = @IpHead[4,5];
$Flags = (hex($IpHead[6]) & 0xe0) >> 5;
$FragOff = ($IpHead[6] & 0x1f) * 0x100 + hex($IpHead[7]);
$TimeToLive = $IpHead[8];
$Protocol = $IpHead[9];
$HeadCkSum = hex($IpHead[10]) * 0x100 + hex($IpHead[11]);
@SourceAddr = @IpHead[12..15];
@DestAddr = @IpHead[16..19];
```

5. Check the protocol field. If it is a known type, print out the type; otherwise, skip to the next packet.

```
if ($Protocol eq "06") {
    print "TCP ";
} elsif ($Protocol eq "11") {
    print "UDP ";
} elsif ($Protocol eq "01") {
    print "ICMP ";
```

```
} else {
    print "Unknown protocol - $Protocol\n";
    next;
}
```

6. Print the from IP address. Use pack to collect the 4 bytes of the address and assign them to a variable. Give that variable to gethostbyaddr to try to get a logical name for the numeric address. If a name is found, print it. Otherwise, print the numeric address in dotted form.

```
print "from ";
$Addr = pack("C4",hex($SourceAddr[0]),hex($SourceAddr[1]),
             hex($SourceAddr[2]),hex($SourceAddr[3]));
($SourceName) = gethostbyaddr($Addr,AF_INET);
if (defined($SourceName)) {
    print "$SourceName ";
} else {
    $Dot ="";
    for $Byte (@SourceAddr) {
        printf "$Dot%d",hex($Byte);
        $Dot = ".";
    }
    print " ";
}
```

7. Print the destination IP address and the length of the IP packet data.

```
print "to ";
$Addr = pack("C4",hex($DestAddr[0]),hex($DestAddr[1]),
             hex($DestAddr[2]),hex($DestAddr[3]));
($DestName) = gethostbyaddr($Addr,AF_INET);
if (defined($DestName)) {
    print "$DestName ";
} else {
    $Dot ="";
    for $Byte (@DestAddr) {
        printf "$Dot%d",hex($Byte);
        $Dot = ".";
    }
    print " ";
}

print $Length - $IpHeadLen, " bytes\n";
```

8. If the packet is a TCP or UDP packet, print the port numbers.

```
if ($Protocol eq "06") {
    $SrcPort = hex($Packet[0]) * 0x100 + hex($Packet[1]);
    $DestPort = hex($Packet[2]) * 0x100 + hex($Packet[3]);
    print "\tFrom port $SrcPort to port $DestPort\n";
} elsif ($Protocol eq "11") {
    $SrcPort = hex($Packet[0]) * 0x100 + hex($Packet[1]);
    $DestPort = hex($Packet[2]) * 0x100 + hex($Packet[3]);
    print "\tFrom port $SrcPort to port $DestPort\n";
}
}
```

9. The entire script follows.

```
use Socket;

$Eof = 0;
PACKET:
while (! $Eof) {
    my(@Packet);
    $i = 0;
    while ($In = <>) {
        chop($In);
        $In =~ s/\s+//g;
        $In =~ /./ || last;
        while ($In =~ s/^..//) {
            $Packet[$i++] = $&;
        }
        if ($In =~ /./) {
            print "Bad packet string - skipping\n";
            next PACKET;
        }
    }
    if (! defined($In)) {
        $Eof = 1;
    }
    $i || next;

    @EtherTo = splice(@Packet,0,6);
    @EtherFrom = splice(@Packet,0,6);
    ($EtherType1,$EtherType2) = splice(@Packet,0,2);
    if ($EtherType1 ne "08" || $EtherType2 ne "00") {
        print "Not an IP packet - skipping\n";
        next;
    }
    $IpHeadLen = 20;
    @IpHead = splice(@Packet,0,$IpHeadLen);
    ($IpVersion,$HeaderLen) = $IpHead[0] =~ /(.)(.)/;
    $HeaderLen = hex($HeaderLen) * 4;
    if ($HeaderLen - 20 > 0) {
        @Options = splice(@Packet,0,$HeaderLen - 20);
        $IpHeadLen = $HeaderLen;
    }
    $TypeOfService = $IpHead[1];
    $Length = hex($IpHead[2]) * 0x100 + hex($IpHead[3]);
    @Ident = @IpHead[4,5];
    $Flags = (hex($IpHead[6]) & 0xe0) >> 5;
    $FragOff = ($IpHead[6] & 0x1f) * 0x100 + hex($IpHead[7]);
    $TimeToLive = $IpHead[8];
    $Protocol = $IpHead[9];
    $HeadCkSum = hex($IpHead[10]) * 0x100 + hex($IpHead[11]);
    @SourceAddr = @IpHead[12..15];
    @DestAddr = @IpHead[16..19];
```

```perl
    if ($Protocol eq "06") {
        print "TCP ";
    } elsif ($Protocol eq "11") {
        print "UDP ";
    } elsif ($Protocol eq "01") {
        print "ICMP ";
    } else {
        print "Unknown protocol - $Protocol\n";
        next;
    }

    print "from ";
    $Addr = pack("C4",hex($SourceAddr[0]),hex($SourceAddr[1]),
                 hex($SourceAddr[2]),hex($SourceAddr[3]));
    ($SourceName) = gethostbyaddr($Addr,AF_INET);
    if (defined($SourceName)) {
        print "$SourceName ";
    } else {
        $Dot ="";
        for $Byte (@SourceAddr) {
            printf "$Dot%d",hex($Byte);
            $Dot = ".";
        }
        print " ";
    }

    print "to ";
    $Addr = pack("C4",hex($DestAddr[0]),hex($DestAddr[1]),
                 hex($DestAddr[2]),hex($DestAddr[3]));
    ($DestName) = gethostbyaddr($Addr,AF_INET);
    if (defined($DestName)) {
        print "$DestName ";
    } else {
        $Dot ="";
        for $Byte (@DestAddr) {
            printf "$Dot%d",hex($Byte);
            $Dot = ".";
        }
        print " ";
    }

    print $Length - $IpHeadLen, " bytes\n";

    if ($Protocol eq "06") {
        $SrcPort = hex($Packet[0]) * 0x100 + hex($Packet[1]);
        $DestPort = hex($Packet[2]) * 0x100 + hex($Packet[3]);
        print "\tFrom port $SrcPort to port $DestPort\n";
    } elsif ($Protocol eq "11") {
        $SrcPort = hex($Packet[0]) * 0x100 + hex($Packet[1]);
        $DestPort = hex($Packet[2]) * 0x100 + hex($Packet[3]);
        print "\tFrom port $SrcPort to port $DestPort\n";
    }
}
```

10. Create a file called ether.in that contains the following data (or copy the file from the CD). There are two IP packets.

```
08 00 20 21 a3 3c 08 00 20 10 2b 33 08 00 45 00
00 d4 d0 da 00 00 3c 11 b8 e9 cc 5f 23 06 c0 0a
01 01 02 af 02 eb 00 c0 00 00 34 62 0b 8c 00 00
00 01 00 00 00 00 00 00 00 00 00 00 00 00 00 00
00 00 00 00 00 01 00 00 00 97 31 39 32 2e 39 2e
31 30 37 2e 37 09 67 61 72 6d 20 67 61 72 6d 2e
69 6c 2e 75 73 2e 73 77 69 73 73 62 61 6e 6b 2e
63 6f 6d 20 67 61 72 6d 2e 73 77 69 73 73 62 61
6e 6b 2e 63 6f 6d 20 77 77 77 2e 73 64 65 2e 73
77 69 73 73 62 61 6e 6b 2e 63 6f 6d 20 73 64 65
2e 73 77 69 73 73 62 61 6e 6b 2e 63 6f 6d 20 77
77 77 2e 74 65 63 68 2e 73 77 69 73 73 62 61 6e
6b 2e 63 6f 6d 20 74 65 63 68 2e 73 77 69 73 73
62 61 6e 6b 2e 63 6f 6d 09 23 20 20 53 54 52 41
54 00

08 00 20 1d c4 5d 00 00 a2 01 cb c0 08 00 45 00
00 b9 e5 ac 00 00 38 06 4c d0 c0 0a 0b 05 cc 5f
23 09 09 ef 08 ec 1e cf 8a 0e 05 99 9b 19 50 18
10 00 a5 01 00 00 00 20 68 65 61 09 ed 42 65 9b 91
ba 1d 44 36 00 79 00 00 00 04 00 00 00 91 20 20
49 4e 54 45 47 45 52 5f 54 59 50 45 0a 20 20 61
63 63 65 73 73 20 30 5f 02 01 00 04 0b 77 65 6c
6c 66 6c 65 65 74 35 31 a4 4d 06 09 2b 06 01 04
01 81 23 03 01 40 0e 31 35 35 2e 31 34 35 2e 31
38 36 2e 32 39 02 01 06 02 01 c9 43 04 30 74 0b
b5 30 24 30 22 06 0c 2b 06 01 04 01 81 23 03 01
03 01 01 04 12 53 4e 4d 50 3a 31 35 35 2e 31 34
35 2e 32 34 36 2e 34
```

11. Run the command.

```
perl ether.pl ether.in
```

12. It will produce output similar to the following. If your host file does not contain the machine names for the IP addresses in the first packet, you will get numeric IP addresses instead.

Output

```
UDP from birdofprey.mcs.com to 192.10.1.1 192 bytes
    From port 687 to port 747
TCP from 192.10.11.5 to 204.95.35.9 165 bytes
    From port 2543 to port 2284
```

End Output

How It Works

The script reads the bytes in a packet one field at a time. This procedure can easily read large and complicated packets.

Comments

The example script prints out some of the major fields of some typical IP protocols. It should be straightforward to add code to print out additional fields and to add new protocols. The two widely available programs for capturing Ethernet packets are etherfind and tcpdump.

This script can run under Perl 5 only. Remove the use of the Socket module and hard-code the AF_INET value to make it run under Perl 4. This may make the script nonportable. If available, the file sys/socket.ph can be used to retrieve the value of AF_INET in a portable way. The Perl 4 script follows.

```perl
$Eof = 0;
PACKET:
while (! $Eof) {
    @Packet = ();
    $i = 0;
    while ($In = <>) {
        chop($In);
        $In =~ s/\s+//g;
        $In =~ /./ || last;
        while ($In =~ s/^..//) {
            $Packet[$i++] = $&;
        }
        if ($In =~ /./) {
            print "Bad packet string - skipping\n";
            next PACKET;
        }
    }
    if (! defined($In)) {
        $Eof = 1;
    }
    $i || next;

    @EtherTo = splice(@Packet,0,6);
    @EtherFrom = splice(@Packet,0,6);
    ($EtherType1,$EtherType2) = splice(@Packet,0,2);
    if ($EtherType1 ne "08" || $EtherType2 ne "00") {
        print "Not an IP packet - skipping\n";
        next;
    }
    $IpHeadLen = 20;
    @IpHead = splice(@Packet,0,$IpHeadLen);
    ($IpVersion,$HeaderLen) = $IpHead[0] =~ /(.)(.)/;
    $HeaderLen = hex($HeaderLen) * 4;
    if ($HeaderLen - 20 > 0) {
        @Options = splice(@Packet,0,$HeaderLen - 20);
        $IpHeadLen = $HeaderLen;
    }
    $TypeOfService = $IpHead[1];
    $Length = hex($IpHead[2]) * 0x100 + hex($IpHead[3]);
    @Ident = @IpHead[4,5];
    $Flags = (hex($IpHead[6]) & 0xe0) >> 5;
    $FragOff = ($IpHead[6] & 0x1f) * 0x100 + hex($IpHead[7]);
    $TimeToLive = $IpHead[8];
    $Protocol = $IpHead[9];
```

continued on next page

continued from previous page

```perl
    $HeadCkSum = hex($IpHead[10]) * 0x100 + hex($IpHead[11]);
    @SourceAddr = @IpHead[12..15];
    @DestAddr = @IpHead[16..19];

    if ($Protocol eq "06") {
        print "TCP ";
    } elsif ($Protocol eq "11") {
        print "UDP ";
    } elsif ($Protocol eq "01") {
        print "ICMP ";
    } else {
        print "Unknown protocol - $Protocol\n";
        next;
    }

    print "from ";
    $Addr = pack("C4",hex($SourceAddr[0]),hex($SourceAddr[1]),
                 hex($SourceAddr[2]),hex($SourceAddr[3]));
    ($SourceName) = gethostbyaddr($Addr,2);
    if (defined($SourceName)) {
        print "$SourceName ";
    } else {
        $Dot ="";
        for $Byte (@SourceAddr) {
            printf "$Dot%d",hex($Byte);
            $Dot = ".";
        }
        print " ";
    }

    print "to ";
    $Addr = pack("C4",hex($DestAddr[0]),hex($DestAddr[1]),
                 hex($DestAddr[2]),hex($DestAddr[3]));
    ($DestName) = gethostbyaddr($Addr,2);
    if (defined($DestName)) {
        print "$DestName ";
    } else {
        $Dot ="";
        for $Byte (@DestAddr) {
            printf "$Dot%d",hex($Byte);
            $Dot = ".";
        }
        print " ";
    }

    print $Length - $IpHeadLen, " bytes\n";

    if ($Protocol eq "06") {
        $SrcPort = hex($Packet[0]) * 0x100 + hex($Packet[1]);
        $DestPort = hex($Packet[2]) * 0x100 + hex($Packet[3]);
        print "\tFrom port $SrcPort to port $DestPort\n";
    } elsif ($Protocol eq "11") {
        $SrcPort = hex($Packet[0]) * 0x100 + hex($Packet[1]);
        $DestPort = hex($Packet[2]) * 0x100 + hex($Packet[3]);
        print "\tFrom port $SrcPort to port $DestPort\n";
    }
}
```

## CHAPTER 19

UNIX SYSTEM ADMINISTRATION

UNIX SYSTEM ADMINISTRATION

How do I...

Perl has gained much of its popularity from the people around the world who like to call themselves "system administrators." The term *system administrator* carries much weight and responsibility, not to mention that it is a totally indefinable job description. When someone introduces himself or herself as a system administrator (*sys-admin,* for short), people pile loads of questions upon the person from all directions. The best analogy I can give is a doctor announcing himself or herself at a hypochondriac convention. The vast amount of work expected of a system administrator is ever expanding, as is the knowledge diversity expected. System administrators are the type of people who use Perl on a daily basis to help them cope with and reduce the workload poured upon them from every direction. This chapter is designed to help the system administrators who have puzzles that keep them up at night and/or have created computer widows/widowers.

19.1   Read the Password File

How to read the password file has to be one of the most frequently asked questions that all system administrators have to answer. This How-To will demonstrate the proper way to read a password file and outline the pitfalls of reading it incorrectly.

19.2   Find All Users Without Passwords

Finding all users without passwords is one of the most common tasks that system administrators face on a regular basis. There is a plethora of shell scripts, C programs, and what not, that accomplish this task. This How-To will show you how easy it is to do this in Perl.

19.3   List All the Groups a User Belongs To

This section will demonstrate the same principles as How-To 19.1 but will use the group file.

19.4   Generate Random Passwords

When you have to create more than 1,000 accounts, the last thing you want to do is create them by hand. This How-To will show you how to generate random passwords.

19.5   Check the Ownership and Permissions

This script is for keeping a tight lid on the mischievous monster named security. This How-To will show you how to make sure that users' accounts are not susceptible to the occasional prankster.

19.6   Determine the Last Time a User Logged In

Unfortunately, some people do things that system administrators don't like. This section will help you call the offender and supply information even the offender didn't know.

19.7 Determine the Number of Times a User Is Logged In

Because some machines don't have the power to support 1,000 people logging in two or three times each, this script will show you how to make imposing login restrictions possible.

19.8 Determine How Much Disk Space a User Is Using

UNIX systems don't have a cornucopia of disk space (much to our chagrin), and disk space quotas can be overhead a system administrator may not have time to establish. This section will help you find what are lovingly known as "disk hogs."

19.9 Determine When a File System Is Getting Full

This script will help you determine when a file system is going to take a turn for the worst before the machine decides to take an unplanned hiatus.

19.10 Find Files Older/Younger Than a Given Age

A weathered system administrator will soon realize that a script that finds files older or younger than a given age can be very helpful indeed when it comes to determining if a cron job ran. This How-To will show you how.

19.11 Find Files Larger/Smaller Than a Given Size

Finding files larger or smaller than a given size is very useful for general housekeeping or hunting for offending files wreaking havoc on a sensitive file system. This section will show you how.

19.12 Compare Two Directory Trees

Comparing two directory trees is one of the most wished for scripts around. There is nothing worse than doing this by hand. This script will show you how to do this using Perl's power.

19.13 Create a Process Tree

Creating a process tree is useful in helping you determine who beget whom. This How-To will show you how to do this.

COMPLEXITY
BEGINNING

19.1   How do I...
Read the password file?

COMPATIBILITY: PERL 4   PERL 5   UNIX

Problem

I want to scan through the password file to get information about each of the users.
How do I do this?

Technique

There are two ways to do this: Open the file and scan through it by hand or use the
password file built-in functions in Perl. The script we wrote uses the password function calls supplied. There are a few very solid reasons for doing so. The first is that
if the password file ever changes format, your code will break and have to be recod-
ed. Of course, the chances of the password file ever changing are slim to none. The
second reason, the most important, applies if the machines are running networked
information services (NIS). If they are, the password information may not come from
the /etc/passwd file; it may come from a different machine altogether. NIS allows machines
to share files, which provides a mechanism to maintain a single master copy of a system file. Figure 19-1 illustrates the concept of file sharing via NIS. We have been
very careful so far not to mention the password file by name because of NIS. If the
password function calls are used, format changes and NIS will not break our code.
Perl supplies a number of commands to parse the password file and retrieve information. This particular script uses only the function getpwent, one of the several
password functions provided with Perl.

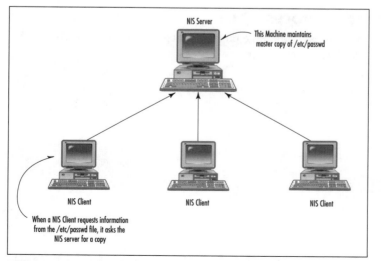

Figure 19-1 File sharing via NIS

Steps

1. Create a new file named readpwd.pl and enter the following script into it.

```perl
#!/usr/local/bin/perl -w

# Purpose:
#   This scans through the entire passwd file and returns
# information for each user found.

# Set the user count.
my $count = 0;

# Do this until there are no more records.
while (($account, $passwd, $uid, $gid, $quota, $comment, $gcos, $home,
$shell) = getpwent())
{
    # Print out the user information.
    write;

    # Increment the user count.
    $count++;
}

# Generate a readable report from the information gathered.
format STDOUT_TOP=
Shell Name            Password             UID  GID  Home
===== ====            ========             ===  ===  ====
.

format STDOUT=
@<<< @<<<<<<<<< @<<<<<<<<<<<<<<<< @<<< @<<< @<<<<<<<<<<<<<<<<<<<<<<<
@<<<<<<<<<<<<
$count,$account,$passwd,$uid,$gid,$home,$shell
.
```

2. Run the script.

```
% chap_19/howto01/readpwd.pl
Shell Name            Password             UID  GID  Home
===== ====            ========             ===  ===  ====
0     root                                 0    0    /root
/bin/tcsh
1     bin            *                     1    1    /bin
2     daemon         *                     2    2    /sbin
3     adm            *                     3    4    /var/adm
4     lp             *                     4    7    /var/spool/lpd
5     sync           *                     5    0    /sbin
/bin/sync
6     shutdown       *                     6    0    /sbin
/sbin/shutdown
7     halt           *                     7    0    /sbin
/sbin/halt
```

continued on next page

continued from previous page

8	mail	*	8	12	/var/spool/mail
9	news	*	9	13	/usr/lib/news
10	uucp	*	10	14	/var/spool/uucppublic
11	operator	*	11	0	/root

/bin/bash

12	games	*	12	100	/usr/games
13	man	*	13	15	/usr/man
14	postmaster	*	14	12	/var/spool/mail

/bin/bash

| 15 | nobody | * | 6553 | 100 | /dev/null |
| 16 | ftp | * | 404 | 1 | /home/ftp |

/bin/bash

| 17 | glover | | 501 | 100 | /home/glover |

/bin/tcsh

| 18 | gizmo | jx3fmf1zs802g | 502 | 100 | /home/gizmo |

/bin/tcsh

As you may notice, we have no password on our account or roots! The account gizmo does, however.

How It Works

This is a very straightforward script. No tricks or hidden features are used. The body of the script rests on the *while* loop. This is not only the data collection element to the script, but also the loop control and termination factor. If the function getpwent returns an empty data set, then the *while* loops fails; otherwise, the getpwent function returns a 9-element array and the commands inside the *while* loop, the write and the counter increment, get read and executed. The following line outlines the general syntax of the getpwent function call.

```
(($account, $passwd, $uid, $gid, $quota, $comment, $gcos, $home, $shell) =
getpwent());
```

The elements returned from the getpwent function call, listed in their respective order, are the login name of the account, the encrypted password, the user's user ID (UID) value, the user's group ID (GID) value, the system quota information, a comment on the user, the gcos value, the home directory of the user, and the user's shell. The gcos value is a field that contains information about the user's phone number, office location, etc. The gcos field is different from the comment field because the comment field usually contains the user's real name. The write command sends the information to the report generator, which in turn prints out the report listed above.

Comments

This script can be retrofitted to take on several personalities without much work. For example, we modified this script to return account information on a given user name. All we needed to do was determine the user name, using either $ARGV[0] or the Getopt::Long module, then call getpwnam with the login ID supplied as the parameter (file chap_19/howto01/readpwd2.pl on the CD-ROM). We also modified this script to accept a UID number by modifying example 2 and changing the call to getpwnam to getpwuid.

COMPLEXITY
BEGINNING

19.2 How do I...
Find all users without passwords?

COMPATIBILITY: PERL 4 PERL 5 UNIX

Problem

I want to find all the users on the system without a password so I can plug up any security holes that hackers could use to compromise the system. How do I do this using Perl?

Technique

The technique used in this How-To is almost exactly the same as that used in How-To 19.1. The only real difference is that the password field is checked. If the password field is empty, then the user's information is printed out in a report-style format.

Steps

1. Create a new file named nopass.pl and enter the following script into it.

```perl
#!/usr/local/bin/perl -w

# Purpose:
#    This finds all users without a password.

# Set the count variable.
my $count = 1;

# Do this until there are no more records.
while (($account, $passwd, $uid, $gid, $quota, $comment, $gcos, $home,
$shell) = getpwent())
{
    # Check if the users password field is empty.
    if ($passwd eq "" || $passwd eq "*")
    {
        # Print out the user information.
        write;

        # Increment the user count.
        $count++;
    }
}
```

continued on next page

continued from previous page
```
# Generate a readable report from the information gathered.
format STDOUT_TOP=
Count Account          UID     GID     Home
=====================================================================
.

format STDOUT=
@>>>> @<<<<<<<<<<<<< @<<<<< @<<<<< @<<<<<<<<<<<<<<<<<<<<<<<<<<<<<<<<<
$count,$account,$uid,$gid,$home
.
```

2. Run the script. We ran this on a home machine.

```
% chap_19/howto02/nopass.pl

Count Account          UID     GID     Home
=====================================================================
    1 root             0       0       /root
    2 bin              1       1       /bin
    3 daemon           2       2       /sbin
    4 adm              3       4       /var/adm
    5 lp               4       7       /var/spool/lpd
    6 sync             5       0       /sbin
    7 shutdown         6       0       /sbin
    8 halt             7       0       /sbin
    9 mail             8       12      /var/spool/mail
   10 news             9       13      /usr/lib/news
   11 uucp             10      14      /var/spool/uucppublic
   12 operator         11      0       /root
   13 games            12      100     /usr/games
   14 man              13      15      /usr/man
   15 postmaster       14      12      /var/spool/mail
   16 nobody           65535   100     /dev/null
   17 ftp              404     1       /home/ftp
   18 glover           501     100     /home/glover
```

Note that on our machine at home, our account has no password (oops).

How It Works

This is a simple script. All it does is scan the password file and look for passwords that are empty. The *if* statement

```
if ($passwd eq "" || $passwd eq "*")
```

checks for two things. It looks for an empty password field and it looks for a password field with an asterisk. The double pipe symbol (||) is a logical OR in Perl; it stands for A or B. The *if* statement listed above checks if the variable *$passwd* (which contains the password of the current user from the password file) is empty. It also checks if the password field contains an asterisk. If the password field has an asterisk, it could mean the account has been disabled, the password is stored in a shadow password file, or anything else. It is dependent on the UNIX system the script is being run on. We are being strict about the definition about "not having a password." Notice the account bin. This account was never meant to be logged into. It just holds a UID and GID value so when an ls -l command is executed, the name bin is displayed instead of the numeric UID/GID of the file being listed.

Comments

This script could easily be modified for many different purposes. For example, at a site where there are a lot of accounts, you may want to find out which accounts are currently under suspension. This would require removing the check for an empty string and leaving the check for the asterisk.

COMPLEXITY
BEGINNING

19.3   How do I...
List all the groups a user belongs to?

COMPATIBILITY:  PERL 4   PERL 5   UNIX

Problem

I want to list all the groups a given user belongs to in order to make sure the user has the correct security. This script actually replicates the UNIX command groups, so little value is added by writing this script. The main difference between this script and the UNIX command is this script also prints out the GID of each group the given user belongs to. Not all UNIX flavors support this option.

Technique

The technique used in this How-To is almost exactly the same as that used in How-To 19.1. The difference is this script reads the group file and uses the functions supplied by Perl to read the group file. The function that this script uses is called getgrent. This function returns information about group definitions from the group file. The function getgrent returns a 4-element array: the group name, a password, the GID, and a list of members in the group. The basic syntax of the getgrent function is

```
($groupName, $passwd, $gid, $memberList) = getgrent()
```

The variable $memberList$ contains a space-separated list of user names that belong to the given group. Once all the groups have been determined, the group list is printed out.

Steps

1. Create a new file named listgrps.pl and enter the following script into it.

```
#!/usr/local/bin/perl -w

# Purpose:
#   This scans through the group file searching for the login Id
# in the group members field.
```

continued on next page

continued from previous page

```perl
# Use $ARGV[0] for the login Id.
my $loginId = $ARGV[0] || die "Usage: $0 UID\n";
my @groupNames = ();
my @groupIds = ();

# Do this until there are no more records.
while (($groupName, $passwd, $gid, $memberList) = getgrent())
{
    # We need to look for the login id in the member list.
    if ($memberList =~ /$loginId/)
    {
        # Add the group name to the group name array
        push (@groupNames, $groupName);

        # Add the GID to the GID array.
        push (@groupIds, $gid);
    }
}

# Only print out results if we found the account name given.
if ($#groupNames >= 0)
{
    # Print out the account name.
    print "Account Name: $loginId\n";

    # Print out the group names and GIDs.
    for ($x=0; $x <= $#groupNames; $x++)
    {
        print "$groupNames[$x]($groupIds[$x]), ";
    }
    print "\n";
}
else
{
    print "No groups found for account $loginId\n";
}
```

2. Run the script.

```
% chap_19/howto03/listgrps.pl
Account Name: glover
sys(3), adm(4), wheel(10), floppy(11), mail(12), news(13), users(100),
```

It also reveals that we like to belong to as many groups as we want. (Hey, it's our machine!)

How It Works

This script is the same simple design that is used in How-To 19.1 and How-To 19.2. It scans the group file, calling the Perl function getgrent. The function getgrent returns a 4-element array, one of which is the group member list, which is the field from the group file that contains all the login IDs of accounts that belong to that group. The script looks in this field for the given account name in the line

```perl
if ($memberList =~ /$loginId/)
```

Notice that the check seems to be backwards. To the novice user, this looks like it is checking if the variable *$memberList* is contained within the scalar $loginId. It actually states, "Does the variable *$memberList* contain the following pattern?", the following pattern being the value of $loginId. If the account is in the member list, then the group name and GID are added onto the end of the group string that is being constructed. Finally, to determine if the account is a member of any group, the group string is checked to see if it is empty.

Comments

Although this type of command exists on every flavor of UNIX, this version also prints out the associated group numbers. This can be very handy in certain cases. Because it was very easy to add that extra little piece of information into the final result, it seemed appropriate.

COMPLEXITY
INTERMEDIATE

19.4 How do I...
Generate random passwords?

COMPATIBILITY: PERL 4 PERL 5 UNIX

Problem

I want to generate random passwords because I have more than 300 new accounts to add to the machine and I don't want to give them passwords that are the same as their login IDs. How do I generate a random series of alphanumeric characters for the passwords?

Technique

Basically, you need to generate each character individually. The only catch is that you don't want to generate nonprintable characters. Do this by looking at the ASCII character chart and picking a contiguous range of alphanumeric characters. Generate characters using this range and add it to the password.

Steps

1. Create a new file named genpw.pl and enter the following script into it.

```perl
#!/usr/local/bin/perl -w

# Purpose:
#    This generates a random password.

# Use long command line options.
use Getopt::Long;

# Parse up the command line.
GetOptions ('l|length=i');

# Set the options from the command line.
```

continued on next page

continued from previous page

```
my $length = $opt_l || 8;
my $password = "";
my $x = 0;

# Plant a new random seed.
srand (time|$$);

# Start generating the password.
for ($x=0; $x < $length; $x++)
{
    # Pick a number. (between 33 to 126)
    my $intval = int (rand(93)) + 33;
    $password .= sprintf ("%c", $intval);
}

# Print out the generated password.
print "Password $password \n";
```

2. Run the script several times to make sure the results are different.

```
% chap_19/howto04/genpw.pl
Password _j^WWO_i
% genpw.pl
Password TIRoDe`v
% genpw.pl
Password <UQ:2g9`
```

How It Works

The user sets the length of the password from the command line, or the program uses a default value. If the command line option -l or --length is not supplied, the default length of 8 is chosen. Then the program plants the seed. If a unique seed is not chosen, then the random number generator will create the same values each time. The seed we used here is the current time since January 1, 1970, supplied by the time command bitwise ORed with the current process number of the running script. This combination would be tough, if not almost impossible, to replicate during another run, so it's a safe number to use. The program generates an ASCII value using the rand function for each character in the password. Notice that the rand function chooses a number between 0 and 93 and then adds 33 to that resulting value. This gives you a range of ASCII characters from 33 to 126 (all which are printable characters). Once the value is chosen, the appropriate ASCII character is added to the end of the password. The translation from number to ASCII character is performed by the line

```
$password .= sprintf ("%c", $intval)
```

sprintf translates the integer value to an ASCII character, which is promptly added to the end of the current password, stored in the variable *$password*. Once the password has been generated, the password is printed out on the screen.

Comments

This script is also very useful for those who administer large institutions where accounts are created in large batches. There is a Perl 4 version of this script with the filename chap_19/howto04/genpw.pl4 on the CD-ROM.

COMPLEXITY
INTERMEDIATE

19.5 How do I...
Check the ownership and permissions?

COMPATIBILITY: PERL 4 | PERL 5 | UNIX

Problem

I want to make sure that the home accounts of all the users on my system are set up correctly. I need to check if the directory exists, if it is owned by the user listed in the password file, if it has the proper group, and if its permissions are set wide open. How can I use Perl to get this information?

Technique

The script reads the password file, as does the one in How-To 19.1, and takes the information returned from the getpwent function call, and checks it against the physical home directory of the user. The syntax of the getpwent function is

```
($name, $passwd, $uid, $gid, $quota, $comment, $gcos, $dir, $shell) =
getpwent()
```

The getpwent function call returns a 13-element array, with each element representing a specific element of a single row from the password file. Table 19-1 lists the elements returned from getpwent in their respective order.

ELEMENT NAME	PURPOSE
Name	This is the login name of the account.
Password	This is the encrypted password of the account.
UID	This is the user's identification number.
GID	This is the account's default group number.
Quota	This contains user quota information. This option is not widely used anymore.
Comment	This contains information about the account holder. This is usually the name of the account holder.
gcos	This is used for personal information about the user: typically, the user's phone number, office number, etc.
Home Directory	This is the home directory of the user.
Login Shell	This is the shell the user will be using when he or she logs in.

Table 19-1 Return elements of the getpwent function call

The checks performed on the home accounts are

● Check if the home directory exists.

● Check if the home directory is a directory.

● Check if the UID of the directory matches the UID of the current user.

● Check if the GID of the directory matches the GID of the current user.

● Check to make sure the permissions of the directory aren't wide open or too restricted.

These checks are performed for each record getpwent returns.

Steps

1. Create a new file named chkperm.pl and enter the following script into it.

```perl
#!/usr/local/bin/perl -w

# Purpose:
#    To check the permissions and ownership of all the
# user accounts in the passwd file.
my ($user, $passwd, $accountuid, $accountgid, $quota, $comment, $gcos,
$home, $shell);

# Start loading up each user from the passwd file.
while (($user, $passwd, $accountuid, $accountgid, $quota, $comment, $gcos,
$home, $shell) = getpwent())
{
    # Check the user's home directory.
    if (! -e $home)
    {
        # The user's home directory does not exist.
        print "The user's <$user> home directory <$home> does not ⇒
exist.\n";
        next;
    }

    # OK, let's start the user's home directory...
    my ($mode, $uid, $gid) = (stat ($home))[2,4,5];

    # Check the user's home directory.
    if (! -d $home)
    {
        # The user's home directory is not a directory.
        print "The user's <$user> home directory <$home> is not a ⇒
directory.\n";
    }
    elsif ($accountuid != $uid)
    {
        # Get the other owner's information.
        my $owner = (getpwuid($uid))[0];

        # The user's home directory is owned by another account.
        print "The user's <$user> home directory <$home> is owned by ⇒
<$owner> ($uid).\n";
    }
```

```
    elsif ($accountgid != $gid)
    {
        # Get the other owners information.
        my $owner = (getgrgid($gid))[0];
        my $real = (getgrgid($accountgid))[0];

        # The user's home directory has group permissions of another group.
        print "The user's <$user> home directory <$home> has group
        permissions of <$owner> instead of <$real>.\n";
    }
    elsif (($mode & 0022) != 0)
    {
        # The owner is allowing others unrestricted access to their
          account.
        my $accmode = ($mode & 0022);
        print "The user <$user> is allowing others unrestricted access to
                their account ($accmode).\n";
    }
    elsif (($mode & 0700) != 0700)
    {
        # The owner has incorrect permissions to their account.
        my $accmode = ($mode & 0022);
        print "The user <$user> does not seem to have the correct
                permissions to use their account ($accmode).\n";
    }
    else
    {
        # Everything seems OK.
        print "The account <$user> seems to OK.\n";
    }
}
```

2. Run the script. Here is the result of running it on our machine.

```
% chap_19/howto05/chkperm.pl
The account <root> seems OK.
The user's <bin> home directory </bin> is owned by <root> (0).
The user's <daemon> home directory </sbin> is owned by <root> (0).
The user's <adm> home directory </var/adm> is owned by <root> (0).
The user's <lp> home directory </var/spool/lpd> is owned by <root> (0).
The user's <sync> home directory </sbin> is owned by <root> (0).
The user's <shutdown> home directory </sbin> is owned by <root> (0).
The user's <halt> home directory </sbin> is owned by <root> (0).
The user's <mail> home directory </var/spool/mail> is owned by <root> (0).
The user's <news> home directory </usr/lib/news> does not exist.
The user <uucp> is allowing others unrestricted access to their account
(18).
The user's <operator> home directory </root> is owned by <root> (0).
The user's <games> home directory </usr/games> is owned by <root> (0).
The user's <man> home directory </usr/man> is owned by <root> (0).
The user's <postmaster> home directory </var/spool/mail> is owned by <root>
(0).
The user's <nobody> home directory </dev/null> is not a directory.
The user's <ftp> home directory </home/ftp> is owned by <root> (0).
The account <glover> seems OK.
The user's <gizmo> home directory </home/gizmo> has group permissions of
<root> instead of <users>.
```

How It Works

As in How-To 19.1, the flow control and data collection are performed by the *while* statement. Because you are scanning through the complete password file, the getpwent function is used once again. The first check makes sure that the user's home directory actually exists. This is performed by the line

```
if (! -e $home)
```

This checks if the file specified in the variable *$home* exists. If it does not, then the *if* statement is satisfied; an error message is printed out and the next record is requested. Once the program understands that the directory exists, then a stat is performed on the directory. This gets the UID, GID, and permissions of the directory. The stat function returns a 13-element array, each element representing a specific element of the file queried. Table 19-2 lists, in order, all the elements returned from a stat function call.

ELEMENT	DESCRIPTION
de	ID of device containing a directory entry for this file.
inode	Inode number.
mode	File permission mode.
nlink	Number of links.
uid	UID of the file's owner.
gid	GID of the file's group.
rdev	ID of device. This is only defined for character or block special files.
size	File size in bytes.
atime	Time of last access in seconds since the epoch.
mtime	Time of last modification in seconds since the epoch.
ctime	Time of last status change in seconds since the epoch.
blksize	Preferred I/O block size. Valid only on BSD-type systems.
blocks	Number of blocks allocated for file. Valid only on BSD systems.

Table 19-2 File statistics returned from the stat command

Notice that stat returns a 13-element array, but you seem to catch only 3—and the correct 3, too!

```
my ($mode, $uid, $gid) = (stat ($home))[2,4,5];
```

This is a standard trick performed by many Perl programmers. The command (stat ($home)) forces the return elements of stat into a temporary array. The [2,4,5] states that only the third, fifth, and sixth elements of that array are wanted. The third, fifth, and sixth elements are the mode, UID, and GID of the home directory, respectively.

Next, check if the file given is a directory. This is performed by the line

```
if (! -d $home)
```

The -d modifier in an *if* statement checks if the file given is a directory. Check the UID and GID values of the directory against what the password file says is correct. The trickiest check is the permissions check. The value returned from the stat on the home directory is not in the standard octal format. To change that, you have to perform a bitwise AND on the file attributes contained in the *$mode* variable. The line

```
elsif (($mode & 0700) != 0700)
```

performs a bitwise AND on *$mode* using the value of 0700, then checks if the return value is 0700. We used the value of 0700, because if the person's directory is anything but 0700, then the person's directory permissions are somewhat open. This section of the script can be enhanced to check for all types of directory permissions.

Comments

The gcos field is given that name because it was used to hold login information needed to submit mainframe batch jobs to a mainframe that had GCOS running. Please do not ask what GCOS actually stands for; we don't know.

COMPLEXITY
BEGINNING

19.6 How do I...
Determine the last time a user logged in?

COMPATIBILITY:

Problem

I want to be able to determine the last time a user logged in and how long he or she was logged in. How can I get this information using Perl?

Technique

This script uses the UNIX command last to retrieve this information. The command is piped via the open function, and the output is parsed as the command runs. If the sought-after user is found, then the output is parsed and the information is printed to the screen. This assures that only the last login time will be displayed, not the last 100 times. When this is done, the *control* loop is exited and the pipe is closed.

Steps

1. Create a new file called lastlog.pl and enter the following script into it.

```perl
#!/usr/local/bin/perl -w

# Purpose:
#    This prints the last time a given user logged in.

# We will use $ARGV[0] for the account name.
my $user = $ARGV[0] || die "Usage: $0 Login\n";

# We need to open a pipe to the UNIX command 'last'
open (LAST, "last|") || die "Could not run command last, $!\n";

# Set up the found flag.
my $found = 0;

# Start looking through the output of last.
while (<LAST>)
{
   next unless /^$user$/;
chomp;

   # We now have the first occurrence of the given user.
   my $tty = substr ($_, 10, 13);
   my $time = substr ($_, 40);

   # Print out the information.
   printf "User: %8s TTY: %16s Time: %s\n", $user, $tty, $time;

   # Set the found flag.
   $found = 1;

   # Exit out.
   last;
}

# If the user was not found, then they have never logged in.
if (!$found)
{
   print "The user $user has never logged in.\n";
}

# Close the pipe.
close (LAST);
```

2. Run the script. Running the script on our machine with the account named glover resulted in

```
% chap_19/howto06/lastlog.pl glover
User:   glover TTY: console          Time: Sun Aug 20 16:30    still
logged in
```

3. Running the script on our machine with the account named gizmo resulted in

```
% chap_19/howto06/lastlog.pl gizmo
User:   gizmo  TTY: console          Time: Sat Aug 12 19:55 - 19:56
(00:01)
```

How It Works

The script opens a pipe to the last command. This is accomplished by the line

```
open (LAST, "last|") || die "Could not run command last, $!\n";
```

When a command is run inside an *open* statement, the output needs to go somewhere. Putting a pipe symbol (|) on the end of the command tells Perl to "pipe," or direct, the output into the script. This means that the script will have access to the output of the command via the filehandle created on the open statement. In the case above, the output of the last command will be accessed via the filehandle LAST. The last command returns a list of information about who logged in, when he or she logged in, if he or she is still logged in, and how long he or she was on. The information is returned in reverse chronological order, meaning the newest entries are printed first. The output is scanned line by line looking for the user's name. The line

```
next if ! /^$user$/;
```

skips all lines that do not begin with the given user's name, which is stored in the variable *$users*. If the user's name is found, the TTY and time are printed out to the screen. You prematurely exit the *while* loop by using the last function. The script also uses a flag to help you find out if the user had ever logged in. The flag is initially set to 0; if the user was found, the variable is set to 1. Outside the loop, if the flag value is still 0, then the user name was not found and a message stating that will be displayed.

Comments

The Perl last function and the UNIX last command are NOT the same. To determine the last time a user logged in, you need to use both the UNIX last command and the Perl last function.

COMPLEXITY
ADVANCED

19.7 How do I...
Determine the number of times a user is logged in?

COMPATIBILITY: PERL 5   UNIX

Problem

The machine(s) I administer has limited resources. I need to be able to determine who is logged in and how many times. How do I do this?

Technique

Many people would write this script using the UNIX commands who or w, then scan the output. This type of approach leads to a very complex and illegible regular expression. Using the /etc/utmp file, you can retrieve the information from the source. (In fact, who and w both use the /etc/utmp file for their information.) The /etc/utmp file maintains a list of current users logged into the machine. The only catch is that the /etc/utmp file is in a binary format, which means you have to be able to read and decode a binary file. The Perl function read can read a binary (or ASCII) file. Just tell the function how much to read, which filehandle to use, and which variable to store the information in. Then convert the information from the read using the Perl function unpack. The only real catch is that to decode the information properly, you need to read the correct number of bytes and know the fields and their lengths to convert them into an ASCII form. Figure 19-2 illustrates the sequence of steps this How-To will follow to read a binary file and convert it into ASCII form. To determine the length of a record in the /etc/utmp file, look at the file /usr/include/utmp.h. This file tells you what fields are defined, their order, and their respective lengths. On our Linux box, the /etc/utmp file states that a record is defined as 56 bytes long. Table 19-3 outlines the details of the /etc/utmp.h file on our Linux box.

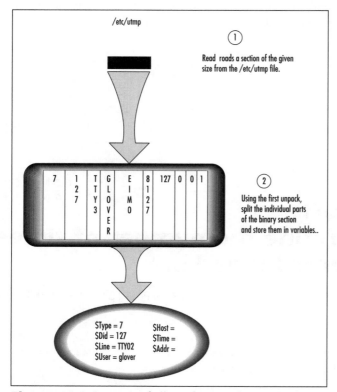

Figure 19-2 Steps to follow for reading a binary file to convert into ASCII

FIELD NAME	DOCUMENTED TYPE	REAL TYPE	LENGTH
UT_TYPE	short	long	4
UT_PID	int	int	4
UT_LINE	char[12]	char[12]	12
UT_ID	char[2]	char[4]	4
UT_TIME	long	long	4
UT_USER	char[8]	char[8]	8
UT_HOST	char[16]	char[16]	16
UT_ADDR	long	long	4
		Total Length	56

Table 19-3 Correct utmp record size for Linux

There is a documented type column and a real type column because there is an error in the documented type in the /usr/include/utmp.h file on the Linux box. This error took a while to find (Thanks, Gord!) and it is worthy of mention. If anyone is going to try to write this script on their Linux box, make note of the error.

Steps

1. Make a directory named Utmp. If it already exists, then skip this step.

2. Create a new file named Utmp/Linux.pm and enter the following script into it.

```
package Utmp::Linux;

#
# This function scans the Linux /etc/utmp file.
#
sub countUsers
{
    # Declare the local variables.
    my ($ut_type, $ut_pid, $ut_line, $ut_id, $ut_time);
    my ($ut_user, $ut_host, $ut_addr);
    my %info = ();
    my $length = 56;
    my $recfields = "lia12a4lA8a16l";
    my $utmp = "";

    # Open the utmp file.
    open (UTMP, "/etc/utmp");

    # Start reading the utmp file.
    while (read (UTMP, $utmp, $length))
    {
        # Read a line from the utmp file.
        ($ut_type, $ut_pid, $ut_line, $ut_id, $ut_time, $ut_user, $ut_host,
        $ut_addr) = unpack ($recfields, $utmp);

        # Save the information in the associative array.
        if ($ut_user ne "" && $ut_type == 7)
        {
```

continued on next page

continued from previous page

```perl
                $info{$ut_user}++;
            }
        }
        close (UTMP);

        # Return the info
        return %info;
    }

1;
```

3. Create a new file named Utmp.pm and enter the following script into it.

```perl
package Utmp;

require Exporter;
require DynaLoader;
require AutoLoader;

@ISA = qw(Exporter DynaLoader);
@EXPORT = qw (countUsers);

#
# This counts the users on the system and determines how many
# times each user is logged in.
#
sub countUsers
{
    # Determine the platform we are using.
    my $os = whichOS();

    # Run the correct function given the operating system.
    if ($os eq "LINUX")
    {
        return Utmp::Linux::countUsers();
    }
    elsif ($os eq "AIX")
    {
        return Utmp::AIX::countUsers();
    }
    elsif ($os eq "HPUX")
    {
        return Utmp::HPUX::countUsers();
    }
    elsif ($os eq "SUNOS")
    {
        return ( Utmp::Sunos::countUsers();
    }
    elsif ($os eq "SOLARIS")
    {
        return Utmp::Solaris::countUsers();
    }
    else
    {
        return Utmp::BSD::countUsers();
    }
}
```

```
#
# This returns a scalar value of which machine it thinks we
# are currently on.
#
sub whichOS
{
    # Determine the platform.
    my ($os, $hostname, $ver) = split (/\s+/, `uname -a`);
    $os = uc $os;

    # Return what we think it is.
    return $os if ($os eq "LINUX");
    return $os if ($os eq "HP-UX");
    return $os if ($os eq "AIX");

    # SunOS and Solaris return the same name from uname, but they
    # are different machines.
    if ($os eq "SUNOS" && $ver =~ /5/)
    {
        return "SOLARIS";
    }
    elsif ($os eq "SUNOS" && $ver =~ /4/)
    {
        return "SUNOS";
    }

    # Return BSD as a default.
    return "BSD";
}

# Load in the other modules.
use Utmp::AIX;
use Utmp::BSD;
use Utmp::HPUX;
use Utmp::Linux;
use Utmp::Solaris;

1;
```

4. Create a new file named countlog.pl and enter the following script into it.

```
#!/usr/local/bin/perl -w

# Purpose:
#    To list all the users on the system and the
# number of times they are logged in. This uses the
# Utmp.pm module.

# Use the Utmp module.
use Utmp;

# Get the information.
my %info = Utmp::countUsers();

# Print out the information.
for $key (sort keys %info)
{
    printf "Login Id: %-20s Logged In %d times.\n", $key, $info{$key};
}
```

5. Run the script countlog.pl.

```
% chap_19/howto07/countlog.pl
Login Id: glover        Logged In 2 times.
Login Id: gizmo         Logged In 1 times.
```

How It Works

The script countlog.pl uses the Utmp.pm module. It does this so it can call the function Utmp::countUsers, which returns an associative array of all the users on the system and their respective login count. The function call

```
my %info = Utmp::countUsers();
```

calls the Utmp::countUsers function and stores the result into the associative array %info.

The module Utmp.pm acts as a director of information. When the Utmp::countUsers function is called, the first thing it does is determine the operating system type. This is done by the following line.

```
my $os = whichOS();
```

The whichOS function returns a scalar string of the name of the operating system. The operating system type is determined by running the UNIX command uname. With the operating system type determined, the correct module function is called. The following lines demonstrate how the correct module function is called.

```
# Run the correct function given the operating system.
return Utmp::Linux::countUsers() if ($os eq "LINUX");
return Utmp::AIX::countUsers() if ($os eq "AIX");
return Utmp::HPUX::countUsers() if ($os eq "HPUX");
return Utmp::Sunos::countUsers() if ($os eq "SUNOS");
return Utmp::Solaris::countUsers() if ($os eq "SOLARIS");
return Utmp::BSD::countUsers();
```

Using the Linux example, if the value of $os is LINUX, then the function Utmp::Linux::countUsers is called. This calls the countUsers function in the Utmp::Linux.pm module. This function actually reads the /etc/utmp file and returns the associative array. The Utmp.pm module creates a single point of entry for all operating system types, which makes the countlog.pl highly portable. At the very end of the Utmp.pm module, you will find the lines

```
# Load in the other modules.
use Utmp::AIX;
use Utmp::BSD;
use Utmp::HPUX;
use Utmp::Linux;
use Utmp::Solaris;
```

These lines load in each operating system type module currently supported. Each module has to be written for each machine, because of inherent differences between operating systems.

All the work is done in the module specific to the operating system. For the rest of the discussion, we will use the Utmp::Linux.pm module, but the theory applies to all of them. The only function each operating system module has is countUsers. This function opens the /etc/utmp file, scans the contents, and returns an associative array of the information found. The /etc/utmp file is opened like a basic ASCII file, with the open command.

```
open (UTMP, "/etc/utmp");
```

The contents of the /etc/utmp file are scanned inside the *while* loop with the read command.

```
while (read (UTMP, $utmp, $length))
```

The read command has the following syntax.

```
read (Filehandle, Variable, Length, Offset);
```

The filehandle is the filehandle created when the file was opened; the variable is the scalar variable the information will be stored in; the length is the length of the section of the file to read in; and the offset states where in the variable to start writing to. The offset parameter is an option; if it's not specified, then the read function writes into the variable at offset zero. If no information can be read, then the read function returns a False value, which exits the *while* loop. In the above example, the variable the information is being read into is *$utmp*; the length is stored in the variable *$length*. The length of a utmp record in Linux is 56 bytes. After the read command has been run, the information is stored in *$utmp*. The information needs to be extracted from *$utmp* into a human readable format. This extraction is performed by the unpack command. The unpack command has the following syntax.

```
List = unpack (Template, Expression);
```

The expression can be anything from a basic scalar value to a complex regular expression. The template field is more complex. This field tells the unpack function what type of characters are stored in what position inside the expression. In this example, the template field looks like lia12a4lA8a16l. This is highly illegible, until it is explained. Table 19-4 outlines the possible template values and what they represent.

CHARACTER	REPRESENTS
a	An unstripped ASCII string.
b	A bit string in low to high order.
c	A signed char.
d	A double precision float.
f	A single precision float.
h	A hexadecimal string, low nibble first.
i	A signed integer.
l	A signed long.
n	A short in network order.
p	A pointer to a string.
s	A signed short.

continued on next page

continued from previous page

CHARACTER	REPRESENTS	
u	Uudecode a string.	
x	Skip forward a byte.	
A	An unterminated ASCII string (i.e., no trailing null character).	
B	A bit string, high to low order.	
C	An unsigned char value.	
H	A hexadecimal string.	
I	An unsigned integer value.	
L	An unsigned long value.	
N	A long in network order.	
S	An unsigned short value.	
X	Skip backwards 1 byte.	
@	Go to the absolute position of a string.	

Table 19-4 unpack template characters

Using Table 19-4, you can outline the details of the Linux /usr/include/utmp.h file and the template string to unpack a record. Table 19-5 lists the unpack template fields, the fields they represent from the /usr/include/utmp.h, and their respective types.

FIELD	FIELD NAME	FIELD TYPE	FIELD TEMPLATE PATTERN	
Login Type	UT_TYPE	long	I	
Process ID	UT_PID	int	i	
Device Name of Terminal	UT_LINE	char[12]	a12	
Abbreviated Device Name	UT_ID	char[2]	a4	
Login Time	UT_TIME	long	I	
User Name	UT_USER	char[8]	A8	
Host Name	UT_HOST	char[16]	a16	
Remote IP Address	UT_ADDR	long	I	

Table 19-5 Linux /etc/utmp unpack template

Given all this information, the /etc/utmp file is read with the line

```
while (read (UTMP, $utmp, $length))
```

A section of the /etc/utmp file is read and stored into the scalar variable *$utmp*. The length is dictated by the value referenced by the variable *$length*. In the Linux case, the length is 56 bytes. The 56-byte segment returned is in binary format, which needs to be translated into human-readable format. This is performed by the unpack function and the unpack template of lia12a4lA8a16l.

```
($ut_type, $ut_pid, $ut_line, $ut_id, $ut_time, $ut_user, $ut_host,
$ut_addr) = unpack ($recfields, $utmp);
```

Once the fields have been unpacked, the login type is determined by checking the value of the ut_type variable. If the value is 7, then the process is an active login on the machine. The following line determines if the record read is an active login record.

```
if ($ut_user ne "" && $ut_type == 7)
```

If the record is an active login record, then a record of the associative array, indexed on the user's login name, is incremented by 1. This keeps track of the number of current logins.

Comments

The only problem with writing scripts that read machine-dependent system files is the format is not consistent from machine to machine. This can cause problems and makes code susceptible to compatibility complications. This example uses only the Linux operating system, but other modules were written. The current operating system modules are Linux, SunOS version 4.1.X, Solaris 2.X, HP-UX version 9.0X, and AIX 3.2.X.

COMPLEXITY
INTERMEDIATE

19.8   How do I...
Determine how much disk space a user is using?

COMPATIBILITY:

Problem

I know users are side-stepping enforced quotas by using /tmp and other publicly writable file systems as personal storage space. I need to know how much true disk space each user is using. How can I check this using Perl?

Technique

This problem cannot be solved merely by running the UNIX command du -s on the user's home directory. Running du on the user's home directory tells you how much space the user is using in his or her home directory. You want the total amount of space used. This script uses the find module to traverse a directory tree and scan all the files in the given tree. As the script traverses the directory tree, the script maintains a tally of the amount of disk space each user is using.

Steps

1. Create a new file called hoglist.pl and enter the following script into it.

```perl
#!/usr/local/bin/perl -w

# Purpose:
#    This determines the total amount of disk space all the
# users on the system are using.

# Load in the modules we need.
require "find.pl";
use Getopt::Long;

# This function does what you need it to do when a file is found.
sub wanted
{
    # Now that we have the file in the var $name, let's start it.
    my ($uid, $size) = (stat($name))[4,7];

    # Keep the information
    $userInfo{$uid} += $size;
}

# Set some global variables.
my %userInfo = ();
my $count = 1;

# Set up command line arguments.
GetOptions ('d|directory=s');

# Parse up the command line.
my $startDirectory = $opt_d || die "Usage: $0 -d Start Directory";

# Traverse desired filesystems.
&find($startDirectory);

# Print out the information.
for $uid (sort keys %userInfo)
{
    # Get the user information from the password file.
    my $username = (getpwuid($uid))[0];
    my $spaceused = $userInfo{$uid};
    write;
}

format STDOUT_TOP=
Count Account         UID      Space Used (Bytes)
================================================
.

format STDOUT=
@>>>> @<<<<<<<<<<<< @<<<<< @<<<<<<<<<<<<<<<<<<
$count,$username,$uid,$spaceused
.
```

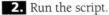 Run the script.

```
% chap_19/howto08/hoglist.pl -d /
Count Account       UID     Space Used (Bytes)
==============================================
    1 root           0      425299637
    2 bin            1      1587799
    3 uucp          10      824828
    4 glover       501      31588745
    5 gizmo        502      14243
```

How It Works

All the intelligence of this script resides in the find.pl package. The find command, from the Perl find.pl package, takes one parameter: the directory to start reading from. The following line starts the directory traversal process.

```
&find($startDirectory);
```

The variable *$startDirectory* is the directory to start the file traversal from. When a file is found, the wanted function is called. The wanted function is where all the file processing takes place. In this example, you run the stat function to get the UID and the size of the file found. The file size information is stored in the global associative array, %userInfo, using the file's UID value as the index value. Each time a file is found, the index value at the UID value is incremented by the file size. This keeps track of all the UID values found and the amount of space each UID is using. Because each user on the machine should have an individual UID value, this approach is safe. The following lines are the desired callback function in the above script.

```
# This is the callback function to the find function.
sub wanted
{
    # Now that we have the file in the var $name, let's stat it.
    my ($uid, $size) = (stat($name))[4,7];

    # Keep the information
    $userInfo{$uid} += $size;
}
```

The variable *$name* is the name of the file and is a variable that the find function creates for the wanted function.

Using the keys function, you extract all the given keys from the associative array %userInfo. The keys function returns a list of the indexes of the associative array, in this case, a list of UIDs found. Using the function getpwuid, you can get the actual login name associated to the UID value. This is done on the following line.

```
my $username = (getpwuid($uid))[0];
```

Then the information is printed out in report format using the write function call and the report format picture at the end of the file.

Comments

This script is a simple find script. It starts at a directory; with every file it finds, it calls the callback function wanted. More complex finds can be constructed easily and quickly by using the find2perl Perl script. This script is an element of the standard Perl package. The find2perl script takes almost all the same command line options as the UNIX find command. Become familiar with the UNIX find command and play with the find2perl script to determine its capabilities.

COMPLEXITY
BEGINNING

19.9 How do I...
Determine when a file system is getting full?

COMPATIBILITY: PERL 4   PERL 5   UNIX

Problem

I want to automate a process that can check if a given file system is getting full. How can I do this using Perl?

Technique

This script captures the output of the UNIX df command into a scalar array. This scalar array is searched looking for the requested file system and its percentage-used column. Once these are found, the script prints out the usage and exits because there is no need to continue. To maintain platform compatibility, this script has been written to run on various platforms. Currently, three different UNIX operating system types are supported.

Steps

1. Edit a new file called checkfs.pl and enter the following script into it.

```perl
#!/usr/local/bin/perl -w

# Purpose:
#   This determines if a given filesystem is
# past a given percentage.

# We are going to use the long command line parameters.
use Getopt::Long;

# Parse the command line options.
GetOptions ('t|threshold=i', 'f|filesystem=s');

# Check the results of the command line options.
```

```perl
my $fsystem = $opt_f || die "Usage: $0 -f Filesystem [-t Threshold]\n";
my $thresh = $opt_t || 95;

# Linux/SunOS/AIX df
chomp (@dfoutput = `df`);

# HP-UX
#chomp (@dfoutput = `bdf`);

# Solaris df
#chomp (@dfoutput = `df -k`);

# Shift the top line off the array.
shift (@dfoutput);

# Start search the output.
foreach $row (@dfoutput)
{
    my ($dev, $blocks, $used, $avail, $cap, $mount) = split (/\s+/, $row);

    # We need the filesystem asked for.
    next if ($mount ne $fsystem);

    # Take the % sign off the capacity percentage.
    $cap =~ s/%$//;

    # Let's see if they are past the threshold.
    if ($cap > $thresh)
    {
        # We are past the threshold.
        print "The filesystem $fsystem is past the threshold of $thresh%.
            (Current: $cap%)\n";

        # Exit with an error.
        exit 1;
    }
    else
    {
        # We are not past the threshold.
        print "The filesystem $fsystem is within the bounds of the
            threshold of ${thresh}%. (Current: ${cap}%)\n";

        # Exit cleanly.
        exit 0;
    }
}
```

2. Uncomment the df command line that corresponds to the system you are running the script on. For example, if you are running on a Linux box, change the line

```perl
#chomp (@dfoutput = `df`);
```

to

```perl
chomp (@dfoutput = `df`);
```

3. Run the script.

```
% chap_19/howto09/checkfs.pl -t 95 -f /local
The file system /local is within the bounds of the threshold of 95%.
(Current: 94%)
% chap_19/howto09/checkfs.pl -t 25 -f /local
The file system /local is past the threshold of 25%. (Current: 94%)
```

How It Works

This is actually a very straightforward script. We carry it with us when we switch job sites because it seems like we need it everywhere we go. All the script does is run the UNIX df command and parse the output. At this point in the book, this script almost seems like a waste of time, but it's not. It is very useful and it demonstrates a couple of subtle tricks that can be used. For example, the line

```
chomp (@dfoutput = `df`)
```

actually chops the last character from the end of each row in the array, which means when you are looping through the array, chopping each row is not necessary. Shifting the top line off the array removes the header from the df output. This is more acceptable than using a counted *for* loop; Larry Wall notes that using the foreach command is more efficient than using a counted *for* loop. For each row from the array, you split up the row on white space and check the current file system name against the file system being checked. We use chomp to remove the percentage sign from the percent used field from the df command; then the script makes a simple arithmetic check. That is all there is to it. Note that when the file system is found from the df command, the script exits. It exits with a 1 on an error and a 0 otherwise, if the script is being run and the output is being ignored, but the return code isn't.

Comments

Different operating systems use different command switches and, in the case of HP, different commands. For the script to be portable, the df command must be modified to run on the given operating system. Table 19-6 lists the equivalent command on the listed operating system. Unfortunately, we cannot say with confidence what the equivalent df command is on a SVR4 operating system. To the best of our knowledge, it is still df, but don't quote us!

OPERATING SYSTEM	EQUIVALENT df COMMAND	
SunOS 4.1.X (BSD)	df	
AIX	df	
HP-UX	bdf	
Solaris (SunOS 5.X)	df -k	
Linux	df	

Table 19-6 Equivalent df commands across UNIX operating systems

COMPLEXITY
INTERMEDIATE

19.10 How do I...
Find files older/younger than a given age?

COMPATIBILITY: PERL 5   UNIX

Problem

I want to find all the files in a given directory older than a given age. This problem creeps up when a file system starts to get too full and I need to do some housecleaning.

Technique

The bulk of the script rests on the Perl time function and the information it returns. Time is a relative thing on all UNIX operating systems. (We can see that statement starting a number of very sophisticated logical discussions.) The epoch time for most UNIX boxes rests around January 1, 1970 (a Thursday, by the way), so all time is kept in seconds relative to then. All time stamps on a UNIX box are kept in that format, so making time comparisons is simple. After verifying that the directory information given to it is valid, the script gets the current time in seconds since January 1, 1970. This is accomplished by the Perl command time. Once the time is obtained, the directory contents are scanned for all files. Each file in that directory is searched for information using the Perl stat command. The time stamp from the file is also in seconds since January 1, 1970, so a simple arithmetic comparison is done to determine the relative age of the file. If the file fits the current requisite, then the file information is printed out using Perl's report-writing facility.

Steps

1. Create a new file named fileage.pl and enter the following script into it.

```
#!/usr/local/bin/perl -w

# Purpose:
#    This finds all files within a given age.
# This script prints the information out on a
# wide screen.

# Use long command line options.
use Getopt::Long;

# Set up the command line arguments.
GetOptions ('a|age=i', 'd|directory=s');

# Declare some variables.
my ($pwd, $diff, $ageInMinutes, $stamp, $date);

# Set up the file age.
```

continued on next page

continued from previous page

```perl
my $age = $opt_a * 60 || die "Usage: $0 -a Age -d Directory\n";
my $dir = $opt_d || die "Usage: $0 -a Age -d Directory\n";

# We need to check the absolute pathname of the directory, so we
# tack on the present working directory if it's not.
if ($dir !~ /^\//)
{
    chomp ($pwd    = `pwd`);
    $dir = "${pwd}/${dir}";
}

# Does the directory exist???
if (! -e $dir)
{
   print "Sorry, but I can't seem to find the directory <$dir>.\n";
   exit 1;
}

# Is the directory really a directory???
if (! -d $dir)
{
   print "The directory <$dir> is not a directory!\n";
   exit 1;
}

# Get the current time.
my $now = time;
chomp ($date = `date`);

# Get a list of all the files under the given directory.
while (glob ($dir/*))
{
    # Keep the filename.
    my $filename = $_;

    # Stat the file.
    my ($size, $ctime) = (stat ($filename))[7,10];

    # Check the differences.
    $diff = $now - $ctime;
    $diff = $diff * -1 if $age < 0;
    if ( $diff > $age)
    {
        $ageInMinutes = abs($diff / 60);
        $stamp = localtime ($ctime);
        write;
    }
}

# Force an exit. (not needed, just here because...)
exit;

# Generate a readable report from the information gathered.
format STDOUT_TOP=
@<<<<<<<<<<<<<<<<<<<<<<<<<<<<<<<<<<<<<<<<<<<<<<
"Current Date: $date"
```

```
                                                              Age
Size        Time
Filename                                                     (Minutes)
(Bytes)     Stamp
============================================================================
.

format STDOUT=
@<<<<<<<<<<<<<<<<<<<<<<<<<<<<<<<<<<<<<<<<<<<<<<<<
@<<<<<<<<<<<< @<<<<<<< @<<<<<<<<<<<<<<<<<<<<<<<
$filename,$ageInMinutes,$size,$stamp
.
```

2. Run the script.

```
% chap_19/howto10/fileage.pl -d /tmp -a 10
Current Date: Sun Aug 20 23:46:49 EDT 1995

                                                              Age
Size        Time
Filename                                                     (Minutes)
(Bytes)     Stamp
============================================================================
/tmp/PQ1161
148336.7666666 15       Tue May  9 23:30:03 1995
/tmp/PQ216                                                   164124.2
               15       Sat Apr 29 00:22:37 1995
/tmp/cron.root.1020                                          77951.8
               40       Tue Jun 27 20:35:01 1995
/tmp/cron.root.2277                                          59741.8
               40       Mon Jul 10 12:05:01 1995
/tmp/cron.root.581                                           30961.8
               40       Sun Jul 30 11:45:01 1995
/tmp/cron.root.9207                                          111241.8
               40       Sun Jun  4 17:45:01 1995
/tmp/cron.root.9208                                          111236.8
               40       Sun Jun  4 17:50:01 1995
/tmp/cron.root.9210                                          111226.8
               40       Sun Jun  4 18:00:01 1995
/tmp/cron.root.9211                                          111216.8
               40       Sun Jun  4 18:10:01 1995
/tmp/passwd                                                  15880.85
               714      Wed Aug  9 23:05:58 1995
/tmp/perl-ea00211
139765.3166666 52       Mon May 15 22:21:30 1995
/tmp/perl-ea00250                                            139764.95
               52       Mon May 15 22:21:52 1995
/tmp/perl-ea00332
139887.2833333 52       Mon May 15 20:19:32 1995
/tmp/perl-ea00347
139764.0333333 53       Mon May 15 22:22:47 1995
/tmp/perl-ea02492                                            79162.2
               74       Tue Jun 27 00:24:37 1995
/tmp/perl-ea06287
81135.68333333 74       Sun Jun 25 15:31:08 1995
```

How It Works

After the command line options are parsed using the GetOptions Perl 5 module, the program verifies the source directory. This check is not really needed, but it is good to have just in case the directory doesn't exist. If the directory does not exist, then nothing would ever get printed out; this can be misleading. After the directory has been verified, the current time is requested using the Perl time function. The line

```
while (glob(dir/*))
```

reads the files in the directory specified by the variable *$dir*. This is a viable replacement for the opendir function. In fact, we prefer using it because we find it more elegant than opendir. Inside the *while* loop, the stat function is called on each of the files to get the file's time stamp. The real tricks are in the time calculation lines. The time specified can be a positive number or negative number. If the files being sought after are younger than a given age, then a negative time reference is needed. This negative value has to be anticipated. Make note of the two lines.

```
$diff = $now - $ctime;
$diff = $diff * -1 if $age < 0;
```

The first line takes the current time stored in the variable *$now* and subtracts the file's creation time, which is stored in $ctime. The second line checks if the value referenced by the variable *$diff* is less than 0. This check needs to be there in case you are looking for a file that is younger than a given age. This situation would cause the value of $age to dip into the negative realm.

Comments

This script could be rewritten to recurse directories, so part of or the entire file system can be traversed. Read How-To 19.8 to learn how to do this.

COMPLEXITY
INTERMEDIATE

19.11 How do I...
Find files larger/smaller than a given size?

COMPATIBILITY: PERL 5   UNIX

Problem

The file systems are reaching a critical state. I need to find all the large files to determine if I can remove them. How can I get this information using Perl?

Technique

This script is almost an exact duplicate of the script introduced in How-To 19.10. The only real difference is that this script does not use the stat function. It uses *if* -s to determine file size, which is more efficient.

Steps

1. Create a new file called filesize.pl and enter the following script into it.

```perl
#!/usr/local/bin/perl -w

# Purpose:
#    This finds all files larger/smaller
# than a given size.

# Use long command line options.
use Getopt::Long;

# Set up the command line arguments.
GetOptions ('s|size=i', 'd|directory=s');

# Set up the file age.
my $filesize = $opt_s || die "Usage: $0 -s Size -d Directory\n";
my $dir = $opt_d || die "Usage: $0 -s Size -d Directory\n";

# We need to check the absolute pathname of the directory, so we
# tack on the present working directory if it's not.
if ($dir !~ /^\//)
{
    chomp ($pwd    = `pwd`);
    $dir = "$pwd/$dir";
}

# Does the directory exist???
if (! -e $dir)
{
    print "Sorry, but I can't seem to find the directory <$dir>\n";
    exit 1;
}

# Is the directory really a directory???
if (! -d $dir)
{
    print "The directory <$dir> is not a directory!\n";
    exit 1;
}

# Get a list of all the files under the given directory.
while (glob ($dir/*))
{
    # Keep the filename
    my $filename = $_;

    # We only want files, not directories.
    if (-f $filename)
    {
        # Get the size of the file.
        my $size = -s $filename;

        # Check the file size.
        if ($filesize < 0)
        {
```

continued on next page

continued from previous page

```
            if ($size <= abs($filesize))
            {
                write;
            }
        }
        else
        {
            if ($size >= $filesize)
            {
                write;
            }
        }
    }
}

# Force an exit.
exit;

# Generate a readable report from the information gathered.
format STDOUT_TOP=
Filename                                                          Size
(Bytes)
=============================================================================
.

format STDOUT=
@<<<<<<<<<<<<<<<<<<<<<<<<<<<<<<<<<<<<<<<<<<<<<<<<<<<<<<<<<<<
@<<<<<<<<<<<
$filename,$size
.
```

2. Run the script.

```
% chap_19/howto11/filesize.pl -d /tmp -s 1000
Filename                                                          Size
(Bytes)
=============================================================================
/tmp/elv_102.1                                                    8192
/tmp/elv_12d9.1                                                   28672
/tmp/elv_19e.1                                                    12288
/tmp/rc.inet1.OLD                                                 1257
```

How It Works

After the command line options are parsed using the GetOptions Perl 5 module, the program verifies the source directory. This check is not really needed, but it is good to have just in case the directory doesn't exist. If the directory does not exist, then nothing would ever get printed out, which might be misleading. The line

```
while (glob($dir/*))
```

reads the files in the directory specified by the variable *$dir*. This is a viable replacement for the opendir function. We prefer using it because we find it more elegant than opendir. Once inside the *while* loop, if the file exists, then the line

```
$size = -s $filename;
```

is run to capture the size of the file referenced by $filename. The use of -s is a little known (or largely forgotten) piece of Perl trivia. Because both the target size and the test size have been acquired, all that is needed is to make sure the sizes fit the requirements. For each file that meets the requirements, the full pathname of the file and its size are printed out using Perl's report-writing facility.

Comments

This script could be rewritten to recurse directories, so part of the entire file system can be traversed. Read How-To 19.8 to learn how to do this.

COMPLEXITY
ADVANCED

19.12 How do I...
Compare two directory trees?

COMPATIBILITY: PERL 5   UNIX

Problem

I just copied a large directory tree and I want to verify that all the files were copied correctly. How would I do this using Perl?

Technique

Even though it may seem that the find function in the find.pl package is best suited to perform this task, it really isn't. Because you are comparing the files under the given directories, you cannot have full filenames stored in the array. Instead of the find function, the script uses the UNIX find command to produce a list of files. After all the file information has been stored in the arrays, the comparison process starts. A controlled loop is started that loops through the authoritative tree. To determine if the secondary tree either has an extra file or is missing a file, compare the file list array's mutually indexed entries. If they are not the same, then the directories are not the same. The problem posed here is that, when the trees are out of sync, it is very difficult to detect if a file is missing or if an extra file is present. This script performs a small trick to detect this.

Steps

1. Create a new file called cmptree.pl and enter the following script into it.

```
#!/usr/local/bin/perl -w

# Purpose:
#   This compares two directory trees to see if the files
# contained in both trees are the same. It notes any difference
# between the two.
```

continued on next page

continued from previous page

```perl
# We will use long command line options.
use Getopt::Long;

# Set up command line arguments.
GetOptions ('a|authority=s', 's|secondary=s');

# Declare global variables.
my @authtree = ();
my @secondtree = ();
my $auth = 0;
my $secondary = 0;

# Parse up the command line.
my $authdir = $opt_a || die "Usage: $0 -a Authoritative Directory -s
Secondary Directory";
my $seconddir = $opt_s || die "Usage: $0 -a Authoritative Directory -s
Secondary Directory";

# Make sure we don't waste our time.
if ($authdir eq $seconddir)
{
    print "The secondary directory is the same as the authoritative
          directory.\n";
    exit 1;
}

# Let's make sure that both directories given are directories.
if (! -e $authdir)
{
    print "The authoritative directory <$authdir> does not exist.\n";
    exit 1;
}
if (! -d $authdir)
{
    print "The authoritative directory <$authdir> is not a directory.\n";
    exit 1;
}
if (! -e $seconddir)
{
    print "The secondary directory <$seconddir> does not exist.\n";
    exit 1;
}
if (! -d $seconddir)
{
    print "The secondary directory <$seconddir> is not a directory.\n";
    exit 1;
}

# Get all the files under both trees.
chomp (@authtree = sort `cd $authdir ; find . -print`);
chomp (@secondtree = sort `cd $seconddir ; find . -print`);

# Start the loop...
while ($auth <= $#authtree)
{
    # Let's check if the filenames are the same.
    if ($authtree[$auth] lt $secondtree[$secondary])
```

```
{
    # The secondary tree may be missing a file.
    print "The secondary tree is missing the file $authtree[$auth]\n";
    $auth++;
}
elsif ($authtree[$auth] gt $secondtree[$secondary])
{
    # The secondary tree contains an extra file.
    print "The secondary tree contains an extra file
        $secondtree[$secondary]\n";
    $secondary++;
}
else
{
    # Both sides have the file.
    print "Both the authoritative and secondary trees contain
        $authtree[$auth]\n";
    $auth++;
    $secondary++;
}
}
```

2. To get ready to test this script, copy a directory from one location to another. For example:

```
% cp -r testdir1 testdir2
```

3. Remove a file from one of the directories. We removed a file named file3 from testdir2.

```
% rm testdir2/file3
```

4. Run the script.

```
% chap_19/howto12/cmptree.pl -a testdir1 -s testdir2
Both the authoritative and secondary trees contain .
Both the authoritative and secondary trees contain ./file1
Both the authoritative and secondary trees contain ./file2
The secondary tree is missing the file ./file3
Both the authoritative and secondary trees contain ./file4
```

How It Works

Once all the checks for the paths are done, the filenames under each tree are collected. As mentioned earlier, the most difficult element of this script is figuring out if a file is missing or if an extra file is present. This problem is overcome by keeping two counters, each of which is an individual counter for an array. The *while* loop will loop if the pointer to the authoritative tree has not gone out of bounds. The heart of the script, the element that detects if a file is missing, is subtle. When you examine the code, notice that the file comparisons are checking for "greater than," "less than," or "equal to." This is the check to see if the current file in the authoritative tree is alphabetically less than the current file in the secondary tree.

```
if ($authtree[$auth] lt $secondtree[$secondary])
```

If the authoritative file is alphabetically less than the secondary directory, then you know that the secondary tree has skipped past the authoritative tree and hence is missing a file. Only the authoritative counter is advanced, not the secondary counter. This is because the authoritative counter needs to "catch up," so the secondary counter needs to "wait." The same goes for the "greater than" check; only the secondary counter is advanced. Of course, if the file is not greater than or less than, then the file must be equal, so both counters are advanced. That's all there is to it. As the files are detected, a message is printed out at each stage.

Comments

This script could be rewritten to check more than two trees; of course, this would be much more complex.

COMPLEXITY
ADVANCED

19.13 How do I...
Create a process tree?

COMPATIBILITY: PERL 5   UNIX

Problem

I want to create a process tree so I can "see" which process spawned which processes. How can I do this in Perl?

Technique

Though it is short, this is a very complicated script. The module Process.pm is the essential element of this script and where most of the work takes place. To collect the process information, the UNIX command ps is run. The output is stored in an array, which is parsed in a controlled loop. This script takes advantage of Perl 5's object-oriented additions, so an object is created for each process found. When the process object is created, it is given some intelligence about itself and its children (this is discussed further in How It Works). When the complete process array has been read, then the process tree is ready to be printed out. This is the tricky element.

Steps

1. Create a new file called Process.pm and enter the following script into it. This module contains two methods: the new method, which creates a new process object, and printSubTree, which prints out a complete child process tree of a given process.

```
package Process;

#
# This creates a new process object.
```

```
#
sub new
{
    my $type = shift;
    my ($ppid, $pid, $uid, $command) = @_;
    my $self = {};

    # Create the new object.
    $self->{'PPID'} = $ppid;
    $self->{'PID'} = $pid;
    $self->{'UID'} = $uid;
    $self->{'Command'} = $command;
    $self->{'Children'} = "";

    # Don't forget to bless ourselves.
    return bless $self;
}


#
# This prints out a subtree to a process object.
#
sub printSubTree
{
    my $self = shift;
    my $space = shift;
    my %processList = @_;
    my $x;

    # Print ourselves out.
    print "$space $self->{'PID'} $self->{'Command'} \n";

    # Make a list of our children.
    my $childrenList = $processList{$self->{'PID'}}->{'Children'};
    my @children = sort split (/,/, $childrenList);

    # Are there any children???
    if ($childrenList ne "")
    {
        # Increment the space holder.
        $space .= "   ";

        # For each child print out its tree.
        for ($x=0; $x <= $#children; $x++)
        {
            my $child = $processList{$children[$x]};
            $child->printSubTree($space, %processList);
        }
    }
    chomp ($space); chomp ($space); chomp ($space);
}

1;
```

2. Create a new file named ptree.pl and enter the following script into it. This
script uses the Process.pm module to complete the task of printing out a
process tree.

```
#!/usr/local/bin/perl -w

# Purpose:
#    This creates a process tree.
# This version works on a Solaris machine.

# We need to use the process module we created.
use Process;

# Declare some global variables.
my %processList = ();

# Get the output from ps.
chomp (@psoutput = `ps -ef`);

# Shift the format line off the top of the array
shift (@psoutput);

# Create an object for each process.
foreach $row (@psoutput)
{
    chomp $row;

    # Strip out the information in the list.
    my $ppid = substr ($row, 15, 5);
    my $pid = substr ($row, 9, 5);
    my $uid = substr ($row, 1, 8);
    my $command = substr ($row, 49);

    # Remove whitespace fromm the PID and PPID.
    $pid =~ s/\s+//g;
    $ppid =~ s/\s+//g;
    $uid =~ s/\s+//g;

    # Create a new object.
    $processList{$pid} = new Process ($ppid, $pid, $uid, $command);

    # Add this child to the parent's child list.
    if (defined $processList{$ppid})
    {
        $processList{$ppid}->{'Children'} .= "$pid,";
    }
}

# Print out the tree.
$processList{1}->printSubTree("", %processList);
```

3. Run the script.

```
% chap_19/howto13/ptree.pl
1 init
    25 /usr/sbin/crond -l10
    41 /usr/sbin/syslogd
    43 /usr/sbin/klogd
    45 (inetd)
    47 /usr/sbin/lpd
    52 sendmail: accepting connections
```

```
   58 (agetty)
   59 (xdm)
      61 /usr/X11R6/bin/X -auth /usr/X11R6/lib/X11/xdm/A:0-a00059
      62 (xdm)
         75 /usr/openwin/bin/olvwm
            106 /usr/bin/X11/color_xterm -sb -sl 500 -j -ls +t -fn 10x20 ⇒
-bg black -fg Green
               107 -tcsh
                  1180 perl ./ex1.pl
                     1181 ps -ajxww
            1097 /usr/openwin/bin/workman
            93 oclock -transparent -hour red -minute green -jewel ⇒
yellow -bd purple -geom -0+0
            95 (olwmslave)
            99 /usr/bin/X11/color_xterm -sb -sl 500 -j -ls +t -fn 10x20 ⇒
-bg black -fg Green
               100 -tcsh
                  1129 vi sec14/sec14.txt
    6 (update)
    7 update (bdflush)
```

How It Works

The process information is gathered with the line

```
chomp (@psoutput = `ps -ef`);
```

Of course, the ps command is completely dependent on your operating system. The process list is cycled through with the foreach command, and each process record is split into its component parts. The two most essential parts of this script are the creation of the process object via the new function and the printing of the process tree. The process object is created by the line

```
$processList{$pid} = new Process ($ppid, $pid, $uid, $command);
```

This line calls the new function in the Process.pm module. This function takes information about the process itself and returns a process object. The object returned is stored into the associative array %processList. The new function creates the process using the following lines of code.

```
# Create the new object.
$self->{'PPID'} = $ppid;
$self->{'PID'} = $pid;
$self->{'UID'} = $uid;
$self->{'Command'} = $command;
$self->{'Children'} = "";

# Don't forget to bless ourselves.
return bless $self;
```

The process object, before it is blessed, is a standard associative array that has index key values of PPID, PID, UID, Command, and Children. The line

```
return bless $self;
```

transforms the associative array reference into an object of the Process package, then returns the object. If the process has a parent, then the object variable *Children*, of the parent object, gets the current process number added to its list of children.

```
if (defined $processList{$ppid})
{
    $processList{$ppid}->{'Children'} .= "$pid,";
}
```

This parent-child relationship is what makes this script possible. If the parent didn't know who its children were, you could not print out the process tree. The parent is notified of a new child in the following lines of the script.

Once all the process objects have been created, the process tree is printed out. This is done by calling the printSubTree method, which is a method made available to all the process objects. The whole print process is initiated with the line

```
$processList{1}->printSubTree("", %processList);
```

The value of 1 is used for the process to start everything off because on a UNIX system, the first process is 1. Because you are printing a process tree, you need to start all the processes from the parent and work to the children. The first parameter to the printSubTree method is the number of spaces to indent the process information; the second number is the associative array %processList, which contains all the process objects. When the printSubTree method is called, the current process information is printed out. Then each child of the current process, if there are any children, calls the printSubTree method. This is performed by the following lines of code.

```
for ($x=0; $x <= $#children; $x++)
{
    my $child = $processList{$children[$x]};
    $child->printSubTree($space, %processList);
}
```

Comments

When using recursive functions, make sure that all the variables in the recursive loop have been defined locally. If not, then each iteration of the function will use the same address space for the variables. This will cause weird and wonderful results. This version of the process works only on a Solaris machine. There is a version for Linux named chap_19/howto13/linux.pl and a version for Sun/OS named chap_19/howto13/sunos.pl.

PERL PRAXIS

PERL PRAXIS

How do I ...

This chapter has less to say about techniques of Perl programming than other chapters in this book. Perl Praxis looks at the products of Perl programming, Perl applications, and the tools used to create and support those applications throughout their lifetime.

Every programmer has a set of favorite tools: editors, debuggers, and the like. Perl Praxis looks at how you can use these tools to create production-quality Perl applications. You can use the information in this chapter to edit Perl scripts more efficiently to optimize code where it matters. You will read about methods of shipping your application to another site, how to store a trace of your program's execution so you can track down problems in the field, how to keep a record of each release of software, and how to guarantee the integrity of your software once you have shipped it to the customer.

20.1   Set Up Emacs to Edit Perl Programs

The most valuable tool any developer can possess is a good editor. This How-To will focus on the Emacs editor, the powerful programmer's editor available for many platforms, and will describe how to install facilities for editing and formatting Perl programs.

20.2   Use Emacs' Perl Mode

Once you have set up Emacs, how do you use it? This How-To will describe the various key strokes and commands available in Emacs' Perl mode.

20.3   Implement Execution Logging

Process tracing can help track down problems in software already running in the field. If a program is running in a complex production environment, you may have difficulties duplicating an error-generating condition in a development environment. By tracing a program's execution, you can get a view of the software running under production conditions. This How-To will describe a technique for implementing execution logging in Perl.

20.4   Trap Potential Errors at Compile Time

C programmers have a tool called lint that checks a program for code that might pass the compiler checks but looks like it may contain an error. You can work in a similar way with Perl if you use the -w flag when you compile and run your code. This How-To will give you a brief guided tour of the -w error messages.

20.5   Write Portable Perl Programs

This How-To will provide some techniques for writing code that work on computers with different architectures, different operating systems, and different environments.

20.6   Profile Perl Code

Best read in conjunction with How-To 20.7 on optimization, this section will describe a method for identifying the areas of your program that are executed most often, areas that may be bottlenecks in the performance of your application.

20.7   Optimize Perl Code

Optimization is the collateral of profiling. Once you have located bottlenecks, you can recode for speed. This How-To will show you how to use a method for measuring speed improvement.

20.8 Ship Perl to Install It on Another System

If you are installing a Perl program at another site, this section will provide some useful advice on ways to bundle up Perl and ship it with your new program.

20.9 Use Revision Control Software with Perl

How do you keep track of each modification of a Perl script? How do you share a set of Perl files between several developers? This How-To will look at ways to use revision control software to coordinate a Perl development project.

20.10 Compile a Perl Script to Binary

Is there a satisfactory way to turn a Perl script into a standalone binary? Just what are the advantages of shipping binaries rather than scripts? This How-To will discuss some methods for gaining the advantages of a binary compilation in a scripting language.

20.11 Protect a Published Perl Script

How can you prevent your Perl scripts from being tampered with once they are released into the field? This section will show you how.

COMPLEXITY
INTERMEDIATE

20.1 How do I...
Set up Emacs to edit Perl programs?

COMPATIBILITY: UNIX DOS

Problem

The Emacs program editor has special facilities to support the development of Perl programs. How do I activate and use Emacs' Perl mode?

Technique

You can configure Emacs to switch into Perl mode automatically whenever you load a Perl program. Emacs is an extraordinarily configurable editor. Virtually every editing function is available in the Emacs command language—a dialect of lisp. So setting up Emacs involves a little Emacs lisp hacking.

In the following steps, we assume you are familiar with the basic facilities of Emacs, in particular, with the conventions for describing Emacs key strokes. Briefly, C-x means hold the (CTRL) key and type (x); M-x means press (ESC) then (x).

Steps

1. To set Perl mode automatically whenever you edit a Perl script, follow the next three steps, run Emacs, and load the file .emacs from your home directory into an Emacs buffer using the C-x C-f sequence.

2. Add the following Emacs lisp command to your .emacs file and save it.

```
; Automatic Perl mode determination
(setq auto-mode-alist
        (append ' (("\\.pl$"   . perl-mode)
                   ("\\.pm$"   . perl-mode))
                   auto-mode-alist))
```

3. To test the new entry, restart Emacs. Quit (C-x C-c) and reinvoke the program. Check for any error messages while the program initializes. If there are any, check the code you inserted in Step 2.

4. If there are no messages, all is well. Load a Perl file with the suffix .pl or .pm. Emacs automatically adopts Perl mode and displays (Perl mode) on the status line.

How It Works

If you are not familiar with lisp, then you may not understand the code above. In lisp, functions and data are represented by lists. A list is delimited by () characters. Emacs keeps a special list called auto-mode-alist that tells it how to map filenames to editing modes. Each element in the list contains a regular expression and a mode name. When Emacs loads a file into an internal buffer, it checks to see if any of the regular expressions matches the filename. If one does, then the associated editing mode is automatically set for that buffer.

The code specifies that if a file ends in .pm or .pl, the associated mode is Perl mode.

Comments

Most Perl files come with .pl or .pm extensions. Beware of any Prolog installations at your site. Prolog systems often expect their source files to have names ending in .pl too. Of course, if you have different rules for naming Perl files, then you must modify the regular expression in the code above.

If you want to look further into Emacs lisp, consult the extensive, some would say immense, GNU-Emacs lisp manual. Good luck.

COMPLEXITY
INTERMEDIATE

20.2 How do I...
Use Emacs' Perl mode?

COMPATIBILITY: UNIX DOS

Problem

The Emacs program editor has special facilities to support the layout and navigation of Perl programs. How do I use Emacs' Perl mode?

Technique

Perl mode provides the Emacs editing commands shown in Table 20-1.

KEY	BINDING
TAB	Perl indent command
DEL	Backward-delete-char-untabify
ESC	Prefix command
:;{}	Electric Perl terminator
ESC C-q	Indent Perl exp
ESC C-h	Mark Perl function
ESC C-e	Perl end of function
ESC C-a	Perl beginning of function

Table 20-1 Emacs' Perl mode key commands

Steps

1. Load a Perl file into an Emacs buffer. If you followed the steps in How-To 20.1, then Emacs should automatically set Perl mode. If Perl mode is not set, set it manually by typing the sequence

```
M-x perl-mode
```

2. View the online Perl mode reference at any time by entering the Emacs command

```
M-x describe-mode
```

3. Type in a new line of Perl code. Terminate the line with a ; character. Emacs automatically aligns the code in relation to the previous statements.

4. To lay out a whole Perl statement, place the cursor somewhere within the expression and press M-C-q. Emacs will format the whole statement.

5. To select a whole Perl function so that it may be cut, pasted, or copied in its entirety, press `M`-`C`-`h`. To cut the function to the Emacs clip buffer, press `C`-`w`; to copy it to the buffer, press `M`-`w`. To paste it, press `C`-`y`.

6. To jump to the beginning of a function definition, press `M`-`C`-`a`. To jump to the end, press `M`-`C`-`e`.

How It Works

The indentation style of Emacs Perl mode is defined by the values of a number of Emacs lisp variables.

perl-indent-level

This variable sets the indentation of Perl statements within surrounding block, that is, the offset of a statement in relation to the line on which the previous enclosing open brace appears. The offset is indicated by the arrow in the code below.

```
sub any {
==>local($foo);
```

perl-continued-statement-offset

This variable determines the extra indentation given to a substatement, a component of a complex statement, such as the then clause of an *if* or the body of a *while*. The indentation is indicated by the arrow in the code below.

```
while ( <>) {
===>$var = $_;
```

perl-continued-brace-offset

This variable sets the extra indentation given to a brace that starts a substatement. This value is added to perl-continued-statement-offset. You can set negative values. The arrow indicates the indentation in the code below.

```
if ($_)
==>{
```

perl-brace-offset

This variable sets extra indentation for a line if it starts with an open brace. The indentation is indicated by the arrow below.

```
sub any
==>{
```

perl-brace-imaginary-offset

This variable determines that an open brace following other text is treated as if it were this far to the right of the start of its line. This variable is generally set to 0.

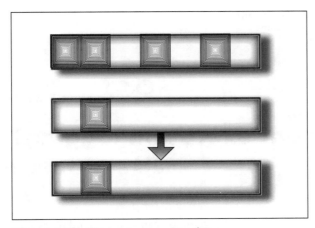

Figure 20-1 Bit vector comparison

perl-label-offset

This variable determines the extra indentation for a line that contains a Perl label. The Emacs editor uses bit vector comparisons, as illustrated in Figure 20-1, to determine indentation.

Comments

Table 20-2 indicates the values of variables for some common Perl layout styles.

VARIOUS INDENTATION STYLES	K&R	BSD	GNU	LW
Perl indent level	5	8	2	4
Perl continued statement offset	5	8	2	4
Perl continued brace offset	0	0	0	-4
Perl brace offset	-5	-8	0	0
Perl brace imaginary offset	0	0	0	0
Perl label offset	-5	-8	-2	-2

Table 20-2 Emacs' Perl mode variable settings for common layout styles

K&R is the classic C language style used by Brian W. Kernigahn and Dennis Richie in *The C Programming Language*. BSD is the popular layout style found in much of the source distribution of the BSD UNIX system. GNU is the GNU standard found in the Emacs' sources. LW is the style used by Perl's creator in his published work.

To set the K&R style, add the following to your .emacs file.

```
(set_variable 'perl-indent-level 2)
(set_variable 'perl-continued-statement-offset 2)
(set_variable 'perl-continued-brace-offset 0)
(set_variable 'perl-brace-offset 0)
(set_variable 'perl-brace-imaginary-offset 0)
(set_variable 'perl-label-offset -2)
```

continued on next page

continued from previous page

```
(set-variable 'perl-tab-always-indent )
(set-variable 'perl-tab-to-comment)
(set_variable 'perl-nochange)
```

COMPLEXITY
INTERMEDIATE

20.3 How do I...
Implement execution logging?

COMPATIBILITY: UNIX DOS

Problem

How can I add execution logging to a Perl program so I can store a record of my program's actions over a period of time? The logging should record significant processing key events in a log file that can be retained for analysis after the program has terminated.

Technique

Long-running programs such as database applications and server daemons often have a facility to log information to a file, storing a record of processing actions while the program executes. This information can later be used for audit, debugging, or informational purposes.

It is straightforward enough to have a program log information to a file while it is running. The problem is that very significant amounts of output can be generated with detailed logging. If you have plenty of disk space, you might find that tolerable. But I/O takes time, and running a program with logging fully active can have a detrimental effect on responsiveness.

What is really required is a mechanism for deactivating most of the *logging* statements and executing only those that relate to a certain class of events or certain areas of the program.

This How-To demonstrates a simple method of logging time-stamped information. Bit vectors and bit vector operations are used to disarm irrelevant *logging* statements.

Steps

1. Create a file called logging.pl and enter the following program. Alternatively, use the example from the CD. The program demonstrates some execution logging techniques.

```
#!/usr/local/bin/perl
# Demonstrate execution logging.

#sub warn_trap {
#   print STDERR "$0-alpha<", localtime(time), ">$_[0]\n";
# }

# $SIG{__WARN__}= \&warn_trap;
```

```
$P_ERRS = 1;
$P_WARN = 2;
$T_ERRS = 3;
$T_WARN = 4;
$L_INFO = 15;

foreach $bit ($P_ERRS, $T_ERRS, $L_INFO) {
    vec($LOGGING, $bit, 1) = 1;
}

warn "P_ERRS logging active\n" if vec($LOGGING,$P_ERRS,1);
warn "P_WARN logging active\n" if vec($LOGGING,$P_WARN,1);
warn "T_ERRS logging active\n" if vec($LOGGING,$T_ERRS,1);
warn "T_WARN logging active\n" if vec($LOGGING,$T_WARN,1);
warn "L_INFO log vector is ", unpack("b*",$LOGGING), "\n"
  if vec($LOGGING,$L_INFO,1);
```

2. Make the program executable and run it. You should see results similar to the following:

Output

```
P_ERRS logging active
T_ERRS logging active
L_INFO logging bit vector is 0101000000000001
```

End Output

3. Remove the comment symbols from the subroutine warn_trap and the assignment to %SIG that follows it.

```
sub warn_trap {
 print STDERR "$0-alpha<", localtime(time), ">$_[0]\n";
}
$SIG{__WARN__}= \&warn_trap;
```

Execute the program again. You will see output similar to before, but each line is tagged with a file and time stamp.

Output

```
logging.pl<10:45:38:17-Aug-95>P_ERRS logging active
logging.pl<10:45:38:17-Aug-95>T_ERRS logging active
logging.pl<10:45:38:17-Aug-95>L_INFO log vector is 0101000000000001
```

End Output

How It Works

The approach is this: Include code in your program to print out as much trace and logging information as you could possibly need. Then make all the *logging* statements conditional on an inexpensive test that determines whether the information is needed. Operations on bit vectors, arrays of 1s and 0s packed into a few bytes, are efficient and a good way of implementing conditional logging.

The code below defines constants with values between 1 and 15. Each represents a class of processing event.

```
$P_ERRS = 1;
$P_WARN = 2;
$T_ERRS = 3;
$T_WARN = 4;
$L_INFO = 15;
```

Constant P_WARN means noncritical processing problems, P_ERRS denotes critical processing errors, T_ERRS means database transaction errors, and so on. You can select sets of these constants to designate the desired level of logging information. When a bit vector is used in this way, it is commonly referred to as a *logging mask*.

Suppose you want to record critical problems in transactions and processing, not less critical problems. To achieve this, set a bit in the mask LOGGING for the constants P_ERRS, T_ERRS, using the Perl vec command.

```
foreach $bit ($P_ERRS, $T_ERRS, $L_INFO) { vec($LOGGING, $bit, 1};
```

You have added the information constant L_INFO to the mask. If the L_INFO bit is set, the program will print out a record of the current mask.

Conditional logging is easily expressed using the Perl postfix *if* statement.

```
warn "P_ERRS logging active\n" if vec($LOGGING, $P_ERRS, 1);
```

This line logs a P_ERRS message only if the P_ERRS bit has the value 1 in the LOGGING mask. In a production program, you would make all P_ERRS log messages conditional on the vec command, logically &&'ed with an internal program status.

```
$P_ERR_NULL_PKT = 'TRUE' unless length($PKT);
warn "Empty packet received\n"
     if vec($LOGGING,$P_ERRS, 1) && $P_ERR_NULL_PKT;
```

Step 2 shows the output generated by the program. Notice how the logging mask has been displayed as a big endian binary string using the unpack b* specification.

The warn function, by default, prints its parameters unadorned to STDERR. Because you wish to prepend time information, you must override the standard warn function by using the Perl warn hook. In Step 3, you uncomment this line:

```
$SIG{__WARN__}= \&warn_trap;
```

Now whenever the warn function is called, Perl sends all the parameters to the subroutine named in the %SIG array under the key __WARN__. In this case, the subroutine warn_trap adds a filename and date stamp to each logged message.

Comments

An interesting extension to this approach enables the desired level of logging to be set dynamically while a process is running. In the example program, the configuration of the logging mask is part of the script. If the program starts to misbehave during execution, the only way to log new information is to stop it, change the logging levels, and restart it.

You can use signals, if your operating system supports them, to manipulate the logging vector of a running program. Under UNIX, the kill command can send any signal to a process. Most implementations of UNIX have two user-defined signals: USR1 and USR2. You can send these signals to, say, process 1999 with this command:

```
kill USR1 1999
```

If process 1999 has defined a handler for $SIG{'USR1'}, then that handler can manipulate the LOGGING vector. A common method is to increment the vector with USR1 and set it to 0 with the USR2 signal.

```
sub usr1_h { warn unpack("b*", ++$LOGGING), "\n";}
sub usr2_h { $LOGGING = 0; warn "$LOGGING\n";}
$SIG{'USR1'} = \&usr1_h;
$SIG{'USR2'} = \&usr2_h;
```

COMPLEXITY
INTERMEDIATE

20.4 How do I...
Trap potential errors at compile time?

COMPATIBILITY: UNIX DOS

Problem

How do I have the Perl compiler look through my code and identify areas where there might be coding mistakes or potentially dangerous idioms?

Technique

Some advice is always good advice. Don't forget a friend's birthday, don't play on the freeway, don't forget to check your Perl with the -w switch. This How-To discusses the -w switch that generates warnings whenever unsafe constructs are found in a Perl program.

Steps

1. Enter the following program or use program wcheck.pl from the CD.

```
#!/usr/local/bin/perl
# Demonstrate warnings with the -w flag.

$P_ERRS = 1;
$P_WARN = 2;
$T_ERRS = 3;
$T_WARN = 4;

foreach $bit ($P_ERRS, $T_ERRS, $L_INFO) {
    vec($LOGGING, $bit, 1) = 1;
}
```

continued on next page

continued from previous page

```
warn "P_ERRS logging active\n" if vec($LOGGING,$P_ERRS,1);
warn "P_WARN logging active\n" if vec($LOGGING,$P_WARN,1);
warn "T_ERRS logging active\n" if vec($LOGGING,$T_ERRS,1);
warn "T_WARN logging active\n" if vec($LOGGING,$T_WARN,1);
warn "L_INFO log vector is ", unpack("b*",$LOGGING), "\n"
  if vec($LOGGING,$L_INFO,1);
```

2. Run it through Perl interpreter with the -w flag set.

```
perl -w wcheck.pl
```

Perl generates the following warnings.

─ Output ───

Use of uninitialized value at logging.pl line 10.

─ End Output ───

This tells you that the value of variable *$L_INFO* is used before it has been assigned. This is a bug.

3. Add the -w flag to the #! Perl line in the program file. This enables the Perl interpreter to pick up some errors that become apparent only at runtime.

How It Works

The messages are classified as follows (listed in increasing order of seriousness):

- (W) A warning (something that might be a problem. Optional—see $^W in the Comments section).

- (D) A deprecation (something that you should not do. Optional—see $^W in the Comments section).

- (S) A severe warning (mandatory).

- (F) A fatal error (trappable by the Perl function eval).

- (P) An internal error you should never see (Perl has malfunctioned but the error is trappable by eval).

- (X) A very fatal error (nontrappable—Perl has totally malfunctioned—extraordinarily rare).

You can locate a list of warnings and error messages, complete with explanations, in the Perldiag 1 man page. To view the manual page on a UNIX system, type

```
man perldiag
```

Non-UNIX users are usually supplied with the Perl manual in text file format. Search through your distribution directories for the man files.

Comments

Sometimes warnings are spurious. If you are sure that your program is working correctly, you can turn warnings off by setting the special variable $^W flag to False and then resetting it again after the line of code that generates spurious error messages.

Program wcheck.pl generates the following warning message when run under the -w flag.

```
Use of uninitialized variable at wcheck.pl line 17.
```

The problem lies in this piece of code (line 17 is the line containing the vec call):

```
foreach $bit ($P_ERRS, $T_ERRS, $L_INFO) {
    vec($LOGGING, $bit, 1) = 1;
}
```

It appears to Perl that the variable *$LOGGING* is supplying an input value to the function vec before *$LOGGING* has been provided with a value by assignment. Because Perl guarantees to initialize any variable to 0 or null automatically, there is no mistake here. The use of the variable *$LOGGING* is quite safe because you are expecting it to start out with the value 0. To stop Perl from complaining, you must insert a line of code before the line that causes the problem and restore $^W afterwards.

```
$^W = 0;
foreach $bit ($P_ERRS, $T_ERRS, $L_INFO) {
    vec($LOGGING, $bit, 1) = 1;
}
$^W = 1;
```

Don't abuse this $^W variable. No error checker is perfect. Perl -w sometimes generates spurious messages. The $^W variable is there so you can run your program under the -w flag but avoid spurious messages.

COMPLEXITY
INTERMEDIATE

20.5 How do I...
Write portable Perl programs?

COMPATIBILITY: UNIX   DOS

Problem

How can I ensure that a Perl script will execute directly on several UNIX architectures and non-UNIX architectures that support Perl?

Technique

The gods are with you! Perl is a great deal more portable than any of the common shell or command languages. Thanks to the Internet volunteer force known as the Perl Porters, the main features of Perl should correspond on any architecture where Perl is available. There are some caveats to that statement: Some OS's just don't have the facilities to support some of Perl's more sophisticated features, such as multitasking. Many Perl functions call POSIX operating-system facilites. If some of your target operating systems are not POSIX compliant, you nullify Perl's guarantee of portability if you use POSIX services in your program.

We recommend that you use each step below to check for possibly nonportable features.

Steps

1. Use the Config array to obtain information about the system executing your script. Use the following program, pconfig.pl, to dump information about your system.

```
#!/usr/local/bin/perl

use Config;
foreach $i (keys %Config) {
    print "$i = $Config{$i}\n";
}
```

The program displays the following interesting values.

pconfig.pl

| Output |

```
archlib = /usr/local/lib/perl5/sun4-sunos
osname = sunos
osvers = 4.1.3_u1
sharpbang = #!
shsharp = true
sig_name = ZERO HUP INT QUIT ILL TRAP ABRT EMT FPE KILL BUS
SEGV SYS PIPE ALRM
so = so
startsh = #!/bin/sh
archname = sun4-sunos
byteorder = 4321
cc = cc
csh = csh
myarchname = sun4-sunos
mydomain =
myhostname = alpha
```

| End Output |

2. Use internal Perl facilities in place of calling out to external programs. For example, if you need to remove a file, use unlink rather than executing system or syscall or rm commands. Don't echo things; use print. Print is more flexible, and you don't have to worry about echo's different behavior on different platforms.

3. If you must use OS commands, then check for the obvious traps. The ps command has different switches and output formats on different systems.

The UNIX mkdir -p command fails on some systems; use the internal mkdir function instead. Use internal functions in place of callouts.

4. If you are assuming Perl 5 features in your script, then add a line like this at or near the start of the program:

```
require 5.000 ;
```

If anyone attempts to execute the script under a Perl 4 interpreter, the program will terminate with an informational message.

5. If you are porting to a DOS environment, check your script for the following:

● Check your use of any multitasking and shell-based featues.

● Work around any attempts to create asynchronous subprocesses.

● Signals or other forms of IPC calls will likely be impossible to port directly.

● System or backquoted commands will not port.

● Shell-related features, quoting, wildcarding, etc., may run into trouble.

6. Be careful with numbers. Float and double values may not survive pack and unpack operations on machines with different byte orders (big endian and little endian machines).

How It Works

In Step 1, you list the contents of the Config array. Perl creates the Config.pm module at install time. It contains the results of the configuration process, which takes place before you build the Perl binaries.

Analyzing the contents of Config array reveals that the local operating system is SunOS v4.1.3.u1. executing on a sun4 sparc processor. It supports at least the 15 named signals. The machine is probably not running NIS because no domain name is set. The hostname alpha is the name of the system on which Perl was compiled. If the Perl executable is on an NFS-mounted disk, then the name of the machine would be different.

Many shell scripts blow up because of assumptions about external programs. Some shells support aliases; these can trip up shell scripts. Common commands may be aliased to be interactive: rm to rm -i, for example. Scripts that try to use the command will stall, waiting for input. If you use the equivalent Perl internal function in place of a call to an external program, you will have much more predictable behavior and you will gain in efficiency.

MS-DOS is still a problematic environment for porting Perl scripts because it is a single-tasking operating system. Pipes and signals are the only form of IPC that DOS supports, but the interrupt signal is available. Running your DOS Perl program under Windows may help. The popular BigPerl implementation of Perl 4 supports virtual memory and the WinSock interface. Windows 95 and Windows NT implementations of Perl 5 are, at the time of writing, immature but promise to develop a near-complete set of features. Some NT Perls support Microsoft's OLE2 interprocess communications standard.

Comments

At the time of writing, Perl 5 has been ported to every major UNIX architecure, NT, Mac, Windows 95, and VMS. Perl 4 is available for DOS, Windows, and MVS platforms.

COMPLEXITY
INTERMEDIATE

20.6   How do I...
Profile Perl code?

COMPATIBILITY: UNIX | DOS

Problem

I wish to increase the efficiency of my Perl program. How can I obtain a profile of its execution? The profile should reveal the areas of the program that are most frequently executed. I can then focus optimization in these areas.

Technique

There is no standard profiler distributed with Perl, but there are several readily available Perl profilers or you can roll your own with the debugger trace command. Because you are going to use the Perl debugger to obtain raw profiling data, you might like to read ahead to Chapter 21, which covers the debugger.

Steps

1. Execute your program this way:

```
perl -d myprog.pl myprog.dat
```

where myprog.pl represents your program and myprog.dat represents any arguments that it might require.

2. At the DB> prompt, enter the command t. The debugger prints out the message

 Output

```
trace mode on
```
End Output

3. To store any further output to a file, type the command

```
open(DB::OUT,">prof.out");
```

where prof.out is the name of an output file in which to store the data.

4. Now you are typing blind because output is going to the file, not to the screen. Enter the command c, which sets the program executing.

5. Create a program called profil.pl or use the code from the CD. This small Perl program will be used to analyze the data generated from the debugger and to report the most frequently executed sections of code.

```perl
#!/usr/local/bin/perl
# profil.pl - simple profile tool
open(OUT, "| sort -rn | head -20")|| die "Can't open output\n";

while(<>){
# input line resembles- module::subroutine(/path/prog1:29): <code>
    m/(.*)::(.*)\((.*):(\d+)\):/;
    $module = $1; $sub = $2; $file = $3; $line = $4;
    $count{"$module\:\:$sub\:$line"}++;
}
# Send the line and execution count to sort.
foreach $i (keys %count) {
    printf OUT "%8d\t%s\n", $count{$i}, $i;
}
```

6. Execute the profile processor on the data created by the debugger.

```
profil.pl prof.out
```

How It Works

In trace mode, the debugger outputs the module, file, and line of each statement of code it is about to execute. By storing this information, you can get a sample of which lines are executed most often in a particular run.

profil.pl works by reading each line of the file, splitting the debugger data into a set of fields that identify each line executed. The fields are interpolated into a string and the string is stored in associative array %count. Each time a particular line is encountered, the value of $count{interpolated_fields} is incremented.

```
$count{"$module\:\:$sub\:$line"}++;
```

Finally, each line and its count are sent to an external sort command. The top 20 lines and the number of times each was executed are printed on STDOUT. If you don't have these external commands available, you can extend the program to sort the data internally.

```
open(OUT, "| sort -rn | head -20")
```

For one particular execution of a pattern-matching program on a large data file, we obtained the following results.

Output

```
8106 main::match_found:53
8106 main::match_found:49
4053 main:::223
4053 main:::217
4053 main:::216
```

continued on next page

continued from previous page

```
4053 main:::215
4053 main:::214
4053 main:::188
4050 main:::221
3872 main:::202
3871 main:::210
1808 main::showline:70
1808 main::showline:67
1808 main::showline:64
1808 main::showline:61
1808 main::showline:58
 543 main:::197
 361 main:::211
 181 main:::200
 181 main:::196
```

End Output

The numbers on the left of the listing show how many times the line of code on the right was executed. The right-hand side is to be interpreted as

```
module_name::sub_routine_if_any:number_of_line_within_file
```

Comments

It's clear from the results above that any optimization should be focused on the routine match_found, two lines of which were executed more than 8,000 times.

COMPLEXITY
INTERMEDIATE

20.7 How do I...
Optimize Perl code?

COMPATIBILITY: UNIX DOS

Problem

My Perl program is not executing with the desired speed. I have run the script through a profiler and identified the bottlenecks. What guidelines should I follow if I want to recode these areas and monitor the increase in performance?

Technique

Optimization is usually a story with a moral: Optimize in a focused way; random optimization is frequently a waste of time and can even be counterproductive.

The first step in optimizing a program is to pinpoint where the program spends its time. If a program executes a few key lines of code or a subroutine many thousands of times, a 1% optimization in those areas will have more impact on the total running time than an optimization of 1000% in an area that is executed only once.

To demonstrate some optimization techniques, we will reexamine program profil.pl. You will modify it in two ways.

Steps

1. Program profil2.pl is a slightly modifed version of program profil.pl. Either take the code file from the CD or modify your version of profil.pl so it is the same as the program listing below.

```perl
#!/usr/local/bin/perl
# profil2.pl - simple profile tool
use Benchmark;

open(OUT, "| sort -rn | head -20")|| die "Can't open output\n";

$t0 = new Benchmark;
while(<>){
# input line resembles-> mod::sub(/home/bin/prog1:29):    $i++;
    m/(.*)::(.*)\((.*):(\d+)\):/;
    $module = $1; $sub = $2; $file = $3; $line = $4;
#   ($module,$x,$sub,$file,$line) = split(/[\(\):]/);
    $count{"$module\:\:$sub\:$line"}++;
}
$t1 = new Benchmark;
$tm = timediff($t1,$t0);
print "Code time:", timestr($tm), "\n";

foreach $i (keys %count) {
    printf OUT "%8d\t%s\n", $count{$i}, $i;
}
```

2. Optimize the pattern-matching code in this block:

```perl
{
    # input line resembles-> mod::sub(/home/bin/prog1:29):    $i++;
    m/(.*)::(.*)\((.*):(\d+)\):/;
    $module = $1; $sub = $2; $file = $3; $line = $4;
    $count{"$module\:\:$sub\:$line"}++;
}
```

Notice that you have coded two forms of the same code: the original version, which uses $1, $2 back references, and a line designed to replace the back-reference code, which uses the split function. For the moment, the line that calls the split function is commented out. Run the program using the large file of profile data generated in How-To 20.6. Record the time it takes to execute.

profil2.pl   prof.out

Output

```
Code time:45 secs (43.80 usr   0.42 sys = 44.22 cpu)
```

End Output

3. Now modify the program to use an alternative coding of the pattern-matching code. The question you are investigating is whether the split function will execute more efficiently than the back-reference code. Delete the two lines that perform the pattern matching and variable assignment immediately after the *while* statement. Insert the line highlighted below.

```
while(<>){
# input line resembles-> mod::sub(/home/bin/prog1:29):    $i++;
    ($module,$x,$sub,$file,$line) = split(/[\(\):]/);
    $count{"$module\:\:$sub\:$line"}++;
}
```

4. Execute the program again and observe the results.

`profil2.pl   prof.out`

```
Code time:38 secs (36.68 usr   0.50 sys = 37.18 cpu)
```

The new version of the program executes faster, 38 seconds as opposed to 45 seconds.

How It Works

This technique of benchmarking code and measuring the optimization is assisted by the Perl 5 library module Benchmark.pm, as shown in Figure 20-2. This module implements a Perl object, a Benchmark. Benchmark objects can be created in the program with calls to the creator function new Benchmark.

`$bm = new Benchmark;`

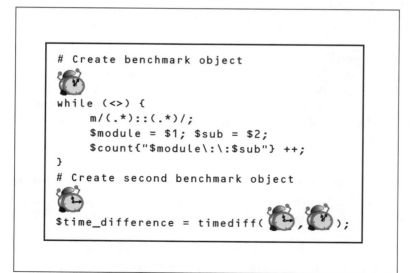

Figure 20-2 Benchmarking Perl code

The technique is to create two Benchmark objects on either side of a block of code and run the program. You can compare the two objects using the routine Benchmark::timediff and determine the time and resources consumed executing the intervening block of code.

```
$t0 = new Benchmark;
# Timed code here ...
$t1 = new Benchmark;
$tm = timediff($t1,$t0);
print "Code time:", timestr($tm), "\n";
```

Benchmark::timestr is used to print out the resulting data in a readable form.

Comments

In reality, you would want to execute the program several times and average the result before you draw too many conclusions about the efficiency of a particular piece of code. Always try to run a benchmark on an otherwise idle machine or on a machine that is evenly loaded over time.

COMPLEXITY
INTERMEDIATE

20.8 How do I...
Ship Perl to install it on another system?

COMPATIBILITY: UNIX   DOS

Problem

I have to deliver a Perl script to a site where either no Perl is installed or the Perl version is in doubt. I don't want to rebuild Perl from the distribution package. How can I take a portable version of Perl with me and install it with my script?

Technique

Under the terms of the Perl license, you are free to distribute Perl binaries and libraries, provided you acknowledge that they are not your own work and place no restrictions on the availability of the source code. The license is designed to place no legal restrictions in distributing Perl, provided you do not attempt to restrict further distribution. Your Perl scripts are your own intellectual property.

The Perl installation is remarkably small. You can pack the full Perl kit for a Sun Sparc machine onto a single floppy disk.

Steps

1. Create an archive of the Perl kit for your target installation environment. For a typical UNIX installation of Perl, where the root directory of the installation is /usr/local, issue the following commands to the C shell.

```
cd /usr/local
tar cvf  perl2go.tar  {lib,bin}/perl5*
compress perl2go.tar && bar cvf  /dev/rfd0c perl2go.tar.Z
```

2. Log in to the target system. Check to see if an installation of Perl already exists.

```
which Perl
```

If this command reveals a version of Perl on your path, go immediately to Step 3.

```
find /usr -name "perl*" -print
```

This command will take some time and resources. If it reveals a version of Perl, go to Step 3.

3. If a Perl installation is present, check to see if it is a version capable of running your script. If the Perl installation shows up under /usr/bin, for example, type

```
/usr/bin/perl -v
```

Output

```
This is perl, version 4.036
```

End Output

4. Assuming the worst, that either there is no version of Perl on site or the version is older than the one you require (remember, your scripts can themselves validate the version of Perl they are running, using the *require* statement), prepare to install from your copy of Perl to go. The easiest way to proceed is to install under the same root directory as on the source system. If that directory is /usr/local, you will now have a privilege problem as any self-respecting system will only allow root write access to the /usr/local/ tree. See if the system administrator will allow you supervised root access to /usr/local while you install Perl. Let the system administrator log you in. Don't ask for the root password—either you will get a blunt no or, if it is provided, every problem with the system during the next six months will be blamed on your brief moment of superuser access.

If you negotiate successfully, go ahead and install from your perl2go kit, as explained in the next step.

5. Check the disk space available on the machine. Under UNIX, use the df command.

Find an area for temporary extraction (we will use /tmp here) and check that there is enough space under the installation root directory for the full installation. Again, we assume your target install root directory is /usr/local.

```
cd /tmp
bar xvf /dev/rfd0c
uncompress perl2go.tar.Z
```

6. Now install your Perl.

```
su  - root
password: *********
cd  /usr/local
tar xvf /tmp/perl2go.tar  .
x ./bin/perl5.001m
...
exit
```

7. Check your installation with the following command

```
perl  -de "require 5.001"
```

where 5.001 is the version of Perl required for your scripts.

8. If you cannot obtain access to a standard Perl installation directory such as /usr/local, you can install Perl in the directory where you install your scripts. You will need to fix the #! lines in your scripts and modify the @INC array to point to your Perl library directory. To modify the @INC array to include the directory /home/perlscripts/lib/perl5.001, add the following commands to your script.

```
BEGIN { unshift(@INC,' /home/perlscripts/lib/perl5.001') }
```

How It Works

The tar command recursively traverses each directory in a specified tree, including each file it finds in an archive file. The tar cvf perl2go.tar {lib,bin}/perl5* command archives the files in each of the directories (the tree that is shown in Figure 20-3) ./lib/perl5.001/ ... and the file bin/perl5.001. Save space by compressing the resulting archive file using the compress command. You could have used the excellent GNU compression utility gzip, but because you have no guarantee that the customer site will have it installed, you would just give yourself the extra problem of having to ship gzip to the customer.

Use the bar command to place the compressed archive file perl2go.tar.Z onto a floppy disk. The advantage of bar over tar is that it handles multiple volumes if the archive file is too large for one floppy disk.

The *BEGIN* {unshift(@INC,' /home/perlscripts/lib/perl5.001')} may need some explanation. The array @INC contains a list of places to search for Perl libraries and files to be used in require, use, and do commands. By placing the local install directory at the front of the array, you ensure that local library files are given precedence over files inserted by other Perl installations. You enclose the *unshift* statement within a *BEGIN* block to ensure that it is evaluated before any *use* statements, which are implicitly enclosed within *BEGIN* blocks.

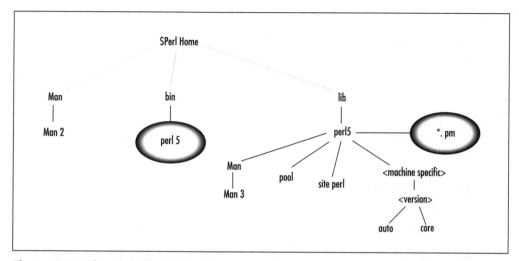

Figure 20-3 The installed Perl directory tree

Comments

Two major problems can happen when you ship a Perl script to a customer location. First, you assume that a version of Perl suitable to run your application is preinstalled. You may arrive on site and find it isn't. This makes you look silly in front of a customer. The second calamity is more serious. You install your own version of Perl and inadvertently overwrite the version of Perl that is already installed and functioning. Don't assume that an older version is an unwanted version. The customer may have scripts in production that assume features of a specific Perl version. You won't be popular if you inadvertently break another system.

Before you proceed with Step 6, check that you are not about to clobber the existing installation. Normally, the Perl executable is stored as perl5.001m, and the file Perl is a link to the file with the version suffix. Be careful. Many installations remove the file with the version suffix, leaving a file with the name Perl that will be overwritten by your new installation. If this is the case, move the existing Perl to perl.NNN, where NNN is the version number, and check whether any existing programs are using the old version of Perl. You may have to fix up their #! lines to use the old version explicitly or check that it still runs correctly with your new installation.

Perl is freely distributable software but not free software. If you are shipping Perl to a new site, ensure that you comply with the Perl licensing agreement: either the Artistic license or the GNU license. Check that the file containing the license is shipped as part of the kit and that the target site agrees with its provisions before a customer uses your software.

COMPLEXITY
INTERMEDIATE

20.9 How do I...
Use revision control software with Perl?

COMPATIBILITY: UNIX DOS

Problem

I need to keep a record of which developer modified Perl sources, why a modification was needed, and when modifications were released for production use. I will use the publically available revision control software (RCS) to manage this information. What approach should I take to integrating Perl scripts into a revision control system?

Steps

1. Add the assignment statement beginning $rcsId = as the first line of file rcs_eg.pl from the CD.

```
#!/usr/local/bin/perl
#
# Test RCS handling of Perl scripts
$rcsId = "\$Id\$";
print "$rcsId\n";
sleep 2;
exit 0;
```

2. Place the file under RCS control by checking the file using the RCS ci command.

```
ci rcs_eg.pl
rcs\rcs_eg.pl  <--  rcs_eg.pl
initial revision: 1.1
enter description, terminated with single '.' or end of file:
NOTE: This is NOT the log message!
>> Initial version.
>> .
done
```

Enter a descriptive comment when prompted, as shown in the dialogue above. Type a stop at the beginning of a line and hit <ENTER> to terminate the description.

3. Retrieve the current version of the file with the RCS check-out command. This copy is for reference only. Make it executable and execute it.

```
co rcs_eg.pl
```

Output

```
rcs\rcs_eg.pl  -->  rcs_eg.pl
revision 1.1
done
```

End Output

rcs_eg.pl

```
$Id: rcs_eg.pl 1.1 1995/1/04 01:21:09 root_dos Exp $
```

4. Now edit the file. Use the co -l option so that the file is checked out locked, ensuring that no other user can simultaneously edit it. Overwrite the existing reference copy of the file.

```
co -l rcs_eg.pl
rcs\rcs_eg.pl   -->   rcs_eg.pl
revision 1.1 (locked)
writable rcs_eg.pl exists; remove it? [ny](n): y
done
```

5. Edit the file. RCS expanded the Id line you inserted into the original file. Don't modify this expanded string, but add the rest of the split statement around it. The file then looks like this:

```
#!/usr/local/bin/perl
#
# Test RCS handling of Perl scripts
($_,$rcsfile,$rcsver,$rcsdate) = split(" ",
    "\$Id: rcs_eg.pl 1.1 1995/1/04 01:21:09 root_dos Exp root_dos $");
print "$rcsfile V$rcsver of $rcsdate\n";
sleep 2;
exit 0;
```

6. Check in the new version of the file. Use the ci -l option so that RCS checks out another editable version immediately after logging the changes. Add a comment in the usual way.

```
ci -l rcs_eg.pl
rcs\rcs_eg.pl   <--   rcs_eg.pl
new revision: 1.2; previous revision: 1.1
enter log message:
(terminate with single '.' or end of file)
>> Added parsing of RCS id message.
>> .
done

Execute the new version of the program.
rcs_eg.pl
rcs_eg.pl V1.2 of 1995/1/04
```

7. Check in the file and display the history of changes. You can show the history of an RCS file using the rlog command.

```
ci -u rcs_eg.pl
rlog rcs_eg.pl
```

```
RCS file: rcs\rcs_eg.pl
```

```
Working file: rcs_eg.pl
head: 1.2
branch:
locks: strict
        root_dos: 1.2
access list:
symbolic names:
comment leader: "% "
keyword substitution: kv
total revisions: 2;     selected revisions: 2
description:
Initial version.
----------------------------
revision 1.2    locked by: root_dos;
date: 1995/1/04 01:38:40;  author: root_dos; state: Exp; lines: +6 -2
added paring of RCS id message.
----------------------------
revision 1.1
date: 1995/1/04 01:21:09;  author: root_dos;  state: Exp;
Initial revision
==================================================================
```

End Output

8. Extend the Perl RCS techniques to handle packages. List files rcs_eg1.pl and rcs_eg1.pm from the CD or enter the code below.

```perl
#!/usr/local/bin/perl
#
# Test RCS handling of Perl scripts

sub print_version {
  local ($message,$rcsid) = @_;
  ($_,$rcsfile,$rcsver,$rcsdate,$@) = split(" ",$rcsId);
  print stderr "$message:: $rcsfile V$rcsver of $rcsdate\n";
}

require "rcs_eg1.pm";

print_version("$0 main", "\$Id$");
sleep 2;
exit 0;
```

9. Check in both files to RCS, reserving a reference copy in the current directory. Use the ci -u option to tell RCS to create a reference copy of the files after checking them in.

```
ci -u rcs_eg1.pl rcs_eg1.pm
```

10. Execute the file and note the initialization information.

```
rcs_eg1.pl
```

Output

```
Package Rcsdemo:: rcs_eg1.pm V1.1 of 1995/1/04
rcs_eg1.pl main:: rcs_eg1.pl V1.2 of 1995/1/04
```

End Output

How It Works

The string Id is special to RCS. When it encounters the string in an input file, RCS interprets it as a special RCS marker; when you check out the file, RCS substitutes a string with the form

```
$Id: filename revision date time author state $
```

in its place. By placing the Id marker in a Perl string, you can capture the information and manipulate it within the Perl program itself. The only catch is the back-slash placed before the initital $ in the marker. This ensures no unexpected Perl substitutions can occur.

Steps 5 and 6 demonstrate how you can parse and manipulate this marker string to produce formatted output identifying the version and date of a file.

Step 8 extends this approach to show how you can use the BEGIN subroutine that is automatically invoked on initialization of Perl 5 packages to force each module in a program to log its version number.

For a more detailed description of the RCS suite, read the man page rcsintro (1).

Comments

RCS is not always shipped as part of the UNIX operating system. UNIX is more commonly shipped with its own source code control system, SCCS. Whereas RCS is available as free software and has been ported to many different architectures, SCCS has languished on UNIX and is not commonly found elsewhere. Modified forms of RCS are available from commercial suppliers. The popular PVCS sytem, available on DOS and OS/2, is an extended commercial-strength version of RCS software.

COMPLEXITY
INTERMEDIATE

20.10 How do I...
Compile a Perl script to binary?

COMPATIBILITY: UNIX | DOS

Problem

Once I have generated a stable Perl script, is there any way to compile it to a binary program that I can ship without the Perl interpreter?

Technique

As of now, the answer is no, not really. There is a documented technique for Perl 4, using a program called undump in which a Perl program can be made to dump a core image of itself to disk by calling the dump function. This core can then be converted to a binary executable using the undump utility. undump is not supplied with Perl 4 or Perl 5 but is available with the distribution of the TeX package.

How It Works

This method of producing a binary has been generally deprecated in the Perl community. Few have reported success with the method, and it is not supported under Perl 5.

Comments

Major Perl figures believe that it is theoretically possible to create a Perl 5 compiler. There is some interest in creating one, although at the time of writing, none exist. Watch the newsgroups and Perl resource channels discussed in Appendix A for announcements.

COMPLEXITY
INTERMEDIATE

20.11 How do I...
Protect a published Perl program?

COMPATIBILITY: UNIX DOS

Problem

If I ship my Perl script, how can I protect my copyright on the code and how can I ensure that I am supporting the released version? Is there any way to render Perl code unmodifiable?

Technique

Compiling a script to binary has a side effect. The user can run the program but, because you can ship the binary without the source, the user can't see how the program works and can't change it.

Neither of these is necessarily an advantage. There are two reasons why you might want to do this. First, you might want to protect some special algorithm or approach in the code as a piece of your intellectual property. Second, you might be concerned with the possibility of the customer modifying a program and then requiring you to support his or her (possibly random) changes. There are three approaches you can take.

First, you can protect any copyrightable code by embedding it in a loadable library built in a compilable language and shipped in binary format.

Second, you can translate your Perl code into a form that is so hard to read that it is effectively binary.

Third, if your concern is the possibility of customers modifying source code and asking you to fix it, you can check-sum the script file so that any modification is easily detectable. You must include a clause in your license agreement that stipulates that only the original installed files will be supported. This is a solution that is often well received by customers. Suppose you have shipped a complex Perl program to a customer. The software can interrogate a database and generate reports. You can

easily extract areas that a user might wish to customize, for example, format statements to separate files. Customers get the option to modify some more cosmetic aspects
of the software, report layouts and the like, but at their own risk.

Steps

1. To record a check-sum of the files in your distribution, issue the following command

```
echo "Warranty void if modified without authorisation."  >  Warranty.txt
echo "File checksums follow" >> Warranty.txt
sum file1.pl file2.pl .... >> Warranty.txt
```

where file<n>.pl is a list of the files you want to check-sum. Make a copy of
the file Warranty.txt for reference.

2. Please see Chapter 26 for details on loading C libraries as Perl modules.

3. Obfuscate the code so that the effort of reading it outweighs the possible
gains. A good Perl obfuscator program is needed. Such a program would
compile Perl source code to equivalent Perl code that performs the same
function yet is so difficult to comprehend that the file is unreadable. There
are free obfuscators for the TCL-script language, but none of the major Perl
code archives contains a decent obfuscator program for Perl 5. A commercial product, ShroudIt, is available for Perl 4, but no such program seems to
be available for Perl 5 as yet. If you are determined, here is how you might
obfuscate a Perl 5 program.

4. Process the source to rename all variables to have nonmeaningful names
systematically. For example, change $user_name to something unreadable
such as $_6789_. Writing a program to do this isn't too hard with Perl 4,
but the inclusion of both local and dynamic scoping of variable names in
Perl 5 makes this a good deal trickier.

5. Remove all the literal strings to an external file and replace them by subroutine calls returning the original string. For example,

```
print "Hello $user_name\n";
```

could be replaced by

```
print txt_12398();
```

where txt_12398() is defined in a required file as

```
sub txt_12398 { return "Hello $v_6789_\n"; }
```

If you have string literals in your program, that is, strings that don't contain
variables, you could encrypt them using the crypt function.

6. Strip out all the clarifying white space from your code. A simple command like

```
perl -pane 's/[\t \n]/ /g'  myfile.txt
```

should do the trick if you have removed all the space-sensitive components such as strings and formats to an external file.

How It Works

The sum command is available on most UNIX platforms and will provide a 16-bit check-sum of the contents of the file.

Comments

Curiously, removing the strings from your program, as described in Step 5, may be a rational thing to do because gathering all the string resources together in one file gives you the chance to internationalize your scripts. If all the natural language output from the program is available in one file, then all you need do to produce alternative language versions of the script is to ship a different strings file.

THE PERL DEBUGGER

THE PERL DEBUGGER

How do I...

The University of Cambridge in Britain has an interesting piece of paper in its archives. It is a printout of a binary dump of program designed for a late-1940s computer. The page is nothing but thousands of 1s and 0s. What distinguishes this listing is an annotation in the handwriting of mathematician and computer pioneer Alan Turing. Turing homes in on two transposed digits, emphasizes them vigorously, and adds the prickly comment "How did this happen?!"

Contemporary programmers regard debugging as part of the software engineering cycle. Ridding a program of flaws is an inescapable and, given some good tools, a satisfying part of software development. Programmers using the standard UNIX shells face the problem that, beyond a crude tracing mechanism, there is very little opportunity to look inside the script while it is executing. DOS shell programmers are not blessed with a tracing mechanism. Isolating the point where problems occur and identifying exactly what is going wrong is far from easy.

With Perl, however, things are different. The Perl interpreter contains an integrated debugger, similar in behavior to the dbx tool used by UNIX C developers.

21.1 Use the Perl Debugger

This section will introduce the Perl debugger and show you how to start Perl in debug mode, step through your program, and examine the values of variables.

21.2 Debug Perl Scripts Containing Subroutines

The debugger has special facilities for navigating through programs containing subroutines. This How-To will show you how to debug a set of subroutines efficiently.

21.3 Set and Unset Breakpoints in My Perl Script

Larger programs may perform a good deal of processing before they reach the section you wish to invesigate. This How-To will show you the Perl debugger breakpoint commands. Breakpoints let you run a program and have it automatically invoke the debugger when execution reaches a designated point.

21.4 Configure the Debugger with Aliases for Common Commands

Some common command sequences can be tedious to type. The debugger allows you to create shorthand names for sets of commands. This section will show you how to use them.

21.5 Execute Perl Commands Interactively Using the Debugger

The debugger will accept any Perl command interactively and execute it. This has applications beyond debugging.This How-To will show you a way to use the debugger like a Perl shell.

21.6 Run the Perl Debugger under Emacs

Visual debuggers automatically update a display window containing executing source code. If you use Perl in combination with Emacs, you can enjoy similar facilities. This section will show you how.

21.7 Redirect Trace Data to a File

The debugger has a trace mode that prints out data about each line before it executes it. This mode produces a lot of data; the results are often more easily examined off-line. This section will show you how to save trace data to a file.

COMPLEXITY:
BEGINNING

21.1 How do I...
Use the Perl debugger?

COMPATIBILITY: UNIX   DOS

Problem

To test and debug a Perl script, I need to be able to run the program under a debug monitor. The facilities required are

- To step through the program line by line

- To allow execution to proceed unhindered up to a specified point

- To inspect the values of variables at any stage of program execution

Technique

Perl is supplied with an integral source-level debugger. The Perl interpreter itself contains built-in support for debugging programs; the Perl library file perldb.pm implements a special command interface so you can input instructions to step through code and inspect variables.

   Perl's debugging monitor is a sophisticated tool and has many commands but is nonetheless easy to learn and use effectively. This How-To takes you through the execution of a Perl program under the debugger and shows you the steps required to master both the basic and the more esoteric debugging facilities.

Steps

1. Create the file ascidump.pl and enter the following code. If you type the command ascidump.pl followed by the name of a file, ascidump.pl lists the text annotated with line numbers, replacing nonprintable characters with the ^ symbol.

```
#!/usr/local/bin/perl -w
# usage ascidump.pl [file]
#
require "ascidrep.pi";

sub print_header {
  print "File: $ARGV[0]\n";
}

sub transform {
  $out = ($data =~ tr/\0-\37\177-\377/^/);
  return $out;
}
```

continued on next page

continued from previous page

```perl
sub process_chunk {
  local($data) = @_;
  transform($data);
  printf "%8.8lx   %s\n", $offset, $data;
  $offset += $LINESIZE;
}

sub process_tail {
  local($data) = @_;
  if ($len) {
    transform($data);
    printf "%8.8lx   %s\n", $offset, $data;
    printf "%8.8lx   %s\n", $offset, "<EOF>"
  }
}

$LINESIZE = 48;
$offset = 0;
$data = "";

open(STDIN, $ARGV[0]) || die "Can't open $ARGV[0]: $!\n"
    if $ARGV[0];
print_header;
while (($len = read(STDIN,$data,$LINESIZE)) == $LINESIZE) {
  process_chunk($data);
}
process_tail($data);
report_stats();

close(STDIN);
```

The included file ascidrep.pl contains a single routine, report_stats.

```perl
# ascidrep.pi
#
sub report_stats {
  printf "Total Bytes %d\n", $offset;
  printf "Total Non-Alphanumeric Characters %d\n", $subs;
}

1;
```

2. Create a data file. Enter the following text and save the file as ascidump.in.

```
Dutch is a Germanic language. The word Dutch itself is a corruption of
the Deutsche, meaning German.  This was a label inaccurately applied
by English sailors to the inhabitants of the Lowlands in the
seventeenth Century. For although the two languages have much in
common the Dutch are at great pains to emphasize the unique identity
of their tongue.
```

3. Invoke Perl directly with the example script as the first argument in the command and the data file ascidump.in as the second command argument.

```
perl ascidump.pl ascidump.in
```

The program is intended to dump a file to screen and report on the contents. Each control character (including new lines) is substituted by a ^ character. The left-hand column displays the hexadecimal byte offset of each line. The program is not working correctly.

It produces the following output.

Output
```
00000000   Dutch is a Germanic language. The word Dutch its
00000030   elf is a corruption of^the Deutsche, meaning Ger
00000060   man.  This was a label inaccurately applied^by E
00000090   nglish sailors to the inhabitants of the Lowland
000000c0   s in the^seventeenth Century. For although the t
000000f0   wo languages have much in^common the Dutch are a
00000120   t great pains to emphasize the unique identity^o
00000150   f their tongue.^
00000150   <EOF>
Total Bytes 336
Total Non-Alphanumeric Characters 0
```
End Output

4. Check the program in the normal way with the Perl -w flag. This flag turns on compiler warnings and other diagnostic information.

```
perl -cw ascidump.pl ascidump.in
```

Output
```
Identifier "main::out" used only once: possible typo
at ascidump.pl line 11.
ascidump.pl syntax OK
```
End Output

5. If the information generated by the -w option is insufficient to isolate the source of a bug, then invoke the Perl debugger. There are two ways to do this. The simplest way is to invoke Perl directly with a -d option. The command looks like this:

```
perl -d ascidump.pl   ascidump.in
```

If you are using a #! line to invoke Perl, edit the file and add a -d option after the name of the Perl interpreter.

6. The Perl interpreter displays the following output.

Output
```
Loading DB routines from $RCSfile: perl5db.pl,v $$Revision: 4.1
$$Date: 92/08/07 18:24:07 $  Emacs support enabled.
Enter h for help.
main::(ascidump.pl:4):        require "ascidrep.pi";
  DB<1>
```
End Output

The first few lines of output display the information about the debugger version and date of creation. The next two lines are more interesting. The output to the left of the colon displays the current module name, the name of the current file, and the number of the first executable line in the file (line 4). The debugger prints out the current line to the left of the colon. The line is a Perl statement requiring an include file.

At this point, Perl has compiled the program and is ready to begin execution of line 4. Keep in mind that the debugger displays the next line to execute, not the last line to have been executed. The line beginning with DB is the debugger prompt, indicating that the debugging monitor is awaiting a user command.

7. Although the debugger will print out each line before the line is executed, you normally need to see the line in the context of the surrounding lines. One solution, if your system supports multiple windows, is to run the debugger in one window while listing the relevant section of the program in another. Even if you don't have those facilities available, the debugger provides a range of commands that list any section of the program source. These commands are summarized in Table 21-1.

DEBUGGER	LISTING COMMANDS
l min+incr	List incr+1 lines starting at min.
l min-max	List lines.
l line	List line.
l	List next window.
-	List previous window.
w line	List window around line.
l subname	List subroutine.
S	List subroutine names.
f filename	Switch to filename.
/pattern/	Search for pattern; final / is optional.
?pattern?	Search backwards for pattern.

Table 21-1 Summary of the listing commands available in the Perl debugger

Enter the command l at the debugger prompt. The debugger prints out a window of 10 lines, starting with the current line.

Enter l again and the debugger increments and prints out the window, displaying the 10 lines following those last listed.

You can specify the window of source lines that the l command should print out. Specify the window as a range of lines. To see the lines surrounding line 10, enter the command l 8-12. The debugger also understands window specifications stated as a starting line and an offset. The command l 8+4 lists lines 8 through 12.

The w command is shorthand for displaying a window of source lines around the current line. The command w 10 gives results similar to the command l 8-12.

8. You are now in a position to begin stepping through the program. Commands to control the execution of a program under the debug monitor are summarized in Table 21-2, and debugger diagnostic command is found in Table 21-3.

COMMAND	DESCRIPTION
n	Execute next line; don't step into subroutine calls.
s	Execute next line; step into subroutine calls.
r	Return from current subroutine.
c	Continue.
c line	Continue up to line, break one time at the given line.
<CR>	Repeat last n or s.
t	Toggle trace mode.
q	Quit.

Table 21-2 Execution control commands available in the Perl debugger

COMMAND	DESCRIPTION
p expr	Evaluate and print the result of expression expr.

Table 21-3 Diagnostic command available in the Perl debugger

Remember, the debugger stated that the current line is line number 4. Type the command w 4 to see line 4 in context. Execute the current line and step to the next line. Type the command n twice. The debugger executes each line, skipping the subroutine definitions and prompts with

```
main::(ascidump.pl:30):        $LINESIZE = 48;
```

indicating that the current line is now line 30. Enter n once more and verify that line 5 executed correctly by printing the current value of the variable *$LINESIZE*. Enter the Perl statement

```
print $LINESIZE;
```

The value is displayed as 48, indicating the assignment succeeded.

Notice that you used a Perl statement here. The debugger will validate nearly all Perl statements and execute them interactively. The debugger commands are just shorthand for more complex Perl statements. The command p is a more concise way of printing out the value of a variable. Enter

```
p $LINESIZE
```

Again the debugger reports the variable's value as 48. The p command is shorthand for print. Notice that you didn't need a ; character to terminate the command.

9. Step ahead to line 36. You can enter n commands or alternatively hit (ENTER). (ENTER) repeats the last stepping command.

The next Perl statement is a *while* loop. Here you could use the n command to step through the code, but if the loop code is repeated many times, this can become tedious. A better approach would be to have the debugger automatically print out the values of interesting variables within the loop and then, after the loop exits, pause, ready to receive more commands.

10. Define an action to be performed automatically by the debugger every time it executes a specific line of code. Enter the following command.

```
a 36 print "*** len is $len ***\n"
```

This action command is executed by the debugger each time it meets line 36.

11. Finally, enter a c, for continue, command to allow the debugger to execute the loop without intervention. Because you want to interact with the debugger again after the loop is complete, qualify the command with a line number. Enter the command

```
c 13
```

This instructs the debugger to execute the program until it reaches line 13, then pause for further commands. The debugger outputs the following:

Output

```
00000000  Dutch is a Germanic language. The word Dutch its
*** len is 48 ***
00000030  elf is a corruption of^the Deutsche, meaning Ger
*** len is 48 ***
00000060  man.  This was a label inaccurately applied^by E
*** len is 48 ***
00000090  nglish sailors to the inhabitants of the Lowland
*** len is 48 ***
000000c0  s in the^seventeenth Century. For although the t
*** len is 48 ***
000000f0  wo languages have much in^common the Dutch are a
*** len is 48 ***
00000120  t great pains to emphasize the unique identity^o
main::(ascidump.pl:38):        process_tail($data);
```

End Output

The debugger has stopped at line 38 awaiting a new command.

12. Type c without a line number and let the program run to termination.

How It Works

This facility represents a considerable advance over other scripting languages such as the Bourne and C shells. If you are used to developing C programs, then you probably expect the Perl debugger to be a separate process, like the dbx debugger. This is not the case. Invoking Perl with the -d option does two things: It tells the interpreter to compile your program with special information to allow debugging and it automatically loads the library module perldb. This library file contains Perl code to implement the debugger command processor.

Comments

Notice in Step 4 that the debugger reports that it supports visual debugging with the Emacs editor. Emacs support is discussed in How-To 21.6. Notice, too, that the debugger prints a command summary in response to the h command. Try it.

COMPLEXITY
BEGINNING

21.2 How do I...
Debug Perl scripts containing subroutines?

COMPATIBILITY: UNIX   DOS

Problem

I need to debug a complex Perl script containing many subroutines. How can I work with the Perl debugger to

- Step through subroutine calls
- Inspect the state of the subroutine stack
- Allow execution to proceed freely up to a specified point
- Inspect the values of variables at any stage of the program execution

Technique

This How-To focuses on traversing subroutine calls in the Perl debugger. It particularly covers the debugger next, step, and return commands.

Steps

1. Start debugging the program ascidump.pl described in How-To 21.1.
The -d option invokes the Perl debugger.

```
perl -d ascidump.pl ascidump.in
```

2. When the debugger starts, use the S command to display all the subroutines in the file.

Then type the following command line.

```
DB<1> c 36
```

The debugger executes up to line 36 and pauses. Line 36 calls a subroutine process_chunk.

```
while (($len = read(STDIN,$data,$LINESIZE)) == $LINESIZE) {
  process_chunk($data);
}
```

You now have a choice: Either enter a next command, n, which will step over the call as if it were any other line, or enter a step command, s, and step into the code of the subroutine. Enter n.

3. The debugger prints out the results of the subroutine call and indicates that the loop has returned to line 36. This time enter an s to step into the subroutine.

```
DB<2> s
main::process_chunk(ascidump.pl:15):    local($data) = @_;
  DB<2> w
12:       }
13:
14:       sub process_chunk {
15:         local($data) = @_;
16:         transform($data);
17:         printf "%8.8lx  %s\n", $offset, $data;
18:         $offset += $LINESIZE;
19:       }
```

The window command reveals that the debugger has jumped into the code of the subroutine process_chunk.

Enter the commands as shown in the next listing.

```
DB<2> s
main::process_chunk(ascidump.pl:16):    transform($data);
  DB<2> s
main::transform(ascidump.pl:11):        $out = ($data =~ tr/\0-\37\177-
  DB<2> w
10:       sub transform {
11:         $out = ($data =~ tr/\0-\37\177-\377/^/);
12:       }
```

Your code has descended through a set of subroutine calls. To see where you are in the hierarchy of subroutines, enter the T command to display the call stack.

```
DB<2> T
$ = main::transform('... the Deutsche...') from ascidump.pl line 16
$ = main::process_chunk('...Deutsche...') from ascidump.pl line 36
```

The stack displays each subroutine call and its parameters.

Comments

In highly layered Perl code, the T command can show whether parameters are being passed down the stack of subroutine calls correctly.

COMPLEXITY
BEGINNING

21.3 How do I...
Set and unset breakpoints in my Perl script?

COMPATIBILITY:

Problem

To debug a Perl script, I need to interrupt the program at certain points during execution and enter the debug monitor. Breaking into the program in this way may be conditional, depending on the value of a variable, or unconditional—the debug monitor should become active every time execution reaches a certain line or subroutine.

Technique

This How-To demonstrates breakpoint control and conditional debugging. A breakpoint is an instruction to the debug monitor to suspend execution of a program at a certain point and allow the programmer to enter debugging commands. Execution can then be resumed or aborted.

Steps

1. Debug the ascidump.pl program that prints a file alongside a margin of character offsets. Either use the example from the CD or type in the listing from How-To 21.1. Invoke the Perl debugger for script ascidump.pl. Issue the command

```
perl -d ascidump.pl ascidump.in
```

2. List the subroutines in the file using the S command and find the line number of the subroutine transform using the // find command.

```
DB<1> main::print_header
main::process_chunk
main::process_tail
```

continued on next page

continued from previous page

```
main::report_stats
main::transform
DB<2> /trans/
10:     sub transform {
```

3. Set a breakpoint at the first line of subroutine transform and then set the program running.

```
DB<3> b transform
DB<4> c
main::transform(ascidump.pl:11):$out=($data =~ tr/\0-\37\177-\377/^/);
DB<4>
```

The DB prompt indicates that the debug monitor has paused at the first line of main::transform. You can now step through the routine and inspect the value of variables.

4. List the active breakpoints.

```
DB<4> L
11:         $out = ($data =~ tr/\0-\37\177-\377/^/);
  break if (1)
```

This output indicates that there is an active breakpoint at line 11, the first line of sub transform. The break if (1) illustrates that the breakpoint is unconditional. 1 is always True.

5. Delete the breakpoint using the d command and the line number.

```
DB<4> d 11
DB<4> L
```

6. Set a conditional breakpoint at line 16, after the return from the transform. The debugger should break only if $out has a value greater than 0.

```
DB<5> b 17 $out > 0
```

7. Run the program and print out the value of $out at each breakpoint.

```
DB<6> c
File: ascidump.in
00000000  Dutch is a Germanic language. The word Dutch its
main::process_chunk(ascidump.pl:17):
        printf "%8.8lx   %s\n", $offset, data;
DB<6> p $out
1
DB<6> c
```

How It Works

Table 21-4 summarizes the commands used in the session.

BREAKPOINT	CONTROL
b	Set breakpoint at the current (next to execute) line.
b [line]	Set breakpoint at the specified line.
b subname	Set breakpoint at first line of subroutine.
b [line|subname] condition	Break at line or subroutine if condition is True.
L	List breakpoints and actions.
d [line]	Delete breakpoint.
D	Delete all breakpoints.

Table 21-4 Breakpoint-related commands in the Perl debugger

Comments

Notice, in Table 21-4, the difference between setting a breakpoint and using the c command with a line number. The command c 17 just means to execute to line 17 one time. If you type c again, execution will proceed and the program will not stop at line 17 again. In contrast, a breakpoint stays around until either it is deleted or the debugger quits. The program will always halt when execution reaches a breakpoint.

From the information printed, you can see that $out is being assigned to rather than incremented. Fix the bug with your editor.

Note that at Step 5, you might have used the D command, which deletes every active breakpoint. This command does not require a line number.

COMPLEXITY
INTERMEDIATE

21.4 How do I...
Configure the debugger with aliases for common commands?

COMPATIBILITY: UNIX DOS

Problem

I want to modify the debugger so I can add custom commands and alias existing commands. How can I do this?

Technique

The debugger alias command = is a hook that allows the user to modify and add to the existing command set. To make modified commands permanently available, modified commands can be added to the Perl debugger initialization file .perldb.

Steps

1. Use the program ascidump.pl, whose listing can be found in How-To 21.1. To add a new command to display the length of a variable, type the following while running the debugger.

```
main::process_chunk(ascidump.pl:15):    local($data) = @_;
DB<1> = size p length($1)
size = p length($1)
DB<2> len $data
64
```

2. Make this alias permanent. Edit or create a .perldb file in your home directory. Add the following line.

```
$DB::alias{size} = 's/^size/p length/';
```

3. Quit the debugger and restart it. Test that the size command is automatically available.

How It Works

The associative array %DB::alias holds a mapping between debugger commands and Perl commands. The debugger's = command adds entries to this associative array. When the debugger reads a user command, it checks the alias table; if the command is present, the debugger applies the substitution to the command.

Aliases can be stored for future sessions in the file .perldb. The debugger module reads this file each time it starts up. The syntax is a little painful.

```
$DB::alias{size} = 's/^size/p length/';
```

The statement creates a new entry in the %DB::alias associative array. The key for the new entry is the name of the command, size. The right-hand side of the assignment, in quotes, is a Perl substitution statement. Consider this substitution statement: The command name, size, is the item to be matched; the replacement is a string that will be substituted whenever size is found in a command. In this case, size is replaced by p length.

Comments

Make sure you include the ^ character in the .perldb entry. This anchors the pattern as the first item on a line. Commands are always the first item of a line. If you forget to do this, any string you enter containing the sequence size will be modified by the alias.

You can build more sophisticated aliases by using submatches. Here is a more exact definition of the size alias that uses $1 to stand for the (*.) submatch on the left-hand side of the s function:

```
$DB::alias{size} = 's/^size(*.)/p length ($1)/';
```

COMPLEXITY

BEGINNING

21.5   How do I ...
Execute Perl commands interactively using the debugger?

COMPATIBILITY: UNIX   DOS

Problem

I would like to test Perl commands interactively, without writing my commands to a file.

Technique

Perl is a programming language rather than a shell. Perl is designed to execute programs stored in files or specified on the command line, rather than accept commands interactively. This is not to say you can't work interactively with Perl. You can easily write a Perl shell or you can use the debugger.

Table 21-5 summarizes the commands that enable you to perform shell-like manipulations of the command history list and create aliases.

COMMAND	MANIPULATION
! number	Redo command (default previous command).
! number	Redo previous command or n'th previous.
H number	Display last number commands (default all).
= [alias value]	Define an alias, or list current aliases.

Table 21-5 Perl debugger history manipulation and aliasing

Steps

1. Execute the following command.

```
perl -de 1
```

2. When the debugger displays its prompt, enter a sequence of arbitrary Perl expressions.

```
perl -de 1
main'(pl000167:1):        1
DB<1> $foo = 127 ; print $foo
127
DB<2> $bar = $foo * 2
DB<3> print $bar
254
```

3. Enter the history command H to see a list of previous commands.

4. Recall a previous command using the ! command. This command is similar to its equivalent in the UNIX C shell.

5. Execute an external command using backquotes.

```
DB<4> $foo = `echo "hello"`
DB<5> print $foo
hello
```

How It Works

In earlier sections of this chapter, we mentioned that the Perl debugger will accept and execute almost any Perl statement. In effect, the debugger provides the facilities of a simple Perl shell. Before you can run the debugger interactively, you must fool it into thinking it is debugging a script. The -e 1 option, supplied on the command line, is the simplest program possible, just an expression with no operators. It evaluates to 1.

Comments

Some would argue that -e 0 is an even simpler program than -e 1. Both work.

COMPLEXITY
BEGINNING

21.6   How do I...
Run the Perl debugger under Emacs?

COMPATIBILITY: [UNIX] [Win95]

Problem

I have to type a list or window command to have the Perl debugger display the lines of code it is executing. Many development environments offer visual debugging, where a window of executing code is automatically displayed and updated by the debugger. How can I execute the Perl debugger so it displays and automatically updates a window of source code around the currently executing statement?

Technique

The Perl debugger is not itself a visual debugging program, but it is designed to work visually with the popular programmer's editor Emacs. Emacs is available for UNIX, Windows 95, and NT platforms. The special Emacs editing mode, Perl mode, is discussed in Chapter 20. When you run the debugger, Perl mode displays two windows on screen. One contains source code; the other is a command window where you can enter commands. Emacs highlights the current line of code and automatically updates the source window as execution progresses.

Steps

1. Invoke Emacs in the usual way and load your source file. If your filename ends in .pl and Emacs is configured correctly, it will automatically recognize the file as Perl source and activate the Emacs Perl mode. If you need to invoke Perl mode yourself, issue the command

```
M-x perl-mode
```

2. Once your file is loaded and you have Perl mode active, invoke the debugger with the following Emacs command:

```
M-x perldb
```

Emacs responds with

```
Run perldb (like this):
```

3. Type the name of the file being debugged and any other flags and arguments you require after the prompt. You don't need the -d flag. Copy this example:

```
Run perldb (like this): perl ascidump.pl ascidump.in
```

4. Press the (ENTER) key. Emacs immediately splits the window into two separate panes, as shown in Figure 21-1. In the lower window, you see the familiar Perl debugger prompt waiting for your commands; in the upper window, you see your source file with the current line indicated by an

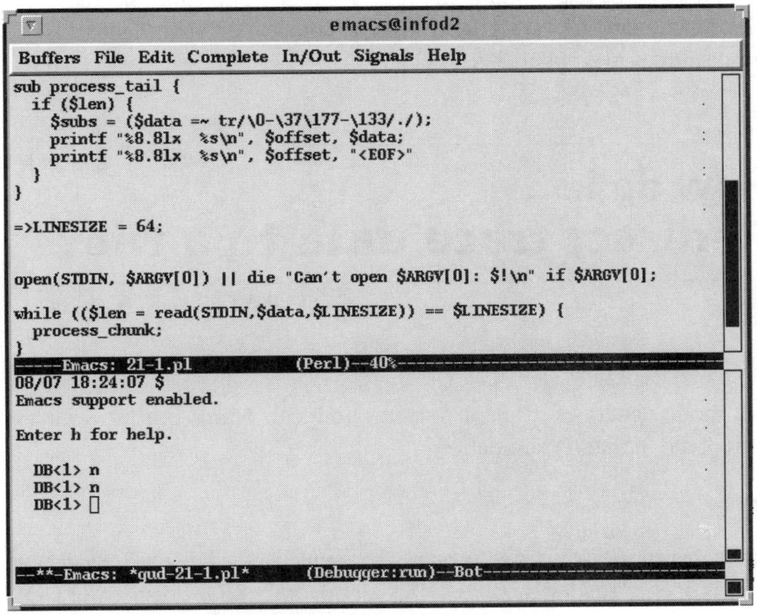

Figure 21-1 Emacs running perldb mode

arrow symbol at the left margin. The upper window mode line displays (Perl), the lower window displays (Debugger:run) mode.

5. Ensure you have the (Debugger:run) mode window active. Step through your program using the usual execution control commands. Notice that the arrow indicator in the (Perl) mode window automatically updates the current line and scrolls as necessary. If your file includes other files, these, too, will be loaded as needed and displayed in the window while execution traverses the source they contain.

How It Works

The Emacs debug mode supports many debuggers for many languages. The Perl debugger library module, which is automatically loaded when you supply the -d flag, contains hooks that drive the Emacs debug mode and tell Emacs how to update the source window.

Comments

The Emacs Perl mode and the perldb support are included in the standard distribution of GNU-Emacs versions 18 and 19. Version 19 supports X-Windows graphical editing for UNIX. There are several versions of Emacs for Mac, DOS, and Windows computers.

If you are not a fan of the Emacs editor, check with the source of your favorite editor to see if it supports the Perl debugger. All the code that drives the Emacs debug mode is contained in the file perl5db.pl in the Perl 5 library. Someone may have contributed a modified version of this file to support your editor. Investigate the Perl information resources in Appendix A.

COMPLEXITY
BEGINNING

21.7   How do I...
Redirect trace data to a file?

COMPATIBILITY: UNIX   DOS

Problem

Debug trace mode generates a lot of output. How can I save output from the debugger into a file for later examination?

Technique

When the debugger starts up, it sends its output to the filehandle DB::OUT. By default, this filehandle is opened to /dev/tty (for UNIX system), or the CON: device (for DOS-derived systems). The debugger does this to keep command interaction and line action output separate from output generated by the program as it runs. But it means you cannot store debugger output by redirecting it to a file because command level redirection operates only on the STDIN, STDOUT, and STDERR streams. The solution is to redirect filehandle DB::OUT to a disk file using the Perl open command.

Steps

1. Start the debugger in the usual way by specifying the -d flag. You can follow the steps using any Perl program. Here, for illustration, we use the ascidump.pl program from How-To 21.1.

```
perl -d ascidump.pl ascidump.in
```

2. If you want to set up line actions, set them up now. When you are ready to trace the program, enter the t command. See How-To 21.1 for how to set up line actions.

```
DB<1> t
```

3. Type the following command. where db.out is the name of the file in which you want to store the trace output.

```
open(DB::OPEN,">&db.out");
```

Once you enter this command, all debugger output will go directly to the disk file db.out. You won't be able to see the DB> prompt on screen anymore.

4. Type c and run the program to completion. If the program produces output, you should still see the output on screen (provided you have not redirected STDOUT).

5. When the debugger terminates, inspect the file db.out in the current directory. It will contain all the trace information that the debugger would normally have sent to the screen.

How It Works

The Perl 5 debugging module is written in Perl. Because the debugger allows you to execute any arbitrary Perl statement at the prompt, you can type commands that modify the behavior of the debugger itself.

Here you use the redirect form of the *open* statement to set the filehandle DB::OPEN to the file db.out. Anything that the debugger writes to that filehandle arrives in the file, not on the screen.

Comments

Once you have the trace data, you can reprocess it to learn more about the behavior of the program. Chapter 20 contains an example of processing trace information to create a simple profiling of an executing program. You can use profiling information to optimize your code.

Finally, be careful; tracing even a small program can produce a megabyte of data in a few seconds. Check to make sure you have sufficient disk space before you try redirecting trace output.

PERL TRICKS

PERL TRICKS

How do I...

The How-To's presented in this chapter don't have any real classification. The examples illustrate various tricks that have been discovered or developed by the ever-growing Perl programming community. The intention of this chapter is twofold: to demonstrate some of the more often repeated tasks and to help you gain an understanding of the flexibility of Perl.

22.1   Add Two Time Values Together

Adding two time values together is one of the most common problems in both Perl programming and quantum mechanics. Because this is a Perl book, we've confined the answer to the one more related to the contents of this book. This How-To will show you how to add two time values together.

22.2   Print Out the Current Time in Standard Time

Daylight saving time is not always the accepted time standard for computer systems. Twice a year, they either lose an hour or skip an hour; this can be quite confusing to the casual observer. This section will show you how to print out the current time in standard time.

22.3   Modify the Contents of a String

String manipulation in Perl is an easier task than most people think. The key is that the substr function not only returns a value but can also accept values and act on them. This How-To will use the substr function to change a string in place.

22.4   Look for an Element in an Array

A common problem no matter what type of script is being written is how to look for an element in an array. This How-To will outline several methods of achieving this task.

22.5   Determine Whether Two Arrays Are the Same

Unfortunately, there are no comparison operators for arrays or hash arrays. This How-To will describe a way to check easily to see if two basic arrays are the same.

22.6   Sort an Associative Array by Value

Sorting an associative array by value is not as simple as it first appears; sorting an associative array is one of the true tricks of Perl programming. This How-To will show you how to do this.

22.7   Expand Tildes in a Filename

The C shell is becoming a more popular shell to use, including tcsh; because of this popularity boost, certain elements of the C shell are being adapted to programs and scripts. One of the more popular elements of the C shell is the tilde (~) user name expansion. This script will demonstrate how to expand a tilde character in a given filename.

22.8   Remove the Comments from C Code

It is easy to strip all the comments from a C source file in Perl 5. This section will show you how.

22.9   Find the Path to All Include Files

When working with C source files, you may want to find out what header files are being included. This How-To will show you how.

COMPLEXITY
INTERMEDIATE

22.1 How do I...
Add two time values together?

COMPATIBILITY: PERL 4 | PERL 5 | UNIX | DOS

Problem

I want to take the current time, add an undetermined number of seconds to it, and get the correct time.

Technique

To do this, you need to translate the current time and the additive time to a basic UNIX time format. This formats the number of seconds since the epoch. Getting the current time in this format is done by calling the function time. The time adjustment from the command line can be translated into seconds with little effort. Once the current time and the additive time are in seconds, the time needs to be translated back into human-readable time. This is performed by the localtime function.

Steps

The script in this How-To accepts the number of hours, minutes, and seconds from the command line, to be added to the current time. The current time and the additive time are added together and the result is printed to the screen in a human-readable format.

1. Create a new file called addtime.pl and type the following script into it.

```perl
#!/usr/local/bin/perl -w

# Purpose:
#        This adds a given amount of time to the current time.

# Use long command line options.
use Getopt::Long;

# Set up the expected command line options.
GetOptions ("d|days:i", "h|hours:i", "m|minutes:i", "s|seconds:i");

# Parse up the command line.
my $days = $opt_d || 0;
my $hours = $opt_h || 0;
my $minutes = $opt_m || 0;
my $seconds = $opt_s || 0;

# Determine the amount to add to the current time.
my $adj = ($days * 86400) + ($hours * 3600) + ($minutes * 60) + $seconds;
```

continued on next page

continued from previous page

```perl
# Get the current time.
my $time = time;
my $currentDate = localtime ($time);
my $future = $time + $adj;
my $futureDate = localtime ($future);

# Print out the date information.
print "$currentDate + ${days}d + ${hours}h + ${minutes}m + ${seconds}s = $futureDate\n";
```

2. Run the script with the following sample input.

```
% addtime.pl -d 1 -h 5 -m 6 -s 55
Wed Aug 23 12:57:44 1995 + 1d + 5h + 6m + 55s = Thu Aug 24 18:04:39 1995
% addtime.pl -h 5 -s 10
Wed Aug 23 12:58:36 1995 + 0d + 5h + 0m + 10s = Wed Aug 23 17:58:46 1995
% addtime.pl -s -10
Wed Aug 23 12:59:27 1995 + 0d + 0h + 0m + -10s = Wed Aug 23 12:59:17 1995
```

Notice that if any of the time fields are set as a negative value, time is subtracted. The following two examples add 4 minutes and 20 seconds to the current time.

```
% addtime.pl -m 4 -s 20
Wed Aug 23 14:50:46 1995 + 0d + 0h + 4m + 20s = Wed Aug 23 14:55:06 1995
% addtime.pl -m 5 -s -40
Wed Aug 23 14:52:01 1995 + 0d + 0h + 5m + -40s = Wed Aug 23 14:56:21 1995
```

How It Works

When the adjustment is passed in from the command line, the time adjustment has to be translated into seconds. The line

```perl
my $adj = ($days * 86400) + ($hours * 3600) + ($minutes * 60) + $seconds;
```

takes the number of days and multiplies it by 86400. This is because there are 86400 seconds in 1 day. The number of hours is multiplied by 3600, because there are 3600 seconds in 1 hour. The call to localtime uses a scalar return variable instead of an array. The function localtime behaves differently, depending upon which variable type is being returned. When the return value of localtime is put into a scalar variable, localtime formats the output much like the UNIX ctime format. An example of the UNIX ctime format follows.

```
Sat Aug 9 10:11:12 1995
```

If localtime is used in array context, then localtime returns a nine-element array of the following values: Seconds, Minutes, Hours, Month day, Month, Month year, Week day, Year day, and a Boolean flag that is set to True if the time is daylight saving time.

The range of the month value that localtime returns is from 0 to 11. This means that June is indexed at 5, not at 6. Figure 22-1 shows a vastly simplified version of this process.

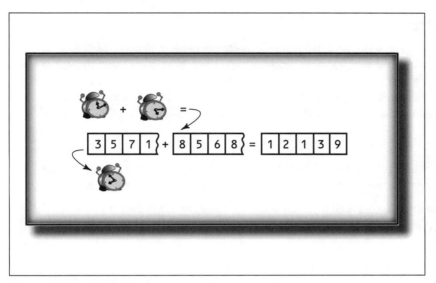

Figure 22-1 Adding two time values together

Comments

If you subtract more seconds than have passed since the UNIX epoch time, then the time will warp ahead to sometime starting in the year 2021. This script does not handle adding or subtracting months. This would require additional knowledge of how many days are in each month of the year.

COMPLEXITY
BEGINNING

22.2 How do I...
Print out the current time in standard time?

COMPATIBILITY:

Problem

I have a database that does not adhere to daylight saving time; I need a script to translate daylight saving time into current local standard time.

Technique

This uses the Perl script localtime again. Unlike the example in How-To 22.1, though, this script uses the nine-element array returned from localtime. One of the values returned from localtime is a Boolean flag. This flag contains a value of True if the given time is during the period of daylight saving time. Using this Boolean flag, you can adjust the current time to reflect the current local standard time.

Steps

The script in this How-To determines the current time using the Perl function time and subtracts one hour from this value if you are currently under daylight saving time.

1. Create a new file, call it standard.pl, and enter the following script into it.

```perl
#!/usr/local/bin/perl -w

# Purpose:
#        Returns the current time in standard time.

# Get the current time.
my $time = time;

# Expand the current time into its element parts.
my ($sec,$min,$hour,$mday,$mon,$year,$wday,$yday,$isdst) = localtime ($time);

# Adjust the time to account for the daylight savings time.
my $newtime = $time - ($isdst * 3600);
my $stdtime = localtime ($newtime);
my $daytime = localtime ($time);

# Print out the result.
print "The current daylight time is: $daytime\n";
print "The current standard time is: $stdtime\n";
```

2. Run the script.

```
% chap_22/howto02/standard.pl
The current daylight time is: Wed Aug 23 16:34:14 1995
The current standard time is: Wed Aug 23 15:34:14 1995
```

How It Works

If localtime is used in array context, then localtime returns a nine-element array of the following values: Seconds, Minutes, Hours, Month day, Month, Month year, Week day, Year day, and a Boolean flag that is set to True if the time is daylight saving time. If the flag comes back as True (1), then a full hour should be removed from the current time. If the current time is not daylight saving time, then the flag is set to False (0). The line

```perl
my $newtime = $time - ($isdst * 3600);
```

makes the time adjustment without having to check the Boolean flag. Because the Boolean flag, $isdst, contains a 1 when in daylight saving time and a 0 otherwise, subtracting ($isdst * 3600) subtracts 3600 seconds when in daylight saving time and nothing otherwise. Then localtime is called in a scalar context to produce a readable time.

Comments

Whenever time is involved on a UNIX operating system, the time is always based on the epoch time, which is the beginning of time for the operating system.

Different UNIX operating systems consider different times to be the epoch time. Most hover around January 1, 1970.

COMPLEXITY
BEGINNING

22.3   How do I...
Modify the contents of a string?

COMPATIBILITY: PERL 4 | PERL 5 | UNIX | DOS

Problem

I have a string and I want to change the value of it, but I do not want to split the string apart and rebuild it.

Technique

To do this, you need to use the Perl substr function. The substr function has not only the ability to return an indexed value, it also has the ability to set it. Knowing this, use the substr function to modify the string. Write the script to accept the word to modify, the replacement word, and an optional argument to set the index location. Cycle through the replacement string and set the contents of the original string to the individual characters of the replacement string.

Steps

1. Create a new file called replace.pl and enter the following script into it.

```
#!/usr/local/bin/perl -w

# Purpose:
#       This script changes the first N characters of a given string.

# Use the Perl5 option parser.
use Getopt::Long;
GetOptions ("w|word=s", "r|replacement=s", "i|index:i");
```

continued on next page

continued from previous page

```perl
# Parse up the command line.
my $word = $opt_w || die "Usage: $0 -w Word -r Replacement [-i Index]\n";
my $replace = $opt_r || die "Usage: $0 -w Word -r Replacement [-i Index]\n";
my $index = $opt_i || 0;

# Print out some user information.
print "Original Word      = <$word>\n";
print "Replacement String = <$replace>\n";
print "Index Value        = <$index>\n";

# Start changing the elements.
for ($x=0; $x < length($replace); $x++)
{
    substr ($word, $x+$index, 1) = substr ($replace, $x, 1);
}

# Print out the result.
print "Resultant Word     = <$word>\n";
```

2. Run the script with the following sample input.

```
% chap_22/howto03/replace.pl -w 'Booga Booga Booga' -r Wooga  -i 6
Original Word      = <Booga Booga Booga>
Replacement String = <Wooga>
Index Value        = <6>
Resultant Word     = <Booga Wooga Booga>
```

How It Works

When the original word and replacement word are passed to the program from the command line, the replacement word is scanned left to right, character by character. Each character in the replacement string is extracted by the statement

```perl
substr ($replace, $x, 1)
```

where $x is the index into the replacement string. For each character "extracted," the character needs to be implanted into the original string. This is also achieved by the substr function. The insertion is performed by the statement

```perl
substr ($word, $x+$index, 1);
```

Notice the variable *$index*. This variable controls where in the new string the character will be placed. Putting the above line segments together

```perl
substr ($word, $x+$index, 1) = substr ($replace, $x, 1);
```

extracts the character from the replacement string and inserts the character into the original string. A graphical version of value string substitution can be found in Figure 22-2.

Comments

Many Perl programmers stumble over similar tasks because they forget that many Perl functions have some sort of side effect, substr included.

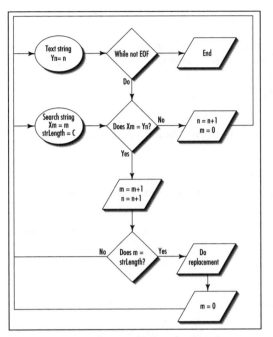

Figure 22-2 Value string substitution

COMPLEXITY
INTERMEDIATE

22.4 How do I...
Look for an element in an array?

COMPATIBILITY: PERL 4 | PERL 5 | UNIX | DOS

Problem

Looking for an entry in a standard array is a matter of performing a linear search on the array: The program cycles through the array, looking at each entry, to see if it matches the value being searched for. The only problem with this is that as the array gets larger, the search takes longer. This response time may become unacceptable.

Technique

To minimize the search for keys on an array, import the array into an associative array. This will require scanning through the standard array once to create the associative array; after that, the searches will take a constant amount of time.

Steps

The script in this How-To takes a standard Perl array and transforms it into an associative array. This reduces the time taken to perform consecutive searches for information on the array. To transform a list to an associative array, construct the associative array using the records of the list as keys for the associative array. Each key record is set to a nonzero value.

1. Edit a new file named srcharry.pl and enter the following script into it.

```perl
#!/usr/local/bin/perl -w

# Purpose:
#    Look for an element in an array. (Using associative arrays)

# Create the array
my @months = qw (Jan Feb Mar April May June July Aug Sept Oct Nov Dec);
my %Months = ();

# Keep the month we are looking for.
my $month = $ARGV[0];

# Translate the array into a hash table.
for ($x=0; $x <= $#months; $x++)
{
    $Months{$months[$x]} = $x;
}

# Look for the month using the associative array.
if (defined $Months{$month})
{
    print "Month $month found in original array position $Months{$month}\n";
}
else
{
    print "Month $month not found.\n";
}
```

2. Run the script with the following sample output.

```
% chap_22/howto04/srcharry.pl June
Month June found in original array position 5
% chap_22/howto04/srcharry.pl Booga
Month Booga not found.
```

How It Works

For each element in the data array, Jan to Dec, an associative array entry is created. In this case, the associative array variable is called *%Months,* so *$Months*{Jan} to *$Months*{Dec} is created. This is achieved by the line

```perl
$Months{$months[$x]} = $x
```

This line takes the array element $months[$x] and uses it as the key to the *%Months* associative array. To determine if an element is contained within the array, check if the element being sought after is defined in the associative array. If it is, then the element exists; if not, then it doesn't. This particular script adds an extra piece of information: the original location of the element. This allows you to index back to the original data array directly, without having to scan through the data array.

Comments

Clearly, this example is slower than simply performing a sequential search for the record. This script is given as an example to demonstrate how to search for an element in an array and how to reduce the search-time overhead at the same time.

COMPLEXITY
INTERMEDIATE

22.5   How do I...
Determine whether two arrays are the same?

COMPATIBILITY: PERL 4 | PERL 5 | UNIX | DOS

Problem

I have two arrays full of data. How do I find out if they contain the same elements?

Technique

This requires taking the arrays and transforming them into scalar variables. Once transformed, the scalars can be compared.

Steps

This script takes two arrays and flattens them into scalar variables. After the scalars have been created, a basic equivalence check is performed. The script provided in this How-To actually does two checks on the arrays: One is to see if the arrays contain the same elements; the other is to see if the arrays are completely the same by taking order into consideration.

1. Create a new file named cmparray.pl and enter the following script into it.

```perl
#!/usr/local/bin/perl

# Purpose:
#    This script determines if two arrays are the same.

# Create the arrays.
my @array1 = qw (Jan Feb Mar April May June July Aug Sept Oct Nov Dec);
```

continued on next page

continued from previous page

```perl
my @array2 = qw (Feb Jan Mar April May June July Aug Sept Oct Nov Dec);

# Check if the same elements are contained in the two arrays.
my $arrayString1 = join (' ', sort @array1);
my $arrayString2 = join (' ', sort @array2);
if ($arrayString1 eq $arrayString2)
{
    # Check if the arrays contain the same elements, in the same order.
    my $arrayString1 = join (' ', @array1);
    my $arrayString2 = join (' ', @array2);
    if ($arrayString1 eq $arrayString2)
    {
        print "The arrays both contain the same elements, and are ordered\n";
    }
    else
    {
        print "The arrays contain the same information, just in a different
                order.\n";
    }
}
else
{
    print "The arrays do not contain the same information.\n";
}
```

2. Run the above script.

```
% chap_22/howto05/cmparray.pl
The arrays contain the same information, just in a different order.
```

How It Works

The script flattens the array into a scalar variable. The "flattening" process is performed by the join on the array. The following line of Perl code flattens an array named @array1 into the scalar variable *$arrayString1*.

```perl
my $arrayString1 = join (' ', @array1);
```

The join function takes two parameters, an expression and a list, and creates a scalar value of the array concatenated using the given expression. In this case, the expression is the space and the list is @array1. Once both arrays have been flattened, a basic scalar equivalence check is performed.

The first time the arrays are flattened, they are sorted before calling the join function. This provides the ability to check to see if the contents of the two arrays are the same, regardless of order. The second check does not sort the array, which makes the check more rigorous.

Comments

You could modify the example to perform checks on the arrays for case insensitivity, alphabetically ordered arrays, and various other equivalence checks.

COMPLEXITY
INTERMEDIATE

22.6 How do I...
Sort an associative array by value?

COMPATIBILITY: PERL 5   UNIX   DOS

Problem

Sorting an associative array by key in Perl is a fairly simple task. All that needs to be done is call the function named keys, which returns an array of keys, and sort the resulting array. The same cannot be done for the values of the associative array. How can I sort my associative array by values instead of by keys?

Technique

You create a subroutine that takes the keys of the associative array and compares successive keys against one another. The subroutine should be generic enough to sort any given associative array. The example in this How-To uses a subroutine that accepts a reference to an associative array. Once the array has been sorted, the new associative array is printed out.

Steps

The bulk of the script lies inside the subroutine named sort_hash. This subroutine takes a reference to an associative array and compares successive values against one another. Because the subroutine takes a reference to an associative array, the subroutine does not need to return anything.

1. Create a new file called sorthash.pl and enter the following script into it.

```perl
#!/usr/local/bin/perl

# Purpose:
#    Sorts an associative array by value. (Using a sort function)

# Load up an associative array.
$assocArray{'Smith,Joe'} = "Nowhere, Special";
$assocArray{'Glover,Mike'} = "Burlington, Ontario";
$assocArray{'Humpreys,Aidan'} = "London, England";
$assocArray{'Weiss,Ed'} = "Paris, France";
$assocArray{'Cook,Gord'} = "Mississauga, Ontario";
$assocArray{'Lopes,Tina'} = "Toronto, Ontario";


#
# This function takes a reference to an associative array, and
# returns a sorted hash.
#
```

continued on next page

continued from previous page

```perl
sub sort_hash
{
    my $x = shift;
    my %array=%$x;

    # Sort the associative array passed in.
    sort { $array{$b} cmp $array{$a}; } keys %array;
}

# Call the sorting function to sort the array.
foreach $key (sort_hash(\%assocArray))
{
    print "Key=<$key> = <$assocArray{$key}>\n";
}
```

2. Run the script.

```
% chap_22/howto06/sorthash.pl
Key=<Lopes,Tina> = <Toronto, Ontario>
Key=<Weiss,Ed> = <Paris, France>
Key=<Smith,Joe> = <Nowhere, Special>
Key=<Cook,Gord> = <Mississauga, Ontario>
Key=<Humpreys,Aidan> = <London, England>
Key=<Glover,Mike> = <Burlington, Ontario>
```

How It Works

The special thing about an associative array is that it has a string as an index value, which is normally called a key. This allows you to create complex data structures using string values as an index instead of just a number. The example given uses an associative array of names and information about the given person. All the work is performed by the line

```perl
sort { $array{$b} cmp $array{$a}; } keys %array;
```

Broken down into its essential elements, there are three elements to this one line of Perl code.

The first element is the call to the keys function on the associative array.

```perl
keys %array
```

This call returns an array of all the keys in the array named %array. The second element is the actual comparison between successive elements of the array. This is performed by the section

```perl
$array{$b} cmp $array{$a}
```

The operation compares the values of the array %array because $a and $b are keys of the array. The last element sorts the final array according to the comparison made with the cmp operator. The array is now sorted.

Comments

The operator cmp performs a stringwise ordering. To perform an ascending numeric sort, change the line

```
sort { $array{$b} cmp $array{$a}; } keys %array;
```
    to the line
```
sort { $array{$b} <=> $array{$a}; } keys %array;
```

To change the sort direction from ascending to descending, swap the variables $a and $b in the sort function.

COMPLEXITY
INTERMEDIATE

22.7 How do I...
Expand tildes in a filename?

COMPATIBILITY: PERL 4   PERL 5   UNIX

Problem

Since the C shell has become more popular, certain elements of its personality have been widely adopted. One of these features is *tilde (~) expansion*. Tilde expansion is for when the tilde character is used as a short form for a user's home directory path. I would like my script to perform tilde expansion, but I cannot seem to get it to work correctly.

Technique

Because many shells currently perform tilde expansion on their own, the script should be written in such a way that the script (not the shell) expands the tilde character. Tilde expansion is for when a pathname is referenced using the tilde character instead of the complete path for a user name. The following example demonstrates the use of tilde expansion.

```
% cd ~glover/tmp
% pwd
/home/glover/tmp
```

We changed directories into the subdirectory named tmp under the account of glover. The home directory of glover is /home/glover, so when the pwd command (present working directory) is issued, it prints out the current directory, in this case, /home/glover/tmp.

Tilde expansion is accomplished by requiring the pathname from inside the script, not the command line. Once the script is given the pathname, it must determine if tilde expansion is possible for the given pathname. If the pathname is a candidate for tilde expansion, then the string directly to the right of the tilde is assumed to be a user name. The user name is searched in the password file. If the user is found, the complete path is printed out; otherwise, an error is printed.

Steps

1. Create a new file called tilde.pl and enter the following script into it.

```perl
#!/usr/local/bin/perl

# Purpose:
#    This expands tildes in a given filename.

# Read in the pathname using read instead of the command line. If
# the pathname comes from the shell, the shell may expand ~ before
# we get a chance to do so.
print "Enter pathname: ";
chop ($pathname = <STDIN>);

# Strip out the user name from the path
if ($pathname =~ /^~(\w*)(\/*.*)/)
{
    # Save the user name and path.
    my $user = $1;
    my $path = $2;

    # Are we expanding just a tilde???
    if ($user eq "")
    {
        # It's our home dir, we'll get it from the password file anyway.
        $user = getlogin;
    }

    # Look for them in the password file.
    my $home = (getpwnam ($user))[7] || die "The user $user is not a valid
            user.\n";

    # Contsruct the full pathname
    my $fullpath = $home . $path;
    print "Full path=<$fullpath>\n";
}
else
{
    print "Full path=<$pathname>\n";
}
```

2. Run the script with the following input.

```
% chap_22/howto07/tilde.pl
Enter pathname: ~glover
Full path=</home/glover>
% chap_22/howto07/tilde.pl
Enter pathname: ~/aaa/bbb/ccc/ddd
Full path=</home/glover/aaa/bbb/ccc/ddd>
% chap_22/howto07/tilde.pl
Enter pathname: ~xxx
The user xxx is not a valid user.
```

How It Works

Most of the work of this script is performed by the line

```
if ($pathname =~ /^~(\w*)(\/*.*)/).
```

This line looks for a tilde at the front of the line /^~ and the user name that follows it (\w*). The rest of the filename is assumed to be a path and is taken as a whole. If the *if* statement succeeds, then the values of the user name and pathname are stored in the global variables $1 and $2, respectively. If the login name is omitted, then the current user is assumed, so getlogin needs to be called. Once the login name is determined, the home directory is determined by a call to getpwnam. Figure 22-3 shows how simple tilde expansion is.

Comments

This script does not work when the tilde is embedded within the filename.

COMPLEXITY
BEGINNING

22.8   How do I...
Remove the comments from C code?

COMPATIBILITY: PERL 4 PERL 5 UNIX DOS

Problem

I would like to count the number of source lines in a C program. How do I remove all the comments so I can do my count?

Technique

Because C comments can span multiple lines, examining the source line by line makes looking for comments much harder. Instead, the entire source file can be read in as one very long string. The comments can then be matched and removed.

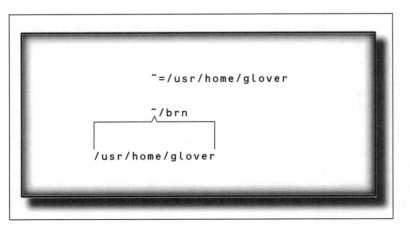

Figure 22-3 Tilde expansion

Steps

The example script reads a C source file and prints out the file with the comments removed.

1. Create a file called comment1.pl. Put the following lines into that file.

```
$File .= $_ while(<>);
$File =~ s%/\*.*?\*/%%sg;
print $File;
```

2. Create a test file called comment1.in. Add the following lines.

```
/* Test comment 1 */

main() {

/*
   Test comment 2
 */

}
```

3. Run the script on the test file. The output follows.

```
main() {



}
```

4. Instead of reading the file line by line and building up a single string, Perl can be told to read in the entire file as one long string. Create a file named comment2.pl and add the following lines.

```
$/ = undef;
$_ = <>;
s%/\*.*?\*/%%sg;
print;
```

5. Run this new script on the test file. The output should be the same as above.

How It Works

The s command matches comments and removes them. The modifiers to the s command are s and g. The s modifier tells the s command to treat the entire string as one string even if there are embedded new-line characters. This will let the regular expression character match any character, including the new-line character. (It does not usually match the new-line character.) The g modifier tells the s command to act globally. This means that it will replace every occurrence of the regular expression it sees. (It normally replaces only the first match.) The regular expression inside the s command says to match the opening comment characters

```
/\*
```

The * is escaped to mean that it should literally match a * character. Then the regular expression says to match any characters it can.

`.*?`

The ? says to do a minimal match. That is, it should match as few characters as possible, but match as many as needed to make the rest of the expression match. In this case, it should match characters until the comment end characters are seen.

`\*/`

The comment that was matched is then deleted. Because the g modifier is given, all the comments are matched and removed.

Comments

The second example undefines the special variable $/. This variable holds the line separator character(s). By undefining it, there is no separator, so the entire file is considered one big line.

Removing comments using Perl 4 is much more complicated. Please refer to the Perl *Frequently Asked Questions (FAQ)* document for the method to accomplish this task. The location of the *FAQ* can be found in Appendix A.

COMPLEXITY
INTERMEDIATE

22.9 How do I...
Find the path to all include files?

COMPATIBILITY: | PERL 4 | PERL 5 | UNIX | DOS |

Problem

I have a complicated C program that includes many header files. How can I list all the headers that are included in a C file?

Technique

Many source files in C include header files. Each header file may include many more header files. Because of this, it is hard to know what files are being included in any source file. The job of finding which header files are included is complicated by the fact that there can be conditional inclusions.

The easiest way to find what header files are being included is to run the C preprocessor on the source file and read its output. The preprocessor adds comment lines telling which header files were included.

In addition to listing which header files are being used by a source file, you may want to see which header is included in which file. Beyond that, it can be useful to search for a string in the preprocessor output to see which file(s) it appears in.

Steps

The first example script starts the C preprocessor on the source file and reads its output. It saves each file seen in an associative array. When all the output is processed, the contents of the associative array are printed. The second script adds the ability to show a tree-like structure of includes. The third script adds the ability to print the line number on which a file is included, as well as the ability to search for a regular expression in the preprocessor output.

1. Create a file called include1.pl. Add the following code to it. First, initialize a variable to hold the program to execute to get the C preprocessor output. Add a loop to gather all the options that can be passed to the command that will affect the output of the preprocessor.

```
$Cpp = "cc -E";
$Defines  = "";
$Includes = "";

while($ARGV[0] =~ /^-/) {
    $Opt = shift;
    if ($Opt eq "-D") {
        $Defines = "$Defines -D " . shift;
    } elsif ($Opt eq "-I") {
        $Includes = "$Includes -I " . shift;
    } else {
        die "Unknown option: $Opt\n";
    }
}
```

2. Add code to loop through each file on the command line and run it through the preprocessor. Examine each line of the output for the comment line that tells that the source of the following output is from a different file. Save the filename in an associative array. When the output ends, print the contents of the associative array.

```
foreach $File (@ARGV) {
    open(FILE,"$Cpp $Defines $Includes $File |") ||
        die "Can't run $Cpp on $File\n";
    while(<FILE>) {

        # cpp lines look like:
        # '# <line number> "filename"'
        # skip everything else

        /^#\s+\d/ || next;
        ($Sharp,$FileLine,$FileName) = split;
        $FileName =~ s/^"(.*)"/$1/;
        $Files{$FileName} = 1;
    }
    foreach $Name (sort keys %Files) {
        print "$Name\n";
    }
}
```

3. The entire script follows.

```
$Cpp = "cc -E";
$Defines  = "";
$Includes = "";

while($ARGV[0] =~ /^-/) {
    $Opt = shift;
    if ($Opt eq "-D") {
        $Defines = "$Defines -D " . shift;
    } elsif ($Opt eq "-I") {
        $Includes = "$Includes -I " . shift;
    } else {
        die "Unknown option: $Opt\n";
    }
}

foreach $File (@ARGV) {
    open(FILE,"$Cpp $Defines $Includes $File |") ||
        die "Can't run $Cpp on $File\n";
    while(<FILE>) {

        # cpp lines look like:
        # '# <line number> "filename"'
        # skip everything else

        /^#\s+\d/ || next;
        ($Sharp,$FileLine,$FileName) = split;
        $FileName =~ s/^"(.*)"/$1/;
        $Files{$FileName} = 1;
    }
    foreach $Name (sort keys %Files) {
        print "$Name\n";
    }
}
```

4. Run the script on a C file from the Perl source.

```
perl include3.pl a2p.c
```

5. The output will look something like the following. (Your output will probably be different, depending on the operating system you are using.)

```
../config.h
/usr/include/_G_config.h
/usr/include/alloca.h
/usr/include/asm/types.h
/usr/include/bytesex.h
/usr/include/ctype.h
/usr/include/endian.h
/usr/include/errno.h
/usr/include/features.h
/usr/include/huge_val.h
/usr/include/libio.h
/usr/include/linux/errno.h
/usr/include/linux/time.h
/usr/include/linux/times.h
```

continued on next page

continued from previous page

```
/usr/include/linux/types.h
/usr/include/math.h
/usr/include/nan.h
/usr/include/stdio.h
/usr/include/stdlib.h
/usr/include/string.h
/usr/include/sys/cdefs.h
/usr/include/sys/time.h
/usr/include/sys/times.h
/usr/include/sys/types.h
/usr/include/time.h
/usr/include/values.h
/usr/lib/gcc-lib/i486-linux/2.6.3/include/float.h
/usr/lib/gcc-lib/i486-linux/2.6.3/include/stddef.h
INTERN.h
a2p.c
a2p.h
a2p.y
a2py.c
handy.h
hash.h
str.h
util.h
y.tab.c
```

6. Create a file called include2.pl. Copy into it the contents of include1.pl. Add a new option for printing out the tree structure of the includes. Add a variable to hold the amount of white space to indent each time a new level of the include tree is seen.

```perl
$Cpp = "cc -E";
$Indent = "    ";
$Defines  = "";
$Includes = "";
$Tree = 0;

while($ARGV[0] =~ /^-/) {
    $Opt = shift;
    if ($Opt eq "-D") {
        $Defines = "$Defines -D " . shift;
    } elsif ($Opt eq "-I") {
        $Includes = "$Includes -I " . shift;
    } elsif ($Opt eq "-t") {
        $Tree = 1;
    } else {
        die "Unknown option: $Opt\n";
    }
}
```

7. Change the code that reads the preprocessor output to support the tree option. If the tree option is selected, print the new file as it is seen. Keep a stack of the currently included files. If the preprocessor output has a filename that is the same as the previous one, it is reporting only a line number change. This can be ignored. If the filename is the same as the one before the current one, the current file has ended and should be popped off the stack.

In any other case, a new file has been included. Keep an associative array of all filenames seen so that multiple inclusions of the same file can be noted.

```
foreach $File (@ARGV) {
    open(FILE,"$Cpp $Defines $Includes $File |") ||
        die "Can't run $Cpp on $File\n";
    while(<FILE>) {

        # cpp lines look like:
        # '# <line number> "filename"'
        # skip everything else

        /^#\s+\d/ || next;
        ($Sharp,$FileLine,$FileName) = split;
        $FileName =~ s/^"(.*)"/$1/;
        if ($Tree) {
            if ($Name[$#Name] eq $FileName) {
                # In the same file, nothing to do
                ;
            } elsif ($Name[$#Name - 1] eq $FileName) {
                # Returning to the previous file
                pop(@Name);
            } else {
                # A new file has been included
                push(@Name,$FileName);
                print $Indent x $#Name;
                print $FileName;
                print "\tAGAIN" if $Files{$FileName}++;
                print "\n";
            }
        } else {
            $Files{$FileName} = 1;
        }
    }
    if (! $Tree) {
        foreach $Name (sort keys %Files) {
            print "$Name\n";
        }
    }
}
```

8. The entire second script follows.

```
$Cpp = "cc -E";
$Indent = "    ";
$Defines  = "";
$Includes = "";
$Tree = 0;

while($ARGV[0] =~ /^-/) {
    $Opt = shift;
    if ($Opt eq "-D") {
        $Defines = "$Defines -D " . shift;
    } elsif ($Opt eq "-I") {
        $Includes = "$Includes -I " . shift;
    } elsif ($Opt eq "-t") {
        $Tree = 1;
```

continued on next page

continued from previous page

```perl
    } else {
        die "Unknown option: $Opt\n";
    }
}


foreach $File (@ARGV) {
    open(FILE,"$Cpp $Defines $Includes $File |") ||
        die "Can't run $Cpp on $File\n";
    while(<FILE>) {

        # cpp lines look like:
        # '# <line number> "filename"'
        # skip everything else

        /^#\s+\d/ || next;
        ($Sharp,$FileLine,$FileName) = split;
        $FileName =~ s/^"(.*)"/$1/;
        if ($Tree) {
            if ($Name[$#Name] eq $FileName) {
                # In the same file, nothing to do
                ;
            } elsif ($Name[$#Name - 1] eq $FileName) {
                # Returning to the previous file
                pop(@Name);
            } else {
                # A new file has been included
                push(@Name,$FileName);
                print $Indent x $#Name;
                print $FileName;
                print "\tAGAIN" if $Files{$FileName}++;
                print "\n";
            }
        } else {
            $Files{$FileName} = 1;
        }
    }
    if (! $Tree) {
        foreach $Name (sort keys %Files) {
            print "$Name\n";
        }
    }
}
```

9. Run the second script.

```
perl include3.pl -t a2p.c
```

10. The output will be something like the following.

```
a2p.c
    a2p.y
        INTERN.h
        a2p.h
            ../config.h
            /usr/include/stdlib.h
                /usr/include/features.h
                    /usr/include/sys/cdefs.h
```

```
                        /usr/include/sys/cdefs.h        AGAIN
                /usr/lib/gcc-lib/i486-linux/2.6.3/include/stddef.h
                /usr/include/errno.h
                        /usr/include/linux/errno.h
                /usr/lib/gcc-lib/i486-linux/2.6.3/include/float.h
                /usr/include/alloca.h
                        /usr/lib/gcc-lib/i486-linux/2.6.3/include/stddef.h AGAIN
        /usr/include/stdio.h
                /usr/include/libio.h
                        /usr/include/_G_config.h
        /usr/include/math.h
                /usr/include/huge_val.h
                        /usr/include/endian.h
                                /usr/include/bytesex.h
                /usr/include/nan.h
                /usr/include/values.h
        /usr/include/sys/types.h
                /usr/include/linux/types.h
                        /usr/include/asm/types.h
        /usr/include/ctype.h
        /usr/include/string.h
                /usr/lib/gcc-lib/i486-linux/2.6.3/include/stddef.h        AGAIN
        /usr/include/sys/time.h
                /usr/include/linux/time.h
                /usr/include/time.h
        /usr/include/sys/times.h
                /usr/include/linux/times.h
        handy.h
        str.h
        hash.h
    y.tab.c
    a2py.c
        util.h
    y.tab.c AGAIN
    y.tab.c AGAIN
```

11. Create a file called include3.pl. Copy the contents of include2.pl into it.
Add two options: one for line numbers and one for searching for regular
expressions.

```perl
$Cpp = "cc -E";
$Indent = "      ";
$Defines  = "";
$Includes = "";
$Tree = 0;
$PrintLines = 0;

while($ARGV[0] =~ /^-/) {
    $Opt = shift;
    if ($Opt eq "-D") {
        $Defines = "$Defines -D " . shift;
    } elsif ($Opt eq "-I") {
        $Includes = "$Includes -I " . shift;
    } elsif ($Opt eq "-t") {
        $Tree = 1;
    } elsif ($Opt eq "-1") {
```

continued on next page

continued from previous page

```
        $PrintLines = 1;
    } elsif ($Opt eq "-m") {
        push(@Patterns,shift);
    } else {
        die "Unknown option: $Opt\n";
    }
}
```

12. Add the following code to create a subroutine to search for all the patterns listed on the command line.

```
$Patterns = 0;
if ($Tree && @Patterns) {
    $Patterns = 1;
    $SubPat = "sub Pat { ";
    foreach $Pattern (@Patterns) {
        if ($PrintLines) {
            $SubPat .= "printf '>> %5d %s', \$Line, \$_ if m$Pattern;";
        } else {
            $SubPat .= "print '>> ', \$_ if m$Pattern;";
        }
    }
    $SubPat .= "}";
    eval $SubPat;
}
```

13. Add code to support the line numbers and to check for patterns. Remember that the line number in the preprocessor output is the line number of the next line, not of the current line.

```
foreach $File (@ARGV) {
    open(FILE,"$Cpp $Defines $Includes $File |") ||
        die "Can't run $Cpp on $File\n";
    $Line = 0;
    while(<FILE>) {
        $Line++;
        &Pat if $Patterns;

        # cpp lines look like:
        # '# <line number> "filename"'
        # skip everything else

        /^#\s+\d/ || next;
        ($Sharp,$FileLine,$FileName) = split;
        $FileName =~ s/^"(.*)"/$1/;
        if ($Tree) {
            if ($Name[$#Name] eq $FileName) {
                # In the same file, nothing to do
                ;
            } elsif ($Name[$#Name - 1] eq $FileName) {
                # Returning to the previous file
                pop(@Name);
            } else {
                # A new file has been included
                push(@Name,$FileName);
                print "    " if $Patterns;
                printf "%5d ", $Line if $PrintLines;
```

```
                        print $Indent x $#Name;
                        print $FileName;
                        print "\tAGAIN" if $Files{$FileName}++;
                        print "\n";
                }
                $Line = $FileLine - 1;
            } else {
                $Files{$FileName} = 1;
            }
        }
    }
    if (! $Tree) {
        foreach $Name (sort keys %Files) {
            print "$Name\n";
        }
    }
}
```

14. The entire third script follows.

```
$Cpp = "cc -E";
$Indent = "    ";
$Defines  = "";
$Includes = "";
$Tree = 0;
$PrintLines = 0;

while($ARGV[0] =~ /^-/) {
    $Opt = shift;
    if ($Opt eq "-D") {
        $Defines = "$Defines -D " . shift;
    } elsif ($Opt eq "-I") {
        $Includes = "$Includes -I " . shift;
    } elsif ($Opt eq "-t") {
        $Tree = 1;
    } elsif ($Opt eq "-1") {
        $PrintLines = 1;
    } elsif ($Opt eq "-m") {
        push(@Patterns,shift);
    } else {
        die "Unknown option: $Opt\n";
    }
}

$Patterns = 0;
if ($Tree && @Patterns) {
    $Patterns = 1;
    $SubPat = "sub Pat { ";
    foreach $Pattern (@Patterns) {
        if ($PrintLines) {
            $SubPat .= "printf '>> %5d %s', \$Line, \$_ if m$Pattern;";
        } else {
            $SubPat .= "print '>> ', \$_ if m$Pattern;";
        }
    }
    $SubPat .= "}";
    eval $SubPat;
}
```

continued on next page

continued from previous page

```
foreach $File (@ARGV) {
    open(FILE,"$Cpp $Defines $Includes $File |") ||
        die "Can't run $Cpp on $File\n";
    $Line = 0;
    while(<FILE>) {
        $Line++;
        &Pat if $Patterns;

        # cpp lines look like:
        # '# <line number> "filename"'
        # skip everything else

        /^#\s+\d/ || next;
        ($Sharp,$FileLine,$FileName) = split;
        $FileName =~ s/^"(.*)"/$1/;
        if ($Tree) {
            if ($Name[$#Name] eq $FileName) {
                # In the same file, nothing to do
                ;
            } elsif ($Name[$#Name - 1] eq $FileName) {
                # Returning to the previous file
                pop(@Name);
            } else {
                # A new file has been included
                push(@Name,$FileName);
                print "    " if $Patterns;
                printf "%5d ", $Line if $PrintLines;
                print $Indent x $#Name;
                print $FileName;
                print "\tAGAIN" if $Files{$FileName}++;
                print "\n";
            }
            $Line = $FileLine - 1;
        } else {
            $Files{$FileName} = 1;
        }
    }
    if (! $Tree) {
        foreach $Name (sort keys %Files) {
            print "$Name\n";
        }
    }
}
```

15. Run the script.

```
perl include3.pl -t -l -m /strlen/ a2p.c
```

16. The output will be similar to the following.

```
 1 a2p.c
 5     a2p.y
12         INTERN.h
13         a2p.h
12             ../config.h
20             /usr/include/stdlib.h
```

```
           26                    /usr/include/features.h
          134                        /usr/include/sys/cdefs.h
          137                        /usr/include/sys/cdefs.h     AGAIN
           32                    /usr/lib/gcc-lib/i486-linux/2.6.3/include/stddef.h
           35                    /usr/include/errno.h
           27                        /usr/include/linux/errno.h
           39                    /usr/lib/gcc-lib/i486-linux/2.6.3/include/float.h
          236                    /usr/include/alloca.h
           24                        /usr/lib/gcc-lib/i486- linux/2.6.3/include/
                                   stddef.h AGAIN
           23                /usr/include/stdio.h
           34                    /usr/include/libio.h
           32                        /usr/include/_G_config.h
           26                /usr/include/math.h
          270                    /usr/include/huge_val.h
           25                        /usr/include/endian.h
           34                            /usr/include/bytesex.h
          274                    /usr/include/nan.h
          278                    /usr/include/values.h
           30                /usr/include/sys/types.h
            4                    /usr/include/linux/types.h
            4                        /usr/include/asm/types.h
           37                /usr/include/ctype.h
           43                /usr/include/string.h
           33                    /usr/lib/gcc-lib/i486-linux/2.6.3/include/stddef.h
                                   AGAIN
>>        127 extern size_t strlen  (__const char *__s)  ;
           69                        /usr/include/sys/time.h
            6                            /usr/include/linux/time.h
           32                        /usr/include/time.h
           77                    /usr/include/sys/times.h
            7                        /usr/include/linux/times.h
           89                handy.h
          294                str.h
          295                hash.h
           19            y.tab.c
          396            a2py.c
           14                util.h
>>        891            len = strlen(ptr);
>>       1152                    newpos += strlen(t);
>>       1153                    d = t + strlen(t);
>>       1171                strcpy(t+strlen(t)-1, "\t#???\n");
          397            y.tab.c        AGAIN
          394            y.tab.c        AGAIN
```

How It Works

Because the C preprocessor includes lines that tell what file was included and what
line number it was at, it is possible to extract useful information from the output.
Just these lines can be examined to see what files are included. By keeping track of
when files are included, you can build a tree of inclusions. By tracking line numbers and searching for patterns, you can extract even more information from the output.

Comments

Each system differs on how to get the output of the C preprocessor. A standard one is

```
cc -E
```

Your system may be different. Add the correct line for your system into the scripts.

By creating one subroutine to search for all the patterns, you can make your program more efficient. Otherwise, for each line in the preprocessor output, each pattern will need to be evaluated to see if it matches the line.

OBJECT-ORIENTED PROGRAMMING

OBJECT-ORIENTED PROGRAMMING

How do I...

23.1   Create a class?

23.2   Create an object?

23.3   Inherit from a class?

23.4   Override a parent method?

23.5   Create a class variable?

23.6   Call a class method directly?

One of the major new features in Perl 5 is the ability to perform *object-oriented programming* (OOP). OOP is a method of encapsulating data and the functions that operate on that data. The entity created from this encapsulation is called an *object*. Objects are usually grouped into a class that defines the behavior of all the objects of the class. There is support in the language for both classes and objects. The OOP features were added with little impact on the existing features. Classes in Perl 5 are nothing more than packages that support objects. Objects are *references* (another new Perl 5 feature) that know what class they belong to. With just a little added syntax, Perl 5 supports objects as easily as it does regular data structures.

Using the OOP features in the language, you can change and extend objects without affecting other parts of the program. Perl 5 also provides *inheritance*. This allows a class to inherit all the functionality of another class without having to write the code over again. The new class, called the *derived class*, needs to supply only the functions that make it different from the class being inherited from. This feature allows code to be reused easily.

23.1   Create a Class

Creating a class in Perl 5 is as easy as creating a package. The subroutines in the package become the class's methods. This section will show you how to create a class.

23.2   Create an Object

You can create objects by telling a reference which class it is an object of. This How-To will demonstrate this method.

23.3   Inherit from a Class

A class can inherit from another class simply by including the class being inherited from in an array. This section will show you how.

23.4   Override a Parent Method

Derived classes can redefine methods defined in a parent class. This How-To will demonstrate how to define the method in the subclass for this to happen.

23.5   Create a Class Variable

Classes as well as objects can have variables. In this way, you can keep data per class instead of per object. This section will show you how to create a class variable.

23.6   Call a Class Method Directly

Class methods can be called explicitly. This can be useful if the derived method will not provide the correct functionality. This How-To will demonstrate how to call a class method directly.

COMPLEXITY
INTERMEDIATE

23.1   How do I...
Create a class?

COMPATIBILITY: PERL 5   UNIX   DOS

Problem

I would like to use the object-oriented features of Perl 5. How do I create a class?

Technique

In object-oriented programming, a class is a structure that encapsulates both data and functions to manipulate that data. These functions are usually called *methods*. A class in Perl 5 is nothing more than a package with subroutines that act as methods. For more information on packages, see Chapter 14. Objects in Perl 5 are references that know what package they come from. An object is created by *bless-*

ing a reference (by way of the bless command). A description of references can be found in Chapter 1.

Because objects know what package they come from, when a method is invoked on an object, the package is examined to find the subroutine that implements the method. This happens even if the object is being used in a different package. (Subroutine names are usually found only in the current package.) When a method is invoked on an object, a reference to the object is passed as the first argument to the method. If arguments are passed to a method, they are all shifted over to allow the reference to be inserted as the first argument.

A class can have a *static method:* a method that is not associated with any particular object. (These methods are sometimes called *class methods.*) These methods are called by using the class name as the "object" that is invoking it. The first argument to these methods is the package name. At least one of these class methods is usually defined for each class. This standard method is new. This is the method that creates and initializes an object of the given class.

A method can be invoked in two ways. The first way is usually used to invoke class methods.

```
$Aobject = new AClass;
```

This is a call to the class method new of the AClass class. Object methods are usually called using a different syntax.

```
$result = $Aobject->Rotate(3);
```

This calls the Rotate method on Aobject, passing it an argument of 3. Both ways of calling methods can be used in Perl scripts. The choice of which one to use should be based on convention and clarity.

Steps

The example script creates a Fruit class. A new class method is defined, as well as some regular methods. The new method creates a Fruit object and initializes it with a few data values. A diagram of the Fruit class and a Fruit object can be seen in Figure 23-1.

1. Create a file called class.pl. First, add a Fruit class to it. Add a new method that creates a reference to an associative array that will be a fruit object. Create three entries in the associative array to hold object-specific data. Store the name, weight, and cost of the fruit. Bless the reference into the package.

```
use strict;

package Fruit;

sub new {
    my $class = shift;
    my $self = {};

    if (defined $_[0]) {
        $self->{Name} = shift;
    }
```

continued on next page

continued from previous page

```
    if (defined $_[0]) {
        $self->{Weight} = shift;
    }
    if (defined $_[0]) {
        $self->{Cost} = shift;
    }
    bless $self, $class;
}
```

2. Create two methods to return the cost and name of a fruit object. These methods do not take any arguments except for the built-in first argument that is a reference to the object.

```
sub Cost {
    my $self = shift;

    $self->{Cost};
}
```

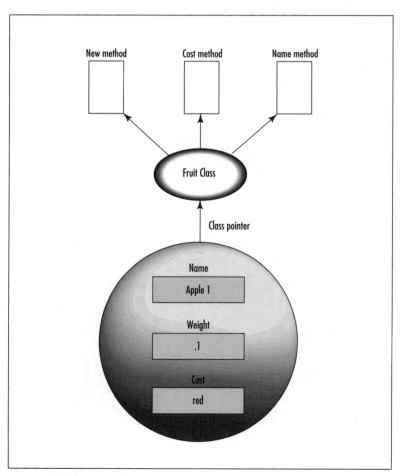

Figure 23-1 The Fruit class and Fruit object

```
sub Name {
    my $self = shift;

    $self->{Name};
}
```

3. Change back to the main package. Create a local reference to a fruit object and initialize it with a call to the new method. Print the object's name and cost by calling the correct methods on the object.

```
package main;

my($apple) = new Fruit("Apple1", .1, .30);

print $apple->Name, " cost = ", $apple->Cost,"\n";

exit(0);
```

4. The entire file should now look like the following.

```
use strict;

package Fruit;

sub new {
    my $class = shift;
    my $self = {};

    if (defined $_[0]) {
        $self->{Name} = shift;
    }
    if (defined $_[0]) {
        $self->{Weight} = shift;
    }
    if (defined $_[0]) {
        $self->{Cost} = shift;
    }
    bless $self, $class;
}

sub Cost {
    my $self = shift;

    $self->{Cost};
}

sub Name {
    my $self = shift;

    $self->{Name};
}

package main;

my($apple) = new Fruit("Apple1", .1, .30);

print $apple->Name, " cost = ", $apple->Cost,"\n";
```

continued on next page

continued from previous page
```
exit(0);
```

5. Run the script.

```
perl class.pl
```

6. The output follows.

Output

```
Apple1 cost = 0.3
```

End Output

How It Works

A class is nothing but a package built to support objects. It usually contains a new method for creating new objects of the class that the package supports. Data variables in an object are stored in the data structure that the reference refers to. This is usually an associative array. By using an associative array, the entries in the array can be used as the variables, with the keys being the variable's names.

Comments

The bless command will work with one argument instead of two. If only one argument is given, the reference is blessed into the current package. It is better to bless it into the package that is passed as the first argument. Usually this is the current package; it does not have to be. The new method could be inherited by a subclass. See How-To 23.3 for more information on inheritance.

The variable *$self* is usually used in a method to hold a reference to the current object. This is only by convention. There is nothing special about *$self*; any variable can be used.

COMPLEXITY
INTERMEDIATE

23.2 How do I...
Create an object?

COMPATIBILITY: PERL 5 UNIX DOS

Problem

I hear that Perl 5 allows you to do object-oriented programming. How do I create an object?

Technique

In Perl, every data structure can be considered an object. Perl 5 adds the ability to tell an object what class it belongs to. (For more information on Perl 5 classes, see How-To 23.1.) Once an object belongs to a class, it can have that class's methods applied to it. Objects in Perl 5 are accessed by using references. (A description of references can be found in Chapter 1.) The bless command is used to tell a reference which class it belongs to.

It is easiest to think of objects as an encapsulation of data. When an object is blessed into a class, the methods of the class can be applied to that data. In some programming languages, the data in an object can be accessed only by using methods. Perl does not have this restriction. An object's data can be accessed by using its reference. To achieve true object-oriented programming, this type of access should not be done.

Steps

Two example scripts are given here. The first has a simple Fruit class that has two methods. One creates a fruit object and one prints a message. The second script is from How-To 23.1. It creates a Fruit class that has each fruit object storing data local to its self. It contains methods to create a fruit object, to return the fruit's name, and to return the fruit's cost.

1. Create a file called object1.pl. Enter the following code into it. First, create a Fruit class with two methods. The new method should create a reference to an empty associative array. Bless this reference into the class. The class name is passed into the method as the first argument. Create a Hi method to print a message.

```perl
use strict;

package Fruit;

sub new {
    my $class = shift;
    my $self = {};

    bless $self, $class;
}

sub Hi {
    print "Hi from Fruit\n";
}
```

2. Change back into the main package. Create a fruit object by calling the new method of the Fruit class. Call that fruit's Hi method.

```perl
package main;

my($fruit) = new Fruit;

$fruit->Hi;

exit(0);
```

3. The entire script follows.

```perl
use strict;
```

continued on next page

continued from previous page

```perl
package Fruit;

sub new {
    my $class = shift;
    my $self = {};

    bless $self, $class;
}

sub Hi {
    print "Hi from Fruit\n";
}

package main;

my($fruit) = new Fruit;

$fruit->Hi;

exit(0);
```

4. Run the script.

```perl
perl object1.pl
```

5. The output follows.

___ Output |————————————————————————————————

```
Hi from Fruit
```

End Output |————————————————————————————————

6. Create a file called object2.pl. Add the following code to it. This script creates a Fruit class. Each fruit object contains its name, weight, and cost. Create two methods to return a fruit's name and cost. Remember that the first argument to a method is a reference to the object that invoked the method. Create a fruit object and use the methods to print information about it.

```perl
use strict;

package Fruit;

sub new {
    my $class = shift;
    my $self = {};

    if (defined $_[0]) {
        $self->{Name} = shift;
    }
    if (defined $_[0]) {
        $self->{Weight} = shift;
    }
    if (defined $_[0]) {
        $self->{Cost} = shift;
    }
    bless $self, $class;
}
```

```
sub Cost {
    my $self = shift;

    $self->{Cost};
}

sub Name {
    my $self = shift;

    $self->{Name};
}

package main;

my($apple) = new Fruit("Apple1", .1, .30);

print $apple->Name, " cost = ", $apple->Cost,"\n";

exit(0);
```

7. Run the script.

```
perl object2.pl
```

8. The output follows.

Output

```
Apple1 cost = 0.3
```

End Output

How It Works

An object is nothing more than a reference that knows what class it belongs to. Methods from the class can be applied to the object. These methods can have arguments, but a first argument is always added. This argument is a reference to the object. This reference can be used to access data internal to the object.

A method can be invoked in two ways. The first way is usually used to invoke class methods.

```
$Aobject = new AClass;
```

This is a call to the class method new of the AClass class. Object methods are usually called using a different syntax.

```
$result = $Aobject->Rotate(3);
```

This calls the Rotate method on Aobject, passing it an argument of 3. Both ways of calling methods can be used in Perl scripts. The choice of which one to use should be based on convention and clarity.

Comments

The object in the examples is always a reference to an associative array. This is usually the case, but it does not have to be. A normal array can be used, as can a scalar value. A scalar can be used when only one value is to be stored in the object. If an array is used, each value to be stored will be associated with an index to the array. Although this can be done, it is not as easy as having a name for the value, as is possible with an associative array.

COMPLEXITY
INTERMEDIATE

23.3 How do I...
Inherit from a class?

COMPATIBILITY: PERL 5 | UNIX | DOS

Problem

I have been able to create and use classes in Perl 5. I would like to be able to create subclasses so I can take advantage of inheritance. How do I do this?

Technique

Inheritance in object-oriented programming is a technique for creating a new class by extending an existing one. The new class is called a *subclass* of the existing class. The subclass inherits all the methods of the parent (existing) class. Inheritance allows this to happen without the programmer having to recode the methods. The subclass can add new methods and redefine existing ones.

It is good object-oriented practice to make the subclass be a specialization of the parent class. The parent class should always be more general. For example, the parent class can be a vehicle, whereas the subclass is a truck.

In Perl 5, a class inherits from a parent class (or base class) by declaring a class array called @ISA. This array contains the name(s) of the parent class(es) of the class. When an object of this class invokes a method, the method is first looked for in the class that the object belongs to. If it is not found, the classes listed in the @ISA array are checked to find the method.

Steps

The example extends the Fruit class from the previous How-To's. This class creates fruit objects that have some local state (the fruit's name, weight, and cost). There are also two methods to return a fruit object's name and cost. A subclass called Grapefruit is created. A grapefruit object also contains a color. The new method of the Fruit class is overridden. This allows it to add the color to a grapefruit object. A diagram of the Fruit class, Grapefruit class, and a Grapefruit object can be seen in Figure 23-2.

1. Create a file called inherit.pl. Add the following code to it. First, copy the Fruit class from the previous How-To's.

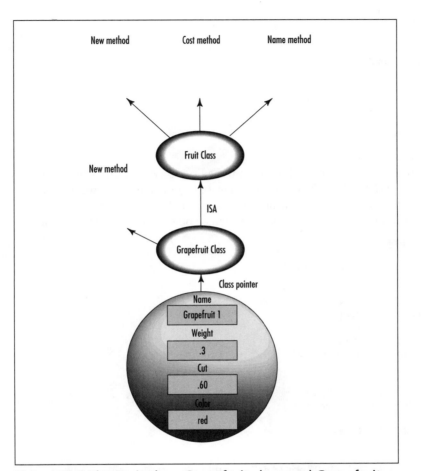

New method   Cost method   Name method

New method

Fruit Class

ISA

Grapefruit Class

Class pointer

Name
Grapefruit 1
Weight
.3
Cut
.60
Color
red

Figure 23-2 The Fruit class, Grapefruit class, and Grapefruit object

```
use strict;

package Fruit;

sub new {
    my $class = shift;
    my $self = {};

    if (defined $_[0]) {
        $self->{Name} = shift;
    }
    if (defined $_[0]) {
        $self->{Weight} = shift;
    }
    if (defined $_[0]) {
        $self->{Cost} = shift;
    }
    bless $self, $class;
}
```

continued on next page

continued from previous page

```perl
sub Cost {
    my $self = shift;

    $self->{Cost};
}

sub Name {
    my $self = shift;

    $self->{Name};
}
```

2. Add a Grapefruit class. Inherit from the Fruit class by creating an array called @ISA that contains Fruit. A fourth argument to the new method will be the color of the grapefruit. The new method should create a fruit object and add the color to it. Bless the modified object into the Grapefruit class.

```perl
package Grapefruit;

@Grapefruit::ISA = qw( Fruit );

sub new {
    my $class = shift;
    my ($self,$color);

    if (defined $_[3]) {
        $color = $_[3];
    }

    $self = new Fruit(@_);
    $self->{Color} = $color;

    bless $self, $class;
}
```

3. Add the creation and use of a grapefruit object to the main package.

```perl
package main;

my($apple) = new Fruit("Apple1", .1, .30);
my($grapefruit) = new Grapefruit("Grapefruit1", .3, .60, "red");

print $apple->Name, " cost = ", $apple->Cost,"\n";
print $grapefruit->Name, " cost = ", $grapefruit->Cost;
print " color = $grapefruit->{Color}\n";

exit(0);
```

4. The entire modified script follows. The changes from the previous How-To's are in bold.

```perl
use strict;

package Fruit;
```

```perl
sub new {
    my $class = shift;
    my $self = {};

    if (defined $_[0]) {
        $self->{Name} = shift;
    }
    if (defined $_[0]) {
        $self->{Weight} = shift;
    }
    if (defined $_[0]) {
        $self->{Cost} = shift;
    }
    bless $self, $class;
}

sub Cost {
    my $self = shift;

    $self->{Cost};
}

sub Name {
    my $self = shift;

    $self->{Name};
}

package Grapefruit;

@Grapefruit::ISA = qw( Fruit );

sub new {
    my $class = shift;
    my ($self,$color);

    if (defined $_[3]) {
        $color = $_[3];
    }

    $self = new Fruit(@_);
    $self->{Color} = $color;

    bless $self, $class;
}

package main;

my($apple) = new Fruit("Apple1", .1, .30);
my($grapefruit) = new Grapefruit("Grapefruit1", .3, .60, "red");
print $apple->Name, " cost = ", $apple->Cost,"\n";
print $grapefruit->Name, " cost = ", $grapefruit->Cost;
print " color = $grapefruit->{Color}\n";

exit(0);
```

5. Run the script.

```
perl inherit.pl
```

6. The output is shown below.

Output

```
Apple1 cost = 0.3
Grapefruit1 cost = 0.6 color = red
```

End Output

How It Works

Inheritance in Perl 5 is achieved by listing the classes that a class inherits from in an array. Multiple classes can be listed in the @ISA array. They are searched in order. The first class and all its base classes are checked for a method before the next class listed is checked. Methods are overridden simply by making them local to the class. The method is then found in the search before any other method with the same name.

The statement

```
print " color = $grapefruit->{Color}\n";
```

breaks the object-orientedness of the script. It is taking advantage of the fact that an object is really only a reference. The correct way to access the color attribute is to create a method that returns the color.

Comments

In the Grapefruit class, a fruit object is created and more data is added to it. The fruit object is then blessed into the Grapefruit class. This reblessing causes the object to forget that it is a fruit object and it becomes a grapefruit object. This is a useful technique when overriding the new method. Be aware that the object completely forgets that it ever was a fruit object. This means that the Grapefruit class needs to perform all cleanup needed when the object is destroyed. The Fruit class will not take care of any of it. (Of course, in this instance, there is nothing that needs to be cleaned up. Cleanup is only necessary if storage needs to be freed, locks need to be released, etc.)

The @ISA array is fully qualified, @Grapefruit::ISA, to pass the strict type-checking. This checking prevents you from accidentally referring to a global variable when you mean a local one. It can prevent one of those hard-to-find errors.

COMPLEXITY
INTERMEDIATE

23.4   How do I...
Override a parent method?

COMPATIBILITY: PERL 5   UNIX   DOS

Problem

I have a subclass in which I would like to override a method in a base class. How can I do this in Perl?

Technique

When creating a new subclass, you may find some of the methods that are inherited from the base class inappropriate. (For more information on inheritance, see How-To 23.3.) The subclass may need to enhance or change the behavior of a method. The technique used to override a base-class method declares that method in the subclass. For all objects of the subclass, the new method is called.

Steps

The example extends the Fruit class from How-To 23.1. This class creates fruit objects that have some local state (the fruit's name, weight, and cost). There are also two methods to return a fruit object's name and cost. In this example, a subclass called Grapefruit is created. For Grapefruit, the cost is not passed into the new method. The cost of a grapefruit is based on its weight. The Cost method is overridden to reflect this.

1. Create a file called override.pl. Add the Fruit class from How-To 23.1.

```
use strict;

package Fruit;

sub new {
    my $class = shift;
    my $self = {};

    if (defined $_[0]) {
        $self->{Name} = shift;
    }
    if (defined $_[0]) {
        $self->{Weight} = shift;
    }
    if (defined $_[0]) {
        $self->{Cost} = shift;
    }
    bless $self, $class;
}

sub Cost {
    my $self = shift;
```

continued on next page

continued from previous page

```
        $self->{Cost};
}

sub Name {
    my $self = shift;

    $self->{Name};
}
```

2. Add a Grapefruit class as a subclass of Fruit. Add a Cost method to override the parent method. The cost is two dollars times the weight of the grapefruit.

```
package Grapefruit;

@Grapefruit::ISA = qw( Fruit );

sub Cost {
    my $self = shift;

    $self->{Weight} * 2.0;
}
```

3. Add the creation of a grapefruit object to the main program. It does not need to be passed a cost argument. Add a line to print the cost of the grapefruit.

```
package main;

my($apple) = new Fruit("Apple1", .1, .30);
my($grapefruit) = new Grapefruit("Grapefruit1", .3);

print $apple->Name, " cost = ", $apple->Cost,"\n";
print $grapefruit->Name, " cost = ", $grapefruit->Cost,"\n";

exit(0);
```

4. The entire script follows. The changes from How-To 23.1 are in bold.

```
use strict;

package Fruit;

sub new {
    my $class = shift;
    my $self = {};

    if (defined $_[0]) {
        $self->{Name} = shift;
    }
    if (defined $_[0]) {
        $self->{Weight} = shift;
    }
    if (defined $_[0]) {
        $self->{Cost} = shift;
    }
    bless $self, $class;
}

sub Cost {
```

```
    my $self = shift;

    $self->{Cost};
}

sub Name {
    my $self = shift;

    $self->{Name};
}

package Grapefruit;

@Grapefruit::ISA = qw( Fruit );

sub Cost {
    my $self = shift;

    $self->{Weight} * 2.0;
}

package main;

my($apple) = new Fruit("Apple1", .1, .30);
my($grapefruit) = new Grapefruit("Grapefruit1", .3);

print $apple->Name, " cost = ", $apple->Cost,"\n";
print $grapefruit->Name, " cost = ", $grapefruit->Cost,"\n";

exit(0);
```

5. Run the script.

```
perl override.pl
```

6. The output follows.

___Output_____

```
Apple1 cost = 0.3
Grapefruit1 cost = 0.6
```
__End Output_____

How It Works

When Perl searches for an object's methods, it first checks the object's class before looking at the base classes. The method needs only to appear first in the search to be overridden. This is easily accomplished by putting the new method in the subclass definition.

Comments

When overriding a method, be sure not to break any functionality of the base class. For example, if an argument to a method is stored as data in the object, this functionality should also be present in the overriding method.

The @ISA array is fully qualified, @Grapefruit::ISA, to pass the strict type-checking. This checking prevents you from accidentally referring to a global variable when you mean a local one. It can prevent one of those hard-to-find errors.

How-To 23.3 shows a technique for overriding the new method.

COMPLEXITY
ADVANCED

23.5 How do I...
Create a class variable?

COMPATIBILITY: PERL 5 UNIX DOS

Problem

I need to keep a variable per class, not per object. I need to have one copy of a value that is shared by all instances of the class. How can I do this in Perl?

Technique

It can be a useful technique to share a variable between all instances of a class. This type of variable is often called a *class variable*. In Perl 5, the technique is to put the variable in the class and not store it into the class objects. This is done by declaring the variable in the body of the package that implements the class and outside of any method.

Steps

These examples extend the Fruit class from How-To 23.1. This class creates fruit objects that have some local state (the fruit's name, weight, and cost). There are also two methods to return a fruit object's name and cost. In this example, two subclasses called Grapefruit and RedGrapefruit are created. For a grapefruit, the cost is based on its weight. For each type of grapefruit, the cost is not passed into the new method.

A class variable is created in each Grapefruit class to store the cost per pound. The Cost method is overridden to use this value in computing the grapefruit's cost. The first example creates a WeightCost method for both Grapefruit classes. This method returns the value of the class variable. The second example shows a method of defining the WeightCost method that works in derived classes. A diagram of the classes with a class variable can be seen in Figure 23-3.

1. Create a file called var1.pl. Add the Fruit class from How-To 23.1.

```
use strict;

package Fruit;

sub new {
    my $class = shift;
    my $self = {};
```

```perl
    if (defined $_[0]) {
        $self->{Name} = shift;
    }
    if (defined $_[0]) {
        $self->{Weight} = shift;
    }
    if (defined $_[0]) {
        $self->{Cost} = shift;
    }
    bless $self, $class;
}

sub Cost {
    my $self = shift;

    $self->{Cost};
}

sub Name {
    my $self = shift;

    $self->{Name};
}
```

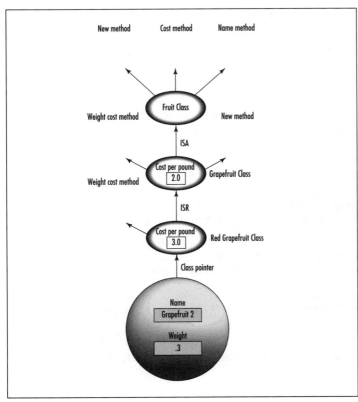

Figure 23-3 The classes with a class variable

2. Create a Grapefruit class that defines a class variable. Override the Cost method to use the class variable to determine the cost. Add a method to return the class variable.

```perl
package Grapefruit;

@Grapefruit::ISA = qw( Fruit );

$Grapefruit::CostPerPound = 2.0;

sub WeightCost {
    $Grapefruit::CostPerPound;
}

sub Cost {
    my $self = shift;

    $self->{Weight} * $self->WeightCost;
}
```

3. Add a RedGrapefruit class that is derived from the Grapefruit class. Add its own class variable and method to return that variable.

```perl
package RedGrapefruit;

@RedGrapefruit::ISA = qw( Grapefruit );

$RedGrapefruit::CostPerPound = 3.0;

sub WeightCost {
    $RedGrapefruit::CostPerPound;
}
```

4. Add two references to hold one of each type of grapefruit. Print the cost of each of the grapefruits. Change the cost per pound of the regular grapefruit and then print the grapefruit object's cost again.

```perl
package main;

my($apple) = new Fruit("Apple1", .1, .30);
my($grapefruit) = new Grapefruit("Grapefruit1", .3);
my($redgrapefruit) = new RedGrapefruit("Grapefruit2", .3);

print $apple->Name, " cost = ", $apple->Cost,"\n";
print $grapefruit->Name, " cost = ", $grapefruit->Cost,"\n";
print $redgrapefruit->Name, " cost = ", $redgrapefruit->Cost,"\n";

$Grapefruit::CostPerPound = 4.0;
print $grapefruit->Name, " cost = ", $grapefruit->Cost,"\n";

exit(0);
```

5. The entire script follows. The changes from How-To 23.1 are shown in bold.

```perl
use strict;
```

```
package Fruit;

sub new {
    my $class = shift;
    my $self = {};

    if (defined $_[0]) {
        $self->{Name} = shift;
    }
    if (defined $_[0]) {
        $self->{Weight} = shift;
    }
    if (defined $_[0]) {
        $self->{Cost} = shift;
    }
    bless $self, $class;
}

sub Cost {
    my $self = shift;

    $self->{Cost};
}

sub Name {
    my $self = shift;

    $self->{Name};
}

package Grapefruit;

@Grapefruit::ISA = qw( Fruit );

$Grapefruit::CostPerPound = 2.0;

sub WeightCost {
    $Grapefruit::CostPerPound;
}

sub Cost {
    my $self = shift;

    $self->{Weight} * $self->WeightCost;
}

package RedGrapefruit;

@RedGrapefruit::ISA = qw( Grapefruit );

$RedGrapefruit::CostPerPound = 3.0;

sub WeightCost {
    $RedGrapefruit::CostPerPound;
}

package main;
```

continued on next page

continued from previous page

```perl
my($apple) = new Fruit("Apple1", .1, .30);
my($grapefruit) = new Grapefruit("Grapefruit1", .3);
my($redgrapefruit) = new RedGrapefruit("Grapefruit2", .3);

print $apple->Name, " cost = ", $apple->Cost,"\n";
print $grapefruit->Name, " cost = ", $grapefruit->Cost,"\n";
print $redgrapefruit->Name, " cost = ", $redgrapefruit->Cost,"\n";

$Grapefruit::CostPerPound = 4.0;
print $grapefruit->Name, " cost = ", $grapefruit->Cost,"\n";

exit(0);
```

6. Run the script.

```perl
perl var1.pl
```

7. The output follows.

| Output |

```
Apple1 cost = 0.3
Grapefruit1 cost = 0.6
Grapefruit2 cost = 0.9
Grapefruit1 cost = 1.2
```

| End Output |

8. Create a file called var2.pl. Copy the contents of var1.pl into it. Change the WeightCost method in the Grapefruit class. Have it return the class variable from the class of the object that called it. The method may be called on behalf of an object or a class. The ref command returns the type of the reference. If the first argument is an object, it will return the object's class. If the return value from the ref command is False, the argument was not an object. In this case, assume it is the class name. (The method can be called as a static method on behalf of the class itself.) Remove the WeightCost method from the RedGrapefruit class.

```perl
sub WeightCost {
    my $class = ref($_[0]);

    unless ($class) {
        $class = $_[0];
    }
    no strict qw(refs);
    return ${"${class}::CostPerPound"};
}
```

9. Add a method to set the class variable of the calling class. It will be called only as a static class method.

```perl
sub SetWeightCost {
    my($class);

    $class = shift;
    no strict qw(refs);
    ${"${class}::CostPerPound"} = $_[0];
}
```

10. Change the main program to use this method.

```
Grapefruit->SetWeightCost(4.0);
```

11. The entire script follows. The changes are in bold.

```perl
use strict;

package Fruit;

sub new {
    my $class = shift;
    my $self = {};

    if (defined $_[0]) {
        $self->{Name} = shift;
    }
    if (defined $_[0]) {
        $self->{Weight} = shift;
    }
    if (defined $_[0]) {
        $self->{Cost} = shift;
    }
    bless $self, $class;
}

sub Cost {
    my $self = shift;

    $self->{Cost};
}

sub Name {
    my $self = shift;

    $self->{Name};
}

package Grapefruit;

@Grapefruit::ISA = qw( Fruit );

$Grapefruit::CostPerPound = 2.0;

sub WeightCost {
    my $class = ref($_[0]);

    unless ($class) {
        $class = $_[0];
    }
    no strict qw(refs);
    return ${"${class}::CostPerPound"};
}

sub SetWeightCost {
    my($class);

    $class = shift;
```

continued on next page

continued from previous page

```
      no strict qw(refs);
      ${"${class}::CostPerPound"} = $_[0];
}

sub Cost {
    my $self = shift;

    $self->{Weight} * $self->WeightCost;
}

package RedGrapefruit;

@RedGrapefruit::ISA = qw( Grapefruit );

$RedGrapefruit::CostPerPound = 3.0;

package main;

my($apple) = new Fruit("Apple1", .1, .30);
my($grapefruit) = new Grapefruit("Grapefruit1", .3);
my($redgrapefruit) = new RedGrapefruit("Grapefruit2", .3);

print $apple->Name, " cost = ", $apple->Cost,"\n";
print $grapefruit->Name, " cost = ", $grapefruit->Cost,"\n";
print $redgrapefruit->Name, " cost = ", $redgrapefruit->Cost,"\n";

Grapefruit->SetWeightCost(4.0);
print $grapefruit->Name, " cost = ", $grapefruit->Cost,"\n";

exit(0);
```

12. Run the script.

```
perl var2.pl
```

13. The output follows.

Output

```
Apple1 cost = 0.3
Grapefruit1 cost = 0.6
Grapefruit2 cost = 0.9
Grapefruit1 cost = 1.2
```

End Output

How It Works

A variable declared in a class (package) automatically becomes a class variable. Only variables that are stored in the objects are local to the objects. The class variables can be accessed using a fully qualified variable name or a static method that accesses the class variable.

The first example needs a WeightCost variable in both Grapefruit classes. This is because it refers to a local class variable. To have the method work in a derived class, the code is changed to

```
return ${"${class}::CostPerPound"};
```

This substitutes the class name of object for the

```
${class}
```

variable and appends on the class variable name. Putting this all in a string returns the fully qualified name for the class variable. The

```
${}
```

around the string causes the value of the appropriate class variable to be retrieved. All this works because the first argument to a method is an object or a class name. If it is an object, its class can be determined by using the ref command. This returns the class of the object even if it is a class derived from the class that is supplying the method being executed.

Comments

The first example directly changes the class variable.

```
$Grapefruit::CostPerPound = 4.0;
```

This is not a very object-oriented thing to do. It is better to create static class methods and use them instead. This is done in the second example.

```
Grapefruit->SetWeightCost(4.0);
```

There are two lines in the script that look like

```
no strict qw(refs);
```

These lines turn off strict checking of references for the rest of the method. Strict reference-checking does not allow you to access a string as a reference.

```
return ${"${class}::CostPerPound"};
```

The strict type-checking can catch hard-to-find errors. If the string used as a reference is misspelled, a new reference will spring into being and the script will continue. This can cause the script to fail in areas of the script that are far away from the source of the error.

If you are not creating large numbers of objects (so space is not a big concern), you may want to store a reference to the class variable in each object. This can make the script more straightforward and more efficient. The class variable could then be accessed directly from the object to read or set it. The method to set the class variable could then be called as a class method or as an object method. The changes to the last script to implement this follow.

```
use strict;

package Fruit;

sub new {
    my $class = shift;
    my $self = {};
```

continued on next page

continued from previous page

```perl
        if (defined $_[0]) {
            $self->{Name} = shift;
        }
        if (defined $_[0]) {
            $self->{Weight} = shift;
        }
        if (defined $_[0]) {
            $self->{Cost} = shift;
        }
        bless $self, $class;
}

sub Cost {
    my $self = shift;

    $self->{Cost};
}

sub Name {
    my $self = shift;

    $self->{Name};
}

package Grapefruit;

@Grapefruit::ISA = qw( Fruit );

$Grapefruit::CostPerPound = 2.0;

sub new {
    my $class = shift;

    my $self = new Fruit(@_);
    no strict qw(refs);
    $self->{WeightCost} = \${"${class}::CostPerPound"};

    bless $self, $class;
}

sub SetWeightCost {
    my $self = $_[0];
    my $class = ref($_[0]);

    if ($class) {
        ${$self->{WeightCost}} = $_[1];
    } else {
        $class = $_[0];
        no strict qw(refs);
        ${"${class}::CostPerPound"} = $_[1];
    }
}

sub Cost {
    my $self = shift;

    $self->{Weight} * ${$self->{WeightCost}};
}
```

```
package RedGrapefruit;

@RedGrapefruit::ISA = qw( Grapefruit );

$RedGrapefruit::CostPerPound = 3.0;

package main;

my($apple) = new Fruit("Apple1", .1, .30);
my($grapefruit) = new Grapefruit("Grapefruit1", .3);
my($redgrapefruit) = new RedGrapefruit("Grapefruit2", .3);

print $apple->Name, " cost = ", $apple->Cost,"\n";
print $grapefruit->Name, " cost = ", $grapefruit->Cost,"\n";
print $redgrapefruit->Name, " cost = ", $redgrapefruit->Cost,"\n";

Grapefruit->SetWeightCost(4.0);
print $grapefruit->Name, " cost = ", $grapefruit->Cost,"\n";

exit(0);
```

COMPLEXITY
BEGINNING

23.6 How do I...
Call a class method directly?

COMPATIBILITY: PERL 5 | UNIX | DOS

Problem

Sometimes I need to call a method in a parent class that has been overridden in a subclass. Can I do this in Perl?

Technique

Every method in Perl can be called directly. This is because each method has a fully qualified name (the package name followed by two colons and then the method name). Using the fully qualified name, you can call any method at any time. If a method is called in this manner, it must be passed the object or class name as the first argument. This is necessary because the object-oriented features of Perl are being bypassed.

Steps

The example in How-To 23.5 is modified to access an overridden base-class method. How-To 23.5 creates a Fruit class. This class creates fruit objects that have some local state (the fruit's name, weight, and cost). There are also two methods to return a fruit object's name and cost. There are two subclasses called Grapefruit and RedGrapefruit. For a grapefruit, the cost is based on its weight.

1. Create a file called direct.pl. Add the script from How-To 23.5. Add a line to call the base class's Cost method directly.

```perl
use strict;

package Fruit;

sub new {
    my $class = shift;
    my $self = {};

    if (defined $_[0]) {
        $self->{Name} = shift;
    }
    if (defined $_[0]) {
        $self->{Weight} = shift;
    }
    if (defined $_[0]) {
        $self->{Cost} = shift;
    }
    bless $self, $class;
}

sub Cost {
    my $self = shift;

    $self->{Cost};
}

sub Name {
    my $self = shift;

    $self->{Name};
}

package Grapefruit;

@Grapefruit::ISA = qw( Fruit );

$Grapefruit::CostPerPound = 2.0;

sub WeightCost {
    my $class = ref($_[0]);

    unless ($class) {
        $class = $_[0];
    }
    no strict qw(refs);
    return ${"${class}::CostPerPound"};
}

sub SetWeightCost {
    my($class);

    $class = shift;
    no strict qw(refs);
```

```
    ${"${class}::CostPerPound"} = $_[0];
}

sub Cost {
    my $self = shift;

    $self->{Weight} * $self->WeightCost;
}

package RedGrapefruit;

@RedGrapefruit::ISA = qw( Grapefruit );

$RedGrapefruit::CostPerPound = 3.0;

package main;

my($apple) = new Fruit("Apple1", .1, .30);
my($grapefruit) = new Grapefruit("Grapefruit1", .3);
my($redgrapefruit) = new RedGrapefruit("Grapefruit2", .3);

print $apple->Name, " cost = ", $apple->Cost,"\n";
print $grapefruit->Name, " cost = ", $grapefruit->Cost,"\n";
print $redgrapefruit->Name, " cost = ", $redgrapefruit->Cost,"\n";

Grapefruit->SetWeightCost(4.0);
print $grapefruit->Name, " cost = ", $grapefruit->Cost,"\n";

print "Grapefruit at Fruit cost = ", &Fruit::Cost($grapefruit), "\n";

exit(0);
```

2. Run the script.

```
perl direct.pl
```

3. The output follows.

Output

```
Apple1 cost = 0.3
Grapefruit1 cost = 0.6
Grapefruit2 cost = 0.9
Grapefruit1 cost = 1.2
Grapefruit at Fruit cost =
```

End Output

How It Works

The Fruit Cost method is directly invoked.

```
&Fruit::Cost($grapefruit)
```

The Cost method is not normally passed an argument. Because the object-oriented call is being bypassed, the object must be explicitly passed to the method. The output of the Cost method is the empty string.

```
Grapefruit at Fruit cost =
```

This is because the grapefruit object was created without a price being passed to it. Therefore, the object does not have a cost key in the associative array.

Comments

It is possible to call a method in an object-oriented fashion and still cause the method to be bypassed. The technique for doing this is to call a member function and tell Perl which class to start looking in for the method. For example, the following code tells Perl to start looking for the Cost method in the Fruit class.

```
print "Grapefruit at Fruit cost = ", $grapefruit->Fruit::Cost, "\n";
```

## CHAPTER 24

GRAPHIC USER INTERFACES

GRAPHIC USER INTERFACES

How do I...

Many die-hard Perl programmers who also know the Tcl/Tk language have been waiting on the edge of their seats for the Tk extension to Perl 5. Tk is an interpreted X Windows-based graphical language. Like Perl, Tk is a tool that allows programmers to create useful programs quickly. The only problem is that one must learn Tcl to use Tk. The Tk extension to Perl allows Perl programmers to create quick X-based scripts in a language they are comfortable with. This chapter outlines how to use the basic widgets and concepts of the Tk extension to Perl 5. The chapter is based on the assumption of some knowledge of the Tk programming language. Because Tk is such a comprehensive language, this chapter can only highlight certain elements of the Tk extension. We cannot dedicate enough page space to all the inner workings of Tk but throughout the chapter, we discuss concepts of Tk to help you create interesting graphic user interfaces. The purpose of this chapter is to get you interested in the Tk extension to Perl and give you a foundation of knowledge to grow from. Do not be discouraged if you do not know Tk. If so, compile the Tk extension into Perl 5 and play with the scripts. They will give you a good idea of what Tk is about. If you want to learn more about the Tk programming language, read the *Tcl and the Tk Toolkit* by John Ousterhout.

24.1 Use the Perl 5 Tk Extension

This How-To will outline the basics needed to use the Perl 5 Tk extension. It will also outline basic concepts of Tk so you can create your own Perl 5 Tk scripts.

24.2 Create a Dialog Box

Creating a dialog box is one of the most useful scripts. This How-To will demonstrate how to create a dialog box, set text in a dialog box, and add a button to a dialog box.

24.3 Create an Entry Field

An entry field is a widget that allows the user to type in information. This How-To will demonstrate how to use the Tk entry widget. It will also introduce the concept of binding events to actions and the use of frames and how they help you create interesting graphical user interfaces.

24.4 Create a Radio List

A radio list is a list that allows only one item in the group to be selected at once. This How-To will demonstrate the Tk radio list widget and how to use it.

24.5 Create a Check List

A check list is a group of items that can be turned off or on via buttons. This How-To will demonstrate the Tk check list widget and how to use it.

24.6 Create a List Box

The Tk list box is a widget that lists items. The list box allows items to be selected and events to be bound to certain actions. This How-To will demonstrate the Tk list box and some of the packing options.

24.7 Create a Scrolling List

Using the script from How-To 24.6, you will add scroll bars to the list box. This chapter will discuss the association of scroll bar widgets to other objects.

24.8 Create a Pull-Down Menu

Building on How-To 24.7, this How-To will add pull-down menus.

24.9 Create a File Viewer

Creating a file viewer is one of the most popular scripts when first learning Tk. This How-To will use a new widget called ScrlListbox, which makes this task very easy.

24.10 Create a File Selector

Creating a file selector is a popular script to write because Tk lacks a built-in file selector widget. For the first significant piece of Perl 5 Tk code, you will create a file selector and file viewer built into one.

24.11 Create a Canvas

One of the most interesting elements of the Tk programming language is the ability to create drawing canvases and manipulate drawn images. This How-To will create a canvas, draw a happy picture, and allow you to modify properties of the image drawn in the canvas.

COMPLEXITY

BEGINNING

24.1 How do I...
Use the Perl 5 Tk extension?

COMPATIBILITY: PERL 5   UNIX

Problem

I want to use the Perl 5 Tk extension but do not know what I need or how to use it. How do I get set up?

Technique

To be able to use the Perl 5 Tk extension, you should have the latest copy of the Tcl/Tk libraries compiled and installed. You also need the Perl 5 Tk extension compiled into Perl 5 and installed. If all the Tk and Perl 5 components are where they are supposed to be, then you are ready to start writing Perl 5 Tk scripts. If you do not know how to compile the Tk extension into Perl 5, look at Appendix B.

Steps

1. To use the Perl 5 Tk extension, use the Tk module. This is done by adding the line

```
use Tk;
```

to the top of the script. Some widgets, like the dialog box widget, require extra modules to be loaded. For example, if a script uses the dialog widget, then the line

```
require Tk::Dialog;
```

is needed at the top of the script.

2. All Tk scripts need a main top-level window. The main top-level window is created by calling the MainWindow->new() method and storing the result into a scalar variable. The following piece of Perl/Tk code demonstrates the creation of the main window.

```
$mainWindow = MainWindow->new();
```

3. Now that the main window exists, you can create any widget as a child of the main top-level window. For example, if you want to create a simple frame widget as a direct child of the main top-level window, you would do the following.

```
$frame = $mainWindow->Frame();
```

4. Add in any Perl/Tk code to complete the script.

5. Call the function MainLoop() so the event handler can handle the X events.

How It Works

When the main top-level window is created, the new method actually returns an object, or reference, to the main window. This object has a number of callable methods with which it can perform many tasks, one of which is to create a widget. Because Perl 5 has an object-oriented design, the Perl/Tk extension team made the Tk extension take advantage of these object-oriented capabilities and create objects with callable methods. A method is nothing more than another name for a function, but a method is not directly callable; it is callable only from the object it is associated with. This makes grouping similar functions together easy. For example, say the variable *$mainWindow* contains a reference to a main window object. Then one method you could call is Frame. The following line calls the method Frame from the *$mainWindow* object.

```
$frame = $mainWindow->Frame();
```

The reference stored in *$frame* is itself an object that has callable methods. Because a frame can have a child, like a top-level window can, the frame must provide the ability to create children from it. The following line calls the Label method from the object referenced in the *$frame* scalar variable.

```
$label = $frame->Label(-text => 'Hello World!', -relief => 'groove');
```

The reference stored in the *$label* variable is an object of type Label, which itself has callable methods. One of these is the method called pack. The pack method is Tk's way to pack widgets within a frame or window.

The following line states that the reference *$label* will pack itself to the top. The top in this case is the top of the frame referenced by the *$frame* variable.

```
$label->pack(-side => 'top');
```

Once all the widgets have been created and packed, control of the events is handed off to the X event handler. The call to MainLoop() performs this. The call to MainLoop() is the last thing that should be done in the script.

Comments

Throughout this chapter, you will see long lines split over several lines. They are still part of the same line but they are split for the sake of readability. The following line

```
$label    = $frame->Label(
    -text => "I like this book so much I\'m going to tell ",
    -relief => 'raised');
```

is exactly the same as

```
$label    = $frame->Label(-text => "I like this book so much I\'m going to
tell ", -relief => 'raised');
```

The former is just easier to read. This is a standard convention in native Tk scripts because widgets can have many options and this style improves readability.

COMPLEXITY
INTERMEDIATE

24.2   How do I...
Create a dialog box?

COMPATIBILITY: PERL 5   UNIX

Problem

I want to create a popup dialog box using the Perl 5 Tk extension but don't know how to do it. How do I make a popup dialog box?

Technique

To create a dialog box using the Perl 5 Tk extension, you need to include the Tk::Dialog extension in the script. If you don't do this, you cannot use the Tk dialog widget. After the Dialog module has been included, create the top-level window. From the top-level window, create the dialog widget. The dialog widget is actually created as a new window, so the dialog message and button are in a new window and not in the top-level window. After you create the dialog widget, call the show method off the dialog widget to activate the widget. This specific example also refines the personality of the dialog object via the configure method.

Steps

1. Edit a new file named dialog.tkp and type the following script into it.

```
#!/usr/local/bin/perl -w

# Require the Tk module.
use Tk;
```

continued on next page

continued from previous page

```
# Require the Tk::Dialog module
require Tk::Dialog;

# Get the message from the command line.
$message = join ("\n", @ARGV);

# Create the main window.
$mainWindow = MainWindow->new;

# Create the dialog window.
$dialog= $mainWindow->Dialog (
        -title => 'Perl5/Tk Dialog Window',
        -text => '',
        -default_button => '1',
        -buttons => ['OK']
        );

# Demonstrate the configure method off the dialog window.
$dialog->configure (
        -wraplength => '6i',
        -justify => 'center',
        -text => $message,
        -bg => 'blue',
        -fg => 'yellow');

# Make sure the dialog gets mapped.
$button = $dialog->show();
print "Button pressed.\n";
```

2. Run the script.

```
% chap_24/howto02/dialog.tkp 'This is a test' 'of the Perl5 Tk' 'Extension'
```

A window resembling Figure 24-1 should appear on the screen.

3. Press the OK button on the dialog box.

How It Works

Whenever a window is created in Tk, you must create a top-level window. How you use this window is, of course, your choice but you must create it. The line

```
$mainWindow = MainWindow->new;
```

Figure 24-1 Perl/Tk
dialog box

creates the main window. The call to MainWindow->new actually creates an object, which in this case is returned to the variable *$mainWindow*. This object is the top-level window for the current script. To create the dialog widget, call the Dialog method off the main window. Because dialog windows are popup standalone windows, the dialog message passed in off the command line is displayed in a new window, not in the top-level window. This is why two windows appear when this script is run. Create the dialog window with the call

```
$dialog= $mainWindow->Dialog (
      -title => 'Perl5/Tk Dialog Window',
      -text => '',
      -default_button => '1',
      -buttons => ['OK']);
```

This line sets the dialog window title to Perl5/Tk Dialog Window with the -title option. It also sets the buttons that are to be on the dialog box, which in this case is simply the OK button. Set the message and colors of the dialog box by the configure method off the dialog object. The following line calls the configure method.

```
$dialog->configure (
      -wraplength => '6i',
      -justify => 'center',
      -text => $message,
      -bg => 'blue',
      -fg => 'yellow');
```

Finally, to display the dialog window, call the show method. The following line maps the dialog window.

```
$button = $dialog->show();
```

Comments

Not every object has the configure method; refer to the Tk manual for more detailed information on which widgets have which methods.

COMPLEXITY
INTERMEDIATE

24.3   How do I...
Create an entry field?

COMPATIBILITY: PERL 5   UNIX

Problem

I need to let the users type information into a field to retrieve the information they entered. How do I do this and what widget do I use?

Technique

The sample script uses the entry widget to get information from a user. This script displays a window and requests the user to type in a small message. After the user has pressed (ENTER), the script prints out the message the user just typed in. The popup window has both a label widget, to display the instruction *Type In A Short Message,* and an entry field, to get the information the user types in. Because this script uses two widgets, we decided to use a frame to maintain order in the window. When a widget is created, it is then packed into the window. When an object is packed, you have to tell Tk how and where to put the object within the window. For example, if you want to create a script that has a label field as a title that spans the window, a label on the bottom-left corner of the window, and an entry field on the bottom right of the window, frames make this task simple. Figure 24-2 is an example of an empty Tk top-level window with nothing in it.

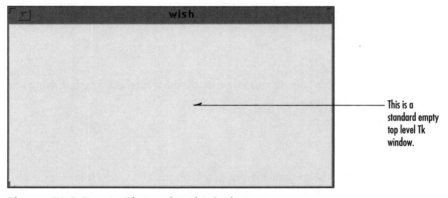

This is a standard empty top level Tk window.

Figure 24-2 Empty Tk top-level window

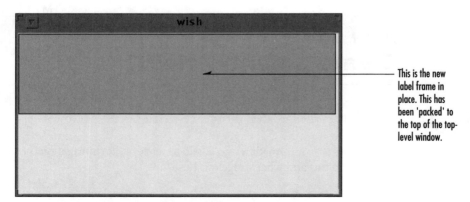

This is the new label frame in place. This has been 'packed' to the top of the top-level window.

Figure 24-3 Label frame packed into place

Using frames makes it easy to pack three objects within the window. The first frame is the frame for the label, which is the title. Figure 24-3 shows how this frame is packed to the top of the window.

Next, create a frame for both the label field and the entry field. This is also packed to the top of the window. Figure 24-4 demonstrates this.

Because the first frame has already been packed to the top, the second frame is packed underneath it. This is what you want because you want the title to go at the top of the window. Next, create the objects and pack them in their frames. The title label gets packed into the top frame, as shown in Figure 24-5.

The entry field label and entry field are packed into the second frame. Because you already established that the label will be on the left, pack the label to the left. Figure 24-6 demonstrates the label field getting packed into its frame.

The last object to be added is the entry widget. It is packed on the right side of the lower frame. Figure 24-7 shows where the final piece fits and what the whole window looks like.

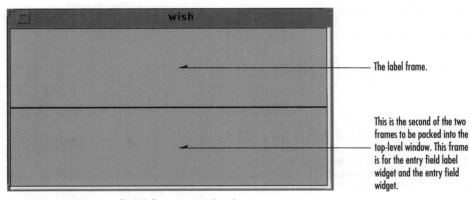

The label frame.

This is the second of the two frames to be packed into the top-level window. This frame is for the entry field label widget and the entry field widget.

Figure 24-4 Entry field frame packed

Figure 24-5 Label widget packed

Figure 24-6 Label widget packed

Figure 24-7 Entry widget packed

This is how using frames can create somewhat complex interfaces. Of course, you could re-create this script without frames, but we prefer to use them in case a last-minute change needs to be made. For example, if you want to put the title on the bottom, then all you would have to do is pack the entry frame first, then the top title frame. Encapsulating associated objects within frames makes it very easy to modify and manipulate the interface.

Steps

1. Edit a new file named entry.tkp and type the following script into it.

```perl
#!/usr/local/bin/perl -w

# Require the Tk module.
use Tk;

# Set the initial value of the entry field from the command line.
$mesg = join (" ", @ARGV) if @ARGV;

# Create the main window.
$mainWindow = MainWindow->new();

# Basic subroutine which prints out a message, then exits.
sub leaveScript
{
    print "You typed in '$mesg'\n";
    exit;
}

# Create a frame to put the label in.
$frame    = $mainWindow->Frame();

# Create and pack the label.
$label    = $frame->Label(-text => 'Type In A Short Message : ');
$label->pack(-side => 'left');

# Create and pack the entry field.
$entry    = $frame->Entry(-textvariable => \$mesg);
$entry->pack(-side => 'right');
$entry->bind ('<Return>' => \&leaveScript );
$entry->configure (-width => 50);

# Now pack the frame.
$frame->pack;

# Let the user interact with the widget...
MainLoop();
```

2. Run this script.

```
% chap_24/howto03/entry.tkp
```

A window resembling Figure 24-8 should appear on the screen.

Figure 24-8 Perl/Tk entry window

Figure 24-9 Perl/Tk entry field

3. Type in a message. The image in Figure 24-9 demonstrates what the entry field looks like after a small message has been typed in.

How It Works

After the top-level window is created, create a frame that contains both the entry field and the label. Create the frame with the line

```
$frame = $mainWindow->Frame();
```

This line states that the frame, which is stored in the variable *$frame*, is associated with the top-level window. More specifically, the frame is a child of the top-level window. The entry field label is created as a child of the frame and is packed to the left side of the frame.

```
$label = $frame->Label(-text => 'Type In A Short Message : ');
$label->pack(-side => 'left');
```

The entry field is also a child of the frame and is packed to the right side of the frame.

```
$entry = $frame->Entry(-textvariable => \$mesg);
$entry->pack(-side => 'right');
```

The parameter -textvariable states which variable will contain the value of the typed input. This gives you access to information in the field of the entry field. The -textvariable message gives you access not only after the information has been typed in but before as well. If you set the value of *$mesg* before the entry field window is drawn, the entry field displays the value given to *$mesg*. This allows you to create a default value within the entry field before the user types anything into it. Notice the line in the script

```
$mesg = join (" ", @ARGV) if @ARGV;
```

This line sets the value of *$mesg* from the command line. This allows you to set the default value of the entry field from the command line. The image in Figure 24-10 demonstrates the above script being run with the following command line options.

```
% chap_24/howto03/entry.tkp This message was passed in from the command
line.
```

Figure 24-10 Perl/Tk entry field

The line

```
$entry->bind ('<Return>' => \&leaveScript );
```

allows you to bind actions to events. The above example states that when the user presses the [ENTER] key, the function named leaveScript is called. A large number of bindings can be made: for each alphanumeric character, for mouse movements, and even for mouse button presses. The function leaveScript prints out the value of the variable *$mesg* and exits the script.

The last line in the script

```
MainLoop();
```

tells the Perl 5 Tk extension to start polling for events. Because X is an event-driven system, the programs need to let X take control of the events. This is what the MainLoop() call does.

Comments

Because the example in this How-To has only two widgets, the frame is excessive. Actually, the objects can be packed directly within the window instead of in the frame.

COMPLEXITY
INTERMEDIATE

24.4 How do I...
Create a radio list?

COMPATIBILITY: PERL 5   UNIX

Problem

I need to create a window that allows me to give the user a list of choices but allows the user to select only one option at a time. How do I do this?

Technique

There is a widget in Tk called Radiobutton that creates a radio list. It's called a *radio list* after the radios in old cars with the push-button channel selectors. These radios allow only one button to be pushed in at a time. When another button is selected, the current button pops out. This script asks a question and provides a radio list for a response. This script has a label at the top of the window that provides the question. The answers are in the radio list. There is also a push button at the bottom of the window to press when selecting an answer. When the answer has been selected and the button at the bottom of the window has been pressed, a response confirming the user's answer is printed out.

Steps

1. Edit a new file named radio.tkp and type the following script into it.

```perl
#!/usr/local/bin/perl -w

# Require the Tk module.
use Tk;

# Create the main window.
$mainWindow = MainWindow->new();

# Create the list of button labels (and values).
@buttonLabels = qw (Great Tremendous Stunning Informative);
$buttonCount = 0;

# Create a frame.
$frame = $mainWindow->Frame();

# Create a label.
$label = $frame->Label(
    -text => 'How Do You Rate This Book?',
    -relief => 'groove');
$label->pack(-side => 'top');

# Set the default button.
$choice = $buttonLabels[0];

# Create the buttons for the radio list...
foreach $button (sort @buttonLabels)
{
    # Create a radio button.
    $buttonList[$buttonCount] = $frame->Radiobutton (
     -text => $button,
     -value => $button,
     -variable => \$choice);

    # Pack the radio button in the main frame.
    $buttonList[$buttonCount]->pack(-side => 'top', -anchor => 'w');

    # Don't forget to increment the button count.
    $buttonCount++;
}

# Create a push button.
$pushButton = $frame->Button(
    -text => 'Push Me',
    -command => sub { print "Thank you! We think it's $choice as well.\n";
$mainWindow->destroy(); exit;} );
$pushButton->pack (
    -side => 'top',
    -expand => 'yes',
```

continued on next page

continued from previous page

```
    -fill => 'x');

# Now pack the frame.
$frame->pack;

# Let the user interact with the widget...
MainLoop();
```

2. Run the script.

```
% chap_24/howto04/radio.tkp
```

A window resembling Figure 24-11 should appear on the screen.

How It Works

The radio buttons are created within the *foreach* loop in the middle of the script. Each radio button object is stored into the array @buttonList. The following line creates each radio button.

```
$buttonList[$buttonCount] = $frame->Radiobutton (
    -text => $button,
    -value => $button,
    -variable => \$choice);
```

Because each radio button is associated with another, a common thread must tie them together. This thread is established with the -variable option. The -variable option accepts a reference to a variable name in which this button will be writing and reading data. In this example, the variable is named *$choice*. The -value option tells you which button is currently highlighted. When a button is pressed, the variable associated with this radio list is assigned a value. The value is given from the value of the -value option from the radio list. The value assigned to the button must be unique from the other buttons. Otherwise, all the buttons that share the same value will appear to be selected when a common button is selected. After being created, the button is then packed in the radio list frame. Just like with the entry field, you can assign a default button by giving the radio list variable an initial value. The script assigns the radio list's default value on the line

```
$choice = $buttonLabels[0];
```

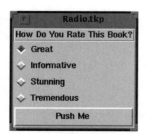

Figure 24-11 Perl/Tk radio list

The push button is created after all the radio list buttons are created. The push button is created with the line

```
$pushButton = $frame->Button(
    -text => 'Push Me',
    -command => sub { print "Thank you! We think it's $choice as well.\n";
$mainWindow->destroy(); exit;} );
```

The -command option happens when the push button is pushed. In this case, the user's choice is affirmed and the top-level window is destroyed using the destroy method. Then the whole script exits.

COMPLEXITY
INTERMEDIATE

24.5 How do I...
Create a check list?

COMPATIBILITY: PERL 5   UNIX

Problem

I need to be able to provide a method so users can pick from a list where more than one choice is acceptable. How do I do this?

Technique

A widget in Tk called Checkbutton provides this capability. The check button widget and the radio button widget are very similar in nature. The check button allows the user to select more than one option. When a button is selected, the button turns a different color than the default unselected color. The script in this How-To asks a question followed by four choices to select from. It also has a push button that allows the user to signify that he or she has made all the selections.

Steps

1. Edit a new file named check.tkp and type the following script into it.

```
#!/usr/local/bin/perl -w

# Require the Tk module.
use Tk;

# Create the main window.
$mainWindow = MainWindow->new();

# Create the list of button labels (and values).
@buttonLabels = ("my friends.", "my parrot Gizmo.", "my grandma, she's a
computer whiz.", "the prime minister.");
@buttonValues = qw (1 0 0 0);
$buttonCount = 0;
```

continued on next page

continued from previous page

```
# A simple subroutine...
sub thankyou
{
    print "Thank you. We appreciate you telling ";

    for ($x=0; $x <= $#buttonLabels; $x++)
    {
        print "$buttonLabels[$x], " if $buttonValues[$x] == 1;
    }
    print "\n";

    # Exit the script.
    $mainWindow->destroy();
    exit;
}

# Create a frame.
$frame    = $mainWindow->Frame();

# Create a label for the window.
$label    = $frame->Label(
    -text => "I like this book so much I\'m going to tell ",
    -relief => 'raised');
$label->pack(-side => 'top', -expand => 'x');

# Create the buttons for the selection list...
foreach $button (@buttonLabels)
{
    # Create the buttons.
    $buttonList[$buttonCount] = $frame->Checkbutton (
     -text => $button,
     -variable => \$buttonValues[$buttonCount]);

    # Pack the buttons
    $buttonList[$buttonCount]->pack(
     -side => 'top',
     -anchor => 'w',
     -expand => 'x');

    # Don't forget to increment the button count.
    $buttonCount++;
}

# Create a push button.
$pushButton = $frame->Button(-text => 'Push Me', -command => \&thankyou );
$pushButton->pack (-side => 'top', -expand => 'yes', -fill => 'x');

# Now pack the frame.
$frame->pack;

# Let the user interact with the widget...
MainLoop();
```

2. Run the script.

```
% chap_24/howto05/check.tkp
```

A window resembling Figure 24-12 should appear on the screen.

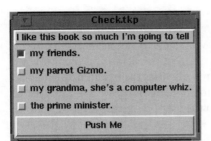

Figure 24-12 Perl/Tk check list

How It Works

Just like the radio list, the main core of the code rests in the *foreach* loop in the center of the script. The check buttons are created on the line

```
$buttonList[$buttonCount] = $frame->Checkbutton (
    -text => $button,
    -variable => \$buttonValues[$buttonCount]);
```

Notice that one very distinct difference between radio lists and check lists is that check lists do not share a common variable. Each check button has its own variable. The check list buttons also do not get a defined alphanumeric value. If the button is selected, its variable is assigned a value of 1; it is assigned 0 otherwise. To assign default buttons to be highlighted, all you need to do is assign each a variable to each button's corresponding variable. The default buttons are set at the top of the script in this instance. The line

```
@buttonValues = qw (1 0 0 0);
```

turns on the first button, which is my friends, by default and leaves the others off.

Comments

Notice the difference in appearance between the buttons on a radio list and those on a check list. The radio list has diamonds by default, whereas check list has squares by default

COMPLEXITY
INTERMEDIATE

24.6   How do I...
Create a list box?

COMPATIBILITY: PERL 5   UNIX

Problem

I need to display a list of items but do not know how to do it. Which Tk widget can I use to do this?

Technique

The list box widget allows you to display a list of items to a user. The script in this How-To allows the user to create a list of items from the command line, which is then displayed in a Tk list box widget. The script also uses the bind function to bind the action of double-clicking on the left button to print out the currently selected item. A push button is also provided so when the user presses the push button, the current selection prints out.

Steps

1. Edit a new file named listbox.tkp and type the following script into it.

```perl
#!/usr/local/bin/perl -w

# Require the needed modules.
use Tk;

# Create the main window.
$mainWindow = MainWindow->new;

# Create the list box.
$listbox = $mainWindow->Listbox();

# Fill in the list.
$listbox->insert('end',@ARGV);
$listbox->configure (-width => 50);

# Create a button.
$pushButton = $mainWindow->Button(
    -text => 'Push Me',
    -command => sub { print "You chose " . $listbox->get('active')."\n"; } );
$pushButton->pack (-side => 'top', -fill => 'x');

# Pack in the list and the button.
$listbox->pack (-side => 'top', -expand => 'yes', -fill => 'both');
$listbox->bind ('<Double-Button-1>' => sub { print "You just double clicked
on " . $listbox->get('active') . "\n"; } );

# Set 1st entry as default.
$listbox->activate(0);

# Let the user interact with the widget...
MainLoop();
```

2. Run the above script

```
% chap_24/howto06/listbox.tkp ~/local/Tk-b8/*
```

A window resembling Figure 24-13 should appear on the screen.

Figure 24-13 Perl/Tk list box

How It Works

The list box widget is created with the line

```
$listbox = $mainWindow->Listbox();
```

Its contents are filled with the line

```
$listbox->insert('end',@ARGV);
```

which fills the list box with the values in the array @ARGV. The line actually fills the list box from the bottom up. This is stated by the end keyword in the insert method. The list box can be emptied with the delete keyword. This method accepts two parameters: the starting point in the list to delete from and the ending point to delete from. An example of deleting the above list box is

```
$listbox->delete ('0', 'end');
```

which states, "delete from the 0th element to the end of the list."

To get the currently selected item from a list box, use the method named get. The following line from the above script binds the action of double-clicking the mouse button to printing out the current selection.

```
$listbox->bind ('<Double-Button-1>' => sub { print "You just double clicked
on " . $listbox->get('active') . "\n"; } );
```

The get method is called with the parameter active, which tells the method to return the currently selected row. It returns the information from the list box, not an index into the list box.

This script (like all the others in this chapter) requires a top-level window. The list box is created within the top-level window, as is the push button. To add some variety to this section, we put the push button at the top of the window instead of the bottom. The list box is packed under the push-button widget. The button is created off the top-level window and is packed to the top of the top-level window. The line

```
$pushButton->pack (-side => 'top', -fill => 'x');
```

states that the push button is packed to the top and fills the x direction of the window. This is apparent by the image supplied above. Another option is used largely in conjunction with the -fill option: the -expand option. You should fully understand this option before using it. The -expand option states that as the window is resized, the widget appropriately expands in both the x and y directions. In some cases, this may be desired; in some, it may not. For example, if you stretch the above window in both the x and y directions, the window will end up looking like Figure 24-14.

The button maintains the full width of the window as dictated by the -fill option. Notice that the -pack option does not use the -expand option on the push button but does on the list box. You want the list box to expand as much as possible to display as much information as possible. On the other hand, the push button does not need to do this, so we omitted this option when packing the button. If the line

```
$pushButton->pack (-side => 'top', -fill => 'x');
```

is changed to

```
$pushButton->pack (-side => 'top', -fill => 'x', -expand => 'yes');
```

and you run the script and stretch the window once again, the result is something like Figure 24-15.

Notice that the push button now has expanded in both the x and y directions, using valuable window real estate. This is why -expand option is not automatic when using the -fill option.

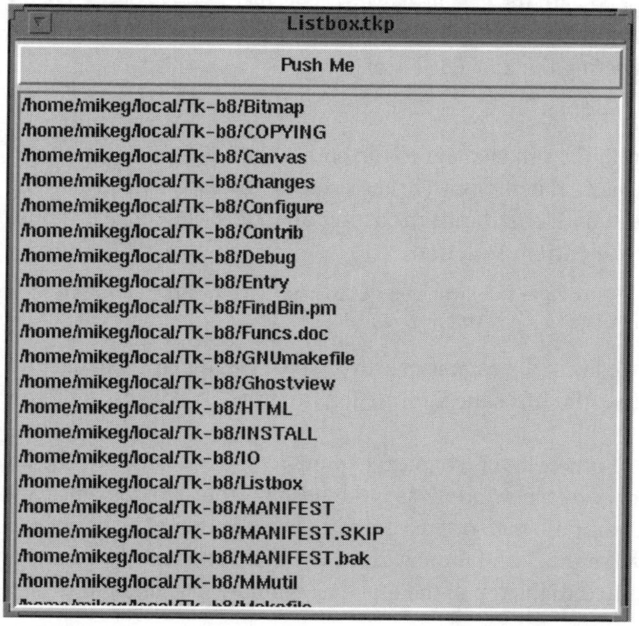

Figure 24-14 Perl/Tk list box

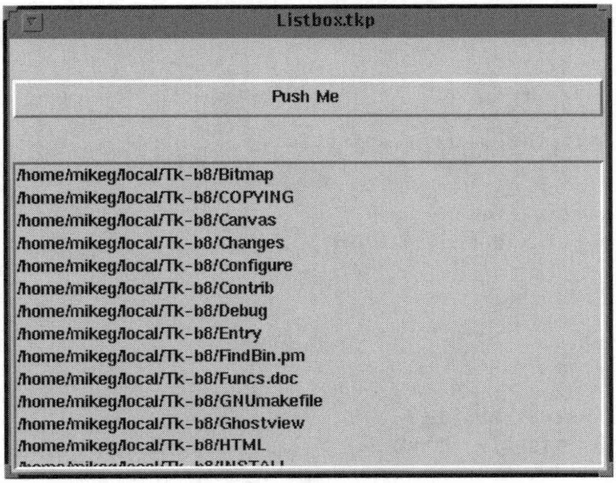

Figure 24-15 Perl/Tk list box

Comments

Notice that the list box displays only as much as it can. The list we supplied to the list box exceeds the displayed information. This list box requires scroll bars. To scan through the complete list box, press and hold mouse button 2 and drag the mouse up and down.

COMPLEXITY
INTERMEDIATE

24.7 How do I...
Create a scrolling list?

COMPATIBILITY: PERL 5   UNIX

Problem

I have a list box with a list of items larger than the window. How do I add a scrolling bar to the list box so the user can easily scroll through the items in the list box?

Technique

To attach a scrolling list to a list box, use the scroll widget. Create the scroll widget and then make an association between the scrolling list and the scrolling object.

Steps

1. Edit a new file named scroll.tkp and type the following script into it.

```perl
#!/usr/local/bin/perl

# Require the Tk module.
use Tk;

# This subroutine prints out the current selection.
sub current
{
    my $file = $listbox->get('active');
    print "You just double clicked on $file \n";
}

# Create the main window.
$mainWindow = MainWindow->new;

# Create the Y axis scroll bar.
$yscrollbar = $mainWindow->Scrollbar();
$yscrollbar->pack(-side => 'right', -fill => 'y');

# Create the list box.
$listbox = $mainWindow->Listbox(
    -yscrollcommand => ['set'=> $yscrollbar],
    -relief => 'sunken',
    -width => 50,
    -height => 20,
    -setgrid => 'yes');

# Fill in the list
$listbox->insert('end',@ARGV);

# Pack in the list
$listbox->pack (-side => 'left', -fill => 'both', -expand => 'yes');

# Bind a double click to an action.
$listbox->bind ('<Double-Button-1>' => \&current );

# Set 1st entry as default.
$listbox->activate(0);

# Configure the scroll bar.
$yscrollbar->configure(-command => ['yview', $listbox]);

# Let the user interact with the widget...
MainLoop();
```

2. Run the script.

```
% chap_24/howto07/scroll.tkp ~/local/Tk-b8/*
```

A window resembling Figure 24-16 should appear on the screen.

If you grab the scroll bar on the right side of the window and drag it to the bottom of the window, you will notice that the items scroll in the list box. If you do this, then you should see something similar to Figure 24-17.

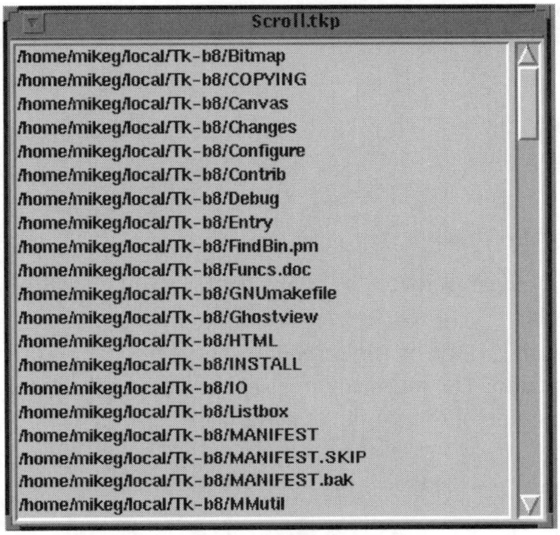

Figure 24-16 Perl/Tk scrolling list

How It Works

The scroll bars are created within the top-level window, as well as within the list box. This means the scroll bar and the list box are two unassociated widgets. An association between the list box and scroll bar has to be made, which is done by telling the list box what commands to issue when the scroll bar is scrolled. The association on the list box side is performed in the creation of the list box object. The option -yscrollcommand tells the list box what to do when the list box is redrawn in the y direction.

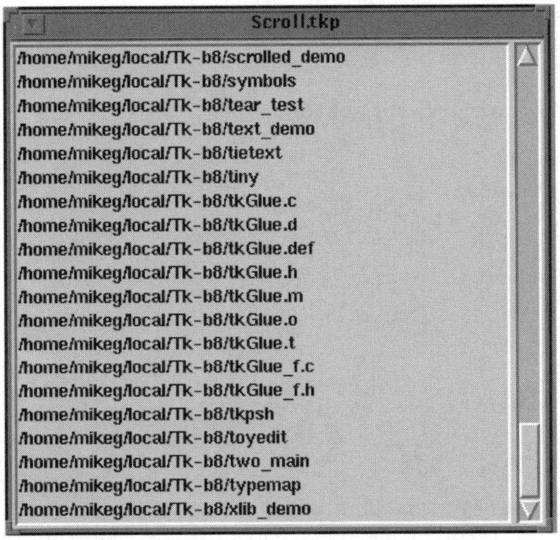

Figure 24-17 Perl/Tk scrolling list

```
$listbox = $mainWindow->Listbox(
        -yscrollcommand => ['set'=> $yscrollbar],
        -relief => 'sunken',
        -width => 50,
        -height => 20,
        -setgrid => 'yes');
```

Specifically, the option

```
-yscrollcommand => ['set'=> $yscrollbar]
```

tells the list box that, on any movement in the y direction, set the scroll bar object referenced by the variable *$yscrollbar*.

The other half of this association is done by the scroll bar. The scroll bar widget is told which widget it is associated to. The following lines of code create the scroll bar object and pack it to the right side of the top-level window.

```
$yscrollbar = $mainWindow->Scrollbar();
$yscrollbar->pack(-side => 'right', -fill => 'y');
```

The association from scroll bar to list box is made on the line

```
$yscrollbar->configure(-command => ['yview', $listbox]);
```

This line specifically states that the scroll bar object referenced by the variable *$yscrollbar* is linked to the yview scroll of the object referenced by the variable *$listbox*. This is the complete link between the scroll bar and the list box.

Comments

A horizontal scroll bar can be added as well. The following script is a modification of the script chap_24/howto07/scroll.tkp. Additions are in bold for clarity.

```
#!/usr/local/bin/perl -w

# Require the Tk module.
use Tk;

# This subroutine prints out the current selection.
sub current
{
    my $file = $listbox->get('active');
    print "You just double clicked on $file \n";
}

# Create the main window.
$mainWindow = MainWindow->new;

# Create the Y axis scroll bar.
$yscrollbar = $mainWindow->Scrollbar();
$yscrollbar->pack(-side => 'right', -fill => 'y');

# Create the X axis scroll bar.
$xscrollbar = $mainWindow->Scrollbar();
$xscrollbar->pack(-side => 'bottom', -fill => 'x', -orient => 'horizontal');
```

```
# Create the list box.
$listbox = $mainWindow->Listbox(
    -yscrollcommand => ['set'=> $yscroll bar],
    -xscrollcommand => ['set'=> $xscroll bar],
    -relief => 'sunken',
    -width => 50,
    -height => 20,
    -setgrid => 'yes');

# Fill in the list.
$listbox->insert('end',@ARGV);

# Pack in the list.
$listbox->pack (-side => 'left', -fill => 'both', -expand => 'yes');

# Bind a double click to an action.
$listbox->bind ('<Double-Button-1>' => \&current );

# Set 1st entry as default.
$listbox->activate(0);

# Configure the scroll bars
$yscrollbar->configure(-command => ['yview', $listbox]);
$xscrollbar->configure(-command => ['xview', $listbox]);

# Let the user interact with the widget...
MainLoop();
```

Running the script should reveal something similar to Figure 24-18.

Figure 24-18 Perl/Tk scrolling list

24.8   How do I...
Create a pull-down menu?

COMPATIBILITY: PERL 5   UNIX

Problem

I want to add pull-down menus to my Tk script. How do I do this?

Technique

To create pull-down menus in Tk scripts, use the menu button widget. This widget allows the user to create pull-down menus and the lists under the buttons. It also allows you to associate actions with the submenus. The script in this section is a modification of the script in How-To 24.7. The additions allow the user to open a file in the list box or quit the script.

Steps

1. Edit a new file named menu.tkp and type the following script into it.

```perl
#!/usr/local/bin/perl -w

# Require the Tk module.
use Tk;

# Turn off buffering.
$|=1;

# This subroutine opens the given file for viewing.
sub openFile
{
    my $filename = $listbox->get('active');

    # Check if this is a text file.
    if ( -d $filename )
    {
        print "File is a directory.\n";
    }
    elsif ( -B $filename )
    {
        print "Cannot display binary files.\n";
    }
    else
    {
        open (FILE, "$filename");
        while (<FILE>)
        {
            print $_;
        }
    }
}
```

```perl
# This displays basic information about this tool.
sub about
{
    print "Written by Mike Glover\n";
}

# Create the main window.
$mainWindow = MainWindow->new;

# Create a menu bar frame.
$menuBar = $mainWindow->Frame;
$menuBar->pack(-side => 'top', -fill => 'x');

# Create a File menu.
$fileMenu = $menuBar->Menubutton(-text => 'File', -underline => 0);
$fileMenu->command( -label => 'Open', -underline => 0, -command => \&openFile
                );
$fileMenu->command( -label => 'Quit', -underline => 0, -command => sub { exit;
                } );
$fileMenu->pack(-side => 'left');

# Create a Help menu.
$helpMenu = $menuBar->Menubutton(-text => 'Help', -underline => 0);
$helpMenu->command( -label => 'About', -underline => 0, -command => \&about );
$helpMenu->pack(-side => 'right');

# Create the Y axis scroll bar.
$yscrollbar = $mainWindow->Scrollbar();
$yscrollbar->pack(-side => 'right', -fill => 'y');

# Create the list box.
$listbox = $mainWindow->Listbox(
    -yscrollcommand => ['set'=> $yscrollbar],
    -relief => 'sunken',
    -width => 50,
    -height => 20,
    -setgrid => 'yes');

# Fill in the list.
$listbox->insert('end',@ARGV);

# Pack in the list.
$listbox->pack (-side => 'left', -fill => 'both', -expand => 'yes');

# Bind a double click to an action.
$listbox->bind ('<Double-Button-1>' => \&openFile );

# Set 1st entry as default.
$listbox->activate(0);

# Configure the scroll bar.
$yscrollbar->configure(-command => ['yview', $listbox]);

# Let the user interact with the widget...
MainLoop();
```

2. Run the script.

```
% chap_24/howto08/menu.tkp ~/local/Tk-b8/*
```

A window resembling Figure 24-19 should appear on the screen.

How It Works

As mentioned before, this script is a modification of the script in How-To 24.7. The additions allow the user to open a file or quit the interface using a pull-down menu. Each pull-down menu is created using the menu button widget; each submenu is then attached to the pull-down menu. The following line from the script creates the File menu.

```
$fileMenu = $menuBar->Menubutton(-text => 'File', -underline => 0);
```

The -underline option is an integer that corresponds to a character in the button label name. This character is the acceleration character, which allows the user to pull down the menu buttons using the keyboard. In the above case, the letter F is underlined, and the key sequence ALT-F displays the pull-down menu under the File menu button. To add the items under the File button, call the method command. The following two lines add two submenus, Open and Quit, to the File menu.

```
$fileMenu->command( -label => 'Open', -underline => 0, -command => \&openFile
);
$fileMenu->command( -label => 'Quit', -underline => 0, -command => sub { exit;
} );
```

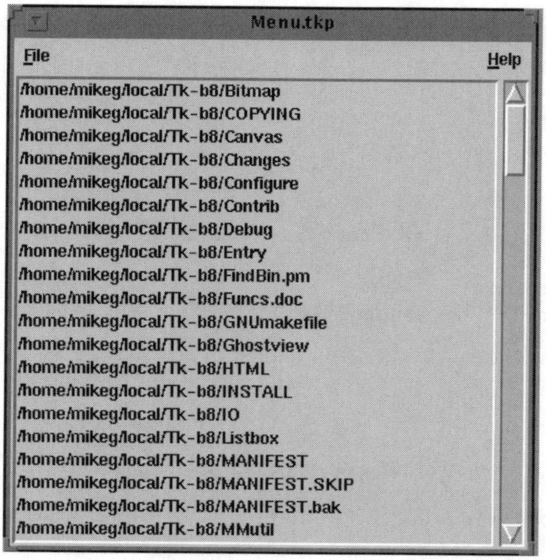

Figure 24-19 Perl/Tk pull-down menus

As with the main menu button, the -underline marks the character to use to accelerate to this option using the keyboard. The -command option states what to do when this option has been selected. Notice that the -command option for the Open submenu is given a reference to a function, whereas the Quit submenu is given a reference to an anonymous subroutine. The File button is then packed to the left side of the window by the line

```
$fileMenu->pack(-side => 'left');
```

The Help submenu is packed to the right side of the window by the line

```
$helpMenu->pack(-side => 'right');
```

If you move the cursor to the File option and pull down, you should see something like Figure 24-20.

Comments

The dotted line you see on the File menu is what Tk calls a *tear-off menu*. If you click the left mouse button on the dotted line and move the mouse, the menu will tear off and get its own window. If you tear off the File menu from Figure 24-20, then you will get a window that looks like Figure 24-21.

Tear-off menus are useful because they provide the ability to keep a menu up all the time. When a menu is torn from the window, it gets its own window and remains up.

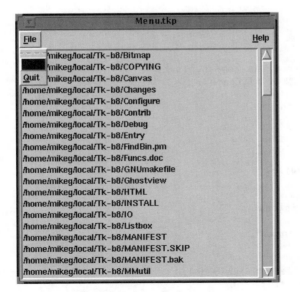

Figure 24-20 Perl/Tk pull-down menus

Figure 24-21
Menu list
tear-off
menu

24.9   How do I...
Create a file viewer?

COMPATIBILITY: PERL 5   UNIX

Problem

I want to create a simple file viewer. I am having problems creating a list box with both x and y axis scroll bars. How can I create a simple file viewer?

Technique

This script accepts a filename from the command line, reads the contents of the file into an array, and then fills the list box with the contents of the array. Instead of using the list box widget to perform this task, use the widget named ScrlListbox. This widget resembles the list box widget, but it is much easier to add scroll bars to this widget. In fact, this widget has an option named -scrollbars that dictates where the scroll bars, if any, are to be. Once the scrolling list box widget is created, the file is read and inserted into the widget.

Steps

1. Edit a new file named fileview.tkp and type the following script into it.

```perl
#!/usr/local/bin/perl -w

# Require the Tk module.
use Tk;

# Get the filename to view from the command line.
$filename = $ARGV[0] || die "$0: filename";

# Open the file and read it in.
open (FILE, "$filename");
@contents = <FILE>;

# Create the main window.
$mainWindow = MainWindow->new();

# Create a scrolling list box.
$scroll = $mainWindow->ScrlListbox(
    -scrollbars => 'se',
    -label => "Viewing: $filename",
    -height => 30,
    -width => 50);
$scroll->configure(-label_relief => 'raised');
$scroll->insert('end', @contents);
$scroll->pack(-side => left, -expand => 1, -fill => 'both');
```

```
# Let the user play...
MainLoop();
```

2. Run the script on itself.

```
% chap_24/howto09/fileview.tkp chap_24/howto09/fileview.tkp
```

A window resembling Figure 24-22 should appear on the screen.

How It Works

All the work in this script is performed by the scrolling list box widget. This one widget makes creating list boxes with scrolling bars easy. The line

```
$scroll = $mainWindow->ScrlListbox(
    -scrollbars => 'se',
    -label => "Viewing: $filename",
    -height => 30,
    -width => 50);
```

creates the scrolling list box widget and assigns the scroll bars in one statement. The option

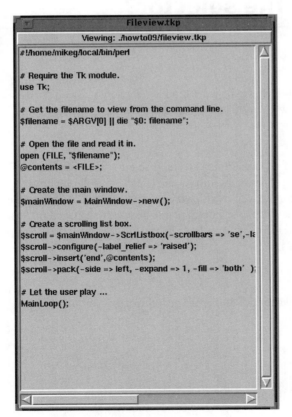

Figure 24-22 Scrolling list window

-scrollbars specifies where the scroll bars are to be placed. In this example, the scroll bars are placed in the south and east walls of the window. This gives you scroll bars on the right wall of the window and the bottom of the window. If you use nw instead, scroll bars are placed on the left wall and the top of the window.

Because this widget is a list box, filling the list box is performed the same way as filling a normal list box. The following line fills the ScrlListbox object with the information from the array @contents.

```
$scroll->insert('end', @contents);
```

Comments

The option -scrollbars can accept values that specify one scroll bar only. The values n, e, s, and w put a scroll bar on the top, right, bottom, and left walls, respectively.

COMPLEXITY
ADVANCED

24.10 How do I...
Create a file selector?

COMPATIBILITY: PERL 5   UNIX

Problem

The standard installation of Tk seems to be lacking a file selection widget. I need to write one but do not know how. How do I write one using the Perl 5 Tk extension?

Technique

This script is a combination of all the scripts presented so far in this chapter. The ScrlListbox widget is used for the files in the current directory. The pull-down menu is managed by the menu button widget; the file viewer is the code taken from the script chap_24/howto09/fileview.tkp. The popup dialog boxes are managed by the popup dialog boxes. All you really need to do to write the file selector is create the correct bindings and call backs.

Steps

1. Edit a new file named selector.tkp and type the following script into it.

```
#!/usr/local/bin/perl -w

# Require the Tk module.
use Tk;

# We need the dialog module.
require Tk::Dialog;
```

```
# This subroutine is a basic popup message displayer.
sub popup
{
    my ($title, $mesgref) = @_;

    # Create the string message.
    $mesg = join ("\n", @$mesgref);

    # Create the dialog box.
    $dialog= $mainWindow->Dialog (-title => "$title", -text => "$mesg", -
default_button => '1', -buttons => ['OK']);

    # Display the dialog box.
    $dialog->show();
}

# This subroutine opens the given file for viewing.
sub openFile
{
    # Get the currently selected filename.
    my $filename = $filelist->get('active');

    # Check if the file is a directory.
    if (-d $filename || -l $filename)
    {
        # Change directories.
        if (! chdir ($filename) )
        {
            # Display an error if we cannot get into the directory.
            popup ("Error", ["Permission denied."]);
            return();
        }

        # Delete the contents of the filelist.
        $filelist->delete ('0', 'end');

        # Open the directory and read in the contents.
        opendir (DIR, ".");
        @contents = readdir (DIR);
        closedir(DIR);

        # Insert the files in the list.
        $filelist->insert('end', @contents);

        # Change the title on the window.
        $directory = qx (pwd);
        $filelist->configure (-label => "Current Directory: $directory");
    }
    elsif ( -B $filename )
    {
        # Display an error.
        popup ("Error", ["Cannot view a binary file."]);
    }
    else
    {
        # Open the file and read in the contents.
```

continued on next page

continued from previous page

```perl
            open (FILE, "$filename");
            @contents = <FILE>;

            # Create a top-level window.
            my $mw = $mainWindow->Toplevel;
            $mw->configure (-title => 'View File');

            # Create the scrolling list.
            my $scroll = $mw->ScrlListbox(-scrollbars => 'se',-label => "Viewing: =>
        ${directory}/${filename}", -height => 20, -width => 50);
            $scroll->configure(-label_relief => 'raised');

            # Fill the list with the contents of the file.
            $scroll->insert('end',@contents);
            $scroll->pack(-side => 'top', -expand => 1, -fill => 'both'  );

            # Create an exit button so we can leave this window.
            my $exitButton = $mw->Button( -text => 'Close', -command => sub
                                        { $mw->destroy;} );
            $exitButton->pack (-side => 'top', -expand => 'yes', -fill => 'x');
    }
}

# This displays basic information about this tool.
sub about
{
    # Self promotion, horrible!
    popup ("About...", ["Perl5 Tk File Viewer", "Written by Mike Glover"]);
}

# Get the directory to open from the command line.
$directory = $ARGV[0] || ".";

# Change directories and get the current full path.
chdir ($directory);
$directory = qx (pwd);

# Open the directory.
opendir (DIR, ".");
@contents = readdir (DIR);
closedir (DIR);

# Create the main window.
$mainWindow = MainWindow->new;

# Create a menu bar frame.
$menuBar = $mainWindow->Frame;
$menuBar->pack(-side => 'top', -fill => 'x');
$menuBar->configure (-fg => 'yellow', -bg => 'blue', -relief => 'raised');

# Create a File menu.
$fileMenu = $menuBar->Menubutton(-text => 'File', -underline => 0);
$fileMenu->command( -label => 'Open', -underline => 0, -command =>
                    \&openFile );
```

```
$fileMenu->command( -label => 'Quit', -underline => 0, -command => sub {
exit;} );
$fileMenu->pack(-side => 'left');
$fileMenu->configure (-fg => 'yellow', -bg => 'blue', -relief => 'raised');

# Create a Help menu.
$helpMenu = $menuBar->Menubutton(-text => 'Help', -underline => 0);
$helpMenu->command( -label => 'About', -underline => 0, -command => \&about );
$helpMenu->pack(-side => 'right');
$helpMenu->configure (-fg => 'yellow', -bg => 'blue', -relief => 'raised');

# Create a scrolling list box.
$filelist = $mainWindow->ScrlListbox (
        -scrollbars => 'se',
        -label => "Current Directory: $directory",
        -labelvariable => $filename,
        -height => 10,
        -width => 30);

# Fill the list with the contents of the directory.
$filelist->insert('end', @contents);
$filelist->pack(-side => 'left', -expand => 1, -fill => 'both');
$filelist->bind ('<Double-Button-1>' => \&openFile);

# Let the user interact with the widget...
MainLoop();
```

2. Run the script.

```
% chap_24/howto10/selector.tkp
```

A window resembling Figure 24-23 should appear on the screen.

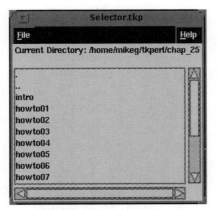

Figure 24-23 File selector

How It Works

The script uses ScrlListbox as the main widget, which displays the current list of files under the current directory. This list box needs to be kept up to date. If the user selects a new directory to change into, then this list must be emptied and refilled. To select a file or directory, the user double-clicks the left button on a filename in the list box. When the user does this, the script does one of two things: tries to open the file or tries to open the directory. Either way, a binding is required. The following line establishes the binding between double-clicking the left mouse button and the attempt to open a file.

```
$filelist->bind ('<Double-Button-1>' => \&openFile);
```

The ScrlListbox widget is referenced by the variable *$filelist*. The action <Double-Button-1> states that the action of double-clicking mouse button 1 causes the script to call the function named openFile. The far left mouse button is button 1, whereas the right mouse button is button 3. The openFile subroutine gets the current selection via the get method.

```
my $filename = $filelist->get('active');
```

Several checks are performed on the file before trying to open the file. For example, if the file is a binary file, then the script does not display its contents. If the file happens to be a directory, then the script must change directories, get the directory contents, and redisplay them in the ScrlListbox. As mentioned before, ScrlListbox and Listbox are related, so emptying and filling these two widgets are done the exact same way. The following line removes the entries from the ScrlListbox.

```
$filelist->delete ('0', 'end');
```

This line states that all the elements from the 0th position to the end are to be deleted. This causes the whole list box to be erased. The following line fills the list box with the files in the current directory.

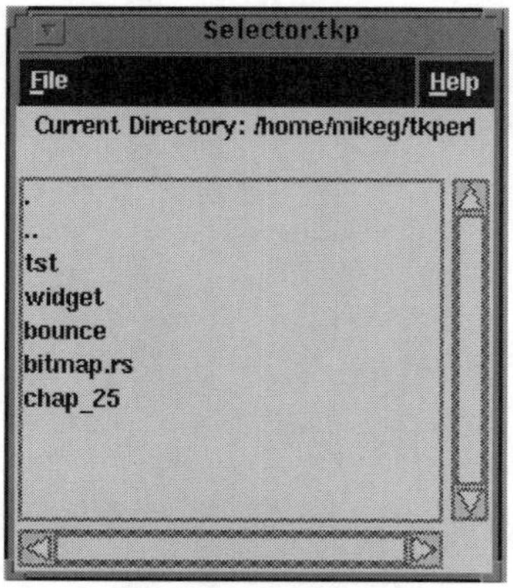

Figure 24-24 File selector

```
$filelist->insert('end', @contents);
```

Figure 24-24 displays the contents of the list box after the user has traversed one directory up.

Of course, the user can perform the same action by using the pull-down menus. If the user selects a file by clicking on it once and selects the Open option under the pull-down menu, the same events will happen. Figure 24-25 demonstrates the user opening a file named tst, using the pull-down menus.

Opening the file results in the window represented in Figure 24-26 being drawn.

The file viewer in this script is taken directly from the script in How-To 24.9. The only difference is that this file viewer has to create a subwindow off the main root window. This is done by the line

```
my $mw = $mainWindow->Toplevel;
```

This statement creates a top-level window that is a child of the main window. The reference to the subwindow is then stored into the variable named $mw. After the subwindow is created, all the widgets are created under this subwindow.

Comments

A file selector widget named FileSelector comes with the Perl/Tk extension package.

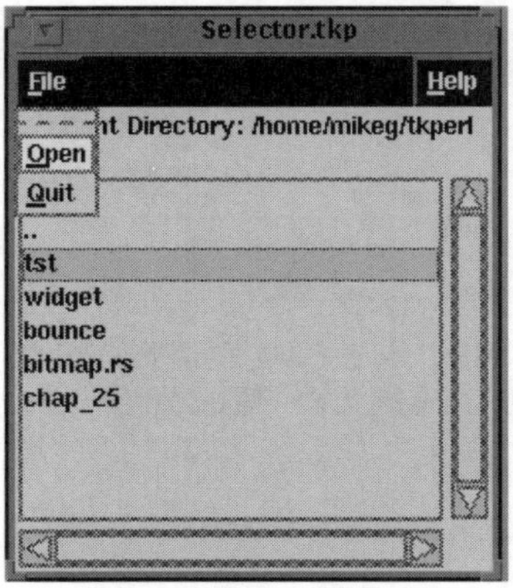

Figure 24-25 File selector

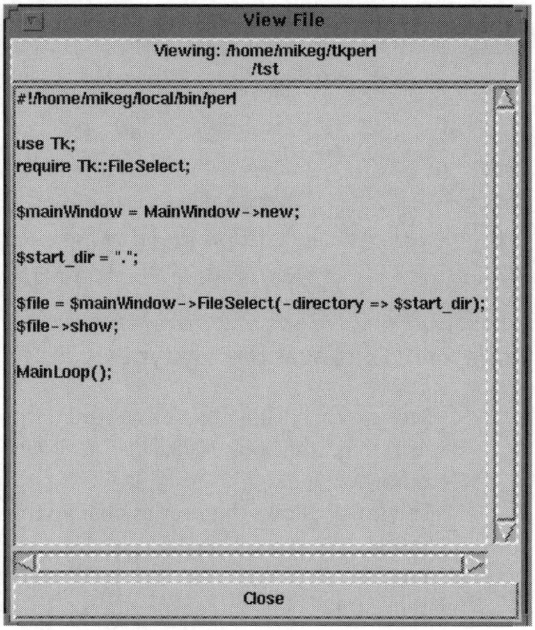

Figure 24-26 File viewer

COMPLEXITY
ADVANCED

24.11 How do I...
Create a canvas?

COMPATIBILITY: PERL 5   UNIX

Problem

I have heard of canvases under Tk, but I do not know how to use them. How do I invoke a canvas with the Perl 5 Tk extension?

Technique

This script creates a canvas and a drawing on the canvas. A canvas in Tk is a widget that displays a drawing surface in which you can place many different object types. Table 24-1 lists all the object types a canvas widget can display.

ITEM NAME	DESCRIPTION
Arcs	Basic curved lines.
Bezier Curves	Basic lines with additional information that states that Bezier cubic splines be drawn instead of a straight line.
Bitmaps	An X Window bitmap can be placed within a Tk canvas.
Circles	Basic circles.
Ellipses	Simple ellipses.
Lines	Lines are considered segments on a Tk canvas, so lines can be associated so that joints can be rounded when segments meet.
Polygons	A simple polygon.
Rectangles	A simple rectangle.
Text	Text can be added to the canvas, and text patterns or segments can be tagged to perform tasks.
Widgets	Any Tk widget can be placed on a canvas so both drawing objects and widgets can interact in the same window.

Table 24-1 Tk canvas display types

Because each Tk widget has a varied number of options, we can't list them all. It is best to get the book *Tcl and the Tk Toolkit* by John Ousterhout or any other notable Tk reference book.

The script allows the user to change the colors of certain features of the drawing inside the canvas. This is accomplished using the concept of *tags*. When an object is drawn on a canvas in Tk, the object is given a tag name. The tag name is used to reference this object under the canvas. To manipulate the object, you must use the tag assigned to it. More than one drawn object can share a tag name. This makes it easy to change a number of items together. This script also demonstrates the use of the tags to make event associations.

Steps

1. Edit a new file named canvas.tkp and type the following script into it.

```perl
#!/usr/local/bin/perl -w

# Require the Tk module.
use Tk;

# This subroutine actually performs the color change.
sub changeObjectColor
{
    my ($itemname, $color) = @_;
    $canvas->itemconfigure ("$itemname" , -fill => $color);
    $mw->destroy();
}

# This changes the color of the given item.
sub changeColor
{
    my ($itemname) = @_;
    my @colors = qw (white yellow orange red purple blue green gray black);
    my $x = 0;

    # Create a top-level window.
    $mw = $mainWindow->Toplevel;
    $mw->configure (-title => 'Change Color');

    # Create the frame for the buttons.
    $frame1 = $mw->Frame();
    $frame2 = $mw->Frame();

    # Pack the frames.
    $frame1->pack (-side => "top", -fill => 'both', -expand => 'yes');
    $frame2->pack (-side => "top", -fill => 'both', -expand => 'yes');

    # Create a label...
    $filltext = $frame1->Label (
     -text => "Pick a new color.",
     -relief => raised);
    $filltext->pack (-side => "top");

    # Create the color buttons.
    foreach $color (@colors)
    {
        # Create the button.
        $button[$x] = $frame2->Button (
         -highlightthickness => 0,
         -text => $color,
         -bg => $color,
         -command => [\&changeObjectColor, $itemname, $color] );
```

continued on next page

continued from previous page

```
            # Pack the button in the window.
            $button[$x]->pack (-side => "top", -expand => 'yes', -fill => 'x');
            $x++;
    }
}


# Create the main window.
$mainWindow = MainWindow->new;
$mainWindow->configure (-title => "Perl5 Tk Canvas Demo");

# Change this line to reflect where the file teapot.xbm resides.
$mainWindow->wm (iconbitmap =>
"@/home/mikeg/tkperl/chap_24/howto11/teapot.xbm");
$mainWindow->wm("minsize",  10, 10);
$mainWindow->wm("geometry", "200x200");
$mainWindow->iconname ("Canvas Demo");

# Create a frame to put the canvas in.
$frame = $mainWindow->Frame();

# Create the canvas.
$canvas = $mainWindow->Canvas("-width" => 200,"-height" => 200);
$canvas->pack("-expand" => 1, "-fill" => "both" );
$canvas->configure (-bg => red);

# Draw a circle.
$head = $canvas->create("oval", 0, 0, 200, 200,
    -tags => head,
    -width => 4,
    -fill => yellow);

# Draw two ovals.
$leye = $canvas->create("oval", 70, 50, 50, 110,
    -tags => righteye,
    -width => 4,
    -fill => black);
$reye = $canvas->create("oval", 150, 50, 130, 110,
    -tags => lefteye,
    -width => 4,
    -fill => black);

# Draw an arc.
$smile = $canvas->create("arc", 40, 170, 160, 80,
    -tags => smile,
    -extent => 180,
    -start => 180,
    -width => 7,
    -outline => black,
    -style => arc);

# Add the tags to the items.
$canvas->bind ('head', '<Button-3>' => sub { changeColor ("head");});
$canvas->bind ('lefteye', '<Button-3>' => sub { changeColor ("lefteye");});
$canvas->bind ('righteye', '<Button-3>' => sub { changeColor ("righteye");});
```

```
# Let the user interact with the widget...
MainLoop();
```

2. Run the script.

```
% chap_24/howto11/canvas.tkp
```

A window resembling Figure 24-27 should appear on the screen.

How It Works

The actual canvas is created with the following command.

```
$canvas = $mainWindow->Canvas("-width" => 200,"-height" => 200);
```

After this, the work is performed by calls to the create methods, which create objects on the canvas. They accept a number of options, one of which specifies what type of object is to be drawn. This specific example creates three ovals and an arc. The three ovals are the eyes and head of a happy face, and the arc is the smile. Each item is given its own individual tag name so you can address each item individually. The following line creates the head, giving it the tag name of head.

```
$head = $canvas->create("oval", 0, 0, 200, 200,
    -tags => head,
    -width => 4,
    -fill => yellow);
```

After the head, the eyes and the smile are created; then the bindings are assigned. Each binding on a canvas has to pass the tag name in the parameter list of the bind function call so the canvas knows which object on the canvas the event is intended for. The following line creates a binding to the item that has the tag name of lefteye.

```
$canvas->bind ('lefteye', '<Button-3>' => sub { changeColor ("lefteye");});
```

The binding states that whenever the third mouse button clicks on this object, the subroutine named changeColor should be called. Notice that the call to the changeColor subroutine is buried within an anonymous function reference. This is

Figure 24-27 Perl/Tk
canvas widget

Figure 24-28 Perl/Tk canvas widget

Figure 24-29
Perl/Tk canvas
widget

done so you can pass the function changeColor a parameter. When a binding or command is given a reference to a function, it passes only the reference, not the parameters. Creating the anonymous function creates a layer in which you can pass variables.

Notice that you do some manipulation to the top-level window. The following lines set the top-level window icon, the minimum size of the canvas window, the start size of the canvas window, and the name of the icon, respectively.

```
$mainWindow->wm (iconbitmap =>
"@/home/mikeg/tkperl/chap_24/howto11/teapot.xbm");
$mainWindow->wm("minsize",  10, 10);
$mainWindow->wm("geometry", "200x200");
$mainWindow->iconname ("Canvas Demo");
```

If you start the script chap_24/howto11/canvas.tkp and then minimize the window, the icon will look like Figure 24-28.

We selected the teapot as the icon graphic in honor of graphics students.

The heart of the script resides in the subroutine named changeColor. This subroutine provides the user with color choices and then changes the colors of the objects within the canvas. When the user presses the right mouse button on an item in the canvas, a window resembling Figure 24-29 should appear on the screen.

This window is nothing more than a second top-level window with a bunch of push buttons. Each button is created in the following *foreach* loop.

```
foreach $color (@colors)
{
    # Create the button.
    $button[$x] = $frame2->Button (
     -highlightthickness => 0,
```

```
    -text => $color,
    -bg => $color,
    -command => [\&changeObjectColor, $itemname, $color] );

    # Pack the button in the window.
    $button[$x]->pack (-side => "top", -expand => 'yes', -fill => 'x');
    $x++;
}
```

The -command option tells the button what to do when the button is pushed. Notice that the -command option is given a reference to an anonymous array. Inside the array is a reference to a function and two scalar variables. This is done so the value in the variable $color is retained at the time the button is created. When the button is pushed, it passes the current value of $color along to the function. If this is not done and the button is pressed, the current value of $color is passed, not the value the button was given. The line that actually performs the change on the drawn object is

```
$canvas->itemconfigure ("$itemname" , -fill => $color);
```

The variable $itemname contains the name of the item. In the above script, it is one of three values: head, lefteye, righteye. The value of $color is the color the item is being set to.

Comments

Additional binds and functions can easily be added to this script so the user can drag the eyes and head around inside the canvas.

## CHAPTER 25

PERL AND THE
WORLD WIDE WEB

PERL AND THE
WORLD WIDE WEB

How do I...

The origins of the Internet lie in the 1970s; many of the protocols and applications that implement the globally connected system date from that period. The reason for the popular conception that the Internet came into existence in the past few years is a phenomenon called the World Wide Web (WWW or the Web). The Web is a set of protocols, servers, documents, and standards that have introduced a new concept to mainstream computing: the concept of hypermedia.

Hypermedia can be defined as the unification of multimedia and hypertext. The Web's implementation of hypermedia has fused together many of the disparate Internet facilities into one coherent, colorful, user-friendly whole. Web documents contain hytertext links that enable the user to leap contents, download applications, and explore multimedia sound and vision at the click of a button.

What role does Perl have in this? Perl has become the language of choice for writing programs that generate dynamic hypertext and translate information held in existing systems into Web pages. Programs with these responsibilities are known as *CGI programs,* named after the Common Gateway Interface standard.

There is no unique relationship between Perl and CGI programming. The CGI specification is language-independent (although it does make some assumptions about the environment in which the CGI program runs). You can create a CGI program in C, FORTRAN, or Visual Basic, for example. Why is Perl the CGI programming tool of choice?

- Its excellent text-processing abilities make it a natural for generating HTML text.

- It is an interpreted language that avoids the need for laborious recompilation in rapidly changing spheres such as the Web.

- Perl's taint check flag (the -T flag) can protect a Web server against hacking and abuse by unscrupulous clients.

The How-To's in this chapter make some assumptions about your knowledge and experience. The focus here is on writing Web-related Perl code rather than providing a tutorial on the Web and its legion of acronyms. We assume that you are familiar with the HTML language and have some knowledge of how a Web server functions and how it can be configured. Table 25-1 presents some of the abbreviations used in this chapter.

ABBREVIATION	MEANING	DEFINITION
URL	Universal resource locator	A hyperlink to another Web resource
WWW	World Wide Web	A set of Internet services based on hypermedia
HTML	Hypertext markup language	A syntax for transforming information to hypertext
HTTP	Hypertext transfer protocol	A protocol used by Web servers to exchange data
CGI	Common Gateway Interface	A standard for interfacing programs and the Web

Table 25-1 WWW glossary

If you lack experience, a huge amount of literature is available on these subjects; much of the software is freely available. Get to know the Web and review this chapter once you are familiar with it.

25.1   Write a CGI Program in Perl

This section will outline the steps involved in setting up a Web environment for developing CGI programs. This section is a prerequisite for the other CGI-related How-To's because it will explain many of the concepts of CGI programming.

COMPLEXITY
INTERMEDIATE

25.1   How do I ...
Write a CGI program in Perl?

COMPATIBILITY: UNIX

Problem

What is CGI and how can I write a CGI program in Perl?

Technique

CGI is a standard for interfacing application programs to information servers such as the HTTP servers that implement the WWW. When you access a universal resource locator (URL) that references a CGI object, the document you retrieve is not a static file. It is an HTML datastream created dynamically by a program associated with the URL. Dynamic information may change on a minute-by-minute basis, like stock market prices, or may be created in response to a specific query from the user.

Programs that create WWW pages dynamically or make information held in traditional information systems accessible through the WWW are referred to as CGI programs.

What are the requirements for presenting dynamic information over the WWW?

First, it is clearly impractical to edit a large number of HTML pages to keep them up to date with information that changes on a daily basis. If the information you wish to present over the WWW is changing second by second, you need to develop ways of generating HTML documents from computer programs.

Second, a CGI program can be written to create HTML data in response to user requests and queries. Because the client's request is received by a WWW server, not the CGI program, an efficient method must exist for communicating the request parameters to the HTML-generating application. The CGI standard specifies a method for achieving this communication through environment variables.

Third, the CGI program should have the power to access information held in any existing information system. The standard is called the Common Gateway Interface because the programs that use CGI often function as gateways between information held in non-WWW systems and the WWW. Imagine that your company has a well-established database system that stores historical stock prices. You want to make this information available to customers over the WWW, but your database system doesn't understand HTTP requests. You need a program that acts as a gateway between the HTTP server and the stock database system. A CGI program can be designed to receive a query from the HTTP user, retrieve data from an established database, and return the requested data to the user via the HTTP server. The data is embellished with HTML markup so it can be displayed, correctly formatted, at the user's browser.

As a consequence of these requirements, a CGI program should be written in a full rights programming language, capable of reading and writing disk files. This implies special security considerations so that unscrupulous client requests cannot fool the CGI program into performing prohibited actions. These are rather different considerations to those that shape applet languages like JavaScript. Applets execute at the client. Consequently, languages such as JavaScript do not need to have full rights to access your computer. CGI programs execute with full rights at the server and must protect themselves from being tricked into abusing server facilities.

Steps

1. We assume your Web server is already set up and running and you have access to the CGI-bin directory defined in the server configuration. If this is not the case, you need to contact your system administrator. Alternatively, you may wish to start a second Web server configured for testing CGI programs. Generally, there is no problem running two Web servers, provided they use separate service addresses. For example, if your production Web server has the URL http://japh.com:80/, your test server could be configured to run as http://japh.com:8080/.

2. Check the default location of your server's HTML files. For convenience, the examples in this chapter are designed to be invoked from a single HTML page. Create the HTML document cgitest.html and enter the listing below. Copy the file to a suitable HTML directory for your site.

```
<HTML><HEAD><TITLE>CGI Perl Test Page</TITLE></HEAD>
<H1>CGI Perl Test Page</H1>
<BR>
<HR>
<H2><I>This Page is under construction</I></H2>
<HR>
<A HREF="/cgi-bin/cgienv.pl/">About you ...</A><P>
<A HREF="/cgi-bin/cgips.pl/">About this server ...</A><P>
<A HREF="/cgi-bin/cgiphone.pl/">Information Gateway</A><P>
<A HREF="/cgi-bin/cgiform.pl/">Customer Feedback form</A><P>
<BR>
</BODY>
</HTML>
```

A system administrator will commonly configure the Web server to allow users to publish HTML files in a subdirectory of their home directory. This subdirectory is frequently named WWW.

3. When you have installed the page check, you can access it. Start up a WWW browser such as Netscape or Mosaic and access the new page's URL. If you are running a test server on a nonstandard port, don't forget that you can specify the port number after the host ID in the URL. Here is an example URL for a test server running on machine japh service port 8080:

```
http://japh:8080/cgitest.html
```

You should see a display resembling Figure 25-1.

4. Create a file called cgienv.pl containing the following Perl code. Make sure the file is executable for your system.

```
#!/usr/local/bin/perl

use FileHandle;
use Env;

autoflush STDOUT 1;
Env::import();

$user_agent_full = $HTTP_USER_AGENT;
($user_agent)    = split(" ",$user_agent_full);
@mime_types = join("<P>", $HTTP_ACCEPT);
```

continued on next page

continued from previous page

```perl
$http_header= <<XXX;
HHTP/1.0 200 OK\r
Content-Type: text/html\r
\r
\r
XXX


$message_body= <<XXX;
<html>
<head>
<title>Client Information</title>
</head>
<body>
<H1>About you ...</H1>
<P>You are $REMOTE_USER host $REMOTE_HOST ($REMOTE_ADDR).
<P>You are reading this page using $user_agent_full.
<P>Your $user_agent browser understands the following data types:
@mime_types.
XXX

$message_tail=<<XXX;
<hr>
<i>webmastered by japh\@www.intern</i>
</body>
</html>
XXX

$not_sup_message = <<XXX;
Content-type: text/html

<H1>Error: Unsupported Method</H1>
<HR>
This script, $0, doesn`t support the $REQUEST_METHOD method of
submitting forms. Please use POST.
XXX

$_ = $REQUEST_METHOD;
SWITCH:{
    /POST|PUT/ && do
    {
        read(STDIN, $query, $CONTENT_LENGTH);
        print $http_header;
        print $message_body;
        print $message_tail;
        last SWITCH;
    };
    /GET/ && do {
        $query = $QUERY_STRING;
        print $http_header;
        print $message_body;
        print $message_tail;
        last SWITCH;
    };
    DEFAULT: {
        print $not_sup_message;
```

```
        exit 1;
    };
}
```

5. CGI programs are normally expected to reside in a specific directory on the server machine. Ascertain the location of the CGI-bin directory for your server. Copy the file cgienv.pl to the CGI bin.

6. If required, edit the URLs contained in the cgitest.html document to point to the appropriate URL for the cgienv.pl program. If you installed cgienv.pl in the default CGI directory, you shouldn't need to change anything.

7. Return to your browser and click on the link About you... You will see a new HTML page that looks similar to Figure 25-2.

8. If your browser allows you to see the HTML page in source form, examine the HTML source for the page. Try to see the relationship between the Perl code, the HTML it generated, and the page displayed on your screen. One sample of HTML generated by the program is listed below.

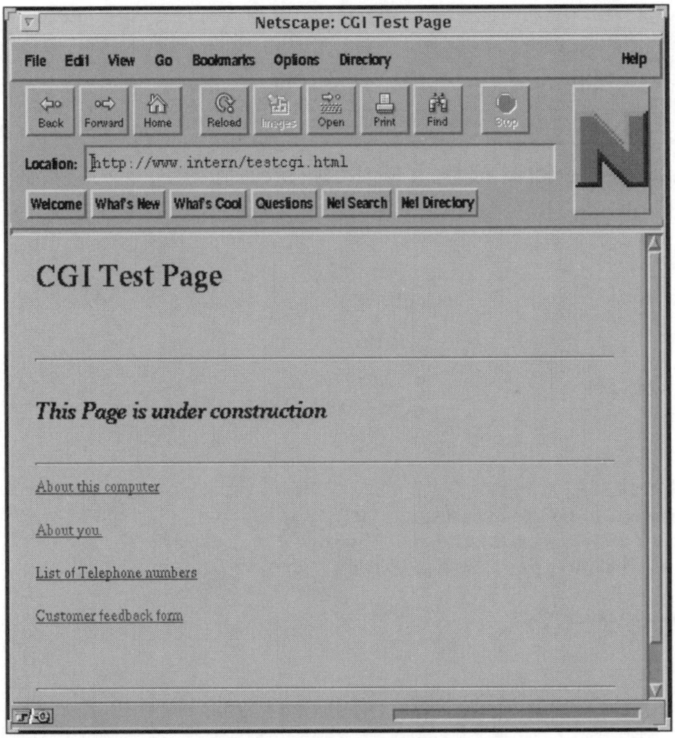

Figure 25-1 The test CGI HTML page, displayed using the Netscape browser

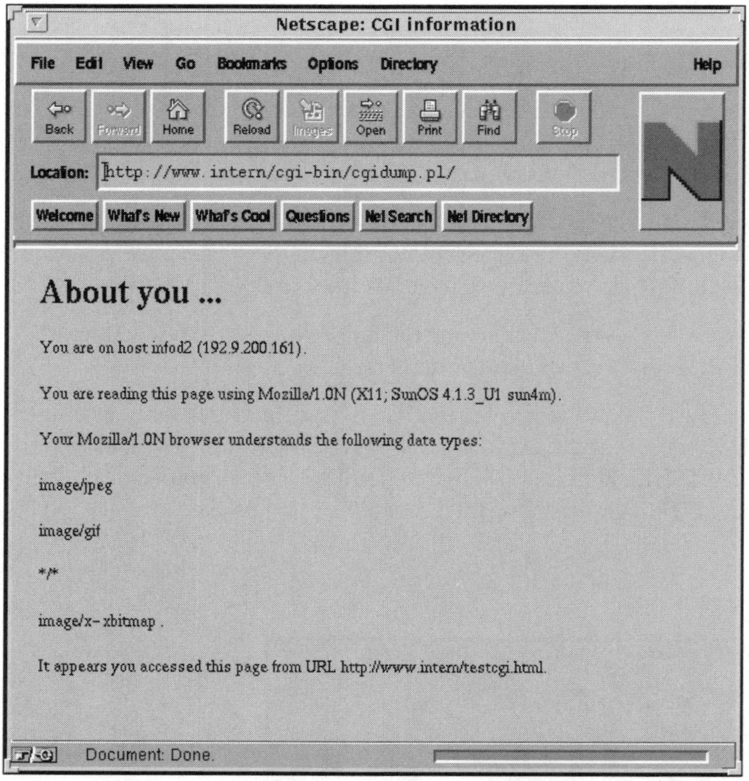

Figure 25-2 An HTML page generated by a Perl CGI program

```
HHTP/1.0 200 OK
Content-Type: text/html


<html>
<head>
<title>Client Information</title>
</head>
<body>
<H1>About you ...</H1>
<P>You are  host pc_01 (192.93.229.25).
<P>You are reading this page using Mozilla/2.0 (Win16; I).
<P>Your Mozilla/2.0 browser understands the following data types:
image/gif, image/x-xbitmap, image/jpeg, image/pjpeg, */*.
<hr>
<i>webmastered by japh@www.intern</i>
</body>
</html>
```

The first few lines before the <html> tag show the HTTP header.

ENVIRONMENT VARIABLE	DESCRIPTION
SERVER_SOFTWARE	The type of Web server running the CGI program
SERVER_NAME	The name of the Web server host
SERVER_PORT	The port address of the Web server
GATEWAY_INTERFACE	The version number of the CGI standard
SERVER_PROTOCOL	The version of HTTP the server is running
REQUEST_METHOD	The method of requesting data specified by the client
QUERY_STRING	Request parameters supplied by the client
SCRIPT_NAME	The resource locator of the CGI program
REMOTE_HOST	The name of the client host
REMOTE_ADDR	The IP address of the client host
AUTH_TYPE	Authorization method, often blank
REMOTE_USER	The name of the user provided by the client
REMOTE_IDENT	An identity for the client user, not often available
REFERER_URL	How the client got here
HTTP_ACCEPT	The MIME types accepted by the client
HTTP_USER_AGENT	The client browser type
CONTENT_TYPE	The MIME type of data supplied with the request

Table 25-2 The environment of a CGI program

How It Works

The name of the cgi-bin directory is defined in the server configuration file. The relevant lines look something like this:

```
# Scripts; URLs starting with /CGI-bin/ will be understood as
# script calls in the directory /your/script/directory
#
Exec    /CGI-bin/*        /user/japh/cgitest/*
```

This indicates that when a user clicks on a URL containing the component / cgibin/cgienv.pl, the local HTTP server will search the directory /user/japh/cgitest/ for an executable file called cgienv.pl. In this case, cgi-bin is an alias for the relative URL /user/japh/cgitest.

When the user clicks on the URL reference in the browser, the request to access the resource is transmitted to the remote Web server using a special application–protocol hypertext transfer protocol, HTTP. This is shown as Stage 1 in Figure 25-2.

The remote server receives the request, parses the URL, and translates the URL element cgi-bin/cgi-envp.pl to the path /usr/japh/cgitest/cgienv.pl according to the rule defined in the configuration file. The server would normally read the resource file but, because the URL specifed a cgi-bin object, the server now prepares to execute the resource as a child process. Remember from Chapter 13 that a child process inherits its environment variables from its parent. Before the server executes the CGI program, it does two things:

● First, it arranges to receive data sent from the STDOUT stream of the child process.

● Second, it sets the value of several environment variables to HTTP parameters transmitted with the user's request.

Several environment variables commonly set by Web servers are listed in Table 25-2. When the CGI program is launched, it can access these values using the Perl %ENV array or, as is the case with cgienv.pl, use the import method of the Env.pm module to import all the environment variables as Perl variables. This is Stage 2 in Figure 25-3.

The STDOUT output of the child CGI program is received by the server. This is shown as Stage 3 in Figure 25-3. If the output contains a valid HTTP header, it is

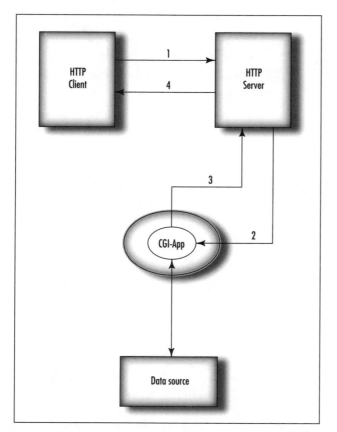

Figure 25-3 The flow of communication in a HTTP exchange involving a CGI program

forwarded on the the client browser, Stage 4 in Figure 25-3. The CGI program terminates.

The client browser receives the HTTP message, parses, and renders the images and HTML contained within it. If the URL cannot be resolved or the program fails, the server returns an HTTP error message to the browser.

Comments

Running a secondary Web server on an internal machine is probably the best solution for the CGI development programmer. Once a program is stable, you can move it to the production HTTP server cgi-bin directory. Consult your system administrator and check to see if running a test server is within the rules at your site.

COMPLEXITY
INTERMEDIATE

25.2   How do I ...
Generate a Web page dynamically from a Perl CGI program?

COMPATIBILITY: UNIX DOS

Problem

How can I write a Perl program capable of dynamically generating a Web page? The information on the page will be automatically kept up to date by the program, avoiding the need to update a static HTML file. The page should be generated on user demand whenever its URL is accessed.

Technique

To demonstrate the generation of Web pages on the fly, you need to have your CGI program generate a Web page that reflects a dynamic situation. If your test HTTP server is running under UNIX, then you can use the UNIX process table, which shows the processes running on the machine at any given time. If you are developing Perl CGI programs on a non-UNIX-based server such as the Mac or Windows 95, you should choose some other dynamic resource in your system to provide input to the CGI program. In the worst case, you could read the system time.

This section is concerned with illustrating the simplest possible way to create an HTML page from a Perl program. The program uses the CGI interface to obtain information about the user request; to obtain its raw data by executing ps, the UNIX process table listing command; to mark up the raw data with HTML; and to return the page to the user via the HTTP server. The program presented here has no intrinsic functionality but illustrates the most direct way of using CGI within a Perl program. Later in this chapter, we will illustrate some superior methods of generating HTML and processing CGI parameters, but let's keep things simple to start with.

Steps

1. List the program cgips.pl and become familiar with its code.

```perl
#!/usr/local/bin/perl -T

use Env;

$succ_message = <<XXX;
HHTP/1.0 200 OK\r
Content-Type: text/html\r
\r
\r
<html>
<head>
<title>Success</title>
</head>
<body>
<h1>Success!</h1>
<HR><IMG SRC="/cpu.gif" alt="IMAGE CPU GAUGE"><P>
You have successfully executed CGI-bin script $0.<p>
<h2>Latest Process Table</h2>
<tt>
<ul>
$pstab
<ul>
</tt>
<hr>
<i>webmastered by japh\@test.com</i>
</body>
</html>
XXX


$not_sup_message = <<XXX;
Content-type: text/html

<H1>Error: Unsupported Method</H1>
<HR>
This script, $0, doesn`t support the $REQUEST_METHOD method of
submitting forms. Please use POST.
XXX


$|=1;
Env::import();

chop( $pstab = `ps auxww`);
$pstab =~ s/\n/\n<li>/g;

$_ = $REQUEST_METHOD;
SWITCH:{
     /POST|PUT/ && do
     {
         read(STDIN, $query, $CONTENT_LENGTH);
         print $succ_message;
         last SWITCH;
```

```
};
/GET/ && do {
    $query = $QUERY_STRING;
    print $succ_message;
    last SWITCH;
};
DEFAULT: {
    print $not_sup_message;
    exit 1;
};
}
```

2. Install the program cgips.pl into the appropriate CGI-bin directory for your site. Make it executable for your system.

3. The HTML page generated by cgips.pl contains a reference to an in-line graphics file, cpu.gif. Copy this GIF file to the appropriate location for your in-line graphic files and edit this line in cgips.pl

```
<IMG SRC="/cpu.gif" ...>
```

to reflect the location of the file at your installation.

4. Now test the program by accessing the resource cgips.pl. Run your WWW browser and access the URL for the resource cgitest.html. Access the link About This Server.

5. You will receive an HTML page resembling Figure 25-4.

6. Reload the page from your browser to see that the information changes dynamically to reflect changes to the server machine process table.

How It Works

The program takes a snapshot of the current state of the process table and holds it in the string scalar $pstab. Then the command s///g is used to append an HTML list item tag <LI> to each line of the listing. You write the output that will use this tag to display the ps data as an HTML list.

As discussed in How-To 25.1, a CGI program obtains information from the HTTP server by accessing the values of a set of environment variables defined by the server when the CGI program is executed. In Perl, you can access environment variables through the predefined associative array %ENV. Accessing each environment variable through this array is somewhat verbose, however. To make the program more succinct, use the Perl library routine Env::import to copy the value of keys %ENV into a similarly named Perl variable. You can then access each piece of CGI environmental information passed by the HTTP server through Perl variables. Hereafter, we will discuss the program as if these Perl variables were set directly by CGI.

Next, the program must parse the CGI query. First, it checks which value was set by CGI for $REQUEST_METHOD. If the request is flagged as a GET method,

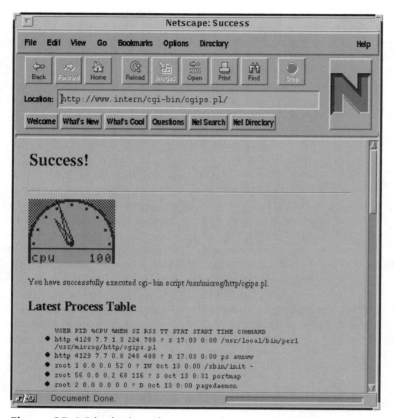

Figure 25-4 Displaying the cgips.pl dynamic HTML page with the Netscape browser

the program expects the query to be set in the variable *$QUERY_STRING*. Because this program responds unconditionally to any request, you need not be concerned with parsing the query parameters supplied in *$QUERY_STRING*. If the request is flagged as a POST or PUT request, then the program expects the query to be supplied through its input stream. The program reads $CONTENT_LENGTH bytes of query data from STDIN.

If $REQUEST_METHOD is set to some other value, then you must respond with a message that the CGI method is unsupported by the program. The program prints the string $not_sup_message on the STDOUT stream. The HTTP server is then responsible for returning this text to the browser that issued the request. CGI programs are not normally interested in talking directly to the requester (although this is possible); they allow the HTTP server to forward STDOUT data on their behalf.

If you use this approach to writing CGI programs, it is very important that you set the STDOUT stream to unbuffered output using the $| = 1 command. If you forget this, your program will buffer its responses to the HTTP daemon, leading to delays or deadlock in the HTTP conversation.

In the case of a successful GET, POST, or PUT, request that the program send the string $succ_message to STDOUT. Notice how the Perl syntax quoting mechanism (the string XXX is a quote) allows you to format the text freely yet take advantage of Perl's variable interpolation to slot the $pstab data into the response.

```
$succ_message = <<XXX;
...
$pstab
...
XXX
```

The $succ_message string itself contains a HTTP header message and an HTML syntax body. If you are familiar with HTML, you should easily understand the body message. It defines a Web page entitled Success, which displays the ps table in a neatly formatted HTML unordered list between two <UL> </UL> markers.

When a HTTP server receives a document, it expects to find the data preceded by a HTTP header message indicating protocol version and the content type of the information. The Comments section discusses the content type field in greater detail.

Comments

It may seem surprising at first that a CGI program, whose job is to generate HTML, has explicitly identified its own output as content type text/html. Don't be misled by the name hypertext transfer protocol. HTTP is capable of transporting many data types, including binary formats for images, video, and sound, not just HTML. Valid content types are defined in another standard—MIME. Table 25-3 lists some data types supported by MIME.

COMMON MIME CONTENT TYPES	ASSOCIATED FILE EXTENSIONS
application/postscript	ai eps ps
application/rtf	rtf
application/zip	zip
application/x-tar	tar
audio/basic	au snd
audio/x-wav	wav
image/gif	gif
image/jpg	jpg
image/tiff	tiff tif
text/plain	txt cc c h
text/html	html htm
video/mpeg	mpeg mpg mpe
video/x-msvideo	avi

Table 25-3 Common data types defined by the MIME standard

The content type field is not strictly necessary because most servers will identify the content type from the file extension or the first few bytes of the data. When you are sending data to an unknown and possibly misconfigured remote entity, it is better practice to label the content type explicitly.

COMPLEXITY
INTERMEDIATE

25.3   How do I ...
Install and use the Perl 5 CGI module?

COMPATIBILITY: UNIX

Problem

Programming a CGI application using explicit HTML is a laborious and repetitious process. How can I install the Perl CGI.pm library module and automate routine CGI coding?

Technique

The CGI.pm module was developed by Lincoln Stein. The package contains the Perl 5-based CGI.pm itself and full documentation in both text and hypertext formats. You can generate documentation from the module itself using the perldoc command.

Steps

1. Copy the file CGI.pm.tar from the CD and expand it in a temporary directory. Install the documentation by copying the file CGI.HTML to a suitable location at your site.

2. Copy the CGI.pm file to the Perl library directory.

How It Works

To use the facilities of CGI.pm, you must include the module in your code with the statement

```
use CGI;
```

To generate HTML, you must first create a CGI object using the new method. All subsequent method calls are performed in relation to this CGI object.

The parsing of URL query parameters is largely transparent. The creation of the object using new initiates the parsing of input from both GET and PUT methods. You can retrieve the tags of each tag value pair through the command

```
@tags = $q->keywords;
```

where $q is your CGI object. Alternatively, you can import the tags as Perl variables using the method import_names. The method will, by default, create the variables in a package called R, so you must access each variable as $R::var1, $R::var2, and so on. If you supply a string as a parameter to the import_names method, then this string will be used instead of R as the package name. Don't import the tags into package Main, as this can be exploited as a security loophole.

Comments

There are a number of alternative CGI- and WWW-related Perl modules, but CGI.pm is one of the most popular, powerful, and flexible.

COMPLEXITY
INTERMEDIATE

25.4   How do I ...
Generate a Web page from data held in another system?

COMPATIBILITY: UNIX

Problem

How can I use CGI.pm to generate an HTML page from raw data taken from another information server or from a file?

Technique

One of the most exciting aspects of Perl CGI is the way the language lends itself to becoming the glue between existing sources of data and the new-era information servers of the World Wide Web. Perl is attuned to developing applications that retrieve data from files or databases and making them available to a Web browser.

The example program here serves two purposes: It introduces high-level CGI programming using the Perl CGI module and it illustrates how a few lines of Perl code can translate raw data into a polished WWW page.

Perl is acting as a gateway between the HTTP server and other sources of data. In a production environment, Perl is capable of translating a user request into an SQL query on a large database, using the Perl 5 DBI interface and returning the results.

The example here is a dynamically created telephone list. This program illustrates how an existing database held in some non-Web-related system can be accessed by a Perl program and translated into a form in which a HTTP server can publish the information.

Steps

1. List the program cgiphone.pl from the CD and become familiar with the code.

```perl
#!/usr/local/bin/perl

BEGIN {
  # Adjust this line to point to the phonelist file
  $PHONETEXT = "/user/japh/ph2/chap25/phoneno.txt";
}
use CGI;

$AGE = int(-M $PHONETEXT);
open(IN,"<$PHONETEXT")|| die "Can't find data file";
while(<IN>){
  chop;
  ($name) = split(",");
   $list{$name} = $_;
}

$q = new CGI;

print $q->header;
print $q->start_html('Telephone List',
                     'japh@test.com',
                     0, 'BGCOLOR="#COCOCO"');
print <<ETX;
<H1>Telephone List</H1>
<table border>
<tr><th>Name<th>Floor<th>Ext<th>Private<th>Mobile</tr>
ETX

for $n (sort keys %list) {
    ($name,$floor,$ext,$home,$mobl) = split(/,/, $list{$n});
    print <<ETX;
<tr>
<td>$name</td><td>$floor</td><td>$ext</td><td>$home</td><td>$mobl</td>
</tr>
ETX
}
print "</table>\n";
print "<br><P>The list was updated $AGE days ago";
print $q->end_html;
```

2. The program references a simple text data file. Adjust the value of the variable *$PHONETEXT*, set in the BEGIN routine, to a path appropriate for your system.

3. Install the program into the test CGI-bin directory and make it executable for your system.

4. Run your browser and access the cgitest.html resource, which will look similar to Figure 25-5.

5. Click the reference Information Gateway. You should see a tabular representation of the data from the file.

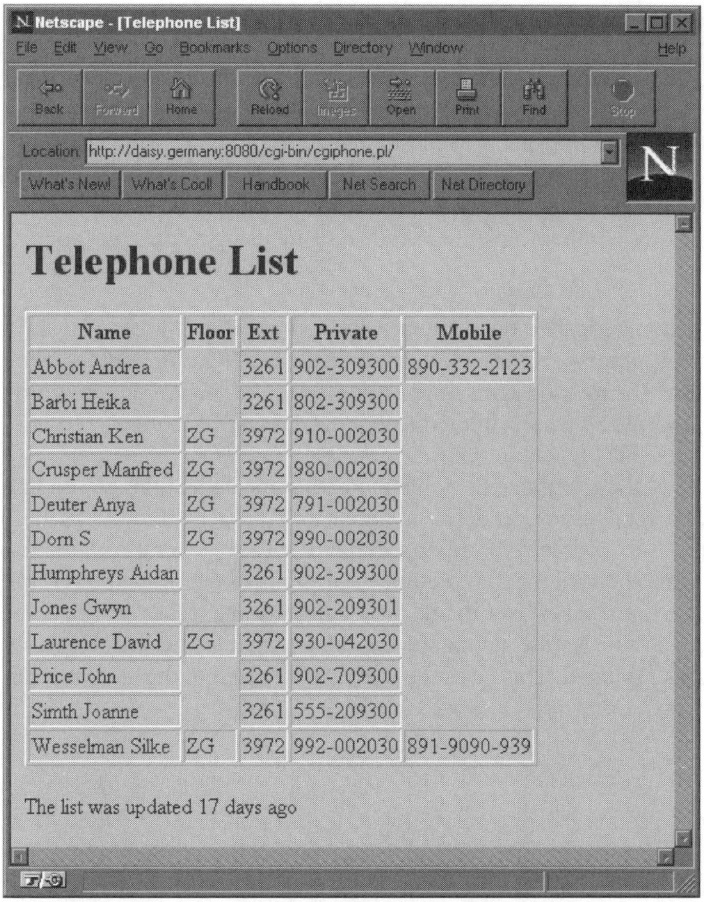

Name	Floor	Ext	Private	Mobile
Abbot Andrea		3261	902-309300	890-332-2123
Barbi Heika		3261	802-309300	
Christian Ken	ZG	3972	910-002030	
Crusper Manfred	ZG	3972	980-002030	
Deuter Anya	ZG	3972	791-002030	
Dorn S	ZG	3972	990-002030	
Humphreys Aidan		3261	902-309300	
Jones Gwyn		3261	902-209301	
Laurence David	ZG	3972	930-042030	
Price John		3261	902-709300	
Simth Joanne		3261	555-209300	
Wesselman Silke	ZG	3972	992-002030	891-9090-939

Figure 25-5 A list formatted with HTML 3 and displayed on the Windows 95 Netscape browser

How It Works

The program uses some of the basic facilities of the CGI module to translate an ASCII text file into an HTML page. Notice how the use of the CGI module removes much of the verbose HTML code that cluttered the raw CGI cgips.pl program. In many cases, large blocks of standard HTML can be replaced by a single method call to a CGI object.

Notice too that you can write CGI programs that accept complex parameter values without effort because the CGI.pm module handles the parameter parsing for you. The collection of CGI parameters is invisible to the application program; there is no need to check the REQUEST_METHOD value to decide if the REQUEST is supported, nor to code a read call on STDIN if the REQUEST_METHOD is a PUT or

POST. All the code that was handled at the application level in How To 25.3 is now invisibly handled in the library.

The structure of cgiphone.pl follows the pattern of many information-processing programs. It initializes itself, reads its input, generates its output, and exits. Initialization consists of importing the CGI module with a *use CGI* statement. Once the CGI code is loaded, the program creates a CGI object using the variable *$q* (for query). Calling a method such as $q->header returns a string of HTML and HTTP elements. You must remember to print the return value using a construct such as

```
print $q->header;
```

Once the program has loaded the comma-delimited telephone list into an associative array, the output phase beings. CGI generates the HTTP header strings using the header method. The method start_html creates an HTML preamble containing the <HTML> and <TITLE> tags. Calling the end_html method creates the balancing </HTML> and </TITLE> tags.

The generation of the telephone list table requires some explicit HTML coding because the CGI object does not yet define methods for table generation. This illustrates that there is no problem in mixing explicit HTML generation and the HTML-generating methods of the CGI module. CGI.pm does not limit your HTML coding in any way; it just takes over many of the burdensome tasks.

Notice the added value feature, telling the user how long it is since the telephone number file was last updated. This gives the user confidence that the list is not out of date.

Comments

The tabular format used in this example employs features of HTML 3. HTML 3, at the time of writing, is not supported by many browsers. We used Netscape 2.0 to display it. If you are still running a pre-Netscape 2 period browser, you might not see the data so neatly formatted. If you are not yet familiar with HTML tables, you may wish to check the meaning of each tag in Table 25-4.

HTML TABLE TAG	MEANING
<TABLE>	Table tag, balanced: <TABLE> starts a table and </TABLE> ends a table.
<TH>	Table heading separator, unbalanced.
<TR>	Table row, balanced. Starts a new line in a table.
<TD>	Table data, balanced. A field within a table row.

Table 25-4 HTML tags for tabular data

If your Web server is accessible by people outside your organization, you might want to publish a set of extension numbers. You certainly would not want to publish a complete telephone list, including private numbers, outside your organization. If you use a static HTML, then you need to maintain two documents. One is the external page accessible from the Internet; the other is the internal list, accessible only within your organization. The second document could contain reserved information such as private telephone numbers. You then create the job of keeping the two documents in step. CGI can avoid this problem by checking the status of the user through the *CGI REMOTE_HOST* variable. If you can determine that the user is accessing the URL from a domain internal to your organization, you can have the program generate the full page. If the user is external, then you can have the Perl program simply omit the confidential fields. You don't need to maintain two documents.

COMPLEXITY
INTERMEDIATE

25.5   How do I ...
Create a form using the Perl 5 CGI module?

COMPATIBILITY: UNIX

Problem

HTML can be used to create Web pages that are interactive forms. How can I create an HTML form using the CGI.pm package?

Technique

This How-To illustrates some advanced features of the CGI.pm package. In particular, we focus on the generation and processing of HTML forms generated by Perl. The example is a common one found on the Web: the customer feedback form.

To understand the features of CGI.pm fully, print out the comprehensive CGI.pm HTML reference manual included in the package. Issue the command

```
perldoc CGI > cgi.doc
```

Then print the file cgi.doc. Have the printed document with you as you read this section. The reference document specifies the use of the many CGI object methods and their parameters. Many parameters take default values and need not always be supplied in the code.

Notice also that you generate an HTML form, process the user response, and generate a reply page, all with one single program in this example. With this powerful method of generating complex HTML documents, you no longer have to struggle to maintain several files containing the HTML for each step in the interaction.

Steps

1. Create an executable file named cgiform.pl and enter the following listing.

```
#!/usr/local/bin/perl
# CGI Feedback Form example.
```

continued on next page

continued from previous page

```
BEGIN {
    $DEBUG = 1;
    $POLL = ['bad','ok','good','excellent'];
    $PAGE = ['Midi','Perl','Graphics'];
    $MAINTAINERS =  ['webmaster', 'midimaster', 'perlmaster',
                     'graphicsmaster'];
}

use CGI;
$q = new CGI;

print $q->header;
print $q->start_html;

#
# Send the customer feedback form
#
unless($q->param) {
    print $q->start_form('User Feedback');
    print "<H1>User Feedback Form</H1><hr>\n";
    print "<P>To:", $q->popup_menu('Recipient',$MAINTAINERS);
    print "From: ",$q->textfield('From', '', 20, 60),
          "(your e-mail address)";

    print "<H2>How did you rate ... ?</H2>";
    print "<PRE>";
    print "<P>Midi Music:", $q->radio_group('Music',    $POLL, 'ok');
    print "<P>Perl       :", $q->radio_group('Perl',     $POLL, 'ok');
    print "<P>Graphics   :", $q->radio_group('Graphics', $POLL, 'ok');
    print "</PRE>";
    print "<H2>Mail me when these pages update</H2>";
    print "<P>", $q->checkbox_group('Mail_me', $PAGE);

    print "<hr>";
    print "<P>", $q->submit('Submit');
    print $q->end_form;
} else {

    #
    # Process the form and confirm
    # receipt of the user comments.
    #
    $customer =  $q->param('From');
    print "<H1>Feedback Form Compete</H1><hr>\n";
    print "<H3>Thank you ",  $customer, " for your feedback ...</H3>";

    print "<P>Your comment that the MIDI page was ", $q->param('Music'),
    ", the Perl page was ", $q->param('Perl'),
    " and the Graphics page was ", $q->param('Graphics'),
    " has been noted.";

    if ($customer && (@interest = $q->param('Mail_me'))) {
        print "<P>You will receive e-mail whenever the ";
        for (@interest) {
          SWITCH:{
                /Midi/ && do {
                    print "Midi ";
```

```
                    # add $customer to Midi mail-list
                    last SWITCH;
                };
                /Perl/ && do {
                    print "Perl ";
                    # add $customer to Perl mail-list
                    last SWITCH;
                };
                /Graphics/ && do {
                    print "Graphics ";
                    # add $customer to Graphics mail-list last SWITCH;
                };
                $x = 1;
            }
        }
        print "pages are next updated.";
    }
    print "<hr>";
    print "<H3>Debug Parameter Dump</H3>", $q->dump, "<hr>" if $DEBUG;
}

print $q->end_html;
```

2. Install the program in the test cgi-bin directory and make it executable for your system.

3. Run your browser and access the cgitest.html resource, as shown in Figure 25-6.

4. Click the reference Customer Feedback form. Your browser will display an interactive form awaiting your feedback.

5. Select a recipient for your comments from the popup list.

6. Type your e-mail address to the text field marked From:

7. Click on one of the radio buttons to provide a rating for each of the three categories: Perl, Graphics, and Midi Music.

8. Select one or more of the checkboxes in the Mail-Me section.

9. Now that you have completed the form, send your assessment back to the server by clicking the Submit button.

10. The server responds with a new page (Figure 25-7) indicating it has processed and acted upon the data you supplied.

11. Return to the test CGI-bin directory and edit the cgiform.pl code so that the variable $DEBUG is set to 1 in the BEGIN subroutine. This activates debugging output.

12. Access the form once more using your browser's reload command. Follow Steps 6 through 9 once more. You can make different choices.

13. Transmit your assessment by clicking on the Submit button.

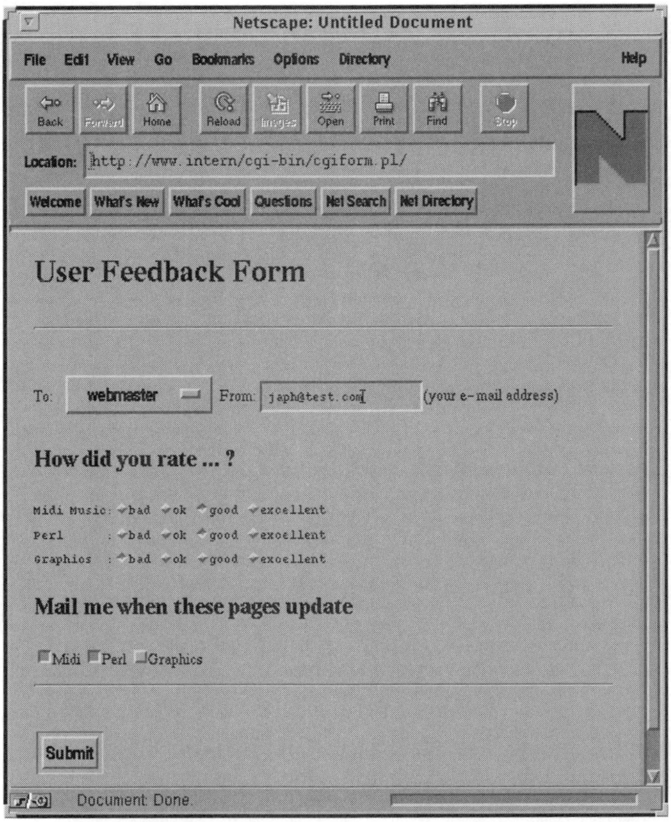

Figure 25-6 An HTML form generated by the CGI.pm Perl module

14. The server responds with a Thank you page that includes debug output from the program, formatted as HTML text, as shown in Figure 25-8. The debug output shows the values parsed from the parameter string by CGI.pm.

How It Works

For form-based CGI programs, the crucial concept to grasp is the stateless nature of the dialog between the client's browser, the server HTTP process, and the CGI program itself.

Generally, when an application program presents the user with a dialog box for data entry, the application stays running on the computer, waiting to react when the

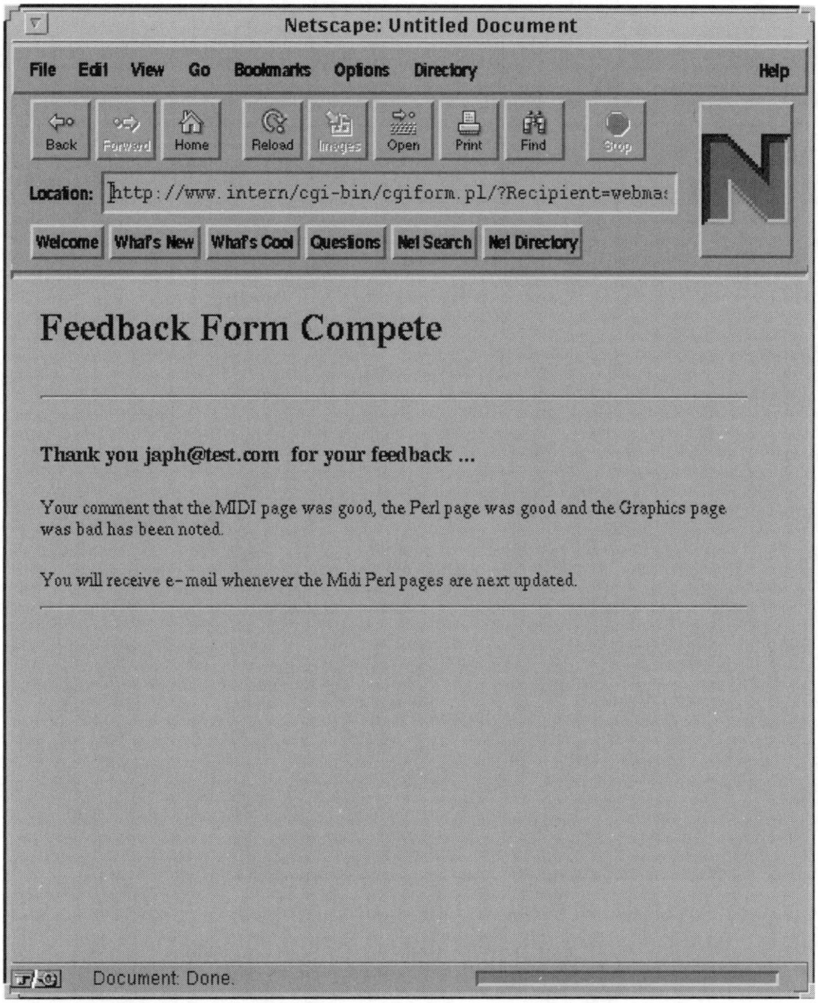

Figure 25-7 A feedback form response generated by a Perl CGI program

user presses the OK button. This is not what is happening in the case of a CGI form. HTTP is a stateless protocol. This means that each download of an HTML page or form is a complete stateless event. The next time you access the server, the server has no information to associate your first request with your second request. Each request is a fresh, context-free transaction.

When you are typing data into an HTML form, it is tempting to think you are talking directly to the CGI program that sent the form mask to the browser. This is not the case. The CGI program that created the form has already terminated when you see the form appear on screen. When you enter data into the fields of the form,

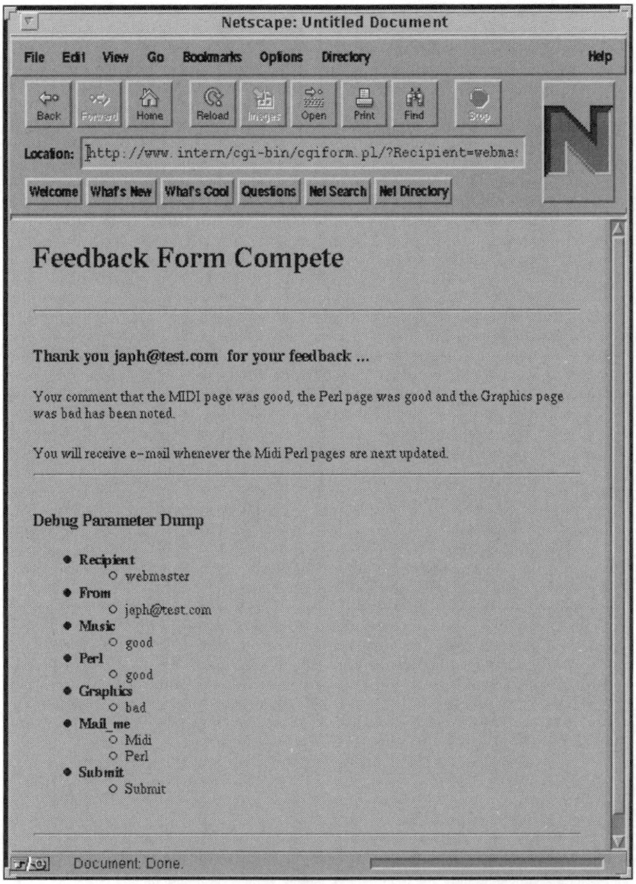

Figure 25-8 A feedback form response displaying a debug translation of the URL parameter string

you are disconnected from the remote server. When you press the Submit button, the data is transmitted back to the remote server in the form of a URL containing a long parameter string. The data processing is not performed by the same processs that transmitted the form, although in this case it is performed by the same script.

The program can behave differently in each step of the dialog only because it checks the parameters that were supplied in the URL. The only method of keeping any kind of state or context in a HTTP dialog is through the URL reference passed back and forth between client and server.

In this case, the first time the program is invoked, the cgiform.pl program is invoked without a parameter list. The program can retrieve the parameter list using the CGI object param method. If param returns a null string, the program deduces that this is a request to send the form to the client. It generates the HTML code to implement the form mask, passes the output to the HTTP server for forwarding, and exits.

The second time the program is invoked, the check on the URL parameter string yields a value. The cgiform.pl program knows that it has received a data transmission from the client and executes the code to process the response. When the response processing is complete, cgiform.pl sends an acknowledgment page back to the client browser.

Comments

Stateless protocols such as HTTP are considerably more efficient than stateful protocols such as FTP. If the HTTP form uses a stateful protocol, then the server machine has to keep the Perl CGI program executing for the entire period that the user completes the data entry. Similarly, the network connection between client and server has to be sustained over long periods. In the case of a popular server servicing several hundred requests every few minutes, the performance of the machine and network would degrade rapidly due to the large number of suspended CGI dialogs waiting for data transmission from the users.

Curiously, for such a fashionable technology, this style of off-line form filling used for HTML forms resembles the transaction-processing idiom used between unfashionable IBM mainframes and their 3270 terminals.

The code for this program demonstrates many of the nice features of the CGI.pm library. Step 14 illustrates the CGI dump method, which is a neat debugging tool. This method displays the parameter string that the program received with the request as part of the response page.

COMPLEXITY
INTERMEDIATE

25.6   How do I...
Use Perl to generate statistics from the common log format?

COMPATIBILITY: PERL 4 PERL 5 UNIX DOS

Problem

How can I generate statistics from the raw data logged by my Web server?

Technique

The WWW server providers have a common log format to save information from accesses to a Web site. A Perl script can be written that understands that format. The log can be read and usage data can be condensed from it. The data gathered can then be sorted to produce interesting statistics such as the top 10 pages being accessed and where most of the accesses are coming from.

Steps

The example script reads an access log file and produces statistics on the number of accesses by machine, number of accesses by resource, number of accesses by time, bytes accessed by machine, and bytes accessed by time.

1. Create a file named log.pl. Enter the following script. First, create an associative array to hold the numeric equivalent for a month. Next, parse each line in the log, saving the number of accesses or byte counts in associative arrays. Not every line will have a byte count. Some accesses will fail or be incorrect.

```perl
%Months = (
            "Jan" => "01",
            "Feb" => "02",
            "Mar" => "03",
            "Apr" => "04",
            "May" => "05",
            "Jun" => "06",
            "Jul" => "07",
            "Aug" => "08",
            "Sep" => "09",
            "Oct" => "10",
            "Nov" => "11",
            "Dec" => "12"
            );

while (<>) {
    chomp;

    # Lines look line: Host Ident AuthUser [Time] "Request" Result Bytes

    $Match = /(\S+)\s+(\S+)\s+(\S+)\s+\[(.*)\]\s+"(.*)"\s+(\S+)\s+(\S+)/;
    if (! $Match) {
        print STDERR "Bad log line - $_\n";
        next;
    }
    $Machine = $1;
    $Ident = $2;
    $AuthUser = $3;
    $Time = $4;
    $Request = $5;
    $Result = $6;
    $Bytes = $7;

    # Time looks like: dd/mm/yyyy:hh:mm:ss

    $Match = $Time =~ m%(..)/(...)/(....):(..):(..):(..)%;
    if (! $Match) {
        print STDERR "Bad time - ($Time) $_\n";
        next;
    }
    $Day = $1;
    $Month = $Months{$2};
    $Year = $3;
```

```
    $Hour = $4;
    $Min = $5;
    $Sec = $6;

    # Requests look like: GET Resource

    $Match = $Request =~ m%\S+\s+(\S+)%;
    if (! $Match) {
        print STDERR "Bad request - ($Request) $_\n";
        next;
    }
    $Resource = $1;

    $AccessByMachine{$Machine}++;
    $AccessByResource{$Resource}++;
    $AccessByTime{"$Year/$Month/$Day $Hour:00"}++;
    if ($Bytes =~ /^\d+$/) {
        $BytesByMachine{$Machine} += $Bytes;
        $BytesByTime{"$Year/$Month/$Day $Hour:00"} += $Bytes;
    }
}
```

2. Create a subroutine for printing out the top 10 users of a specific type. The first argument is a reference to an associative array that holds the data. Sort the keys of the associative array using the value for that key. Print the top 10 keys and their associated value.

```
sub SortedPrint {
    my($Aarray) = $_[0];
    my(@Sorted);

    @Sorted = sort { $Aarray->{$b} <=> $Aarray->{$a} }
        keys %$Aarray;

    for $i (0..9) {
        if (defined($Sorted[$i])) {
            printf "%-30s %10d\n",
                $Sorted[$i], $Aarray->{$Sorted[$i]};
        }
    }
}
```

3. Print the top 10 users in each category.

```
print "\n\tTop Accesses By Machine\n\n";
print "Machine                         Count\n\n";
&SortedPrint(\%AccessByMachine);

print "\n\tTop Accesses by Resource\n\n";
print "Resource                        Count\n\n";
&SortedPrint(\%AccessByResource);

print "\n\tTop Accesses by Time\n\n";
print "Time                            Count\n\n";
&SortedPrint(\%AccessByTime);

print "\n\tTop Byte Count By Machine\n\n";
```

continued on next page

continued from previous page

```perl
print "Machine                                    Count\n\n";
&SortedPrint(\%BytesByMachine);

print "\n\tTop Byte Count by Time\n\n";
print "Time                                       Count\n\n";
&SortedPrint(\%BytesByTime);
```

4. The entire script follows.

```perl
%Months = (
            "Jan" => "01",
            "Feb" => "02",
            "Mar" => "03",
            "Apr" => "04",
            "May" => "05",
            "Jun" => "06",
            "Jul" => "07",
            "Aug" => "08",
            "Sep" => "09",
            "Oct" => "10",
            "Nov" => "11",
            "Dec" => "12"
            );

while (<>) {
    chomp;

    # Lines look line: Host Ident AuthUser [Time] "Request" Result Bytes

    $Match = /(\S+)\s+(\S+)\s+(\S+)\s+\[(.*)\]\s+"(.*)"\s+(\S+)\s+(\S+)/;
    if (! $Match) {
        print STDERR "Bad log line - $_\n";
        next;
    }
    $Machine = $1;
    $Ident = $2;
    $AuthUser = $3;
    $Time = $4;
    $Request = $5;
    $Result = $6;
    $Bytes = $7;

    # Time looks like: dd/mm/yyyy:hh:mm:ss

    $Match = $Time =~ m%(..)/(...)/(....):(..):(..):(..)%;
    if (! $Match) {
        print STDERR "Bad time - ($Time) $_\n";
        next;
    }
    $Day = $1;
    $Month = $Months{$2};
    $Year = $3;
    $Hour = $4;
    $Min = $5;
    $Sec = $6;

    # Requests look like: GET Resource
```

```
    $Match = $Request =~ m%\S+\s+(\S+)%;
    if (! $Match) {
        print STDERR "Bad request - ($Request) $_\n";
        next;
    }
    $Resource = $1;

    $AccessByMachine{$Machine}++;
    $AccessByResource{$Resource}++;
    $AccessByTime{"$Year/$Month/$Day $Hour:00"}++;
    if ($Bytes =~ /^\d+$/) {
        $BytesByMachine{$Machine} += $Bytes;
        $BytesByTime{"$Year/$Month/$Day $Hour:00"} += $Bytes;
    }
}

sub SortedPrint {
    my($Aarray) = $_[0];
    my(@Sorted);

    @Sorted = sort { $Aarray->{$b} <=> $Aarray->{$a} }
        keys %$Aarray;

    for $i (0..9) {
        if (defined($Sorted[$i])) {
            printf "%-30s %10d\n",
                $Sorted[$i], $Aarray->{$Sorted[$i]};
        }
    }
}

print "\n\tTop Accesses By Machine\n\n";
print "Machine                          Count\n\n";
&SortedPrint(\%AccessByMachine);

print "\n\tTop Accesses by Resource\n\n";
print "Resource                         Count\n\n";
&SortedPrint(\%AccessByResource);

print "\n\tTop Accesses by Time\n\n";
print "Time                             Count\n\n";
&SortedPrint(\%AccessByTime);

print "\n\tTop Byte Count By Machine\n\n";
print "Machine                          Count\n\n";
&SortedPrint(\%BytesByMachine);

print "\n\tTop Byte Count by Time\n\n";
print "Time                             Count\n\n";
&SortedPrint(\%BytesByTime);
```

5. Create an input file called log.in. Add the following data to it.

```
localhost - - [02/Nov/1995:21:35:59 -0600] "GET / HTTP/1.0" 200 292
localhost - - [02/Nov/1995:21:36:00 -0600] "GET /icons/blank.xbm ⇐
HTTP/1.0" 404 -
localhost - - [02/Nov/1995:21:36:00 -0600] "GET /icons/menu.xbm ⇐
```

continued on next page

continued from previous page

```
HTTP/1.0" 404 -
localhost - - [02/Nov/1995:21:36:06 -0600] "GET / HTTP/1.0" 200 292
localhost - - [02/Nov/1995:21:37:14 -0600] "GET /cgi-bin/calendar ⇐
HTTP/1.0" 200 246
localhost - - [02/Nov/1995:21:38:16 -0600] "GET /cgi-bin/calendar?1995 ⇐
HTTP/1.0" 200 1966
localhost - - [02/Nov/1995:21:39:01 -0600] "GET /cgi-bin/date HTTP/1.0" ⇐
200 29
localhost - - [02/Nov/1995:21:39:22 -0600] "GET /cgi-bin/test-cgi ⇐
HTTP/1.0" 200 450
localhost - - [02/Nov/1995:21:39:55 -0600] "GET /cgi-bin/test-env ⇐
HTTP/1.0" 200 512
localhost - - [02/Nov/1995:21:41:21 -0600] "GET /cgi-bin/date HTTP/1.0" ⇐
200 29" 200 29
localhost - - [02/Nov/1995:21:41:36 -0600] "GET /cgi-bin/date HTTP/1.0" ⇐
200 29" 200 29
localhost - - [02/Nov/1995:21:41:45 -0600] "GET /cgi-bin/date HTTP/1.0" ⇐
200 29" 200 29
localhost - - [02/Nov/1995:21:42:17 -0600] "GET /cgi-bin/date" 200 29
xcel - - [05/Nov/1995:14:06:01 -0600] "GET / HTTP/1.0" 200 292
xcel - - [05/Nov/1995:14:06:02 -0600] "GET /icons/blank.xbm HTTP/1.0" ⇐
404 -
xcel - - [05/Nov/1995:14:06:02 -0600] "GET /icons/menu.xbm HTTP/1.0" ⇐
404 -
xcel - - [05/Nov/1995:14:06:41 -0600] "GET /date HTTP/1.0" 404 -
xcel - - [05/Nov/1995:14:07:16 -0600] "GET /cgi-bin/date HTTP/1.0" 200 ⇐
29
xcel - - [05/Nov/1995:14:10:05 -0600] "GET /cgi-bin/test-env HTTP/1.0" ⇐
200 512
```

6. Run the script with this command:

```
perl log.pl log.in
```

── Output ──

Top Accesses By Machine

Machine	Count
localhost	13
xcel	6

Top Accesses by Resource

Resource	Count
/cgi-bin/date	6
/	3
/icons/menu.xbm	2
/cgi-bin/test-env	2
/icons/blank.xbm	2
/cgi-bin/calendar?1995	1
/cgi-bin/calendar	1
/date	1
/cgi-bin/test-cgi	1

```
            Top Accesses by Time

Time                    Count
1995/11/02 21:00           13
1995/11/05 14:00            6

            Top Byte Count By Machine

Machine Count

localhost                3903
xcel                      833

            Top Byte Count by Time

Time                    Count

1995/11/02 21:00         3903
1995/11/05 14:00          833
```

End Output

How It Works

The basic idea behind the script is simple: Use an associative array to store each type of statistic desired. Each key of the associative array represents a different item of the type being counted (e.g., a machine). The value of the array element is the accumulated count for that key (the number of bytes retrieved by the machine). The associative array can then be sorted to give useful information (the machine retrieving the most bytes).

Comments

The print subroutine could be made more general. It could take the heading and the number of elements to be printed.

COMPLEXITY
INTERMEDIATE

25.7 How do I...
Use Perl to generate a usage graph for my WWW site?

COMPATIBILITY: PERL 4 | PERL 5 | UNIX | DOS

Problem

How can I create graphic representations of the number of accesses logged at my Web site?

Technique

Perl does not have any built-in graphing functions, but this How-To explains a method for creating simple character-based graphs. The program sorts the usage data, determines the range of the data, and prints character sequences proportional to the value of each data point.

Steps

The example script is based on How-To 25.6, which shows how to collect usage data from the access logs. The data collection portion of the script from How-To 25.6 is copied unmodified. The data collected by the script is then used to produce simple graphs.

1. Create a file called graph.pl. Add the data collection portion of How-To 25.6 to it.

```perl
%Months = (
            "Jan" => "01",
            "Feb" => "02",
            "Mar" => "03",
            "Apr" => "04",
            "May" => "05",
            "Jun" => "06",
            "Jul" => "07",
            "Aug" => "08",
            "Sep" => "09",
            "Oct" => "10",
            "Nov" => "11",
            "Dec" => "12"
            );

while (<>) {
    chomp;

    # Lines look line: Host Ident AuthUser [Time] "Request" Result Bytes

    $Match = /(\S+)\s+(\S+)\s+(\S+)\s+\[(.*)\]\s+"(.*)"\s+(\S+)\s+(\S+)/;
    if (! $Match) {
        print STDERR "Bad log line - $_\n";
        next;
    }
    $Machine = $1;
    $Ident = $2;
    $AuthUser = $3;
    $Time = $4;
    $Request = $5;
    $Result = $6;
    $Bytes = $7;

    # Time looks like: dd/mm/yyyy:hh:mm:ss

    $Match = $Time =~ m%(..)/(...)/(....):(..):(..):(..)%;
    if (! $Match) {
        print STDERR "Bad time - ($Time) $_\n";
```

```
        next;
    }
    $Day = $1;
    $Month = $Months{$2};
    $Year = $3;
    $Hour = $4;
    $Min = $5;
    $Sec = $6;

    # Requests look like: GET Resource

    $Match = $Request =~ m%\S+\s+(\S+)%;
    if (! $Match) {
        print STDERR "Bad request - ($Request) $_\n";
        next;
    }
    $Resource = $1;

    $AccessByMachine{$Machine}++;
    $AccessByResource{$Resource}++;
    $AccessByTime{"$Year/$Month/$Day $Hour:00"}++;
    if ($Bytes =~ /^\d+$/) {
        $BytesByMachine{$Machine} += $Bytes;
        $BytesByTime{"$Year/$Month/$Day $Hour:00"} += $Bytes;
    }
}
```

2. Define a global variable to hold the maximum number of characters that can be used in showing the data. Add a subroutine that takes a reference to an associative array. Sort the associative array by the values stored in the array to find the maximum value in the array. This value is used to determine the size of a unit (one character in the graph). Sort the associative array by key field so the graph presents the data in an ordered fashion. Print the key field, a number of * characters based on the data value, and the data value.

```
$Xlen = 50;

sub Graph {
    my($Aarray) = $_[0];
    my($High, $Unit, @SortedTimes, $Time);

    $High = (sort { $b <=> $a } values %$Aarray)[0];
    $Unit = $High / $Xlen;

    @SortedTimes = sort { $a cmp $b } keys %$Aarray;

    for $Time (@SortedTimes) {
        print "$Time ";
        print "*" x (int($Aarray->{$Time} / $Unit) + 1);
        print "  $Aarray->{$Time}\n";
    }
}
```

3. Use the associative arrays created from the access logs as arguments to the subroutine.

```
print "\n\tAccesses by Time\n\n";
&Graph(\%AccessByTime);

print "\n\tByte Count by Time\n\n";
&Graph(\%BytesByTime);
```

4. Here is the entire script.

```
%Months = (
                "Jan" => "01",
                "Feb" => "02",
                "Mar" => "03",
                "Apr" => "04",
                "May" => "05",
                "Jun" => "06",
                "Jul" => "07",
                "Aug" => "08",
                "Sep" => "09",
                "Oct" => "10",
                "Nov" => "11",
                "Dec" => "12"
                );

while (<>) {
    chomp;

    # Lines look line: Host Ident AuthUser [Time] "Request" Result Bytes

    $Match = /(\S+)\s+(\S+)\s+(\S+)\s+\[(.*)\]\s+"(.*)"\s+(\S+)\s+(\S+)/;
    if (! $Match) {
        print STDERR "Bad log line - $_\n";
        next;
    }
    $Machine = $1;
    $Ident = $2;
    $AuthUser = $3;
    $Time = $4;
    $Request = $5;
    $Result = $6;
    $Bytes = $7;

    # Time looks like: dd/mm/yyyy:hh:mm:ss

    $Match = $Time =~ m%(..)/(...)/(....):(..):(..):(..)%;
    if (! $Match) {
        print STDERR "Bad time - ($Time) $_\n";
        next;
    }
    $Day = $1;
    $Month = $Months{$2};
    $Year = $3;
    $Hour = $4;
    $Min = $5;
    $Sec = $6;
```

```
    # Requests look like: GET Resource

    $Match = $Request =~ m%\S+\s+(\S+)%;
    if (! $Match) {
        print STDERR "Bad request - ($Request) $_\n";
        next;
    }
    $Resource = $1;

    $AccessByMachine{$Machine}++;
    $AccessByResource{$Resource}++;
    $AccessByTime{"$Year/$Month/$Day $Hour:00"}++;
    if ($Bytes =~ /^\d+$/) {
        $BytesByMachine{$Machine} += $Bytes;
        $BytesByTime{"$Year/$Month/$Day $Hour:00"} += $Bytes;
    }
}

$Xlen = 50;

sub Graph {
    my($Aarray) = $_[0];
    my($High, $Unit, @SortedTimes, $Time);

    $High = (sort { $b <=> $a } values %$Aarray)[0];
    $Unit = $High / $Xlen;

    @SortedTimes = sort { $a cmp $b } keys %$Aarray;

    for $Time (@SortedTimes) {
        print "$Time ";
        print "*" x (int($Aarray->{$Time} / $Unit) + 1);
        print "   $Aarray->{$Time}\n";
    }
}

print "\n\tAccesses by Time\n\n";
&Graph(\%AccessByTime);

print "\n\tByte Count by Time\n\n";
&Graph(\%BytesByTime);
```

5. Create a file called graph.in. Add the following access log data to it.

```
localhost - - [02/Nov/1995:21:35:59 -0600] "GET / HTTP/1.0" 200 292
localhost - - [02/Nov/1995:21:36:00 -0600] "GET /icons/blank.xbm ⇐
HTTP/1.0" 404 -
localhost - - [02/Nov/1995:21:36:00 -0600] "GET /icons/menu.xbm ⇐
HTTP/1.0" 404 -
localhost - - [02/Nov/1995:21:36:06 -0600] "GET / HTTP/1.0" 200 292
localhost - - [02/Nov/1995:21:37:14 -0600] "GET /cgi-bin/calendar ⇐
HTTP/1.0" 200 246
localhost - - [02/Nov/1995:21:38:16 -0600] "GET /cgi-bin/calendar?1995 ⇐
HTTP/1.0" 200 1966
localhost - - [02/Nov/1995:21:39:01 -0600] "GET /cgi-bin/date HTTP/1.0" ⇐
200 29
localhost - - [02/Nov/1995:21:39:22 -0600] "GET /cgi-bin/test-cgi ⇐
```

continued on next page

continued from previous page

```
HTTP/1.0" 200 450
localhost - - [02/Nov/1995:21:39:55 -0600] "GET /cgi-bin/test-env ⇐
HTTP/1.0" 200 512
localhost - - [02/Nov/1995:21:41:21 -0600] "GET /cgi-bin/date HTTP/1.0" ⇐
200 29" 200 29
localhost - - [02/Nov/1995:21:41:36 -0600] "GET /cgi-bin/date HTTP/1.0" ⇐
200 29" 200 29
localhost - - [02/Nov/1995:21:41:45 -0600] "GET /cgi-bin/date HTTP/1.0" ⇐
200 29" 200 29
localhost - - [02/Nov/1995:21:42:17 -0600] "GET /cgi-bin/date" 200 29
xcel - - [05/Nov/1995:14:06:01 -0600] "GET / HTTP/1.0" 200 292
xcel - - [05/Nov/1995:14:06:02 -0600] "GET /icons/blank.xbm HTTP/1.0" ⇐
404 -
xcel - - [05/Nov/1995:14:06:02 -0600] "GET /icons/menu.xbm HTTP/1.0" ⇐
404 -
xcel - - [05/Nov/1995:14:06:41 -0600] "GET /date HTTP/1.0" 404 -
xcel - - [05/Nov/1995:14:07:16 -0600] "GET /cgi-bin/date HTTP/1.0" 200 ⇐
29
xcel - - [05/Nov/1995:14:10:05 -0600] "GET /cgi-bin/test-env HTTP/1.0" ⇐
200 512
```

6. Run the script in this way:

```
perl graph.pl graph.in
```

─ Output ───

```
Accesses by Time

1995/11/02 21:00 ************************************************  13
1995/11/05 14:00 ************************  6

          Byte Count by Time

1995/11/02 21:00 ************************************************  3903
1995/11/05 14:00 ***********  833
```

─ End Output ───

How It Works

The graph is a simple representation of the data as a series of * characters. The number of characters is based on the value of the data point. The maximum value of the data to be graphed, plus the maximum number of characters that can be printed, gives the value that each * represents. With this information, you can graph each collected data point with the appropriate number of characters printed.

The statement

```
$High = (sort { $b <=> $a } values %$Aarray)[0];
```

sorts the values of the associative array and returns a list in descending order. The

```
[0]
```

removes the first value from the list and returns it. In this case, it is the largest value in the array.

The x operator is a repeat operator. The statement

```perl
print "*" x 20;
```

prints 20 stars.

Comments

Character graphs are a simple but informative method of analyzing this type of data. For a sophisticated presentation, you can arrange to pass the data to a dedicated graphing program.

EXTENDING
PERL 5

EXTENDING PERL 5

How do I...

One of the most useful features of Perl 5 is its ability to have external libraries linked into it. Through this, Perl allows people to add new commands to Perl's command set. Currently, programmers are working on extending Sybase and Oracle into Perl so people can write Perl scripts that interact with Sybase and Oracle databases. Other projects have already extended Perl to include graphical libraries such as curses and Tk. Chapter 24 outlines how to write Perl 5 Tk programs. This chapter outlines the steps, considerations, and information needed to extend Perl.

Before moving on, we should discuss how all the elements in this chapter relate to Perl, extending Perl, and the process of adding an extension. Following is a list of the steps to be taken when extending Perl 5.

- Run the script h2xs on the header file of the library. This creates the extension directory in the Perl source tree and any subsequent files needed for the extension.

- Modify the typemap file to tell Perl how to manipulate any special data types the library uses.

- Edit the .pm and .xs files created.

- Edit the Makefile.PL file, created to set any compile time options needed.

- Run the Configure script in the Perl 5 source tree. This modifies any makefile that will compile in the new extension.

If all the steps are completed correctly, the new functions should be available in the newly compiled version of the Perl binary. This chapter outlines each of the preceding steps and more. Once you read this chapter, you will have enough information to extend your own functions into Perl.

Each How-To in this chapter builds on knowledge gained from the preceding How-To. To avoid a lot of forward or backward referencing, read the How-To's in this chapter in their sequential order.

26.1   Use the Perl Script h2xs

A script called h2xs is used to help reduce the amount of effort required when adding an extension to Perl 5. This How-To will demonstrate how to use the h2xs script to enhance your efforts of extending Perl.

26.2   Make Perl Understand My Data Types

Because your new extension might have many new data types, telling Perl how to use them and how they behave is important. This How-To will outline the use of the typemap file and how it helps Perl understand your data types.

26.3   Transform a Reference to a Char **

Knowing how to translate C data types to Perl data types is an essential piece of information in extending Perl. This How-To demonstrates one of the most common translations that can occur.

26.4   Extend Perl to Include My Function

This How-To demonstrates what steps are required in telling Perl about your new function.

26.5   Return More Than One Value from a Function

A lot of Perl functions return more than one element from a function. This How-To shows how to do this.

26.6   Have Perl Automatically Deallocate My Variables

When extending Perl, the last thing you want is to create a huge memory leak. Perl has an internal memory management convention so variables will automatically get deallocated when they go out of scope. This How-To will show you how to do this.

26.7   Set Default Values for Parameters in My XSUB Routines

Many of Perl's built-in functions assume a value if one is not passed. This How-To will show you how to do the same with your new function calls.

26.8   Create Variable-Length Parameter Lists

Setting a default value in the parameter list may not be enough. A variable-length parameter list may be the only way to set dynamic value variables without making them mandatory in the function call. This How-To will demonstrate how to do this.

26.9   Create a Callback Function in Perl

Having Perl call a C library is one thing, but what happens when the C function has to talk back to the Perl script? This How-To will show you the other side of the Perl-to-C communication channel.

26.10   Compile My Extension into Perl

Once everything has been written and added, what do I do so Perl will incorporate my new function calls? This How-To will show you the basic steps to compile your new extension.

For this chapter to be of assistance, you must have the latest copy of Perl. As of this writing, the latest released version of Perl is 5.001 patch level m.

COMPLEXITY
BEGINNING

26.1   How do I...
Use the Perl script h2xs?

COMPATIBILITY: PERL 5   UNIX

Problem

I want to extend Perl to include my libraries. I know that the Perl script h2xs helps, but how?

Technique

The Perl script h2xs is a tool that Larry Wall gave the rest of Perl programmers to aid them in extending Perl. The h2xs script reads the given C header file and creates the extension directory and the extension files needed for adding a new extension to Perl. Four files are created: a template for the XSUB routines (.xs), the module that is the file that will be included to make use of the extension (.pm), a makefile (Makefile.PL) that tells Perl how to compile the new extension, and a manifest of all the files created. As an example, this How-To uses the password function library header file, which is /usr/include/pwd.h.

Steps

1. From the shell, change directories to the Perl source directory.

2. Run the h2xs Perl script on your header file.

```
$ h2xs /usr/include/pwd.h
```

This will result in the following being printed to the screen.

Output

```
Writing ext/Pwd/Pwd.pm
Writing ext/Pwd/Pwd.xs
Writing ext/Pwd/Makefile.PL
```

End Output

We are using the header file /usr/include/pwd.h only as an example. If your header file is called gizmo.h and it resides in /home/gizmo/src/include, then you should type in

```
$ h2xs /home/gizmo/src/include/gizmo.h
```

and the following will be printed to the screen.

Output

```
Writing ext/Gizmo/Gizmo.pm
Writing ext/Gizmo/Gizmo.xs
Writing ext/Gizmo/Makefile.PL
```

End Output

3. Examine the files created.

```
use ExtUtils::MakeMaker;
# See lib/ExtUtils/MakeMaker.pm for details of how to influence
# the contents of the Makefile that is written.
WriteMakefile(
    'NAME'      => 'Pwd',
    'VERSION'   => '0.1',
    'LIBS'      => [''],    # e.g., '-lm'
```

```
    'DEFINE'    => '',     # e.g., '-DHAVE_SOMETHING'
    'INC'       => '',     # e.g., '-I/usr/include/other'
);
package Pwd;

require Exporter;
require DynaLoader;
require AutoLoader;

@ISA = qw(Exporter DynaLoader);
# Items to export into callers namespace by default. Note: do not export
# names by default without a very good reason. Use EXPORT_OK instead.
# Do not simply export all your public functions/methods/constants.
@EXPORT = qw(
);

sub AUTOLOAD {
    # This AUTOLOAD is used to 'autoload' constants from the constant()
    # XS function. If a constant is not found, then control is passed
    # to the AUTOLOAD in AutoLoader.

    local($constname);
    ($constname = $AUTOLOAD) =~ s/.*:://;
    $val = constant($constname, @_ ? $_[0] : 0);
    if ($! != 0) {
    if ($! =~ /Invalid/) {
        $AutoLoader::AUTOLOAD = $AUTOLOAD;
        goto &AutoLoader::AUTOLOAD;
    }
    else {
        ($pack,$file,$line) = caller;
        die "Your vendor has not defined Pwd macro $constname, used at $file
line $line.
";
    }
    }
    eval "sub $AUTOLOAD { $val }";
    goto &$AUTOLOAD;
}

bootstrap Pwd;

# Preloaded methods go here.

# Autoload methods go after __END__, and are processed by the autosplit
program.

1;
__END__


#include "EXTERN.h"
#include "perl.h"
#include "XSUB.h"
```

continued on next page

continued from previous page

```
#include <pwd.h>

static int
not_here(s)
char *s;
{
    croak("%s not implemented on this architecture", s);
    return -1;
}

static double
constant(name, arg)
char *name;
int arg;
{
    errno = 0;
    switch (*name) {
    case '_':
    if (strEQ(name, "__need_FILE"))
#ifdef __need_FILE
        return __need_FILE;
#else
        goto not_there;
#endif
    break;
    }
    errno = EINVAL;
    return 0;

not_there:
    errno = ENOENT;
    return 0;
}

MODULE = Pwd        PACKAGE = Pwd

double
constant(name,arg)
    char *      name
    int         arg
```

How It Works

The Perl script h2xs reads the given header file and creates four files: MANIFEST, Makefile.PL, the .xs file, and the .pm file. The Makefile.PL, the .xs file, and the .pm file are used to tie the new extension into Perl. The .xs file contains function prototypes that Perl can use to call the new functions. The .xs file contains all the new functions that will be compiled into Perl. This file's main purpose is to act as an interpreter between the library being extended into Perl and Perl itself. The .pm file is the module file that will be used by the Perl scripts that wish to take advantage of the new extension. If the .pm module is not used, then the extension may not work properly (or work at all!). Another file created is the Makefile.PL. This file is used to tell the compiler how to compile the new extension into Perl. The details of the Makefile.PL file are discussed in How-To 26.10.

The Perl script h2xs reads the header file looking for functions, constants, and defined variables. It then creates the .xs file based on the contents of the header file. It does this so that any defines created in the C program are available in the Perl scripts. For example, if one C define is defined in a C header file as follows

```
#define IMACDEFINE 10
```

use the same define name in the Perl code. The h2xs script maintains this compatibility by using the function constant inside the .xs file. When the string IMACDEFINE is found in a script, Perl examines it and asks a few questions, one of the most important questions being, "What is this value?" Let's say the following lines of code are in a Perl script.

```
if ($myVariable eq IMACDEFINE)
{
    print "C define found.\n";
}
```

The Perl parser will evaluate the line and try to determine if it knows what IMACDEFINE is. The Perl internal parser checks to see if it knows what the string IMACDEFINE is by calling the constant function. If the constant function recognizes it, then the True value, in this case 10, is returned. If the value is not found, then the value is taken as a scalar. (If your Perl script uses the -w flag, then you will get a warning about the possible use of a future reserved word.)

Comments

Once the h2xs script has been run, the framework is in place to extend Perl. We say "framework" because h2xs does not include any of the functions prototyped in the header file. This is the responsibility of you, the programmer.

COMPLEXITY
ADVANCED

26.2 How do I...
Make Perl understand my data types?

COMPATIBILITY: PERL 5   UNIX

Problem

I have a special data type and I want Perl to understand it. How do I do this?

Technique

For Perl to understand your data type, you need to add the data type to the typemap file. For Perl to understand different data types in relation to Perl's own internal data types, there must be some method, or file, to make the connection. This is the purpose of the typemap file. The typemap file allows for new data types to become, or become related to, an internal Perl data type. The first thing to determine is the type of the newly introduced data type. Table 26-1 outlines standard C data types and their related Perl typedefs.

PERL TYPEMAP TYPE	C DATA TYPE	DESCRIPTION
T_IV	int	Integer type.
T_CHAR	char	Single character. This type represents a single byte, not a character array.
T_DOUBLE	double	Double precision floating point.
T_ENUM	enum	Use this if the type represents an enumerated type.
T_LONG	long int	Long integer.
T_FLOAT	float	Single precision floating point.
T_SHORT	short int	Short integer.
T_PTR	void *	Use this when the type represents a pointer to void.
T_PTROBJ	structure	Use this when the type represents a pointer to a structure. The T_PTROBJ type requires the object be blessed.
T_PTRREF	structure	Use this when the type represents a pointer to a structure. The T_PTRREF type does not require that the object be blessed.
T_U_CHAR	unsigned char	Unsigned single byte.
T_U_LONG	unsigned long int	Unsigned long integer.
T_U_SHORT	unsigned short int	Unsigned short integer.

Table 26-1 Internal Perl data types

If you look at the file lib/ExtUtils/typemap under the Perl 5 source tree, you will see all the standard C data types linked to a Perl internal data type. This global typemap file saves you from having to define all the standard C types in every new extension to Perl. The typemap file in the extension directory is for personal data types that Larry Wall could not predict.

Steps

1. Copy the files Pwd.xs, Pwd.pm, and Makefile.PL from How-To 26.1 into the current directory.

2. The first step in defining a data type is to determine what Perl data type your C data type is. Using the /usr/include/passwd.h file once again, use the structure passwd that is defined in the password header file. In our header file, the passwd structure is defined as follows.

```
struct passwd
{
```

```
    char *pw_name;        /* Username.      */
    char *pw_passwd;      /* Password.      */
    __uid_t pw_uid;       /* User ID.       */
    __gid_t pw_gid;       /* Group ID.      */
    char *pw_gecos;       /* Real name.     */
    char *pw_dir;         /* Home directory. */
    char *pw_shell;       /* Shell program. */
};
```

The structure does not create a new data type; it defines a group of common entities labeled under the structure name. In this case, the structure name is passwd. You want Perl to understand the structure, so you need to create a new type via the typedef command in C. Define the type in the Pwd.xs file. Edit the Pwd.xs file and add the following lines. Additions are in bold for clarity.

```
#include "EXTERN.h"
#include "perl.h"
#include "XSUB.h"

#include <pwd.h>

/*
 * Create a new type named Passwd.
 */
typedef struct passwd Passwd;

static int
not_here(s)
char *s;
{
    croak("%s not implemented on this architecture", s);
    return -1;
}

static double
constant(name, arg)
char *name;
int arg;
{
    errno = 0;
    switch (*name) {
    }
    errno = EINVAL;
    return 0;

not_there:
    errno = ENOENT;
    return 0;
}

MODULE = Pwd          PACKAGE = Pwd
```

continued on next page

continued from previous page

```
double
constant(name,arg)
    char *     name
    int      arg
```

Now that you have defined a new type named Passwd, decide what Perl type Passwd is most closely related to. Using Table 26-1, determine that Passwd is a typedef to a structure and the best definition is T_PTROBJ. If a type was already defined for the passwd structure, then you would use the one defined instead of creating your own.

3. Edit a file named typemap and add the following line to the TYPEMAP section of the typemap file. If the typemap file does not already exist or the TYPEMAP section is not defined, do not worry. Just add the line; the TYPEMAP section is assumed if one has not been added.

```
Passwd   *   T_PTROBJ
```

Be very careful when adding information to the typemap file because the format is very specific. The preceding entry was typed in as follows.

```
Passwd<space>*<tab>T_PTROBJ
```

How It Works

The typemap file is used as a database for all the data types introduced by the extension. The file that introduces Perl to the library's data types is the .xs file. The new data types are introduced when the .xs file is converted into a .c file via the .xs to .c compiler, which is called xsubpp. If xsubpp does not know how to manipulate a data type, it returns an error. For example, if the extension name is Cdk and there is a data type named BOO *, then xsubpp might return the following error message

```
Error: 'BOO *' not in typemap in Cdk.xs, line 1357
make[1]: *** [Cdk.c] Error 1
make[1]: Leaving directory `/opt/perl5.001m/ext/Cdk'
```

if the data type BOO * is not listed in the typemap file. There are actually three sections to the typemap file: INPUT, OUTPUT, and TYPEMAP. Table 26-2 explains each section in the typemap file.

SECTION NAME	DESCRIPTION	
INPUT	Tells the compiler how to translate Perl values into C variables.	
OUTPUT	Tells the compiler how to translate C values into Perl variables.	
TYPEMAP	Maps a C type to a Perl value.	

Table 26-2 Typemap file directives

Following is an example of a typemap file that uses all three directives.

```
SV *      T_SVREF
AV *      T_AVREF
```

```
HV *        T_HVREF
CV *        T_CVREF

INPUT
T_SVREF
    if (sv_isa($arg, \"${ntype}\"))
        $var = (SV*)SvRV($arg);
    else
        croak(\"$var is not of type ${ntype}\")
T_AVREF
    if (sv_isa($arg, \"${ntype}\"))
        $var = (AV*)SvRV($arg);
    else
        croak(\"$var is not of type ${ntype}\")
T_HVREF
    if (sv_isa($arg, \"${ntype}\"))
        $var = (HV*)SvRV($arg);
    else
        croak(\"$var is not of type ${ntype}\")
T_CVREF
    if (sv_isa($arg, \"${ntype}\"))
        $var = (CV*)SvRV($arg);
    else
        croak(\"$var is not of type ${ntype}\")

OUTPUT
T_SVREF
    $arg = newRV((SV*)$var);
T_AVREF
    $arg = newRV((SV*)$var);
T_HVREF
    $arg = newRV((SV*)$var);
T_CVREF
    $arg = newRV((SV*)$var);
```

The TYPEMAP directive does not have to be listed; it is assumed if it is not found.

Comments

To get a better understanding of the format of the typemap file, look at the global typemap file.

COMPLEXITY
ADVANCED

26.3 How do I...
Transform a reference to a char **?

COMPATIBILITY: PERL 5   UNIX

Problem

I have a Perl reference C function that takes a char ** as a parameter. I do not know how to translate it into something Perl would understand.

Technique

To do this, create a macro in the .xs file that will transform a Perl reference into a C character array (char **). To do this, you must first understand what data types are available in Perl. Table 26-3 outlines the internal data types available and what they mean.

PERL TYPEDEF	DATA TYPE	PURPOSE
SV	Scalar Value	The standard Perl variable. A typical scalar variable is $age=27, where $age is the scalar variable.
AV	Array Value	The standard Perl array. A typical array variable is $pet[0] = "Parrot", where @pet is the array variable.
HV	Hash Value	The standard Perl hash. A typical hash variable is $name{'Parrot'} = "Gizmo", where %name is the hash variable.
IV	Integer Value	An internal data type that Perl uses. Its main purpose is to hold either an integer or a pointer.
I32	Integer Value	A typedef, which is always a 32-bit integer.
I16	Integer Value	A typedef, which is always a 16-bit integer.

Table 26-3 Internal Perl data types

Now that you understand the data types that Perl understands, you need to convert the Perl data type to the C data type. To do this, you must draw parallels between the C data type and the Perl data type. The Perl reference can be assumed to point to a list of lists. This means the reference can point to an AV * type, where each element points to an AV *. Each element of the subarray points to a scalar value, SV *. A char ** C type is actually a pointer to an array of char *. A char * is a pointer to an array of char. With this parallel drawn, you need a way to convert Perl pointers into C pointers. To help you, Table 26-4 lists all the functions needed to perform this task.

SV FUNCTION PROTOTYPE	DESCRIPTION
SvRV (SV *)	This macro dereferences the SV reference into the casted type.
SvPV (PV *, int strlen)	This macro dereferences the SV into a char *.
av_len (AV *)	This determines the length of the given AV.
av_fetch (AV *, I32 index, I32 lvalue)	This function gets the value at the index. If the lvalue is nonzero, then the value is set to the lvalue.

Table 26-4 Internal Perl functions

Steps

1. Copy the files Pwd.xs, Pwd.pm, Makefile.PL, and typemap from How-To 26.2 into the current directory.

2. Edit the Pwd.xs file created by h2xs and add the following lines. Additions are in bold for clarity.

```
#include "EXTERN.h"
#include "perl.h"
#include "XSUB.h"

#include <pwd.h>

/*
 * Create a new type named Passwd.
 */
typedef struct passwd Passwd;

/*
 * This converts a Perl reference into a char ** C data type.
 */
#define MAKE_CHAR_MATRIX(START,INPUT,NEWARRAY,ARRAYSIZE,ARRAYLEN)             \
    do {                                                                      \
        AV *array    = (AV *)SvRV((INPUT));                                   \
        int x, y;                                                             \
                                                                             \
        (ARRAYLEN)   = av_len ( array );                                      \
                                                                             \
        for (x = 0; x <= (ARRAYLEN); x++)                                     \
        {                                                                     \
            SV *tmp          = *av_fetch(array,x,FALSE);                      \
            AV *subArray     = (AV *)SvRV(tmp);                               \
            int subLen       = av_len (subArray);                            \
            (ARRAYSIZE)[x+(START)] = subLen + 1;                             \
                                                                             \
            for (y=0; y <= subLen; y++)                                       \
            {                                                                 \
                SV *sv   = *av_fetch(subArray,y,FALSE);                       \
                (NEWARRAY)[x+(START)][y+(START)] = strdup((char *)SvPV(sv,na)); \
            }                                                                 \
        }                                                                     \
        (ARRAYLEN)++;                                                         \
    } while (0)

static int
not_here(s)
char *s;
{
    croak("%s not implemented on this architecture", s);
    return -1;
}

static double
constant(name, arg)
```

continued on next page

continued from previous page

```
char *name;
int arg;
{
    errno = 0;
    switch (*name) {
    }
    errno = EINVAL;
    return 0;

not_there:
    errno = ENOENT;
    return 0;
}


MODULE = Pwd        PACKAGE = Pwd

double
constant(name,arg)
    char *       name
    int    arg
```

How It Works

The macro MAKE_CHAR_MATRIX takes five parameters: START, INPUT, NEWARRAY, ARRAYSIZE, and ARRAYLEN. The START parameter allows you to start the matrix at 0,0 or 1,1 or X,X. This is in case the Perl matrix and the C matrix don't start at the same location. INPUT is the SV * reference. The NEWARRAY parameter is the array where the information is stored; ARRAYSIZE is the size of the array being translated. The last parameter, ARRAYLEN, is an array that contains the lengths of each row in the matrix. This is just in case the matrix is not a perfect rectangle. Given these variables, the transformation may now begin.

The first line of the macro

```
AV *array = (AV *)SvRV((INPUT));
```

takes the initial SV reference and creates an AV *. This is actually the matrix itself. You can get the height of the matrix using the function av_len, which is what is done on the line

```
(ARRAYLEN) = av_len (array);
```

Notice that the length of the AV * is stored in the variable *ARRAYLEN*. Once you have the height of the matrix, each row of the matrix can be converted into a C type.
Inside the *for* loop, the line

```
SV *tmp = *av_fetch(array,x,FALSE);
```

creates a pointer of SV * from the AV *, created from the SV reference. The SV * just created is converted into an AV * using the function SvRV.

```
AV *subArray = (AV *)SvRV(tmp);
```

Of course, you need to keep the length of this row in the matrix. This is done on the line

```
int subLen = av_len (subArray);
```

Now you have the ability to scan through each row in the matrix. Using the logic from above, reapply it against each row in the matrix and start again, on a lesser level. You need another *for* loop so you can cycle through each record of each row from the matrix.

Each record in the row has to be fetched from the row pointer. This is done by

```
SV *sv = *av_fetch(subArray,y,FALSE);
```

Finally, the SV * returned from above is casted into a char * and copied into a cell in the matrix. This is done by the line

```
(NEWARRAY)[x+(START)][y+(START)] = strdup((char *)SvPV(sv,na));
```

Comments

This macro has to be defined before the first MODULE keyword. When the .xs to .c converter, xsubpp, converts the .xs file, it takes everything up to the first MODULE keyword as strict C code. This means that no conversion is performed on any code before the first MODULE keyword. This is useful if you need to add a function into the .xs function, which should not be converted.

COMPLEXITY
ADVANCED

26.4   How do I...
Extend Perl to include my function?

COMPATIBILITY: PERL 5   UNIX

Problem

I do not know what to do so my new command will be native to Perl. What do I do to make this happen?

Technique

Add the definition of the extended subroutine (XSUB) in the .xs file. In this example, you add the definition to the file Pwd.xs. For example, say you are adding a new password function called getuseruid. This function will accept a login name and return the user ID (UID) value back. We assume that the directory ext/Pwd has been created and all the files under the directory exist.

Steps

1. Copy the files Pwd.xs, Pwd.pm, Makefile.PL, and typemap from How-To 26.3 into the current directory.

2. Edit the Pwd.xs file and add the following lines. The new additions are in bold for clarity. Make sure the new lines are added after the first occurrence of the MODULE keyword.

```
#include "EXTERN.h"
#include "perl.h"
#include "XSUB.h"

#include <pwd.h>

/*
 * Create a new type named Passwd.
 */
typedef struct passwd Passwd;

/*
 * This converts a Perl reference into a char ** C data type.
 */
#define MAKE_CHAR_MATRIX(START,INPUT,NEWARRAY,ARRAYSIZE,ARRAYLEN)           \
    do {                                                                   \
        AV *array  = (AV *)SvRV((INPUT));                                  \
        int x, y;                                                          \
                                                                           \
        (ARRAYLEN) = av_len ( array );                                     \
                                                                           \
        for (x = 0; x <= (ARRAYLEN); x++)                                  \
        {                                                                  \
            SV *tmp             = *av_fetch(array,x,FALSE);                \
            AV *subArray        = (AV *)SvRV(tmp);                         \
            int subLen          = av_len (subArray);                       \
            (ARRAYSIZE)[x+(START)] = subLen + 1;                           \
                                                                           \
            for (y=0; y <= subLen; y++)                                    \
            {                                                              \
                SV *sv  = *av_fetch(subArray,y,FALSE);                     \
                (NEWARRAY)[x+(START)][y+(START)] = strdup((char *)SvPV(sv,na)); \
            }                                                              \
        }                                                                  \
        (ARRAYLEN)++;                                                      \
    } while (0)

static int
not_here(s)
char *s;
{
    croak("%s not implemented on this architecture", s);
    return -1;
}

static double
constant(name, arg)
char *name;
int arg;
{
```

```
    errno = 0;
    switch (*name) {
    }
    errno = EINVAL;
    return 0;

not_there:
    errno = ENOENT;
    return 0;
}

MODULE = Pwd        PACKAGE = Pwd

double
constant(name,arg)
    char *      name
    int     arg

int
getuserid(loginId)
    char * loginId
    CODE:
    {
        /* Get the password record.      */
        Passwd * record = getpwnam (loginId);

        /* Return the value if it exists, -1 otherwise. */
        if (record != (Passwd *)NULL)
        {
            RETVAL = record->pw_uid;
        }
        else
        {
            RETVAL = -1;
        }
    }
    OUTPUT:
        RETVAL
```

3. Edit the Pwd.pm file and add the new function into the export list. The
additions are in bold for clarity.

```
package Pwd;

require Exporter;
require DynaLoader;
require AutoLoader;

@ISA = qw(Exporter DynaLoader);

# Items to export into callers namespace by default. Note: do not export
# names by default without a very good reason. Use EXPORT_OK instead.
# Do not simply export all your public functions/methods/constants.
@EXPORT = qw(getuserid);
```

continued on next page

continued from previous page

```perl
sub AUTOLOAD {
    # This AUTOLOAD is used to 'autoload' constants from the constant()
    # XS function.  If a constant is not found, then control is passed
    # to the AUTOLOAD in AutoLoader.

    local($constname);
    ($constname = $AUTOLOAD) =~ s/.*:://;
    $val = constant($constname, @_ ? $_[0] : 0);
    if ($! != 0) {
    if ($! =~ /Invalid/) {
        $AutoLoader::AUTOLOAD = $AUTOLOAD;
        goto &AutoLoader::AUTOLOAD;
    }
    else {
        ($pack,$file,$line) = caller;
        die "Your vendor has not defined Pwd macro $constname, used at $file
line $line.
";
    }
    }
    eval "sub $AUTOLOAD { $val }";
    goto &$AUTOLOAD;
}

bootstrap Pwd;

# Preloaded methods go here.

# Autoload methods go after __END__, and are processed by the autosplit
program.

1;
__END__
```

4. Recompile Perl so the new additions can be incorporated into Perl. If you
do not know how to do this, read How-To 26.10.

5. Edit a file named getuser.pl and type the following script into it.

```perl
#!/usr/local/bin/perl -w

# Use our Pwd.pm module.
use Pwd;

# Get the current login name.
my $login = getlogin();

# Call our new function.
my $uid = getuserid($login);

# Print out the results.
print "Login $login has UID $uid\n";
```

6. Run the getuser.pl script.

```
% getuser.pl
Login glover has UID 100
```

How It Works

When a new extended subroutine (XSUB) is being added to the .xs file, a specific format has to be adhered to or else the script xsubpp (the .xs to .c converter) will complain.

 The parameter list of the subroutine definition cannot have any white space; the following is incorrect.

```
int
getuserid( loginId )
    char *    loginId
```

 The return value and the prototype must be on separate lines; the following is incorrect.

```
int getuserid( loginId )
    char *    loginId
```

The parameter list has to be in one of the following formats.

```
<TAB>type *<TAB>variable
<TAB>type<TAB>&variable
<TAB>type<TAB>variable
```

The new subroutine has to be defined after the first occurrence of the MODULE keyword because the .xs to .c converter (xsubpp) takes everything it finds before the first MODULE keyword as strict C code.

Inside an .xs file, several directives control the way XSUBs work and what they return. Three of the directives, CODE, OUTPUT, and RETVAL, control the way the function behaves. Table 26-5 outlines the directives and their purpose.

DIRECTIVE NAME	PURPOSE
CODE	This is usually written when the XSUB is too complex. It is usually written when the C-to-Perl interface is not the same.
PPCODE	This is usually written when the XSUB returns more than one value.
OUTPUT	The output actually has a dual purpose. It can be used to control which of the parameter variables should be updated within the function, and it can be used to designate which variable will be the output of the function when the function exits.
RETVAL	This is the return value of the function.

Table 26-5 XSUB keywords

The modifications to the Pwd.pm file export the new function, so you can call the function is if it were native to Perl. If you had not exported the function getuserid, then you would have had to call the function with the module name attached to it. The following example demonstrates what the getuser.pl script would look like if you had not exported the function.

```
#!/usr/local/bin/perl -w

# Use our Pwd.pm module.
use Pwd;

# Get the current login name.
my $login = Pwd::getlogin();

# Call our new function.
my $uid = getuserid($login);

# Print out the results.
print "Login $login has UID $uid\n";
```

Comments

To understand more about Perl's API, read the perlapi online manual page.

COMPLEXITY
ADVANCED

26.5 How do I...
Return more than one value from a function?

COMPATIBILITY: PERL 5   UNIX

Problem

I have a function that needs to return more than one value. How do I do this?

Technique

Perl returns more than one variable by using a stack pointer. This stack pointer is manipulated with the macros outlined in Table 26-6.

FUNCTION	PURPOSE
PUSHs (SV*)	Pushes a SV * pointer onto the stack pointer. There must be enough room for the SV * or this will fail.
PUSHi(IV)	Pushes a IV type variable onto the stack pointer. There must be enough room for the IV or this will fail.
PUSHn(double)	Pushes a double precision integer onto the stack pointer. There must be enough room for the double or this will fail.
PUSHp(char *, I32)	Pushes a char * pointer onto the stack pointer. The I32 parameter is the length of the char * pointer. There must be enough room for the char * or this will fail.

FUNCTION	PURPOSE
XPUSHs (SV*)	Pushes a SV * pointer onto the stack pointer. If there is not enough room for this pointer, the macro will expand the stack pointer to accommodate the new item.
XPUSHi(IV)	Pushes a IV type variable onto the stack pointer. If there is not enough room for this pointer, the macro will expand the stack pointer to accommodate the new item.
XPUSHn(double)	Pushes a double precision integer onto the stack pointer. If there is not enough room for this pointer, the macro will expand the stack pointer to accommodate the new item.
XPUSHp(char *, I32)	Pushes a char * pointer onto the stack pointer. The I32 parameter is the length of the char * pointer. If there is not enough room for this pointer, the macro will expand the stack pointer to accommodate the new item.
dSP	Declares and initializes a local copy of the stack pointer.

Table 26-6 Perl's stack functions

In this example, the function you are adding returns a list of user names that matches the given group number. Because the list you are returning is filled with char * pointers, use the macro XPUSHs to push the values onto the stack.

Steps

1. Copy the files Pwd.xs, Pwd.pm, Makefile.PL, and typemap from How-To 26.4 into the current directory.

2. Edit Pwd.xs and add the following lines into the file. The additions are in bold for clarity.

```
#include "EXTERN.h"
#include "perl.h"
#include "XSUB.h"

#include <pwd.h>

/*
 * Create a new type named Passwd.
 */
typedef struct passwd Passwd;

/*
 * This converts a Perl reference into a char ** C data type.
 */
#define MAKE_CHAR_MATRIX(START,INPUT,NEWARRAY,ARRAYSIZE,ARRAYLEN)        \
    do {                                                                \
        AV *array  = (AV *)SvRV((INPUT));                               \
        int x, y;                                                       \
                                                                        \
        (ARRAYLEN) = av_len ( array );                                  \
                                                                        \
        for (x = 0; x <= (ARRAYLEN); x++)                               \
```

continued on next page

continued from previous page

```
        {                                                                    \
            SV *tmp              = *av_fetch(array,x,FALSE);                  \
            AV *subArray         = (AV *)SvRV(tmp);                          \
            int subLen           = av_len (subArray);                        \
            (ARRAYSIZE)[x+(START)] = subLen + 1;                            \
                                                                             \
            for (y=0; y <= subLen; y++)                                      \
            {                                                                \
                SV *sv  = *av_fetch(subArray,y,FALSE);                       \
                (NEWARRAY)[x+(START)][y+(START)] = strdup((char *)SvPV(sv,na)); \
            }                                                                \
        }                                                                    \
        (ARRAYLEN)++;                                                        \
    } while (0)

static int
not_here(s)
char *s;
{
    croak("%s not implemented on this architecture", s);
    return -1;
}

static double
constant(name, arg)
char *name;
int arg;
{
    errno = 0;
    switch (*name) {
    }
    errno = EINVAL;
    return 0;

not_there:
    errno = ENOENT;
    return 0;
}

MODULE = Pwd        PACKAGE = Pwd

double
constant(name,arg)
    char *     name
    int        arg

int
getuserid(loginId)
    char * loginId
    CODE:
    {
        /* Get the password record.       */
        Passwd * record = getpwnam (loginId);

        /* Return the value if it exists, -1 otherwise. */
        if (record != (Passwd *)NULL)
```

```
        {
            RETVAL = record->pw_uid;
        }
        else
        {
            RETVAL = -1;
        }
    }
    OUTPUT:
        RETVAL

void
getgidlist(GID)
    int     GID
    PPCODE:
    {
        Passwd * record = getpwent();
        while (record != (Passwd *)NULL)
        {
            if (record->pw_gid == GID)
            {
                XPUSHs (sv_2mortal(newSVpv(record->pw_name, strlen(record-
                    >pw_name))));
            }
            record = getpwent();
        }
    }
```

3. Edit Pwd.pm and add the following lines into the file. The additions are in bold for clarity.

```
package Pwd;

require Exporter;
require DynaLoader;
require AutoLoader;

@ISA = qw(Exporter DynaLoader);
# Items to export into callers namespace by default. Note: do not export
# names by default without a very good reason. Use EXPORT_OK instead.
# Do not simply export all your public functions/methods/constants.
@EXPORT = qw(getuserid getgidlist);

sub AUTOLOAD {
    # This AUTOLOAD is used to 'autoload' constants from the constant()
    # XS function.  If a constant is not found, then control is passed
    # to the AUTOLOAD in AutoLoader.

    local($constname);
    ($constname = $AUTOLOAD) =~ s/.*:://;
    $val = constant($constname, @_ ? $_[0] : 0);
    if ($! != 0) {
    if ($! =~ /Invalid/) {
        $AutoLoader::AUTOLOAD = $AUTOLOAD;
        goto &AutoLoader::AUTOLOAD;
    }
```

continued on next page

continued from previous page

```
    else {
        ($pack,$file,$line) = caller;
        die "Your vendor has not defined Pwd macro $constname, used at $file
line $line.
";
    }
    }
    eval "sub $AUTOLOAD { $val }";
    goto &$AUTOLOAD;
}

bootstrap Pwd;

# Preloaded methods go here.

# Autoload methods go after __END__, and are processed by the autosplit
program.

1;
__END__
```

4. Recompile Perl so the new additions can be incorporated into Perl. If you do not know how to do this, read How-To 26.10.

5. Edit a file named getgids.pl and type the following script into it.

```
#!/usr/local/bin/perl -w

# Use our Pwd.pm module.
use Pwd;

# Get the GID from the command line.
my $gid = $ARGV[0] || die "$0 GID\n";

# Call our new function.
my @userList = getgidlist($gid);

print "The following users have GID $uid\n";

# Print out each user found.
foreach $user (@userList)
{
    print "User $user\n";
}
```

6. Run the getgids.pl script.

```
% getgids.pl
```

Output

```
The following users have GID 100
User glover
User gizmo
User elmo
```

End Output

How It Works

The function getpwent is actually a C function from the C library, not a Perl function. Though the functions have the same name and perform the same task, the above code is written in C, not Perl. The variable record is a pointer to type Passwd, which is defined at the top of the Pwd.xs file. The *while* loop is the control loop for this code segment. When the variable record is null, the *while* loop exits and the function exits, leaving what you have pushed on the stack where it is. Each iteration of the loop means you have a new nonnull record from the passwd file. Each record is checked to see if the GID of the record equals the GID passed into the function. If it does, then the login ID has to be pushed onto the stack, which is performed by the statement

```
XPUSHs (sv_2mortal(newSVpv(record->pw_name, strlen (record->pw_name))));
```

There are three elements to this line. The first, innermost element is the creation of the SV * pointer. This is done by the function newSVpv. The newSVpv function creates and loads a SV * type. It takes two arguments: the char * to load and the number of characters of the char * you want loaded. The resulting SV * is then passed to sv_2mortal. The sv_2mortal function takes an existing SV * and makes it mortal. The concept of *mortal* means that when the Perl code leaves the current context, the memory is automatically freed. The last element is XPUSHs. XPUSHs is a macro that pushes elements onto the stack.

While this function is running, it keeps pushing SV * elements onto the stack. When the function exits, the elements pushed onto the stack are now accessible. This is how Perl returns more than one variable from a function call. Notice that the return type of this function is defined as void. This is because you do not explicitly return anything from the function. This is standard with PPCODE functions like the one you created.

Comments

This example uses the XPUSHs macro because you do not know how many values will be returned. If you did know how many values were to be returned, you could initialize the stack with the dSP macro and use the PUSHs macro.

COMPLEXITY
ADVANCED

26.6   How do I...
Have Perl automatically deallocate my variables?

COMPATIBILITY: PERL 5   UNIX

Problem

I want to be able to tell Perl how to free up any memory that my data types are using safely. How do I do this?

Technique

Create something the C++ language likes to call *destructors*. A destructor is a method specifically designed for cleaning up after an object. This can involve everything from freeing up the memory used to closing file descriptors to possibly nothing at all. The convenience of a destructor is that you never need to call it directly. Once the variable goes out of scope, the destructor is called to clean up after the object. Perl uses the same concept, only it uses packages to create the illusion of a destructor.

Steps

1. Copy the files Pwd.xs, Pwd.pm, Makefile.PL, and typemap from How-To 26.5 into the current directory.

2. Edit the Pwd.xs file and add the following lines to the file. The additions are in bold for clarity.

```
#include "EXTERN.h"
#include "perl.h"
#include "XSUB.h"

#include <pwd.h>

/*
 * Create a new type named Passwd.
 */
typedef struct passwd Passwd;

/*
 * This converts a Perl reference into a char ** C data type.
 */
#define MAKE_CHAR_MATRIX(START,INPUT,NEWARRAY,ARRAYSIZE,ARRAYLEN)        \
    do {                                                                 \
        AV *array   = (AV *)SvRV((INPUT));                               \
        int x, y;                                                        \
                                                                         \
        (ARRAYLEN) = av_len ( array );                                   \
                                                                         \
        for (x = 0; x <= (ARRAYLEN); x++)                                \
        {                                                                \
            SV *tmp        = *av_fetch(array,x,FALSE);                   \
            AV *subArray   = (AV *)SvRV(tmp);                            \
            int subLen     = av_len (subArray);                          \
            (ARRAYSIZE)[x+(START)] = subLen + 1;                         \
                                                                         \
            for (y=0; y <= subLen; y++)                                  \
            {                                                            \
                SV *sv   = *av_fetch(subArray,y,FALSE);                  \
                (NEWARRAY)[x+(START)][y+(START)] = strdup((char *)SvPV(sv,na)); \
            }                                                            \
        }                                                                \
```

```
        (ARRAYLEN)++;                                              \
    } while (0)

static int
not_here(s)
char *s;
{
    croak("%s not implemented on this architecture", s);
    return -1;
}

static double
constant(name, arg)
char *name;
int arg;
{
    errno = 0;
    switch (*name) {
    }
    errno = EINVAL;
    return 0;

not_there:
    errno = ENOENT;
    return 0;
}


MODULE = Pwd        PACKAGE = Pwd


double
constant(name,arg)
    char *      name
    int      arg

int
getuserid(loginId)
    char * loginId
    CODE:
    {
        /* Get the password record.      */
        Passwd * record = getpwnam (loginId);

        /* Return the value if it exists, -1 otherwise. */
        if (record != (Passwd *)NULL)
        {
            RETVAL = record->pw_uid;
        }
        else
        {
            RETVAL = -1;
        }
    }
    OUTPUT:
        RETVAL
```

continued on next page

continued from previous page

```
void
getgidlist(GID)
    int GID
    PPCODE:
    {
        Passwd * record = getpwent();
        while (record != (Passwd *)NULL)
        {
            if (record->pw_uid == GID)
            {
                XPUSHs (sv_2mortal(newSVpv(record->pw_name, strlen(record-
                    >pw_name))));
            }
            record = getpwent();
        }
    }


MODULE = Pwd         PACKAGE = PasswdPtr    PREFIX=pwd_
void
pwd_DESTROY(object)
    Passwd *    object
    CODE:
    {
        free (object);
    }
```

3. Recompile Perl so the new additions can be incorporated into Perl. If you do not know how to do this, read How-To 26.10.

How It Works

When the function getpasswdrec() is called, Perl considers the C pointer Passwd * to be a blessed object because the typedef file specifies the Passwd type to be of type T_PTROBJ. When the variable goes out of scope and needs to be destroyed, Perl looks for the destroy method. If it does not exist, then nothing is done and a memory leak could occur. Because you set up the DESTROY function, Perl finds it and calls it. Perl does not care whether the reference it passes to the DESTROY function is a blessed reference or a C structure. The responsibility for cleaning up the memory belongs to the XSUB DESTROY function, not to Perl. This means the responsibility for cleaning up the memory lies with the programmer and the code written and placed in the CODE: fragment of the DESTROY function.

Comments

This example uses the Passwd pointer for consistency, but this pointer does not have to be destroyed unless an explicit copy of the pointer has been made.

COMPLEXITY
INTERMEDIATE

26.7 How do I...
Set default values for parameters in my XSUB routines?

COMPATIBILITY: PERL 5   UNIX

Problem

I know I can set default values for some of the parameters to my XSUBs. How do I do this?

Technique

For each parameter that is going to get a default value, you need to declare the parameter, then follow it with an equal sign and a value. The syntax of this is

```
functionName (variable1=value1,variable2=value2);
```

This is very much like assigning an initial value to a variable inside a Perl subroutine.

Steps

 Copy the files Pwd.xs, Pwd.pm, Makefile.PL, and typemap from How-To 26.6 into the current directory.

2. Edit the Pwd.xs file and add the following lines to the file. The additions are in bold for clarity.

```
#include "EXTERN.h"
#include "perl.h"
#include "XSUB.h"

#include <pwd.h>

/*
 * Create a new type named Passwd.
 */
typedef struct passwd Passwd;

/*
 * Use a global variable to hold the current password filename.
 */
char *  PASSWD_FILE = (char *)NULL;

/*
 * This converts a Perl reference into a char ** C data type.
 */
#define MAKE_CHAR_MATRIX(START,INPUT,NEWARRAY,ARRAYSIZE,ARRAYLEN)     \
    do {                                                             \
```

continued on next page

continued from previous page

```
            AV *array   = (AV *)SvRV((INPUT));                              \
            int x, y;                                                       \
                                                                            \
            (ARRAYLEN) = av_len ( array );                                  \
                                                                            \
            for (x = 0; x <= (ARRAYLEN); x++)                               \
            {                                                               \
                SV *tmp        = *av_fetch(array,x,FALSE);                  \
                AV *subArray   = (AV *)SvRV(tmp);                           \
                int subLen     = av_len (subArray);                         \
                (ARRAYSIZE)[x+(START)] = subLen + 1;                        \
                                                                            \
                for (y=0; y <= subLen; y++)                                 \
                {                                                           \
                    SV *sv  = *av_fetch(subArray,y,FALSE);                  \
                    (NEWARRAY)[x+(START)][y+(START)] = strdup((char *)SvPV(sv,na)); \
                }                                                           \
            }                                                               \
            (ARRAYLEN)++;                                                   \
        } while (0)

static int
not_here(s)
char *s;
{
    croak("%s not implemented on this architecture", s);
    return -1;
}

static double
constant(name, arg)
char *name;
int arg;
{
    errno = 0;
    switch (*name) {
    }
    errno = EINVAL;
    return 0;

not_there:
    errno = ENOENT;
    return 0;
}

MODULE = Pwd         PACKAGE = Pwd

double
constant(name,arg)
    char *      name
    int         arg

int
getuserid(loginId)
    char * loginId
    CODE:
    {
```

```
        /* Get the password record.      */
        Passwd * record = getpwnam (loginId);

        /* Return the value if it exists, -1 otherwise. */
        if (record != (Passwd *)NULL)
        {
            RETVAL = record->pw_uid;
        }
        else
        {
            RETVAL = -1;
        }
    }
    OUTPUT:
        RETVAL

void
getgidlist(GID)
    int GID
    PPCODE:
    {
        Passwd * record = getpwent();
        while (record != (Passwd *)NULL)
        {
            if (record->pw_uid == GID)
            {
                XPUSHs (sv_2mortal(newSVpv(record->pw_name, strlen(record-
                        >pw_name))));
            }
            record = getpwent();
        }
    }

void
setpwfile(filename="/etc/passwd")
    char * filename
    CODE:
    {
        if (PASSWD_FILE != (char *)NULL)
        {
            free (PASSWD_FILE);
        }

        PASSWD_FILE = strdup (filename);
    }

char *
getpwfile()
    CODE:
    {
        RETVAL = PASSWD_FILE;
    }
    OUTPUT:
        RETVAL

MODULE = Pwd    PACKAGE = PasswdPtr    PREFIX=pwd_
```

continued on next page

continued from previous page

```
void
pwd_DESTROY(object)
    Passwd *   object
    CODE:
    {
        free (object);
    }
```

3. Edit Pwd.pm and add the following lines into the file. The additions are in bold for clarity.

```
package Pwd;

require Exporter;
require DynaLoader;
require AutoLoader;

@ISA = qw(Exporter DynaLoader);
# Items to export into callers namespace by default. Note: do not export
# names by default without a very good reason. Use EXPORT_OK instead.
# Do not simply export all your public functions/methods/constants.
@EXPORT = qw(getuserid getgidlist setpwfile getpwfile);

sub AUTOLOAD {
    # This AUTOLOAD is used to 'autoload' constants from the constant()
    # XS function.  If a constant is not found, then control is passed
    # to the AUTOLOAD in AutoLoader.

    local($constname);
    ($constname = $AUTOLOAD) =~ s/.*:://;
    $val = constant($constname, @_ ? $_[0] : 0);
    if ($! != 0) {
    if ($! =~ /Invalid/) {
        $AutoLoader::AUTOLOAD = $AUTOLOAD;
        goto &AutoLoader::AUTOLOAD;
    }
    else {
        ($pack,$file,$line) = caller;
        die "Your vendor has not defined Pwd macro $constname, used at
$file line $line.
";
    }
     }
     eval "sub $AUTOLOAD { $val }";
     goto &$AUTOLOAD;
}

bootstrap Pwd;

# Preloaded methods go here.

# Autoload methods go after __END__, and are processed by the autosplit
program.

1;
__END__
```

4. Recompile Perl so the new additions can be incorporated into Perl. If you do not know how to do this, read How-To 26.10.

5. Edit a file named setpw.pl and type the following script into it.

```
#!/usr/local/bin/perl -w

# Use our Pwd.pm module.
use Pwd;

# Get the password file from the command line.
my $file = $ARGV[0] || die "$0 filename\n";

# Set the password file without a name.
setpwfile();

# Get the name of the password file.
my $passwdFile = getpwfile();

# Print out what the value is.
print "Password file is <$passwdFile>\n";

# Set the password file to the name given off the command line.
setpwfile($file);

# Get the name of the password file.
my $passwdFile = getpwfile();

# Print out what the value is.
print "Password file is <$passwdFile>\n";
```

6. Run the script.

```
% setpw.pl /dev/null
```

Output

```
Password file is </etc/passwd>
Password file is </dev/null>
```

End Output

How It Works

When the script h2xs translates the .xs file into the .c file, it has the intelligence to translate a defaulted parameter and match it with the correct value. It does this by using the variable items that the xsubpp script provides to each function in the .xs file. This variable holds a count of all the parameters passed to the function. The actual C code generated then checks the value of items and determines if the defaulted variable should be set to the value passed in or to the default value. To help clear this up, the following code segment is what the setpwfile function looks like after xsubpp is run on the preceding copy of Pwd.xs.

```
XS(XS_Pwd_setpwfile)
{
    dXSARGS;
    if (items < 0 || items > 1) {
        croak("Usage: Pwd::setpwfile(filename=\"/etc/passwd\")");
    }
    {
        char *  filename;

        if (items < 1)
            filename = "/etc/passwd";
        else {
            filename = (char *)SvPV(ST(0),na);
        }
```

Notice that, after the declaration of the filename char pointer, the number of elements passed to the function is checked via the items variable. Because you have only one parameter to this function, items is checked to see if it is less than 1. If so, then nothing is passed to the function. Therefore, the default value /etc/passwd should be used. If the value of items is greater than 1, then use the value passed to the function, in this case, the value that is currently sitting in the function stack, ST, at index 0.

A warning flag should be raised at this point because the order of the defaulted parameters against the nondefaulted parameters is important. Because the parameter list works like a stack (in fact, it is a stack) if the defaulted parameters and nondefaulted parameters are interleaved together, then weird and wonderful things are to be expected when you start omitting parameter values for their defaulted values. For example, say the function above actually takes four parameters: user, time, date, and filename. Create the setpwfile prototype with the assigned defaulted parameters.

```
void
setpwfile(user=root,time,date,filename="/etc/passwd")
    char * user
    char * time
    char * date
    char * filename
```

If this function is called with only two values, the time and date

```
setpwfile ("17:00:00", "June 1 1968");
```

the values of time and date are not set correctly. In fact, the result of calling this function this way sets the variables to the following values.

```
user="17:00:00"
time="June 1 1968"
date=""
filename="/etc/passwd"
```

This is because there is no way to bind the value from the parameter list to the value that is supposed to be assumed when the function starts manipulating the variables and the values. To avoid this, put all the defaulted items at the end of the parameter list in the order of least likely to be defaulted to most likely. The above function fit to this rule would look like this:

```
void
setpwfile(time,date,user=root,filename="/etc/passwd")
```

```
char * time
char * date
char * user
char * filename
```

The user name is more of a dynamic value than the filename of the password file.

Comments

You can use quotes in the default assignments for clarity.

COMPLEXITY
INTERMEDIATE

26.8 How do I...
Create variable-length parameter lists?

COMPATIBILITY: PERL 5   UNIX

Problem

I understand there is a way to have variable-length parameter lists for my XSUBs. How do I do this?

Technique

The XSUB declaration accepts an ellipsis (...) type token, which is akin to the ANSI C ellipsis. The ellipsis states that more parameters may or may not follow at this point, which means that the ellipsis has to be the last element in the function prototype list. To demonstrate this point, the following definition is correct

```
functionName (variable1, variable2, ...)
```

whereas the following is not.

```
functionName (variable1, variable2, ..., variable3)
```

Inside the CODE fragment, the predefined variable items are used to determine if a variable is passed in on the command line. If a value is passed into the function, you have to transform the Perl SV pointer into a C char pointer because the C function getpwnam takes a C char * pointer. To transform the SV pointer to a char pointer, use the SvPV macro. Table 26-7 outlines all the macros provided that manipulate SV types.

FUNCTION	PURPOSE
SvIV (SV*)	Takes a SV pointer and returns an integer.
SvNV (SV*)	Takes a SV pointer and returns a double.
SvPV (SV*, I32)	Takes a SV pointer and an integer. The length of the returned char pointer is
	stored in the integer supplied.

continued on next page

continued from previous page

FUNCTION	PURPOSE	
SvTRUE (SV*)	Returns True if the value of the SV is True.	
SvGROW (SV*, int)	Expands the SV if the macro determines the SV needs more memory.	
SvOK (SV *)	Tells you if the SV pointer has been defined.	
SvIOK (SV *)	Tells you if the SV is an integer.	
SvNOK (SV *)	Tells you if the SV is a double.	
SvPOK (SV *)	Tells you if the SV is a pointer to char.	
SvIOKp (SV *)	Tells you if the SV is an integer. This is considered a private macro and performs a more strict type-check than the macro SvIOK.	
SvNOKp (SV *)	Tells you if the SV is a double. This is considered a private macro and performs a more strict type-check than the macro SvNOK.	
SvPOKp (SV *)	Tells you if the SV is a pointer to char. This is considered a private macro and performs a stricter type-check than the macro SvPOK.	
SvCUR (SV *)	Returns the length of the given SV pointer.	
SvCUR_set (SV *)	Sets the length of the given SV pointer.	

Table 26-7 SV macros

Steps

1. Copy the files Pwd.xs, Pwd.pm, Makefile.PL, and typemap from How-To 26.7 into the current directory.

2. Edit the Pwd.xs file and add the following lines to the file. The additions are in bold for clarity.

```
#include "EXTERN.h"
#include "perl.h"
#include "XSUB.h"

#include <pwd.h>

/*
 * Create a new type named Passwd.
 */
typedef struct passwd Passwd;

/*
 * Use a global variable to hold the current password.
 */
char *  PASSWD_FILE = (char *)NULL;

/*
 * This converts a Perl reference into a char ** C data type.
 */
#define MAKE_CHAR_MATRIX(START,INPUT,NEWARRAY,ARRAYSIZE,ARRAYLEN)       \
    do {                                                               \
        AV *array  = (AV *)SvRV((INPUT));                              \
```

```
            int x, y;                                                           \
                                                                                \
            (ARRAYLEN) = av_len ( array );                                      \
                                                                                \
            for (x = 0; x <= (ARRAYLEN); x++)                                   \
            {                                                                   \
                SV *tmp         = *av_fetch(array,x,FALSE);                     \
                AV *subArray    = (AV *)SvRV(tmp);                             \
                int subLen      = av_len (subArray);                           \
                (ARRAYSIZE)[x+(START)] = subLen + 1;                           \
                                                                                \
                for (y=0; y <= subLen; y++)                                     \
                {                                                               \
                    SV *sv  = *av_fetch(subArray,y,FALSE);                     \
                    (NEWARRAY)[x+(START)][y+(START)] = strdup((char *)SvPV(sv,na)); \
                }                                                               \
            }                                                                   \
            (ARRAYLEN)++;                                                       \
        } while (0)
static int
not_here(s)
char *s;
{
    croak("%s not implemented on this architecture", s);
    return -1;
}

static double
constant(name, arg)
char *name;
int arg;
{
    errno = 0;
    switch (*name) {
    }
    errno = EINVAL;
    return 0;

not_there:
    errno = ENOENT;
    return 0;
}

MODULE = Pwd          PACKAGE = Pwd

double
constant(name,arg)
    char *      name
    int         arg

int
getuserid(...)
    CODE:
    {
        char *loginId;
```

continued on next page

continued from previous page

```
        Passwd *record;

        /* Check the parameter list.        */
        if (items>0)
        {
            loginId=(char *)SvPV(ST(0),na);
        }
        else
        {
            loginId=getlogin();
        }

        /* Get the password record.         */
        record = getpwnam (loginId);

        /* Return the value if it exists, -1 otherwise. */
        if (record != (Passwd *)NULL)
        {
            RETVAL = record->pw_uid;
        }
        else
        {
            RETVAL = -1;
        }
    }
    OUTPUT:
        RETVAL

void
getgidlist(GID)
    int GID
    PPCODE:
    {
        Passwd * record = getpwent();
        while (record != (Passwd *)NULL)
        {
            if (record->pw_uid == GID)
            {
                XPUSHs (sv_2mortal(newSVpv(record->pw_name, strlen(record-
                    >pw_name))));
            }
            record = getpwent();
        }
    }

void
setpwfile(filename="/etc/passwd")
    char * filename
    CODE:
    {
        if (PASSWD_FILE != (char *)NULL)
        {
            free (PASSWD_FILE);
        }

        PASSWD_FILE = strdup (filename);
    }
```

```
char *
getpwfile()
    CODE:
    {
        RETVAL = PASSWD_FILE;
    }
    OUTPUT:
        RETVAL

MODULE = Pwd    PACKAGE = PasswdPtr    PREFIX=pwd_
void
pwd_DESTROY(object)
    Passwd *    object
    CODE:
    {
        free (object);
    }
```

3. Recompile Perl so the new additions can be incorporated into Perl. If you do not know how to do this, read How-To 26.10.

4. Edit a file named getuser.pl and enter the following script into it.

```
#!/usr/local/bin/perl -w

# Use the Pwd.pm module.
use Pwd;
my $UID;

# If users want the UID of a specific user, they can pass it
# in on the command line. Otherwise their UID will be printed.
if (defined $ARGV[0])
{
    $UID = getuserid($ARGV[0]);
}
else
{
    $UID = getuserid();
}
print "User Id: $UID\n"
```

5. Run the script getuser.pl.

```
% getuser.pl
```

Output

```
User Id: 100
```

End Output

```
% getuser.pl glover
```

Output

```
User Id: 100
```

End Output

```
% getuser.pl gizmo
```

Output

```
User Id: 101
```

End Output

How It Works

The most important element in the getuserid function is the assignment of the variable loginId from the function stack. The function stack, ST, is a stack of all the values passed to the function. To get the value from the stack and put it into the correct variable, you need to transform the value from the stack data type into the receiving variable data type. The line

```
loginId=(char *)SvPV(ST(0),na);
```

takes the element in the first element of the ST stack pointer and passes it to the macro SvPV. This macro, as outlined in Table 26-7, takes two parameters: a pointer to SV and an integer. The integer supplied contains the length of the char pointer returned from the SvPV macro. If you do not care about the length, then you can use the global variable *na*. The returning pointer from the SvPV macro is then cast to the correct type; in this case, the correct type is a pointer to char.

Comments

There is an assortment of other macros for both pointers to lists and hashes. To find out more, read the online manual page perlguts.

COMPLEXITY
INTERMEDIATE

26.9   How do I...
Create a callback function in Perl?

COMPATIBILITY: PERL 5   UNIX

Problem

I have a callback function in my C code and I need to have the C code call the Perl script to act on the callback. How do I do this?

Technique

To do this, a call-back routine in the C library must catch the callback and perform the C functions on it, as well as the Perl function . The path of a callback in Perl starts

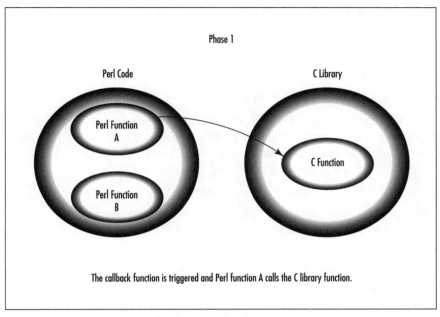

Figure 26-1 Phase one of a Perl callback

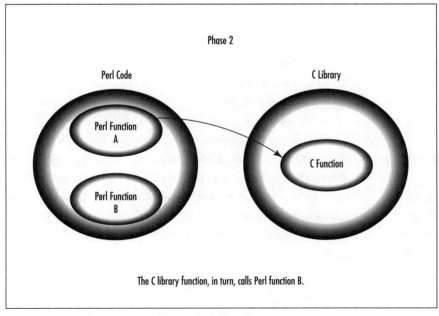

Figure 26-2 Phase two of a Perl callback

at the calling Perl function, which calls the C function. In turn, the C function must call a Perl function to act on the initial callback. Figure 26-1 illustrates the first phase of a Perl callback. Figure 26-2 illustrates the second phase. Four functions in Perl allow you to call Perl subroutines.

The first of the four functions is perl_call_sv; it is prototyped as

```
I32 perl_call_sv(SV* sv, I32 flags);
```

The parameter sv is a pointer to a SV that contains either a name of a subroutine or a reference to a subroutine. The flags parameter indicates how the Perl subroutine is to be called. More detail about the flags field is given in Table 26-8.

The second of the four functions is perl_call_pv; it is prototyped as

```
I32 perl_call_pv(char *subname, I32 flags);
```

The char pointer subname is the name of the Perl subroutine to call.

The third of the four functions is perl_call_pv; it is prototyped as

```
I32 perl_call_method(char *methname, I32 flags);
```

The char pointer methname is the name of the method to call. The class of the method is pushed onto the stack.

The last of the four functions is perl_call_argv; it is prototyped as

```
I32 perl_call_argv(char *subname, I32 flags, register char **argv);
```

The char pointer subname is the name of the Perl subroutine to call, whereas the parameter argv is a null-terminated list of char pointers that get passed to the subroutine when called.

The flags parameter in each of the functions is a bit mask that tells Perl how to call the given subroutine. Table 26-8 lists all the legal values for this field.

FLAG NAME	DESCRIPTION
G_SCALAR	Calls the Perl subroutine in a scalar context. This means the calling subroutine can return only a scalar variable.
G_ARRAY	Calls the Perl subroutine in a list context.
G_DISCARD	If the Perl subroutine puts information on the stack, this flag removes it.
G_NOARGS	Does not return anything from the called subroutine. There is a slight warning when using this flag. When using this flag, you must know that the @_ array remains intact from the previous function. To get a better understanding of what we mean, read the perlcall manual page.
G_EVAL	Traps for an unexpected die from the called routine.

Table 26-8 Perl callback function flags

Every function also returns an integer representing the number of values returned from the Perl subroutine. The returned elements are pushed onto the stack. Using any one of these functions, the C function has the ability to call a Perl subroutine. This example uses the simplest of the four, perl_call_sv.

Steps

1. Copy the files Pwd.xs, Pwd.pm, Makefile.PL, and typemap from How-To 26.8 into the current directory.

2. Edit the Pwd.xs file and add the following lines to the file. The additions are in bold for clarity.

```c
#include "EXTERN.h"
#include "perl.h"
#include "XSUB.h"

#include <pwd.h>

/*
 * Create a new type named Passwd.
 */
typedef struct passwd Passwd;

/*
 * Use a global variable to hold the current password.
 */
char *  PASSWD_FILE = (char *)NULL;

/*
 * This converts a Perl reference into a char ** C data type.
 */
#define MAKE_CHAR_MATRIX(START,INPUT,NEWARRAY,ARRAYSIZE,ARRAYLEN)          \
    do {                                                                  \
        AV *array  = (AV *)SvRV((INPUT));                                 \
        int x, y;                                                         \
                                                                          \
        (ARRAYLEN) = av_len ( array );                                    \
                                                                          \
        for (x = 0; x <= (ARRAYLEN); x++)                                 \
        {                                                                 \
            SV *tmp           = *av_fetch(array,x,FALSE);                 \
            AV *subArray      = (AV *)SvRV(tmp);                          \
            int subLen        = av_len (subArray);                        \
            (ARRAYSIZE)[x+(START)] = subLen + 1;                         \
                                                                          \
            for (y=0; y <= subLen; y++)                                   \
            {                                                             \
                SV *sv  = *av_fetch(subArray,y,FALSE);                    \
                (NEWARRAY)[x+(START)][y+(START)] = strdup((char *)SvPV(sv,na)); \
            }                                                             \
        }                                                                 \
        (ARRAYLEN)++;                                                     \
    } while (0)

static int
not_here(s)
char *s;
```

continued on next page

continued from previous page

```
{
    croak("%s not implemented on this architecture", s);
    return -1;
}

static double
constant(name, arg)
char *name;
int arg;
{
    errno = 0;
    switch (*name) {
    }
    errno = EINVAL;
    return 0;

not_there:
    errno = ENOENT;
    return 0;
}

MODULE = Pwd        PACKAGE = Pwd

double
constant(name,arg)
    char *      name
    int     arg

int
getuserid(...)
    CODE:
    {
        char *loginId;
        Passwd *record;

        /* Check the parameter list.      */
        if (items>0)
        {
            loginId=(char *)SvPV(ST(0),na);
        }
        else
        {
            loginId=getlogin();
        }

        /* Get the password record.       */
        record = getpwnam (loginId);

        /* Return the value if it exists, -1 otherwise. */
        if (record != (Passwd *)NULL)
        {
            RETVAL = record->pw_uid;
        }
        else
        {
            RETVAL = -1;
        }
    }
```

```
    OUTPUT:
        RETVAL

void
getgidlist(GID)
    int GID
    PPCODE:
    {
        Passwd * record = getpwent();
        while (record != (Passwd *)NULL)
        {
            if (record->pw_uid == GID)
            {
                XPUSHs (sv_2mortal(newSVpv(record->pw_name, strlen(record-
                    >pw_name))));
            }
            record = getpwent();
        }
    }

void
setpwfile(filename="/etc/passwd")
    char * filename
    CODE:
    {
        if (PASSWD_FILE != (char *)NULL)
        {
            free (PASSWD_FILE);
        }

        PASSWD_FILE = strdup (filename);
    }

char *
getpwfile()
    CODE:
    {
        RETVAL = PASSWD_FILE;
    }
    OUTPUT:
        RETVAL

void
callbackTest(subName)
    SV *    subName
    CODE:
    {
        perl_call_sv (subName, G_NOARGS);
    }

MODULE = Pwd    PACKAGE = PasswdPtr    PREFIX=pwd_
void
pwd_DESTROY(object)
    Passwd *    object
    CODE:
    {
        free (object);
    }
```

3. Recompile Perl so the new additions can be incorporated into Perl. If you do not know how to do this, read How-To 26.10.

4. Edit a file named callback.pl and enter the following script into it.

```
#!/usr/bin/local/perl -w

# Use the Pwd.pm module.
use Pwd;

sub function1 { print "Inside function 1\n"; }
sub function2 { print "Inside function 2\n"; }

# Call the subroutine called 'function1'
callbackTest ("function1");

# Create a reference to the subroutine called 'function2'
my $functionRef = \&function2;

# Call the subroutine called 'function2'
callbackTest ($functionRef);
```

5. Run the script callback.pl

```
% callback.pl
```

___Output_____

```
Inside function 1.
Inside function 2.
```

___End Output_____

How It Works

When the function callbackTest is called, it is passed a pointer to a SV. This pointer can contain either a C string name of the subroutine or a reference to the call-back subroutine. Notice that you called the subroutines with the flag G_NOARGS. This means that you don't want the return values from the called subroutines. When using this flag, keep in mind that the stack does not get modified.

Comments

The example provided in this How-To is light compared to the rest of the chapter. We did not want to spend too much time on this information because it is still a rough area of Perl 5 extensions. The perlcall manual page states this and provides the following warning.

"WARNING: This document is still under construction. There are bound to be a number of inaccuracies, so tread very carefully for now."

This means the information provided here may be revamped or incorrect. The example does work, so you can rely on the information provided.

COMPLEXITY
BEGINNING

26.10 How do I...
Compile my extension into Perl?

COMPATIBILITY: PERL 5   UNIX

Problem

I have extended Perl, added my functions to my .xs file, modified the typemap file appropriately, and rerun the make. I still can't seem to call my functions from Perl. Why not?

Technique

You need to rerun Configure to tell the makefiles about the new extension. If you do not do this, the makefile will not make the files in the extension directory, which means they will not be compiled into Perl. Before a new extension can be compiled into Perl correctly, the Makefile.PL file has to be edited. If the Makefile.PL file is not edited, then the extension may not compile into Perl correctly. Five default directives are provided in the Makefile.PL file after h2xs has created it. Table 26-9 outlines each directive.

DIRECTIVE	PURPOSE
NAME	This is a text name of the extension. This is a noncritical directive.
VERSION	This is a version number of the extension. This is a noncritical directive.
LIBS	This tells the compiler which libraries are required to compile this extension.
	Both the -L and -I flags are supplied in this directive.
DEFINE	This tells the compiler which defines you want set when compiling in this extension.
INC	This tells the compiler which paths to use to look for header files that
	may be required.

Table 26-9 Makefile.PL default directives

Steps

1. Edit the Makefile.PL file to make sure the contents are correct. Our example of the Pwd extension does not require that Makefile.PL be changed.

2. Change directories into the root directory of the Perl source tree.

3. Run the script Configure.

 Configure

4. Answer all the questions that are appropriate to your particular system and setup. Because running the Configure script is a lengthy process, we show only the questions that relate directly to compiling the new extension. To learn more about compiling Perl, read Appendix B.

5. During the configuration, look for the following message.

— Output

```
Looking for extensions...
A number of extensions are supplied with perl5. You may choose to
compile these extensions for dynamic loading (the default), compile
them into the perl5 executable (static loading), or not include
them at all. Answer "none" to include no extensions.
```

End Output

When the above message is displayed, you will be asked if you want to link your extension dynamically or statically. If your operating system does not support dynamic linking, then you will be asked only which extension you want to link in statically. Following is what will appear if your machine supports dynamic linking.

— Output

```
What extensions do you wish to load dynamically?
[Devel/DProf Fcntl NDBM_File ODBM_File POSIX SDBM_File Socket]
```

End Output

Following is what will appear if your machine supports only static linking.

— Output

```
What extensions do you wish to load statically?
[Devel/DProf Fcntl NDBM_File ODBM_File POSIX SDBM_File Socket]
```

End Output

6. When the preceding question appears, check to make sure your extension is listed. If it is not, then you have to add it. In our case, the extension name is Pwd and it is not in the list.

7. Add the name of the extension to the list. You can retype the whole line and add your extension name at the end, or you can use the special variable $* and your extension name. The following example uses the $* variable. What we typed in is in bold for clarity.

— Output

```
What extensions do you wish to load dynamically?
[Devel/DProf Fcntl NDBM_File ODBM_File POSIX SDBM_File Socket]
```

End Output

$* Pwd

Output

```
*** Substitution done -- please confirm.
What extensions do you wish to load dynamically?
[Devel/DProf Fcntl NDBM_File ODBM_File POSIX SDBM_File Socket Pwd]
What extensions do you wish to load statically? []
```

End Output

8. Answer the rest of the questions and recompile Perl. After the compilation, your extension should be available. To recompile Perl, type in the following in the root of Perl's source tree.

```
% make
```

To recompile and install Perl, type in the following in the root of Perl's source tree.

```
% make install
```

How It Works

Configure needs to be rerun because all the make dependencies and system configurations need to updated. The Configure script re-creates a file called config.sh, which holds all the answers you supplied from the run of the Configure. Once Configure has finished running, your extension should be available.

Comments

Read the README file in the Perl source directory. It will guide you in rebuilding Perl.

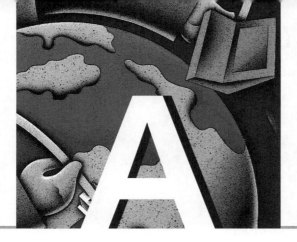

INTERNET RESOURCES

This appendix outlines resources currently available via the Internet. There are seven sections, each of which outlines various methods to get, submit, or read information about Perl and Perl 5. Most of the sites listed have been checked for authentication, but we can't make any promises about whether the sites will still be active by the time you get a chance to try them. We can only hope that they survive the test of time.

A.1 Where do I...
Get the latest copy of Perl from the Internet?

Due to the sheer number of machines on the Net that mirror or maintain a copy of the Perl 5 sources, we have to restrict the list to the three most reliable sites of the Perl sources. The best sites to go to are sites that mirror Comprehensive Perl Archive Network (CPAN). All the sites listed can be accessed using ftp and anonymous login. The sites listed in Tables A-1, A-2, and A-3 are in order of most comprehensive first.

SITE NAME	IP ADDRESS	DIRECTORY	
ftp.netlabs.com	192.94.48.152	/pub/outgoing/perl5.0	
ftp.cis.ufl.edu	128.227.100.198	/pub/perl/CPAN/src/5.0	
ftp.metronet.com	192.245.137.1	/pub/perl/source	

Table A-1 North American Perl 5 ftp sites

SITE NAME	IP ADDRESS	DIRECTORY	
ftp.funet.fi	128.214.248.6	/pub/languages/perl/CPAN/src/5.0	
sunsite.doc.ic.ac.uk	155.198.1.40	/pub/computing/programming/languages/perl/perl.5.0	
ftp.cs.ruu.nl	131.211.80.17	/pub/PERL/perl5.0/src	

Table A-2 European Perl 5 ftp sites

SITE NAME	IP ADDRESS	DIRECTORY	
coombs.anu.edu.au	150.203.76.2	/pub/perl/CPAN/src/5.0	
sungear.mame.mu.oz.au	128.250.209.2	/pub/perl/src/5.0	

Table A-3 Australian Perl 5 ftp sites

A.2   Where do I...
Get the Perl 5 extension libraries?

Due to the sheer number of machines on the Net that mirror or maintain a copy of the Perl 5 sources, we had to restrict the list to the three most reliable sites from which you can get the Perl sources. All the sites listed can be accessed using ftp and anonymous login. The sites listed in Tables A-4, A-5, and A-6 are listed in order of most comprehensive first.

SITE NAME	IP ADDRESS	DIRECTORY	
ftp.cis.ufl.edu	128.227.100.198	/pub/perl/CPAN/modules/by-module	
ftp.metronet.com	192.245.137.6	/pub/perl/perl5/extensions	
ftp.khoros.unm.edu	198.59.155.28	/pub/perl/extensions	

Table A-4 North American Perl 5 extension sites

SITE NAME	IP ADDRESS	DIRECTORY
ftp.funet.fi	128.214.248.6	/pub/languages/perl/CPAN/modules/by-module
sunsite.doc.ic.ac.uk	155.198.1.40	/pub/computing/programming/languages/perl/collections/
		cis.ufl/CPAN/modules/by-module
ftp.cs.ruu.nl	131.211.80.17	/pub/PERL/perl5.0/ext

Table A-5 European Perl 5 extension sites

SITE NAME	IP ADDRESS	DIRECTORY
coombs.anu.edu.au	150.203.76.2	/pub/perl/CPAN/modules/by-module

Table A-6 Australian Perl 5 extension sites

A.3 Where do I...
Find Perl information using USENET?

There are three Perl newsgroups so far: comp.lang.perl.misc, comp.lang.perl.announce, and comp.lang.perl.tk.

The heaviest traffic is in the newsgroup comp.lang.perl.misc. This is a general forum newsgroup, where anyone can post a question asking Perl gurus for advice or help. Of course, we strongly advise you to read the *Frequently Asked Questions* (FAQ) before you post a question here. Even if you don't plan on asking a question, the FAQ can help answer questions before they keep you up at night. The Perl FAQ is a very well maintained and organized list; it has become a very useful reference page for many Perl programmers, ourselves included. If you are relying on USENET for Perl information, you will have to wait until someone, such as the group moderator, posts the FAQ. The FAQ is posted on a fairly regular basis, so you shouldn't have to wait long. If you have ftp access, then any of the sites listed in this appendix will have a copy of the FAQ.

The newsgroup comp.lang.perl.announce is where everyone posts extensions, patches, modules, scripts, and other interesting elements related to Perl.

The last of the three newsgroups, comp.lang.perl.tk, is where the Tk extension to Perl is discussed.

For those who want access to the newsgroup comp.lang.perl but do not have USENET access, there is a mailing list named "Perl-Users" that is the mailing list version of the comp.lang.perl newsgroup. To make posts to the newsgroup, use one of the following e-mail addresses:

Perl-Users@UVAARPA.VIRGINIA.EDU
PERL-USERS@VIRGINIA.EDU

To get added to the mailing list, e-mail one of the two following addresses:

Perl-Users-Request@uvaarpa.Virginia.EDU
Perl-Users-Request@Virginia.EDU

These mailing lists are maintained by Marc Rouleau, who can be reached at mer6g@VIRGINIA.EDU.

A.4 Where do I...
Find Perl information using WWW?

Because the World Wide Web is expanding at astronomical proportions, we can't show even a tenth of all the possible sites. Some of the more notable sites are listed in Table A-7.

URL	DESCRIPTION
http://www.metronet.com/perlinfo/perl5.html	Probably the best Perl 5 Web site we have found. This site is beyond description; it must be visited if you are serious about Perl 5. It has many links to other Perl 5 Web sites.
Http://www.perl.com	This is Tom Christiansen's Web page. It has a lot of information for the more serious Perl programmer. He has some nice links from basic Perl FAQs to CPAN.
http://www.cis.ufl.edu/perl	A nice starting point, but not really a full-blown Perl WWW site. Can be downloaded from the UFL script archive.
http://www.eecs.nwu.edu/perl/perl.html	Very nice reference page. References web.nexor.co.uk and www.metronet.com quite a bit. Worth checking out. For those interested in writing WWW scripts in Perl, follow the WWW-project link.

Table A-7 Perl 5 WWW site list

A.5 Where do I...
Find a Perl script site?

There are two main mechanisms to get publicly available Perl scripts: via ftp and by using a Web browser. The sites described in Tables A-8 and A-9 seem to have the most comprehensive Perl script archive available. The entries in Table A-8 are arranged in the order of most comprehensive first.

SITE NAME	IP ADDRESS	DIRECTORY
ftp.funet.fi	128.214.248.6	/pub/languages/perl/CPAN/scripts
ftp.cis.ufl.edu	128.227.100.198	/pub/perl/CPAN/scripts
coombs.anu.edu.au	150.203.76.2	/pub/perl/CPAN/scripts

Table A-8 Perl script sites (ftp)

Using a Web browser, the sites in Table A-9 maintain an archive of scripts.

URL	DESCRIPTION
http://worldwidemart.com/scripts	CGI Perl script archive.
http://www.metronet.com/1h/perlinfo	Very well-organized script archive. Broken into subject of the script.
http://www.seas.upenn.edu/~mengwong/perlhtml.html	This page contains links to other Perl CGI script archives.

Table A-9 Perl script sites (http)

A.6   Where do I...
Obtain a copy of the Perl *Frequently Asked Questions* (FAQ)?

The FAQ is currently archived on ftp.cis.ufl.edu (128.227.100.198) in the file /pub/perl/doc/FAQ, as well as on rtfm.mit.edu (18.181.0.24) in the subdirectory /pub/usenet/comp.lang.perl. The machine rtfm.mit.edu archives a lot of USENET newsgroups, so the file may be broken up into four or five parts as it was posted; take care when getting the FAQ from rtfm.mit.edu.

A.7   Where do I...
Find Perl mailing lists?

There are quite a few mailing lists for Perl. We have not verified any of these mailing lists; if we did, we would be swamped with mail, so we cannot guarantee that these will work.

Mac Perl

A mailing list pertaining to Mac Perl users. To get information, e-mail mpw-perl-request@iis.ee.ethz.ch.

Database-Independent Interface Query

Buzz Moschetti (buzz@bear.com) has organized a project to create an independent database interface. The main goal of the project is to create a generic database-independent interface to any backend database engine. If you wish to become involved in this project, or have questions, mail perldb-interest-request@vix.com and ask to be placed on the 'perldb-interest' mailing list.

Perl Database Extensions

To join the DBI mailing list, send your request to perldb-interest-request@vix.com.

COMPILING PERL AND THE TK-PERL EXTENSION

B.1 How do I...
Compile Perl on UNIX platforms?

COMPATIBILITY:

Introduction

This appendix describes how to obtain the latest version of Perl and shows you how to approach solving any problems that may occur during the compilation.

Perl is normally distributed in the form of a compressed archive file containing source code, documentation, and the information needed to configure and compile Perl for any supported platform. More recently, it has become possible to obtain pre-built versions of Perl for specific platforms from vendors or Internet locations. If you are working on a platform without a bundled compiler, such as a DOS or Windows PC, then Perl is almost always supplied as a precompiled binary. Installing a pre-built version of Perl may be easier but it takes the fun out of building and configuring Perl for your own machine.

Technique

The steps involved in building Perl are as follows.

● Obtain the latest version from an FTP archive server.

● Decompress the distribution file.

● Expand the distribution into the temporary directories.

● Read the documentation.

● Configure the build software.

● Build the programs in a temporary directory.

● Run the test suite.

● Install the Perl binaries, libraries, and documentation into the production directories.

Steps

1. Obtain the latest version from an FTP-archive server. If you have a WWW browser, obtaining Perl is a simple process. You can download the latest Perl distribution from many sites at the click of a mouse button. A good starting point if you live in North America is Metronet (URL http://www.metronet.com/perlinfo/source/), which lists several sites that hold the latest Perl distribution ready for FTP downloads. European residents can try SunSITE Northern Europe URL http://ftp.doc.ic.ac.uk/.

If you have plain old FTP access, then you need to obtain the address of your nearest server using an Internet location service such as Archie or Gopher and initiate an FTP session to the site. Here you are accessing http://ftp.doc.ic.ac.uk/, the SunSITE FTP archive at Imperial College London. Be sure to reduce bandwidth by using a server in your region. Access the site using the user ID anonymous or FTP. Type

```
ftp ftp@ftp.doc.ic.ac.uk

331-(----GATEWAY CONNECTED TO ftp.doc.ic.ac.uk----)
331-(220 sunsite.doc.ic.ac.uk FTP server ready.)
331 Guest login OK, send your complete e-mail address as password.
Password:
```

Type your e-mail address as a password at the password prompt.

The Perl distribution is held in the /gnu directory at this site. The location will vary from site to site. You may need to retrieve the site INDEX file to locate the exact directory at your FTP server.

Change to the appropriate directory for your site and read the README file. Use the FTP command get README - . The - sign indicates that transfer should send data to stdout, which is usually defined as the terminal screen.

```
ftp> cd /gnu
250-Please read the file README
250-   it was last modified on Wed Jun 14 16:59:00 1995 - 142 days ago

ftp> get README -
150 Opening ASCII mode data connection for README (979 bytes).
...
226 Transfer complete.
```

List the Perl-related files in the directory.

```
ftp> ls perl*
150 Opening ASCII mode data connection for file list.
perl-4.036.tar.gz
perl5.001.pat.gz
perl5.001m.tar.gz
perlref-5.000.0.tar.gz
remote: perl*
226 Transfer complete.
79 bytes received in 0.026 seconds (3 Kbytes/s)
```

The Perl distribution is contained in a file named perl5.NNNp.tar.gz (where NNNp is the version number and patch level). The latest version available here is contained in the file perl5.001m.tar.gz. Before you download it, set the transfer mode to binary using the command bin.

```
ftp> bin
200 Type set to I.
```

You are now ready to transfer the Perl distribution using the get command. If you want to watch the progress of the transfer, set hash printing on using the hash command.

```
ftp> hash
Hash mark printing on (8192 bytes/hash mark).
```

Now initiate the transfer with the command get perl5.001m.tar.gz.

```
ftp> get perl5.001m.tar.gz
200 PORT command successful.
150 Opening BINARY mode connection for perl5.001.tar.gz (1130765 bytes).
##### ...
226 Transfer complete.
```

When the transfer is complete, terminate the session with the quit command.

```
ftp> quit
```

2. Now decompress and unarchive the distribution. To conserve disk space at the FTP-server site, the distribution file is always held in compressed form. Once you have downloaded the distribution file, the next step is to decompress it. There are two common compression formats used with free software for UNIX: compress format and GNU-ZIP format. The former provides the fewest problems because you will find the uncompress software on every standard UNIX system.

Although compress .Z compression is a UNIX standard, it is rapidly being replaced in the FTP-archive world by GNU-ZIP compression. The GNU-ZIP program gzip generally offers higher compression ratios than the compress program. If you find that your server holds the Perl kit in a file with a .gz suffix, the first step is to obtain the gzip program for your system. Fortunately, any archive holding .gz file will also hold the gzip distribution; it may even hold gzip in binary format for specific systems.

To expand a .Z file, issue this command:

```
zcat perl5.001m.tar.Z | tar xvf -
```

To expand a .gz file, issue this command:

```
gzip -dc perl5.001m.tar.gz | tar xvf -
```

You will see output in a format similar to this; the files and directories from the distribution will be created within your current directory.

```
x perl5.001m/Artistic, 6112 bytes, 12 tape blocks
x perl5.001m/Changes, 55793 bytes, 109 tape blocks
x perl5.001m/Changes.Conf, 5302 bytes, 11 tape blocks
x perl5.001m/Configure, 184010 bytes, 360 tape blocks ...
```

3. Change to the top-level distribution directory with the following command.

```
cd perl5.001m
```

and list the directory

```
ls
Artistic      INTERN.h       av.c          configpm      dosish.h
Changes       MANIFEST       av.h          configure     dump.c
Changes.Conf  Makefile.SH    c2ph.SH       cop.h         eg
Configure     README         c2ph.doc      cv.h
Copying       README.vms     cflags.SH     deb.c
Doc           Todo           config_H      doio.c
EXTERN.h      XSUB.h         config_h.SH   doop.c
```

The next step is to read any documentation in the README file. Note any information in the installation section.

4. Because the distribution is generic and designed to be built on any platform, the first step in the build process is to configure the build tools using the Configure program in the top-level directory. It is a bad idea to issue the command Configure because you may have other configure programs on your path. Qualify the command with a ./ to pick up the script in the current directory.

```
./Configure
 Beginning of configuration questions for perl5.

Checking echo to see how to suppress newlines...
```

```
...using -n.
The star should be here-->*

First let's make sure your kit is complete.   Checking...
Looks good...
```

This program will probe around your system, identifying the machine type, the operating-system version, other software on the system, and various features of the environment. When it is complete, it will write a file, config.sh, that contains a database of system information. The file will be consulted by the build tools when you create the software.

The Configure program can be run in interactive mode (where it will ask you questions) or default mode (where it will attempt to identify the features of the system by itself). If your system has a common architecture/operating system combination, you should have no problem if you let the Configure software run noninteractively.

```
./Configure -d
```

After the script has finished, it will prompt

```
Run make depend now [y]
```

Answer yes. After the dependency file has been created, the script terminates with the line

```
Now you must run a make.
```

5. To build Perl for your machine, start the make process by typing

```
make
```

The compilation and build process begins. This will take 10 to 30 minutes, depending on the speed of your machine. You will see output similar to the following.

```
`sh   cflags libperl.a miniperlmain.o`   miniperlmain.c
         CCCMD =   cc -c   -O
`sh   cflags libperl.a perl.o`   perl.c
         CCCMD =   cc -c   -O
```

6. Even though the configuration tools are mature and more knowledgeable about the system than most system administrators, there is no guarantee that the build will succeed the first time through. What can you do if your build fails? First, don't be daunted. The solution to build problems is usually not as complex as the obscure compiler error messages suggest. Try to narrow down the problem.

● Is the make itself tool failing or complaining about implausible syntax errors in the Makefile?

Your manufacturer's implementation of the make program may be somewhat lacking. One solution is to get hold of the excellent GNU-make tool gmake and build that. Then use gmake in place of your standard make program.

● Is the compiler complaining that it cannot find an include file?

This is probably due to identifying the location of system header files incorrectly during the configuration stage. Locate the missing file on your system using the find command. Here is an example that searches the /usr/include directory tree.

```
find /usr/include -name "missing.file" -print
```

Rerun the configure program interactively and supply the correct location when the question comes around.

● Is the compiler complaining about redefinition of functions or conflicting data definitions?

Take a look in the file that is failing to compile; check the system header files that are included by the file. When you identify the cause of the double definition, make a reasonable judgment about how to resolve it. If the definitions look fundamentally compatible, then remove the second definition in the Perl distribution. Try restarting the build by retyping `make`. If the build continues, make sure the final resulting programs are error-free by running the test suite.

If you are really stuck with a build problem, there are two options: Find a C programmer to help you out or consult the Perl newsgroup comp.lang.perl.misc for messages that might have been posted by others experiencing the same problems. As a last resort, post to the newsgroup explaining your problem as clearly as you can. Chances are that some helpful Perl hacker will have some good advice for you within a few hours.

7. When the build completes successfully, the next step is to check the integrity of the new Perl by running the test suite. Use the following command.

```
make test
```

Perl will then run a series of tests using the newly built programs. Normally, a successful build will pass all the tests without a problem. If you get a failure for no obvious reason, don't install the software. Follow the advice given above for build problems.

8. The final step is to install the software in the production directory. If you are upgrading from a previous version of Perl, then you may wish to take some steps to ensure that old Perl binaries are not overwritten. The normal installation will create binaries perl5 and perl. If you have renamed your previous version binary perl, you may wish to make a copy of it. The new Perl 5 libraries will be written to .../lib/Perl5; this should cause no problems. Type the install command as

```
make install
```

Check that the software is installed and on the path by issuing the command

```
perl -v
```

The version number displayed should be the same as the new distribution.

9. Once the installation is complete, you can delete the temporary directory with the following command.

```
rm -fr perl5.001m
```

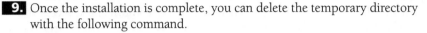

COMPLEXITY
INTERMEDIATE

B.2   How do I...
Build the Tk-Perl extension for UNIX?

COMPATIBILITY: UNIX

The Perl-Tk module is discussed in Chapter 26. In this appendix, we describe how to compile the various software components needed to build the Tk-Perl extension.

At the time of writing, the latest version of Tk-Perl is Tk-8b. The Perl Tk extension requires that Perl 5, Tcl, and Tk be installed on the system. You don't need Tcl or Tk once you have built Tk-Perl, but you need the Tcl and Tk libraries for the compilation of Tk-Perl.

Technique

Here is an overview of the build process:

- Obtain the latest version of Tk-Perl from an FTP archive server or download it from the Web. Consult the README file in the Tk-Perl distribution to discover which versions of Tcl and Tk are compatible with Tk-Perl. Obtain compatible versions of Tcl and Tk.

- Build and install Tcl.

- Build and install Tk.

- Build Tk-Perl in a temporary directory.

- Run the test suite.

- Install the Tk-Perl library and documentation into the production directories.

Steps

1. Obtain the latest version of Tk-Perl from an FTP archive server in your region. See Appendix A for a list of Perl-related Internet resources. You should be able to discover the latest version from any Internet information service, the Perl module list, or the Perl FAQ. Follow the example of the FTP session in Appendix B.1.

2. Determine the compatible version of Tcl and Tk by reading the README, INSTALL, and Changes files. When you have the information, access your local FTP server and download these programs. Most sites that carry Perl or Tk-Perl also carry Tcl and Tk.

3. Expand the Tcl distribution using the techniques covered in Appendix B.1. Once the kit is fully expanded in a temporary directory, cd to the top-level directory in the distribution. Then run the configure program. (Note that configure for Tcl and Tk is spelled with a lowercase c; the equivalent command for Perl and the Perl-Tk extension is spelled Configure.)

```
./configure
loading cache ./config.cache
checking for a BSD compatible install... (cached) //bin/install -c
checking for ranlib... (cached) ranlib
creating ./config.status
...
creating Makefile
```

Install Tcl and Tk under the /usr/local directory, unless you have a concrete reason not to. This directory is the default location; selecting the default location simplifies the installation of Tk-Perl.

4. Start the build process by issuing the command

```
make
```

When the build completes successfully, check the resulting binaries and libraries by running the test suite. Type the command

```
make test
```

When the tests complete successfully, install Tcl with the command

```
make install
```

If you are installing into /usr/local, most systems will require root permission to write to the directory. You may need your system administrator to perform this step.

5. Next, install Tk using a similar method as for the installation of Tcl. Expand the distribution into a temporary directory, cd to the top distribution directory, and run the configure command. Select /usr/local as the default directory location for the installed Tk.

```
./configure
loading cache ./config.cache
checking for a BSD compatible install... (cached) //bin/install -c
checking for ranlib... (cached) ranlib
...
creating ./config.status
creating Makefile
```

Start the build.

make

Now run the tests. You will need an X-windows display for this step. Check that your display variable DISPLAY is set to your local screen.

```
echo $DISPLAY
alpha:0.0
```

Run the test suite (this step may be more entertaining than you expect).

```
make test
...
```

Finally, install Tk in /usr/local using the command

make install

6. Build the Tk extension by expanding the distribution into a temporary directory, cd to the top-level directory in the distribution, and run the Configure program.

```
./Configure
/usr/local/bin/perl Makefile.PL PERL=/usr/local/bin/perl
Using -L/usr/openwin/lib to find /usr/openwin/lib/libX11.so.4.3
Using -I/usr/openwin/include to find /usr/openwin/include/X11/Xlib.h
Checking if your kit is complete...
Looks good
...
`config' is up to date.
```

Run make.

```
make
cd Bitmap && make config INSTALLPRIVLIB="/usr/local/lib/perl5
INSTALLARCHLIB="/usr/local/lib/perl5/sun4-sunos"
INSTALLBIN="/usr/local/bin" LIBPERL_A="libperl.a" LINKTYPE="dynamic"
...
```

Run the test suite.

make test

Check that you have permission to write to /usr/local if that is your production directory and install the new Tk-Perl with the following command.

make install

You should now be able to run the programs and examples given in Chapter 26.

GNU GPL AND LGPL

GNU General Public License Version 2, June 1991

Copyright (C) 1989, 1991 Free Software Foundation, Inc. 675 Mass Ave, Cambridge, MA 02139, USA

Everyone is permitted to copy and distribute verbatim copies of this license document, but changing it is not allowed.

Preamble

The licenses for most software are designed to take away your freedom to share and change it. By contrast, the GNU General Public License is intended to guarantee your freedom to share and change free software – to make sure the software is free for all its users. This General Public License applies to most of the Free Software Foundation's software and to any other program whose authors commit to using it. (Some other Free Software Foundation software is covered by the GNU Library General Public License instead.) You can apply it to your programs, too.

When we speak of free software, we are referring to freedom, not price. Our General Public Licenses are designed to make sure that you have the freedom to distribute copies of free software (and charge for this service if you wish), that you receive source code or can get it if you want it, that you can change the software or use pieces of it in new free programs; and that you know you can do these things.

To protect your rights, we need to make restrictions that forbid anyone to deny you these rights or to ask you to surrender the rights. These restrictions translate to certain responsibilities for you if you distribute copies of the software, or if you modify it.

For example, if you distribute copies of such a program, whether gratis or for a fee, you must give the recipients all the rights that you have. You must make sure that they, too, receive or can get the source code. And you must show them these terms so they know their rights.

We protect your rights with two steps: (1) copyright the software, and (2) offer you this license which gives you legal permission to copy, distribute and/or modify the software.

Also, for each author's protection and ours, we want to make certain that everyone understands that there is no warranty for this free software. If the software is modified by someone else and passed on, we want its recipients to know that what they have is not the original, so that any problems introduced by others will not reflect on the original authors' reputations.

Finally, any free program is threatened constantly by software patents. We wish to avoid the danger that redistributors of a free program will individually obtain patent licenses, in effect making the program proprietary. To prevent this, we have made it clear that any patent must be licensed for everyone's free use or not licensed at all.

The precise terms and conditions for copying, distribution and modification follow.

Terms and Conditions for Copying, Distribution and Modification

1. This License applies to any program or other work which contains a notice placed by the copyright holder saying it may be distributed under the terms of this General Public License. The "Program", below, refers to any such program or work, and a "work based on the Program" means either the Program or any derivative work under copyright law: that is to say, a work containing the Program or a portion of it, either verbatim or with modifications and/or translated into another language. (Hereinafter, translation is included without limitation in the term "modification".) Each licensee is addressed as "you". Activities other than copying, distribution and modification are not covered by this License; they are outside its scope. The act of running the Program is not restricted, and the output from the Program is covered only if its contents constitute a work based on the Program (independent of having been made by running the Program). Whether that is true depends on what the Program does.

2. You may copy and distribute verbatim copies of the Program's source code as you receive it, in any medium, provided that you conspicuously and appropriately publish on each copy an appropriate copyright notice and disclaimer of warranty; keep intact all the notices that refer to this License and to the absence of any warranty; and give any other recipients of the Program a copy of this License along with the Program. You may charge a fee for the physical act of transferring a copy, and you may at your option offer warranty protection in exchange for a fee.

3. You may modify your copy or copies of the Program or any portion of it, thus forming a work based on the Program, and copy and distribute such modifications or work under the terms of Section 1 above, provided that you also meet all of these conditions:

1. You must cause the modified files to carry prominent notices stating that you changed the files and the date of any change.

2. You must cause any work that you distribute or publish, that in whole or in part contains or is derived from the Program or any part thereof, to be licensed as a whole at no charge to all third parties under the terms of this License.

3. If the modified program normally reads commands interactively when run, you must cause it, when started running for such interactive use in the most ordinary way, to print or display an announcement including an appropriate copyright notice and a notice that there is no warranty (or else, saying that you provide a warranty) and that users may redistribute the program under these conditions, and telling the user how to view a copy of this License. (Exception: if the Program itself is interactive but does not normally print such an announcement, your work based on the Program is not required to print an announcement.)

These requirements apply to the modified work as a whole. If identifiable sections of that work are not derived from the Program, and can be reasonably considered independent and separate works in themselves, then this License, and its terms, do not apply to those sections when you distribute them as separate works. But when you distribute the same sections as part of a whole which is a work based on the Program, the distribution of the whole must be on the terms of this License, whose permissions for other licensees extend to the entire whole, and thus to each and every part regardless of who wrote it. Thus, it is not the intent of this section to claim rights or contest your rights to work written entirely by you; rather, the intent is to exercise the right to control the distribution of derivative or collective works based on the Program. In addition, mere aggregation of another work not based on the Program with the Program (or with a work based on the Program) on a volume of a storage or distribution medium does not bring the other work under the scope of this License.

4. You may copy and distribute the Program (or a work based on it, under Section 2) in object code or executable form under the terms of Sections 1 and 2 above provided that you also do one of the following:

1. Accompany it with the complete corresponding machine-readable source code, which must be distributed under the terms of Sections 1 and 2 above on a medium customarily used for software interchange; or,

2. Accompany it with a written offer, valid for at least three years, to give any third party, for a charge no more than your cost of physically performing source distribution, a complete machine-readable copy of the corresponding source code, to be distributed under the terms of Sections 1 and 2 above on a medium customarily used for software interchange; or,

3. Accompany it with the information you received as to the offer to distribute corresponding source code. (This alternative is allowed only for noncommercial distribution and only if you received the program in object code or executable form with such an offer, in accord with Subsection b above.)

The source code for a work means the preferred form of the work for making modifications to it. For an executable work, complete source code means all the source code for all modules it contains, plus any associated interface definition files, plus the scripts used to control compilation and installation of the executable. However, as a special exception, the source code distributed need not include anything that is normally distributed (in either source or binary form) with the major components (compiler, kernel, and so on) of the operating system on which the executable runs, unless that component itself accompanies the executable. If distribution of executable or object code is made by offering access to copy from a designated place, then offering equivalent access to copy the source code from the same place counts as distribution of the source code, even though third parties are not compelled to copy the source along with the object code.

5. You may not copy, modify, sublicense, or distribute the Program except as expressly provided under this License. Any attempt otherwise to copy, modify, sublicense or distribute the Program is void, and will automatically terminate your rights under this License. However, parties who have received copies, or rights, from you under this License will not have their licenses terminated so long as such parties remain in full compliance.

6. You are not required to accept this License, since you have not signed it. However, nothing else grants you permission to modify or distribute the Program or its derivative works. These actions are prohibited by law if you do not accept this License. Therefore, by modifying or distributing the Program (or any work based on the Program), you indicate your acceptance of this License to do so, and all its terms and conditions for copying, distributing or modifying the Program or works based on it.

7. Each time you redistribute the Program (or any work based on the Program), the recipient automatically receives a license from the original licensor to copy, distribute or modify the Program subject to these terms and conditions. You may not impose any further restrictions on the recipients' exercise of the rights granted herein. You are not responsible for enforcing compliance by third parties to this License.

8. If, as a consequence of a court judgment or allegation of patent infringement or for any other reason (not limited to patent issues), conditions are imposed on you (whether by court order, agreement or otherwise) that contradict the conditions of this License, they do not excuse you from the conditions of this License. If you cannot distribute so as to satisfy simultaneously your obligations under this License and any other pertinent obligations, then as a consequence you may not distribute the Program at all. For example, if a patent license would not permit royalty-free redistribution of the Program by all those who receive copies directly or indirectly through you, then the only way you could satisfy both it and this License would be to refrain entirely from distribution of the Program. If any portion of this section is held invalid or unenforceable under any particular circumstance, the balance of the section is intended to apply and the section as a whole is intended to apply in other circumstances. It is not the purpose of this section to induce you to infringe any patents or other property right claims or to contest validity of any such claims; this section has the sole purpose of protecting the integrity of the free software distribution system, which is implemented by public license practices. Many people have made generous contributions to the wide range of software distributed through that system in reliance on consistent application of that system; it is up to the author/donor to decide if he or she is willing to distribute software through any other system and a licensee cannot impose that choice. This section is intended to make thoroughly clear what is believed to be a consequence of the rest of this License.

9. If the distribution and/or use of the Program is restricted in certain countries either by patents or by copyrighted interfaces, the original copyright holder who places the Program under this License may add an explicit geographical distribution limitation excluding those countries, so that distribution is permitted only in or among countries not thus excluded. In such case, this License incorporates the limitation as if written in the body of this License.

10. The Free Software Foundation may publish revised and/or new versions of the General Public License from time to time. Such new versions will be similar in spirit to the present version, but may differ in detail to address new problems or concerns. Each version is given a distinguishing version number. If the Program specifies a version number of this License which applies to it and "any later version", you have the option of following the terms and conditions either of that version or of any later version published by the Free Software Foundation. If the Program does not specify a version number of this License, you may choose any version ever published by the Free Software Foundation.

11. If you wish to incorporate parts of the Program into other free programs whose distribution conditions are different, write to the author to ask for permission. For software which is copyrighted by the Free Software Foundation, write to the Free Software Foundation; we sometimes make exceptions for this. Our decision will be guided by the two goals of preserving the free status of all derivatives of our free software and of promoting the sharing and reuse of software generally.

No Warranty

12. BECAUSE THE PROGRAM IS LICENSED FREE OF CHARGE, THERE IS NO WARRANTY FOR THE PROGRAM, TO THE EXTENT PERMITTED BY APPLICABLE LAW. EXCEPT WHEN OTHERWISE STATED IN WRITING THE COPYRIGHT HOLDERS AND/OR OTHER PARTIES PROVIDE THE PROGRAM "AS IS" WITHOUT WARRANTY OF ANY KIND, EITHER EXPRESSED OR IMPLIED, INCLUDING, BUT NOT LIMITED TO, THE IMPLIED WARRANTIES OF MERCHANTABILITY AND FITNESS FOR A PARTICULAR PURPOSE. THE ENTIRE RISK AS TO THE QUALITY AND PERFORMANCE OF THE PROGRAM IS WITH YOU. SHOULD THE PROGRAM PROVE DEFECTIVE, YOU ASSUME THE COST OF ALL NECESSARY SERVICING, REPAIR OR CORRECTION.

13. IN NO EVENT UNLESS REQUIRED BY APPLICABLE LAW OR AGREED TO IN WRITING WILL ANY COPYRIGHT HOLDER, OR ANY OTHER PARTY WHO MAY MODIFY AND/OR REDISTRIBUTE THE PROGRAM AS PERMITTED ABOVE, BE LIABLE TO YOU FOR DAMAGES, INCLUDING ANY GENERAL, SPECIAL, INCIDENTAL OR CONSEQUENTIAL DAMAGES ARISING OUT OF THE USE OR INABILITY TO USE THE PROGRAM (INCLUDING BUT NOT LIMITED TO LOSS OF DATA OR DATA BEING RENDERED INACCURATE OR LOSSES SUSTAINED BY YOU OR THIRD PARTIES OR A FAILURE OF THE PROGRAM TO OPERATE WITH ANY OTHER PROGRAMS), EVEN IF SUCH HOLDER OR OTHER PARTY HAS BEEN ADVISED OF THE POSSIBILITY OF SUCH DAMAGES.

END OF TERMS AND CONDITIONS

How to Apply These Terms to Your New Programs

If you develop a new program, and you want it to be of the greatest possible use to the public, the best way to achieve this is to make it free software that everyone can redistribute and change under these terms.

To do so, attach the following notices to the program. It is safest to attach them to the start of each source file to most effectively convey the exclusion of warranty, and each file should have at least the "copyright" line and a pointer to where the full notice is found.

```
one line to give the program's name and an idea of what it does.
Copyright (C) 19yy  name of author

This program is free software; you can redistribute it and/or modify it
```

under the terms of the GNU General Public License as published by the Free Software Foundation; either version 2 of the License, or (at your option) any later version.

This program is distributed in the hope that it will be useful, but WITHOUT ANY WARRANTY; without even the implied warranty of MERCHANTABILITY or FITNESS FOR A PARTICULAR PURPOSE. See the GNU General Public License for more details.

You should have received a copy of the GNU General Public License along with this program; if not, write to the Free Software Foundation, Inc., 675 Mass Ave, Cambridge, MA 02139, USA.

Also, add information on how to contact you by electronic and paper mail.

If the program is interactive, make it output a short notice like this when it starts in an interactive mode:

Gnomovision version 69, Copyright (C) 19yy **name of author**
Gnomovision comes with ABSOLUTELY NO WARRANTY; for details type 'show w'. This is free software, and you are welcome to redistribute it under certain conditions; type 'show c' for details.

The hypothetical commands 'show w' and 'show c' should show the appropriate parts of the General Public License. Of course, the commands you use may be called something other than 'show w' and 'show c'; they could even be mouse-clicks or menu items—whatever suits your program.

You should also get your employer (if you work as a programmer) or your school, if any, to sign a "copyright disclaimer" for the program, if necessary. Here is a sample; alter the names:

Yoyodyne, Inc., hereby disclaims all copyright interest in the program 'Gnomovision' (which makes passes at compilers) written by James Hacker.

signature of Ty Coon, 1 April 1989
Ty Coon, President of Vice

This General Public License does not permit incorporating your program into proprietary programs. If your program is a subroutine library, you may consider it more useful to permit linking proprietary applications with the library. If this is what you want to do, use the GNU Library General Public License instead of this License.

GNU Library General Public License Version 2, June 1991

Copyright (C) 1991 Free Software Foundation, Inc.
675 Mass Ave, Cambridge, MA 02139, USA

Everyone is permitted to copy and distribute verbatim copies of this license document, but changing it is not allowed.

[This is the first released version of the library GPL. It is numbered 2
because it goes with version 2 of the ordinary GPL.]

Preamble

The licenses for most software are designed to take away your freedom to share and change it. By contrast, the GNU General Public Licenses are intended to guarantee your freedom to share and change free software – to make sure the software is free for all its users.

This license, the Library General Public License, applies to some specially designated Free Software Foundation software, and to any other libraries whose authors decide to use it. You can use it for your libraries, too.

When we speak of free software, we are referring to freedom, not price. Our General Public Licenses are designed to make sure that you have the freedom to distribute copies of free software (and charge for this service if you wish), that you receive source code or can get it if you want it, that you can change the software or use pieces of it in new free programs; and that you know you can do these things.

To protect your rights, we need to make restrictions that forbid anyone to deny you these rights or to ask you to surrender the rights. These restrictions translate to certain responsibilities for you if you distribute copies of the library, or if you modify it.

For example, if you distribute copies of the library, whether gratis or for a fee, you must give the recipients all the rights that we gave you. You must make sure that they, too, receive or can get the source code. If you link a program with the library, you must provide complete object files to the recipients so that they can relink them with the library, after making changes to the library and recompiling it. And you must show them these terms so they know their rights.

Our method of protecting your rights has two steps: (1) copyright the library, and (2) offer you this license which gives you legal permission to copy, distribute and/or modify the library.

Also, for each distributor's protection, we want to make certain that everyone understands that there is no warranty for this free library. If the library is modified by someone else and passed on, we want its recipients to know that what they have is not the original version, so that any problems introduced by others will not reflect on the original authors' reputations.

Finally, any free program is threatened constantly by software patents. We wish to avoid the danger that companies distributing free software will individually obtain patent licenses, thus in effect transforming the program into proprietary software. To prevent this, we have made it clear that any patent must be licensed for everyone's free use or not licensed at all.

Most GNU software, including some libraries, is covered by the ordinary GNU General Public License, which was designed for utility programs. This license, the

GNU Library General Public License, applies to certain designated libraries. This license is quite different from the ordinary one; be sure to read it in full, and don't assume that anything in it is the same as in the ordinary license.

The reason we have a separate public license for some libraries is that they blur the distinction we usually make between modifying or adding to a program and simply using it. Linking a program with a library, without changing the library, is in some sense simply using the library, and is analogous to running a utility program or application program. However, in a textual and legal sense, the linked executable is a combined work, a derivative of the original library, and the ordinary General Public License treats it as such.

Because of this blurred distinction, using the ordinary General Public License for libraries did not effectively promote software sharing, because most developers did not use the libraries. We concluded that weaker conditions might promote sharing better.

However, unrestricted linking of non-free programs would deprive the users of those programs of all benefit from the free status of the libraries themselves. This Library General Public License is intended to permit developers of non-free programs to use free libraries, while preserving your freedom as a user of such programs to change the free libraries that are incorporated in them. (We have not seen how to achieve this as regards changes in header files, but we have achieved it as regards changes in the actual functions of the Library.) The hope is that this will lead to faster development of free libraries.

The precise terms and conditions for copying, distribution and modification follow. Pay close attention to the difference between a "work based on the library" and a "work that uses the library". The former contains code derived from the library, while the latter only works together with the library.

Note that it is possible for a library to be covered by the ordinary General Public License rather than by this special one.

Terms and Conditions for Copying, Distribution and Modification

1. This License Agreement applies to any software library which contains a notice placed by the copyright holder or other authorized party saying it may be distributed under the terms of this Library General Public License (also called "this License"). Each licensee is addressed as "you". A "library" means a collection of software functions and/or data prepared so as to be conveniently linked with application programs (which use some of those functions and data) to form executables. The "Library", below, refers to any such software library or work which has been distributed under these terms. A "work based on the Library" means either the Library or any derivative work under copyright law: that is to say, a work containing the Library or a portion of it, either verbatim or with modifications and/or translated straightforwardly into another language. (Hereinafter, translation is included without limitation in the term "modification".) "Source code" for a work means the preferred form of the work for making modifications to it. For a library, complete source code means all the source code for all modules it contains, plus any associated interface definition files, plus the scripts used to control compilation and installation of the library. Activities other than copying, distribution and modification are not covered by this License; they are outside its scope. The act of running a program using the Library is not restricted, and output from such a program is covered only if its contents constitute a work based on the Library (independent of the use of the Library in a tool for writing it). Whether that is true depends on what the Library does and what the program that uses the Library does.

2. You may copy and distribute verbatim copies of the Library's complete source code as you receive it, in any medium, provided that you conspicuously and appropriately publish on each copy an appropriate copyright notice and disclaimer of warranty; keep intact all the notices that refer to this License and to the absence of any warranty; and distribute a copy of this License along with the Library. You may charge a fee for the physical act of transferring a copy, and you may at your option offer warranty protection in exchange for a fee.

3. You may modify your copy or copies of the Library or any portion of it, thus forming a work based on the Library, and copy and distribute such modifications or work under the terms of Section 1 above, provided that you also meet all of these conditions:

1. The modified work must itself be a software library.

2. You must cause the files modified to carry prominent notices stating that you changed the files and the date of any change.

3. You must cause the whole of the work to be licensed at no charge to all third parties under the terms of this License.

4. If a facility in the modified Library refers to a function or a table of data to be supplied by an application program that uses the facility, other than as an argument passed when the facility is invoked, then you must make a good faith effort to ensure that, in the event an application does not supply such function or table, the facility still operates, and performs whatever part of its purpose remains meaningful. (For example, a function in a library to compute square roots has a purpose that is entirely well-defined independent of the application. Therefore, Subsection 2d requires that any application-supplied function or table used by this function must be optional: if the application does not supply it, the square root function must still compute square roots.)

These requirements apply to the modified work as a whole. If identifiable sections of that work are not derived from the Library, and can be reasonably considered independent and separate works in themselves, then this License, and its terms, do not apply to those sections when you distribute them as separate works. But when you distribute the same sections as part of a whole which is a work based on the Library, the distribution of the whole must be on the terms of this License, whose permissions for other licensees extend to the entire whole, and thus to each and every part regardless of who wrote it. Thus, it is not the intent of this section to claim rights or contest your rights to work written entirely by you; rather, the intent is to exercise the right to control the distribution of derivative or collective works based on the Library. In addition, mere aggregation of another work not based on the Library with the Library (or with a work based on the Library) on a volume of a storage or distribution medium does not bring the other work under the scope of this License.

4. You may opt to apply the terms of the ordinary GNU General Public License instead of this License to a given copy of the Library. To do this, you must alter all the notices that refer to this License, so that they refer to the ordinary GNU General Public License, version 2, instead of to this License. (If a newer version than version 2 of the ordinary GNU General Public License has appeared, then you can specify that version instead if you wish.) Do not make any other change in these notices. Once this change is made in a given copy, it is irreversible for that copy, so the ordinary GNU General Public License applies to all subsequent copies and derivative works made from that copy. This option is useful when you wish to copy part of the code of the Library into a program that is not a library.

5. You may copy and distribute the Library (or a portion or derivative of it, under Section 2) in object code or executable form under the terms of Sections 1 and 2 above provided that you accompany it with the complete corresponding machine-readable source code, which must be distributed under the terms of Sections 1 and 2 above on a medium customarily used for software interchange. If distribution of object code is made by offering access to copy from a designated place, then offering equivalent access to copy the source code from the same place satisfies the requirement to distribute the source code, even though third parties are not compelled to copy the source along with the object code.

6. A program that contains no derivative of any portion of the Library, but is designed to work with the Library by being compiled or linked with it, is called a "work that uses the Library". Such a work, in isolation, is not a derivative work of the Library, and therefore falls outside the scope of this License. However, linking a "work that uses the Library" with the Library creates an executable that is a derivative of the Library (because it contains portions of the Library), rather than a "work that uses the library". The executable is therefore covered by this License. Section 6 states terms for distribution of such executables. When a "work that uses the Library" uses material from a header file that is part of the Library, the object code for the work may be a derivative work of the Library even though the source code is not. Whether this is true is especially significant if the work can be linked without the Library, or if the work is itself a library. The threshold for this to be true is not precisely defined by law. If such an object file uses only numerical parameters, data structure layouts and accessors, and small macros and small inline functions (ten lines or less in length), then the use of the object file is unrestricted, regardless of whether it is legally a derivative work. (Executables containing this object code plus portions of the Library will still fall under Section 6.) Otherwise, if the work is a derivative of the Library, you may distribute the object code for the work under the terms of Section 6. Any executables containing that work also fall under Section 6, whether or not they are linked directly with the Library itself.

7. As an exception to the Sections above, you may also compile or link a "work that uses the Library" with the Library to produce a work containing portions of the Library, and distribute that work under terms of your choice, provided that the terms permit modification of the work for the customer's own use and reverse engineering for debugging such modifications. You must give prominent notice with each copy of the work that the Library is used in it and that the Library and its use are covered by this License. You must supply a copy of this License. If the work during execution displays copyright notices, you must include the copyright notice for the Library among them, as well as a reference directing the user to the copy of this License. Also, you must do one of these things:

1. Accompany the work with the complete corresponding machine-readable source code for the Library including whatever changes were used in the work (which must be distributed under Sections 1 and 2 above); and, if the work is an executable linked with the Library, with the complete machine-readable "work that uses the Library", as object code and/or source code, so that the user can modify the Library and then relink to produce a modified executable containing the modified Library. (It is understood that the user who changes the contents of definitions files in the Library will not necessarily be able to recompile the application to use the modified definitions.)

2. Accompany the work with a written offer, valid for at least three years, to give the same user the materials specified in Subsection 6a, above, for a charge no more than the cost of performing this distribution.

3. If distribution of the work is made by offering access to copy from a designated place, offer equivalent access to copy the above specified materials from the same place.

4. Verify that the user has already received a copy of these materials or that you have already sent this user a copy.

For an executable, the required form of the "work that uses the Library" must include any data and utility programs needed for reproducing the executable from it. However, as a special exception, the source code distributed need not include anything that is normally distributed (in either source or binary form) with the major components (compiler, kernel, and so on) of the operating system on which the executable runs, unless that component itself accompanies the executable. It may happen that this requirement contradicts the license restrictions of other proprietary libraries that do not normally accompany the operating system. Such a contradiction means you cannot use both them and the Library together in an executable that you distribute.

8. You may place library facilities that are a work based on the Library side-by-side in a single library together with other library facilities not covered by this License, and distribute such a combined library, provided that the separate distribution of the work based on the Library and of the other library facilities is otherwise permitted, and provided that you do these two things:

1. Accompany the combined library with a copy of the same work based on the Library, uncombined with any other library facilities. This must be distributed under the terms of the Sections above.

2. Give prominent notice with the combined library of the fact that part of it is a work based on the Library, and explaining where to find the accompanying uncombined form of the same work.

9. You may not copy, modify, sublicense, link with, or distribute the Library except as expressly provided under this License. Any attempt otherwise to copy, modify, sublicense, link with, or distribute the Library is void, and will automatically terminate your rights under this License. However, parties who have received copies, or rights, from you under this License will not have their licenses terminated so long as such parties remain in full compliance.

10. You are not required to accept this License, since you have not signed it. However, nothing else grants you permission to modify or distribute the Library or its derivative works. These actions are prohibited by law if you do not accept this License. Therefore, by modifying or distributing the Library (or any work based on the Library), you indicate your acceptance of this License to do so, and all its terms and conditions for copying, distributing or modifying the Library or works based on it.

11. Each time you redistribute the Library (or any work based on the Library), the recipient automatically receives a license from the original licensor to copy, distribute, link with or modify the Library subject to these terms and conditions. You may not impose any further restrictions on the recipients' exercise of the rights granted herein. You are not responsible for enforcing compliance by third parties to this License.

12. If, as a consequence of a court judgment or allegation of patent infringement or for any other reason (not limited to patent issues), conditions are imposed on you (whether by court order, agreement or otherwise) that contradict the conditions of this License, they do not excuse you from the conditions of this License. If you cannot distribute so as to satisfy simultaneously your obligations under this License and any other pertinent obligations, then as a consequence you may not distribute the Library at all. For example, if a patent license would not permit royalty-free redistribution of the Library by all those who receive copies directly or indirectly through you, then the only way you could satisfy both it and this License would be to refrain entirely from distribution of the Library. If any portion of this section is held invalid or unenforceable under any particular circumstance, the balance of the section is intended to apply, and the section as a whole is intended to apply in other circumstances. It is not the purpose of this section to induce you to infringe any patents or other property right claims or to contest validity of any such claims; this section has the sole purpose of protecting the integrity of the free software distribution system which is implemented by public license practices. Many people have made generous contributions to the wide range of software distributed through that system in reliance on consistent application of that system; it is up to the author/donor to decide if he or she is willing to distribute software through any other system and a licensee cannot impose that choice. This section is intended to make thoroughly clear what is believed to be a consequence of the rest of this License.

13. If the distribution and/or use of the Library is restricted in certain countries either by patents or by copyrighted interfaces, the original copyright holder who places the Library under this License may add an explicit geographical distribution limitation excluding those countries, so that distribution is permitted only in or among countries not thus excluded. In such case, this License incorporates the limitation as if written in the body of this License.

14. The Free Software Foundation may publish revised and/or new versions of the Library General Public License from time to time. Such new versions will be similar in spirit to the present version, but may differ in detail to address new problems or concerns. Each version is given a distinguishing version number. If the Library specifies a version number of this License which applies to it and "any later version", you have the option of following the terms and conditions either of that version or of any later version published by the Free Software Foundation. If the Library does not specify a license version number, you may choose any version ever published by the Free Software Foundation.

15. If you wish to incorporate parts of the Library into other free programs whose distribution conditions are incompatible with these, write to the author to ask for permission. For software which is copyrighted by the Free Software Foundation, write to the Free Software Foundation; we sometimes make exceptions for this. Our decision will be guided by the two goals of preserving the free status of all derivatives of our free software and of promoting the sharing and reuse of software generally.

No Warranty

16. BECAUSE THE LIBRARY IS LICENSED FREE OF CHARGE, THERE IS NO WARRANTY FOR THE LIBRARY, TO THE EXTENT PERMITTED BY APPLICABLE LAW. EXCEPT WHEN OTHERWISE STATED IN WRITING THE COPYRIGHT HOLDERS AND/OR OTHER PARTIES PROVIDE THE LIBRARY "AS IS" WITHOUT WARRANTY OF ANY KIND, EITHER EXPRESSED OR IMPLIED, INCLUDING, BUT NOT LIMITED TO, THE IMPLIED WARRANTIES OF MERCHANTABILITY AND FITNESS FOR A PARTICULAR PURPOSE. THE ENTIRE RISK AS TO THE QUALITY AND PERFORMANCE OF THE LIBRARY IS WITH YOU. SHOULD THE LIBRARY PROVE DEFECTIVE, YOU ASSUME THE COST OF ALL NECESSARY SERVICING, REPAIR OR CORRECTION.

17. IN NO EVENT UNLESS REQUIRED BY APPLICABLE LAW OR AGREED TO IN WRITING WILL ANY COPYRIGHT HOLDER, OR ANY OTHER PARTY WHO MAY MODIFY AND/OR REDISTRIBUTE THE LIBRARY AS PERMITTED ABOVE, BE LIABLE TO YOU FOR DAMAGES, INCLUDING ANY GENERAL, SPECIAL, INCIDENTAL OR CONSEQUENTIAL DAMAGES ARISING OUT OF THE USE OR INABILITY TO USE THE LIBRARY (INCLUDING BUT NOT LIMITED TO LOSS OF DATA OR DATA BEING RENDERED INACCURATE OR LOSSES SUSTAINED BY YOU OR THIRD PARTIES OR A FAILURE OF THE LIBRARY TO OPERATE WITH ANY OTHER SOFTWARE), EVEN IF SUCH HOLDER OR OTHER PARTY HAS BEEN ADVISED OF THE POSSIBILITY OF SUCH DAMAGES.

END OF TERMS AND CONDITIONS

How to Apply These Terms to Your New Libraries

If you develop a new library, and you want it to be of the greatest possible use to the public, we recommend making it free software that everyone can redistribute and change. You can do so by permitting redistribution under these terms (or, alternatively, under the terms of the ordinary General Public License).

To apply these terms, attach the following notices to the library. It is safest to attach them to the start of each source file to most effectively convey the exclusion of warranty; and each file should have at least the "copyright" line and a pointer to where the full notice is found.

```
one line to give the library's name and an idea of what it does.
Copyright (C) year   name of author

This library is free software; you can redistribute it and/or modify it
under the terms of the GNU Library General Public License as published by
the Free Software Foundation; either version 2 of the License, or (at your
option) any later version.

This library is distributed in the hope that it will be useful, but WITHOUT
ANY WARRANTY; without even the implied warranty of MERCHANTABILITY or
FITNESS FOR A PARTICULAR PURPOSE.  See the GNU Library General Public
License for more details.

You should have received a copy of the GNU Library General Public License
along with this library; if not, write to the Free Software Foundation,
Inc., 675 Mass Ave, Cambridge, MA 02139, USA.
```

Also, add information on how to contact you by electronic and paper mail.

You should also get your employer (if you work as a programmer) or your school, if any, to sign a "copyright disclaimer" for the library, if necessary. Here is a sample; alter the names:

```
Yoyodyne, Inc., hereby disclaims all copyright interest in the library
'Frob' (a library for tweaking knobs) written by James Random Hacker.

signature of Ty Coon, 1 April 1990
Ty Coon, President of Vice
```

That's all there is to it!

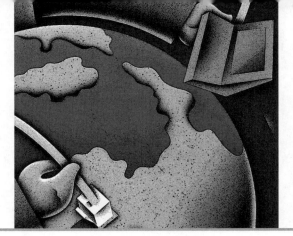

INDEX

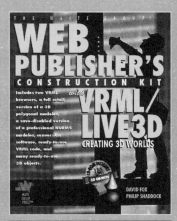

SOFTWARE LICENSE AGREEMENT

SATISFACTION REPORT CARD

Please fill out this card if you wish to know of future updates to
Perl 5 How-To, **or to receive our catalog.**

SATISFACTION CARD

First Name: _____ **Last Name:** _____

Address: _____

Street: _____

City: _____ **State:** _____ **Zip:** _____

Daytime Telephone: (   ) _____

E-Mail Address: _____

Date product was acquired: Month _____ **Day** _____ **Year** _____ **Your Occupation:** _____

Overall, how would you rate *Perl 5 How-To?*
- ☐ Excellent   ☐ Very Good   ☐ Good
- ☐ Fair   ☐ Below Average   ☐ Poor

What did you like MOST about this book? _____
_____
_____

What did you like LEAST about this book? _____
_____
_____

Please describe any problems you may have encountered with installing or using the disk: _____
_____

How did you use this book (problem-solver, tutorial, reference...)?
_____

What is your level of computer expertise?
- ☐ New   ☐ Dabbler   ☐ Hacker
- ☐ Power User   ☐ Programmer   ☐ Experienced Professional

What computer languages are you familiar with? _____
_____

Please describe your computer hardware:
Computer _____ Hard disk _____
5.25" Disk drives _____ 3.5" Disk drives _____
Video card _____ Monitor _____
Printer _____ Peripherals _____
Sound board _____ CD-ROM_____

Where did you buy this book?
- ☐ Bookstore (name): _____
- ☐ Discount store (name): _____
- ☐ Computer store (name): _____
- ☐ Catalog (name): _____
- ☐ Direct from WGP   ☐ Other _____

What price did you pay for this book? _____

What influenced your purchase of this book?
- ☐ Recommendation   ☐ Advertisement
- ☐ Magazine review   ☐ Store display
- ☐ Mailing   ☐ Book's format
- ☐ Reputation of Waite Group Press   ☐ Other

How many computer books do you buy each year? _____

How many other Waite Group books do you own? _____

What is your favorite Waite Group book? _____
_____

Is there any program or subject you would like to see Waite Group Press cover in a similar approach? _____
_____

Additional comments? _____
_____

Please send to: Waite Group Press
                200 Tamal Plaza
                Corte Madera, CA 94925

☐ **Check here for a free Waite Group catalog**

STOP!

BEFORE YOU OPEN THE DISK OR CD-ROM PACKAGE ON THE FACING PAGE, CAREFULLY READ THE LICENSE AGREEMENT.

Opening this package indicates that you agree to abide by the license agreement found in the back of this book. If you do not agree with it, promptly return the unopened disk package (including the related book) to the place you obtained them for a refund.